SCHAUM'S OUTLINE OF

THEORY AND PROBLEMS

OF

PROGRAMMING
with
STRUCTURED COBOL

.

by

LAWRENCE R. NEWCOMER, M.S.
Assistant Professor of Computer Science
Pennsylvania State University

.

SCHAUM'S OUTLINE SERIES
McGRAW-HILL BOOK COMPANY

New York   St. Louis   San Francisco   Auckland   Bogotá   Guatemala   Hamburg   Johannesburg
Lisbon   London   Madrid   Mexico   Montreal   New Delhi   Panama   Paris
San Juan   São Paulo   Singapore   Sydney   Tokyo   Toronto

To Deirdre and Caitlin

LAWRENCE R. NEWCOMER is an Assistant Professor of Computer Science at Pennsylvania State University. He holds a B.A. in English from Wesleyan University (Conn.), an M.S. in Psychology from Millersville State University, and an M.S. in Computer Science from Pennsylvania State University. In addition to teaching computer science business applications, Professor Newcomer has published articles on computer science education, produced several licensed program products, and conducted numerous industry workshops and seminars.

Schaum's Outline of Theory and Problems of
PROGRAMMING WITH STRUCTURED COBOL

Copyright © 1984 by McGraw-Hill, Inc. All rights reserved. Printed in the United States of America. Except as permitted under the Copyright Act of 1976, no part of this publication may be reproduced or distributed in any form or by any means, or stored in a data base or retrieval system, without the prior written permission of the publisher.

2 3 4 5 6 7 8 9 10 11 12 13 14 15 16 17 18 19 20 SHP SHP 8 9 8 7 6 5 4

ISBN 0-07-037998-X

Sponsoring Editor, David Beckwith
Editing Supervisor, Marthe Grice
Production Manager, Nick Monti

Library of Congress Cataloging in Publication Data

Newcomer, Lawrence.
  Schaum's outline of theory and problems of programming with structured COBOL.

  (Schaum's outline series)
  Includes index.
  1. COBOL (Computer program language)--Problems,
exercises, etc. 2. Structured programming--Problems,
exercises, etc. I. Title.
QA76.73.C25N48   1984   001.64′24   83-17547
ISBN 0-07-037998-X

Preface

This Outline teaches COBOL (as defined by the American National Standards Institute in 1974) from the *structured programming* point of view. It covers most, although not all, of the techniques that have enabled programmers to become more productive in the development of *individual programs*. We stress the use of *top-down*, *modular design*, along with the application of numerous COBOL *coding standards*.

The book aims to be both thorough and concise, allowing the reader to progress quickly. By the end of Chapter 2, the reader is ready to write simple COBOL programs. Since learning to program a computer is like learning to swim (you have to jump in and do it), the reader is urged to implement as many of the Programming Assignments as possible on an actual machine. Chapter 9, which covers debugging, is designed so that it can be read any time after Chapter 2; consult Chapter 9 whenever you have trouble with a Programming Assignment.

Where *extensions* to ANS COBOL '74 appear, they will be IBM OS/VS COBOL extensions and will be clearly identified as such. All examples and problems were tested on Pennsylvania State University's IBM 3081 computer system with IBM OS/VS COBOL. Where information varies from system to system, we give material pertinent to IBM 370-type systems, with OS/VS-type operating systems. The American National Standards Institute is presently working on a 1980 version of ANS COBOL. The changes which are likely to be included in COBOL '80 are given in Appendix C.

I wish to thank Diane Anderson, who was extraordinarily helpful in preparing the manuscript; Marge Johnson, for her constant help in communications; Mike Perelman, for his unflagging enthusiasm; Bob Rodgers and Carol Miller, for their helpful comments; and Debby Lord, for many useful suggestions and several programming assignments. It was a pleasure to work with David Beckwith, Marthe Grice, and the rest of the McGraw-Hill staff. Special thanks are due my parents, who helped educate me, and—most of all—my wife, who made it all possible.

LAWRENCE NEWCOMER

Acknowledgment

The following extract from Government Printing Office Form Number 1965-0795689 is presented for the information and guidance of the user:

Any organization interested in reproducing the COBOL report and specifications in whole or in part, using ideas taken from this report as the basis for an instruction manual or for any other purpose is free to do so. However, all such organizations are requested to reproduce this section as part of the introduction to the document. Those using a short passage, as in a book review, are requested to mention "COBOL" in acknowledgment of the source, but need not quote this entire section.

COBOL is an industry language and is not the property of any company or group of companies, or of any organization or group of organizations.

No warranty, expressed or implied, is made by any contributor or by the COBOL Committee as to the accuracy and functioning of the programming system and language. Moreover, no responsibility is assumed by any contributor, or by the committee, in connection therewith.

Procedures have been established for the maintenance of COBOL. Inquiries concerning the procedures for proposing changes should be directed to the Executive Committee of the Conference of Data Systems Languages.

The authors and copyright holders of the copyrighted material used herein

FLOW-MATIC (Trademark of Sperry Rand Corporation), Programming for the UNIVAC® I and II, Data Automation Systems copyrighted 1958, 1959, by Sperry Rand Corporation; IBM Commercial Translator, Form No. F28-8013, copyrighted 1959 by IBM; FACT, DSI 27A5260-2760, copyrighted 1960 by Minneapolis-Honeywell

have specifically authorized the use of this material in whole or in part, in the COBOL specifications. Such authorization extends to the reproduction and use of COBOL specifications in programming manuals or similar publications.

Contents

CONTENTS

CONTENTS

Chapter 1

Data Processing Concepts

1.1 How a Computer System Works

The physical devices which make up a *computer system* are referred to as *hardware*. From the programmer's point of view, a computer system has the functional components shown in Fig. 1-1.

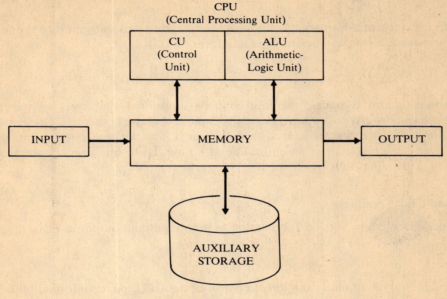

Fig. 1-1

1.2 Input

Input devices are machines which transmit information from the outside world into computer memory. In most cases, we first have to put the information into a form suitable for use by the input device, usually by some form of typing. The documents from which the information is *keyed* (typed) are called *source documents*. The three principal input devices are as follows.

Card Readers

A *keypunch*, or *card punch*, is first used to record information as holes in standard-sized cards. The deck of cards is then placed in the card reader, which electromechanically or photomechanically senses the holes in the cards and transmits the information to computer memory.

Key-to-Disk

The key-to-disk system is conceptually similar to card systems, but it records data magnetically on either a *floppy disk* or a *hard disk*. The disk is then placed in a *disk drive*, which is able to sense the magnetically encoded information and transmit it to computer memory. The disk drive reads data much faster than a card reader. Also, unlike cards, the floppy or hard disk can be reused for different data.

1

Hard Copy and CRT Terminals

Terminals can be attached to the computer so that their *keyboards* serve as an input device. Whenever a key is struck, the character corresponding to that key is transmitted to computer memory. *Intelligent terminals* have a *microprocessor* (a tiny computer on an integrated-circuit chip) and some memory built into the terminal, so that the terminal is capable of storing up characters as they are typed and transmitting them to the computer memory in groups (rather than one at a time). Intelligent terminals may also be able to do some local processing of information within the terminal itself. Both intelligent and *dumb* terminals also have output devices as part of the terminal: *hard copy* terminals have a typewriterlike printer, while *cathode-ray tube* (*CRT*) terminals have a video screen.

1.3   Output

Output devices receive information from computer memory and transmit it to the outside world, either in *human-readable* or in *machine-readable* form.

Printers

These devices record computer memory contents as printed characters on paper. In *impact printers*, an inked ribbon strikes the paper; *nonimpact printers* may use thermal, electrostatic, laser, or other techniques to form character images on the paper. *Character printers* print one character at a time, while faster *line printers* print an entire line at a time. Laser line printers are now capable of rates exceeding 20 000 lines/min.

Hard Copy and CRT Terminals

The devices described in Section 1.2 function as both input and output devices.

Card Punches

These devices, operating under the direct control of the CPU, punch information into cards.

Magnetic Disk

Disk drives which input information from floppy or hard disks can also record information on the disks.

1.4   Auxiliary Storage

Devices capable of both input and output can serve as *auxiliary storage devices*, which are needed because: (i) even the largest computer memory could not hold all the information needed by a relatively small business, and (ii) modern computer memories are wiped clean if the power is shut off, so that even if all needed information would fit in memory, it would be an unacceptable risk to keep it there.

Hard Disk

In this, the most important auxiliary storage device, a disk drive is utilized to read data from or write data onto a *disk pack*. A disk pack consists of a stack of flat aluminum platters, coated with a magnetic material, on a central spindle (Fig. 1-2). An *access arm* housing a set of *read/write heads* (one head for each surface) can be moved in and out. In a stopping position, the access arm puts the heads opposite a set of circular *tracks* on the surfaces of the rotating disk pack; data are recorded along these tracks. Tracks are organized into sets called *cylinders*, the group of tracks accessible at any one stopping position of the access mechanism.

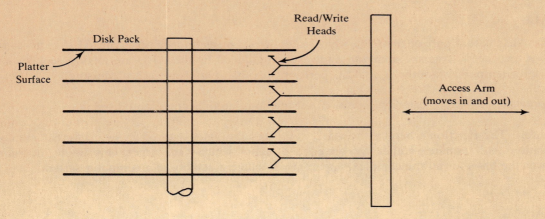

Fig. 1-2

The average time to move the access arm to a desired cylinder (*access time*) falls in the 16–60 millisecond range (a *millisecond*, ms, is 1/1000 of a second). To this time must be added the *rotational delay* (the time for the desired spot on the track to be spun under the chosen head) and the (small) time needed to transfer the data to or from memory. The overall *retrieval time* is of the order of 30 ms for IBM disks.

Some disks (called *fixed head-per-track*) have a read/write head for every track of the disk pack, thereby reducing the access time to zero.

Magnetic Tape

Computer tape is similar in principle to audio recording tape, and can be packaged in reels or cassettes. Information is recorded magnetically along the length of the tape.

A major disadvantage of tape as auxiliary storage is that the tape drive must read through all the information in front of a desired piece of information in order to get to that piece. Hence, tape is efficient only if we process the information in the same sequence in which it is physically stored on the tape (*sequential processing*). Information stored on disk can be processed in any order we desire (*random processing*).

1.5   Memory

Computer memory is made up of electronic components each of which can store one *binary digit* (*bit*) of information. Since a bit can only have the value zero or one, bits are grouped into units of (usually) eight, called *bytes*. One byte is enough computer memory to hold one *character* of information.

Memory bytes are numbered $0, 1, 2, 3, \ldots$; the unique number assigned to identify a byte is called its *address*. Random access to a given address can be accomplished in a matter of *nanoseconds* (ns, 1/1 000 000 000 of a second).

Memory and auxiliary storage capacity is measured in terms of KB (*kilobyte*, roughly a thousand bytes) and MB (*megabyte*, roughly a million bytes). A memory of roughly 128 000 bytes would be called a 128K memory, while a memory of roughly 2 000 000 bytes would be called a 2M memory. Typical disk packs might hold between 29 MB and 1260 MB, depending on the model.

The constant flow of information into memory from input devices and/or auxiliary storage devices, the processing of information while it's in memory, and the final transfer of results either to output devices or to auxiliary storage (for permanent storage in a form easily accessible to the computer)—all this constitutes the *input-process-output cycle* characteristic of almost all business data processing.

1.6   ALU

The ALU is that part of the CPU which actually processes information. The ALU receives the data it is to process from the memory, and results produced by the ALU are in turn sent back to memory for temporary storage. The ALU performs two basic kinds of data processing:

Arithmetic.   The operations of addition, subtraction, multiplication, and division.

Logic.   The function whereby the ALU compares the values stored in two different memory locations to determine whether they are equal or, if not, which is the larger. This simple "decision" forms the basis for all the complex, apparently intelligent activity of a computer system.

1.7   CU

Modern computers operate on the concept of a *stored program*, which allows us to change the task the computer performs (e.g., payroll versus inventory) simply by inputting a different succession of instructions (the program) into its memory. The control unit is designed to *execute* the stored program, as follows:

(1)   The first thing the CU does is to *fetch* the stored instruction whose address is in a special storage area called the IAR (Instruction Address Register).

(2)   The CU next *decodes* the instruction fetched from memory; i.e., it analyzes the instruction to determine what is to be done (what *operation* is to be carried out) and what data are to be used in the operation (what are the memory addresses of the *operands*).

(3)   The CU now replaces the address in the IAR with that of the *next* stored instruction.

(4)   Finally, the CU sends signals to the rest of the system to ensure that the indicated operation is carried out. Thus, for an addition operation, the control unit would arrange for the memory to send copies of the values to be added to the ALU. It would then cause the ALU to actually perform the addition and send the sum back to the desired memory location. For an input or output operation, the CU would activate the indicated *I/O device* and the memory, causing proper transfer of data.

When these four phases of control unit operation are completed, the cycle simply starts over again at step 1. (The IAR was reset in step 3.)

The programmer can alter this normal *sequential execution* by putting *branch instructions* in his or her program. A branch instruction changes the IAR so that it contains an address other than that of the physically next instruction, thus causing the computer to resume normal sequential execution at the indicated branch address.

We measure the speed with which modern computers can execute instructions in *MIPS* (millions instructions·per second). Computers now on the market operate at from 0.2 to 11.0 MIPS; these typical figures can be expected constantly to increase.

1.8   Programming Languages

As stored in computer memory and executed by the CPU, program instructions have the form of strings of binary digits; we say that they are expressed in *machine language*. Humans, however, find it more convenient to write (and read) programs in some *higher-level language*, such as COBOL. The necessary translation of the higher-level language program (the *source program*) into the machine-language equivalent (the *object program*) is done by the computer itself, under the control of a special program called a *compiler*. Compilers are usually written by the company which produces the hardware and are kept in auxiliary storage, in machine-language form.

The process of compilation (of a source program written in COBOL) is diagrammed in Fig. 1-3. If the compiler detects errors in construction (*syntax errors*) in the source program, it will also cause *diagnostic error messages* to be printed on the source listing.

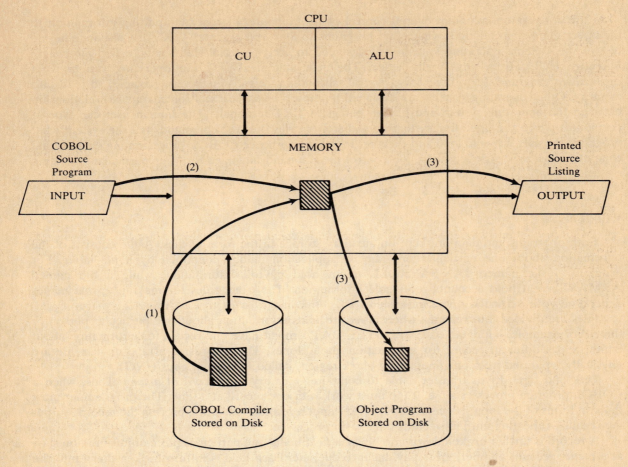

(1)   The compiler is brought from auxiliary storage into memory.
(2)   The compiler is executed by the computer, causing the COBOL source program to be read and translated.
(3)   Instructions in the compiler cause the object program to be placed on disk (for later use) and the *source listing*, a copy of the source program, to be printed.

Fig. 1-3

If syntax errors were detected, the programmer must correct them and recompile the modified source program. This new source program (or the original source program, if no syntax errors were found) must now be *debugged*; that is, it must be run with a set of input data for which the correct corresponding output data are known in advance. This procedure is designed to detect any *logic errors* in the program; e.g., telling the machine to add (instead of multiply) hours worked and hourly wage rate to calculate gross pay. During debugging, the source program will have to be recompiled each time it is modified to eliminate a logic error.

After the program has been debugged, the final version of the object program is permanently saved on auxiliary storage so that it can be read into computer memory and executed as needed.

1.9   Operating Systems

Rather than give slow, human *operators* the responsibility for *loading* object programs into memory for execution, computer manufacturers and other specialists have written programs called *operating systems* which allow the computer itself to take over this task, at machine speeds. These operating-system programs are permanently stored in machine-language form on disk.

Human operators maintain overall control of the computer system by inputting information to the operating system telling it what other programs to load and execute. This is usually done in one of two ways. Some operating systems are designed to accept special statements, called *job control language* (JCL), from any input device. The JCL statements tell the operating system what *applications programs* (e.g., inventory, payroll, accounts receivable, accounts payable) to load into memory. Other operating systems are designed to allow a *conversational* (or *interactive*) relationship between the operating system and human beings at CRT terminals. The human user can type in *commands* which the operating system immediately carries out; the commands tell the system what programs the user wants to load and execute. In order to practice COBOL programming on an actual computer, you must first learn the job control or command language for your particular operating system.

1.10   Files

Both programs and data are kept on auxiliary storage in the form of files. A *file* consists of the information about one particular program or application, and is identified by a *file name*. For example, a file named JAN.PAYROLL might hold payroll information, while a file named ARMAST might hold accounts receivable information. The exact rules for making up file names depend on your particular operating system.

Files are divided into records, where a *record* holds information about one particular person or thing. For example, a file named EMPLOYEE.DATA might have one record for information about Smith, and a different record for information about Jones. The records in a tape or disk file are physically separated from one another by blank regions called *interrecord gaps* (IRG).

Disk and tape drives transfer a file to computer memory *one record at a time*. Thus, when a COBOL program processes a file, it too must work with one record at a time. The programmer must think in terms of the input-process-output cycle: input a record from a file, process the record, output the results—repeating until all records have been processed.

A record is further broken down into fields, a *field* being one particular piece of information such as a name, account number, gross pay, balance due, etc. Each field is in turn broken down into the individual *bytes* (or *characters*) which make it up. The file/record/field/character hierarchy is illustrated in Fig. 1-4.

Most operating systems maintain a *file label* for each file on a tape or disk. The file label is a special record that contains such fields as the name of the file, when it was created, how long it should be retained, where the file is located (on disk), the size of the file, password information which secures the file from unauthorized access, etc. Tape file labels immediately precede and follow the file

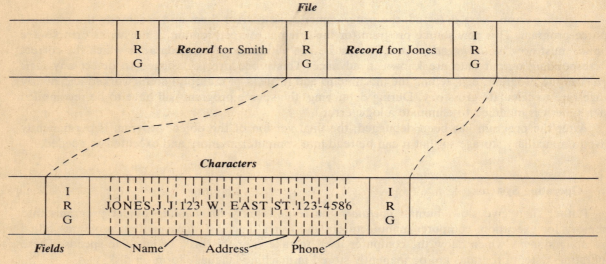

Fig. 1-4

itself on the tape; disk file labels are usually grouped together in what is called a *volume table of contents* (*VTOC*) or *directory*. The operating system can locate any file on a disk pack by searching the directory for its file label. The use of file labels helps ensure that programs process the right files.

1.11 Data Codes

The fundamental unit of memory and auxiliary storage is, as we know, the binary digit, or bit. Any information stored in these parts of the system must be *coded* as a string of binary digits. For purposes of coding, it is convenient to classify data as follows:

Alphanumeric (or *alphameric*) data may be made up of any characters from an input keyboard or an output video screen or printer. This class includes all the *letters* of the alphabet, the *digits* 0 to 9, and all other *special characters* such as @, #, $, %, &, *, (,), -, +, blank space, etc. The field "John W. Doe" is alphanumeric (note the special character "."), as is "238-9761" (note the special character "-").

Alphabetic data are made up of the letters of the alphabet along with the character blank space. "John W Doe" is alphabetic, as is "N SPRINT ST"; "John W. Doe" and "43 N SPRINT ST" are not.

Numeric data consist of the digits 0 to 9 along with an optional + or − sign. In some cases numeric data may include a decimal point ("."), but often decimal points are just *assumed* to be present. Examples of numeric data are "1278", "−53", "1.28", and "1͵28" (where ͵ represents an assumed decimal point).

The following *codes* are used to represent alphanumeric, alphabetic, and numeric data as binary numbers suitable for storage within a computer system:

DISPLAY (*EBCDIC* and *ASCII*).   EBCDIC (Extended Binary-Coded Decimal Interchange Code) and ASCII (American Standard Code for Information Interchange) are the two most common codes used to represent alphanumeric data. Both codes represent each alphanumeric character (including the blank space) as an 8-bit binary number (hence each character requires one byte of memory or auxiliary storage). The full codes are listed in Appendix B.

Printers, card readers, and hard copy and CRT terminals are all designed to transmit either EBCDIC or ASCII to/from memory. In COBOL, EBCDIC- or ASCII-coded data are said to be in *DISPLAY* format.

COMP-3 (*packed-decimal*).   Packed-decimal is a code used strictly for numeric data in memory or auxiliary storage; it is *not* used by any input or output devices, nor is it available on all computers. In COBOL, packed-decimal numbers are said to be in *COMP-3* format. Packed-decimal coding has the following advantages over EBCDIC and ASCII: (i) the ALU can directly calculate with packed-decimal numbers (if numbers entering a calculation are EBCDIC or ASCII, the object program must temporarily *convert* them to packed-decimal for the computation, then reconvert the result to the original EBCDIC or ASCII); (ii) packed-decimal numbers take fewer bytes than the same numbers represented in EBCDIC or ASCII.

COMP (*binary-twos-complement*).   Binary-twos-complement has the same application and advantages as packed-decimal; in COBOL, binary-twos-complement numbers are said to be in *COMP* format.

Almost every computer will support some version of binary-twos-complement; some will support packed-decimal also. See Chapter 5 for a discussion of when to use each of the above codes.

Chapter 2

COBOL Overview

One of COBOL's important features is that it is largely *self-documenting*: a programmer can understand most of a COBOL program simply by reading the program code itself. Examine the complete COBOL program of Example 2.1, which will be referred to repeatedly in this chapter.

EXAMPLE 2.1

```
00001              IDENTIFICATION DIVISION.
00002
00003              PROGRAM-ID. QUARTER.
00004              AUTHOR. LARRY NEWCOMER.
00005              INSTALLATION.  PENN STATE UNIVERSITY--YORK CAMPUS.
00006              DATE-WRITTEN.  MAY 1983.
00007              DATE-COMPILED. MAY  9,1983.
00008              SECURITY.   THERE ARE NO SECURITY CONSIDERATIONS FOR QUARTER.
00009         *
00010         *OVERVIEW OF PROGRAM QUARTER--
00011         *
00012         *    QUARTER READS A FILE CONTAINING SALESPERSON MONTHLY
00013         *    SALES FOR THE 3 MONTHS IN A QUARTER ALONG WITH THE
00014         *    SALESPERSON´S NAME AND QUARTERLY QUOTA SALES AMOUNT.
00015         *    IT PRINTS A REPORT SHOWING SALESPERSON:
00016         *
00017         *       NAME      QUARTERLY SALES        QUOTA
00018         *
00019         *       JONES      $42,000.98         $40,000.00
00020         *       SMITH      $59,000.67         $60,000.00
00021         *       YOST       $47,893.00         $45,000.00
00022         *
00023
00024              ENVIRONMENT DIVISION.
00025
00026              CONFIGURATION SECTION.
00027              SOURCE-COMPUTER. IBM-370.
00028              OBJECT-COMPUTER. IBM-370.
00029
00030              INPUT-OUTPUT SECTION.
00031              FILE-CONTROL.
00032                  SELECT SALES-FILE         ASSIGN TO SALES.
00033                  SELECT QUARTERLY-REPORT ASSIGN TO SALESRPT.
00034
00035              DATA DIVISION.
00036
00037              FILE SECTION.
00038
00039              FD SALES-FILE
00040                  LABEL RECORDS ARE STANDARD
00041                  RECORD CONTAINS 80 CHARACTERS
00042                  .
00043              01  SALES-RECORD.
00044                  05  SALES-RECORD-NAME            PIC X(15).
00045                  05  SALES-RECORD-MONTH-1-SALES   PIC S9(4)V99.
00046                  05  SALES-RECORD-MONTH-2-SALES   PIC S9(4)V99.
00047                  05  SALES-RECORD-MONTH-3-SALES   PIC S9(4)V99.
00048                  05  SALES-RECORD-QUOTA           PIC S9(5)V99.
00049                  05  FILLER                       PIC X(40).
```

```
00050
00051            FD   QUARTERLY-REPORT
00052                 LABEL RECORDS ARE OMITTED
00053                 RECORD CONTAINS 132 CHARACTERS
00054                 .
00055            01   QUARTERLY-REPORT-LINE               PIC X(132).
00056
00057        WORKING-STORAGE SECTION.
00058
00059            01   SWITCHES-AND-TOTALS.
00060                 05   SALES-FILE-END                 PIC X.
00061                 05   QUARTERLY-TOTAL                PIC S9(5)V99      COMP-3.
00062            01   WORKING-REPORT-LINE.
00063                 05   WORKING-NAME                   PIC X(15).
00064                 05   FILLER                         PIC X(5)      VALUE SPACES.
00065                 05   WORKING-TOTAL                  PIC $$$,$$$.99.
00066                 05   FILLER                         PIC X(5)      VALUE SPACES.
00067                 05   WORKING-QUOTA                  PIC $$$,$$$.99.
00068                 05   FILLER                         PIC X(87)     VALUE SPACES.
00069
00070        PROCEDURE DIVISION.
00071
00072            010-EXECUTIVE-PARA.
00073                PERFORM 020-INITIALIZE-AND-SET-UP
00074                PERFORM 040-PRINT-REPORT-LINES
00075                    UNTIL SALES-FILE-END = "T"
00076                PERFORM 050-TERMINATION-AND-WIND-UP
00077                STOP RUN
00078                .
00079
00080            020-INITIALIZE-AND-SET-UP.
00081                OPEN  INPUT  SALES-FILE
00082                       OUTPUT QUARTERLY-REPORT
00083                MOVE "F" TO SALES-FILE-END
00084                PERFORM 030-READ-SALES-FILE
00085                .
00086
00087            030-READ-SALES-FILE.
00088                READ SALES-FILE
00089                    AT END
00090                         MOVE "T" TO SALES-FILE-END
00091                .
00092
00093            040-PRINT-REPORT-LINES.
00094                MOVE SALES-RECORD-NAME TO WORKING-NAME
00095                COMPUTE QUARTERLY-TOTAL =   SALES-RECORD-MONTH-1-SALES
00096                                        +  SALES-RECORD-MONTH-2-SALES
00097                                        +  SALES-RECORD-MONTH-3-SALES
00098                MOVE QUARTERLY-TOTAL TO WORKING-TOTAL
00099                MOVE SALES-RECORD-QUOTA TO WORKING-QUOTA
00100                WRITE QUARTERLY-REPORT-LINE
00101                    FROM WORKING-REPORT-LINE
00102                PERFORM 030-READ-SALES-FILE
00103                .
00104
00105            050-TERMINATION-AND-WIND-UP.
00106                CLOSE   SALES-FILE
00107                        QUARTERLY-REPORT
00108                .
```

2.1 The COBOL DIVISIONs

A COBOL program always consists of four main parts, called DIVISIONs, in the following order: IDENTIFICATION, ENVIRONMENT, DATA, and PROCEDURE. At the beginning of each DIVISION is a special COBOL statement called a *division header*.

EXAMPLE 2.2   The division headers in Example 2.1 are

> line 1:   IDENTIFICATION DIVISION.
> line 24:   ENVIRONMENT DIVISION.
> line 35:   DATA DIVISION.
> line 70:   PROCEDURE DIVISION.

The IDENTIFICATION DIVISION provides the name of the program, who wrote it, when and where it was written, when it was compiled, and what security precautions (if any) should be taken to restrict access to the program or to the files it processes. The DIVISION should end with a set of English sentences giving a brief overview of what the program does (lines 9 through 22 in Example 2.1).

The ENVIRONMENT DIVISION contains information about the computer(s) on which the COBOL program will be compiled and on which the resulting machine-language program will be run. It also gives a COBOL name to each file to be processed and assigns each file to a specified I/O device. This information defines the *hardware environment* in which the program will run.

EXAMPLE 2.3   In Example 2.1:

●   line 27:   SOURCE-COMPUTER. IBM-370.
specifies the computer used to compile the source program;

●   line 28:   OBJECT-COMPUTER. IBM-370.
specifies the computer used to execute the resulting object program;

●   lines 32–33:   SELECT SALES-FILE ASSIGN TO SALES.
>   SELECT QUARTERLY-REPORT ASSIGN TO SALESRPT.
assign files to their respective I/O devices.

The DATA DIVISION gives a brief description of each file to be processed, and then gives a detailed layout for the records in the file. Each field in a record is described in terms of its length and its type of data. The DATA DIVISION also describes data fields used by the program that are not in file records; such fields are stored in a memory area called WORKING-STORAGE. *All data fields* (in file records or in WORKING-STORAGE) *must be described* in the DATA DIVISION.

EXAMPLE 2.4   Lines 39–49 of Example 2.1 describe the input sales file and the records it contains:

```
FD   SALES-FILE
     LABEL RECORDS ARE STANDARD
     RECORD CONTAINS 80 CHARACTERS

01   SALES-RECORD.
     05   SALES-RECORD-NAME            PIC X(15).
     05   SALES-RECORD-MONTH-1-SALES   PIC S9(4)V99.
     05   SALES-RECORD-MONTH-2-SALES   PIC S9(4)V99.
     05   SALES-RECORD-MONTH-3-SALES   PIC S9(4)V99.
     05   SALES-RECORD-QUOTA           PIC S9(5)V99.
     05   FILLER                       PIC X(40).
```

Lines 57–68 describe WORKING-STORAGE data items which are not part of any file records:

```
WORKING-STORAGE SECTION.

01    SWITCHES-AND-TOTALS.
      05   SALES-FILE-END      PIC X.
      05   QUARTERLY-TOTAL     PIC S9(5)V99   COMP-3.
```

```
01    WORKING-REPORT-LINE.
      05   WORKING-NAME               PIC X(15).
      05   FILLER                     PIC X(5)  VALUE SPACES.
      05   WORKING-TOTAL              PIC $$$,$$$.99.
      05   FILLER                     PIC X(5)  VALUE SPACES.
      05   WORKING-QUOTA              PIC $$$,$$$.99.
      05   FILLER                     PIC X(87) VALUE SPACES.
```

It is in the PROCEDURE DIVISION that the computer is actually instructed as to what processing is to be carried out. The directions closely resemble English sentences.

EXAMPLE 2.5   The following PROCEDURE DIVISION statements are taken from Example 2.1.

●   PERFORM 020-INITIALIZE-AND-SET-UP

(line 73) causes all the statements in the COBOL *paragraph* named "020-INITIALIZE-AND-SET-UP" (lines 80–85) to be executed once before the computer goes on to execute the statement following "PERFORM 020-INITIALIZE-AND-SET-UP" (i.e., line 74).

●   PERFORM 040-PRINT-REPORT-LINES UNTIL SALES-FILE-END = "T"

(lines 74–75) causes the computer to execute the statements in the paragraph named "040-PRINT-REPORT-LINES" (lines 93–103) over and over, in sequence, until the data item named "SALES-FILE-END" contains the value "T". When this has occurred, the computer goes on to the next statement (i.e., line 76).

●   OPEN INPUT SALES-FILE OUTPUT QUARTERLY-REPORT

(lines 81–82) The OPEN statement prepares a file for processing and indicates whether the file will be used for input or output. A file must be OPENed before it can be used by the program.

●   MOVE SALES-RECORD-NAME TO WORKING-NAME

(line 94) The MOVE statement copies the contents of one storage location (in this case, the location assigned to the data item SALES-RECORD-NAME) into another storage location (here, that assigned to the data item WORKING-NAME).

●   COMPUTE QUARTERLY-TOTAL = SALES-RECORD-MONTH-1-SALES
                               + SALES-RECORD-MONTH-2-SALES
                               + SALES-RECORD-MONTH-3-SALES

(lines 95–97) The COMPUTE statement is used to carry out a numeric computation. The result of the computation is stored in the data item (i.e., in the memory location assigned to that data item) named on the left-hand side of the equals sign.

2.2   SECTIONs and Paragraphs

Each DIVISION of a COBOL program is broken down into *SECTION*s, beginning in special lines called *section headers*, and each SECTION in turn is broken down into *paragraphs*.

EXAMPLE 2.6   The section headers in Example 2.1 are:

```
line 26:   CONFIGURATION SECTION.
line 30:   INPUT-OUTPUT SECTION.
line 37:   FILE SECTION.
line 57:   WORKING-STORAGE SECTION.
```

Section headers consist of the name of the section followed by the word "SECTION" and a period. SECTION names in the ENVIRONMENT and DATA DIVISIONs are a fixed part of the COBOL language and cannot be changed (such words are called *reserved words*). SECTIONs are optional in the PROCEDURE DIVISION; when they are used, their names must follow the rules for COBOL words (such names are *programmer-defined names*). The IDENTIFICATION DIVISION has no SECTIONs.

Paragraphs in COBOL may be part of a SECTION or can stand alone within their DIVISION. In all cases, paragraphs are identified by a *paragraph header*, which consists solely of the name of the paragraph followed by a period. Paragraph names in the IDENTIFICATION, ENVIRONMENT, and DATA DIVISIONs are a fixed part of COBOL and cannot be changed. Paragraphs in the PROCEDURE DIVISION are optional and their names are made up by the programmer.

EXAMPLE 2.7 The IDENTIFICATION DIVISION consists only of paragraphs (no SECTIONs). The paragraph names used in the IDENTIFICATION DIVISION of Example 2.1 are

PROGRAM-ID   AUTHOR   INSTALLATION   DATE-WRITTEN   DATE-COMPILED
SECURITY

These paragraph names are a fixed part of the COBOL language.

EXAMPLE 2.8 The PROCEDURE DIVISION of a COBOL program may or may not be composed of SECTIONs. Example 2.1 uses only paragraphs in the PROCEDURE DIVISION, their programmer-defined names being

010-EXECUTIVE-PARA   020-INITIALIZE-AND-SET-UP   030-READ-SALES-FILE
040-PRINT-REPORT-LINES   050-TERMINATION-AND-WIND-UP

Although it is not a requirement of the COBOL language, these paragraph names all start with numbers—a practice that makes it much easier to find a desired paragraph in a program listing (*assuming the numbers are kept in order*).

Use of the Period

Paragraphs in the PROCEDURE DIVISION are made up of sentences, and, just as in English, sentences are defined by use of the period. Although COBOL allows a period at the end of every statement, it is a good idea to use periods in the PROCEDURE DIVISION only when absolutely necessary. Observe that in the PROCEDURE DIVISION of Example 2.1, periods are given their own lines. This use of the period (the *structured period*) is recommended because it makes the period stand out visually, allows the insertion of new statements in front of the period, and helps to eliminate logic errors.

EXAMPLE 2.9 In COBOL, periods should be used at the end of every paragraph. Sometimes they are also needed to separate one statement from another within a paragraph. The PROCEDURE DIVISION in Example 2.1 uses (i) a period after the DIVISION header (line 70); (ii) a period after each paragraph header (lines 72, 80, 87, 93, and 105); and (iii) a structured period at the end of each paragraph (lines 78, 85, 91, 103, and 108).

EXAMPLE 2.10 Lines 42 and 54 of Example 2.1 contain structured periods. These are parts of the DATA DIVISION that may require the addition or deletion of COBOL lines as changes are made to the program; the structured period facilitates such changes. However, the usual rule is that, outside the PROCEDURE DIVISION, periods are placed on the same line as the entry they terminate.

2.3 Rules for Typing COBOL Programs

COBOL programmers usually write their programs on special, pre-printed, *COBOL coding forms* (Fig. 2-1). Columns 1–6 of each line are used for sequence numbers, which make it easier to put the program back together again in case lines are accidently shuffled. Columns 73–80 of each line are used for program identification; an abbreviation of the program name is typed in these columns. Sequence numbers and identification were important when programs were punched into cards, because card decks could be dropped. Now that programs are usually typed on CRT terminals and stored on disk, there is less concern with sequencing and identification.

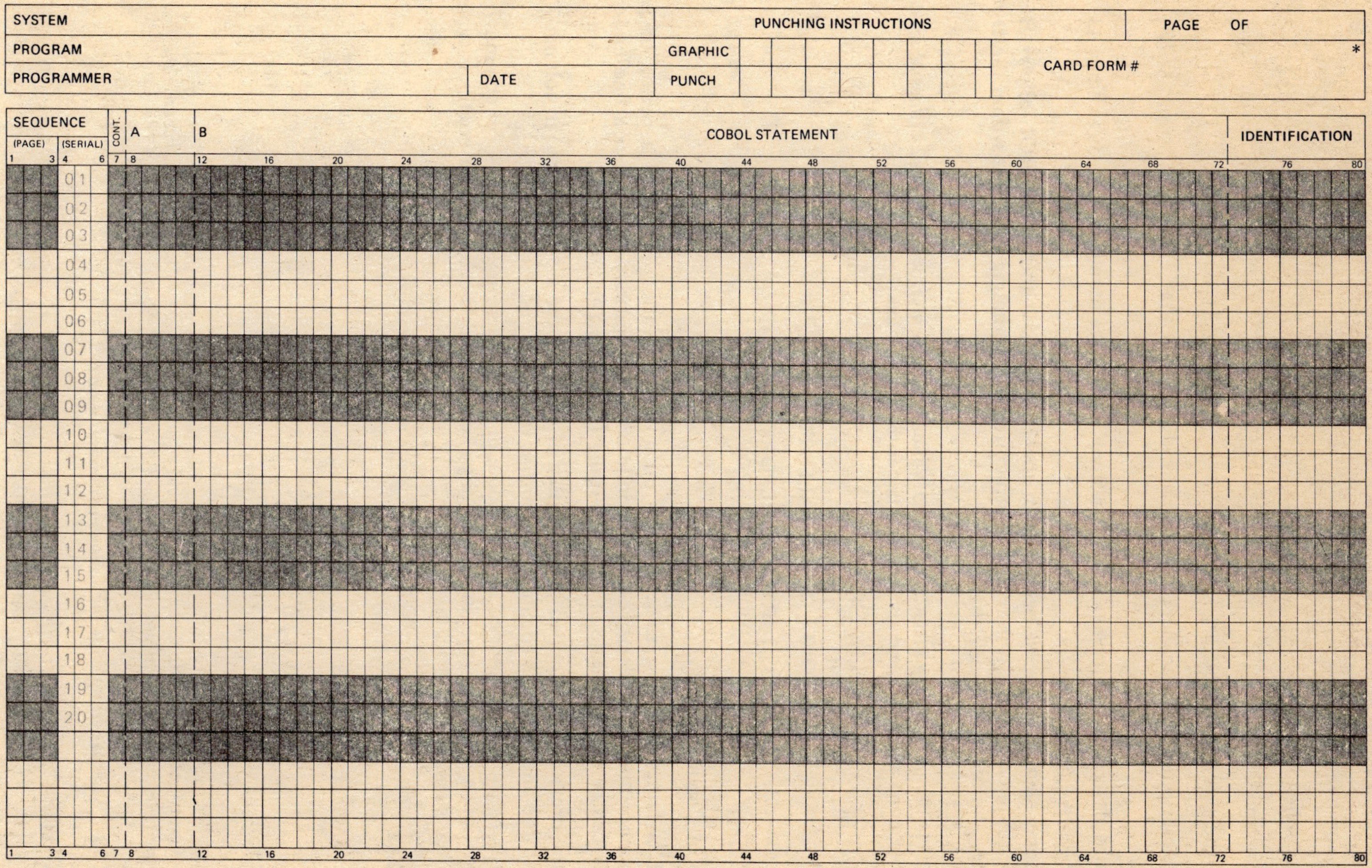
SYSTEM
PUNCHING INSTRUCTIONS
PAGE OF
PROGRAM
GRAPHIC
CARD FORM #
*
PROGRAMMER
DATE
PUNCH
SEQUENCE
(PAGE)
(SERIAL)
CONT.
A
B
COBOL STATEMENT
IDENTIFICATION
01
02
03
04
05
06
07
08
09
10
11
12
13
14
15
16
17
18
19
20

Fig. 2-1

COBOL statements themselves are typed in columns 8–72. Columns 8–11 make up the *A margin*, and columns 12–72 the *B margin*. The following items should begin in the A margin:

- division headers

- section headers

- paragraph headers

and, within the DATA DIVISION,

- file description entry headers (starting with the letters "FD", as in lines 39 and 51 of Example 2.1)

- record description entry headers (data items with level number "01", as in lines 43, 55, 59, and 62 of Example 2.1)

All other items should be typed beginning in the B margin. Although COBOL allows B margin entries to begin in column 12, it is crucial in structured programming to indent within the B margin, to clarify the relationships among the lines.

EXAMPLE 2.11   In the following PROCEDURE DIVISION statements from Example 2.1, lines which continue a statement begun on a previous line are indented under the original line:

- lines 88–90:   READ SALES-FILE
                            AT END
                                MOVE "T" TO SALES-FILE-END

- lines 100–101:   WRITE QUARTERLY-REPORT-LINE
                                FROM WORKING-REPORT-LINE

Special Uses of Column 7

COBOL assumes that a statement keeps on going, line after line, until a period or another statement is encountered. Special rules for continuation are needed only when a line ends in the middle of a word or in the middle of a *quoted string* (Section 5.19):

(1) If the previous line stopped in the middle of a word, type a "-" (hyphen) in column 7 of the next line and continue spelling the word in the B margin.

(2) If the previous line stopped in the middle of a quoted string, type a "-" in column 7 of the next line, repeat the opening quote anywhere in the B margin, and continue typing the quoted string.

EXAMPLE 2.12

```
          MOVE "THANK YOU FOR YOUR
     -           "PROMPT PAYMENT" TO
                 CUSTOMER-MESSAGE
     col.  col.  col.
      7    12    16
```

While displaying proper continuation, the above would produce many unwanted blanks, *because the first line of the quoted string is assumed to go all the way to column 72* (and no further).

EXAMPLE 2.13   What is wrong with the following continuation?

```
          MOVE "OVER
     -           "PAYMENT" TO NEGATIVE-BALANCE-MESSAGE
     col.  col.  col.
      7    12    16
```

(*a*) The continuation could have been avoided in the first place:

            MOVE "OVERPAYMENT"

                TO NEGATIVE-BALANCE-MESSAGE

(*b*) Because the first line extends all the way to column 72, the message would actually look like

            "OVER   PAYMENT"

which is not what was intended.

When a "*" is typed in column 7, the rest of the line is treated as a COBOL *comment*. This means that although the compiler prints the line on the source listing, it does not translate the line into the object program. Comments are used to explain what a program is doing and/or how it does it. They are intended for other COBOL programmers, who may have to make changes in the program. Remember: to the extent that COBOL really is a self-documenting language, comments are superfluous—use them only when further clarification is truly necessary.

EXAMPLE 2.14 Comments are illustrated by lines 9–22 of Example 2.1.

Column 7 is also used to insert *debugging lines* into a COBOL program. Debugging lines are simply COBOL statements with a "D" typed in column 7. As their name implies, they are used to help locate and correct the errors in a program. (See Section 4.2.)

Blank Lines

Blank lines may appear in a COBOL program; they are used to make the source listing more readable. (Lines 2, 23, 25, 29, . . . , 104 make Example 2.1 more readable.)

Some programmers prefer *blank comment lines* (lines with only a "*" in column 7), because the compiler can process a comment line faster than a totally blank line. However, the advantage is minuscule, and we shall employ totally blank lines.

2.4 Programmer-Defined Names and Reserved Words

The individual words which make up a COBOL program are formed according to the following rules:

(1) No more than 30 characters in length

(2) Allowed characters are the letters A through Z, the digits 0 through 9, and the hyphen

(3) Must not begin or end with a hyphen

(4) No embedded blanks

Some of the words in a COBOL program are considered as peculiar to the COBOL language and as serving one and only one predefined purpose. These *reserved words* include "IDEN-TIFICATION", "DIVISION", "DATE-WRITTEN", "INPUT-OUTPUT", "SECTION", "WORKING-STORAGE", "MOVE", "OPEN", and "COMPUTE"; for a complete list see Appendix A. Programmer-defined names, constructed according to the above rules, *may not* duplicate the spelling of any reserved word. Among programmer-defined words are:

- file names used in SELECT statements and file descriptions (FDs) (see lines 32, 33, 39, and 51 of Example 2.1)

- names of records, and fields within records in the DATA DIVISION (lines 43–49, 55, 59–68)

- names of paragraphs and SECTIONs in the PROCEDURE DIVISION (lines 72, 80, 87, 93, 105)

EXAMPLE 2.15

(*a*) Compare the following pairs of programmer-defined names:

- YTDAS or YEAR-TO-DATE-AVERAGE-SALES

- GPA or CUMULATIVE-GRADE-POINT-AVERAGE

- EXTRA or YEAR-END-BONUS-PAY

When in doubt, spell it out—it's hard to go wrong being too descriptive.

(*b*) The following programmer-defined names are invalid or undesirable:

- RECORD (invalid: duplicates a reserved word)

- STUDENT-BODY-CUMULATIVE-GRADE-POINT-AVERAGE (invalid: more than 30 characters)

- -OUT-OF-STOCK (invalid: begins with a hyphen)

- N (undesirable: not descriptive)

- TOTAL-$SALES (invalid: contains a forbidden character)

2.5 Getting Started

We have at this point barely scratched the surface of COBOL programming. However, *any* programming language is best learned by *doing*. The two COBOL programs that follow will serve as guides in carrying out the Programming Assignments given at the end of this chapter. To actually test the programs you will write, you will have to consult an instructor or experienced programmer about the job-control or command-language statements needed on your computer system.

EXAMPLE 2.16 A complete COBOL program. All comments are presented as part of the program (using comment lines). Sample output follows this actual source listing.

```
00001          IDENTIFICATION DIVISION.
00002
00003          PROGRAM-ID. PHONELST.
00004
00005          AUTHOR.   LARRY NEWCOMER.
00006          INSTALLATION.   PENN STATE UNIVERSITY--YORK CAMPUS.
00007
00008          DATE-WRITTEN.   MAY 1983.
00009          DATE-COMPILED. MAY  9,1983.
00011     *    PHONELST PRODUCES A PRINTED LISTING OF ALL EMPLOYEE
00012     *    NAMES AND PHONE NUMBERS.   NAMES AND PHONE NUMBERS ARE
00013     *    INPUT FROM A CARD FILE WHICH IS MAINTAINED IN ALPHABETICAL
00014     *    ORDER BY EMPLOYEE NAME.   THE ONLY OUTPUT IS A PRINTED
00015     *    COPY OF NAMES AND PHONE NUMBERS -- SINGLE SPACED, WITH
00016     *    NO HEADINGS, PAGE NUMBERS, ETC. (KEEP IT SIMPLE)

00018          ENVIRONMENT DIVISION.

00020          CONFIGURATION SECTION.

00022     *    THE CONFIGURATION SECTION DESCRIBES THE COMPUTER SYSTEM
00023     *    TO BE USED TO COMPILE THE COBOL PROGRAM
00024     *    (SOURCE-COMPUTER), AND THE COMPUTER SYSTEM TO BE USED TO
00025     *    EXECUTE THE RESULTING OBJECT PROGRAM (OBJECT-COMPUTER).
00026
00027          SOURCE-COMPUTER. IBM-370.
00028          OBJECT-COMPUTER. IBM-370.
```

```
00030          INPUT-OUTPUT SECTION.

00032           FILE-CONTROL.

00034     *     THE FILE-CONTROL PARAGRAPH OF THE INPUT-OUTPUT SECTION
00035     *     BEGINS TO DEFINE THE FILES TO BE PROCESSED BY THIS PROGRAM:
00036
00037           SELECT CARD-FILE                ASSIGN TO CARDS.
00038           SELECT PRINT-FILE               ASSIGN TO PRINTER.
00039
00040     *     THESE STATEMENTS GIVE COBOL NAMES TO THE FILES TO BE
00041     *     PROCESSED.  IN THIS CASE THE INPUT FILE IS KNOWN AS
00042     *     CARD-FILE AND THE OUTPUT FILE IS KNOWN AS PRINT-FILE.
00043
00044     *     THE SELECT STATEMENTS ALSO ASSIGN EACH FILE TO A JOB
00045     *     CONTROL LANGUAGE STATEMENT WHICH WILL PROVIDE FURTHER
00046     *     INFORMATION REGARDING THE ACTUAL I/O DEVICE TO BE USED.
00047     *     CONSULT YOUR INSTRUCTOR OR AN EXPERIENCED PROGRAMMER
00048     *     REGARDING WHAT JOB CONTROL LANGUAGE IS NEEDED TO RUN
00049     *     A COBOL PROGRAM ON YOUR SYSTEM.

00051           DATA DIVISION.

00053     *         THE DATA DIVISION DESCRIBES ALL DATA ITEMS TO BE
00054     *         PROCESSED BY THIS PROGRAM.
00055
00056           FILE SECTION.

00058     *         THE FILE SECTION PROVIDES ADDITIONAL INFORMATION FOR
00059     *         EACH FILE NAMED IN A SELECT STATEMENT.  NOTICE THAT
00060     *         THE SELECT FILE NAME AND THE "FD" FILE NAME ARE THE
00061     *         SAME.  THERE MUST BE A FILE DESCRIPTION ("FD") FOR
00062     *         EACH FILE.
00063
00064        FD  CARD-FILE
00065            RECORD CONTAINS 80 CHARACTERS
00066            LABEL RECORDS ARE OMITTED
00067
00068     *         THE "FD" INDICATES THE NUMBER OF CHARACTERS IN A RECORD
00069     *         AND WHETHER OR NOT THE FILE HAS FILE LABELS.  FOR A
00070     *         STANDARD SIZE CARD, THE LENGTH IS 80 COLUMNS.
00071     *         FILE LABELS ARE NOT PERMITTED FOR CARD FILES.
00072
00073     *         THE REST OF THE "FD" DESCRIBES THE RECORD CONTENTS.
00074     *         "PIC X(80)" MEANS EACH RECORD IS 80 ALPHANUMERIC
00075     *         CHARACTERS.
00076
00077
00078        01  NAME-PHONE-INPUT              PIC X(80).

00080     *         THE "FD" FOR A PRINT FILE MUST INDICATE NO FILE LABELS.
00081     *         MOST PRINTERS PRINT UP TO 132 CHARACTER LINES.
00082
00083        FD  PRINT-FILE
00084            RECORD CONTAINS 132 CHARACTERS
00085            LABEL RECORDS ARE OMITTED
00086            .
00087
00088     *         A "RECORD" FOR A PRINT FILE IS A PRINTED LINE.  IN
00089     *         THIS CASE EACH LINE CONSISTS OF 132 ALPHANUMERIC
00090     *         CHARACTERS ("PIC X(132)").
00091
00092        01  PRINT-LINE                    PIC X(132).

00094          WORKING-STORAGE SECTION.
```

```
00096        *          WORKING-STORAGE AREAS ARE NOT PART OF FILE RECORDS.
00097        *          HERE WE DEFINE A PROGRAM SWITCH WHICH CAN HOLD 3
00098        *          ALPHANUMERIC CHARACTERS ("PIC X(3)").   THE SWITCH
00099        *          CONTAINS THE VALUE "NO " AS LONG AS THERE ARE MORE
00100        *          INPUT RECORDS TO BE PROCESSED.  WHEN THERE ARE NO
00101        *          MORE INPUT RECORDS LEFT, THE SWITCH IS SET TO "YES".
00102
00103        01   END-OF-CARDS-SWITCH          PIC X(3).

00105        *          THIS AREA HOLDS AN INPUT CARD WITH AN EMPLOYEE'S
00106        *          NAME AND PHONE NUMBER -- NAME IS 20 ALPHANUMERIC
00107        *          CHARACTERS; PHONE IS 8 ALPHANUMERIC CHARACTERS.
00108        *          "FILLER" IS USED TO DEFINE ANY PART OF A RECORD WHICH
00109        *          WILL NOT BE PROCESSED BY THE PROGRAM.
00110
00111        01   NAME-PHONE-CARD.
00112             05   EMPLOYEE-NAME           PIC X(20).
00113             05   EMPLOYEE-PHONE-NUMBER   PIC X(8).
00114             05   FILLER                  PIC X(52).

00116        *         THIS AREA IS WHERE WE PUT TOGETHER A LINE TO BE PRINTED.
00117        *          NOTICE THERE ARE SOME AREAS BETWEEN DATA ITEMS WHICH
00118        *          HAVE BEEN NAMED "FILLER" AND SET TO BLANK SPACES
00119        *          WITH "VALUE SPACES".   THESE AREAS SEPARATE FIELDS
00120        *          ON THE PRINTED LINE.
00121
00122        01   NAME-PHONE-LINE.
00123             05   PRINT-NAME              PIC X(20).
00124             05   FILLER                  PIC X(5)        VALUE SPACES.
00125             05   PRINT-PHONE-NUMBER      PIC X(8).
00126             05   FILLER                  PIC X(99)       VALUE SPACES.

00128        PROCEDURE DIVISION.

00130        *          THE PROCEDURE DIVISION CONTAINS THE INSTRUCTIONS
00131        *          WHICH TELL THE COMPUTER WHAT TO DO.
00132
00133        000-PRODUCE-PHONE-LISTING.

00135             MOVE "NO " TO END-OF-CARDS-SWITCH
00136
00137        *          SETS END-OF-CARDS-SWITCH TO "NO".
00138
00139        *          THE OPEN STATEMENT MUST BE USED BEFORE A FILE CAN
00140        *          BE PROCESSED IN ANY WAY.   IT TELLS WHETHER THE FILE
00141        *          IS TO BE USED FOR INPUT OR OUTPUT.
00142
00143             OPEN    INPUT           CARD-FILE
00144                     OUTPUT          PRINT-FILE
00145
00146             PERFORM 100-INPUT-A-RECORD
00147
00148        *          THE PERFORM STATEMENT CAUSES ALL STATEMENTS
00149        *          IN THE PARAGRAPH NAMED "100-INPUT-A-RECORD" TO BE
00150        *          EXECUTED. NOTE THAT THIS CAUSES THE FIRST RECORD
00151        *          OF THE FILE TO BE INPUT.  THE "PRODUCE-NAME-PHONE-
00152        *          LISTING" PARAGRAPH EXECUTED NEXT BEGINS BY
00153        *          PROCESSING THIS FIRST RECORD.   WHEN IT IS DONE
00154        *          PROCESSING THE RECORD, IT THEN PERFORMS THE
00155        *          100-INPUT-A-RECORD PARAGRAPH TO OBTAIN THE NEXT
00156        *          RECORD IN THE FILE.
00157
00158
00159
```

```
00160                     PERFORM 200-PRODUCE-NAME-PHONE-LIST
00161                         UNTIL END-OF-CARDS-SWITCH IS EQUAL TO "YES"
00162
00163            *                   THIS VERSION OF PERFORM CAUSES THE ENTIRE
00164            *                   PARAGRAPH NAMED "200-PRODUCE-NAME-PHONE-LIST"
00165            *                   TO BE EXECUTED REPEATEDLY.   THE REPEATED
00166            *                   INVOKING OF THE PARAGRAPH CONTINUES UNTIL
00167            *                   END-OF-CARDS-SWITCH CONTAINS THE VALUE "YES".
00168
00169
00170                 CLOSE   CARD-FILE
00171                         PRINT-FILE
00172
00173            *                   THE CLOSE STATEMENT MUST BE USED WHEN THE PROGRAM
00174            *                   IS DONE PROCESSING A FILE.   IT "DISCONNECTS" THE
00175            *                   FILE FROM THE COBOL PROGRAM.
00176
00177                 STOP RUN
00178
00179            *                   THE STOP STATEMENT TELLS THE COMPUTER TO STOP
00180            *                   EXECUTING INSTRUCTIONS IN THIS PROGRAM.
00181
00182                     .


00184             100-INPUT-A-RECORD.
00185
00186            *                   THIS PARAGRAPH INPUTS A CARD.    THE READ
00187            *                   STATEMENT INPUTS THE NEXT CARD IN THE FILE AND
00188            *                   MOVES THE CONTENTS OF THE CARD INTO THE
00189            *                   WORKING-STORAGE AREA NAMED "NAME-PHONE-CARD".
00190            *                   IF THERE ARE NO MORE CARDS TO BE READ
00191            *                   ("AT END"), END-OF-CARDS-SWITCH IS SET
00192            *                   TO "YES".   THIS CAUSES THE CLOSE AND STOP
00193            *                   RUN STATEMENTS TO BE EXECUTED.
00194
00195                 READ CARD-FILE RECORD
00196                     INTO NAME-PHONE-CARD
00197                     AT END
00198                         MOVE "YES" TO END-OF-CARDS-SWITCH
00199                     .


00201             200-PRODUCE-NAME-PHONE-LIST.
00202
00203            *                   THIS PARAGRAPH MOVES THE DATA FROM NAME-PHONE-CARD
00204            *                   TO THE AREA FROM WHICH A LINE OF THE REPORT WILL BE
00205            *                   PRINTED.   THE "WRITE" STATEMENT PRINTS A LINE WHOSE
00206            *                   CONTENTS ARE IN "NAME-PHONE-LINE".   HAVING PROCESSED
00207            *                   ONE EMPLOYEE'S INFORMATION, "PERFORM 100-INPUT-A-RECORD"
00208            *                   CAUSES THE READ STATEMENT IN PARAGRAPH 100-INPUT-A-RECORD
00209            *                   TO BE EXECUTED, BRINGING THE NEXT RECORD INTO MEMORY
00210            *                   FOR PROCESSING.
00211
00212                 MOVE EMPLOYEE-NAME             TO PRINT-NAME
00213                 MOVE EMPLOYEE-PHONE-NUMBER   TO PRINT-PHONE-NUMBER
00214
00215                 WRITE PRINT-LINE
00216                     FROM NAME-PHONE-LINE
00217
00218                 PERFORM 100-INPUT-A-RECORD
00219                     .
```

```
ABEL FRED                    123-4567
BAKER SUE                    111-2222
CHARLIE SUE                  453-7822
PERELMAN BARNEY              UNLISTED
PERELMAN MIKE                UNKNOWN
RODGERS BOB                  234-5678
RODGERS BOBB                 345-6789
RODGERS LEE                  456-7890
FOLKERS DICK                 567-8901
FOLKERS RUTH                 678-9012
SUE PEGGY                    231-7856
ZOTZ ZAPPA                   999-9999
```

EXAMPLE 2.17   Similar to Example 2.16; we comment only on those features which are new.

```
00001             IDENTIFICATION DIVISION.
00002
00003             PROGRAM-ID. TIMELIST.
00004
00005             AUTHOR.  LARRY NEWCOMER.
00006             INSTALLATION.  PENN STATE UNIVERSITY--YORK CAMPUS.
00007
00008             DATE-WRITTEN.  MAY 1983.
00009             DATE-COMPILED. MAY  9,1983.
00011      *    TIMELIST PRINTS ONE LINE FOR EACH EMPLOYEE SHOWING:
00012      *    NUMBER OF REGULAR HOURS WORKED, NUMBER OF OVERTIME
00013      *    HOURS WORKED, AND TOTAL HOURS WORKED. AT THE END OF THE
00014      *    REPORT, IT ALSO PRINTS A COUNT OF THE NUMBER OF
00015      *    EMPLOYEES PROCESSED.  INPUT IS FROM A DECK OF TIME
00016      *    CARDS, KEPT IN SEQUENCE BY EMPLOYEE NAME.

00018             ENVIRONMENT DIVISION.

00020             CONFIGURATION SECTION.

00022             SOURCE-COMPUTER. IBM-370.
00023             OBJECT-COMPUTER. IBM-370.

00025             INPUT-OUTPUT SECTION.

00027             FILE-CONTROL.

00029                 SELECT CARD-FILE            ASSIGN TO CARDS.
00030                 SELECT PRINT-FILE           ASSIGN TO PRINTER.

00032             DATA DIVISION.

00034             FILE SECTION.

00036             FD  CARD-FILE
00037                 RECORD CONTAINS 80 CHARACTERS
00038                 LABEL RECORDS ARE OMITTED
00039                 .
00040
00041             01  TIME-CARD-INPUT            PIC X(80).

00043             FD  PRINT-FILE
00044                 RECORD CONTAINS 132 CHARACTERS
00045                 LABEL RECORDS ARE OMITTED
00046                 .
00047
00048             01  PRINT-LINE                 PIC X(132).

00050             WORKING-STORAGE SECTION.

00052      *    OBSERVE THAT THERE ARE SEVERAL NUMERIC FIELDS DEFINED
```

```
00053          *       IN WORKING-STORAGE USING "PIC 99" OR "PIC 999".  EACH
00054          *       "9" IN THE DESCRIPTION OF A NUMERIC ITEM REPRESENTS
00055          *       ONE DECIMAL DIGIT POSITION. THUS "PIC 99" DESCRIBES
00056          *       A DATA ITEM WHICH CAN HOLD A 2-DIGIT NUMBER.
00057
00058          01  END-OF-CARDS-SWITCH              PIC X(3).

00060          01  WORKING-TIME-CARD.
00061
00062          *       HOLDS INFORMATION INPUT FROM THE TIME CARD FILE
00063
00064              05  WORKING-NAME                PIC X(20).
00065              05  WORKING-REGULAR-HOURS       PIC 99.
00066              05  WORKING-OVERTIME-HOURS      PIC 99.
00067              05  FILLER                      PIC X(56).

00069          01  TIME-LISTING-LINE.
00070
00071          *       AREA USED TO CONSTRUCT A LINE TO BE PRINTED ON THE REPORT
00072
00073              05  LISTING-NAME                PIC X(20).
00074              05  FILLER                      PIC X(5)        VALUE SPACES.
00075              05  LISTING-REGULAR-HOURS       PIC 99.
00076              05  FILLER                      PIC X(5)        VALUE SPACES.
00077              05  LISTING-OVERTIME-HOURS      PIC 99.
00078              05  FILLER                      PIC X(5)        VALUE SPACES.
00079              05  LISTING-TOTAL-HOURS         PIC 999.
00080              05  FILLER                      PIC X(90)       VALUE SPACES.

00082          01  EMPLOYEE-TOTAL-LINE.
00083
00084          *       AREA USED TO CONSTRUCT THE LINE TO BE PRINTED AT END OF
00085          *       THE REPORT.   CONTAINS COUNTER FOR NUMBER OF EMPLOYEES
00086          *       PROCESSED.
00087
00088              05  FILLER                      PIC X(25)
00089                                              VALUE "NUMBER OF EMPLOYEES IS".
00090              05  NUMBER-OF-EMPLOYEES         PIC 999.
00091              05  FILLER                      PIC X(104)      VALUE SPACES.

00093          PROCEDURE DIVISION.

00095          000-PRODUCE-HOURS-REPORT.
00096
00097          *           PROGRAM SWITCHES AND COUNTERS MUST BE INITIALIZED
00098          *           AT THE START OF PROGRAM EXECUTION.  THE SWITCH IS
00099          *           SET TO "NO " WHILE THE COUNTER FOR NUMBER OF
00100          *           EMPLOYEES IS INITIALLY SET TO ZERO.  ONE WILL BE
00101          *           ADDED EACH TIME AN EMPLOYEE IS PROCESSED (SEE
00102          *           200-PRODUCE-TIME-LISTING PARAGRAPH).
00103
00104              MOVE "NO " TO END-OF-CARDS-SWITCH
00105              MOVE ZERO TO NUMBER-OF-EMPLOYEES
00106
00107              OPEN    INPUT               CARD-FILE
00108                      OUTPUT              PRINT-FILE
00109
00110             PERFORM 100-INPUT-A-RECORD
00111
00112             PERFORM 200-PRODUCE-TIME-LISTING
00113                 UNTIL END-OF-CARDS-SWITCH IS EQUAL TO "YES"
00114
00115          *           AFTER ALL INPUT CARDS HAVE BEEN PROCESSED (I.E.,
00116          *           WHEN END-OF-CARDS-SWITCH HAS BEEN CHANGED TO
00117          *           "YES"), A LINE CONTAINING A COUNT OF ALL
00118          *           EMPLOYEES PROCESSED MUST BE PRINTED.
```

```
00119          *                    "WRITE PRINT-LINE FROM EMPLOYEE-TOTAL-LINE" PRINTS
00120          *                    THE CONTENTS OF EMPLOYEE-TOTAL-LINE.
00121
00122               WRITE PRINT-LINE
00123                   FROM EMPLOYEE-TOTAL-LINE
00124
00125               CLOSE    CARD-FILE
00126                        PRINT-FILE
00127               STOP RUN
00128                   .

00130          100-INPUT-A-RECORD.
00131
00132               READ CARD-FILE RECORD
00133                   INTO WORKING-TIME-CARD
00134                   AT END
00135                       MOVE "YES" TO END-OF-CARDS-SWITCH
00136                   .

00138          200-PRODUCE-TIME-LISTING.
00139
00140          *                    INCREMENT COUNTER EACH TIME AN EMPLOYEE IS PROCESSED
00141
00142               ADD 1 TO NUMBER-OF-EMPLOYEES
00143
00144          *                    MOVE DATA FROM INPUT CARD TO AREA WHERE LINE IS BUILT
00145
00146               MOVE WORKING-NAME            TO LISTING-NAME
00147               MOVE WORKING-REGULAR-HOURS   TO LISTING-REGULAR-HOURS
00148               MOVE WORKING-OVERTIME-HOURS  TO LISTING-OVERTIME-HOURS
00149
00150          *                    CALCULATE TOTAL HOURS BY ADDING REGULAR, OVERTIME.
00151          *                    NOTE THAT RESULT IS PLACED IN TIME-LISTING-LINE.
00152
00153               ADD WORKING-REGULAR-HOURS  WORKING-OVERTIME-HOURS
00154                   GIVING LISTING-TOTAL-HOURS
00155
00156               WRITE PRINT-LINE
00157                   FROM TIME-LISTING-LINE
00158
00159               PERFORM 100-INPUT-A-RECORD
00160
```

```
ABEL FRED                  40      03      043
BAKER SUE                  30      00      030
CHARLIE CHUCK              40      12      052
FLECKSTEINER CINDY         40      00      040
FLECKSTEINER DON           40      20      060
FLECKSTEINER STACY         15      00      015
PERELMAN BARNEY            40      15      055
PERELMAN MIKE              03      00      003
NUMBER OF EMPLOYEES IS     008
```

Review Questions

2.1   What is meant by saying that COBOL is self-documenting?

2.2   What are the four DIVISIONs of a COBOL program?

2.3   What is the general purpose of the IDENTIFICATION DIVISION?

2.4   What is the general purpose of the ENVIRONMENT DIVISION?

2.5   What is the general purpose of the DATA DIVISION?

2.6   What is WORKING-STORAGE?

2.7   Which DIVISION specifies the actual processing to be done?

2.8   What is a COBOL SECTION?

2.9   What are COBOL paragraphs?

2.10   Why is it suggested that PROCEDURE DIVISION paragraph names contain sequence numbers as part of the name?

2.11   What is a structured period?

2.12   Explain the COBOL A and B margins.

2.13   What items should be typed starting in margin A?

2.14   Explain the importance of indentation within the B margin.

2.15   Explain the COBOL continuation rules.

2.16   Explain the rules for typing a COBOL program.

2.17   What are the special uses of column 7 in COBOL?

2.18   What are COBOL reserved words?

2.19   What are the rules for COBOL programmer-defined names?

2.20   Explain the function of blank lines in a COBOL program.

Solved Problems

2.21   What kinds of data items belong in WORKING-STORAGE?

WORKING-STORAGE is used for data items which are not fields in file records. Such items are usually calculated by the program or used as temporary work areas during processing. Normally assigned to WORKING-STORAGE are:

Counters, or memory locations used to hold numeric data representing a count (e.g., number of employees). Counters are usually initialized to zero.

Accumulators, or memory locations used to accumulate a total (e.g., total balance due). Accumulators are usually initialized to zero.

Program flags, switches. These are memory locations holding information indicating whether certain events have occurred during program execution. Flags and switches often have true/false-type values (e.g., whether or not all the records in a given file have been processed). Flags are set and reset as needed during program execution.

Line image areas. It is often convenient to construct a line of information in WORKING-STORAGE, then move it to the record area of the print file before finally printing it out with the WRITE statement.

2.22 What will the computer do when it executes the machine-language version of "PERFORM 090-CALCULATE-TAX"?

The computer will branch to the first instruction in the machine-language version of the paragraph named "090-CALCULATE-TAX". It will then proceed to execute all other instructions in the paragraph, one after the other, and will finally branch back to the instruction which immediately follows "PERFORM 090-CALCULATE-TAX".

2.23 What will the computer do when it executes the machine-language version of "MOVE INVENTORY-ON-HAND-AMOUNT TO INVENTORY-REPORT-AMOUNT"?

In general terms, it will copy the contents of the memory location (*sending field*) "INVENTORY-ON-HAND-AMOUNT" into the memory location (*receiving field*) "INVENTORY-REPORT-AMOUNT". The value of INVENTORY-ON-HAND-AMOUNT will remain unchanged. The exact contents of the receiving field will depend on the DATA DIVISION descriptions of the two items.

2.24 Indicate whether the following names are incorrect, correct but poor in terms of programming style, or completely acceptable: (*a*) INPUT, (*b*) INPUT-INVENTORY-RECORD, (*c*) B-INPUT-INVENTORY-RECORD-040, (*d*) PROCESS-DATA.

(*a*)   Incorrect: programmer-defined name duplicates a reserved word.

(*b*)   Correct (could be improved by adding a sequence number to the name).

(*c*)   Correct: the combination of sequence letters and/or numbers, together with a name that describes what the paragraph does, is optimal.

(*d*)   Correct, but the name is so vague it is not descriptive of what the paragraph actually does.

2.25 Explain the following special uses of column 7:

(*a*)   MOVE SPACES TO WORKING-NAME-ADDR
            -        ESS-LINE

(*b*)   *   THE FOLLOWING PARAGRAPH COMPUTES STATE TAX

(*c*)   MOVE "THE PENNSYLVANIA STATE UNIVERSITY BO ←col. 72
            -        "OKSTORE" TO REPORT-HEADING

(*d*)   D   EXHIBIT NAMED NUMBER-OF-EMPLOYEES-PROCESSED
            ↑   ↑
         col. 7   B Margin

(*a*)   Since WORKING-NAME-ADDRESS-LINE is split between lines, the "-" in column 7 is needed to indicate continuation. Note that the continuation should have been avoided:

            MOVE SPACES TO
            WORKING-NAME-ADDRESS-LINE

(b) The "*" in column 7 indicates that the rest of the line is a comment, used to explain what a given part of the program is doing and/or how it does it.

(c) The "-" in column 7 is used here to continue a quoted string (*nonnumeric literal*) from one line to the next. Note that there is no closing quote on the first line (which ends in column 72), and that the opening quote is repeated in the B margin of the continuation line. It might have been possible to avoid this continuation by typing:

> MOVE
>> "THE PENNSYLVANIA STATE UNIVERSITY BOOKSTORE"
>> TO REPORT-HEADING

(d) The "D" in column 7 marks the line as a debugging line, used to find errors in the program. Debugging lines are in effect removed once the program has been debugged (see Section 4.2).

2.26   Comment on the following programmer-defined names for data items: (*a*) TNWI, (*b*) TOTAL-NET-WORTH-OF-INVENTORY-FOR-JULY, (*c*) PHONE NUMBER, (*d*) #-ON-HAND, (*e*) ON-HAND-.

(*a*)   Data names *must* be descriptive. Although TNWI is legal, TOTAL-NET-WORTH-OF-INVENTORY is much better.

(*b*)   Programmer-defined names are limited to 30 characters; hence this one is illegal and constitutes a syntax error.

(*c*)   Programmer-defined names must not contain embedded blanks (nor any characters other than letters, digits, and hyphens): syntax error.

(*d*)   Illegal character "#": syntax error.

(*e*)   Cannot begin or end with hyphen: syntax error.

Supplementary Problems

2.27   Interview a professional COBOL programmer. Discuss his or her organization's coding standards with respect to (*a*) comment lines, (*b*) continuation, (*c*) programmer-defined names, (*d*) structured period, (*e*) indentation, (*f*) blank lines.

2.28   Reread Example 2.1 and see if you can now understand most of what is in the program. Could you understand the program *without* comments? blank lines? indentation? descriptive data and paragraph names?

Programming Assignments

In the following, assume that all money amounts are given in round dollars (see Chapter 5 for treatment of dollars and cents).

2.29   Write, test, and debug a complete COBOL program to print the following report. Make up your own test data and verify that your output is correct.

1. A line of the report is 132 characters, in the following sequence: customer number—5 alphanumeric characters; 10 spaces; customer name—30 alphanumeric characters; 10 spaces; item number—7 alphanumeric characters; 5 spaces; quantity ordered—4 digits; 5 spaces; quantity shipped—4 digits; rest of line blank.

2. Input data are punched into cards as follows: customer number—first 5 columns; customer name—next 30 columns; item number—next 7 columns; quantity ordered—next 4 columns; quantity shipped—next 4 columns; rest of card—unused.

3. At the end of the report, print a line showing the total number of items ordered (for all customers) and the total number of items shipped (to all customers).

4. Do not worry about titles, page numbers, extra spaces between lines, etc.

2.30 Write, test, and debug a complete COBOL program to print the following report:

customer number: 8 characters	5 spaces	old balance: 5 digits	5 spaces	payment amount: 4 digits	5 spaces	new balance: 5 digits

Input is punched into cards as follows:

customer number: 8 characters	old balance: 5 digits	payment amount: 4 digits	63 columns unused

New balance is calculated as old balance minus payment.

At the end, print a line showing the total payments.

2.31 Write, test, and debug a complete COBOL program to print the following report:

Output consists of the following fields, spaced appropriately: part number—8 characters; on hand—5 digits; on order—5 digits; quantity available—6 digits.

Input is punched into cards as follows: part number—first 8 columns; on hand—5 columns; on order—5 columns; rest of card—unused.

Quantity available is calculated as on-hand + on-order.

At the end, print a line showing total quantity on hand (for all parts) and total quantity on order (for all parts).

2.32 Write, test, and debug a complete COBOL program to print the following report:

Output (spaced appropriately): general ledger account number—4 characters; description—20 characters; credit amount—5 digits; debit amount—5 digits.

Input is punched into cards which are ordered by general ledger account number: general ledger account number—4 characters; description—20 characters; credit amount—5 digits; debit amount—5 digits; rest of card—unused.

At the end, print a line showing total credit and total debit amounts.

2.33 Write, test, and debug a program to print the following listing from an employee master file:

Output consists of the following fields, with 5 spaces between each field: employee ID—6 characters; number of deductions—2 digits; last year's annual salary—5 digits; this year's annual salary—5 digits.

Input is punched into cards as follows: employee ID—cols. 1–6; number of deductions—cols. 7–8; last year's annual salary—cols. 9–13; this year's annual salary—cols. 14–18.

At the end of the report, print a line showing total salaries for this year and last year, and number of employees processed.

2.34 Write, test, and debug a program to print the following listing from an accounts payable file:

Output (with 8 spaces between each field): invoice number—4 characters; invoice date (mmyydd)—6 digits; invoice amount—5 digits; discount amount—4 digits; amount due (less discount)—5 digits.

Input is punched into card columns as follows: invoice number, 1–4; invoice amount, 5–9; discount amount, 10–13; invoice date (mmyydd), 14–19.

At the end of the report, print a line showing total invoice amount, total discounts, and total amounts less discounts.

2.35 Print a report showing the following fields from a university's student file:

> Student #   Name   Year   # Credits Completed

Input is punched into card columns as follows: student number, 1–9; name, 10–29; year (1, 2, 3, or 4), 30; number of credits completed, 31–33.

At the end, print the total number of credits completed and the total number of students.

2.36 Print mailing labels of the form

>   M. MOUSE
>   1031 EDGECOMB AVE.
>   YORK, PA 17403

Input is punched into card columns as follows: name, 1–20; street, 21–40; city, 41–51; state, 52–53; zip code, 54–58.

[*Hints*: (1) You will need *three* output line image areas (Problem 2.21). (2) Each input record will generate three lines of output. (3) Use

>   WRITE PRINT-LINE
>   FROM WORKING-NAME-LINE
>   AFTER ADVANCING 2 LINES

to leave a blank line between labels.]

2.37 Write a program to print checks of the form

> _____
>
>   CHECK #
> _____   _____
>   PAYEE   AMOUNT (dollars)

Input is punched into cards and consists of the payee name in columns 1–20 and the amount [PIC 9(5)] in columns 21–25. Check numbers are *generated by the program*, starting with check # 100, then 110, 120, 130, etc. After all checks have been printed, print a line showing the total amount disbursed.

2.38 Write a program which prints a banking report from the following card input: customer name, 1–20; savings account balance, 21–25; checking account balance, 26–30; certificates of deposit balance, 31–35. The output should consist of a line for each customer, showing the customer name and the various balances. At the end of the report, print a line showing total savings, total checking, and total certificate balances. The precise layout of the report is up to you.

Chapter 3

Identification Division

3.1 Syntax Notation

This section applies not only to the IDENTIFICATION DIVISION, but to a COBOL program in its entirety.

Syntax refers to the grammatical structure of a language. For example, the English sentence "dog the chaxed cat the" has several *syntax errors* involving spelling and word order. If a COBOL program contains (COBOL) syntax errors, the compiler will not be able to translate the invalid statement(s), and there will be no object program to execute. Diagnostic error messages, printed as part of the source listing, help the programmer to find and correct all syntax errors.

A common notation has been developed to show the correct syntax for COBOL statements. It uses the following conventions:

(1) *Square brackets* [ ] enclose a set of one or more *optional* items. You may choose *any one* from the set, *or none.*

(2) *Braces* { } enclose a set of one or more items. You *must* choose *exactly one* of the items.

(3) *Uppercase letters* are used for reserved words and *lowercase letters* for programmer-defined names.

(4) Reserved words (uppercase) which are underlined must appear as shown in the item; reserved words which are not underlined may be omitted.

(5) Ellipsis (. . .) is used to identify items which may be repeated any number of times.

EXAMPLE 3.1 Consider the following notation of a PROCEDURE DIVISION MOVE statement:

$$\underline{\text{MOVE}} \left\{ \begin{array}{l} \text{identifier-1} \\ \text{literal} \end{array} \right\} \underline{\text{TO}} \text{ identifier-2 [identifier-3] } \ldots$$

The word "MOVE" is underlined and not in square brackets; it is therefore required. Next, the programmer can use *either* an identifier *or* a literal (the only literals discussed so far are quoted strings). Since both these items are in lowercase, the programmer may make up an identifier or literal at pleasure. Following the identifier (or literal) is the required "TO", which in turn is followed by a required identifier (to be made up by the programmer). This in turn may be followed by any number (including none) of optional programmer-defined identifiers.

EXAMPLE 3.2 We comment on several realizations of the statement of Example 3.1.

●   MOVE INPUT-CUSTOMER-NAME TO OUTPUT-CUSTOMER-NAME
Correct: of the form "MOVE identifier-1 TO identifier-2".

●   MOVE "OVERPAID" TO INVOICE-MESSAGE-AREA TYPE-OF-ACCOUNT
Correct: of the form "MOVE literal TO identifier-2 identifier-3".

●   MOVE DISCOUNT-AMOUNT TO INVOICE-DISCOUNT AND SHIPPING-DISCOUNT
Incorrect: "AND" should not appear between the identifiers INVOICE-DISCOUNT and SHIPPING-DISCOUNT.

●   MOVE GREETING TO "HELLO"
Incorrect: although "HELLO" is a valid literal, literals may not follow "TO".

●   MOVE "HELLO" GROSS-SALES TO GREETING SALES-TOTAL
Incorrect: only *one* identifier or literal may appear between "MOVE" and "TO".

3.2 IDENTIFICATION DIVISION Syntax

The IDENTIFICATION DIVISION, whose function was described in Section 2.1, has the syntactical form shown in Fig. 3-1.

<u>IDENTIFICATION DIVISION</u>.
<u>PROGRAM-ID</u>. program-name.
[<u>AUTHOR</u>. comment.]
[<u>INSTALLATION</u>. comment.]
[<u>DATE-WRITTEN</u>. comment.]
[<u>DATE-COMPILED</u>.]
[<u>SECURITY</u>. comment.]

Fig. 3-1

Note that the DIVISION header and PROGRAM-ID paragraph are the only required items.

EXAMPLE 3.3   Compare lines 1–8 of Example 2.1 with the syntactical model, Fig. 3-1.

3.3 PROGRAM-ID Paragraph

The PROGRAM-ID paragraph is used to assign a name to the object program. When this program, in its final debugged form, is placed on a permanent disk file (a *program library*), it is identified by its PROGRAM-ID name (kept in the library *directory*). Under this name, it can be accessed for rerunning, without compilation.

The PROGRAM-ID should generally conform to the rules for programmer-defined names (Section 2.5). However, on IBM OS/VS and other systems, the COBOL compiler will automatically convert a COBOL-type PROGRAM-ID into a program library-type name. Therefore, to avoid confusion, it is best to restrict PROGRAM-IDs to the rules for program library names. For IBM OS/VS COBOL: (i) no more than 8 characters, (ii) letters and digits only, (iii) first character a letter.

EXAMPLE 3.4   On IBM systems:

● INVENTORY-REPORT would become INVENTOR
(only 8 characters allowed; compiler truncates name)

● INVRPT would not be changed

● PRINT-PAYCHECKS would become PRINT0PA
(only 8 characters; hyphen not allowed, so compiler transforms it to a zero)

● 1-UPDATE-RECEIVABLES would become A0UPDATE
(only 8 characters; hyphens transformed to zeros; must begin with a letter, so "1" is replaced by the letter "A")

● RECVUPDT would not be changed

3.4 Optional Paragraphs

The remaining paragraphs in the IDENTIFICATION DIVISION are all optional, and the sentences in each paragraph are treated as comments. Because these paragraphs may contain anything the programmer wishes to write, the paragraph names should clearly reflect the kind of information to be presented.

EXAMPLE 3.5

● INSTALLATION. RESEARCH AND DEVELOPMENT.
The INSTALLATION paragraph will indicate at what computer center the program was developed (a large organization may have many computer systems in various geographical locations).

- DATE-COMPILED.

The DATE-COMPILED paragraph is special because the compiler, not the programmer, fills in the entry.

- SECURITY. AUTHORIZED PERSONNEL ONLY—SEE POLICY MANUAL 301.

The SECURITY paragraph will set forth any security considerations which apply to this program or the files it processes.

Following the various paragraphs of the IDENTIFICATION DIVISION, it is strongly suggested that the programmer include a set of comment cards ("*" in column 7) giving a brief overview of what the program does. This will save time and money when, subsequently, another programmer has to make changes to your COBOL program (called *maintenance programming*). The purpose of all good program documentation is to make the program easier to read, understand, and modify.

EXAMPLE 3.6 Criticize the following IDENTIFICATION DIVISION of a program to be run on an IBM OS/VS computer system:

```
PROGRAM-ID. PRINT-MAILING-LABELS.
DATE-WRITTEN. OCT 1983.
```

Technically, the only thing wrong is that the division header ("IDENTIFICATION DIVISION") is missing. However: (1) PRINT-MAILING-LABELS is not in program library form; the compiler will transform it into PRINT0MA. (2) The omission of AUTHOR, INSTALLATION, DATE-COMPILED, SECURITY, and the comment statements giving a brief overview of the program, is very poor practice. Good documentation is an essential part of any COBOL program.

Review Questions

3.1   What is the purpose of the IDENTIFICATION DIVISION?

3.2   Define: (*a*) syntax, (*b*) syntax errors, (*c*) diagnostic error messages.

3.3   Explain the syntax notation used in this book.

3.4   Give the syntax of the IDENTIFICATION DIVISION.

3.5   Which parts of the IDENTIFICATION DIVISION are required?   which optional?

3.6   Explain the rules for typing the IDENTIFICATION DIVISION.

3.7   What is the function of a program library?

3.8   What are the rules for PROGRAM-ID on IBM systems?

3.9   Explain what information is given in each of the optional paragraphs of the IDENTIFICATION DIVISION.

3.10 What is maintenance programming? How does it relate to the IDENTIFICATION DIVISION?

Solved Problems

3.11 Given the following model for the PROCEDURE DIVISION PERFORM statement:

$$\underline{PERFORM} \left\{ \begin{array}{l} \text{paragraph-name-1} \\ \text{section-name-1} \end{array} \right\} \left[\left\{ \begin{array}{l} \underline{THROUGH} \\ \underline{THRU} \end{array} \right\} \left\{ \begin{array}{l} \text{paragraph-name-2} \\ \text{section-name-2} \end{array} \right\} \right]$$

$$\left\{ \begin{array}{l} \text{identifier-1} \\ \text{integer-1} \end{array} \right\} \underline{TIMES}$$

indicate whether the following are syntactically correct:

(*a*) PERFORM CALCULATE-DISCOUNT-AMOUNT 10 TIMES

(*b*) PERFORM READ-EMPLOYEE-RECORD THROUGH PRINT-PAYCHECKS
      NUMBER-OF-EMPLOYEES TIMES

(*c*) PERFORM CHECK-DEPENDENT-STATUS TO COMPUTE-DEDUCTIONS
      NUMBER-OF-DEPENDENTS TIMES

(*d*) PERFORM THRU VALIDATE-ZIP-CODE 9 TIMES

(*e*) PERFORM CHECK-DEPARTMENT-CODE THROUGH CODE-COUNT TIMES

(*f*) PERFORM PRINT-INVOICE-LINE 7

    (*a*) Correct. (*b*) Correct. (*c*) Incorrect: "THROUGH" or "THRU" must be used, not "TO". (*d*) Incorrect: either paragraph-name-1 or section-name-1 is required (PERFORM VALIDATE-NAME THRU VALIDATE-ZIP-CODE 9 TIMES). (*e*) Incorrect: either paragraph-name-2 or section-name-2 must follow THROUGH or THRU (PERFORM CHECK-DEPARTMENT-CODE THRU PRINT-DEPARTMENT-TOTAL CODE-COUNT TIMES. (*f*) Incorrect: "TIMES" is required (PERFORM PRINT-INVOICE-LINE 7 TIMES).

3.12 Which of the following are suitable PROGRAM-IDs?

    (*a*) MONTHLY-SALES-REPORT

    (*b*) PRINT-ACCOUNTS-RECEIVABLE-AGED-TRIAL-BALANCE

(*a*) Correct: the name is properly descriptive of what the program does. The IBM COBOL compiler would transform it into "MONTHLY0", so it would be better to use an 8-character abbreviation in the first place (e.g., "SALESRPT").

(*b*) Incorrect: PROGRAM-ID must be a valid programmer-defined name (limited to 30 characters).

3.13 Write the IDENTIFICATION DIVISION for a COBOL program to print paychecks. All information for the checks is on a disk file created by another payroll program.

    In the following solution, note the use of blank lines to set off the PROGRAM-ID.

```
IDENTIFICATION DIVISION.

PROGRAM-ID. PRNTCHCK.

AUTHOR. MIKE PERELMAN, JUNIOR PROGRAMMER, PAYROLL APPLICATIONS.
INSTALLATION. XYZ COMPANY, BALTIMORE, MD.
DATE-WRITTEN. 7 SEPT., 1983.
DATE-COMPILED.
SECURITY. SEE POLICY MANUAL 7A3 REGARDING HANDLING OF
          COMPANY CHECKS.
```

* PRNTCHCK PRINTS EMPLOYEE PAYCHECKS BY COPYING THE PAYROLL
* INFORMATION ALREADY ON DISK FILE PAYCHECK.IMAGE ONTO
* PRE-PRINTED CHECKS IN THE PRINTER. THE OPERATOR HAS
* THE CAPABILITY TO STOP OR BACK-UP PRINTING IN CASE OF
* DIFFICULTY WITH THE FORMS AND/OR PRINTER. PRNTCHCK ALSO
* LOGS THE FOLLOWING CONTROL INFORMATION: # CHECKS PRINTED,
* # CHECKS BACKED-UP, TOTAL $ AMOUNT OF CHECKS.

Programming Assignments

3.14–3.23 Modify Problems 2.29–2.38 to reflect your expanded knowledge of the IDENTIFICATION DIVISION.

Chapter 4

Environment Division

4.1 ENVIRONMENT DIVISION Syntax

The ENVIRONMENT DIVISION, whose general function was described in Section 2.1, has the syntactical form shown in Fig. 4-1. (Line numbers have been inserted for convenient reference.) It is seen that the ENVIRONMENT DIVISION is made up of the CONFIGURATION SECTION and the INPUT-OUTPUT SECTION. The former includes the SOURCE-COMPUTER, OBJECT-COMPUTER, and SPECIAL-NAMES paragraphs; the latter has the single FILE-CONTROL paragraph. Recall that the division header (line 1 in Fig. 4-1), section headers (lines 2 and 14), and paragraph headers (lines 3, 4, 6, and 15) should all be typed starting in the A margin; other entries should start in the B margin. Sometimes paragraph entries are typed on the same line as the paragraph header, sometimes not. Good visual appearance should be your guide (see Example 4.1). Only entries applicable to sequentially organized files (Section 4.5) are discussed here.

```
(1)   ENVIRONMENT DIVISION.
(2)   CONFIGURATION SECTION.
(3)   SOURCE-COMPUTER. computer-name [WITH DEBUGGING MODE].
(4)   OBJECT-COMPUTER. computer-name
(5)       [PROGRAM COLLATING SEQUENCE IS alphabet-name].
(6)   [SPECIAL-NAMES.
(7)       [function-name IS cobol-name] . . .
(8)       ⎡alphabet-name IS                                        ⎤
(9)       ⎢      STANDARD-1                                        ⎥
(10)      ⎢      NATIVE                                            ⎥
                      ⎡⎧THROUGH⎫         ⎤
(11)      ⎨   literal-1 ⎢⎨THRU   ⎬ literal-2⎥ . . . ⎬
                      ⎣⎩       ⎭         ⎦
                      ⎣ ALSO literal-3 [ALSO literal-4]⎦
                      ⎡⎧THROUGH⎫         ⎤
(12)      ⎢   literal-5 ⎢⎨THRU   ⎬ literal-6⎥ . . . ⎥
                      ⎣⎩       ⎭         ⎦
                      ⎣ ALSO literal-7 [ALSO literal-8]⎦
(13)      ·]
(14)  [INPUT-OUTPUT SECTION.
(15)  FILE-CONTROL.
(16)      SELECT file-name
(17)          ASSIGN TO external-name
(18)          [ORGANIZATION IS SEQUENTIAL]
(19)          [ACCESS MODE IS SEQUENTIAL]
(20)          [FILE STATUS IS data-name]      ·
(21)          ⎡RESERVE integer ⎡AREAS⎤⎤
                              ⎣AREA ⎦
(22)          ·]
```

Fig. 4-1

33

EXAMPLE 4.1

```
00031          ENVIRONMENT DIVISION.
00032
00033          CONFIGURATION SECTION.
00034
00035          SOURCE-COMPUTER.  IBM-370 WITH DEBUGGING MODE.
00036          OBJECT-COMPUTER.  IBM-370
00037                          PROGRAM COLLATING SEQUENCE IS
00038                             CUSTOMER-NUMBER-CODE-SEQUENCE.
00039          SPECIAL-NAMES.
00040
00041             C01 IS TOP-OF-PAGE
00042             CUSTOMER-NUMBER-CODE-SEQUENCE IS
00043                "3" THRU "9"
00044                "2"
00045                "0" THRU "1"
00046                .
00047
00048          INPUT-OUTPUT SECTION.
00049
00050          FILE-CONTROL.
00051
00052             SELECT CUSTOMER-SALES-FILE
00053                ASSIGN TO CUSTSALE
00054                ORGANIZATION IS SEQUENTIAL
00055                ACCESS IS SEQUENTIAL
00056                FILE STATUS IS CUST-SALES-FILE-STATUS
00057                .
00058
00059             SELECT SALES-REPORT
00060                ASSIGN TO SALERPT
00061                ORGANIZATION IS SEQUENTIAL
00062                ACCESS IS SEQUENTIAL
00063                FILE STATUS IS SALES-REPORT-STATUS
00064                .
```

4.2 CONFIGURATION SECTION: SOURCE-COMPUTER Paragraph

The CONFIGURATION SECTION describes the computer system(s) used to compile and execute the program. The SOURCE-COMPUTER paragraph begins with a "computer-name" which specifies the computer used for compilation. This entry is treated as a comment by the compiler and serves merely as program documentation. The form of the "computer-name" varies from one computer system to another; for IBM 370-type systems, just "IBM-370" is acceptable.

The SOURCE-COMPUTER paragraph also has the *optional* entry "WITH DEBUGGING MODE" (line 3, Fig. 4-1). If this entry occurs, all debugging lines (marked by a "D" in column 7) are translated into the object program and are therefore carried out by the computer during the execution of the object program. If this entry does not occur, debugging lines are treated as comments (i.e., although they are printed on the source listing, they are *not* translated into the object program and therefore *have no effect* during execution). Debugging will be fully treated in Chapter 9.

EXAMPLE 4.2

●   SOURCE-COMPUTER. IBM-370-158.

Computer model number "158" is optionally appended to "IBM-370". Since WITH DEBUGGING MODE is not specified, statements typed with a "D" in column 7 will be treated as comments and therefore will have no effect at execution. Computer name is treated as a comment.

●   SOURCE-COMPUTER. IBM-370
                    WITH DEBUGGING MODE.

Debugging lines will be translated into object program (like regular statements) and will be executed. Clause is typed on its own line for visual appearance.

4.3 CONFIGURATION SECTION:
OBJECT-COMPUTER Paragraph

The OBJECT-COMPUTER paragraph indicates the computer used to execute the object program. The computer-name serves merely as program documentation; it is usually the same as that in the SOURCE-COMPUTER entry.

Recall that computers store information by representing each alphanumeric character by a unique binary number. When these numbers are ranged from smallest to largest, there results an ordering of the corresponding characters called the *collating sequence*. The collating sequence depends, of course, on the binary code being used; the EBCDIC and ASCII collating sequences are exhibited in Appendix B.

EXAMPLE 4.3   In the EBCDIC collating sequence,

$$\text{space} < \$ < \# < A < B < Z < 0 < 9$$

The same characters are ordered in the ASCII collating sequence as

$$\text{space} < \# < \$ < 0 < 9 < A < B < Z$$

Both EBCDIC and ASCII retain the normal alphabetical order; e.g., "ZAG" < "ZIG".

The OBJECT-COMPUTER paragraph has an optional entry (line 5, Fig. 4-1) which allows the programmer to choose a collating sequence for use during program execution. If the entry is omitted from the program, the default sequence for the computer system is in effect (and, since the default is almost always the desired collating sequence, the entry usually is omitted). The collating sequence determines the results when alphanumeric items are compared or sorted.

EXAMPLE 4.4   Refer to Example 4.1. In the OBJECT-COMPUTER paragraph (lines 36–38), "IBM-370" is treated as a comment, while "CUSTOMER-NUMBER-CODE-SEQUENCE" is prescribed as the collating sequence to be used in the program. This sequence is *defined* by lines 42–45 of the SPECIAL-NAMES paragraph to be

$$3 < 4 < 5 < 6 < 7 < 8 < 9 < 2 < 0 < 1$$

4.4 CONFIGURATION SECTION:
SPECIAL-NAMES Paragraph

This paragraph has three main functions, which we treat individually.

Naming Carriage Control Channels

When output data are printed on a continuous sheet of paper, or *continuous form*, the positions of the various data items along the form are defined by *carriage control channels*. In Fig. 4-2 these channels are indicated as holes in a paper tape that travels along with the form; more likely, in modern printers, the channel positioning would be achieved electronically. In any case, line 7 of Fig. 4-1 is used to assign a COBOL name to a carriage control channel for a printer. In IBM OS/VS COBOL the "function-name" for a channel consists of the letter "C" followed by a two-digit channel number: C01, C02, . . . , C12. The "cobol-name" for a channel can be any programmer-defined name.

EXAMPLE 4.5

```
C01  IS  TOP-OF-INVOICE
C02  IS  INVOICE-DATE-AREA
C03  IS  CUSTOMER-ADDRESS-AREA
C04  IS  LINE-ITEM-AREA.
```

Here, channels 1–4 are associated with programmer-defined names that will be used in the PROCEDURE DIVISION to control the position of printed output. Note that there is only *one period* for the whole SPECIAL-NAMES paragraph (line 13 of Fig. 4-1)—do not use periods between entries. Note also the descriptive character of the programmer-defined names.

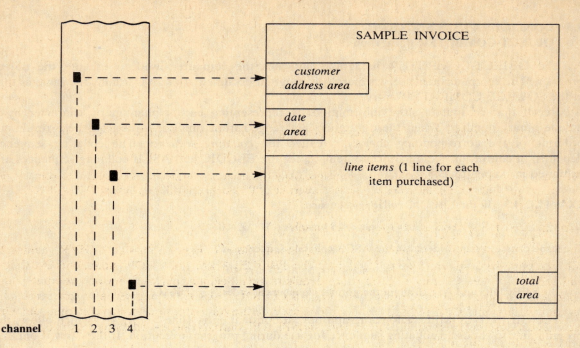

Fig. 4-2

Defining the Collating Sequence(s)

If a nondefault collating sequence is specified in the **OBJECT-COMPUTER** paragraph, this collating sequence must be defined in the **SPECIAL-NAMES** paragraph (lines 8–12 of Fig. 4-1). The alphabet-name (line 8) in **SPECIAL-NAMES** should be the same as that in **OBJECT-COMPUTER** (line 5). The collating sequence associated with alphabet-name is then defined as *one* of the following:

●   STANDARD-1
(line 9, Fig. 4-1), indicating ASCII collating sequence

●   NATIVE
(line 10, Fig. 4-1), indicating EBCDIC collating sequence (the default for IBM 370-type systems)

●   programmer-defined
(lines 11–12, Fig. 4-1). The programmer can define his or her own collating sequence by writing a series of characters in the desired order. Ranges of characters may be specified for brevity ("literal-1 THROUGH literal-2"); equality of two characters is indicated with the "ALSO" option.

Again we point out that, regardless of the number of carriage control channels and collating sequences defined in the **SPECIAL-NAMES** paragraph, there is only one period, at the end of the whole paragraph.

EXAMPLE 4.6

· ·

OBJECT-COMPUTER. IBM-370 COLLATING SEQUENCE IS RUSH-ORDER-CODES.
SPECIAL-NAMES.

C01 IS TOP-OF-FORM
C02 IS MAILING-ADDRESS-AREA

RUSH-ORDER-CODES IS

"I" THRU "N"
"D" "G" "F" "E"
"A" THRU "C"
"H" ALSO "O"

Here, SPECIAL-NAMES defines the prescribed collating sequence RUSH-ORDER-CODES as follows:

$$I < J < K < L < M < N < D < G < F < E < A < B < C < H = O$$

"H" and "O" are considered equal in this sequence. Any characters not specified are assumed to come at the end (after "H" and "O") in their normal default order; i.e., "P" would immediately follow "H" and "O".

Naming SYSIN, SYSOUT, and Operator's Console

The SPECIAL-NAMES paragraph can optionally (line 7, Fig. 4-1) assign COBOL names to certain specialized system files processed by the PROCEDURE DIVISION statements ACCEPT and DISPLAY (see Chapter 6). The exact details of this mechanism vary from one computer and operating system to the next, but in IBM OS/VS COBOL "ACCEPT" inputs one record from the *operator's console* (a CRT or hard copy terminal used by the computer operator to communicate with the operating system) or from the file SYSIN. "DISPLAY" outputs one record, either to the operator's console or to the file SYSOUT.

EXAMPLE 4.7

SPECIAL-NAMES.
    C01 IS TOP-OF-INVOICE
    CONSOLE IS OPERATOR-MESSAGE-DEVICE.

The function-name "CONSOLE" is an IBM reserved word. "OPERATOR-MESSAGE-DEVICE" is the name by which the rest of the COBOL source program will refer to the computer operator's console terminal in ACCEPT and DISPLAY statements:

DISPLAY . . . UPON OPERATOR-MESSAGE-DEVICE
ACCEPT . . . FROM OPERATOR-MESSAGE-DEVICE

EXAMPLE 4.8

SPECIAL-NAMES.
    C01 IS HEADING-AREA
    C02 IS TOTAL-AREA
    SYSIN IS FUNCTION-SELECT-INPUT
    BACK-ORDER-CODING-SEQUENCE IS STANDARD-1

"FUNCTION-SELECT-INPUT" is chosen as the COBOL name for the special input file SYSIN (an IBM reserved word). "FUNCTION-SELECT-INPUT" will be used in PROCEDURE DIVISION ACCEPT statements:

ACCEPT . . . FROM FUNCTION-SELECT-INPUT

EXAMPLE 4.9

SPECIAL-NAMES.
    SYSOUT IS ERROR-LOG.

Output from the PROCEDURE DIVISION DISPLAY statement will go to the special system output file SYSOUT (an IBM COBOL reserved word). The COBOL name for SYSOUT will be "ERROR-LOG"; e.g.,

DISPLAY . . . UPON ERROR-LOG

4.5 INPUT-OUTPUT SECTION

All COBOL data processing is based on the concept of manipulating *records* in *files*. Input information (regardless of the actual input device involved) is thought of as consisting of *input records* from an *input file*. Output information (regardless of the actual output device used) is thought of as discrete *output records* going to an *output file*. Because of their ability to access any record in a matter of milliseconds (Section 1.4), auxiliary storage devices such as disk (generically called *direct-access devices*) can support files whose records are both input and output by the same COBOL program (*input-output files*). A direct-access record could be input, modified, and then output to its original location on the disk. Such an operation is called an *update in place*.

EXAMPLE 4.10 A COBOL program to print employee paychecks would probably process at least 3 files:

(1) An input file whose records (time cards) contained the fields employee ID and weekly hours worked.

(2) Paycheck information would be output to the printer and printed on pre-printed check forms. Each line printed is considered a record in an output print file.

(3) Wage rate information for each employee would probably be input from an employee master disk file. As each employee's time card is input, his or her employee master record would also be located and input from the disk file. It is likely that some employee master fields would be modified as a result of payroll processing; e.g., year-to-date gross pay would have this week's gross pay added to the total. The *updated* employee master record would then be output back to its original location on the disk (erasing the previous record contents, which are now out of date). Thus the disk file would serve as both an input and an output file for the payroll program. This is a common situation for files on auxiliary storage devices.

Structurally, the INPUT-OUTPUT SECTION consists of one COBOL paragraph, the FILE-CONTROL paragraph, which must contain a SELECT statement for every file (input, output, or input-output) to be processed by the program. Each SELECT statement consists of several clauses and ends with a period (see lines 16–22, Fig. 4-1).

SELECT file-name   (Line 16)

The "file-name" is a programmer-defined COBOL name. It should be as descriptive as possible; e.g., "EMPLOYEE-MASTER-FILE" rather than "FILE-1". It is used to refer to the file in all other program statements.

EXAMPLE 4.11

```
INPUT-OUTPUT SECTION.
FILE-CONTROL.
    SELECT CUSTOMER-SALES-FILE ...
    SELECT SALES-REPORT ...
```

(cf. Example 4.1). This program would process exactly two files (since there are exactly two SELECT statements), referred to in the rest of the COBOL source program as CUSTOMER-SALES-FILE and SALES-REPORT.

ASSIGN TO external-name   (Line 17)

The ASSIGN TO clause assigns files to I/O devices. Each file is given an "external-name" which associates the COBOL file with *job-control-language statements* or *operating-system commands* that further describe the file and the I/O device to the computer's *operating system* (see Section 1.9 and Problem 4.45). The content and format of job control statements and commands vary tremendously from one computer and operating system to the next; *find out at this time how to write the external-name for your computer system*. In IBM OS/VS COBOL, the external-name must be made up of 1–8 letters and/or digits, with the first character a letter. It is to the COBOL programmer's advantage to learn as much as possible about job control language.

EXAMPLE 4.12

```
    INPUT-OUTPUT SECTION.
    FILE-CONTROL.
        SELECT CUSTOMER-SALES-FILE
            ASSIGN TO CUSTSALE...
        SELECT SALES-REPORT
            ASSIGN TO SALERPT...
```

(cf. Example 4.1). Here, CUSTOMER-SALES-FILE is assigned the external-name CUSTSALE, and SALES-REPORT is given the external-name SALERPT. These external-names will appear in job control statements or operating system commands which provide further information about the I/O devices needed to process these files.

ORGANIZATION IS SEQUENTIAL   (Line 18; Optional)
ACCESS MODE IS SEQUENTIAL   (Line 19; Optional)

The COBOL language is built around the concept of processing file records *one at a time*. There is flexibility, however, regarding which record is processed first, which second, etc. There are two fundamental modes of *file processing*, or *access*:

Sequential access (processing). The records are processed according to their physical order on the I/O device. No information is needed in the file beyond the actual data records themselves. This type of processing can be done for files on any kind of I/O device.

Random access (processing). The records are processed in an order determined by the program, which may differ from the order in which records are physically stored on the I/O device. This type of processing is possible only for files on direct-access devices. It may require that the file contain extra information, used to help locate the data records requested by the program.

File organization refers to the method used to store records (and any extra information needed to help locate individual records) in a file. Standard COBOL offers the programmer a choice of three file organizations:

Sequential organization. Sequentially organized files can be placed on any type of I/O device. The file consists only of actual data records, which must be processed in their order of placement on the I/O device.

Indexed organization. Indexed files must be placed on direct-access-type devices. They may be processed either sequentially or randomly. When they are processed sequentially, records are retrieved in ascending order according to a predefined *key* (a field whose contents uniquely identify each record in the file; e.g., part number, account number). When they are processed randomly, records are identified using the same key. The file consists not only of actual data records, but also includes *index records* which contain information regarding the location of each data record in the file. If a data record's key field is known, its location can be quickly ascertained by searching through the index records in the file. This is what makes random processing possible.

Relative organization. Relative files are not as frequently used as sequential or indexed files. The file consists only of actual data records, which are numbered 1, 2, 3, . . . , and by means of this *record number* the file may be processed randomly. Since businesses are accustomed to identifying the information kept in records by *key, not record number*, relative files are used only when extremely fast access is essential. Relative files must be placed on direct-access-type devices.

The SELECT statement provides a means for the COBOL programmer to choose a file organization and access mode for each file to be processed by the program. This choice is a crucial one. Usually, files which require random processing are created with indexed organization; files which require only sequential processing are created with sequential organization; and files which require both sequential and random processing are created with indexed organization (which provides for both processing modes). Sequential file processing is described in detail in Chapter 11; indexed and relative files are beyond the scope of this Outline.

EXAMPLE 4.13

```
INPUT-OUTPUT SECTION.
FILE-CONTROL.
    SELECT CUSTOMER-SALES-FILE
        ASSIGN TO CUSTSALE
        ORGANIZATION IS SEQUENTIAL
        ACCESS IS SEQUENTIAL...
    SELECT SALES-REPORT
        ASSIGN TO SALERPT
        ORGANIZATION IS SEQUENTIAL
        ACCESS IS SEQUENTIAL...
```

(cf. Example 4.1). There are SELECT statements for two files, CUSTOMER-SALES-FILE (external-name, CUSTSALE) and SALES-REPORT (external-name, SALERPT).

●   ORGANIZATION IS SEQUENTIAL

This entry may be omitted, because sequential file organization is the default. Other possibilities are ORGANIZATION IS INDEXED and ORGANIZATION IS RELATIVE.

●   ACCESS MODE IS SEQUENTIAL

This entry may also be omitted, because sequential access is the default. The other possibilities are ACCESS MODE IS RANDOM and ACCESS MODE IS DYNAMIC. Sequentially organized files may only be accessed sequentially; other accessing modes require INDEXED or RELATIVE organization.

FILE STATUS IS data-name   (Line 20; Optional)

Conceptually, the PROCEDURE DIVISION manipulation of file records in COBOL is quite simple. A READ statement brings one record from an input or auxiliary storage device into CPU memory for processing; WRITE transfers a record from CPU memory to the output or auxiliary storage device holding the file. Before READ or WRITE can be used to process the records in a file, the statement "OPEN..." must be used to prepare the file for processing (see Example 2.5). Similarly, the statement "CLOSE..." should be used to deactivate a file after all READs and WRITEs have been executed.

In real life, however, it is all too easy for things to go wrong. For instance, an OPEN operation may fail because the description of the file in the COBOL source program is inconsistent with the description in the associated job control statements. Or a WRITE to add a record to a sequentially organized file on disk may fail because there is no more disk space available. Indeed, the expectation that certain statements *will* fail is built into COBOL programs. Thus, to process the records in a sequential file, we so design the program that it keeps READing a record, processing the record, and outputting results until the READ fails because all the records in the file have *already been* READ (this is called an *end of file* condition).

Programs should be so written as to handle the *exception conditions* which can arise during file processing. The SELECT statement provides a means to obtain *feedback* about the success or failure of every operation attempted with a file. This feedback is provided in the form of a data area into which a code is moved after every OPEN, CLOSE, READ, or WRITE statement for the file. The code tells whether the statement was successful or not—and if not, why not.

EXAMPLE 4.14

```
    INPUT-OUTPUT SECTION.
    FILE-CONTROL.
        SELECT MONTHLY-SALES-FILE
            ASSIGN TO MSALES
            FILE STATUS IS MONTHLY-SALES-FILE-STATUS
```

In the FILE STATUS clause the programmer has chosen the name "MONTHLY-SALES-FILE-STATUS" for the data area which will be used to provide feedback regarding the results of every PROCEDURE DIVISION operation (OPEN, READ, WRITE, CLOSE) performed on the file. "MONTHLY-SALES-FILE-STATUS" must be defined in the DATA DIVISION as an area which can hold a 2-digit code registering the success or failure of any given operation on the file. Consult your vendor manual for the meaning of FILE STATUS on your system.

Many experienced COBOL programmers will not bother to define a FILE STATUS area for sequentially organized files, since there are other ways to check on the successful completion of I/O operations (see Chapter 11).

RESERVE integer AREAS   (Line 21; Optional)

This clause can be used to speed file processing when ACCESS IS SEQUENTIAL (see "Multiple Buffers", Section 5.8).

4.6 ENVIRONMENT DIVISION Examples

EXAMPLE 4.15

```
    ENVIRONMENT DIVISION.
    CONFIGURATION SECTION.
    SOURCE-COMPUTER. IBM-370.
    OBJECT-COMPUTER. IBM-370.
    INPUT-OUTPUT SECTION.
    FILE-CONTROL.
        SELECT OLD-INVENTORY-MASTER-FILE
            ASSIGN TO OLDMAST.
        SELECT NEW-INVENTORY-MASTER-FILE
            ASSIGN TO NEWMAST.
        SELECT TRANSACTION-FILE
            ASSIGN TO TRANS.
```

This is an ENVIRONMENT DIVISION for a sequential file update program. Records of TRANSACTION-FILE will be used to update the information in the records of OLD-INVENTORY-MASTER-FILE. Records containing the updated information will be placed on the NEW-INVENTORY-MASTER-FILE. All three files are sequential (the default when ORGANIZATION IS . . . is omitted) and are processed sequentially (the default when ACCESS MODE IS . . . is omitted). Since all files are sequential, FILE STATUS code areas are optional and are not used (testing for exceptional conditions during I/O operations will be done using other PROCEDURE DIVISION methods). The collating sequence is the default for the computer system (EBCDIC for IBM 370-type systems). Since DEBUGGING MODE is not specified, lines with a "D" in column 7 will be treated as comments and will have no effect during program execution. The ASSIGN TO names have the correct format for IBM OS/VS systems ("OLDMAST", "NEWMAST", and "TRANS" consist of 1–8 characters, letters and/or digits, the first of which is a letter).

EXAMPLE 4.16

```
        ENVIRONMENT DIVISION.
        CONFIGURATION SECTION.
        SOURCE-COMPUTER. IBM-370
            WITH DEBUGGING MODE.
        OBJECT-COMPUTER. IBM-370.
        SPECIAL-NAMES.
            C01 IS TOP-OF-CHECK
            C02 IS PAYEE-AREA
            C05 IS AMOUNT-AREA

        INPUT-OUTPUT SECTION.
        FILE-CONTROL.
            SELECT PAYROLL-FILE
                ASSIGN TO PAYROLL
                ORGANIZATION IS SEQUENTIAL
                ACCESS MODE IS SEQUENTIAL
                FILE STATUS IS PAYROLL-STATUS-CODE

            SELECT PAYCHECK-FILE
                ASSIGN TO CHECKS
                ORGANIZATION IS SEQUENTIAL
                ACCESS MODE IS SEQUENTIAL
                FILE STATUS IS CHECK-STATUS-CODE
```

Comments:

(1) DEBUGGING MODE is "on", so lines with a "D" in column 7 will be translated and will have an effect during execution.

(2) Note the use of the structured periods to end SPECIAL-NAMES and each SELECT statement.

(3) Channels 1, 2, and 5 of the printer carriage control mechanism will be used to position the printer to the three areas on the paychecks to be printed by this program.

(4) The program uses two files. Using the information input from PAYROLL-FILE, it prints paychecks on the PAYCHECK-FILE. The external names for the files (PAYROLL and CHECKS) have IBM OS/VS format.

(5) The ORGANIZATION and ACCESS MODE clauses are specified, even though they have the default value SEQUENTIAL. This is done to provide explicit program documentation.

(6) Both files have associated FILE STATUS code areas which can be tested after every file operation in the PROCEDURE DIVISION. PAYROLL-STATUS-CODE and CHECK-STATUS-CODE must be further defined in the DATA DIVISION. FILE STATUS areas could have been omitted and exception conditions handled in other ways (see Chapter 11).

Review Questions

4.1   Describe the syntax of the ENVIRONMENT DIVISION.

4.2   What is the purpose of the CONFIGURATION SECTION?

4.3   What is the purpose of the INPUT-OUTPUT SECTION?

4.4   Describe the rules for typing the ENVIRONMENT DIVISION.

4.5 Explain the purpose of "debugging lines". How are they affected by the SOURCE-COMPUTER paragraph?

4.6 What is meant by "collating sequence"?

4.7 How is the default collating sequence implemented?

4.8 What must be done in order to use a nondefault collating sequence?

4.9 What are the three functions of the SPECIAL-NAMES paragraph?

4.10 What are "continuous forms"?

4.11 What is a printer carriage control tape?

4.12 Explain how carriage control channels relate to areas on continuous forms.

4.13 What do some modern printers use instead of an actual carriage control tape?

4.14 On IBM systems, what collating sequence is identified by STANDARD-1? by NATIVE?

4.15 What is the computer operator's console terminal?

4.16 What do the PROCEDURE DIVISION statements ACCEPT and DISPLAY do? How do they relate to the SPECIAL-NAMES paragraph of the ENVIRONMENT DIVISION?

4.17 Give the meanings of the following "function-names" in IBM OS/VS COBOL: (*a*) SYSIN, (*b*) CONSOLE, (*c*) SYSOUT, (*d*) C01, (*e*) C04.

4.18 What are direct-access devices?

4.19 What is an "update in place" operation?

4.20 Give some examples of records and files.

4.21 Describe each part of the SELECT statement and explain what it does.

4.22 What is job control language (JCL)?

4.23 What is operating system command language?

4.24 How does the ASSIGN TO clause of the SELECT statement relate to job control language?

4.25 Explain sequential file access (or processing).

4.26 Explain random file access (or processing).

4.27 Define "file organization".

4.28 Briefly explain sequential file organization.

4.29 Briefly explain indexed file organization.

4.30 Briefly explain relative file organization.

4.31 Why is the choice of a file organization so important?

4.32   Relate the need for sequential versus random access to the choice of a file organization.

4.33   Briefly explain the purpose of the PROCEDURE DIVISION statements OPEN, READ, WRITE, CLOSE.

4.34   List some "exception conditions" which may arise during file processing.

4.35   How does the FILE STATUS clause of the SELECT statement relate to handling exception conditions?

4.36   What is an "end of file" condition?

Solved Problems

4.37   Write the CONFIGURATION SECTION of a program to be tested on an IBM 370 computer system. Debugging lines are to be translated into the object program and the EBCDIC collating sequence is to be used:

```
        CONFIGURATION SECTION.
        SOURCE-COMPUTER. IBM-370 WITH DEBUGGING MODE.
        OBJECT-COMPUTER.  IBM-370.
or
        CONFIGURATION SECTION.
        SOURCE-COMPUTER. IBM-370
                    WITH DEBUGGING MODE.
        OBJECT-COMPUTER.  IBM-370
                    PROGRAM COLLATING SEQUENCE IS EBCDIC-ORDER.
        SPECIAL-NAMES.
                    EBCDIC-ORDER IS NATIVE.
```

4.38   Give all the legal variations of line 5, Fig. 4-1.

(1) PROGRAM COLLATING SEQUENCE IS alphabet-name; (2) PROGRAM SEQUENCE IS alphabet-name; (3) PROGRAM SEQUENCE alphabet-name; (4) COLLATING SEQUENCE IS alphabet-name; (5) SEQUENCE IS alphabet-name; (6) PROGRAM COLLATING SEQUENCE alphabet-name; (7) COLLATING SEQUENCE alphabet-name; (8) SEQUENCE alphabet-name; (9) blank line.

4.39   Checks are to be printed by computer. Carriage control channels are set to match up with areas on the checks, as follows: channel 1, date; channel 2, payee; channel 5, amount. The program also displays on the operator's console the total number of checks printed. Write the SPECIAL-NAMES paragraph for such a program.

```
        SPECIAL-NAMES.
            C01 IS CHECK-DATE-AREA
            C02 IS CHECK-PAYEE-AREA
            C05 IS CHECK-AMOUNT-AREA
            CONSOLE IS CHECK-CONTROL-COUNT-DEVICE
```

4.40   Write the CONFIGURATION SECTION for a program using the following collating sequence: B, J, A, K, . . . , W, C, . . . , I, 7, 1, 0, 2, . . . , 6, 9. The program is already fully debugged and is to be compiled and executed on an IBM 370 computer.

        CONFIGURATION SECTION.

        SOURCE-COMPUTER. IBM-370.

        OBJECT-COMPUTER. IBM-370
                    COLLATING SEQUENCE IS
                      WAREHOUSE-BIN-ORDER.

        SPECIAL-NAMES.

          WAREHOUSE-BIN-ORDER IS
            "B" "J" "A"
            "K" THRU "W"
            "C" THRU "I"
            "7" "1" "0"
            "2" THRU "6"
            "9"

4.41   Write the CONFIGURATION SECTION for a program to be run on an IBM 370 computer with the ASCII collating sequence rather than the default EBCDIC sequence. Debugging lines should be translated.

        CONFIGURATION SECTION.
        SOURCE-COMPUTER. IBM-370 DEBUGGING MODE.
        OBJECT-COMPUTER. IBM-370 SEQUENCE ASCII-ORDER.
        SPECIAL-NAMES.
          ASCII-ORDER IS STANDARD-1.

4.42   Card readers, printers, and card punches are often termed *unit record devices*. Explain the file, record, and field concepts in relation to (*a*) a deck of cards; (*b*) a sales analysis report printed on continuous forms.

    (*a*)   Each card is a *record*; the entire deck makes up a card *file*; each separate piece of information keypunched on a card is a *field* (e.g., part #, quantity on order).

    (*b*)   The collection of all printed lines in the report is a *file*; each line is a *record*; each piece of information on a line is a *field* (including separative blanks).

4.43   Describe how an update in place of a disk record might figure in a bank's savings account operations.

      Consider a bank which has online teller terminals (i.e., the terminals are connected to the bank's computer system, either by in-house cable or by telecommunications). If a customer wishes to make a deposit or withdrawal from a savings account, the teller types on the terminal the account number, the kind of transaction, and the amount. This information is input by a computer program which will randomly access a disk file record holding the savings account balance for this customer (to allow random processing, the file would probably be indexed by savings account number). The program then updates the account balance by adding or subtracting the transaction amount. The updated customer record is finally written back to its original location on disk.

4.44   Classify the following COBOL file names:

> (*a*)   SELECT REPORT ASSIGN TO . . .
>
> (*b*)   SELECT REPORT-FILE ASSIGN TO . . .
>
> (*c*)   SELECT OUT-OF-STOCK-ITEMS-REPORT ASSIGN TO . . .
>
> (*d*)   SELECT INPUT-FILE ASSIGN TO . . .

as correct, correct but poor, or incorrect.

(*a*) Incorrect: "REPORT" is a reserved word. (*b*) Correct but poor: "REPORT-FILE" is not very descriptive. (*c*) Correct. (*d*) Correct but poor: there will probably be several input files.

4.45   Each file processed by a COBOL program must be described with a SELECT statement in the INPUT-OUTPUT SECTION. What is the purpose of ASSIGN TO . . . in the SELECT statement?

The ENVIRONMENT DIVISION (since it deals with the hardware environment of the program) is the part of a COBOL program *most likely to change* as you go from one computer system to another. We give two examples:

(*a*)   IBM OS/VS COBOL (for IBM 370-type systems) requires that each file must be additionally described in a job control statement called a *DD* (data-definition) *statement*. The ASSIGN TO name is the common link between the DD statement and the information in the COBOL source program. Thus, for

> SELECT INVENTORY-MASTER ASSIGN TO INVMAST . . .

the associated DD statement would be of the form:

DD statement	*Explanation*
//INVMAST DD UNIT=DISK,	actual device is a disk
// VOL=SER=ABC123,	disk pack named ABC123
// DISP=OLD,	file already exists
// DSNAME=INVNTRY.MASTER.A17	name of file in file label

The presence of the ASSIGN TO name ("INVMAST") at the beginning of the DD statement is mandatory.

(*b*)   Burroughs COBOL (for the B1910 computer system) employs operating system command language instead of job control language. A user at a CRT terminal can type in a COBOL source program, and then type in a command language statement that causes the program to be compiled. Suppose the source program has the following SELECT:

> SELECT INVENTORY ASSIGN TO DISK

B1910 file names are limited to 10 characters ("INVENTORY"). "DISK" in the ASSIGN TO name is a reserved word which indicates to the system that "INVENTORY" is on a magnetic disk device. In B1910 COBOL it is the file name "INVENTORY" that serves as a link between the file definition in the program and command language statements which further define the file. If the PROGRAM-ID is "INVUPDATE", the following command could be typed to execute the compiled program:

> EXECUTE INVUPDATE; FILE INVENTORY NAME INVMASA17

The EXECUTE command tells the operating system to execute the indicated object program. The FILE clause matches the file called "INVENTORY" in the COBOL program with the file actually named "INVMASA17" on the disk. When the program executes, it will update the disk file INVMASA17.

4.46   Indicate your choices of file organization and access mode for the following applications: (*a*) a credit limit master file for a company that allows other merchants to phone in and retrieve the credit limit for a customer's credit card; (*b*) a tape file of names and addresses to be used to print mailing labels; (*c*) an accounts receivable disk file with records of the customers' outstanding balances.

(*a*)   Organization: indexed (by credit card number). Access: random.

(*b*)   Organization: sequential (the only choice for a non-direct-access device). Access: sequential (the only choice for tape).

(*c*)   Organization: either indexed (by customer number) or sequential (sorted by customer number).
        Access: The file must be updated with information about payments and new purchases. If organization is indexed, this could be done randomly. If the payments and purchases file is also sorted by customer number, the update could be accomplished with either random or sequential access. Printing reports (such as an aged trial balance) would be done using sequential access.

4.47   What is an end of file condition?

The "end of file" concept applies when a file is being processed sequentially for input. The first record in the file is read first; the second, second; etc. If the file has 7000 records, "end of file" occurs when the 7001st read is attempted and fails.

4.48   Write a complete ENVIRONMENT DIVISION for a program which prints paychecks. It uses an input tape file of weekly time records, sorted by employee #, and an input disk file of employee master records, also sorted by employee #. All file processing is sequential, and the program is debugged. Carriage control channels are not used by this program, although some messages may be printed on the computer operator's console.

```
ENVIRONMENT DIVISION.

CONFIGURATION SECTION.

SOURCE-COMPUTER. IBM-370.

OBJECT-COMPUTER.  IBM-370.

SPECIAL-NAMES.

    CONSOLE IS OPERATOR-MESSAGES-DEVICE


INPUT-OUTPUT SECTION.

FILE-CONTROL.

    SELECT WEEKLY-TIME-FILE
        ASSIGN TO WKLYTIME
        ORGANIZATION IS SEQUENTIAL
        ACCESS IS SEQUENTIAL
        FILE STATUS IS TIME-FILE-STATUS

    SELECT EMPLOYEE-MASTER-FILE
        ASSIGN TO EMPMAST
        ORGANIZATION IS SEQUENTIAL
        ACCESS IS SEQUENTIAL

    SELECT PAYCHECK-FILE
        ASSIGN TO CHECKS
        ORGANIZATION IS SEQUENTIAL
        ACCESS IS SEQUENTIAL
```

(Did you forget that the printed checks constitute a file and hence require a SELECT statement?) *Note*: (i) the blank lines and structured periods; (ii) the omission of DEBUGGING MODE and COLLATING SEQUENCE; (iii) the association of COBOL name "OPERATOR-MESSAGES-DEVICE" with system CONSOLE; (iv) that WEEKLY-TIME-FILE has been assigned an area (called TIME-FILE-STATUS and further defined in the DATA DIVISION) into which a feedback code will be placed, after every operation on the file.

Programming Assignments

4.49–4.58 Modify Problems 2.29–2.38 to reflect your expanded knowledge of the ENVIRONMENT DIVISION.

Chapter 5

Data Division

5.1 DATA DIVISION Structure

Figure 5-1 indicates the broad structure of the DATA DIVISION, whose general function was described in Section 2.1.

<u>DATA DIVISION</u>.
[<u>FILE SECTION</u>.
[file description entry
 record description entry] . . .
[<u>WORKING-STORAGE SECTION</u>.
[data item or "record" description entry] . . .

Fig. 5-1

Both the FILE SECTION and WORKING-STORAGE SECTION are optional. In practice they are usually both needed, since almost every program uses at least one file and some WORKING-STORAGE counters, flags, work areas, etc. An actual DATA DIVISION, corresponding to the ENVIRONMENT DIVISION of Example 4.1, is given in Example 5.1.

EXAMPLE 5.1

```
00066        DATA DIVISION.
00067
00068        FILE SECTION.
00069
00070        FD   CUSTOMER-SALES-FILE
00071             BLOCK CONTAINS 0 RECORDS
00072             RECORD CONTAINS 80 CHARACTERS
00073             LABEL RECORDS ARE STANDARD
00074             .
00075
00076        01   CUSTOMER-SALES-RECORD.
00077             05   CUST-SALES-CUSTOMER-NO    PIC X(4).
00078             05   CUST-SALES-SALES-ID       PIC X(6).
00079             05   CUST-SALES-AMOUNT         PIC S9(7)V99.
00080             05   FILLER                    PIC X(61).
00081
00082        FD   SALES-REPORT
00083             RECORD CONTAINS 132 CHARACTERS
00084             LABEL RECORDS ARE OMITTED
00085             .
00086
00087        01   SALES-REPORT-LINE             PIC X(132).
00088
00089        WORKING-STORAGE SECTION.
00090
00091        01   END-OF-FILE-AND-STATUS-AREA.
00092
00093             05   CUSTOMER-SALES-FILE-END  PIC X.
00094                  88   NO-MORE-CUSTOMER-RECORDS          VALUE "T".
00095             05   CUST-SALES-FILE-STATUS   PIC XX.
00096             05   SALES-REPORT-STATUS      PIC XX.
00097
```

```
00098        01   TOTAL-AND-COMPARISON-AREAS.
00099
00100             05   OLD-CUSTOMER-NO          PIC X(4).
00101             05   CUSTOMER-TOTAL           PIC S9(9)V99   COMP-3.
00102             05   GRAND-TOTAL              PIC S9(9)V99   COMP-3.
00103
00104        01   COUNTER-AREA.
00105
00106             05   LINE-COUNT               PIC S9(3)      COMP-3.
00107             05   PAGE-COUNT               PIC S9(5)      COMP-3.
00108             05   LINE-SKIP                PIC S9(3)      COMP-3.
00109
00110        01   HEADING-LINE.
00111
00112             05   FILLER                   PIC X(10)      VALUE SPACES.
00113             05   FILLER                   PIC X(20)
00114                                           VALUE "SALES BY CUSTOMER".
00115             05   FILLER                   PIC X(10)      VALUE SPACES.
00116             05   OUTPUT-PAGE-COUNT         PIC ZZ,ZZ9.
00117             05   FILLER                   PIC X(86)      VALUE SPACES.
00118
00119        01   ERROR-LINE.
00120
00121             05   ERROR-CUSTOMER-NO        PIC X(4).
00122             05   FILLER                   PIC X(2)       VALUE SPACES.
00123             05   FILLER                   PIC X(22)
00124                                           VALUE "** OUT OF SEQUENCE **".
00125             05   FILLER                   PIC X(104)     VALUE SPACES.
00126
00127        01   OUTPUT-TOTAL-LINE.
00128
00129             05   FILLER                   PIC X(30)      VALUE SPACES.
00130             05   OUTPUT-CUSTOMER-TOTAL     PIC $$$$,$$$,$$$.99-.
00131             05   FILLER                   PIC XX         VALUE " *".
00132             05   GRAND-TOTAL-FLAG          PIC X.
00133             05   FILLER                   PIC X(83)      VALUE SPACES.
00134
00135        01   OUTPUT-LINE.
00136
00137             05   OUTPUT-CUSTOMER-NO       PIC X(4).
00138             05   FILLER                   PIC X(10)      VALUE SPACES.
00139             05   OUTPUT-SALES-ID          PIC X(6).
00140             05   FILLER                   PIC X(10)      VALUE SPACES.
00141             05   OUTPUT-AMOUNT            PIC $$,$$$,$$$.99-.
00142             05   FILLER                   PIC X(88)      VALUE SPACES.
```

5.2 FILE SECTION

The FILE SECTION must contain a *file description entry* ("FD") for each file named in a SELECT statement of the ENVIRONMENT DIVISION.

EXAMPLE 5.2 In Example 4.1,

        line 52:   SELECT CUSTOMER-SALES-FILE
        line 59:   SELECT SALES-REPORT

name the two files to be processed by the program. The corresponding FD entries in Example 5.1 begin on lines 70 and 82.

Following the FD information, each file must have at least one level-01 *record description entry*, describing the layout of the records in the file. The syntactical structure of an FD entry is displayed in Fig. 5-2.

FD   file-name

$$\left[\underline{\text{BLOCK}} \text{ CONTAINS } [\text{integer-1 } \underline{\text{TO}}] \text{ integer-2 } \left\{ \begin{array}{l} \text{CHARACTERS} \\ \underline{\text{RECORDS}} \end{array} \right\} \right]$$

$$[\underline{\text{RECORD}} \text{ CONTAINS } [\text{integer-3 } \underline{\text{TO}}] \text{ integer-4 CHARACTERS}]$$

$$\underline{\text{LABEL}} \left\{ \begin{array}{l} \underline{\text{RECORD}} \text{ IS} \\ \underline{\text{RECORDS}} \text{ ARE} \end{array} \right\} \left\{ \begin{array}{l} \underline{\text{STANDARD}} \\ \underline{\text{OMITTED}} \end{array} \right\}$$

$$\left[\underline{\text{DATA}} \left\{ \begin{array}{l} \underline{\text{RECORD}} \text{ IS} \\ \underline{\text{RECORDS}} \text{ ARE} \end{array} \right\} \text{ data-name-3 [data-name-4]} \dots \right]$$

$$\left[\underline{\text{LINAGE}} \text{ IS } \left\{ \begin{array}{l} \text{data-name-5} \\ \text{integer-5} \end{array} \right\} \text{ LINES} \right.$$

$$\left[\text{WITH } \underline{\text{FOOTING}} \text{ AT } \left\{ \begin{array}{l} \text{data-name-6} \\ \text{integer-6} \end{array} \right\} \right]$$

$$\text{LINES AT } \underline{\text{TOP}} \left\{ \begin{array}{l} \text{data-name-7} \\ \text{integer-7} \end{array} \right\}$$

$$\left. \text{LINES AT } \underline{\text{BOTTOM}} \left\{ \begin{array}{l} \text{data-name-8} \\ \text{integer-8} \end{array} \right\} \right]$$

Fig. 5-2

The file description header ("FD") must be typed beginning in the A margin; all other entries are typed in the B margin. The "file-name" (same as in the SELECT statement for the file) must be the first entry. The remaining entries may be typed in any order. Blank lines (or blank comment lines) and indentation should be used for readability. There is *only one period*, placed at the end of the entire FD (best to make it a structured period).

EXAMPLE 5.3

DATA DIVISION.

FILE SECTION.

FD   WEEKLY-PERSONNEL-REPORT

　　　　BLOCK CONTAINS 1 RECORD
　　　　RECORD CONTAINS 132 CHARACTERS
　　　　LABEL RECORDS ARE OMITTED
　　　　DATA RECORD IS PERSONNEL-REPORT-RECORD
　　　　LINAGE IS 50 LINES
　　　　　　WITH FOOTING AT 45
　　　　　　LINES AT TOP 8
　　　　　　LINES AT BOTTOM 8

.

　　01   PERSONNEL-REPORT-RECORD...

Note use of blank lines, indentation, and structured period. The record description entry following the FD will describe each field in the file records. The FD name ("WEEKLY-PERSONNEL-REPORT") must be the same as that used in the SELECT statement for the file.

In Sections 5.3–5.7 which follow, we discuss the FD clauses, as shown in Fig. 5-2, one by one. Keep in mind that the purpose of each clause is to provide information regarding how file records are stored on an actual device.

5.3 FD BLOCK CONTAINS...

Files stored on disk or tape are often *blocked* to achieve more efficient space utilization and to speed file processing. In blocking, we distinguish between a *logical record* (processed one at a time by the program) and a *physical record* (the unit of information transferred in or out by an I/O device).

EXAMPLE 5.4 An *unblocked file* on tape or disk consists of *logical records* separated by *interrecord gaps*:

In a *blocked file*, the logical records are grouped into *physical records*, or *blocks*, separated by *interblock gaps*:

The indicated blocked file has three logical records in each physical record; we say that it has a *blocking factor* of 3 (BF = 3), relative to the corresponding unblocked file (BF = 1). For either file, all characters between successive gaps are read in or written out as a unit. Thus, in sequential processing, the blocked file would require only 1/3 as many I/O operations as would the unblocked file—with the consequence that total tape or disk positioning time would be cut down to (very nearly) 1/3 for the blocked file. Since the blocked file has only 1/3 as many gaps, it also takes less file space.

EXAMPLE 5.5 Suppose it is desired to *randomly process* a nonsequential file of 20 000 inventory records. Further, suppose that on the average only half the records in the file are processed during any given computer run. If the file was unblocked, it would require about 10 000 input operations to obtain the 10 000 logical records to be processed.

If the file had a blocking factor of 10, it would still require roughly 10 000 input operations to obtain the desired 10 000 logical records (because, with random processing, the next logical record needed is not likely to be in the block just read). The data transfer time for the "extra" (unprocessed) records in the blocks would thus be wasted. Although blocking can significantly speed sequential file processing, it will slightly slow random processing. However, randomly processed files may still be blocked to save disk space.

The BLOCK CONTAINS clause indicates whether the file is blocked or unblocked, and specifies the blocking factor. The operating system will automatically assemble logical records into blocks on output and analyze blocks into logical records on input. Hence the PROCEDURE DIVISION *is always written to work with individual logical records, regardless of the BF* (see Section 5.8). Three possibilities exist:

File is unblocked.   In this case, the BLOCK CONTAINS clause is omitted from the FD:

            FD   WEEKLY-PERSONNEL-REPORT
                  RECORD CONTAINS 132 CHARACTERS
                  LABEL RECORDS ARE OMITTED
                        .
            01   PERSONNEL-REPORT-RECORD . . .

As blocking applies only to magnetic media, card and printer files are unblocked.

Blocks of fixed length.   Use BLOCK CONTAINS integer-2 CHARACTERS:

            FD   MASTER-INVENTORY-FILE
                  BLOCK CONTAINS 500 CHARACTERS
                  RECORD CONTAINS 100 CHARACTERS
                  LABEL RECORDS ARE STANDARD
                        .

or use BLOCK CONTAINS integer-2 RECORDS:

            FD   MASTER-INVENTORY-FILE
                  BLOCK CONTAINS 5 RECORDS
                  RECORD CONTAINS 100 CHARACTERS
                  LABEL RECORDS ARE STANDARD
                        .

In the first example, the implied BF is

$$\frac{500 \text{ bytes/block}}{100 \text{ bytes/record}} = 5 \text{ records/block}$$

while in the second example the implied block length is

$$(5 \text{ records/block})(100 \text{ bytes/record}) = 500 \text{ bytes/block}$$

The two forms are thus completely equivalent.

Blocks of variable length (which occur when logical records in a file are of different lengths). Use

BLOCK CONTAINS integer-1 TO integer-2 CHARACTERS
RECORD CONTAINS integer-3 TO integer-4 CHARACTERS

(see Example 5.6) or use

BLOCK CONTAINS integer-2 RECORDS
RECORD CONTAINS integer-3 TO integer-4 CHARACTERS

(see Example 5.7).

EXAMPLE 5.6

FD   MASTER-CUSTOMER-FILE
     BLOCK CONTAINS 220 TO 420 CHARACTERS
     RECORD CONTAINS 50 TO 100 CHARACTERS
     LABEL RECORDS ARE STANDARD

Figure 5-3 indicates the structure of one of the variable-length blocks (assuming BF = 3), under IBM OS/VS COBOL.

. . .	gap	BDW	RDW	Logical Record	RDW	Logical Record	RDW	Logical Record	gap	. . .

> BDW ≡ *block descriptor word* (automatically
> inserted by the compiler), which specifies
> the length of the block, including
> the 4-byte BDW itself
>
> RDW ≡ *record descriptor word* (automatically
> inserted by the compiler), which specifies
> the length of the logical record it
> precedes, including the 4-byte RDW
> itself

Fig. 5-3

The RECORD CONTAINS clause *excludes* the RDW, but the BLOCK CONTAINS . . . CHARACTERS clause *includes* the BDW and the RDWs. Thus, a shortest block of our file contains

$$\frac{220 - 4}{50 + 4} = 4 \text{ records}$$

and a longest block contains

$$\frac{420 - 4}{100 + 4} = 4 \text{ records}$$

In short, BF = 4 for the file.

EXAMPLE 5.7

```
FD   MASTER-CUSTOMER-FILE
     BLOCK CONTAINS 4 RECORDS
     RECORD CONTAINS 50 TO 100 CHARACTERS
     LABEL RECORDS ARE STANDARD
```

Here, in contradistinction to Example 5.6, the blocking factor is stated explicitly: BF = 4. The minimum and maximum block lengths are then

$$4(50 + 4) + 4 = 220 \text{ bytes} \qquad 4(100 + 4) + 4 = 420 \text{ bytes}$$

and it is seen that this FD is precisely equivalent to that of Example 5.6.

5.4 FD RECORD CONTAINS . . .

The application of this clause to fixed-length and to variable-length records has already been covered in Section 5.3. The clause is optional because the compiler can determine the record length from the level-01 record description (which includes the size of each field). However, it is a good idea always to use RECORD CONTAINS . . . , since it is useful program documentation and since some compilers will generate a warning message if the field sizes do not sum to the RECORD CONTAINS . . . value.

BLOCK/RECORD CONTAINS 0 CHARACTERS

In IBM OS/VS COBOL, it is valid to specify

$$\text{BLOCK CONTAINS } 0 \begin{Bmatrix} \text{CHARACTERS} \\ \text{RECORDS} \end{Bmatrix} \qquad \text{or} \qquad \text{RECORD CONTAINS } 0 \text{ CHARACTERS}$$

This is an *extension* of the ANS standard, which requires a positive number of characters or records. In IBM COBOL, the use of zero indicates that the block or record size should be taken from the job control language statements which further describe the file (see Section 4.5). Although RECORD CONTAINS 0 CHARACTERS has little practical application in COBOL, BLOCK CONTAINS 0 . . . can and *should* be used to make a COBOL program *independent of* the blocking factor (so that changing the blocking factor will not necessitate changing and recompiling the COBOL source program). (Recall that card and printer files cannot be blocked.)

EXAMPLE 5.8

```
FD   OPEN-INVOICE-FILE
     BLOCK CONTAINS 0 CHARACTERS
     RECORD CONTAINS 250 CHARACTERS
     LABEL RECORDS ARE STANDARD
```

The block length will be taken from the job control statement associated with the file at execution time. If the file already exists and has a file label, the block length could also be taken from the file label (thus eliminating the need to specify it on the job control language statement).

5.5 FD LABEL RECORDS . . .

Recall from Section 1.10 that each file on a direct-access device has a *file label* (automatically supplied by the operating system) which indicates the name by which the file is known to the operating system, the file organization (sequential, indexed, or relative), the location of the index area (if present), the location of the data records, the block size, the type of record (fixed- or variable-length) and the record length, any passwords required to access the file, how long the file should be protected from deletion, etc. The file labels on a disk pack are grouped together in a special operating system file called the *volume table of contents* (*VTOC*) or *directory*.

File labels are optional for magnetic tape files, but because of their many benefits they are almost always used. File labels are not possible for unit record I/O devices (card readers, punches, and printers).

LABEL RECORDS... is the only *required* FD entry. Use

LABEL RECORDS ARE OMITTED

if the file is on a unit record I/O device, or if the file is on magnetic tape but does not have file labels. Use

LABEL RECORDS ARE STANDARD

if the file is on a direct-access device (disk, drum, floppy disk, etc.), or if the file is on a magnetic tape with file labels.

5.6 FD DATA RECORDS...

The DATA RECORDS clause lists the programmer-defined names by which the records in the file will be referred to in the PROCEDURE DIVISION. This clause is of limited utility, especially for fixed-length records, since the COBOL record names immediately follow the FD (they are the first entry in the level-01 record description). The level-01 record name(s) must match the name(s) in the DATA RECORDS clause. DATA RECORDS... is always optional.

EXAMPLE 5.9

```
FD   WEEKLY-TIME-FILE
     BLOCK CONTAINS 436 TO 1636 CHARACTERS
     RECORD CONTAINS 50 TO 200 CHARACTERS
     LABEL RECORDS ARE STANDARD
     DATA RECORDS ARE CLERICAL-TIME-RECORD
                       LAWYER-TIME-RECORD

01   CLERICAL-TIME-RECORD.
        (description of 50-byte logical record)
01   LAWYER-TIME-RECORD.
        (description of 200-byte logical record)
```

Assuming IBM OS/VS COBOL, the blocking factor for WEEKLY-TIME-FILE is 8.

Card files (necessarily unblocked) often have more than one kind of record because all needed fields won't fit on one card. When this occurs, the information is usually *split* across several cards and each card in the group is *coded* to indicate what fields it contains. The *card code* is often placed in the first or last byte of the record (card).

EXAMPLE 5.10 It is desired to place mailing label information on standard 80-column cards. Because the data require more than 80 characters, the file will contain three record types. The file (FD) and record (level-01) descriptions for such a file might be:

```
FD   MAILING-LABEL-FILE
     RECORD CONTAINS 80 CHARACTERS
     LABEL RECORDS ARE OMITTED
     DATA RECORDS ARE RECORD-TYPE-1-NAME
                       RECORD-TYPE-2-CITY
                       RECORD-TYPE-3-BUSINESS
```

```
01    RECORD-TYPE-1-NAME.
      05   CODE-1              PIC X.
      05   ID-1                PIC X(9).
      05   NAME-1              PIC X(30).
      05   STREET-1            PIC X(30).
      05   FILLER              PIC X(10).
01    RECORD-TYPE-2-CITY.
      05   CODE-2              PIC X.
      05   ID-2                PIC X(9).
      05   PHONE-2             PIC X(8).
      05   CITY-2              PIC X(30).
      05   STATE-2             PIC X(2).
      05   ZIP-2               PIC X(9).
      05   FILLER              PIC X(21).
01    RECORD-TYPE-3-BUSINESS.
      05   CODE-3              PIC X.
      05   ID-3                PIC X(9).
      05   BUSINESS-3          PIC X(70).
```

Note that BLOCK CONTAINS . . . is omitted for an unblocked card file. RECORD CONTAINS . . . is used in order that the compiler issue a warning message should any level-01 record not sum to 80 characters (a useful check, since the intent is certainly not to have variable-length records, but to have three kinds of records all of which are of the same length). LABEL RECORDS . . . is omitted for a card file. DATA RECORDS . . . serves as program documentation, making it easy to determine how many different kinds of records there are in the file. Can you name the fields in each type of logical record?

5.7   FD LINAGE . . .

The LINAGE clauses are used only for output print files, and are always optional. When used, they define a *logical page* which includes a *top margin*, a *bottom margin*, and a *page body* within which actual printing takes place. An area at the bottom of the page body may optionally be defined as a *footing area*. LINAGE . . . can be used *instead of* carriage control channels (Section 4.4); the two methods may *not both* be used for the same file. The LINAGE clause is not available with all compilers. See Prob. 8.30 for techniques to control pagination without LINAGE.

EXAMPLE 5.11

```
FD   SALES-BY-SALESPERSON-REPORT
     RECORD CONTAINS 132 CHARACTERS
     LABEL RECORDS ARE OMITTED
     LINAGE IS 54 LINES
          WITH FOOTING AT 44
          LINES AT TOP 6
          LINES AT BOTTOM 6
```

The print file is unblocked, with no file label. LINAGE clauses define a logical page as indicated in Fig. 5-4. All printing will be positioned within the page body (shaded).

The top and bottom margins of a logical page are always left blank, so margins serve only to separate one page body from the next. Both "LINES AT TOP . . ." and "LINES AT BOTTOM . . ." are optional; if either is omitted, the corresponding margin is assumed to contain zero lines.

The footing area within the page body might be used for: (1) printing page totals for certain fields, (2) printing a message when part of a report crosses a page boundary and thus must be continued on the next page body, or (3) ensuring that there is enough room at the end of the page body to finish whatever material has been started (thus eliminating the possibility of something being continued on the next page). The footing area is optional, and if "WITH FOOTING AT . . ." is omitted, the footing is assumed to consist of zero lines at the end of the page body.

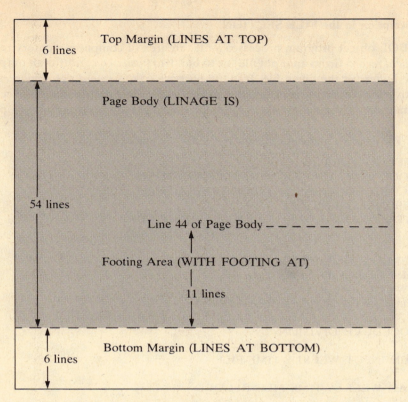

Fig. 5-4

The page body is where the normal report lines are printed. See Chapter 6 for a discussion of PROCEDURE DIVISION considerations when using the WRITE statement to output to a file with LINAGE . . . .

EXAMPLE 5.12

●   FD   OUT-OF-STOCK-REPORT
              RECORD CONTAINS 132 CHARACTERS
              LABEL RECORDS ARE OMITTED
              LINAGE IS 66 LINES
              .

Each page body is 66 lines long and immediately adjoins the next page body. The footing area is zero lines (i.e., it does not exist on the page), but the detection of a footing area will be signaled to the WRITE statement when the bottom of the page body is reached.

●   FD   SALES-BY-CUSTOMER-REPORT
              RECORD CONTAINS 132 CHARACTERS
              LABEL RECORDS OMITTED
              LINAGE 50 LINES
                 LINES AT TOP SIZE-TOP-MARGIN
                 LINES AT BOTTOM 5
              .

Any or all of the LINAGE clauses can specify a value that has been placed in storage before the file is OPENed (prepared for processing, see Example 2.5). In this case, the unsigned integer contained in location SIZE-TOP-MARGIN when SALES-BY-CUSTOMER-REPORT is OPENed will be the width of the top margin. This feature allows the program to *input* or *calculate* the width of any of the LINAGE areas.

5.8 Record Description in the FILE SECTION

When a COBOL object program processes a file, an area of computer memory must be set aside to receive a *physical record* (from an input file) or to build a *physical record* (for an output file); such an area is called the *buffer* for the given file. It is the purpose of the *record description entry* to describe the currently active *logical record* as it appears in the buffer. In other words, the record description entry specifies that part of the buffer which holds the logical record currently being processed.

EXAMPLE 5.13   The program segment of Example 5.9 has the following continuation:

```
FD   WEEKLY-TIME-FILE
     BLOCK CONTAINS 436 TO 1636 CHARACTERS
     RECORD CONTAINS 50 TO 200 CHARACTERS
     LABEL RECORDS ARE STANDARD
     DATA RECORDS ARE CLERICAL-TIME-RECORD
                        LAWYER-TIME-RECORD
     .
01   CLERICAL-TIME-RECORD.
     (description of 50-byte logical record)
01   LAWYER-TIME-RECORD.
     (description of 200-byte logical record)
     . . .
     PROCEDURE DIVISION.
     . . .
     OPEN INPUT WEEKLY-TIME-FILE
     . . .
     READ WEEKLY-TIME-FILE RECORD
     . . .
```

The PROCEDURE DIVISION statements illustrate how to prepare a file for input ("OPEN INPUT WEEKLY-TIME-FILE") and how actually to input a record from the file ("READ WEEKLY-TIME-FILE RECORD"). The READ statement accomplishes the following:

(1) If the buffer is empty, it inputs a physical record into the buffer and makes the first logical record in that physical record available to the program.

(2) If the buffer currently holds a physical record of which all logical records have already been processed, it brings about the same action as in (1).

(3) If the buffer is holding a physical record of which not all logical records have been processed, it makes the *next* (unprocessed) logical record available to the program.

In any event, after the READ statement, there is a *logical record* available to the program. *It is up to the programmer to make sure that the program recognizes which kind of logical record this one is.* The usual procedure is to reserve a certain byte in each kind of record for a *record code*. Thus, the first byte of all clerical records might contain a "C", while the first byte of all lawyer records might contain an "L". A "C-record" would then be given "C-processing" by the program, and an "L-record" would be given "L-processing".

Level Numbers

As an essential part of record description, the fields in a logical record are assigned *level numbers* from 01 to 49. Level number 01 is reserved for the name of the record itself. If the level number increases in going from one field to the next, the second field is said to be a *subfield* of the first.

EXAMPLE 5.14

```
FD   PAYMENT-FILE
     BLOCK CONTAINS 100 RECORDS
     RECORD CONTAINS 33 CHARACTERS
     LABEL RECORDS ARE STANDARD
```

```
01   PAYMENT-RECORD.
     05   CUSTOMER-NUMBER          PIC  X(5).
     05   CUSTOMER-REGION          PIC  X(2).
     05   PAYMENT-DUE-DATE.
          10   DUE-MONTH           PIC  X(2).
          10   DUE-DAY             PIC  X(2).
          10   DUE-YEAR            PIC  X(2).
     05   PAYMENT-RECEIVED-DATE.
          10   RECEIVED-MONTH      PIC  X(2).
          10   RECEIVED-DAY        PIC  X(2).
          10   RECEIVED-YEAR       PIC  X(2).
     05   PREVIOUS-BALANCE         PIC  S9(5)V99.
     05   PAYMENT-AMOUNT           PIC  S9(5)V99.
```

Level number 01, typed in the A margin, indicates the start of a record description entry. The other level numbers, here 05 and 10, are typed in the B margin. Note the use of indentation in the DATA DIVISION. Although not required by the compiler, it is an *extremely* important coding standard, which elucidates the record structure.

The structure defined by the level numbers of the present example is diagrammed in Fig. 5-5.

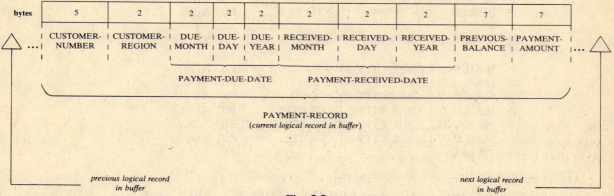

Fig. 5-5

Fields which possess subfields are called *group items*; fields which have no subfields are called *elementary items.*

EXAMPLE 5.15   In Example 5.14:

group items	PAYMENT-RECORD
	PAYMENT-DUE-DATE
	PAYMENT-RECEIVED-DATE
elementary items	CUSTOMER-NUMBER
	CUSTOMER-REGION
	DUE-MONTH
	DUE-DAY
	DUE-YEAR
	RECEIVED-MONTH
	RECEIVED-DAY
	RECEIVED-YEAR
	PREVIOUS-BALANCE
	PAYMENT-AMOUNT

Notice that the elementary items have a "PIC" clause which describes the length and type of data for the item. Group items do not have such descriptions, because they are completely defined by their component elementary items. *The programmer-defined names for group and elementary items always refer to the currently active logical record in the buffer.*

It is a recommended coding standard that an abbreviation of the record name (level-01 name) and/or file name (FD name) be *prefixed* to each data name in the record. It will then be obvious to which file and/or record a given item belongs.

EXAMPLE 5.16

```
FD   MAILING-LABEL-FILE
     RECORD CONTAINS 76
     LABEL RECORDS OMITTED
     DATA RECORDS MAILING-LABEL-NAME-STREET-REC
                  MAILING-LABEL-CITY-STATE-REC


01   MAILING-LABEL-NAME-STREET-REC.

     05   MAILING-LABEL-NAME-ST-CODE          PIC X.
     05   MAILING-LABEL-NAME-ST-ID            PIC X(5).
     05   MAILING-LABEL-NAME-ST-NAME          PIC X(30).
     05   MAILING-LABEL-NAME-ST-STREET        PIC X(30).
     05   FILLER                              PIC X(10).


01   MAILING-LABEL-CITY-STATE-REC.

     05   MAILING-LABEL-CITY-STATE-CODE       PIC X.
     05   MAILING-LABEL-CITY-STATE-ID         PIC X(5).
     05   MAILING-LABEL-CITY-STATE-PHONE      PIC X(8).
     05   MAILING-LABEL-CITY-STATE-CITY       PIC X(30).
     05   MAILING-LABEL-CITY-STATE-STATE      PIC X(2).
     05   MAILING-LABEL-CITY-STATE-ZIP        PIC X(9).
     05   FILLER                              PIC X(21).
```

There are actually two levels of prefixes used in this example:

(1) Every record name and field name starts with "MAILING-LABEL", which is an abbreviation of the file name "MAILING-LABEL-FILE". Any data name starting with "MAILING-LABEL" is thereby known to be associated with the MAILING-LABEL-FILE. This makes it possible to read the PROCEDURE DIVISION without having constantly to refer back to the DATA DIVISION to find out which record and file contains a given field. (When there is more than one level-01 entry for an FD, the logical record descriptions are said to implicitly redefine one another.)

(2) The name of every field in the MAILING-LABEL-NAME-STREET-REC contains the secondary prefix "NAME-ST", which is an abbreviation of "NAME-STREET-REC" (e.g., MAILING-LABEL-NAME-ST-CODE is associated with the MAILING-LABEL-FILE and, in particular, is a field of the record MAILING-LABEL-NAME-STREET-REC in that file). Likewise, every field in the record MAILING-LABEL-CITY-STATE-REC has the secondary prefix "CITY-STATE" in its name.

EXAMPLE 5.17 In Example 5.16 there are two level-01 descriptions for the currently active logical record in the buffer; these two descriptions are visualized in Fig. 5-6.

Note that *both* record descriptions *agree* on the interpretation of the first 6 bytes of the logical record. As MAILING-LABEL-NAME-ST-CODE and MAILING-LABEL-CITY-STATE-CODE both refer to the same memory location (namely, the first byte of the logical record), these two data names may be treated as synonyms in the rest of the program. Likewise, MAILING-LABEL-NAME-ST-ID and MAILING-LABEL-CITY-STATE-ID both refer to bytes 2 through 6 of the logical record, so that interchanging the use of these data names in the PROCEDURE DIVISION will not affect the execution of the program. The first byte of the logical record (which can be referred to either as MAILING-LABEL-NAME-ST-CODE or as MAILING-LABEL-CITY-STATE-CODE) could be used to contain a record code identifying it as a name/street record or as a city/state record. (See Example 5.13 and Problem 5.80.)

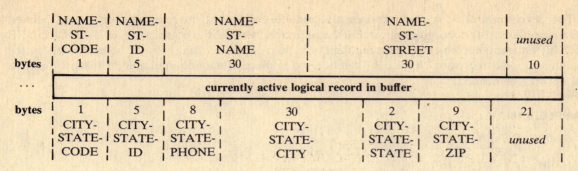

Fig. 5-6

Multiple Buffers

For a sequentially accessed file, it can be advantageous to have two (or more) buffers: the contents of one can be undergoing processing in the CPU at the same time that the other is being fed the *next* block from an I/O device. In IBM OS/VS COBOL, the default number of buffers for a sequentially accessed file is two; the default for randomly accessed files is one buffer. ANS COBOL has an additional clause in the SELECT statement which allows the programmer to specify the number ("integer") of buffers for a file:

$$\underline{SELECT} \ldots \underline{ASSIGN} \text{ TO} \ldots \left[\underline{RESERVE} \text{ integer} \begin{bmatrix} \text{AREA} \\ \text{AREAS} \end{bmatrix} \right] \ldots$$

Unless you are intimately familiar with the computer system and its I/O structure, it is probably best to omit the RESERVE clause and accept the default number of buffers supplied by the compiler.

5.9 Data Description Syntax

The purpose of a data description entry in the FILE SECTION is to describe in full a field of a logical record. Figure 5-7 indicates the general syntax of a data description entry.

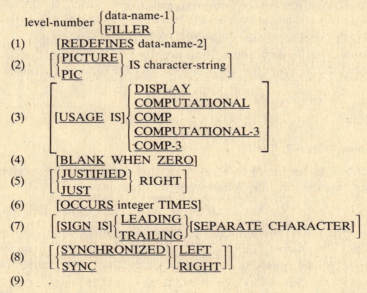

Fig. 5-7

The level-number must be between 01 and 49, where 01 is reserved for record names. "Data-name-1" is the programmer-defined name for the field, to be used in PROCEDURE DIVISION statements which process the field. If a field is present that will *not* be processed by the program, the reserved word "FILLER" can be used in place of a made-up name. "FILLER" may be used as often as needed.

EXAMPLE 5.18

```
FD   PAYMENT-FILE
     LABEL RECORDS ARE STANDARD.
01   PAYMENT-RECORD.
     05   CUSTOMER-NAME              PIC X(20).
     05   PAYMENT-AMOUNT             PIC S9(5)V99.
FD   WEEKLY-RECEIPTS-REPORT
     LABEL RECORDS ARE OMITTED.
01   WEEKLY-RECEIPTS-RECORD.
     05   CUSTOMER-NAME              PIC X(20).
     05   FILLER                     PIC X(5).
     05   PAYMENT-AMOUNT             PIC ZZ,ZZZ.99−.
     05   FILLER                     PIC X(65).
```

. . . .

```
PROCEDURE DIVISION.
```

. . . .

```
     READ PAYMENT-FILE RECORD
     MOVE CUSTOMER-NAME OF PAYMENT-RECORD
         TO CUSTOMER-NAME OF WEEKLY-RECEIPTS-RECORD
     MOVE PAYMENT-AMOUNT OF PAYMENT-RECORD
         TO PAYMENT-AMOUNT OF WEEKLY-RECEIPTS-RECORD
```

The COBOL language rules permit duplication of data-names: "CUSTOMER-NAME" and "PAYMENT-AMOUNT" each appear in two different records in this example. When a duplicated data-name is used in the PROCEDURE DIVISION, it must be *qualified*; i.e., it must be subordinated to a unique group name (thus: "PAYMENT-AMOUNT OF PAYMENT-RECORD" and "CUSTOMER-NAME OF WEEKLY-RECEIPTS-RECORD").

We recommend the use of unique data-names with file/record name prefixes (Example 5.16) over the use of duplicate data-names with PROCEDURE DIVISION qualification.

If used, the REDEFINES . . . clause must directly follow "level-number . . ."; the other clauses may appear in any order. In the succeeding Sections 5.10–5.17 we discuss the clauses in the order of decreasing frequency of use. (Except for the position of REDEFINES . . . , this is the order indicated in Fig. 5-7.)

5.10   PICTURE Clause (Fig. 5-7, line 2)

This clause describes the format of an elementary item; it may not be specified for a group item. The "character-string" may involve the following *picture characters*:

$$ A \quad B \quad P \quad S \quad V \quad X \quad Z \quad 0 \quad 9 \quad / \quad , \quad . \quad + \quad - \quad CR \quad DB \quad * \quad \$ $$

The character-string specifies (1) the number of character positions in the elementary item; (2) the kind of data (numeric, alphanumeric, alphabetic) that will occupy the character positions; and (3) whether or not the item will be *edited* for good visual appearance when printed out or displayed on a video screen.

The PICTURE clause is complicated because so many variations are possible. We discuss each picture character individually below. Remember: *every elementary item must have a PICTURE clause.*

A

Each "A" in "character-string" represents a character position (byte) which can contain only a letter or a space.

EXAMPLE 5.19

        01   EMPLOYEE-NAME.
            05   EMPLOYEE-LAST-NAME   PIC A(15).
            05   EMPLOYEE-FIRST-NAME   PIC A(10).
            05   EMPLOYEE-MIDDLE-INITIAL PIC A.

Comments: (1) Group item EMPLOYEE-NAME has no PICTURE. (2) All elementary items have descriptive PICTURE clauses. (3) The use of a *repetition* or *duplication factor* simplifies typing the PICTURE:

        "A(10)" is an abbreviation for "AAAAAAAAAA" (ten A's)
        "A(4)" is an abbreviation for "AAAA" (four A's)

(4) EMPLOYEE-LAST-NAME occupies 15 character positions (bytes); EMPLOYEE-FIRST-NAME, 10 bytes; EMPLOYEE-MIDDLE-INITIAL, 1 byte. (5) All three data items will consist of letters of the alphabet and/or blank spaces. (6) Use of "PIC" rather than "PICTURE IS" is common.

B (Editing Character)

Each "B" in a PICTURE string represents one byte into which a blank space will be inserted when data are moved into the field. "B" is an example of an *editing character*, which causes data to be rearranged or reformatted when moved into the field having the edit PICTURE.

EXAMPLE 5.20

●   01   GREETING   PIC AABA(5).

Comments: (1) GREETING is an 8-byte field: 2 letters/spaces ("AA"), followed by a space ("B"), followed by 5 letters/spaces ["A(5)"]. (2) 'MOVE "HITHERE" TO GREETING' would produce the following contents in GREETING:

        "HI THERE"

The "B" causes a blank space to be inserted between the first two letters and the last five letters.

●   01   EMPLOYEE-INITIALS.
            05   COMPRESSED-INITIALS   PIC A(3).
            05   SEPARATED-INITIALS   PIC ABABAB.

Comments: (1) *Groups* of picture characters cannot be repeated except by writing them out. ["AB(3)" would give "ABBB", *not* "ABABAB".] (2) If COMPRESSED-INITIALS contained "DAF", then

        MOVE COMPRESSED-INITIALS TO
          SEPARATED-INITIALS

would place "D A F " in SEPARATED-INITIALS.

X

This heavily used picture character represents a byte that can contain *any* character in the character set of the computer system (e.g., EBCDIC for IBM 370-type systems). Often X is used in the PICTURE clause that must accompany a 01-level record that is not divided into fields.

EXAMPLE 5.21

        . . . .
        05   INPUT-SOCIAL-SECURITY-NUMBER   PIC X(9).

        . . . .
        05   PRINT-SOCIAL-SECURITY-NUMBER   PIC XXXBXXBXXXX.

        . . . .

INPUT-SOCIAL-SECURITY-NUMBER might hold a value input from disk such as "111223333", a worker's social security number without unnecessary spacing or punctuation. "PIC X(9)" sets aside enough space to hold any 9 characters. When the social security number is to be printed, however, we will want to *edit* the value to make it more readable. This can be done by inserting blank spaces via the "B" picture character, yielding the printout "111 22 3333".

In general, when numeric data are used for identification rather than computation (e.g., social security numbers, telephone numbers), it is best to use "PIC X".

9

Each "9" in a PICTURE represents the position of a decimal digit (0 to 9). Unlike "A", "B", and "X", however, a "9" does not always require one byte (or character position) of memory. The actual size of a numeric item, which depends upon the data code, will be treated in Section 5.18. While it is invalid in COBOL to program calculations using "numbers" with "PIC X", "PIC 9" is specifically designed for computation. "PIC 9" does not cause any editing of a numeric data item; in particular, it does not insert punctuation or remove *leading zeros*.

EXAMPLE 5.22

```
01   EMPLOYEE-INFORMATION-RECORD.
. . . . . . . . . . . . . . . . . . . . . . . . . . . . .
     05   EMPLOYEE-INFO-SOCIAL-SECURITY        PIC X(9).
     05   EMPLOYEE-INFO-DEPENDENTS             PIC 99.
     05   EMPLOYEE-INFO-SICK-DAYS-LEFT         PIC 9(3).
     05   EMPLOYEE-INFO-VACATION-LEFT          PIC 9(3).
. . . . . . . . . . . . . . . . . . . . . . . . . . . . .
01   SAVINGS-ACCOUNT-RECORD.
     05   SAVINGS-ACCT-NUMBER-DEPOSITS         PIC 9(5).
     05   SAVINGS-ACCT-NUMBER-WITHDRAWS        PIC 9(5).
     05   SAVINGS-ACCT-NUMBER                  PIC X(7).
. . . . . . . . . . . . . . . . . . . . . . . . . . . . .
01   INVENTORY-MASTER-RECORD.
     05   INVENTORY-MAST-QUANTITY-ONHAND       PIC 9(7).
```

EMPLOYEE-INFO-SOCIAL-SECURITY and SAVINGS-ACCT-NUMBER are used for identification, not computation, and so are given "PIC X". All other fields might take part in calculations and so are given "PIC 9". Note that if 52 were moved to the QUANTITY-ONHAND field, it would be stored as "0000052".

S

The "S" picture character indicates the presence of an *operational sign* in a number. An operational sign takes *no extra* storage space, because it is incorporated into the internal data representation for the digits (see Sections 1.11 and 5.11). Binary-twos-complement (COMP) and packed-decimal (COMP-3) have operational signs built into the data representation; so, for these USAGEs, omitting the "S" from a picture string is equivalent to requesting the *absolute value*. DISPLAY (EBCDIC and ASCII) representations automatically reserve space for an operational sign as part of the representation of the rightmost digit, but whether or not the space is actually used depends on whether or not "S" is specified in the PICTURE.

EXAMPLE 5.23

```
05   SECONDS-BEFORE-LAUNCH       PIC S9(5).
```

Comments:

(1) If "S" is used, it must be the *first character* in the PICTURE.

(2) When DISPLAY numbers with operational signs are printed, *the rightmost digit prints as a letter or a blank*. Thus, under EBCDIC (Table 5-1), if SECONDS-BEFORE-LAUNCH is printed 17 seconds before

Table 5-1

Rightmost Digit	With + Sign Prints As	With − Sign Prints As
0	*blank*	*blank*
1	A	J
2	B	K
3	C	L
4	D	M
5	E	N
6	F	O
7	G	P
8	H	Q
9	I	R

launch, it will print as 0001G; whereas if it is printed 12 seconds after launch, it will print as 0001K.

(3) Numbers with operational signs should be moved to *edited fields* and printed in their edited version to avoid difficulty in interpreting printed output.

EXAMPLE 5.24

    05   TOTAL-BALANCE-DUE   PIC 9(5).

Without the "S" in the PICTURE for a numeric item, the computer will always generate a + sign for the number, in effect giving its absolute value. Not only does this require extra machine-language instructions every time the field is manipulated, but also it can be dangerous. For instance, suppose TOTAL-BALANCE-DUE contains 00015, indicating that a customer owes $15. If the customer pays $20 and the value 20 is subtracted from TOTAL-BALANCE-DUE, the following occurs: 00015 minus 00020 gives −00005, which, since there is no "S" in the PICTURE, is stored as +00005. Thus it appears that the customer still owes $5, when in reality the customer has overpaid by $5!

Unless the absolute value is expressly desired, it is best to sign numeric PICTUREs:

    05   TOTAL-BALANCE-DUE   PIC S9(5).

V

The "V" picture character is used to indicate the presence of an *assumed decimal point* in a numeric item. It is used in conjunction with the "9" picture character and may appear *only once* in a given PICTURE. If "V" is omitted, the decimal point is assumed to follow the rightmost digit of the number. Since an assumed decimal point is not actually present in the internal representation of the item, it does not take any extra storage space. Assumed decimal points are used to align numeric items for purposes of editing or computation.

EXAMPLE 5.25   Given that the fields

    05   HOURS-WORKED-THIS-WEEK   PIC S99V9.
    05   TOTAL-HOURS-FOR-YEAR   PIC S9(4).

presently contain +42.5 and +0063. respectively (a fraction of an hour is significant compared to a week, but not to a year). If the computer is to add the weekly hours to the yearly hours, it must be told where the decimal points are supposed to be:

	Incorrect		*Correct*
weekly hours =	425	weekly hours =	42.5
yearly hours =	0603	yearly hours =	0603.
SUM	1028	SUM	0645.5

If the (correct) result is to be stored in TOTAL-HOURS-FOR-YEAR, either the fractional part (.5) must be *truncated* (chopped off) or the number must be *rounded*. If 0645.5 is truncated to PIC S9(4), the result is +0645. Rounding adds 1 to the rightmost digit to be retained if the leftmost digit to be dropped is 5 or more. Hence, if 0645.5 is rounded to PIC S9(4), the result is +0646.

Z (Editing Character)

The "Z" picture character is used in place of "9" to represent the position of a decimal digit which is to be replaced with a blank space if that digit is a leading zero. Fields with editing characters (including "Z") may not be used *in* a computation, although they may receive the result *of* a computation.

EXAMPLE 5.26

●   05   PRICE   PIC ZZZZ9.

If PRICE contains the value two hundred three and is part of a record output to the printer, it would print as *bb*203 (*b* ≡ a blank space). The first two "Z"s in the PICTURE correspond to leading zeros in the value to be printed, so the corresponding positions in the record are filled with blank spaces. The fourth "Z" corresponds to a zero in the value also, but since it is not a *leading* zero (i.e., does not precede all the nonzero digits), it *is* printed. (If PRICE contained zero, *bbbb*0 would print, since PIC "9" always represents the digit, whether it is a leading zero or not.)

●   05   PRICE   PIC ZZZZ.

If PRICE contains zero and is printed, the result is *bbbb*.

. (Period—Editing Character)

The "." (period, decimal point) represents the position of an *actual* decimal point in a field (as against "V", which represents an assumed decimal point). The "." takes one byte of memory in the field and appears when the field is printed or displayed. "." is considered an editing character, so fields with "." in the PICTURE may *not* be used in a calculation. Further, "." may not be the last character in the PICTURE.

EXAMPLE 5.27

```
01   INVOICE-DETAIL-LINE.
     05   INVOICE-PART-NUMBER            PIC X(5).
     05   FILLER                         PIC X(8).
     05   INVOICE-PART-DESCRIPTION       PIC X(20).
     05   FILLER                         PIC X(5).
     05   INVOICE-QUANTITY-PURCHASED     PIC ZZ9.
     05   FILLER                         PIC X(3).
     05   INVOICE-UNIT-PRICE             PIC ZZZ.99.
     05   FILLER                         PIC X(10).
     05   INVOICE-TOTAL-PRICE            PIC ZZZZZZ.99.
```

Comments:

(1) Group item (level-01) does not have PICTURE.

(2) INVOICE-PART-NUMBER is a numeric field used only for identification, so it is given a "PIC X(5)".

(3) FILLER is a reserved word, used in place of a data-name for a field that will not be processed in the PROCEDURE DIVISION. Here it is used to name blank fields that will separate actual data items when these are printed or displayed on a CRT.

(4) INVOICE-QUANTITY-PURCHASED is edited for printing. It is a 3-digit field (two "Z"s and one "9"), and the first two digits will be blanked if they contain leading zeros.

(5) INVOICE-UNIT-PRICE and INVOICE-TOTAL-PRICE are edited for printing. This includes blanking leading zeros and printing an actual decimal point. Note the use of "9"s instead of "Z"s after the "." in the PIC. This is to ensure that the decimal point always prints; punctuation characters surrounded by "Z"s in a PIC are blanked if both "Z"s represent leading zeros.

, (Comma—Editing Character)

The "," represents one byte of storage in which the code for a comma will be placed. Like the ".", a comma between two "Z"s is replaced with a blank if both "Z"s are blanked (because they represent leading zeros). The comma is also replaced with a blank *if there are only blanks to its left*. Numeric fields with "," in the PIC may not be used in calculations (although they may receive the results of a calculation).

EXAMPLE 5.28

PICTURE	Value	Prints As
ZZ,ZZZ.99	00010.05	*bbbb*10.05
ZZ,ZZZ.99	00123.45	*bbb*123.45
ZZ,ZZZ.99	01000.00	*b*1,000.00
ZZ,ZZZ.99	98765.43	98,765.43
ZZ,ZZZ.ZZ	00000.00	*bbbbbbbb*
ZZ,ZZZ.ZZ	00000.03	*bbbbbbb*3
		(falsified)
ZZ,ZZZ.99	00000.03	*bbbbbb*.03
		(correct version of above)

$ (Editing Character)

The "$" picture character can be used to insert a *fixed dollar sign* that prints immediately to the left of the first digit *position*.

EXAMPLE 5.29

PICTURE	Value	Prints As
$Z,ZZZ.99	0072.15	$*bbb*72.15
$Z,ZZZ.99	9876.54	$9,876.54

The "$" may also indicate a *floating dollar sign* that prints immediately to the left of the first *significant character* (which is the first significant *digit* of the numeric item or, possibly, a decimal point). For this use, more than one "$" is needed in the PICTURE: the leftmost "$" represents a place for the dollar sign itself, the remaining "$"s represent digit positions in the field.

EXAMPLE 5.30

	PICTURE	Value	Prints As
(*a*)	$$,$$$.99	0001.23	*bbbb*$1.23
(*b*)	$$,$$$.99	0845.79	*bb*$845.79
(*c*)	$$,$$$.99	9876.54	$9,876.54
(*d*)	$$,$$$.99	12345.67	$2,345.67
(*e*)	$$,$$$.99	−0000.05	*bbbbb*$.05

Comments: (*a*)–(*c*) The dollar sign "floats" over to the highest figure of the edited value. (*d*) There are only 6 digit positions in the PICTURE (the 4 "$"s after the first, plus the two "9"s). Thus the 7-digit value is truncated *on the left*. (*e*) There is no provision for algebraic sign in the PICTURE, so the value is printed as if positive. Here, the first significant character is the decimal point, and the dollar sign floats up to it.

Remember that a floating dollar sign requires *one more* "$" in the PICTURE than there are digit positions to be edited. Items with "$" in their PIC may not be used in computations.

CR, DB, −, + (Sign Control Editing Characters)

These characters are used chiefly in the editing of negative numerical values.

EXAMPLE 5.31 The picture characters "CR" (or "DB") may be used at the right-hand end of a numeric picture to indicate a negative "credit" (or "debit").

	PICTURE	Value	Prints As
(a)	$Z,ZZZ.99CR	0010.56	$bbb10.56bb
(b)	$Z,ZZZ.99CR	−1435.72	$1,435.72CR
(c)	$$,$$$.99BDB	−3476.52	$3,476.52 DB

Comments: (a)–(b) If the value is negative, "CR" (or "DB") prints; otherwise, it is replaced with blanks. (c) Here, the "B" causes a blank space between the last printed digit and "DB" (or "CR").

The other two sign control characters, "+" and "−", also function identically, except in one respect: the "+" always causes the sign of the number to print (whether it is positive or negative), whereas the "−" causes an explicit sign only when the value being edited is negative. These PICTURE characters may be used in a *leading position* (immediately preceding the first digit position) or a *trailing position* (immediately following the last digit position). They are also used in *fixed* and *floating* modes, exactly as the "$".

EXAMPLE 5.32

	PICTURE	Value	Prints As
(a)	$$,$$$.99−	−2345.67	$2,345.67−
(b)	$$,$$$.99−	0023.78	bbb$23.78b
(c)	ZZZ.9+	−763.7	763.7−
(d)	−ZZ.9	23.7	b23.7
(e)	−ZZ.9	−00.7	−bb.7
(f)	+ZZ9	−005	−bb5
(g)	++,+++.9	0003.7	bbbb+3.7
(h)	−−,−−9	0000	bbbbb0
(i)	−−,−−9	−0100	bb−100
(j)	++,++9	0000	bbbb+0

Comments: (a) The trailing minus is frequently employed in business reports to highlight negative numbers. (b) The trailing minus position is set blank for a positive value. (c) The trailing plus position contains the sign of the value. (d) The fixed leading minus is set blank for a nonnegative value. (e) The fixed leading minus always prints in the first position. (f) The fixed leading plus always puts the sign in the first position. (g) The floating plus moves over to the first significant character. (h) The floating minus prints only if the value is negative; ending the PIC with "9" forces "0" to print. (i) The floating minus prints when the value is negative. (j) Zero is considered positive.

In business reporting, sign control is usually handled either by the trailing "−" or by the (trailing) "CR" and "DB". As with the other editing characters, fields with sign control characters may not be used in computation.

* (Asterisk—Editing Character)

Check protection refers to the practice of filling leading-zero positions in a number with asterisks, so that the amount field on a check can be protected from tampering: $***23.54. Check protection is implemented with the picture character "*".

EXAMPLE 5.33

	PICTURE	Value	Prints As
(a)	$*,***.99	12345.67	$2,345.67
(b)	$*,***,***.99	0001234.56	$****1,234.56
(c)	$*,***.**	0000.00	$*****.**

Comments: (a) Four "*"s and two "9"s can accommodate only 6 digits; truncation is on the left. (b) Leading zeros and leading commas are replaced with "*"s; significant digits and significant commas remain. (c) The decimal point always prints when using check protection, even for a zero value.

0 (Zero—Editing Character)

The picture character "0" is used to reserve a position within the edited result into which a "0" will be inserted.

EXAMPLE 5.34

A typical use of the "0" picture character is to supply zero cents so that an item which is kept as dollars in computer memory can be printed as dollars and cents.

PICTURE	Value	Prints As
$ZZ,ZZZ.00	01205	$b1,205.00
$ZZ,ZZZ.00	00002	$bbbbb2.00
$$$,$$$.00	00002	bbbbb$2.00

/ (Slash—Editing Character)

The "/" picture character is used to reserve a byte in the edited result which will always hold a slash (/). "/" is particularly useful when editing numbers which represent dates (e.g., 102383 is edited to 10/23/83 by PIC 99/99/99).

P

A string of "P"s is used to indicate the location of an *assumed* decimal point when the location falls outside the range of digits being kept in memory. "P" is *not* an editing character and is used to define numeric fields which will be used in computations. "P" does not take any extra storage space in a field, it merely indicates the position of an assumed decimal point. "P" may appear only at the left or right end of a numeric field. The only characters which may precede "P" on the left are "S" and "V"; the only character which may follow "P" on the right is "V".

EXAMPLE 5.35

	PICTURE	Value in Memory	Value Used in Computation
(a)	PP99	12	.0012
(b)	99PP	12	1200.
(c)	PP99PP	—	—
(d)	SPPP999	735	+.000735
(e)	SVPPP999	735	+.000735
(f)	SPP999	1234	+.00234
(g)	S9(3)P(4)	538	+5380000.
(h)	SP99	03	+.003

Comments: (a), (b), (g) The assumed decimal point is as many places to the left of the first digit (to the right of the last digit) as there are "P"s on the left (right) of the field. (c) *Invalid*: "P" may not appear on both ends. (d) "S" may precede "P" on the left. (e) "V" is redundant here, because the assumed decimal point is already fixed immediately to the left of the leftmost "P". (f) If the value in memory has more digits than there are "9"s in the PIC, the value is truncated on the left and the assumed decimal point in the truncated value is located by the "P"s. (h) It does not matter to the functioning of the "P" that the leftmost digit is a zero.

5.11   USAGE Clause (Fig. 5-7, line 3)

This clause, which specifies the internal representation to be used for a data item, is often omitted from data descriptions since DISPLAY usage, the default, is the most frequently appropriate.

USAGE IS DISPLAY

Under DISPLAY, a data item is represented in the computer system's character code (either EBCDIC or ASCII), in which each alphanumeric character is represented by a binary code requiring one byte of memory. **DISPLAY is mandatory** if the data item is (1) alphanumeric (PIC X); (2) alphabetic (PIC A); (3) any type of field in a card file record (either input or output); (4) any type of field in a record to be output to a printer; (5) any type of field to be input or output to a CRT or hard-copy terminal; (6) a numeric field whose PICTURE involves one or more editing characters; (7) any type of field *input* from a file where it was *already* DISPLAY. **DISPLAY is recommended** if the data item is a numeric field used only for identification, not computation (it could be in WORKING-STORAGE or on any kind of I/O or auxiliary storage device).

EXAMPLE 5.36 After each field we list the reason(s) why it must be DISPLAY, using the above numberings.

```
01   INPUT-TIME-CARD-RECORD.
     05   TIME-CARD-ID        PIC X(5)       USAGE IS DISPLAY.   (1, 3, 7)
     05   TIME-CARD-NAME      PIC A(20)      USAGE DISPLAY.      (2, 3, 7)
     05   TIME-CARD-HOURS     PIC S9(2)V9.                       (3, 7)
```

USAGE IS COMPUTATIONAL (abbreviated COMP)

COMP is the ANS Standard COBOL USAGE for numeric items to be used in computations. The exact data representation used for COMP data may vary from machine to machine (it is usually some variation of binary-twos-complement). Although the computer can carry out calculations with COMP numbers more efficiently than with DISPLAY numbers, the novice programmer is advised to bear in mind the following. **Don't use COMP** if the data item is (1) properly DISPLAY; (2) nonnumeric or edited; (3) a field associated with a unit record device or a hard copy or CRT terminal; (4) numeric but used for identification only (use PIC X DISPLAY instead). **Use COMP** if the data item is (i) a numeric field in a record *input* from a tape or disk file where it was *already* COMP; (ii) numeric, is used in calculations, and is a field in a record to be *output* to a *tape or disk file* from which it will later be input and used in further computation; (iii) in WORKING-STORAGE (not a file record field) and is numeric, not edited, and used in a calculation.

EXAMPLE 5.37

```
01   DISK-OUTPUT-RECORD.
     05   DISK-CUSTOMER-NUMBER   PIC X(6).
     05   DISK-CUSTOMER-NAME     PIC X(30).
     05   DISK-LAWYER-NUMBER     PIC X(3).
     05   DISK-JOB-NUMBER        PIC X(4).
     05   DISK-JOB-HOURS         PIC S9(3)V9    COMP.
     05   DISK-JOB-RATE          PIC S9(3)V99   COMP.
```

Customer number, lawyer number, and job number are all numbers used solely for identification and so are defined as PIC X DISPLAY (remember: DISPLAY is the default). Customer name is an alphanumeric item and so must be PIC X DISPLAY. Job hours and job rate are two numeric fields which will be used in computations. It is thus more efficient to store them on the disk in COMP form. Later they will be input into COMP data items and used to compute customer invoice amounts, etc.

EXAMPLE 5.38

```
     . . . . . . . . . . . . . . . . . .
     05   ORIGINAL-PRICE      PIC S9(3)V99.
     05   DISCOUNT            PIC S9(3)V99.
     05   DISCOUNTED-PRICE    PIC S9(3)V99.
     . . . . . . . . . . . . . . . . . .

     PROCEDURE DIVISION.
     . . . . . . . . . . . . . . . . . .

          SUBTRACT DISCOUNT FROM ORIGINAL-PRICE GIVING
             DISCOUNTED-PRICE
```

Since all three data items are DISPLAY, the compiler recognizes that they must be converted to COMP (or COMP-3) for purposes of carrying out the calculation. The result will then be converted back to DISPLAY. A typical machine-language translation of the above SUBTRACT might be:

(1) convert ORIGINAL-PRICE to COMP form and place result in temporary memory location T1

(2) convert DISCOUNT to COMP form and place result in temporary memory location T2

(3) subtract contents of memory location T2 from contents of location T1; place difference in temporary memory location T3

(4) convert contents of temporary memory location T3 to DISPLAY form and place result in DISCOUNTED-PRICE

If the three data items had been defined as USAGE COMP, the translation would be more economical:

(1) subtract contents of DISCOUNT from ORIGINAL-PRICE; place difference in location DISCOUNTED-PRICE

USAGE IS COMPUTATIONAL-3 (abbreviated COMP-3)

COMP-3 is an extension of ANS COBOL available on some but not all computer systems. COMP-3 is similar to COMP in that the CPU is capable of doing arithmetic with both COMP and COMP-3 numbers; also, both codes take less memory to represent a given numeric value than DISPLAY does. When COMP-3 is available, it may be a better choice than COMP for numeric items involved in business-type calculations (consult your vendor manuals). *Exception*: Do not use COMP-3 for subscripts (see Chapter 10).

EXAMPLE 5.39 In Example 5.38, replacing "PIC S9(3)V99." by "PIC S9(3)V99 COMP-3." would give the most efficient object program on an IBM-370-type computer. Using COMP for all three data items would give the next-most efficient translation; using DISPLAY (as in Example 5.38) gives the least efficient translation.

5.12 BLANK Clause (Fig. 5-7, line 4)

BLANK WHEN ZERO causes a data item to be set to blank spaces whenever a zero value would have been moved into the item. The clause may be used only with numeric items that do not have check protection. A data item with BLANK WHEN ZERO is automatically considered to be edited, hence its USAGE must be DISPLAY.

EXAMPLE 5.40

```
01   ACCOUNTS-RECEIVABLE-LINE.
     05   A-R-CUSTOMER-NAME      PIC X(30).
     05   FILLER                 PIC X(5).
     05   A-R-TYPE-PAYMENT       PIC XBX.
     05   FILLER                 PIC X(4).
     05   A-R-DAYS-PAST-DUE      PIC ZZ9        BLANK WHEN ZERO.
     05   FILLER                 PIC X(7).
     05   A-R-AMOUNT-PAST-DUE    PIC $$,$$$.99   BLANK WHEN ZERO.
```

If the value zero is moved into A-R-DAYS-PAST-DUE, it will print as *bbb* (instead of as *bb*0). If zero is moved into A-R-AMOUNT-PAST-DUE, it will print as *bbbbbbbbb* (instead of as *bbbbb*$.00). The result is that only nonzero values print on the report, thus confining the user's attention to those customers who are actually past due.

EXAMPLE 5.41   A report produced in Example 5.40 might, without use of BLANK WHEN ZERO, appear as follows:

NAME	TYPE	PAYMENT	DAYS PAST	AMOUNT PAST
FRANK	A	7	0	$.00
ACE	A	7	0	$.00
CARTER	B	3	5	$25.32
SMITH	A	7	0	$.00
PERELMAN	B	5	63	$587.00
CONVERSE	A	7	0	$.00
GETZ	B	3	0	$.00

Observe how significant data requiring human attention "get lost" in the maze of zeros.

5.13   JUSTIFIED Clause (Fig. 5-7, line 5)

The JUSTIFIED clause may be used only for alphanumeric (PIC X) or alphabetic (PIC A) items. Normally (i.e., by default), alphanumeric and alphabetic data are *left-justified* in the field; the clause causes such data to be *right-justified*. This clause is little used.

EXAMPLE 5.42

```
05   FIELD-A    PIC X(5).
05   FIELD-B    PIC X(5)    JUSTIFIED RIGHT.
```

Suppose that the value "CAT" is moved to both FIELD-A and FIELD-B. Then:

Field	*Prints As*
FIELD-A	CAT*bb*
FIELD-B	*bb*CAT

EXAMPLE 5.43

```
05   FIELD-A    PIC X(3).
05   FIELD-B    PIC X(3)    JUSTIFIED RIGHT.
```

Suppose that the value "SMILES" is moved to both FIELD-A and FIELD-B. Then:

	Field	*Prints As*
(*a*)	FIELD-A	SMI
(*b*)	FIELD-B	LES

Comments: (*a*) If a value is too long for the receiving field, PIC X and PIC A items are truncated on the same side where padding occurs if the value is too short. Since the default is left-justification, truncation occurs on the right and the leftmost 3 characters are moved into the field. (*b*) The JUSTIFIED clause causes right-justification. Hence the rightmost 3 characters of the value are moved into the PIC X(3) field.

5.14   OCCURS Clause (Fig. 5-7, line 6)

The OCCURS clause allows the programmer to create a data structure commonly called a *table* or *array*; we discuss COBOL Table Handling in Chapter 10.

EXAMPLE 5.44

```
01   ITEM-DESCRIPTION-RECORD.
     05   ITEM-NUMBER              PIC X(7).
     05   ITEM-WAREHOUSE-BIN       PIC X(2).
     05   ITEM-ON-HAND             PIC S9(5)              COMP-3.
     05   ITEM-SUPPLIERS                       OCCURS 10 TIMES.
          10   ITEM-SUPPLIER-NAME  PIC X(20).
          10   ITEM-SUPPLIER-ID    PIC X(5).
          10   ITEM-SUPPLIER-COST  PIC S9(5)V99           COMP-3.
     05   ITEM-PRICE               PIC S9(5)V99           COMP-3.
```

The group item ITEM-SUPPLIERS is repeated 10 times in the record, thus constituting a *table*. In the PROCEDURE DIVISION, the programmer must use a *subscript* or an *index* to indicate which table entry is to be processed:

> MOVE 'NUTS AND BOLTS, INC.' TO ITEM-SUPPLIER-NAME (WHICH-SUPPLIER)

WHICH-SUPPLIER, a numeric item with a value between 1 and 10, indicates which of the 10 table entries is being processed. Such subscripts should be defined with USAGE COMP:

> 05   WHICH-SUPPLIER   PIC S9(2)   COMP.

5.15   SIGN Clause (Fig. 5-7, line 7)

The SIGN clause may be used only for numeric items having an "S" in the PICTURE and having USAGE DISPLAY. The following options exist:

●   SIGN IS TRAILING
The operational sign is part of the internal representation of the rightmost digit and does not require any extra storage space. This is the default for IBM OS/VS COBOL.

●   SIGN IS LEADING
The operational sign is part of the internal representation of the leftmost digit. It does not require any extra storage space.

●   SIGN IS TRAILING SEPARATE CHARACTER
The EBCDIC (or ASCII) code for a "+" or a "−" is appended to the internal representation of the number. In this instance, the "S" picture character *does* represent an extra byte of storage required for the item. If the sign is not present in a value placed in this data item during program execution, the program will terminate abnormally.

●   SIGN IS LEADING SEPARATE CHARACTER
The EBCDIC (or ASCII) code for a "+" or a "−" is prefixed to the internal representation of the number. Again, the "S" picture character *does* represent an extra byte of storage required. A LEADING, SEPARATE sign corresponds to the way in which human beings normally write negative numbers. If the sign is not present in a value moved into this item during execution, the program will terminate abnormally.

EXAMPLE 5.45   Given

> DATA-ITEM   PIC S9(3)

with a value of +123, Fig. 5-8 shows the internal representation of DATA-ITEM for various SIGN . . . clauses. Each rectangular box represents one byte of memory:

SIGN IS TRAILING: | 1 | 2 | 3+ | (3 bytes)

SIGN IS LEADING: | +1 | 2 | 3 | (3 bytes)

SIGN IS TRAILING SEPARATE CHARACTER: | 1 | 2 | 3 | + | (4 bytes)

SIGN IS LEADING SEPARATE CHARACTER: | + | 1 | 2 | 3 | (4 bytes)

Fig. 5-8

The "SEPARATE CHARACTER" and "LEADING" options will result in a less efficient object program for IBM 370-type computers. In general, it is best to omit "SIGN . . ." and accept the default implementation of the operational sign, on any computer system.

5.16   SYNCHRONIZED Clause (Fig. 5-7, line 8)

On some computers (such as the IBM 370) numeric items with USAGE COMP can be manipulated somewhat more efficiently if the memory locations assigned to the item are *aligned* on the proper *boundary*. For example, a 2-byte COMP item can be processed more efficiently if the address of the first of the two bytes is itself divisible by 2; a 4-byte COMP field can be more efficiently processed if it starts at a byte whose address is divisible by 4.

The SYNCHRONIZED (abbreviated SYNC) clause causes the compiler to assign a location to a COMP item so that it is aligned on the most efficient boundary. This may require the insertion of some *slack bytes* between the previous field in the record and the field being aligned; these are automatically supplied by the compiler.

EXAMPLE 5.46   Given the record description

Length in Bytes

	01	ORDER-RECORD.	
4	05	ORDER-NUMBER	PIC X(4).
5	05	ORDER-CUSTOMER-ID	PIC X(5).
6	05	ORDER-ITEM-NO	PIC X(6).
2	05	ORDER-QUANTITY	PIC S9(4) COMP SYNC.
4	05	ORDER-UNIT-PRICE	PIC S9(5)V99 COMP SYNC.

the memory layout for ORDER-RECORD would be as follows (the leftmost byte has address 0):

4 bytes	5 bytes	6 bytes	1 byte	2 bytes	2 bytes	4 bytes
Order #	Customer ID	Item #	*slack*	Quantity	*slack*	Unit Price

Because the slack bytes are wasteful of storage and can lead to errors determining record lengths, it is recommended that COMP SYNC be used only for subscripts, on IBM 370-type systems.

EXAMPLE 5.47   In Example 5.44, WHICH-SUPPLIER is best defined as:

       05   WHICH-SUPPLIER   PIC S9(2)   COMP SYNC.

It should be noted that in IBM OS/VS COBOL, the specification of "LEFT" or "RIGHT" in the SYNCHRONIZED clause is ignored by the compiler.

5.17   REDEFINES Clause (Fig. 5-7, line 1)

The REDEFINES clause is used to provide an alternative description of a group or elementary data item. When REDEFINES . . . is used, it must be the first clause following the level-number and data-name:

       level-number   data-name-1   REDEFINES data-name-2

"Data-name-1" is the alternative name for the data area, while "data-name-2" is its previous name. The level-number of data-name-1 must be the same as that of data-name-2.

EXAMPLE 5.48

       FD   CUSTOMER-MASTER-FILE
            RECORD CONTAINS 105 CHARACTERS
            LABEL RECORDS ARE STANDARD

```
01    CUSTOMER-MASTER-RECORD.

      05   CUSTOMER-ID                        PIC X(6).
      05   CUSTOMER-NAME                      PIC X(30).
      05   CUSTOMER-ADDRESS                   PIC X(30).
      05   CUSTOMER-REGULAR-DATA.
           10   CUSTOMER-BILLING-TYPE         PIC XX.
           10   CUSTOMER-CREDIT-LIMIT         PIC S9(5)V99    COMP-3.
           10   CUSTOMER-WEIGHT-LIMIT         PIC S9(3)V9     COMP-3.
      05   CUSTOMER-PREFERRED-DATA
           REDEFINES CUSTOMER-REGULAR-DATA.
           10   PREFERRED-DISCOUNT-RATE       PIC SV99        COMP-3.
           10   PREFERRED-LOCATION-CODE       PIC X(3).
           10   PREFERRED-SHIPPING-MODE       PIC X(3).
           10   PREFERRED-BILLING-TYPE        PIC X.
      05   CUSTOMER-CITY-STATE-ZIP.
           10   CUSTOMER-CITY                 PIC X(19).
           10   CUSTOMER-STATE                PIC X(2).
           10   CUSTOMER-ZIP                  PIC X(9).
```

Since the file is kept on disk, COMP-3 can be used for numeric items entering calculations. This not only saves disk space, but results in the most efficient object code. The REDEFINES clause causes CUSTOMER-REGULAR-DATA and CUSTOMER-PREFERRED-DATA to occupy exactly the same memory locations (since this is an FD, these locations would be part of the currently active logical record in the file buffer). Thus there is a 9-byte area of the currently active logical record which can have two quite different interpretations (Fig. 5-9). It is up to the programmer to work with the data-names which correctly match the actual contents of the memory at a given point in program execution. For example, preferred customers might all be given CUSTOMER-IDs which end in zero. After reading a CUSTOMER-MASTER-RECORD, the program could check the last character of the CUSTOMER-ID. If it were not zero, the CUSTOMER-REGULAR-DATA items would be processed; if it were zero, the CUSTOMER-PREFERRED-DATA items would be processed.

CUSTOMER-PREFERRED-DATA

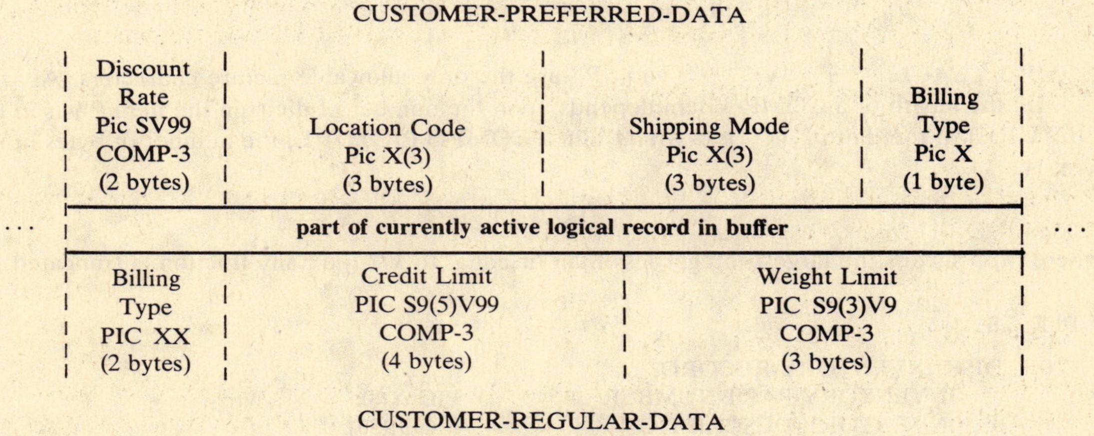

Fig. 5-9

Note that there is complete freedom to REDEFINE an area in terms of PICTURE, USAGE, etc. The only restriction is that *the length of the item being redefined and the length of the redefining item must be the same*. Note, too, that REDEFINES must be taken into account when figuring the record length: the length of CUSTOMER-MASTER-RECORD is 105, not 114, bytes.

EXAMPLE 5.49   In the program of Example 5.16, the statement

```
01   MAILING-LABEL-CITY-STATE-REC
     REDEFINES MAILING-LABEL-NAME-STREET-REC.
```

would cause a syntax error (and would be unnecessary, since the two level-01 items *implicitly redefine* each other). Level-01 items in the FILE SECTION may *not* be explicitly REDEFINED. Level-01 items may, however, be REDEFINED in WORKING-STORAGE.

EXAMPLE 5.50 It is often helpful when checking input fields for correctness (input *validation*) to be able to refer to a given numeric field as either PIC X or PIC 9. REDEFINES . . . allows the programmer to have it both ways:

. . . .

```
05   NUMERIC-INPUT-FIELD                        PIC S9(3)V99.
05   NUMERIC-INPUT-FIELD-AS-X
        REDEFINES NUMERIC-INPUT-FIELD           PIC X(5).
```

5.18 Determining the Length of a Data Item

The amount of memory required to store a given data item is codetermined by its PICTURE and its USAGE. Since the length of a group item is the sum of the lengths of the elementary items which make it up, it suffices to know how to find the length of an elementary item.

DISPLAY USAGE.   Each picture character (with the exception of "P", "S", and "V") requires one byte of storage; "P", "S", and "V" do not take any extra storage.

COMP USAGE.   Since COMP items may not be edited, "S", "V", "9", and "P" are the only allowable picture characters. As with DISPLAY items, "S", "V", and "P" do not contribute to the amount of memory required. Unfortunately, the number of "9"s in a COMP PICTURE does not by itself determine the length. For IBM 370-type systems:

Number of "9"s in PIC	Length of Item in Bytes
1 to 4	2
5 to 9	4
10 to 18	8

COMP-3 USAGE.   "S", "V", "9", and "P" are the only allowable picture characters. As with COMP, the length of a COMP-3 item depends upon the number of digits in the item ("9"s in the PICTURE). If there are k ($1 \le k \le 18$) "9"s in a COMP-3 PICTURE, the number of bytes in the item is

$$[k/2] + 1$$

where $[k/2]$ means the largest integer less than or equal to $k/2$ (i.e., any fraction is truncated).

EXAMPLE 5.51

```
01   DISK-INVENTORY-RECORD.
     05   INVENTORY-PART-NUMBER              PIC X(8).
     05   INVENTORY-DESCRIPTION              PIC X(30).
     05   INVENTORY-ON-HAND                  PIC S9(5)        COMP.
     05   INVENTORY-ON-ORDER                 PIC S9(4)        COMP.
     05   INVENTORY-DISCOUNT                 PIC S9(3)V99     COMP.
     05   INVENTORY-PRICE-WE-CHARGE          PIC S9(5)V99     COMP.
     05   INVENTORY-ORDERED-DATE.
          10   INVENTORY-ORDERED-MONTH       PIC XX.
          10   INVENTORY-ORDERED-DAY         PIC XX.
          10   INVENTORY-ORDERED-YEAR        PIC XX.
     05   INVENTORY-PERCENT-SCRAPPED         PIC SVP9         COMP.
```

On an IBM 370-type system, we should have:

Data Name	Length in Bytes	Comment
DISK-INVENTORY-RECORD	60	record length is sum of field lengths
INVENTORY-PART-NUMBER	8	one byte for each PIC X
INVENTORY-DESCRIPTION	30	one byte for each PIC X
INVENTORY-ON-HAND	4	5 to 9 digits COMP: 4 bytes
INVENTORY-ON-ORDER	2	1 to 4 digits COMP: 2 bytes
INVENTORY-DISCOUNT	4	5 to 9 digits COMP: 4 bytes
INVENTORY-PRICE-WE-CHARGE	4	5 to 9 digits COMP: 4 bytes
INVENTORY-ORDERED-DATE	6	field length is sum of subfield lengths
INVENTORY-ORDERED-MONTH	2	one byte for each PIC X
INVENTORY-ORDERED-DAY	2	one byte for each PIC X
INVENTORY-ORDERED-YEAR	2	one byte for each PIC X
INVENTORY-PERCENT-SCRAPPED	2	1 to 4 digits COMP: 2 bytes (note only one 9 in PIC)

With COMP-3 used instead of COMP, the following changes would occur in the above field lengths:

Data Name	Length in Bytes	Comment
DISK-INVENTORY-RECORD	58	2 bytes saved by using COMP-3
INVENTORY-ON-HAND	$[5/2] + 1 = 3$	saves 1 byte versus COMP; there are five "9"s in PICTURE
INVENTORY-ON-ORDER	$[4/2] + 1 = 3$	takes 1 extra byte versus COMP; there are four "9"s in PICTURE
INVENTORY-DISCOUNT	$[5/2] + 1 = 3$	saves 1 byte versus COMP
INVENTORY-PRICE-WE-CHARGE	$[7/2] + 1 = 4$	same as COMP
INVENTORY-PERCENT-SCRAPPED	$[1/2] + 1 = 1$	saves 1 byte versus COMP

5.19 WORKING-STORAGE SECTION

The WORKING-STORAGE SECTION of the DATA DIVISION allows the programmer to define main storage data areas which are needed by the program but which are not part of any logical record processed by the program (see Problem 2.21). Data description in the WORKING-STORAGE SECTION is quite similar to that in the FILE SECTION, with the following differences:

(1) Since WORKING-STORAGE fields are not part of logical records, there are no FD entries in the WORKING-STORAGE SECTION.

(2) There is a new level number (77) for use in defining WORKING-STORAGE fields which are not part of a record structure.

(3) There is a new data description clause ("VALUE..."), which specifies the value a WORKING-STORAGE SECTION item should have at the start of program execution.

Level-77

While all fields in the FILE SECTION are either logical records or parts of logical records, many WORKING-STORAGE SECTION fields are *independent items*, standing in no evident relationship to other fields in WORKING-STORAGE. The independent items may each be given level number 77 and put at the beginning of WORKING-STORAGE. However, we recommend that, so far as possible, independent items be grouped into WORKING-STORAGE "records", with level-01 record description entries (just as in the FILE SECTION). This makes for easier program debugging and maintenance.

EXAMPLE 5.52 Compare the following two versions of a WORKING-STORAGE SECTION:

```
●   77   NUMBER-OF-CHECKS-PRINTED          PIC S9(5)        COMP-3.
    77   NUMBER-OF-OVERTIME-WORKERS        PIC S9(5)        COMP-3.
    77   TAX-TABLE-SUBSCRIPT               PIC S9(4)        COMP SYNC.
    77   ALL-RECORDS-PROCESSED-SW          PIC X.
    77   DEDUCTION-TABLE-SUBSCRIPT         PIC S9(4)        COMP SYNC.
    77   BELONGS-CREDIT-UNION-SW           PIC X.


    01   PAYROLL-REPORT-LINE-AREA.
         05   PAYROLL-EMPLOYEE-ID          PIC X(5).
         05   FILLER                       PIC X(3)         VALUE SPACES.
         05   PAYROLL-EMPLOYEE-NAME        PIC X(20).
         05   FILLER                       PIC X(4)         VALUE SPACES.
         05   PAYROLL-GROSS-PAY            PIC $$$,$$$.99.

●   01   WORKING-COUNTERS.
         05   WORKING-NUMBER-CHECKS-PRINTED    PIC S9(5)    COMP-3.
         05   WORKING-NUM-OVERTIME-WORKERS     PIC S9(5)    COMP-3.

    01   WORKING-PROGRAM-SWITCHES.
         05   ALL-RECORDS-PROCESSED-SW     PIC X.
         05   BELONGS-CREDIT-UNION-SW      PIC X.

    01   WORKING-TABLE-SUBSCRIPTS.
         05   TAX-TABLE-SUBSCRIPT          PIC S9(4)        COMP SYNC.
         05   DEDUCTION-TABLE-SUBSCRIPT    PIC S9(4)        COMP SYNC.

    01   PAYROLL-REPORT-LINE-AREA.
         05   PAYROLL-EMPLOYEE-ID          PIC X(5).
         05   FILLER                       PIC X(3)         VALUE SPACES.
         05   PAYROLL-EMPLOYEE-NAME        PIC X(20).
         05   FILLER                       PIC X(4)         VALUE SPACES.
         05   PAYROLL-GROSS-PAY            PIC $$$,$$$.99.
```

In the second version, the six original level-77 items have been grouped into three classes: counters, program switches, and subscripts. Each group of items has been treated as a set of fields in a level-01 entry. The level-01 data-name is descriptive of the class of data items being defined. This second version is much better organized than the first.

EXAMPLE 5.53 Although the PICTURE clause is invalid for a group item, USAGE... and SYNCHRONIZED... may be specified at the group level, in which case they apply to all items in the group. We feel that this practice should be used sparingly, if at all, since it increases the probability that a maintenance programmer will not recognize the correct USAGE for an item. A relatively "safe" place to employ group USAGE would be in the groupings of what would otherwise be level-77 items in WORKING-STORAGE (e.g., in Ex. 5.52, "01 WORKING-COUNTERS   COMP-3").

VALUE Clause

When

$$\left[\underline{\text{VALUE}} \text{ IS } \left\{ \begin{array}{l} \text{literal} \\ \text{figurative constant} \end{array} \right\} \right]$$

is used, it indicates the value of a WORKING-STORAGE data item at the start of program execution. If the VALUE clause is not used, data items have totally unpredictable starting contents; programmers say that such data items contain *garbage* or are *undefined*. Many times, the initial contents of a data item are of no importance because the logic of the program injects meaningful data (erasing the garbage) before attempting to use the contents of the location.

There are two kinds of literals and six types of figurative constants:

Nonnumeric literals. A nonnumeric literal consists of any string of characters inside quotes (called a *quoted string* in Section 2.3). If it is desired to represent a quote in a nonnumeric literal, two quotes next to each other are used; only one of the quotes is considered part of the literal.

EXAMPLE 5.54

    05 CUSTOMER-NAME PIC X(15) VALUE """"KWIK"" CLEAN".

specifies the value "KWIK" CLEAN (each *pair* of double quotes within the literal represents one double quote in the value).

    Some compilers use the single quote (or apostrophe) instead of the double quote. The ANS 74 Standard specifies the use of double quotes, but the programmer should, of course, conform to his or her computer system:

    05 CUSTOMER-NAME PIC X(15) VALUE 'PERELMAN''S PETS'.

Numeric literals are composed of the digits 0 through 9, + (plus sign), − (minus sign), and the decimal point. The maximum value of a numeric literal will depend on your computer system; in IBM OS/VS COBOL it is $10^{18} - 1$ (i.e., 18 digits). When a sign is not specified, numeric literals are assumed to be positive. If a numeric literal does not have a decimal point, it is said to be an *integer*.

Figurative constants. A figurative constant is a reserved word which stands for a constant value and can be used anywhere in a program in place of the corresponding literal. Table 5-2 displays the figurative constants of IBM OS/VS COBOL.

Table 5-2

Reserved Word	Type of Literal Replaced	Value
ZERO ZEROS (or ZEROES)	numeric	0 (repeated an appropriate number of times; compiler adjusts for DISPLAY zero or COMP zero)
SPACE SPACES	nonnumeric	a blank space (appropriately repeated)
HIGH-VALUE HIGH-VALUES	nonnumeric	the highest character in the collating sequence (appropriately repeated)
LOW-VALUE LOW-VALUES	nonnumeric	the lowest character in the collating sequence (appropriately repeated)
QUOTE QUOTES	nonnumeric	the (single or double) quotation marks in use (appropriately repeated)
ALL literal	nonnumeric	"literal" may be any string of characters enclosed in quotes (string appropriately repeated)

EXAMPLE 5.55   Observe the use of literals and figurative constants in the following:

. . . .

```
        WORKING-STORAGE SECTION.
        01   ALL-WORKING-STORAGE.
             05   FILLER                    PIC X(30)
                                            VALUE "WORKING-STORAGE BEGINS HERE".
             05   LAST-RECORD-FLAG          PIC X(3)
                                            VALUE HIGH-VALUES.
             05   UNDERLINE-AREA            PIC X(100)    VALUE ALL "-".
             05   BLANK-LINE-AREA           PIC X(100)    VALUE SPACES.
             05   INVALID-RECORD-COUNT      PIC S9(4)     COMP-3   VALUE ZERO.
```

. . . .

```
        PROCEDURE DIVISION.
             MOVE SPACES TO OUTPUT-MESSAGE-AREA
             MOVE "INVALID PART NUMBER" TO OUTPUT-MESSAGE
             MOVE 200.95 TO DAILY-QUOTA
             MOVE ALL "*" TO PAID-OUT-MESSAGE-AREA
             MOVE LOW-VALUES TO EMPLOYEE-MASTER-ID
```

Note especially the use of a nonnumeric literal to mark the beginning of WORKING-STORAGE. This can make it easier to find WORKING-STORAGE in a *dump* (see Section 9.2).

VALUE . . . versus MOVE . . .

As we have seen, the VALUE clause can be used to initialize a WORKING-STORAGE item:

```
        05   INVALID-RECORD-COUNT   PIC S9(4)   COMP-3   VALUE ZERO.
```

Now, a PROCEDURE DIVISION MOVE statement at the beginning of program execution could also be used to initialize the item:

```
        MOVE ZERO TO INVALID-RECORD-COUNT
```

We offer the following suggestions regarding these two techniques:

(1)   If the item being initialized will retain its initial value throughout program execution, use the VALUE clause.

(2)   If the value of the data item will change during program execution and the program logic requires that the item have a definite starting value, use the MOVE statement.

(3)   If the item is not in WORKING-STORAGE (with the exception of level-88 items; see Section 7.8), the VALUE clause may *not* be used.

(4)   If the starting value of the data item is irrelevant to the program, don't initialize the item.

5.20   Coding Standards

We here recapitulate the recommended coding standards for the IDENTIFICATION, ENVIRONMENT, and DATA DIVISIONS.

1.   The IDENTIFICATION DIVISION paragraphs were included in the ANS Standard because the information they represent is important. Don't skimp on IDENTIFICATION DIVISION entries.

2.   There is considerable flexibility in the typing of the IDENTIFICATION DIVISION: aim to keep it readable.

3.   Use comment lines at the end of the IDENTIFICATION DIVISION to summarize what the program is all about.

4. Use structured periods when an entry has several clauses (e.g., SPECIAL-NAMES, FD).

5. Increment level numbers by more than 01, allowing insertions later on. (In this Outline 01, 05, 10, 15, 20, . . . is used.)

6. Indent to show structure of level numbers.

7. Each data-name should have a short prefix (or suffix) which associates it with the record of which it is a part.

8. The rest of the data-name should be as descriptive as possible (remember that you have up to 30 characters).

9. Code the SELECT statements in some standard order (e.g., input files first, then input/output files, then output files) and use the same order for the FDs.

10. Do not use level-77 items in WORKING-STORAGE; instead, group items into meaningful categories under descriptive level-01 names.

11. Use some standard order for coding items in WORKING-STORAGE, which include: program switches, flags, counters, figurative constants and literals, total areas (accumulators), subscripts, tables, and working copies of logical records for files. These last should be ordered as in the FDs; for print files define working copies of heading lines first, body lines next, then total and footing lines last.

12. So far as possible, align PIC, USAGE, SYNC, and VALUE clauses in columns.

13. If possible, indicate the function of a data item in the data-name; e.g., make all program switches end in "-SWITCH" or "-SW", all flags in "-FLAG", all total areas in "-TOTAL", all counters in "-COUNT" or "-COUNTER".

14. Some compilers provide extensions to ANS COBOL which allow the programmer to separate items on the printed source listing, for greater readability. For instance, in IBM OS/VS COBOL, "EJECT", typed anywhere in margin B of a line, causes the next line of the listing to start at the top of a new page. "SKIP1", "SKIP2", or "SKIP3", typed anywhere in margin B of a line, causes the compiler to skip the indicated number of lines in the listing. These features can be used to ensure that each DIVISION and SECTION begins on a new page of the listing, and that paragraphs are separated from one another (with the paragraph name set off by blank lines). SKIP1, SKIP2, and SKIP3 can be processed faster by the compiler than totally blank lines inserted in the program for spacing purposes.

Review Questions

5.1 What is the purpose of the DATA DIVISION? of the FILE SECTION? of the WORKING-STORAGE SECTION?

5.2 What kinds of data items are likely to be found in WORKING-STORAGE?

5.3 What is the purpose of a level-01 entry in the DATA DIVISION?

5.4 Explain the relationship between FDs and SELECT statements.

5.5 What information is specified in an FD?

5.6 Explain how blocking saves space on disk or tape.

5.7 Differentiate between physical and logical records.

5.8   Define *blocking factor.*

5.9   What are interrecord and interblock gaps?

5.10   Explain how blocking can speed sequential file processing for a disk or tape.

5.11   Explain the effect of blocking on random file processing.

5.12   Explain how variable-length records are handled by IBM OS/VS systems.

5.13   Explain how to calculate the BLOCK CONTAINS . . . values for variable-length records.

5.14   Why is RECORD CONTAINS . . . optional? When should it be used?

5.15   Explain how to calculate the RECORD CONTAINS . . . values for variable-length records.

5.16   What is the special meaning of "BLOCK CONTAINS 0 RECORDS" in IBM OS/VS COBOL?

5.17   Explain the use of file labels for tape and disk files.

5.18   What is a VTOC or directory?

5.19   What is the only required entry in an FD?

5.20   Which files are likely to have file labels?   which are not?

5.21   Why is DATA RECORDS . . . used so infrequently? When might it be useful?

5.22   Give an example of a file with more than one type of logical record. Explain how *record codes* could be used to distinguish between the various types.

5.23   Define the following terms associated with the LINAGE clause: (*a*) logical page, (*b*) page body, (*c*) footing area, (*d*) top margin, (*e*) bottom margin.

5.24   For what type of file should the LINAGE clause be used?

5.25   What is an *I/O area* or *buffer*?

5.26   Explain the relationship between level-01 entries in the FD for a file and the file's buffers.

5.27   What are the valid level numbers?

5.28   What is special about level number 01?

5.29   Explain how level numbers are used to show record structure.

5.30   What is the importance of indentation in the DATA DIVISION?

5.31   Define: (*a*) group item, (*b*) elementary item.

5.32   Give some suggestions for inventing names for data items.

5.33   When a file has more than one type of logical record, why is it that both types generally agree in a particular byte or bytes?

5.34   Explain how multiple buffers can speed sequential file processing.

5.35 What is the use of "FILLER"?

5.36 Describe what is meant by *editing*.

5.37 What is the purpose of the PICTURE clause?

5.38 How may a picture character be easily repeated in a PICTURE?

5.39 Explain the use of picture characters "A" and "B".

5.40 Why is "X" such a frequently used picture character?

5.41 Discuss what PICTUREs should be used to represent "numbers".

5.42 Explain the use of "S", "9", and "V" in representing numbers. Differentiate between these and PIC "X".

5.43 Define: (*a*) truncation, (*b*) rounding.

5.44 Why do "S" and "V" not require any storage space in a data item?

5.45 When should "S" be used, and why? When should it be omitted?

5.46 What would be the result if a numeric item with PIC "S", "9", and "V" were printed "as is" on an IBM system?

5.47 Explain numeric editing with: "Z", period, comma, "$", "CR", "DB", "−", "+".

5.48 Explain check protection.

5.49 Explain the difference between "fixed" and "floating" editing.

5.50 In what format are negative numbers usually printed in business reports?

5.51 Explain the use of PIC "0", "/", and "P".

5.52 Give the USAGEs available with IBM OS/VS COBOL, and tell when each ought, or ought not, to be used.

5.53 When must an item be DISPLAY?

5.54 Why is COMP or COMP-3 more efficient for fields in computations?

5.55 What are some advantages of using COMP or COMP-3 for numeric fields in disk or tape records?

5.56 Explain how to determine the length of a data item which is (*a*) DISPLAY, (*b*) COMP, (*c*) COMP-3.

5.57 Explain the use of BLANK WHEN ZERO.

5.58 Explain the function of JUSTIFIED . . . .

5.59 What does the OCCURS clause do?

5.60 Discuss the various options for SIGN IS . . . .

5.61 Explain what SYNCHRONIZED . . . does.

5.62   What are slack bytes? Relate them to the question of when SYNC should and should not be used.

5.63   Explain the use of REDEFINES . . . . Give a concrete example.

5.64   What should be used in place of level-77 in WORKING-STORAGE?

5.65   What is *garbage*?

5.66   Give the rules for forming COBOL literals and figurative constants.

5.67   Explain the use of the VALUE clause.

5.68   When should a data item be initialized with a VALUE clause?   with a PROCEDURE DIVISION MOVE statement?

Solved Problems

5.69   What is wrong with the following WORKING-STORAGE SECTION entry?

        05   MAXIMUM-TOTAL-SALES   PIC S9(5)V99   VALUE HIGH-VALUES.

    HIGH-VALUES and LOW-VALUES are nonnumeric figurative constants; they may be used only with PIC X, and never in calculations.

5.70   Given

      SELECT CUSTOMER-ORDER-FILE   ASSIGN TO ORDERS.
      SELECT ORDER-EDIT-REPORT   ASSIGN TO EDITLOG.
      SELECT CUSTOMER-MASTER-FILE   ASSIGN TO CUSTMAST.

what FD names would be used in the FILE SECTION?

      FILE SECTION.

      FD   CUSTOMER-ORDER-FILE
      . . . .
      FD   ORDER-EDIT-REPORT
      . . . .
      FD   CUSTOMER-MASTER-FILE
      . . . .

5.71   Suppose the CUSTOMER-ORDER-FILE in Problem 5.70 to consist of 65-byte records, with a blocking factor of 40. They are currently stored on disk. Give the complete FD.

      FD   CUSTOMER-ORDER-FILE
         BLOCK CONTAINS 40 RECORDS
         RECORD CONTAINS 65 CHARACTERS
         LABEL RECORDS ARE STANDARD

    Since the file is on disk, standard file labels are required. On IBM systems, it would have been better to use "BLOCK CONTAINS 0 RECORDS" so that the blocking factor might be taken from the already-existing file label.

5.72 If the file in Problem 5.71 contains 2000 logical records, how many disk input operations would be required to sequentially process the file?

With 40 logical records per block, 2000 logical records require 2000/40 or 50 blocks. Since each disk input transfers an entire block, only 50 input operations would be required.

Had the file been unblocked, there would have been one logical record per physical record. Hence there would have been one disk I/O operation per logical record, for a total of 2000 I/O operations.

5.73 Why is the number of "disk I/O operations" an important measure of the speed with which the file can be processed?

Unlike accessing data in computer memory, which can be done in nanoseconds (10^{-9} s) or less, accessing data on disk *sometimes* involves access arm movement (unless the disk is fixed head per track or unless the movable arm already happens to be where it's needed) and *always* involves rotational delay while the desired block spins around under the head. These are mechanical operations, which are very slow compared to computer electronic operations: for an IBM 3380-model disk, the average access motion time is 16 ms and the average rotational delay is 8.3 ms. If file processing involves a large number of physical disk accesses, these millisecond times can add up.

5.74 How does blocking affect the utilization of space on a tape or disk?

Blocking saves disk and tape space by eliminating some of the interrecord gaps. For instance, the file in Problem 5.72 requires 4 tracks on a model 3380 disk, if BF = 40. If BF = 1, the same file would require 25 tracks.

5.75 Suppose that ORDER-EDIT-REPORT in Problem 5.70 is to be output on a printer that prints 132 characters per line. Give the complete FD for this file.

```
FD   ORDER-EDIT-REPORT
     RECORD CONTAINS 132 CHARACTERS
     LABEL RECORDS ARE OMITTED
     LINAGE IS 60
         WITH FOOTING AT 55
         LINES AT TOP 3
         LINES AT BOTTOM 3
```

BLOCK CONTAINS . . . is omitted, to indicate that the print file is unblocked. LABEL RECORDS ARE OMITTED for printer files. The LINAGE clause makes it easier for PROCEDURE DIVISION "WRITE" statements to control the position of lines on the page. Carriage control channels may not be used with this file, since LINAGE is specified.

5.76 Suppose that the CUSTOMER-MASTER-FILE in Problem 5.70 has two kinds of logical records: REGULAR-CUSTOMER-RECORDS are 200 bytes long, while PREFERRED-CUSTOMER-RECORDS are 350 bytes long. Give the complete FD, if the blocking factor is 40. Use BLOCK CONTAINS . . . RECORDS.

```
FD   CUSTOMER-MASTER-FILE
     BLOCK CONTAINS 40 RECORDS
     RECORD CONTAINS 200 TO 350 CHARACTERS
     LABEL RECORDS ARE STANDARD
     DATA RECORDS ARE
         REGULAR-CUSTOMER-RECORD
         PREFERRED-CUSTOMER-RECORD

01   REGULAR-CUSTOMER-RECORD . . .

01   PREFERRED-CUSTOMER-RECORD . . .
```

5.77   Work Problem 5.76 using BLOCK CONTAINS . . . CHARACTERS.

        FD   CUSTOMER-MASTER-FILE
             BLOCK CONTAINS 8164 TO 14164 CHARACTERS
             RECORD CONTAINS 200 TO 350 CHARACTERS
             LABEL RECORDS ARE STANDARD
             DATA RECORDS ARE
                 REGULAR-CUSTOMER-RECORD
                 PREFERRED-CUSTOMER-RECORD

RECORD CONTAINS . . . does not include bytes used for the record and block descriptor words; but, when the CHARACTERS option is used, BLOCK CONTAINS . . . must include these 4-byte areas. 8164 is the number of bytes required to hold a minimum-sized block: forty 200-byte logical records, plus forty 4-byte record descriptor words, plus one 4-byte block descriptor word. Similarly, 14164 is the number of bytes required to hold a maximum-sized block.

        In IBM OS/VS COBOL, it would be better to specify "BLOCK CONTAINS 0 CHARACTERS", so that the block size could be taken from the file label (since this is an already-existing file with standard labels).

5.78   If a file *does not exist*, but is to be created by the program, may "BLOCK CONTAINS 0 . . ." be used?

        Yes, but in this case the job control language statement which defines the file must specify the block size, or an error will occur.

5.79   Classify the I/O devices discussed in this book, with respect to whether or not they support file labels.

Label Records Omitted	*Label Records Standard*
1. card reader	1. movable-head disk
2. card punch	2. fixed-head disk and drums
3. printer	3. magnetic tape (reel)
	4. magnetic tape (cassette)
	5. floppy disk

Labels are required for all types of disk files. Labels are generally used for all types of tape files because of the safeguards and convenience they provide.

5.80   Write PROCEDURE DIVISION statements, involving record codes, which will print a mailing label from the file of Examples 5.16 and 5.17.

        READ MAILING-LABEL-FILE RECORD
        IF MAILING-LABEL-NAME-ST-CODE IS EQUAL TO "1"
            MOVE MAILING-LABEL-NAME-ST-NAME   TO LABEL-NAME
            MOVE MAILING-LABEL-NAME-ST-STREET   TO LABEL-STREET
        ELSE
            IF MAILING-LABEL-NAME-ST-CODE IS EQUAL TO "2"
                MOVE MAILING-LABEL-CITY-STATE-CITY   TO LABEL-CITY
                MOVE MAILING-LABEL-CITY-STATE-STATE   TO LABEL-STATE
                MOVE MAILING-LABEL-CITY-STATE-ZIP   TO LABEL-ZIP
            ELSE
                DISPLAY "ERROR -- INVALID RECORD CODE: IGNORED"

The READ statement first inputs a logical record from the MAILING-LABEL-FILE. Recall from Example 5.17 that the first byte of the logical record is occupied by a record code which identifies its type. Suppose that name/street records have a "1" in the first byte, and city/state/zip records have a "2".

Since the first byte of each type of record is described as PIC X, it doesn't matter by which data-name the programmer refers to it (both MAILING-LABEL-NAME-ST-CODE and MAILING-LABEL-CITY-STATE-CODE access the first byte of the logical record and interpret it as "PIC X").

After the READ statement, the program uses an IF statement to check whether the first byte of the logical record is a "1". If it is, the name and street are moved into the label area; if it is not, the first byte of the logical record is checked to see whether it is a "2". If the first byte is neither a "1" nor a "2", the program prints an error message and ignores the logical record. Notice how the data-names used in the MOVE statements depend completely on the record code.

5.81 Both PIC A and PIC X can be used for alphabetic data. Which is better?

Many COBOL programmers use PIC X instead of PIC A for alphabetic data. There are no disadvantages in doing this, and in fact there are some advantages: certain PROCEDURE DIVISION statements are valid for PIC X but not PIC A. (See Chapters 6 and 7.)

5.82 Classify the data items whose PICTUREs follow as (i) alphabetic, (ii) alphanumeric, (iii) numeric, or (iv) numeric edited:

(a)	AABAAA	(e)	99/99/99	(i)	A(10)
(b)	XXBXXX	(f)	$ZZ,ZZZ.99	(j)	9(3)V99
(c)	S9(3)V99	(g)	S99PP	(k)	$$$,$$$.99BCR
(d)	S9(3).99	(h)	X(7)	(l)	Z999

(a) i; (b) ii; (c) iii; (d) iv (the operational sign "S" and the editing character "." are incompatible); (e) iv; (f) iv; (g) iii; (h) ii; (i) i; (j) iii; (k) iv; (l) iv.

5.83 Give an appropriate PICTURE, and a USAGE if not DISPLAY, for each of the following data items (if more than one choice is possible, list the best choice first): (a) a social security number (without hyphens); (b) an amount up to $1,000 on a check; (c) a social security number (with hyphens); (d) a last name (up to 20 characters); (e) number of hours of overtime (to nearest tenth)—tape file; (f) number of widgets in the warehouse (up to 99,999)—disk file; (g) balance due on a mortgage (up to 500,000.00)—card file; (h) balance due on a mortgage (up to 500,000.00)—disk file; (i) balance due on a mortgage (up to 500,000.00)—printed report; (j) number of hours of overtime (nearest .1)—card file; (k) number of hours of overtime (nearest .1)—printed report; (l) number of widgets in the warehouse (up to 99,999)—card file; (m) number of widgets in the warehouse (up to 99,999)—printed report; (n) freight charges per pound (nearest .1 cent)—card file; (o) freight charges per pound (nearest .1 cent)—disk file; (p) freight charges per pound (nearest .1 cent)—printed report; (q) a date in the form yymmdd (no hyphens)—card file; (r) a date in the form yymmdd (no hyphens)—disk file; (s) a date in the form yymmdd, edited for printing; (t) a one-digit record code—card file; (u) a one-digit record code—disk file; (v) a one-digit record code—printed report; (w) shipping instructions (up to 70 characters)—card/disk/printer; (x) a part number (7 digits)—card file; (y) a part number (7 digits)—disk file; (z) the salary you would like to earn (and could express in IBM OS/VS COBOL)—printed report.

(a) PIC X(9) or PIC 9(9) (b) PIC $*,***.99 (c) PIC X(11) (d) PIC X(20) or PIC A(20) (e) PIC S99V9 or PIC 99V9 with COMP-3 or COMP (f) PIC S9(5) or PIC 9(5) with COMP-3 or COMP (g) PIC S9(6)V99 or PIC 9(6)V99 (h) PIC S9(6)V99 or PIC 9(6)V99 with COMP-3 or COMP (i) PIC $$$$,$$$.99− (j) PIC S99V9 or PIC 99V9 (k) PIC ZZ.9 (l) PIC S9(5) or PIC 9(5) (m) PIC ZZ,ZZ9− or PIC ZZ,ZZ9 (n) PIC S9(3)V999 or PIC 9(3)V999 (o) PIC S9(3)V999 or PIC 9(3)V999 with COMP-3 or COMP (p) PIC ZZZ.999 (q) PIC X(6) or PIC 9(6) (r) PIC X(6) or PIC 9(6) (s) PIC XX/XX/XX or PIC 99/99/99 (t) PIC X or PIC 9 (u) PIC X or PIC 9 (v) PIC X or PIC 9 (w) PIC X(70) (x) PIC X(7) or PIC 9(7) (y) PIC X(7) or PIC 9(7) (z) PIC $$,$$$,$$$,$$$.99

5.84   Give the length, in bytes, of each data item defined in Problem 5.83. (Assume an IBM OS/VS COBOL system; where appropriate, give lengths for both COMP-3 and COMP.)

(*a*)   9 (with DISPLAY, each PIC character except "S" and "V" requires 1 byte)
(*b*)   9 (with DISPLAY, each PIC character except "S" and "V" requires 1 byte)
(*c*)   11
(*d*)   20
(*e*)   COMP-3:   2   [PIC has 3 digits, so takes (3/2) + 1 = 2 bytes]
     COMP   :   2   (can hold 1 to 4 digits)
(*f*)   COMP-3:   3   [PIC has 5 digits, so takes (5/2) + 1 = 3 bytes]
     COMP   :   4   (can hold 5 to 9 digits)
(*g*)   8 (with DISPLAY, each PIC character except "S" and "V" requires 1 byte)
(*h*)   COMP-3:   5   [PIC has 8 digits, so takes (8/2) + 1 = 5 bytes]
     COMP   :   4   (holds 5 to 9 digits)
(*i*)   12
(*j*)   3 ("S" and "V" require no extra space)
(*k*)   4 (period "." represents an actual decimal point and takes 1 byte)
(*l*)   5
(*m*)   7 with trailing minus, 6 without
(*n*)   6 ("S" and "V" require no extra space)
(*o*)   COMP-3:   4   [PIC has 6 digits, so takes (6/2) + 1 = 4 bytes]
     COMP   :   4   (holds 5 to 9 digits)
(*p*)   7   (*r*)   6   (*t*)   1   (*v*)   1   (*x*)   7
(*q*)   6   (*s*)   8   (*u*)   1   (*w*)   70   (*y*)   7
(*z*)   17 (each PIC character in an edited picture requires 1 byte)

5.85   Given the statement MOVE ZEROS TO SAMPLE-DATA-ITEM, show the results when SAMPLE-DATA-ITEM is defined as:

(*a*)   PIC S9(3)V99 COMP-3   (*b*)   PIC S9(3)V99   (*c*)   PIC ZZ.ZZ
(*d*)   PIC $**,***.**   (*e*)   PIC $**,***.**   (*f*)   PIC Z,ZZZ.99
                           BLANK WHEN ZERO
(*g*)   PIC Z,ZZZ.Z9   (*h*)   PIC Z,ZZZ.99   (*i*)   PIC X(4)
                           BLANK WHEN ZERO
(*j*)   PIC A(4)   (*k*)   PIC XX/XX/XX   (*l*)   PIC XXBXXBXX

(*a*)   +000 00 (COMP-3 form)
(*b*)   +000 00 (DISPLAY form)
(*c*)   *bbbbb*
(*d*) $******.** ("." always prints with check protection)
(*e*)   *Invalid*: BLANK WHEN ZERO may not be used with check protection.
(*f*)   *bbbbb*.00
(*g*)   *bbbbbbb*0
(*h*)   *bbbbbbbb*
(*i*)   0000 (EBCDIC zeros)
(*j*)   *Invalid*: PIC A holds only letters and spaces.
(*k*)   00/00/00
(*l*)   00*b*00*b*00

5.86   Given the statement MOVE SPACES TO SAMPLE-DATA-ITEM, show the results when SAMPLE-DATA-ITEM is defined as:

(*a*)   PIC X(3)   (*b*)   PIC A(4)   (*c*)   PIC 9(3)   (*d*)   PIC S9(4)V99
(*e*)   PIC XXX/XX

(*a*)   *bbb*   (*b*)   *bbbb*   (*c*)   *invalid*   (*d*)   *invalid*   (*e*)   *bbb*/*bb*

(Remember that "PIC 9" can only hold a digit.)

5.87   Given the statement MOVE "ABCDE" TO SAMPLE-DATA-ITEM, show the results when SAMPLE-DATA-ITEM is defined as:

> (a)   PIC X(3)   (b)   PIC X(3) JUSTIFIED RIGHT   (c)   PIC XX/XX
> (d)   PIC X(8)   (e)   PIC X(8) JUSTIFIED RIGHT

(a)   ABC   (truncates on right)
(b)   CDE   (truncates on left because of JUSTIFIED RIGHT clause)
(c)   AB/CD   (truncates on right; inserts "/")
(d)   ABCDE*bbb*   (pads with blanks on right)
(e)   *bbb*ABCDE   (JUSTIFIED RIGHT clause causes value to move to right side of field; pads with blanks on left)

5.88   How important is the use of SYNC with COMP items?

The importance of SYNCHRONIZING COMP items depends on the architecture of the computer system being used and on the actual implementation of COMP items. On IBM-370 computer systems, the savings in execution time is likely to be insignificant. Because of the insertion of slack bytes (Section 5.16), SYNC should generally not be used for COMP items that are in logical records.

5.89   What is the result of the statement MOVE ZEROS TO A-GROUP-ITEM, where the item is defined as:

> 01   A-GROUP-ITEM.
>   05   A   PIC X(2).
>   05   B   PIC S9(3)V99.
>   05   C   PIC S9(5)V99   COMP-3.
>   05   D   PIC S9(4)   COMP.

When group items are manipulated in the PROCEDURE DIVISION, they are always treated as *one* (large) *PIC X field*. Since the length of A-GROUP-ITEM is 13 bytes $(2 + 5 + 4 + 2)$, the MOVE statement treats A-GROUP-ITEM as if it had been defined PIC X(13). Hence, 13 DISPLAY zero bytes are moved into the item. These bytes will correctly zero items A and B, because A and B are DISPLAY (by default). However, C requires COMP-3 zeros and D requires COMP zeros, *not* DISPLAY zeros. The result is that locations C and D do not contain valid data; in fact, manipulation of fields C and D will cause incorrect results and possible abnormal termination of program.

5.90   Given

> 01   SAMPLE-ITEM.
>   05   A   PIC 9(4)V99.
>   05   B REDEFINES A.
>   10   C   PIC 9(2)V9.
>   10   D   PIC 9(3).

What are the contents of C and of D after the statement MOVE 12.34 TO A has been executed?

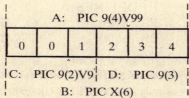

Fig. 5-10

Because of the MOVE, A contains 0012ᵥ34. Because of the REDEFINES, however, C and D refer to exactly the same computer memory locations as does A. The situation is shown in Fig. 5-10. It is seen that C contains the left half of A, which (from the standpoint of item C) is 00.1; D contains 234 (the right half of A). B, being a group item, would contain 001234 and would be treated as PIC X(6) DISPLAY.

5.91   Given

```
01   SAMPLE-ITEM.
     05   A              PIC X(8)      VALUE "ABCDEFGH".
     05   B REDEFINES A.
          10   C         PIC X(3).
          10   D         PIC X(2).
          10   E         PIC X(3).
```

what is in C?   in D?   in E?   in B?

Since B redefines A, we have the situation shown in Fig. 5-11.

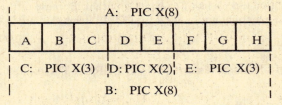

Fig. 5-11

Because B is a group item, it is the equivalent of PIC X(8). Notice that the REDEFINING item must be the same length as the redefined item. C contains "ABC", D contains "DE", and E contains "FGH". B contains "ABCDEFGH", since it refers to exactly the same memory locations as does data item A.

5.92   Define a field which shall be part of a printed line. The field contains either (1) the amount of money (maximum, 50,000.00) tied up in stocking a certain item, or (2) the message "STOCK-OUT" if the company has none of this item on hand.

```
05   VALUE-OF-INVENTORY          PIC ZZ,ZZZ.99.
05   OUT-OF-STOCK-MESSAGE-AREA   REDEFINES VALUE-OF-INVENTORY
                                 PIC X(9).
```

This problem illustrates the need for, and the means of obtaining, both a numeric and an alphanumeric PICTURE for the same field of a record. "MOVE "STOCK-OUT" TO VALUE-OF-INVENTORY" would cause a syntax error, since only numeric data may be moved to a numeric edited item. "MOVE "STOCK-OUT" TO OUT-OF-STOCK-MESSAGE-AREA" is valid and accomplishes exactly what is wanted.

5.93   What is wrong with the following?

```
01   SAMPLE-ITEM.
     05   A           PIC X(5).
     05   B           REDEFINES A.
          10   C      PIC S9(5)       COMP-3.
          10   D      PIC S9(4)       COMP.
```

Nothing is wrong. The length of B is $3 + 2 = 5$ bytes, which matches the length of A, as required. The programmer is free to change completely the layout of subfields, PICTUREs, USAGEs, etc., when REDEFINES is used. The only stipulations are: (i) the lengths must be the same, (ii) REDEFINES cannot be used for level-01 items in the FILE SECTION, and (iii) the redefined and redefining items must have the same level.

5.94   What is wrong with the following?

```
01   SAMPLE-ITEM      PIC X(5).
01   OTHER-ITEM       REDEFINES SAMPLE-ITEM.
     05  A            PIC X(4).
     05  B            PIC X(3).
     04  C            PIC X(2) REDEFINES B.
```

(1)   REDEFINES is used for level-01 items: okay in WORKING-STORAGE, but an error in the FILE SECTION.

(2)   Length of OTHER-ITEM is not the same as that of SAMPLE-ITEM.

(3)   Length of C is not the same as that of B.

(4)   For item C, REDEFINES must be the *first* clause of the item description.

(5)   Level number of redefining item C is not the same as that of redefined item B.

5.95   What is wrong with the following?

```
WORKING-STORAGE SECTION.
01   PROGRAM-COUNTERS.
     05  NUMBER-UNPAID-INVOICES    PIC S9(5)    COMP-3.

PROCEDURE DIVISION.

    ADD 1 TO NUMBER-UNPAID-INVOICES
```

The ADD statement takes the current contents of NUMBER-UNPAID-INVOICES, adds 1, and places the result back in NUMBER-UNPAID-INVOICES. But what are the current contents of NUMBER-UNPAID-INVOICES when the program begins executing? Since the programmer has not put an initial value in this data item, its contents at the time of the ADD will be *undefined* or *garbage*. This is an extremely common error for beginning programmers; the consequences will be a totally incorrect count or a program ABEND (*abnormal end*).

5.96   What can be done to fix the error in Problem 5.95?

The data item should be initialized to zero. Since its value will change during program execution, the preferred way of initializing it would be with a PROCEDURE DIVISION MOVE statement:

```
PROCEDURE DIVISION.
    MOVE ZERO TO NUMBER-UNPAID-INVOICES
. . . . . . . . . . . . . . . . . . . . . . . . . . . . . .
    ADD 1 TO NUMBER-UNPAID-INVOICES
```

Since NUMBER-UNPAID-INVOICES is defined in WORKING-STORAGE, an alternative method would be to use the VALUE clause:

```
05  NUMBER-UNPAID-INVOICES  PIC S9(5)  COMP-3  VALUE ZERO.
```

which will ensure that NUMBER-UNPAID-INVOICES contains zero (instead of garbage) at the start of program execution. (Some companies' coding standards reserve the VALUE clause for those items whose contents don't change during program execution.)

5.97   Many programmers prefer not to write detailed descriptions of logical records in the FILE SECTION. Instead, they define a WORKING-STORAGE area which is the same size as a logical record. As soon as a logical record is input from a file (using the READ statement), the program moves a copy of the logical record into this WORKING-STORAGE area. All manipulation of data is then done using the WORKING-STORAGE copy. Similarly, output records are put together in a WORKING-STORAGE area of the appropriate size and description, then moved to the logical record area for the file (level-01 in the FD) before the WRITE statement is executed.

Take the FILE SECTION entry given below and modify it so that record processing can be done in WORKING-STORAGE.

```
FILE SECTION.

FD   TIME-CARD-INPUT-FILE
     BLOCK CONTAINS 0 CHARACTERS
     RECORD CONTAINS 21 CHARACTERS
     LABEL RECORDS ARE STANDARD
     .

01   TIME-RECORD.
     05   TIME-EMPLOYEE-ID               PIC X(5).
     05   TIME-REGULAR-HOURS             PIC 99V9.
     05   TIME-OVERTIME-HOURS            PIC 99V9.
     05   TIME-EXPENSES                  PIC S9(4)V99.
     05   TIME-SICK-LEAVE                PIC 99.
     05   TIME-VACATION                  PIC 99.


FILE SECTION.

FD   TIME-CARD-INPUT-FILE
     BLOCK CONTAINS 0 CHARACTERS
     RECORD CONTAINS 21 CHARACTERS
     LABEL RECORDS ARE STANDARD
     .

01   TIME-RECORD                         PIC X(21).

WORKING-STORAGE SECTION.

01   WORKING-TIME-RECORD-AREA.
     05   WORKING-EMPLOYEE-ID            PIC X(5).
     05   WORKING-REGULAR-HOURS          PIC 99V9.
     05   WORKING-OVERTIME-HOURS         PIC 99V9.
     05   WORKING-EXPENSES               PIC S9(4)V99.
     05   WORKING-SICK-LEAVE             PIC 99.
     05   WORKING-VACATION               PIC 99.
```

Notice that the record description in the FILE SECTION has become trivial—just PIC X(21), where 21 is the record length. The detailed description of each record field has been moved to the WORKING-STORAGE SECTION. Notice that REGULAR-HOURS, OVERTIME-HOURS, SICK-LEAVE, and VACATION have not been given operational signs. This does not affect the efficiency of the object program *so long as these items never receive the result of a calculation and are never supposed to be negative* (which, without PIC "S", is impossible). A conservative programmer might choose to use PIC "S" for these items, just to be safe.

5.98   The WORKING-STORAGE approach discussed in Problem 5.97 is almost always used for printer output files, as their records hold much constant information, such as page titles, column headings, etc. The VALUE clause can be used in WORKING-STORAGE to set up such records. Revise the entry given below so that the records are set up in WORKING-STORAGE. Also, create a record for printing column headings over the information shown.

```
FILE SECTION.

FD   PAYROLL-REGISTER-FILE
     RECORD CONTAINS 132 CHARACTERS
     LABEL RECORDS ARE OMITTED
     .

01   PAYROLL-REGISTER-LINE.
     05   REGISTER-EMPLOYEE-ID              PIC X(5).
     05   FILLER                            PIC X(10).
     05   REGISTER-REGULAR-HOURS            PIC ZZ.9.
     05   FILLER                            PIC X(10).
     05   REGISTER-OVERTIME-HOURS           PIC ZZ.9.
     05   FILLER                            PIC X(99).


FILE SECTION.

FD   PAYROLL-REGISTER-FILE
     RECORD CONTAINS 132 CHARACTERS
     LABEL RECORDS ARE OMITTED
     .

01   PAYROLL-REGISTER-LINE                  PIC X(132).

WORKING-STORAGE SECTION.

01   WORKING-REGISTER-LINE.
     05   WORKING-LINE-EMPLOYEE-ID      PIC X(5).
     05   FILLER                        PIC X(10)     VALUE SPACES.
     05   WORKING-LINE-REGULAR-HOURS    PIC ZZ.9.
     05   FILLER                        PIC X(10)     VALUE SPACES.
     05   WORKING-LINE-OVERTIME-HOURS   PIC ZZ.9.
     05   FILLER                        PIC X(99)     VALUE SPACES.

01   WORKING-HEADING-LINE.
     05   FILLER                        PIC X(15)
                                        VALUE "EMPLOYEE ID".
     05   FILLER                        PIC X(14)
                                        VALUE "REGULAR HOURS".
     05   FILLER                        PIC X(103)
                                        VALUE "OVERTIME HOURS".
```

Notice that PAYROLL-REGISTER-LINE is now simply defined as PIC X(132) and all the real description is done in WORKING-REGISTER-LINE. The "FILLER" areas, for separating printed data on a line, can be set to SPACES using the VALUE clause (which could *not* be used when the description was in the FILE SECTION). WORKING-HEADING-LINE has nothing but FILLER entries with VALUE clauses to generate the appropriate column headings. Satisfy yourself that each column heading begins above the first character of information for the column. (Note, however, that they are *not* *centered*.)

Programming Assignments

5.99–5.108 Modify Problems 2.29–2.38 to reflect your expanded knowledge of the DATA DIVISION. Change all dollar amounts to dollars and cents, modifying record layouts where necessary. Edit all printed output, and do calculations as efficiently as possible.

Chapter 6

Procedure Division

6.1 Introduction; Coding Standards

The IDENTIFICATION, ENVIRONMENT, and DATA DIVISIONs serve as a kind of prologue to the PROCEDURE DIVISION, in which the programmer specifies the instructions which the computer is to carry out. In this chapter it will be assumed that these instructions have to do with the input, processing, and output of *sequentially organized files* (that are *accessed sequentially*).

Structurally, the PROCEDURE DIVISION is composed of SECTIONs and/or paragraphs. The division header ("PROCEDURE DIVISION") is typed in the A margin; SECTION and paragraph headers also begin in the A margin. Paragraphs and SECTIONs are composed of *sentences* which are delimited by periods. Each sentence can consist of one or more *statements*, which are valid PROCEDURE DIVISION instructions beginning with a COBOL *verb*.

PROCEDURE DIVISION Coding Standards

1. Type only one statement per line.
2. Paragraph and SECTION headers should have their own lines.
3. Each paragraph or SECTION should have a well-defined purpose; the name should describe that purpose.
4. Sequence paragraph and SECTION headers by attaching prefixes or suffixes to the names.
5. Indent (a fixed amount, starting from column 12) to show the continuation of a statement over more than one line and/or to clarify the relationships among statements.
6. Use blank lines, blank comment lines, or (best if available) EJECT, SKIP1, SKIP2, and SKIP3, to leave plenty of space between paragraphs/SECTIONs and to set off the headers.
7. Use periods only when absolutely necessary, and make them structured.
8. Use commas only when absolutely necessary.
9. Avoid using SECTIONs unless required to do so (stick to paragraphs).
10. Keep everything as simple and straightforward as possible.

6.2. Input/Output: OPEN Statement

Each file *must* be successfully OPENed before any other PROCEDURE DIVISION statements are used to process the file. (i) OPEN . . . obtains main memory space for file buffers. (ii) OPEN . . . processes file labels if they exist (if LABEL RECORDS ARE STANDARD is specified in FD):

Input or input-output file.   Existing label records are checked to ensure that all information is available and file is accessible and correctly identified.

Output file.   Label records for file are created.

(iii) OPEN . . . positions the file for logical record access—usually at the beginning (first logical record) of the file.

The general syntax of the OPEN statement is displayed in Fig. 6-1. As the braces indicate, at least one of the four OPEN modes must be specified; as many files as desired may be OPENed for each mode.

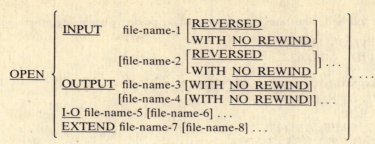

Fig. 6-1

INPUT mode. File is opened for input *only*; file must already exist and be accessible, or program will abnormally terminate. "READ", the only applicable verb, is used to input a logical record.

OUTPUT mode.   File is opened for output *only*; "WRITE" is the only applicable verb. If file already exists, the old version of the file is entirely deleted, and a new version is created by using WRITE to output logical records. If file does not exist, a file is created by using WRITE to output logical records.

I-O mode.   File is opened for *both* input and output; file must already exist and be accessible, or program will abnormally terminate. Applicable verbs are "READ", "WRITE", and "REWRITE"; for a file on a direct-access device, REWRITE verb can be used to write a changed version of a logical record back to its original location in the file (an update in place).

EXTEND mode.   File is OPENed for *output only*, and is positioned at the end (*after* the last logical record). Thus, when the WRITE statement is used to output logical records, they are added to the physical end of the file, succeeding any already existing logical records.

The "REVERSED" and "WITH NO REWIND" options are rather rarely used; they apply only to files on magnetic tape.

REVERSED option.   REVERSED may be used only with tape files OPENed for INPUT. It specifies that the file will be positioned at the last logical record and will be read backwards (not all tape drives have this capability).

WITH NO REWIND option.   This option may be used only for tape files OPENed for INPUT or for OUTPUT. It specifies that the file *should not be positioned* during OPEN processing. Thus the file remains positioned wherever it was when the OPEN statement was executed.

EXAMPLE 6.1 All file names used in the following OPEN statement must correspond to those used in the SELECT and FD:

```
OPEN    INPUT     EDITED-TIME-FILE
                  EMPLOYEE-MASTER-FILE-OLD
        OUTPUT    PAYROLL-REGISTER-REPORT
                  EMPLOYEE-MASTER-FILE-NEW
        EXTEND    TIME-RECORD-SUMMARY-FILE
```

Notice the coding standard for typing the OPEN statement: all file names typed in the same column; all OPEN modes typed in the same column, with appropriate indentation.

As an alternative, each file could have a separate OPEN statement. In general, opening many files with one OPEN statement will take more computer memory for OPEN processing, but will allow the opening to be completed more quickly.

EXAMPLE 6.2 The following illustrates a common mistake made by beginning programmers:

```
        IDENTIFICATION DIVISION.
        PROGRAM-ID.  MISTAKE.

        ENVIRONMENT DIVISION.
        INPUT-OUTPUT SECTION.
        FILE-CONTROL.
            SELECT TIME-CARD-FILE
                ASSIGN TO WKLYTIME
                .
            SELECT PAYROLL-EDIT-REPORT
                ASSIGN TO TIMEEDIT
                .

        DATA DIVISION.
        FILE SECTION.
        FD  TIME-CARD-FILE
            LABEL RECORDS ARE OMITTED
            .
        01   TIME-CARD-RECORD.
             05 TIME-CARD-ID            PIC X(6).
             . . . . . . . . . . . . .

        FD  PAYROLL-EDIT-REPORT
            LABEL RECORDS ARE OMITTED
            RECORD CONTAINS 132 CHARACTERS
            .
        01   EDIT-LINE.
             05  EDIT-ID               PIC X(6).
             05  FILLER                PIC X(5).
             . . . . . . . . . . . . .

        PROCEDURE DIVISION.
            MOVE ALL "*" TO EDIT-LINE
            WRITE EDIT-LINE
                AFTER ADVANCING PAGE
            OPEN    OUTPUT    PAYROLL-EDIT-REPORT
            OPEN    INPUT     TIME-CARD-FILE
            . . . . . . . . . . . . . . . . . . . . .
```

Look closely at the PROCEDURE DIVISION. EDIT-LINE, the logical record area for PAYROLL-EDIT-REPORT, *must not* be manipulated or used until after the file is OPENed. As things stand, "MOVE ALL "*" TO EDIT-LINE" will have unpredictable results, and "WRITE EDIT-LINE . . ." will cause an ABEND.

EXAMPLE 6.3 Suppose a FILE STATUS clause (Section 4.5) in the (corrected) program of Example 6.2:

```
        . . . . . . . . . . . . . . . . . . . .
        FILE-CONTROL.
            SELECT TIME-CARD-FILE
                ASSIGN TO WKLYTIME
                FILE STATUS IS TIME-CARD-STATUS
                .

            . . . . . . . . . . . . . . . . . . . .
        WORKING-STORAGE SECTION.
        01  TIME-CARD-STATUS          PIC XX.
        . . . . . . . . . . . . . . . .
        PROCEDURE DIVISION.
        . . . . . . . . . . . . .
            OPEN INPUT TIME-CARD-FILE
            IF TIME-CARD-STATUS NOT EQUAL "00"
            . . . . . . . . . . . . . . . . . . .
```

TIME-CARD-STATUS is defined to be a two-byte area (PIC XX). After the OPEN statement has been executed, this area should contain the nonnumeric literal "00", if the execution was successful. If TIME-CARD-STATUS had instead been defined PIC 99, then a *numeric* literal (or equivalent figurative constant) would be used in the test:

> IF TIME-CARD-STATUS NOT EQUAL 0 . . .

or

> IF TIME-CARD-STATUS NOT EQUAL ZERO . . .

6.3　Input/Output: CLOSE Statement

The CLOSE statement terminates the processing of a file by (i) releasing memory space used for buffers, (ii) completing any necessary label processing for files with standard labels, and (iii) generally *undoing* everything OPEN did. Every file that has been OPENed should be CLOSEd before the program terminates; forgetting to do so can lead to serious errors on some systems. The syntax of the CLOSE statement is displayed in Fig. 6-2.

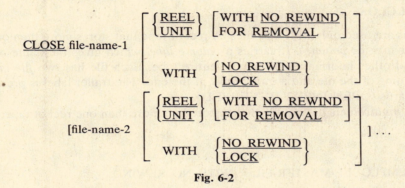

Fig. 6-2

Main Version of CLOSE . . .

The most frequently needed version of the CLOSE statement is simply the verb followed by one or more file names. Files may be CLOSEd individually (taking less memory) or collectively (taking less time), and in any order (independent of the order of OPENing). Whatever version of CLOSE is used, if FILE STATUS . . . has been specified for a file being CLOSEd, the CLOSE operation will cause a status code to be placed in the FILE STATUS data item, thus indicating the success or failure of the CLOSE attempt.

EXAMPLE 6.4

> PROCEDURE DIVISION.
> . . . .
> OPEN　　OUTPUT　　INVENTORY-MASTER-FILE
> . . . .
> 　　(*use WRITE to add records to INVENTORY-MASTER-FILE*)
> . . . .
> CLOSE INVENTORY-MASTER-FILE
> OPEN　　INPUT　　　　INVENTORY-MASTER-FILE
> . . . .
> 　　(*use READ to input logical records from INVENTORY-MASTER-FILE*)
> . . . .
> CLOSE INVENTORY-MASTER-FILE
> OPEN　　I-O　　　　　INVENTORY-MASTER-FILE
> . . . .
> 　　(*use READ and REWRITE to update logical records from INVENTORY-MASTER-FILE*)
> . . . .
> CLOSE INVENTORY-MASTER-FILE

Once a file is closed, it can be reopened for further processing. Here a file is opened for output, some records are added, then the file is closed. Next it is opened for input, logical records are retrieved (for example, to print a report), and it is closed. Finally, it is opened again for I-O, some logical records are updated, and the file is closed again.

EXAMPLE 6.5

PROCEDURE DIVISION.
. . . .
    OPEN   I-O   EMPLOYEE-MASTER-FILE
. . . .
    CLOSE EMPLOYEE-MASTER-FILE   WITH LOCK

When a file is CLOSED WITH LOCK, it may not be OPENed again during the current execution of the program. Of course, the file may be OPENed by other programs, or by this program if it is executed again.

Minor Versions of CLOSE . . .

These versions are used only with tape files. A reel of tape that stores more than one file is called a *multifile reel* (or *tape* or *volume*). It carries a *volume label* which gives the name of the reel (the *volume name*) and other information about the entire tape. Each file has two *file labels*: a *header label* at the beginning of the file and a *trailer label* at the end. The trailer label is present in case the file is read backwards (OPEN INPUT REVERSED).

Conversely, a *multivolume file* is a file that is stored on more than one reel of tape (or disk pack).

EXAMPLE 6.6

CLOSE   EMPLOYEE-MASTER-FILE   WITH NO REWIND

Normally, when a tape file is CLOSEd, the tape is rewound to the beginning of the file. Here: (i) EMPLOYEE-MASTER-FILE is on a multifile reel, and we want to leave the tape in position for the OPENing of the *next* file on the tape; or (ii) EMPLOYEE-MASTER-FILE is going to be reOPENed for INPUT REVERSED, and so we want to leave it positioned at its end.

EXAMPLE 6.7

PROCEDURE DIVISION.
. . . .
    OPEN   OUTPUT   JOB-COSTING-HISTORY-FILE
. . . .
    WRITE JOB-COSTING-HISTORY-RECORD
. . . .
    CLOSE JOB-COSTING-HISTORY-FILE   UNIT
. . . .
    WRITE JOB-COSTING-HISTORY-RECORD
. . . .
    CLOSE JOB-COSTING-HISTORY-FILE

The above program creates a multivolume JOB-COSTING-HISTORY-FILE, which is OPENed OUTPUT. The first WRITE statement is used to output records to the file. The CLOSE . . . UNIT statement (or the exactly equivalent CLOSE . . . REEL) does not actually close the file, but automatically ensures that the *next* WRITE statement will output a record to the *next* reel or pack of the file. (This is called a *volume switch*.) Notice that when all logical records have been written, the file is closed normally.

For a multivolume file OPENed INPUT, a READ statement after CLOSE . . . UNIT would input a record from the next reel or pack.

If, in the above program, the first CLOSE statement were replaced with

CLOSE JOB-COSTING-HISTORY-FILE   UNIT   FOR REMOVAL

then the operating system would not only effect the volume switch but would "know" that the "unit" being closed will not be needed again. This would free the I/O device for other employment. The closed "unit" *could*, however, be accessed again if the file were CLOSEd normally, then reOPENed.

Other Input/Output Statements

Besides OPEN . . . and CLOSE, there is the REWRITE statement, for which see Chapter 11.

6.4   Input: READ Statement

The READ statement may be used only for files that have been successfully opened INPUT or I-O. Its general format is:

READ file-name RECORD [INTO data-name]
   [AT END imperative-statement-1 [imperative-statement-2] . . .]

The "file-name" must be the same as that used in the SELECT statement and FD for the file. Assuming, as always, sequential organization, READ makes the physically next logical record available in the logical record area for the file [level-01 record description(s) in FD]. If a FILE STATUS area has been defined for the file, READ sets the status key contents to indicate the results of READ execution.

EXAMPLE 6.8   The syntax of READ . . . requires the use of the *file* name rather than the logical record name. Exactly the opposite holds true for WRITE . . . (see Section 6.5). To avoid confusion, remember the COBOL slogan: "Read a File, Write a Record".

When READ is executed and there are no more logical records available, an *end of file* condition is said to exist. The statement(s) in the AT END clauses are executed *only* when end of file exists; otherwise, the clause is ignored by the computer. When end of file is reached, the file must be closed and reopened before any further processing is attempted.

EXAMPLE 6.9

```
          . . . . . . . . . . . . . . . . . . . . . . . . . . . .
          ENVIRONMENT DIVISION.

               SELECT SALES-FILE   ASSIGN TO SALES.

          DATA DIVISION.
          FILE SECTION.

          FD   SALES-FILE
                    BLOCK CONTAINS 0 RECORDS
                    RECORD CONTAINS 39 CHARACTERS
                    LABEL RECORDS ARE STANDARD


          01   SALES-RECORD.
                    05   SALES-RECORD-NAME                  PIC X(15).
                    05   SALES-RECORD-MONTH-1-SALES         PIC S9(4)V99.
                    05   SALES-RECORD-MONTH-2-SALES         PIC S9(4)V99.
                    05   SALES-RECORD-MONTH-3-SALES         PIC S9(4)V99.
                    05   SALES-RECORD-QUOTA                 PIC S9(4)V99

          WORKING-STORAGE SECTION.

          01   WORK-AREAS.
                    05   SALES-FILE-END-SW                  PIC X.
                    05   QUARTERLY-TOTAL                    PIC S9(5)V99 COMP-3.
```

```
PROCEDURE DIVISION.

OPEN  INPUT  SALES-FILE
MOVE "F" TO SALES-FILE-END-SW
. . . . . . . . . . . . . . . . . . . . . . . . . . . . . . . . . . . . . . .
READ SALES-FILE
    AT END
        MOVE "T" TO SALES-FILE-END-SW

IF SALES-FILE-END-SW EQUAL "F"
    ADD   SALES-RECORD-MONTH-1-SALES
          SALES-RECORD-MONTH-2-SALES
          SALES-RECORD-MONTH-3-SALES
                              GIVING QUARTERLY-TOTAL


. . . . . . . . . . . . . . . . . . . . . . . . . . . . . . . . . . . . . .
```

After SALES-FILE is OPENed for INPUT, the switch SALES-FILE-END-SW is initialized to "F" (for false). The program then attempts to read a SALES-FILE logical record. If there are no logical records available, AT END . . . is executed, setting the switch to "T" (for true). If a record is successfully READ, AT END . . . is ignored and the switch remains set to "F". Notice that the program tests that SALES-FILE is not AT END *before* attempting to ADD . . . . Also notice the use of a structured period to mark the conclusion of the AT END clause. This is necessary, since the clause is assumed to continue until a period is encountered.

EXAMPLE 6.10   Consider the program segment

```
READ SALES-FILE RECORD
    AT END
        MOVE "T" TO SALES-FILE-END-SW
MOVE SALES-RECORD-QUOTA TO SALES-REPORT-QUOTA
MOVE "NO" TO SALES-INPUT-ERROR-FLAG
WRITE . . .
```

First, we notice that the programmer has, by forgetting to place a period after the AT END clause, rendered MOVE . . . , MOVE . . . , and WRITE . . . ineffective before end of file (the indentation notwithstanding). Second, and perhaps less obvious, he has forgotten that if the READ . . . does hit end of file, the logical record area SALES-RECORD will contain garbage; hence garbage will be moved to SALES-REPORT-QUOTA, causing incorrect output and possibly other errors. *Do not process a logical record after AT END . . . is executed* (unless the file has been closed and reopened).

READ . . . INTO Option

The INTO . . . option of the READ . . . statement causes the logical record which is input to be copied from the logical record area into another data item. Thus,

```
READ SALES-FILE INTO WORKING-COPY
```

and

```
READ SALES-FILE
MOVE SALES-RECORD TO WORKING-COPY
```

are exactly equivalent. READ . . . INTO . . . is heavily used to provide WORKING-STORAGE copies of logical records (see Problems 5.97 and 5.98). Under '74 ANS COBOL, the option may be exercised only for fixed-length records (see Appendix C for COBOL '80).

6.5   Output: WRITE Statement

WRITE . . . may be used only for a file that has been OPENed for OUTPUT, I-O, or EXTEND. Execution of the statement releases the contents of the current logical record area (level-01) for output, and at the same time *changes the reference of the level-01 record name to a currently unused buffer area* associated with the file. (Review "Multiple Buffers" in Section 5.8 and "blocking" in Section 5.3; the new buffer segment, which at this point contains garbage, can be used for building the *next* logical record to be output.) As a consequence, the logical record just written *is no longer accessible to the program.*

WRITE . . . for Nonprinter Files

Here the syntax is

WRITE logical-record-name [FROM data-name]

The FROM option is often used by programmers who elect to do all record processing using WORKING-STORAGE copies of logical records) cf. READ . . . INTO . . . ; Section 6.4).

        WRITE INVOICE-TO-BE-PAID-RECORD
            FROM WS-INVOICE-TO-BE-PAID-REC

has exactly the same machine language translation as

        MOVE WS-INVOICE-TO-BE-PAID-REC
            TO INVOICE-TO-BE-PAID-RECORD
        WRITE INVOICE-TO-BE-PAID-RECORD

The "logical-record-name" must be the name of a level-01 item in the FD for the file. When the FROM option is used, "data-name" is usually defined in WORKING-STORAGE. If a FILE STATUS area has been defined for the file, WRITE . . . places a 2-byte code in the status key area to indicate the results of WRITE execution.

EXAMPLE 6.11

```
    FD   PENDING-INVOICE-FILE
         BLOCK CONTAINS 0 RECORDS
         RECORD CONTAINS 32 CHARACTERS
         LABEL RECORDS ARE STANDARD
         .
    01   PENDING-INVOICE-RECORD              PIC X(32).

    FD   PAYABLE-INVOICE-FILE
         BLOCK CONTAINS 0 RECORDS
         RECORD CONTAINS 16 CHARACTERS
         LABEL RECORDS ARE STANDARD
         .
    01   PAYABLE-INVOICE-RECORD              PIC X(16).

    WORKING-STORAGE SECTION.

    01   WS-PENDING-INVOICE REC.
         05  WS-PENDING-CODE                 PIC X.
         05  WS-PENDING-VENDOR-ID            PIC X(7).
         05  WS-PENDING-INVOICE-NUMBER       PIC X(4).
         05  WS-PENDING-INVOICE-DATE         PIC 9(6).
         05  WS-PENDING-INVOICE-DUE-DATE     PIC 9(6).
         05  WS-PENDING-INVOICE-AMOUNT       PIC S9(5)V99   COMP-3.
         05  WS-PENDING-INVOICE-DISCOUNT     PIC S9(5)V99   COMP-3.

    01   WS-PAYABLE-INVOICE-REC.
         05  WS-PAYABLE-CODE                 PIC X.
         05  WS-PAYABLE-VENDOR-ID            PIC X(7).
         05  WS-PAYABLE-INVOICE-NUMBER       PIC X(4).
         05  WS-PAYABLE-AMOUNT               PIC S9(5)V99   COMP-3.
```

```
PROCEDURE DIVISION.

    OPEN    INPUT      PENDING-INVOICE-FILE
            OUTPUT     PAYABLE-INVOICE-FILE
    . . . . . . . . . . . . . . . . . . . . . . . . . . . . . . . . . . .
    READ PENDING-INVOICE-FILE
        INTO WS-PENDING-INVOICE-REC
        AT END
            MOVE "T" TO WS-END-OF-FILE-SW
        .
    IF WS-END-OF-FILE-SW NOT EQUAL "T"
        MOVE WS-PENDING-CODE              TO WS-PAYABLE-CODE
        MOVE WS-PENDING-VENDOR-ID         TO WS-PAYABLE-VENDOR-ID
        MOVE WS-PENDING-INVOICE-NUMBER    TO WS-PAYABLE-INVOICE-NUMBER

        SUBTRACT WS-PENDING-INVOICE-DISCOUNT
            FROM WS-PENDING-INVOICE-AMOUNT
                GIVING WS-PAYABLE-AMOUNT

        WRITE PAYABLE-INVOICE-RECORD FROM WS-PAYABLE-INVOICE-REC

    . . . . . . . . . . . . . . . . . . . . . . . . . . . . . . . . . . .

    CLOSE PENDING-INVOICE-FILE
          PAYABLE-INVOICE-FILE
    . . . . . . . . . . . . . . . . . . . . . . . . . . . . . . . . . . .
```

This program illustrates file processing using WORKING-STORAGE copies of logical records. PENDING-INVOICE-RECORD and PAYABLE-INVOICE-RECORD are described merely as PIC X(32) and PIC X(16), respectively, since they are not going to be processed in the logical record area of the buffer. READ PENDING-INVOICE-FILE INTO WS-PENDING-INVOICE-REC is used to input a logical record and move a copy of it to WORKING-STORAGE. The MOVE and SUBTRACT statements are used to construct a logical record in WS-PAYABLE-INVOICE-REC. Then, WRITE PAYABLE-INVOICE-RECORD FROM WS-PAYABLE-INVOICE-REC is used to move this record from WORKING-STORAGE to the logical record area in the buffer and release it for output.

After the WRITE statement, PAYABLE-INVOICE-RECORD no longer contains the data just output; rather it refers to the next available empty buffer segment, which can be used to construct the *next* logical record. However, WS-PAYABLE-INVOICE-REC *still contains* the logical record just written; this constitutes another advantage of doing all record processing in WORKING-STORAGE.

Like "READ . . . INTO . . .", "WRITE . . . FROM . . ." should never be used with variable-length records (see Appendix C for COBOL '80 considerations). The WORKING-STORAGE approach for such records would require coupled MOVE and WRITE statements:

```
MOVE WS-PAYABLE-INVOICE-REC TO PAYABLE-INVOICE-RECORD
WRITE PAYABLE-INVOICE-RECORD
```

WRITE . . . for Printer Files

The syntax is as indicated in Fig. 6-3. The various options all have to do with controlling the spacing of printed output.

$$\underline{\text{WRITE}}\text{ record-name }[\underline{\text{FROM}}\text{ identifier}]$$

$$\left[\left\{ \begin{matrix} \underline{\text{BEFORE}} \\ \underline{\text{AFTER}} \end{matrix} \right\} \text{ADVANCING} \left[\left\{ \begin{matrix} \text{identifier-2} \\ \text{integer} \\ \{\text{mnemonic-name}\} \\ \underline{\text{PAGE}} \end{matrix} \right\} \left[\begin{matrix} \text{LINE} \\ \text{LINES} \end{matrix} \right] \right] \right]$$

$$\left[\underline{\text{AT}} \left\{ \begin{matrix} \underline{\text{END-OF-PAGE}} \\ \underline{\text{EOP}} \end{matrix} \right\} \text{ imperative-statement-1 [imperative-statement-2] . . .} \right]$$

Fig. 6-3

EXAMPLE 6.12

```
FD   TIME-CARD-FILE
     BLOCK CONTAINS 0 RECORDS
     RECORD CONTAINS 33 CHARACTERS
     LABEL RECORDS ARE STANDARD
         .
01   TIME-CARD-RECORD                          PIC X(33).

FD   TIME-CARD-EDIT-REPORT
     RECORD CONTAINS 132 CHARACTERS
     LABEL RECORDS ARE OMITTED
         .
01   TIME-CARD-EDIT-LINE                        PIC X(132).

WORKING-STORAGE SECTION.

01   WS-TIME-CARD-REC.
     05   WS-TIME-CARD-ID                       PIC X(6).
     05   WS-TIME-CARD-NAME                     PIC X(20).
     05   WS-TIME-CARD-DEPARTMENT               PIC X(4).
     05   WS-TIME-CARD-HOURS                    PIC S99V9.

01   WS-TIME-EDIT-LINE.
     05   WS-TIME-EDIT-ID                       PIC X(6).
     05   FILLER                                PIC X(4)     VALUE SPACES.
     05   WS-TIME-EDIT-NAME                     PIC X(20).
     05   FILLER                                PIC X(10)    VALUE SPACES.
     05   WS-TIME-EDIT-DEPARTMENT               PIC X(4).
     05   FILLER                                PIC X(6)     VALUE SPACES.
     05   WS-TIME-EDIT-HOURS                    PIC ZZ.9−.
     05   FILLER                                PIC X(77)    VALUE SPACES.

01   NUMBER-TO-SKIP                             PIC S9(3)    COMP-3.

PROCEDURE DIVISION.

     OPEN     INPUT      TIME-CARD-FILE
              OUTPUT     TIME-CARD-EDIT-REPORT

     READ TIME-CARD-FILE
          INTO WS-TIME-CARD-REC
          AT END...
              .
     MOVE WS-TIME-CARD-ID                  TO WS-TIME-EDIT-ID
     MOVE WS-TIME-CARD-NAME                TO WS-TIME-EDIT-NAME
     MOVE WS-TIME-CARD-DEPARTMENT          TO WS-TIME-EDIT-DEPARTMENT
     MOVE WS-TIME-CARD-HOURS               TO WS-TIME-EDIT-HOURS

     WRITE TIME-CARD-EDIT-LINE FROM WS-TIME-EDIT-LINE
           BEFORE ADVANCING 3 LINES
```

"WRITE...BEFORE ADVANCING 3 LINES" causes the current contents of WS-TIME-EDIT-LINE, via TIME-CARD-EDIT-LINE, to be printed wherever the paper is positioned in the printer. After the line has been printed, the paper is advanced three lines. Therefore if WRITE... is executed over and over, the result will be to leave two blank lines between printed lines.

This example exploits the WORKING-STORAGE approach, in that the VALUE clause is used to set the FILLER areas (which separate fields on the printed report) to blank spaces. If we were building TIME-EDIT-LINE in the FILE SECTION (where "VALUE..." is illegal), we should have to use the MOVE statement to move SPACES into the logical record area prior to moving in the information to be printed.

If the clause "BEFORE ADVANCING 3 LINES" were absent from the above program, the default, "AFTER ADVANCING 1 LINE", would be in effect. Thus there would be no blank lines between printed lines.

EXAMPLE 6.13 To illustrate the use of the option

WRITE . . . BEFORE/AFTER ADVANCING identifier-2 LINES

suppose that as in Example 6.12 we define a data item NUMBER-TO-SKIP which must have a numeric PICTURE with no decimal point. Then:

```
. . . . . . . . . . . . . . . . . . . . . . . . . . . .
MOVE 3 TO NUMBER-TO-SKIP
. . . . . . . . . . . . . . . . . . . . . . . . . . . .
WRITE  TIME-CARD-EDIT-LINE
    FROM WS-TIME-EDIT-LINE
    AFTER ADVANCING NUMBER-TO-SKIP LINES
```

The contents of NUMBER-TO-SKIP could be an arbitrary integer input by the program or resulting from a programmed calculation. WRITE . . . AFTER ADVANCING . . . causes the paper to be advanced the indicated number of lines, then the output line to be printed.

EXAMPLE 6.14 The BEFORE/AFTER ADVANCING PAGE option moves the paper to the top of the next page. If the LINAGE clause is specified in the FD for the file, the paper is positioned to the top of the page body of the next logical page (see Section 5.7). Otherwise, the paper is positioned to channel 1 of the printer carriage-control mechanism (which generally corresponds to line 1 of the next page; see Section 4.4).

EXAMPLE 6.15 "BEFORE/AFTER ADVANCING mnemonic-name" allows the paper to be positioned at a carriage-control channel defined in the SPECIAL-NAMES paragraph of the ENVIRONMENT DIVISION (review Section 4.4).

```
ENVIRONMENT DIVISION.
CONFIGURATION SECTION.
SPECIAL-NAMES.
    C01 IS TOP-OF-FORM
    C02 IS HEADING-AREA
    C05 IS TOTAL-AREA
        .

. . . . . . . . . . . . . . . . . . . .
PROCEDURE DIVISION.
    WRITE REPORT-LINE
        FROM WS-PAGE-NUMBER-DATE-LINE
        AFTER ADVANCING TOP-OF-FORM
    WRITE REPORT-LINE
        FROM WS-HEADING-LINE
        AFTER ADVANCING HEADING-AREA
    WRITE REPORT-LINE
        FROM WS-TOTAL-LINE
        AFTER ADVANCING TOTAL-AREA
```

Here, "AFTER ADVANCING TOP-OF-FORM" advances the paper to carriage-control channel 1, then prints the current contents of WS-PAGE-NUMBER-DATE-LINE; etc. *Before the program is allowed to execute, the computer operator must set up the printer so that the carriage-control channels used by the program match up with the appropriate parts of the continuous forms.* If this is not done, printer spacing will not be correct.

The use of carriage-control channels defined in SPECIAL-NAMES and the use of the LINAGE clause in the FD are *mutually exclusive.*

In Fig. 6-3, "AT END-OF-PAGE" and "AT EOP" are equivalent. They may be used only when the LINAGE clause is specified in the FD; in that case, the COBOL compiler automatically causes the object program to maintain a LINAGE-COUNTER which counts all lines printed or skipped on a logical page. Whenever a new logical page is started, the LINAGE-COUNTER is automatically reset to 1.

The statements specified in the AT END-OF-PAGE option are executed *only when* the execution of WRITE...BEFORE/AFTER ADVANCING... would cause LINAGE-COUNTER to exceed (1) the value specified in WITH FOOTING AT... (but *not* the size of the page body as prescribed by LINAGE IS...), or (2) the size of the page body.

Case 1. The WRITE statement is executed as it normally would be, the statement(s) in the AT END-OF-PAGE clause is (are) executed, and then normal execution of statements resumes.

Case 2. If BEFORE ADVANCING... is specified, the line is printed, then the paper is advanced to the start of the next logical page body; if AFTER ADVANCING... is specified, the paper is advanced to the start of the next logical page body, then the line is printed. Then the AT END-OF-PAGE statement(s) is (are) executed.

EXAMPLE 6.16 Case 2 is termed *automatic page overflow*. Suppose that for REPORT-FILE

```
LINAGE IS 60
    WITH FOOTING AT 53
    LINES AT TOP 3
    LINES AT BOTTOM 3
```

and that the paper is currently positioned at line 52 within the page body. Execution of

```
WRITE REPORT-LINE
    FROM WS-CHECK-REQUEST-EDIT-LINE
    AFTER ADVANCING 10 LINES
    AT END-OF-PAGE
        MOVE WS-RUNNING-TOTAL TO WS-OUTPUT-RUNNING-TOTAL
        WRITE REPORT-LINE FROM WS-RUNNING-TOTAL-LINE
            AFTER ADVANCING 5 LINES
```

is designed to print a running total in the footing area at the bottom of each page body. However, since "AFTER ADVANCING 10 LINES" causes a page overflow (52 + 10 is 62, which exceeds the page body size of LINAGE 60), the following occurs: (i) the paper is advanced to the first printable line of the *next* logical page; (ii) the contents of WS-CHECK-REQUEST-EDIT-LINE are printed; (iii) since an automatic page overflow has occurred, AT END-OF-PAGE... causes the paper to be advanced another 5 lines and the contents of WS-RUNNING-TOTAL-LINE to be printed.

Thus, the running total line winds up near the top of the page body, mixed in with regular report lines—clearly an undesirable situation.

EXAMPLE 6.17 The programmer can eliminate difficulties with AT END-OF-PAGE routines by properly coordinating BEFORE/AFTER ADVANCING... values with the WITH FOOTING AT... value and the AT END-OF-PAGE routine.

Let the LINAGE clause be the same as in Example 6.16. Suppose also that at the top of each page body a heading is printed which leaves the paper positioned at line 10 of the page body. Finally, suppose that it is desired to print report lines with two blank lines in between. Consider the following WRITE statement:

```
WRITE REPORT-LINE
    FROM WS-CHECK-REQUEST-EDIT-LINE
    AFTER ADVANCING 3 LINES
    AT END-OF-PAGE
        MOVE WS-RUNNING-TOTAL TO WS-OUTPUT-RUNNING-TOTAL
        WRITE REPORT-LINE
            FROM WS-RUNNING-TOTAL-LINE
            AFTER ADVANCING 5 LINES
        WRITE REPORT-LINE
            FROM WS-FIRST-TITLE-LINE
            AFTER ADVANCING PAGE
        WRITE REPORT-LINE
            FROM WS-SECOND-TITLE-LINE
            AFTER ADVANCING 9 LINES
```

The first time this WRITE ... is executed, let the paper be positioned at the end of the heading (line 10). Hence (AFTER ADVANCING 3 LINES) the first report line will be on line 13; the second report line, on line 16; ... ; the 14th report line, on line 52. The 15th execution of the WRITE statement will then bring about the following: (i) the 15th report line is printed on line 55; (ii) since the LINAGE-COUNTER (now 55) exceeds the footing area boundary (WITH FOOTING AT 53), the AT END-OF-PAGE routine causes the paper to be advanced to line 60 (AFTER ADVANCING 5 LINES), the contents of WS-RUNNING-TOTAL-LINE to be printed on line 60 (the last line of the page body), the first line of the title for the next page to be written on line 1 of the next page body (AFTER ADVANCING PAGE), and, finally, the rest of the title to be written on line 10 (AFTER ADVANCING 9 LINES from line 1).

Notice how the AT END-OF-PAGE routine not only prints the running total in the footing area of each page, but also advances the paper to the next logical page and prints the title. The paper is left positioned at line 10, so that the entire cycle can begin again.

Like AT END ... (Section 6.4), AT END-OF-PAGE ... is assumed to continue until a period is encountered.

EXAMPLE 6.18

```
      READ CHECK-REQUEST-FILE
         AT END
               MOVE "T" TO CHECK-REQUEST-END-SW
      MOVE CHECK-REQUEST-VENDOR-ID   TO  WS-VENDOR-ID
      MOVE CHECK-REQUEST-AMOUNT         TO   WS-AMOUNT
      WRITE CHECK-REQUEST-EDIT-LINE
         FROM WS-EDIT-LINE
         AFTER ADVANCING 2 LINES
         AT END-OF-PAGE
               WRITE CHECK-REQUEST-EDIT-LINE
                  FROM CHECK-REQUEST-EDIT-TITLE
                  AFTER ADVANCING PAGE
      ADD 1 TO NUMBER-CHECK-REQUESTS
```

This program segment requires a structured period after "MOVE "T" ...", and another after "AFTER ADVANCING PAGE". As it stands, *indentation notwithstanding*, the AT END routine extends to the end of the segment. It therefore includes the first WRITE statement. But this WRITE statement is a *conditional* statement, because it contains a clause (AT END-OF-PAGE) that is executed only under certain conditions. AT END ... thus embodies a syntax error, for (see Section 6.4) it may legally contain only *imperative* (unconditional) statements.

6.6 Input: ACCEPT Statement

The ACCEPT statement is used for certain specialized input.

ACCEPTing Information from the Operating System

The syntax for transferring special operating system information to the COBOL object program is:

$$\underline{\text{ACCEPT}} \text{ identifier } \underline{\text{FROM}} \begin{Bmatrix} \underline{\text{DATE}} \\ \underline{\text{DAY}} \\ \underline{\text{TIME}} \end{Bmatrix}$$

where "identifier" is an appropriately defined data-name from the DATA DIVISION.

EXAMPLE 6.19

●   WORKING-STORAGE SECTION.
       01   SAMPLE-ACCEPTED-DATE   PIC 9(6).

       PROCEDURE DIVISION.
           ACCEPT SAMPLE-ACCEPTED-DATE FROM DATE

The operating system places the current date in data item SAMPLE-ACCEPTED-DATE. The appropriate PICTURE for DATE is PIC 9(6). The date is in the form yymmdd; e.g., February 12, 1983, would be represented by the 6-digit number 830212.

●   01   SAMPLE-ACCEPTED-DAY   PIC 9(5).
           ACCEPT SAMPLE-ACCEPTED-DAY FROM DAY

The operating system places the *Julian date* in data item SAMPLE-ACCEPTED-DAY. The appropriate PICTURE for DAY is PIC 9(5). The Julian date is a 5-digit number of the form yyddd, where yy is the year and ddd is the day of the year (where days are numbered from 1 to 365). February 12, 1983, would be represented by 83043.

●   01   SAMPLE-ACCEPTED-TIME   PIC 9(8).
           ACCEPT SAMPLE-ACCEPTED-TIME FROM TIME

The operating system places the time of day in data item SAMPLE-ACCEPTED-TIME. The appropriate PICTURE for TIME is PIC 9(8). The time of day is an 8-digit number of the form HHmmsshh, where HH is the hour (0 to 23), mm is the minute of the hour (0 to 59), ss is the second of the minute (0 to 59), and hh is the hundredth of the second (0 to 99). Thus 3:24 P.M. would be represented by 15240000.

ACCEPTing Data from SYSIN or the Operator's Console Terminal

The other version of the ACCEPT statement can be used to input small amounts of information from a special system file or, more frequently, from the computer operator's console terminal. The syntax is:

        ACCEPT identifier [FROM special-name]

"Special-name" must be defined in the SPECIAL-NAMES paragraph of the ENVIRONMENT DIVISION (Section 4.4). The exact details of this version of ACCEPT vary from system to system, but in IBM OS/VS COBOL the two allowable SPECIAL-NAMES entries for ACCEPT are CONSOLE and SYSIN:

        SPECIAL-NAMES.
            CONSOLE IS OPERATOR-MESSAGE-DEVICE
            SYSIN   IS BATCH-CONTROL-CARD
            .

CONSOLE is an IBM reserved word which signifies the computer operator's console terminal. The console terminal is used for communication with the operating system and with other executing programs *through* the operating system. SYSIN is an IBM reserved word which signifies a special file of 80-byte records. If the programmer desires to use the SYSIN file, a job-control-language statement must be supplied to define it. In general, using ACCEPT to input from the SYSIN file should be avoided, unless the amount of information involved is extremely small. It is better to set up a regular input file with a SELECT statement, FD, OPEN, and READ.

EXAMPLE 6.20

        SPECIAL-NAMES.
            CONSOLE IS OPERATOR-MESSAGE-DEVICE
        . . . .
        WORKING-STORAGE SECTION.
        01 NUMBER-OF-LABELS-ACROSS   PIC 9   DISPLAY.
        . . . .
        PROCEDURE DIVISION.
            ACCEPT NUMBER-OF-LABELS-ACROSS FROM OPERATOR-MESSAGE-DEVICE

When mailing labels, checks, or other small forms are printed by computer, it can speed the printing considerably if several forms are printed per line. The above excerpt from a program illustrates how the computer operator might be enabled to indicate the number of labels that should be printed across the page on this particular execution of the program. When the ACCEPT statement is executed, execution of the rest of the program is temporarily suspended until the computer operator types the needed information on the console terminal's keyboard. The information is then placed in the data item indicated in the ACCEPT statement (NUMBER-OF-LABELS-ACROSS). Since the data ACCEPTed come from a CRT or hard copy terminal, DISPLAY usage is called for. *The computer operator must type the information according to the PICTURE(S) in the COBOL program, otherwise errors will occur.*

EXAMPLE 6.21 One of the few practical uses of ACCEPT from SYSIN might be to supply control card input. *Control cards* are records (often punched into cards) which specify the program options that are to be in effect for the current computer run. Suppose that a mailing label program may sort the labels either by zip code or by name, and that it may optionally include or exclude company employees.

```
        SPECIAL-NAMES.
            SYSIN IS OPTION-INPUT-DEVICE
. . . . . . . . . . . . . . . . . . . . . . . . .

        WORKING-STORAGE SECTION.
        01   OPTIONS-FOR-THIS-RUN.
             05   TYPE-OF-SORT            PIC X(4)
             05   INCLUDE-EMPLOYEES       PIC X(3).
. . . . . . . . . . . . . . . . . . . . . . . . .

        PROCEDURE DIVISION.
            ACCEPT OPTIONS-FOR-THIS-RUN FROM OPTION-INPUT-DEVICE
```

A control card might contain

$$\underline{\text{N A M E N O } b} \qquad \text{or} \qquad \underline{\text{Z I P } b \text{ Y E S}}$$
$$\text{X(4) \quad X(3)} \qquad\qquad\qquad \text{X(4) \quad X(3)}$$

to cause the program, respectively, to sort labels by name with omission of employees from the mailing, or to sort by zip code with employees included. Each execution of ACCEPT . . . would input another logical record from the SYSIN file. Note that although SYSIN records are 80 bytes, there is no need to account for the extra $80 - (4 + 3) = 73$ bytes in the description of OPTIONS-FOR-THIS-RUN.

6.7   Output: DISPLAY Statement

DISPLAY . . . is designed to produce low-volume printed output on special system files or the computer operator's console. Like its counterpart, ACCEPT . . . , its exact details vary from system to system. For IBM OS/VS COBOL, the syntax of the statement is

$$\underline{\text{DISPLAY}} \begin{Bmatrix} \text{identifier-1} \\ \text{literal-1} \end{Bmatrix} \begin{bmatrix} \text{identifier-2} \\ \text{literal-2} \end{bmatrix} \dots [\underline{\text{UPON}} \text{ special-name}]$$

where "special-name" must be defined in the SPECIAL-NAMES paragraph (Section 4.4). The valid entries in SPECIAL-NAMES for DISPLAY are:

```
        SPECIAL-NAMES.
            CONSOLE IS . . .
            SYSOUT IS . . .
```

Here, "CONSOLE" is as in Section 6.6, and "SYSOUT" is the output analog of "SYSIN".

EXAMPLE 6.22 DISPLAY can be used (in conjunction with ACCEPT) for interaction with the computer operator via the operator's console:

```
        SPECIAL-NAMES.
            CONSOLE IS OPERATOR-MESSAGE-DEVICE

        WORKING-STORAGE SECTION.
```

```
01   WS-OPERATOR-REPLIES.
     05   WS-NUMBER-OF-LABELS-ACROSS      PIC 9.
     05   WS-EMPLOYEES-INCLUDED           PIC X(3).

PROCEDURE DIVISION.

     DISPLAY "PLEASE SET UP PRINTER FOR MAILING LABELS"
         UPON OPERATOR-MESSAGE-DEVICE

     DISPLAY "WHEN READY, ENTER NUMBER OF LABELS ACROSS (1 DIGIT)"
         UPON OPERATOR-MESSAGE-DEVICE

     ACCEPT WS-NUMBER-OF-LABELS-ACROSS
         FROM OPERATOR-MESSAGE-DEVICE

     DISPLAY "EMPLOYEES INCLUDED? ('YES' OR 'NO')"
         UPON OPERATOR-MESSAGE-DEVICE

     ACCEPT WS-EMPLOYEES-INCLUDED
         FROM OPERATOR-MESSAGE-DEVICE
```

The printed *prompts* on the operator's console direct the operator to perform certain actions or guide the operator in entering information for ACCEPT statements.

It should be borne in mind that when nonnumeric literals (such as the above prompts) are DISPLAYed on an output device that accommodates lines of, say, 100 characters, the output will be broken into 100-character chunks, with the breaks falling where they fall. In the case of figurative constants, one character is printed ("DISPLAY SPACES" outputs *one* space). DISPLAY . . . automatically converts COMP or COMP-3 items to DISPLAY format before printing. In IBM OS/VS COBOL, plus signs are automatically removed but operational minus signs are not (see Table 5-1). PIC "V" decimal points do not print.

EXAMPLE 6.23   A second major use of DISPLAY is in *debugging lines* (see Section 4.2):

```
     SPECIAL-NAMES.
D        SYSOUT IS DEBUGGING-DEVICE

     PROCEDURE DIVISION.
D        DISPLAY "STARTING VALUE OF WS-NUMBER-OF-CLIENTS IS "
D            WS-NUMBER-OF-CLIENTS
D            UPON DEBUGGING-DEVICE
. . . . . . . . . . . . . . . . . . . . . . . . . . . . .
D        DISPLAY "WHEN ID INVALID, EMPLOYEE NAME IS "
D            EMPLOYEE-MASTER-NAME
D            UPON DEBUGGING-DEVICE
```

When SOURCE-COMPUTER specifies WITH DEBUGGING MODE, the debugging lines ("D" in column 7) are translated into the object program and cause valuable information about the contents of data items to print on the SYSOUT file. Note that the nonnumeric literals include an extra space (before the close quote) to separate items in the DISPLAY line; DISPLAY . . . does not automatically provide separating spaces.

EXAMPLE 6.24   The third major use of DISPLAY is to print error and/or exception messages on the SYSOUT print file, so that human attention can be directed to the errors and/or exceptional conditions detected during program execution. (This use should not be made when a significant number of errors/exceptions are expected. Thus, keyed input is usually processed by an *edit program*, whose main functions are to detect errors in input data and to print an error report giving enough information so that the errors can be corrected. In these cases, error information should be printed on a regular file, which is set up with a SELECT, FD, etc.)

```
     SPECIAL-NAMES.
         SYSOUT IS ERROR-MESSAGE-LOG
. . . . . . . . . . . . . . . . . . . . . . . . . . . . .
     PROCEDURE DIVISION.
. . . . . . . . . . . . . . . . . . . . . . . . . . . . .
```

```
      OPEN   INPUT   CHECK-REQUEST-FILE
      IF CHECK-REQUEST-STATUS-CODE NOT EQUAL "00"
          DISPLAY "UNABLE TO OPEN CHECK REQUEST FILE"
              UPON ERROR-MESSAGE-LOG
```

If the UPON option is not elected in the DISPLAY statement, the IBM OS/VS COBOL default is

```
      DISPLAY . . . UPON SYSOUT
```

6.8 Processing: MOVE Statement

"MOVE" is a misleading verb, for the effect of the MOVE statement is to *copy* the contents of one data item into another data item or items. The *sending field* is unchanged by the execution of a MOVE statement. The *receiving field*(*s*) have their original contents replaced with the contents of the sending field; the original contents of the receiving field(s) are annihilated. The MOVE statement also causes data to be *converted* from the sending field USAGE to the receiving field USAGE, if the latter differs from the former. Furthermore, if the lengths of the sending and receiving fields are different, MOVE . . . may result in *padding* or *truncation* at the receiving end. Finally, the MOVE statement will cause numeric data to be *edited* if the receiving PICTURE contains editing characters.

The MOVE statement has the following syntax:

$$\underline{\text{MOVE}} \begin{Bmatrix} \text{identifier-1} \\ \text{literal} \end{Bmatrix} \underline{\text{TO}} \text{ identifier-2 [identifier-3]} \ldots$$

(An alternate syntax, which will not be treated in this book, is mentioned in Example 6.31.)

EXAMPLE 6.25 Given

```
      01   SAMPLE-MOVE-ITEMS.
           05   A     PIC X(5).
           05   B     PIC X(5).
           05   C     PIC X(3).
           05   D     PIC X(7).
```

suppose that field A contains "HELLO". Then:

● MOVE A TO B
copies the contents of data item A ("identifier-1") into data item B ("identifier-2"). Since A and B have the same PICTURE and USAGE, they both contain "HELLO" after the MOVE. The original contents of item B are lost.

● MOVE A TO C
copies the contents of item A into item C. Since C is PIC X(3), the value "HELLO" is truncated on the right: after the MOVE, A contains "HELLO" and C contains "HEL".

● MOVE A TO D
copies the contents of item A into item D. Since D is PIC X(7), the value "HELLO" is padded on the right with spaces: after the MOVE, A contains "HELLO" and D contains "HELLO*bb*".

● MOVE A TO B C D
copies the contents of data item A into data items B, C, and D. It generates exactly the same machine language as the preceding set of three MOVE statements.

● MOVE SPACES TO A
copies 5 blank spaces (here, "literal" is the figurative constant SPACES) into data item A ("identifier-2"), which is defined PIC X(5).

● MOVE ZEROS TO A C
sets A to "00000" and C to "000", the zeros being DISPLAY zeros.

● MOVE ALL "-" TO C D
sets C to "---" and D to "-------". Again notice that the use of a figurative constant (ALL "-") automatically supplies the correct number and type of characters.

EXAMPLE 6.26   Given

> 01   SAMPLE-NUMERIC-ITEMS.
>   05   A   PIC S9(5)   VALUE +12345.
>   05   B   PIC S9(5).
>   05   C   PIC S9(3).
>   05   D   PIC S9(7).

●   MOVE A TO B

Since A and B are both PIC S9(5) DISPLAY, they will contain the same value after the move: +12345.

●   MOVE A TO C

For numeric items, truncation is on the left. C would contain +345 [PIC S9(3)]; A would remain unchanged.

●   MOVE A TO D

For numeric items, padding is on the left with zeros. A would remain unchanged; D would contain +0012345.

EXAMPLE 6.27   Given

> 01   SAMPLE-NUMERIC-ITEMS.
>   05   A   PIC S9(3)V99   COMP-3   .VALUE +123.45.
>   05   B   PIC S9(3)V99   DISPLAY.
>   05   C   PIC S9(3)V99   COMP.
>   05   D   PIC S9(5)V99   COMP-3.
>   05   E   PIC S9(5)V9   DISPLAY.
>   05   F   PIC S9(5)V999   COMP.
>   05   G   PIC S9(2)V9   COMP-3.

●   MOVE A TO B

A and B have the same PICTUREs but different USAGEs. The COMP-3 value in A is converted to DISPLAY as it is copied into B. Thus, both A and B contain +123.45 after the MOVE, but the value in A is stored in COMP-3 form, while the value in B is stored in DISPLAY form.

●   MOVE A TO D

Here the USAGEs are the same, but the PICTUREs are different. The decimal points are aligned, then the receiving field is padded with zeros on the left. A remains unchanged; D contains +00123.45 in COMP-3 form. Decimal points in sending and receiving fields are always kept aligned.

●   MOVE A TO E

An automatic conversion will be made from COMP-3 to DISPLAY. In addition, the integer part of the value will be padded with zeros (on the left). Since E has only one decimal place, E will contain DISPLAY +00123.4 after the MOVE. Note that *rounding* is *not* performed by the MOVE statement, and that decimal points are kept aligned.

●   MOVE A TO F

Here, there is an automatic conversion from COMP-3 to COMP. The integer part of the value is padded with zeros (on the left). Since the receiving field specifies more decimal places than the sending field, the receiving field is also padded with zeros (on the right). A is unchanged after the move; F contains COMP +00123.450.

●   MOVE A TO G

Both USAGEs are COMP-3, so that no conversion is performed. However, since G is PIC S9(2)V9, truncation will be performed on both the left and the right. The result in G will be COMP-3 +23.4.

●   MOVE A TO B D E F G

This statement produces exactly the same machine language as the collection of five MOVE statements discussed above.

●   MOVE ZEROS TO A B C

Since A, B, and C all have the same PICTURE, they all contain +000.00. However, each field will contain a *different kind* of "ZERO": A will be COMP-3, B will be DISPLAY, and C will be COMP. When figurative constants are used in a MOVE statement or VALUE clause, they always represent the *correct amount* of data and the *correct USAGE*.

EXAMPLE 6.28 Given

```
01   SAMPLE-NUMERIC-ITEMS.
     05   A            PIC S9(5)V99      VALUE +00010.08.
     05   A-EDITED   PIC $$$,$$$.99-.
```

●   MOVE A TO A-EDITED

Whenever a numeric item is moved to a field with editing characters, part of the execution of the MOVE statement involves editing the value in the receiving field. The value in A remains unchanged; the value in A-EDITED after the MOVE is:

$$bbbb\$10.08b$$

EXAMPLE 6.29 (Invalid MOVEs)   COBOL classifies data items into six *categories of data*. Letting "identifier-1" and "identifier-2" name certain pairs of these categories, we have the following list of all 14 invalid MOVEs:

●   MOVE ALPHABETIC-DATA TO NUMERIC-INTEGER-DATA

●   MOVE ALPHABETIC-DATA TO NUMERIC-NONINTEGER-DATA

●   MOVE ALPHABETIC-DATA TO NUMERIC-EDITED-DATA

●   MOVE ALPHANUMERIC-EDITED-DATA TO NUMERIC-INTEGER-DATA

●   MOVE ALPHANUMERIC-EDITED-DATA TO NUMERIC-NONINTEGER-DATA

●   MOVE ALPHANUMERIC-EDITED-DATA TO NUMERIC-EDITED-DATA

●   MOVE NUMERIC-INTEGER-DATA TO ALPHABETIC-DATA

●   MOVE NUMERIC-NONINTEGER-DATA TO ALPHABETIC-DATA

●   MOVE NUMERIC-NONINTEGER-DATA TO ALPHANUMERIC-DATA

●   MOVE NUMERIC-NONINTEGER-DATA TO ALPHANUMERIC-EDITED-DATA

●   MOVE NUMERIC-EDITED-DATA TO ALPHABETIC-DATA

●   MOVE NUMERIC-EDITED-DATA TO NUMERIC-INTEGER-DATA

●   MOVE NUMERIC-EDITED-DATA TO NUMERIC-NONINTEGER-DATA

●   MOVE NUMERIC-EDITED-DATA TO NUMERIC-EDITED-DATA

Note that every illegal combination is of an alphabetic/alphanumeric/edited data item and a numeric data item. Any combination not listed above is valid.

EXAMPLE 6.30   So far, all MOVEs illustrated have been from one elementary item to another. Consider the following attempted *group MOVE*:

```
01   INPUT-INVOICE-RECORD.
     05   INPUT-VENDOR-ID          PIC  X(5).
     05   INPUT-INVOICE-ID         PIC  X(4).
     05   INPUT-NUMBER-ITEMS       PIC  S9(4).
     05   INPUT-AMOUNT             PIC  S9(5)V99.

01   PAYABLE-INVOICE-RECORD.
     05   PAYABLE-VENDOR-ID        PIC  X(5).
     05   PAYABLE-INVOICE-ID       PIC  X(4).
     05   PAYABLE-NUMBER-ITEMS     PIC  S9(4)      COMP-3.
     05   PAYABLE-AMOUNT           PIC  S9(5)V99   COMP-3.
```

MOVE INPUT-INVOICE-RECORD TO PAYABLE-INVOICE-RECORD

When a group item (at any level) is MOVEd or receives a MOVE, it is treated as one large PIC X (alphanumeric) item. Here, all fields in INPUT-INVOICE-RECORD are DISPLAY; so the group item is 20 bytes long (5 + 4 + 4 + 7) and it is MOVEd as if it were defined PIC X(20). PAYABLE-INVOICE-RECORD is 16 bytes long $(5+4+3+4$; note the difference caused by the COMP-3 USAGE for the numeric items); hence, for purposes of the MOVE, it is treated as if it were defined PIC X(16). Execution of the MOVE statement (i) does *not* convert the subfields INPUT-NUMBER-ITEMS and INPUT-AMOUNT from DISPLAY to COMP-3 before moving them respectively to PAYABLE-NUMBER-ITEMS and PAYABLE-AMOUNT, and (ii) *truncates* the rightmost 4 bytes of INPUT-INVOICE-RECORD [in going from PIC X(20) to PIC X(16)]. The result is garbage in PAYABLE-NUMBER-ITEMS and PAYABLE-AMOUNT, which will cause a program ABEND if these fields are referenced.

EXAMPLE 6.31   From Example 6.30 we infer that a group MOVE is unsafe unless

(1)   all subfields in both the sending and receiving item have USAGE DISPLAY, and any effects due to differences in length or order of subfields are anticipated and desired by the programmer;

or else

(2)   not all subfields are DISPLAY, but the sending item and the receiving item correspond exactly in terms of each subfield's position, PICTURE, and USAGE.

Consider the group items

```
01   PENDING-INVOICE-RECORD.
     05   PENDING-INVOICE-ID          PIC  X(4).
     05   PENDING-VENDOR-ID           PIC  X(5).
     05   PENDING-AMOUNT-DUE          PIC  S9(5)V99.
     05   PENDING-NUMBER-ITEMS        PIC  S9(4).

01   PAYABLE-INVOICE-RECORD.
     05   PAYABLE-VENDOR-ID           PIC  X(5).
     05   PAYABLE-AMOUNT-DUE          PIC  S9(5)V99.
     05   PAYABLE-INVOICE-ID          PIC  X(4).
     05   PAYABLE-NUMBER-ITEMS        PIC  S9(4).
```

Since condition (1) above is not satisfied,

MOVE PENDING-INVOICE-RECORD TO PAYABLE-INVOICE-RECORD

would not work. Because of the differing *orders* of the subfields in the two group items, PENDING-INVOICE-ID (4 bytes) and the *first* byte of PENDING-VENDOR-ID would be moved to PAYABLE-VENDOR-ID (5 bytes); etc. This would, of course, result in errors when PAYABLE-INVOICE-RECORD fields are referenced.

The only correct way to achieve the desired results is to MOVE the subfields individually:

```
MOVE   PENDING-INVOICE-ID      TO   PAYABLE-INVOICE-ID
MOVE   PENDING-VENDOR-ID       TO   PAYABLE-VENDOR-ID
MOVE   PENDING-AMOUNT-DUE      TO   PAYABLE-AMOUNT-DUE
MOVE   PENDING-NUMBER-ITEMS    TO   PAYABLE-NUMBER-ITEMS
```

(On some installations, certain group MOVEs may be effected by a statement of the form

MOVE CORRESPONDING identifier-1 TO identifier-2

We strongly recommend the method of individual MOVEs instead.)

6.9   Terminating Program Execution: STOP Statement

STOP RUN

STOP RUN causes the object program to turn control of the computer back to the operating system. This action permanently terminates this particular execution of the program. *All files must be CLOSEd before executing STOP RUN*; otherwise, serious errors may occur during later file processing. Each program should have at least one STOP RUN, and many installation's coding standards demand *exactly one*.

STOP literal

This version of the STOP statement (i) causes the value of "literal" to be displayed upon the computer operator's console terminal; and (ii) causes object program execution to be *temporarily suspended* (while the operator changes tapes, printer forms, etc.) until the operator signals the operating system, via the console terminal, that execution of the object program may be resumed.

EXAMPLE 6.32

```
PROCEDURE DIVISION.
    OPEN  INPUT  PAYABLE-INVOICE-FILE
    STOP "PLEASE MOUNT PREPRINTED CHECK FORMS IN PRINTER"
    OPEN  OUTPUT  PAID-INVOICE-CHECK-FILE
```

After reading the message "PLEASE MOUNT . . ." on the console terminal, the operator will presumably ready the printer to print checks, and will then restart the program at "OPEN OUTPUT . . .".

6.10   Controlled Execution of a Paragraph: PERFORM Statement

The PERFORM statement allows an entire paragraph to be executed one or more times from a point in the program other than that at which the paragraph would be executed during normal sequential execution of statements. The simplest version of the PERFORM statement is:

> PERFORM paragraph-name

where "paragraph-name" is the programmer-defined name of a paragraph in the PROCEDURE DIVISION. Execution of this version causes *all statements* in the indicated paragraph to be executed in normal sequential fashion (first to last). Normal sequential execution of instructions then resumes with the statement immediately following the PERFORM statement.

EXAMPLE 6.33

```
PROCEDURE DIVISION.

    OPEN    INPUT     TIME-CARD-FILE
            OUTPUT    TIME-CARD-LISTING

    PERFORM INITIALIZE-COUNTERS-SWITCHES

    WRITE LISTING-LINE
        FROM WS-LISTING-LINE-HEADING
        AFTER ADVANCING PAGE

    PERFORM INPUT-TIME-RECORD

    MOVE WS-TIME-CARD-ID TO WS-LISTING-ID
. . . . . . . . . . . . . . . . . . . . . . . .
INITIALIZE-COUNTERS-SWITCHES.

    MOVE "F" TO TIME-CARD-END-SW
    MOVE ZEROS TO WS-EMPLOYEE-COUNTER
                  WS-AMOUNT-OVERTIME
                  WS-TOTAL-HOURS
```

INPUT-TIME-RECORD.

    READ TIME-CARD-FILE
        INTO WS-TIME-CARD-RECORD
        AT END
            MOVE "T" TO TIME-CARD-END-SW

Owing to the presence of the two PERFORM statements, the order of execution of the above is: (1) OPEN . . . , (2) PERFORM INITIALIZE- . . . , (3) MOVE "F" . . . , (4) MOVE ZEROS . . . , (5) WRITE . . . , (6) PERFORM INPUT- . . . , (7) READ . . . , (8) MOVE WS- . . . .

Most business programs need to repeat the input-process-output cycle for each logical record in an input file. This means that the *program logic* must contain a *loop*, whereby a set of instructions is executed over and over. The COBOL statement most useful for programming loops has the syntax

    <u>PERFORM</u> paragraph-name <u>UNTIL</u> condition

When such a statement is executed, the indicated paragraph is "PERFORMed" over and over again until the specified "condition" is met. "Conditions" will be discussed fully in Chapter 7; for now, a condition has the form "data-name EQUAL literal".

EXAMPLE 6.34

    PROCEDURE DIVISION.

        OPEN   INPUT   TIME-CARD-FILE
                  OUTPUT   TIME-CARD-LISTING

        MOVE "F" TO TIME-CARD-END-SW

        PERFORM PRODUCE-TIME-LISTING-LINE
            UNTIL TIME-CARD-END-SW EQUAL "T"

        CLOSE TIME-CARD-FILE
            TIME-CARD-LISTING

        STOP RUN

    PRODUCE-TIME-LISTING-LINE.

        READ TIME-CARD-FILE
            INTO WS-TIME-RECORD
            AT END
                MOVE "T" TO TIME-CARD-END-SW

        IF TIME-CARD-END-SW EQUAL "F"

        MOVE WS-TIME-REC-ID   TO   WS-LISTING-ID
        MOVE WS-TIME-REC-NAME   TO   WS-LISTING-NAME
        MOVE WS-TIME-REC-HOURS TO   WS-LISTING-HOURS

        WRITE TIME-CARD-LISTING-LINE
            FROM WS-LISTING-LINE
            AFTER ADVANCING 2 LINES

Let us suppose that there are only two logical records in TIME-CARD-FILE. The logical order in which statements will be executed is:

1. OPEN . . .
2. MOVE "F" TO TIME-CARD-END-SW
3. PERFORM PRODUCE-TIME-LISTING-LINE UNTIL . . .
    (*Since TIME-CARD-END-SW is not "T", paragraph is PERFORMed first time.*)

1st PERFORM of PRODUCE-TIME-LISTING-LINE

4. READ TIME-CARD-FILE . . . AT END MOVE "T" TO TIME-CARD-END-SW
    (*Inputs first logical record; switch remains "F".*)
5. IF TIME-CARD-END-SW EQUAL "F"
    (*Since condition is* true, *all statements up to period are executed.*)
6. MOVE WS-TIME-REC-ID . . .
7. MOVE WS-TIME-REC-NAME . . .
8. MOVE WS-TIME-REC-HOURS . . .
9. WRITE TIME-CARD-LISTING-LINE FROM . . .
    (*After last statement in paragraph, condition is evaluated. Since switch is not "T", paragraph is PERFORMed again.*)

2nd PERFORM

10. READ TIME-CARD-FILE . . . AT END MOVE "T" TO TIME-CARD-END-SW
    (*Inputs second logical record; switch remains "F".*)
11. IF TIME-CARD-END-SW EQUAL "F"
    (*Since condition is* true, *all statements up to period are executed.*)
12. MOVE WS-TIME-REC-ID . . .
13. MOVE WS-TIME-REC-NAME . . .
14. MOVE WS-TIME-REC-HOURS . . .
15. WRITE TIME-CARD-LISTING-LINE FROM . . .
    (*After last statement in paragraph, condition is evaluated. Since switch is not "T", paragraph is PERFORMed again.*)

3rd PERFORM

16. READ TIME-CARD-FILE . . . AT END MOVE "T" TO TIME-CARD-END-SW
    (*Upon this third READ of a file with only two logical records, end of file occurs. AT END . . . is executed making switch contain "T"; PERFORM still continues to end of paragraph.*)
17. IF TIME-CARD-END-SW EQUAL "F"
    (*Switch is now "T", so all statements up to the period that ends IF . . . are* skipped. *This period also ends paragraph, making IF . . . the* last *statement executed in paragraph.*)

18. CLOSE . . .
    (*After executing last statement in PERFORMed paragraph, computer tests switch. As it now contains "T", execution of PERFORM statement halts and next statement, CLOSE . . . , is executed.*)
19. STOP RUN
    (*After STOP RUN is executed, no more program statements are carried out.*)

Notice how the logic of the program carefully avoids processing a record after end of file has occurred (cf. Example 6.10).

EXAMPLE 6.35 Having illustrated looping, we are now in a position to look at a complete COBOL program. Consider a payroll application in which employees fill out weekly time sheets with their identification number, name, and total hours worked for the week. These time sheets are signed by a supervisor and sent to data processing, where the information is entered using key-to-disk equipment. It is desired to have an *edit program* print a hard copy listing of weekly time records for visual inspection and correction.

The source listing for such an edit program is given below. It is hoped that the reader will be able to identify the applications of the principles of COBOL programming discussed so far in this Outline. In particular:

1. ORGANIZATION and ACCESS clauses in SELECT statements, though redundant (since the default is SEQUENTIAL), are specified for program documentation.

2. Use of IBM "BLOCK CONTAINS 0 . . ." for the input disk file.

3. Omission of BLOCK CONTAINS clause for print file.

4. LABEL RECORDS ARE STANDARD for the disk file, OMITTED for the printer file.

5. All record processing is actually done in WORKING-STORAGE using "READ...INTO..." and "WRITE...FROM..."; record descriptions in the FILE SECTION are just PIC X(80) and PIC X(132), since actual record layout is specified for the WORKING-STORAGE copy.

6. WORKING-STORAGE items are grouped under level-01 categories; items are listed in a systematic manner.

7. VALUE clause is used to set up both heading lines and ID/name/hours lines in WORKING-STORAGE.

8. "FILLER" is used for all data items which are not referenced in the PROCEDURE DIVISION.

9. PROCEDURE DIVISION makes heavy use of PERFORM... and PERFORM UNTIL... for controlling program logic flow and setting up the fundamental input-process-output loop.

10. Satisfy yourself that this program *does not* process a garbage record after hitting end of file (and that it *does* process *all* logical records in the time sheet disk file).

11. Observe the indentation in the PROCEDURE DIVISION, and the indentation and column alignment in the DATA DIVISION.

```
00001          IDENTIFICATION DIVISION.

00003          PROGRAM-ID. HRVERIFY.
00004
00005          AUTHOR.  LARRY NEWCOMER.
00006          INSTALLATION.  PENN STATE UNIVERSITY, YORK CAMPUS.
00007
00008          DATE-WRITTEN.  MAY 1983.
00009          DATE-COMPILED. MAY  9,1983.

00011          SECURITY.  NONE.
00012
00013      *   HRVERIFY PRODUCES A PRINTED LISTING OF THE WEEKLY PAYROLL
00014      *   TIME FILE (PREPARED BY KEY-TO-DISK OPERATORS USING WEEKLY
00015      *   TIME SHEETS).  THIS LISTING IS USED TO VISUALLY VERIFY
00016      *   THE CORRECTNESS OF EMPLOYEE ID NUMBERS, EMPLOYEE NAMES,
00017      *   AND EMPLOYEE WEEKLY HOURS WORKED AS TYPED BY DATA ENTRY.
00018      *   THE ONLY OUTPUT IS THIS VISUAL EDIT REPORT.


00020          ENVIRONMENT DIVISION.

00022          CONFIGURATION SECTION.

00024          SOURCE-COMPUTER.  IBM-3081.
00025          OBJECT-COMPUTER.  IBM-3081.

00027          INPUT-OUTPUT SECTION.
00028
00029          FILE-CONTROL.

00031              SELECT TIME-SHEET-INPUT-FILE
00032                  ASSIGN TO TIMECARD
00033                  ORGANIZATION IS SEQUENTIAL
00034                  ACCESS IS SEQUENTIAL
00035                  .
00036
00037              SELECT VER1FY-TIME-REPORT
00038                  ASSIGN TO TIMELIST
00039                  ORGANIZATION IS SEQUENTIAL
00040                  ACCESS IS SEQUENTIAL
00041                  .


00043          DATA DIVISION.
```

```
00045                FILE SECTION.

00047           FD   TIME-SHEET-INPUT-FILE
00048                BLOCK CONTAINS 0 RECORDS
00049                RECORD CONTAINS 80 CHARACTERS
00050                LABEL RECORDS ARE STANDARD
00051                .
00052
00053           01   TIME-SHEET-INPUT-RECORD      PIC X(80).

00055           FD   VERIFY-TIME-REPORT
00056                RECORD CONTAINS 132 CHARACTERS
00057                LABEL RECORDS ARE OMITTED
00058                LINAGE IS 50
00059                    WITH FOOTING AT 45
00060                    LINES AT TOP 8
00061                    LINES AT BOTTOM 8
00062                .
00063
00064           01   VERIFY-TIME-LINE             PIC X(132).


00066           WORKING-STORAGE SECTION.

00068           01   PROGRAM-FLAGS-AND-SWITCHES.
00069                05  WS-TIME-SHEET-END-SW     PIC X.

00071           01   WORKING-INPUT-RECORD-AREAS.

00073                05  WS-TIME-SHEET-REC.
00074                    10  WS-TIME-SHEET-ID     PIC X(4).
00075                    10  WS-TIME-SHEET-NAME   PIC X(20).
00076                    10  WS-TIME-SHEET-HOURS  PIC S9(2)V9.
00077                    10  FILLER               PIC X(53).

00079           01   WORKING-OUTPUT-RECORD-AREAS.

00081                05  WS-VERIFY-HEADING.
00082                    10  FILLER               PIC X(4)      VALUE "-ID-".
00083                    10  FILLER               PIC X(4)      VALUE SPACES.
00084                    10  FILLER               PIC X(20)     VALUE "NAME".
00085                    10  FILLER               PIC X(4)      VALUE SPACES.
00086                    10  FILLER               PIC X(5)      VALUE "HOURS".
00087                    10  FILLER               PIC X(95)     VALUE SPACES.

00089                05  WS-VERIFY-LINE.
00090                    10  WS-VERIFY-ID         PIC X(4).
00091                    10  FILLER               PIC X(4)      VALUE SPACES.
00092                    10  WS-VERIFY-NAME       PIC X(20).
00093                    10  FILLER               PIC X(4)      VALUE SPACES.
00094                    10  WS-VERIFY-HOURS      PIC Z9.9-.
00095                    10  FILLER               PIC X(95)     VALUE SPACES.


00097           PROCEDURE DIVISION.

00099                PERFORM INITIALIZE-FILES-AND-SWITCHES
00100
00101                PERFORM PRODUCE-VERIFY-LINE
00102                    UNTIL WS-TIME-SHEET-END-SW EQUAL "T"
00103
00104                CLOSE   TIME-SHEET-INPUT-FILE
00105                        VERIFY-TIME-REPORT
00106
```

```
00107                     STOP RUN
00108                         .

00110               INITIALIZE-FILES-AND-SWITCHES.

00112                   MOVE "F" TO WS-TIME-SHEET-END-SW
00113                   OPEN    INPUT    TIME-SHEET-INPUT-FILE
00114                           OUTPUT   VERIFY-TIME-REPORT
00115                   PERFORM READ-TIME-SHEET-FILE
00116                   WRITE VERIFY-TIME-LINE
00117                       FROM WS-VERIFY-HEADING
00118                       AFTER ADVANCING PAGE
00119                         .

00121               READ-TIME-SHEET-FILE.

00123                   READ TIME-SHEET-INPUT-FILE
00124                       INTO WS-TIME-SHEET-REC
00125                       AT END
00126                           MOVE "T" TO WS-TIME-SHEET-END-SW
00127                         .

00129               PRODUCE-VERIFY-LINE.

00131                   MOVE WS-TIME-SHEET-ID        TO WS-VERIFY-ID
00132                   MOVE WS-TIME-SHEET-NAME      TO WS-VERIFY-NAME
00133                   MOVE WS-TIME-SHEET-HOURS     TO WS-VERIFY-HOURS
00134                   WRITE VERIFY-TIME-LINE
00135                       FROM WS-VERIFY-LINE
00136                       AFTER ADVANCING 3 LINES
00137                       AT END-OF-PAGE
00138                           WRITE VERIFY-TIME-LINE
00139                               FROM WS-VERIFY-HEADING
00140                               AFTER ADVANCING PAGE
00141                         .
00142                   PERFORM READ-TIME-SHEET-FILE
00143                         .
```

An output line of the above program would look like:

0027   FOLKERS DEIRDRE   45.6

6.11 Processing: ADD Statement

The ADD statement causes the contents of two or more numeric data items to be added and the sum placed in one or more data items. There are two main versions of the statement, ADD . . . TO . . . and ADD . . . GIVING . . . (a third version, ADD CORRESPONDING . . . , is not recommended and will be omitted from this book).

ADD . . . TO . . .

This option has the syntax indicated in Fig. 6-4.

$$\underline{ADD} \left\{ \begin{array}{l} \text{identifier-1} \\ \text{literal-1} \end{array} \right\} \left[\begin{array}{l} \text{identifier-2} \\ \text{literal-2} \end{array} \right] \ldots$$

$$\underline{TO}\ \text{identification-m}\ [\underline{ROUNDED}]\,[\text{identification-n}\ [\underline{ROUNDED}]]$$

$$[\text{ON}\ \underline{SIZE\ ERROR}\ \text{imperative-statement}]$$

Fig. 6-4

EXAMPLE 6.36

●   ADD WEEKLY-HOURS TO TOTAL-HOURS

The current contents of WEEKLY-HOURS are added to the current contents of TOTAL-HOURS, and the sum replaces the original contents of TOTAL-HOURS; WEEKLY-HOURS is unchanged. Both items must be numeric (and not edited). The compiler automatically generates extra machine language to handle aligning decimal points and converting from one USAGE to another.

●   ADD ITEM-A ITEM-B TO ITEM-C

The contents of ITEM-A, ITEM-B, and ITEM-C are added together, and the sum replaces the original contents of ITEM-C; ITEM-A and ITEM-B are unchanged. All data items must be numeric (and not edited).

●   ADD ITEM-A ITEM-B ITEM-C TO ITEM-D ITEM-E

The sum of ITEM-A, ITEM-B, ITEM-C, and ITEM-D replaces the original contents of ITEM-D; the sum of ITEM-A, ITEM-B, ITEM-C, and ITEM-E replaces the original contents of ITEM-E. ITEM-A, ITEM-B, and ITEM-C remain unchanged.

●   ADD 1 TO NUMBER-OVERTIME-EMPLOYEES

One is added to the current contents of NUMBER-OVERTIME-EMPLOYEES (which is thus *incremented by 1*). The use of numeric literals in calculations is common.

ADD . . . GIVING . . .

This option has the syntax indicated in Fig. 6-5.

$$\underline{ADD} \begin{Bmatrix} identifier\text{-}1 \\ literal\text{-}1 \end{Bmatrix} \begin{Bmatrix} identifier\text{-}2 \\ literal\text{-}2 \end{Bmatrix} \begin{bmatrix} identifier\text{-}3 \\ literal\text{-}3 \end{bmatrix} \dots$$

GIVING identifier-m [$\underline{ROUNDED}$] [identifier-n [$\underline{ROUNDED}$]] . . .

[ON $\underline{SIZE\ ERROR}$ imperative-statement]

Fig. 6-5

EXAMPLE 6.37

●   ADD REGULAR-HOURS OVERTIME-HOURS GIVING TOTAL-HOURS

The GIVING option requires at least two items to the left of the word "GIVING" and at least one item to the right. The current contents of REGULAR-HOURS and those of OVERTIME-HOURS are added together and the sum replaces the original contents of TOTAL-HOURS. REGULAR-HOURS and OVERTIME-HOURS are unchanged. The original contents of TOTAL-HOURS are *not* included in the sum. Data items to the left of "GIVING", which are added together, must be numeric and not edited. Data items to the right of "GIVING" receive the result of the addition but are themselves not added; so, although they also must be numeric, they *may be edited*.

●   ADD   PAYABLE-INVOICE-AMOUNT
              PAYABLE-INVOICE-FREIGHT
              PAYABLE-INVOICE-SPECIAL
                        GIVING   OUTPUT-CHECK-AMOUNT

Style of typing improves readability and modifiability. All PAYABLE-INVOICE fields must be numeric and not edited. They are added and their sum replaces the original contents of OUTPUT-CHECK-AMOUNT (which does not participate in the sum). OUTPUT-CHECK-AMOUNT is edited for printing.

●   ADD   STATE-TAX
           FEDERAL-TAX GIVING PAYROLL-REPORT-TOTAL-TAX
                          EMPLOYEE-MASTER-TOTAL-TAX

All fields must be numeric; however, PAYROLL-REPORT-TOTAL-TAX is edited (valid when receiving result). STATE-TAX and FEDERAL-TAX are added and their sum replaces the original contents of PAYROLL-REPORT-TOTAL-TAX and those of EMPLOYEE-MASTER-TOTAL-TAX.

EXAMPLE 6.38 (Common ADD Errors)

●   ADD STATE-TAX TO FEDERAL-TAX GIVING TOTAL-TAX

A syntax error: the TO and GIVING options are mutually exclusive.

●   ADD FREIGHT-CHARGES TO INVOICE-AMOUNT AND SHIPPING-TOTAL

"AND" is invalid in both versions of ADD . . . .

●   ADD DAILY-HOURS GIVING WEEKLY-HOURS MONTHLY-HOURS

The GIVING option requires at least two values to the left of "GIVING". Presumably, the intention was:

    ADD DAILY-HOURS TO WEEKLY-HOURS MONTHLY-HOURS

The use of the ROUNDED option and the ON SIZE ERROR clause, which occur in both versions of ADD . . . , will be explained in Sections 6.12 and 6.13.

6.12 Processing: Truncation and the ROUNDED Option

All arithmetic statements (ADD, SUBTRACT, MULTIPLY, DIVIDE, and COMPUTE) automatically generate machine language instructions to (i) align the decimal points of values being added or subtracted; (ii) convert from one USAGE to another and back. It is possible that the result of a calculation will have more decimal places than a field which is to receive the result. In this case, the default action is to chop off (*truncate*) the necessary number of digits on the right.

To modify the truncation process, the word "ROUNDED" may be placed after the name of any field that is to receive the result of an arithmetic calculation (review Figs. 6-4 and 6-5). With ROUNDED specified:

  (1)   if the leftmost digit to be truncated is 5 or more, 1 is added to the rightmost digit to be retained (*rounding up*);

  (2)   if the leftmost digit to be truncated is 4 or less, the result is simply truncated, with no change of the rightmost retained digit (*rounding down*).

EXAMPLE 6.39

    05   ANSWER   PIC S99V9

    . . . .

    ADD X Y Z GIVING ANSWER

If the sum of X, Y, and Z is 54.34999, the last four decimal places in the result are dropped, and ANSWER will contain 54.3.

    . . . .

    ADD X Y Z GIVING ANSWER ROUNDED

With the specification of ROUNDED, we still get 54.3 in ANSWER; the leftmost digit to be truncated being 4, the result is *not* rounded up to 54.4.

EXAMPLE 6.40

    ADD HOURS-WORKED TO WEEKLY-TOTAL

                      MONTHLY-TOTAL ROUNDED

                      YEARLY-TOTAL   ROUNDED

It is permissible to specify ROUNDED for only some of the receiving fields in a calculation.

6.13 Processing: Overflow and the ON SIZE ERROR Clause

If the *integer part* of a calculated number will not fit in a receiving field, *overflow* or a *SIZE ERROR* is said to occur. The ON SIZE ERROR clause allows the programmer to specify a set of statements that are executed only in the event of a SIZE ERROR.

EXAMPLE 6.41

```
    ADD WEEKLY-HOURS TO YEARLY-TOTAL-HOURS
        ON SIZE ERROR
            MOVE EMPLOYEE-ID    TO ERROR-LINE-ID
            MOVE WEEKLY-HOURS TO ERROR-LINE-HOURS
            MOVE "YEARLY HOURS OVERFLOW--HOURS NOT INCLUDED IN TOTAL"
                TO ERROR-LINE-MESSAGE
            WRITE REPORT-LINE
                FROM ERROR-LINE
                AFTER ADVANCING 3 LINES

    PERFORM COMPUTE-GROSS-PAY
. . . . . . . . . . . . . . . . . . . . . . . . . . . . . . . . .
```

If the result of ADDing WEEKLY-HOURS to YEARLY-TOTAL-HOURS will fit in YEARLY-TOTAL-HOURS, the ON SIZE ERROR . . . statements will be ignored for this execution of the ADD statement. Observe that the ON SIZE ERROR clause (like AT END . . . and AT END-OF-PAGE . . .) is ended by a period. Omission of the structured period preceding the PERFORM statement would cause the PERFORM to become part of the ON SIZE ERROR clause, with the result that it would be executed *only when* a SIZE ERROR occurs, rather than *every time*, as intended.

EXAMPLE 6.42   Given

```
    05  A  PIC S99V99   VALUE +50.34.
    05  B  PIC S99V99   VALUE +50.23.
    05  C  PIC S99V9    VALUE +12.3.
```

- ADD A B GIVING C

Since the sum of A and B is +100.57, the integer part of the result is too large to fit into the receiving field, C. Without an ON SIZE ERROR clause, the computer simply truncates the integer part of the result (on the left) and keeps on going. Thus C would contain +00.5, which, of course, is incorrect.

- ADD A B GIVING C
      ON SIZE ERROR
          DISPLAY "SIZE ERROR FOR C--C IS UNCHANGED"

With ON SIZE ERROR . . . specified, the truncated sum is *not* moved into C; C continues to hold +12.3. Furthermore, DISPLAY . . . prints an error message (on the special system file SYSOUT for IBM OS/VS COBOL).

Guidelines Concerning ON SIZE ERROR . . .

1. If possible, size the PICTURES of numeric data items large enough so that, for the calculations being done by the program, overflow is mathematically impossible. This allows the ON SIZE ERROR clause to be omitted without danger.

2. If there is the slightest possibility that a SIZE ERROR could occur, use the ON SIZE ERROR clause.

3. When used, ON SIZE ERROR . . . routines should (*a*) print an error message with enough information to allow human beings to "patch things up"; (*b*) arrange that processing of the logical record(s) causing the SIZE ERROR be partially or completely by-passed; (*c*) allow normal processing of remaining logical records to continue (don't STOP the whole program run).

6.14 Processing: SUBTRACT Statement

Figure 6-6 gives the two main formats of the SUBTRACT statement. Because SUBTRACT . . . FROM . . . is analogous in every respect to ADD . . . TO . . ., we need only illustrate the handling of SUBTRACT . . . FROM . . . GIVING . . . .

$$\underline{SUBTRACT} \begin{Bmatrix} \text{identifier-1} \\ \text{literal-1} \end{Bmatrix} \begin{bmatrix} \text{identifier-2} \\ \text{literal-2} \end{bmatrix} \dots$$

$$\underline{FROM} \text{ identifier-m } [\underline{ROUNDED}] \text{ [identifier-n } [\underline{ROUNDED}]] \dots$$

$$[\text{ON } \underline{SIZE ERROR} \text{ imperative-statement}]$$

(a)

$$\underline{SUBTRACT} \begin{Bmatrix} \text{identifier-1} \\ \text{literal-1} \end{Bmatrix} \begin{bmatrix} \text{identifier-2} \\ \text{literal-2} \end{bmatrix} \dots$$

$$\underline{FROM} \begin{Bmatrix} \text{identifier-m} \\ \text{literal-m} \end{Bmatrix}$$

$$\underline{GIVING} \text{ identifier-n } [\underline{ROUNDED}] \text{ [identifier-o } [\underline{ROUNDED}]] \dots$$

$$[\text{ON } \underline{SIZE ERROR} \text{ imperative-statement}]$$

(b)

Fig. 6-6

EXAMPLE 6.43

●   SUBTRACT DISCOUNT-AMOUNT FROM CURRENT-PRICE GIVING NEW-PRICE
Current contents of DISCOUNT-AMOUNT are subtracted from current contents of CURRENT-PRICE, and the difference replaces the original contents of NEW-PRICE. NEW-PRICE may be an edited field, since it does not itself take part in the calculation. DISCOUNT-AMOUNT and CURRENT-PRICE are unaffected by the subtraction.

●   SUBTRACT 10 FROM A-GRADE-CUTOFF GIVING B-GRADE-CUTOFF
Numeric literals are often used in arithmetic statements.

●   SUBTRACT   STATE-TAX
                   FEDERAL-TAX
                   FICA-AMOUNT   FROM GROSS-PAY
                   GIVING NET-PAY   ROUNDED
NET-PAY is the only data item whose contents are changed. The sum of STATE-TAX, FEDERAL-TAX, and FICA-AMOUNT is subtracted from GROSS-PAY; the difference is placed in NET-PAY, after being ROUNDED.

●   SUBTRACT   A   B   C
       FROM D
       GIVING   E   F   ROUNDED   G
       ON SIZE ERROR
            PERFORM OVERFLOW-ROUTINE.
The sum of A, B, and C is subtracted from D; a copy of the result is placed in E; a copy is rounded and placed in F; and a copy is placed in G. If a SIZE ERROR occurs during any of the above, the paragraph named OVERFLOW-ROUTINE is PERFORMed once before the computer goes on to the next statement.

●   01   SAMPLE-DATA.
         05   A   PIC S9(3)V9.
         05   B   PIC S9V99   COMP-3.
         05   C   PIC ZZZ.99.

     SUBTRACT B FROM C GIVING A
The SUBTRACT is invalid, for it attempts to involve an edited item (C) in a calculation.

●   SUBTRACT   A   B   FROM   C   D   GIVING   E   F
A syntax error: only one data item can directly follow "FROM".

6.15 Processing: MULTIPLY Statement

The MULTIPLY statement, used to multiply two numeric items, has two formats.

MULTIPLY . . . BY . . .

The syntax of this statement is shown in Fig. 6-7.

$$\text{MULTIPLY} \begin{Bmatrix} \text{identifier-1} \\ \text{literal-1} \end{Bmatrix} \underline{\text{BY}} \text{ identifier-2 } [\underline{\text{ROUNDED}}] \text{ [identifier-3 } [\underline{\text{ROUNDED}}]] \dots$$
$$[\text{ON } \underline{\text{SIZE ERROR}} \text{ imperative-statement}]$$

Fig. 6-7

EXAMPLE 6.44

●   MULTIPLY QUANTITY-PURCHASED BY UNIT-COST

The current contents of QUANTITY-PURCHASED are multiplied by the current contents of UNIT-COST, and the product replaces the contents of UNIT-COST. QUANTITY-PURCHASED is unchanged.

●   MULTIPLY QUANTITY-PURCHASED
         BY UNIT-COST   ROUNDED
         ON SIZE ERROR
            PERFORM EXTENDED-COST-TOO-LARGE

The product is rounded before being placed in UNIT-COST. If a SIZE ERROR occurs, the paragraph named EXTENDED-COST-TOO-LARGE is executed once before the computer goes on to execute the statement following the MULTIPLY . . . .

●   MULTIPLY .90 BY WHOLESALE-PRICE
                RETAIL-PRICE   ROUNDED

The contents of WHOLESALE-PRICE are multiplied by .90 and the result replaces the original contents of WHOLESALE-PRICE (excess decimal places are truncated); then the contents of RETAIL-PRICE are multiplied by .90 and the (ROUNDED) product replaces the original contents of RETAIL-PRICE.

●   MULTIPLY CURRENT-PRICE BY .90

A *very* common error (since it reads so well in English). Unfortunately, it directs the computer to multiply the contents of CURRENT-PRICE by .90 and place the result *in the literal .90*—which is impossible. Correct would be

      MULTIPLY .90 BY CURRENT-PRICE

provided the programmer did not mind losing the original contents of CURRENT-PRICE.

MULTIPLY . . . BY . . . GIVING . . .

The syntax of this statement is given in Fig. 6-8.

$$\text{MULTIPLY} \begin{Bmatrix} \text{identifier-1} \\ \text{literal-1} \end{Bmatrix} \underline{\text{BY}} \begin{Bmatrix} \text{identifier-2} \\ \text{literal-2} \end{Bmatrix}$$
$$\underline{\text{GIVING}} \text{ identifier-3 } [\underline{\text{ROUNDED}}] \text{ [identifier-4 } [\underline{\text{ROUNDED}}]] \dots$$
$$[\text{ON } \underline{\text{SIZE ERROR}} \text{ imperative-statement}]$$

Fig. 6-8

EXAMPLE 6.45

●   MULTIPLY UNIT-PRICE BY QUANTITY-PURCHASED
         GIVING EXTENDED-PRICE

The current contents of UNIT-PRICE and those of QUANTITY-PURCHASED are multiplied, and the product replaces the original contents of EXTENDED-PRICE. All other data items are unchanged. All data items must be numeric; EXTENDED-PRICE may be edited, since it only receives the result of the calculation and does not take part in it.

●   MULTIPLY A BY B
         GIVING C
             D   ROUNDED
             E
         ON SIZE ERROR
            PERFORM FIX-UP-ROUTINE

The contents of A are multiplied by the contents of B; the product replaces the original contents of C (extra decimal places truncated), of D (with rounding), and of E (with truncation). If a SIZE ERROR occurs during any of the foregoing, FIX-UP-ROUTINE is PERFORMed before the computer goes on to the next statement.

●   MULTIPLY HOURS-WORKED PAY-RATE BY OVERTIME-FACTOR
        GIVING OVERTIME-PAY

A syntax error: this does *not* multiply HOURS-WORKED, PAY-RATE, and OVERTIME-FACTOR together—nor would

      MULTIPLY HOURS-WORKED PAY-RATE BY OVERTIME-FACTOR

Unlike ADD . . . and SUBTRACT . . . , MULTIPLY . . . *can multiply only two values at a time.* One solution to the problem would be:

      MULTIPLY HOURS-WORKED BY PAY-RATE GIVING TEMP
      MULTIPLY TEMP   BY OVERTIME-FACTOR
        GIVING OVERTIME-PAY

where TEMP is a WORKING-STORAGE area defined by the programmer. For a better solution, see Section 6.17.

6.16   Processing: DIVIDE Statement

The DIVIDE statement is used to divide the contents of one numeric data item into the contents of another numeric data item. It has three formats, one of which gives *two* results, the quotient and the remainder. No format allows division by zero. An attempted division by zero causes a program ABEND unless the ON SIZE ERROR clause is specified, in which case it always causes a SIZE ERROR.

DIVIDE . . . INTO . . .

The syntax is displayed in Fig. 6-9.

$$\underline{\text{DIVIDE}} \left\{ \begin{array}{l} \text{identifier-1} \\ \text{literal-1} \end{array} \right\}$$
$$\underline{\text{INTO}} \text{ identifier-2 } [\underline{\text{ROUNDED}}] \text{ [identifier-3 } [\underline{\text{ROUNDED}}]] \ldots$$
$$[\text{ON } \underline{\text{SIZE ERROR}} \text{ imperative-statement}]$$

Fig. 6-9

EXAMPLE 6.46

●   DIVIDE 100 INTO PERCENTAGE-SCRAPPED

The numeric literal 100 is divided into the current contents of PERCENTAGE-SCRAPPED, which contents are replaced by the result of the division. PERCENTAGE-SCRAPPED must be numeric and not edited.

●   DIVIDE A INTO B
            C ROUNDED
            D
     ON SIZE ERROR
       PERFORM ERROR-MESSAGE-ROUTINE

A is divided into B, and the result (possibly truncated on the right) replaces the original contents of B; A is divided into C, and the result (with rounding) replaces the original contents of C; A is divided into D, and the (truncated) result replaces the original contents of D. If a SIZE ERROR occurs in any of the above, the PERFORM statement is executed; otherwise it is skipped.

●   DIVIDE A B C INTO D

A syntax error: only one identifier is allowed on either side of "INTO". (MULTIPLY . . . and DIVIDE . . . do *not* have the same syntax as ADD . . . and SUBTRACT . . . .)

DIVIDE . . . INTO/BY . . . GIVING . . .

The syntax is given in Fig. 6-10.

$$\underline{DIVIDE} \begin{Bmatrix} \text{identifier-1} \\ \text{literal-1} \end{Bmatrix} \begin{Bmatrix} \underline{INTO} \\ \underline{BY} \end{Bmatrix} \begin{Bmatrix} \text{identifier-2} \\ \text{literal-2} \end{Bmatrix}$$
$$\underline{GIVING} \text{ identifier-3 } [\underline{ROUNDED}] \text{ [identifier-4 } [\underline{ROUNDED}]] \dots$$
$$[\text{ON } \underline{SIZE\ ERROR} \text{ imperative-statement}]$$

Fig. 6-10

EXAMPLE 6.47

●   DIVIDE 100 INTO PERCENTAGE-SCRAPPED GIVING FRACTION-SCRAPPED

The value of the literal 100 is divided into the current contents of PERCENTAGE-SCRAPPED, and the result replaces the original contents of FRACTION-SCRAPPED. All items must be numeric; FRACTION-SCRAPPED may be edited, since it does not take part in the calculation but merely receives the result.

●   DIVIDE PERCENTAGE-SCRAPPED BY 100 GIVING FRACTION-SCRAPPED

Identical in effect to the preceding statement.

●   DIVIDE NUMBER-EMPLOYEES INTO TOTAL-SALARIES
        GIVING AVERAGE-SALARY
     ON SIZE ERROR
        PERFORM PRINT-ERROR-MESSAGE

The current contents of NUMBER-EMPLOYEES is divided into the current contents of TOTAL-SALARIES, and the result replaces the contents of AVERAGE-SALARY (which may be an edited item). NUMBER-EMPLOYEES and TOTAL-SALARIES are unchanged. If a SIZE ERROR occurs, PRINT-ERROR-MESSAGE is performed.

●   DIVIDE B BY A GIVING C
               D   ROUNDED
               E
     ON SIZE ERROR
      PERFORM ERROR-ROUTINE

The current contents of B are divided by those of A; the result replaces the original contents of C (with truncation of the fractional part if needed), of D (possibly with rounding), and of E (possibly with truncation). If a SIZE ERROR occurs during any of the foregoing, the paragraph named ERROR-ROUTINE is PERFORMed. A and B are unchanged; C, D, and E may be edited, if desired.

●   DIVIDE A INTO B ROUNDED GIVING C

Invalid: "ROUNDED" may be used only with fields that receive the quotient.

DIVIDE . . . INTO/BY . . . GIVING . . . REMAINDER . . .

This version has the syntax shown in Fig. 6-11.

$$\underline{DIVIDE} \begin{Bmatrix} \text{identifier-1} \\ \text{literal-1} \end{Bmatrix} \begin{Bmatrix} \underline{INTO} \\ \underline{BY} \end{Bmatrix} \begin{Bmatrix} \text{identifier-2} \\ \text{literal-2} \end{Bmatrix}$$
$$\underline{GIVING} \text{ identifier-3 } [\underline{ROUNDED}]$$
$$\underline{REMAINDER} \text{ identifier-4}$$
$$[\text{ON } \underline{SIZE\ ERROR} \text{ imperative-statement}]$$

Fig. 6-11

EXAMPLE 6.48

●   DIVIDE A INTO B GIVING C REMAINDER D

All data items must be numeric; C and D may be edited. The current contents of A are divided into those of B, and the *quotient* replaces the original contents of C; the *remainder* replaces the original contents of D. By the "quotient" is meant the result of the division to as many decimal places as are specified in the PICTURE of C; the "remainder" is then defined by

$$\text{remainder} = \text{dividend} - (\text{quotient} \times \text{divisor})$$

For example, if A contains 3.3, B contains 10.2, and C can accommodate two decimal places, then

$$\text{quotient} = 3.09 \qquad \text{remainder} = 10.2 - (3.09)(3.3) = .003$$

If "ROUNDED" is specified for the "GIVING" data item (which receives the quotient), the remainder is calculated *before* the rounding is done. If ON SIZE ERROR . . . is specified and a SIZE ERROR occurs for the quotient (GIVING item), then *both* the GIVING and REMAINDER data items are *unchanged* and the ON SIZE ERROR routine is executed. If a SIZE ERROR occurs *just* for the REMAINDER, then the GIVING item is replaced by the quotient but the REMAINDER field is *unchanged*. The programmer can decide whether the quotient or remainder caused the SIZE ERROR by checking whether the quotient field is *changed* (remainder caused SIZE ERROR) or *unchanged* (quotient caused SIZE ERROR). Remember: if the ON SIZE ERROR clause is not specified, the computer just goes on to the next statement, even when incorrect results are stored in the GIVING and/or REMAINDER fields.

●   DIVIDE B BY A GIVING C REMAINDER D
This is precisely equivalent to the preceding statement.

●   DIVIDE 24 INTO TOTAL-HOURS GIVING NUMBER-OF-DAYS
                            REMAINDER HOURS-LEFT-OVER
The quotient is the number of complete days represented by TOTAL-HOURS; the remainder represents any left-over part of a day, in hours.

●   DIVIDE BALANCE-DUE BY AMOUNT-EACH-PAYMENT
        GIVING   NUMBER-OF-FULL-PAYMENTS
        REMAINDER   AMOUNT-OF-LAST-PAYMENT
In commercial credit applications the last payment on a loan is usually different from the rest. The DIVIDE statement computes the *number* of regular payments to be made and the *amount* of the final (smaller) payment.

●   DIVIDE A INTO B GIVING C ROUNDED REMAINDER D ROUNDED
A syntax error: "ROUNDED" may be used only with the "GIVING" item, *not* with the REMAINDER field.

●   DIVIDE PAYMENT-AMOUNT INTO BALANCE-DUE
        REMAINDER LAST-PAYMENT
This is a common error: the GIVING option must be used when REMAINDER is specified. If the quotient really is of no interest, the following technique may be used:

    DIVIDE PAYMENT-AMOUNT INTO BALANCE-DUE
      GIVING DUMMY-FIELD
      REMAINDER LAST-PAYMENT

where DUMMY-FIELD is defined in WORKING-STORAGE (but is never used).

6.17   Processing: COMPUTE Statement

The COMPUTE statement allows many arithmetic operations to be specified at once. It usually results in a more efficient object program than when the same calculations are written out using several ADD, SUBTRACT, MULTIPLY, and DIVIDE statements. Hence, any calculation involving more than a single arithmetic operation should be programmed using COMPUTE . . . .

The COMPUTE statement has only one format (Fig. 6-12).

COMPUTE identifier-1 [ROUNDED]
     [identifier-2 [ROUNDED]] . . .
       = arithmetic-expression
     [ON SIZE ERROR imperative-statement(s)]

Fig. 6-12

The "arithmetic-expression" in the COMPUTE statement is similar to the expressions occurring in elementary algebra. It is formed of numeric data items and/or numeric literals, combined by one or more of the five COBOL *arithmetic operators*

+	*Addition*	/	*Division*
−	*Subtraction*	**	*Exponentiation* (raising to a power)
*	*Multiplication*		

These are *binary operators*, because they require *two operands* on which to operate. COBOL also allows the use of a *unary minus sign*, to negate a numeric value. Items on the right side of the "=", which enter the computation, may not be edited; data items on the left side, which receive the result, may be edited. In COMPUTE statements, each arithmetic operator should be preceded and followed by a blank space, or preceded by ")" and followed by "(".

EXAMPLE 6.49

●   COMPUTE A = B + C

is the equivalent of

    ADD B C GIVING A

●   COMPUTE A = B − C

is the equivalent of

    SUBTRACT C FROM B GIVING A

●   COMPUTE A = B * C

is the equivalent of

    MULTIPLY B BY C GIVING A

●   COMPUTE A = B / C

is the equivalent of

    DIVIDE B BY C GIVING A

●   COMPUTE A = B ** C

has no equivalent in another statement. "B ** C" represents "B raised to the power C"; i.e., B^C. For example, B ** 3 is B cubed.

●   COMPUTE A = − B

(the unary minus) is the equivalent of

    SUBTRACT B FROM ZERO GIVING A

Parentheses may be used to control the order of operations within a COMPUTE statement: operations in the innermost parentheses are done first, then operations in the next-innermost parentheses, etc. In the absence of parentheses, the compiler follows these rules:

    (1)   all unary minus signs are done first, on a left-to-right basis;

    (2)   all ** are done next, on a left-to-right basis;

    (3)   all * and / are done next, on a left-to-right basis;

    (4)   all + and − are done last, on a left-to-right basis.

EXAMPLE 6.50

●   COMPUTE A ROUNDED = (B + C) * (D + E)

In order: (i) the sum of B and C is calculated, (ii) the sum of D and E is calculated, (iii) the results of (i) and (ii) are multiplied together, (iv) the product is rounded, and (v) the rounded product replaces the original contents of A. Items B, C, D, and E must be numeric and not edited; A may be edited.

●   COMPUTE A ROUNDED

            B

            C   = A + B * C / D

      ON SIZE ERROR

        PERFORM PRINT-ERROR-MESSAGE

In the absence of parentheses, the following occurs: (i) B * C is calculated, (ii) the result in (i) is divided by D, (iii) the result of (ii) is added to A, (iv) the result of (iii) replaces the current contents of A (with rounding), (v) the result of (iii) replaces the current contents of B (with truncation), (vi) the result of (iii) replaces the current contents of C (with truncation). If a SIZE ERROR occurs during the storing of the result in A, B, or C, PRINT-ERROR-MESSAGE is PERFORMed.

- COMPUTE GROSS-PAY = (40 * RATE) +
                                          (1.5 * RATE * (HOURS-WORKED − 40))

This is a typical formula in the case of overtime. The normal rate is paid for the first 40 hours ("40 * RATE"). One-and-a-half times the normal rate ("1.5 * RATE") is paid for hours in excess of 40 ("HOURS-WORKED − 40"). GROSS-PAY is the sum of the two payments.

- COMPUTE NUMBER-EMPLOYEES = NUMBER-EMPLOYEES + 1

This strange-looking statement is the equivalent of

    ADD 1 TO NUMBER-EMPLOYEES

- COMPUTE QUANTITY-ON-HAND =   QUANTITY-ON-HAND   (100)
                                          + QUANTITY-RECEIVED   (10)
                                          + QUANTITY-RETURNED-TO-US (20)
                                          − QUANTITY-SHIPPED   (30)
                                          − QUANTITY-SCRAPPED   (40)

The current contents of QUANTITY-ON-HAND has QUANTITY-RECEIVED and QUANTITY-RETURNED-TO-US added to it, then that result has QUANTITY-SHIPPED and QUANTITY-SCRAPPED subtracted from it. The final result is put back in QUANTITY-ON-HAND, destroying the original contents. If each data item had the *starting* contents shown in parentheses, the *final* contents of QUANTITY-ON-HAND would be 60. All other data items would be unchanged.

- COMPUTE AVERAGE-PAY =
          (SALARIED-TOTAL + NONSALARIED-TOTAL) / NUMBER-EMPLOYEES

The use of parentheses is essential here. Without them, NONSALARIED-TOTAL would be divided by NUMBER-EMPLOYEES, and the result added to SALARIED-TOTAL; this would produce a false value for the average pay.

- COMPUTE CLEARANCE-PRICE   ROUNDED   =
          REGULAR-PRICE − .15 * REGULAR-PRICE

Parentheses are not needed here, since multiplication precedes subtraction anyway. A simpler version of the same calculation is:

    COMPUTE CLEARANCE-PRICE   ROUNDED   = .85 * REGULAR-PRICE

- COMPUTE C = (A ** 2 + B ** 2) ** .5

Raising to the .5 power is the same as taking the square root, so this amounts to computing "the square root of the quantity A squared plus B squared". In algebraic notation,

$$c = \sqrt{a^2 + b^2}$$

EXAMPLE 6.51 Suppose that a monthly payment is made on a loan. It is desired to calculate the amount paid on the principal, the amount paid for interest, and the new balance.

    COMPUTE INTEREST-PAID = OLD-BALANCE * (ANNUAL-INTEREST-RATE / 12)
    COMPUTE PRINCIPAL-PAID = PAYMENT-AMOUNT − INTEREST-PAID
    COMPUTE NEW-BALANCE = OLD-BALANCE − PRINCIPAL-PAID

Note that the annual interest rate is divided by 12 to obtain the monthly interest rate.

EXAMPLE 6.52   (Incorrect uses of COMPUTE)

(*a*) A common beginner's mistake is failure to leave at least one space before and after each arithmetic operator and that is not surrounded by ")" and "(", or before and after each "=":

    COMPUTE A = B+C
    COMPUTE A = B + C*D
    COMPUTE A = (A+B)/(A−B)

are all incorrect, although "COMPUTE A = (A + B)/(A − B)" is valid.

(*b*) Lack of surrounding spaces will make a minus sign look like a hyphen:

COMPUTE A = B−C

The compiler looks for a data item *named* "B-C"; it does not interpret this as a subtraction.

(*c*) A frequent error is failure to obtain the desired computation because of missing parentheses. There is absolutely *no disadvantage to using parentheses*—so if there is any doubt as to whether they are needed, *use them and be sure.*

COMPUTE NEW-BALANCE =   OLD-BALANCE
                       − PAYMENT-AMOUNT
                       + OLD-BALANCE *
                         ANNUAL-INTEREST-RATE / 12

happens to be correct. However, the following is also correct and is just as efficient:

COMPUTE NEW-BALANCE =
    OLD-BALANCE
   − (PAYMENT-AMOUNT
       − (OLD-BALANCE * (ANNUAL-INTEREST-RATE / 12)))

Observe how the parentheses fall into balanced pairs; failure to balance "(" and ")" is a common syntax error.

6.18 Efficiency in Arithmetic Calculations

In general a more efficient object program is obtained when:

1. Data items involved in a calculation together have PICTUREs with decimal points already aligned

2. Data items involved in a calculation together have the same USAGE

3. Data items used in arithmetic have USAGE COMP or COMP-3

4. (In IBM OS/VS COBOL) COMP-3 fields have an odd number of digits (especially when ON SIZE ERROR . . . is used)

5. If a field in a logical record is DISPLAY and is involved in several calculations, the field is MOVEd to a WORKING-STORAGE area which is COMP or COMP-3, and this WORKING-STORAGE copy is used in the calculations (i.e., one conversion of USAGE rather than many)

6. "S" is used for numeric PICTUREs involved in arithmetic (unless absolute value is desired)

7. Specification of ON SIZE ERROR . . . is avoided by careful choice of PICTUREs

6.19 Additional PROCEDURE DIVISION Coding Standards (cf. Section 6.1)

11. Use only *one* STOP RUN in a program.

12. Break long statements at the start of a clause and indent the next line.

13. Place clauses such as AT END . . ., AT END-OF-PAGE . . ., and ON SIZE ERROR . . . indented on their own lines.

14. Vertically align similar statements or parts of statements.

15. Use a literal only if you are sure that it will never have to be changed during the lifetime of the program.

EXAMPLE 6.53

● MOVE ZERO TO NUMBER-OF-EMPLOYEES

As NUMBER-OF-EMPLOYEES is always set to zero at the start of program execution, the use of the literal (figurative constant) ZERO is proper.

● MULTIPLY REGULAR-PRICE BY .08 GIVING EMPLOYEE-DISCOUNT

The employee discount rate might change from .08 to something else; the literal should not have been used. Instead, the programmer should define a WORKING-STORAGE data item:

WORKING-STORAGE SECTION.

```
01   PROGRAM-CONSTANTS.
     05   EMPLOYEE-DISCOUNT-RATE       PIC SV99
                                       VALUE +.08.
. . . . . . . . . . . . . . . . . . . . . . . . . . . . . . . .
```

and should replace the above MULTIPLY . . . by

MULTIPLY REGULAR-PRICE BY EMPLOYEE-DISCOUNT-RATE GIVING
    EMPLOYEE-DISCOUNT

Now, if the employee discount rate should change, only a single VALUE would have to be altered, rather than the literal in every one of its occurrences in the PROCEDURE DIVISION.

Review Questions

6.1   What is the purpose of the PROCEDURE DIVISION?

6.2   Explain the PROCEDURE DIVISION structure by defining: SECTION, paragraph, sentence, statement, and verb.

6.3   Discuss the coding standards for typing the PROCEDURE DIVISION.

6.4   What is the function of the OPEN statement?

6.5   Explain each of the OPEN modes: INPUT, OUTPUT, I-O, and EXTEND.

6.6   Discuss the use of one OPEN statement to open all files, as against a separate OPEN statement for each file.

6.7   What happens if a program refers to the logical record area for a file before the file is opened *or* after the file is closed?

6.8   What is the function of the CLOSE statement?

6.9   Compare closing all files with one CLOSE statement to closing each file with a separate CLOSE statement.

6.10   Discuss how a file might be opened and closed several times by the same program.

6.11   What is the function of "WITH LOCK" in a CLOSE statement?

6.12   What is a multifile tape?

6.13   Explain the use of STANDARD LABELS for a multifile tape.

6.14   What is a multivolume file?

6.15   What is meant by "volume switching"?

6.16 What is the purpose of the READ statement?

6.17 Explain the purpose of an AT END clause in a READ statement.

6.18 What is an end of file condition? When does it occur?

6.19 Why is it essential not to process a logical record after end of file has occurred?

6.20 Why do some programmers choose to do all logical record processing using WORKING-STORAGE copies of logical records?

6.21 Explain the use of READ . . . INTO . . . .

6.22 What is meant by "Read a file, write a record"?

6.23 What is the purpose of the WRITE statement?

6.24 What is in the logical record area for a file immediately after a successful WRITE?

6.25 What are some of the advantages of building logical records in a WORKING-STORAGE area and then using WRITE . . . FROM . . to move them to the buffer for output?

6.26 If READ . . . INTO . . . and WRITE . . . FROM . . . cannot be used with variable-length records, how can a program process such records in WORKING-STORAGE areas?

6.27 Discuss the various means of controlling printer spacing for files output to a printer.

6.28 What happens if a WRITE to a printer file does not include any printer spacing clauses?

6.29 Give some examples of when a data item should be used to specify the number of lines in the BEFORE/AFTER ADVANCING option of the WRITE statement.

6.30 What are the possible meanings of BEFORE/AFTER ADVANCING PAGE?

6.31 Explain how the carriage-control channels specified in the SPECIAL-NAMES paragraph can be used to control printer spacing with a WRITE statement.

6.32 Explain the areas of a logical page defined by the LINAGE clause.

6.33 State the *two* conditions under which the AT END-OF-PAGE routine will be executed as part of a WRITE statement.

6.34 What can happen if the LINAGE clause, BEFORE/AFTER ADVANCING values, and the AT END-OF-PAGE routine are not properly coordinated?

6.35 What is automatic page overflow?

6.36 Define "conditional statement" and "imperative statement".

6.37 When is a READ statement conditional? imperative?

6.38 When is a WRITE statement conditional? imperative?

6.39 What kind of operating system information can be obtained with an ACCEPT statement? How might this information be used?

6.40   Give some examples of when the ACCEPT statement might be used to input information from the computer operator's console terminal.

6.41   When should ACCEPT . . . *not* be used instead of setting up a regular file with a SELECT, FD, OPEN, READ, and CLOSE?

6.42   What are control cards?

6.43   How may the DISPLAY statement be used to debug a program?

6.44   When might DISPLAY . . . be used for error messages (instead of a regular printed output file with SELECT, FD, OPEN, WRITE, CLOSE)?

6.45   Give some examples of when DISPLAY . . . might be used to communicate with the computer operator via the console terminal.

6.46   In addition to "moving" data, what are the functions which may be carried out by a MOVE statement?

6.47   Define: (*a*) sending field, (*b*) receiving field, (*c*) conversion, (*d*) padding, (*e*) truncation, (*f*) editing.

6.48   What padding and truncation rules apply when (*a*) numeric data, (*b*) nonnumeric data, are MOVEd?

6.49   What happens in COBOL when a group item is MOVEd? What are some common errors incurred in group MOVEs?

6.50   When is it safe to execute a group MOVE?

6.51   Characterize the combinations of elementary items which are invalid in a MOVE statement. Give several concrete examples of invalid elementary MOVEs.

6.52   What is the function of STOP RUN?

6.53   Why should all files be closed before executing a STOP RUN?

6.54   What does the statement 'STOP "GIVE ME A KISS" ' bring about?

6.55   What is the purpose of the PERFORM statement?

6.56   Differentiate between the "physical order" of PROCEDURE DIVISION statements and their "logical order".

6.57   What is a program loop?

6.58   Explain in detail how a simple PERFORM statement works.

6.59   Explain in detail how a PERFORM . . . UNTIL . . . statement works.

6.60   What happens if the condition for ending a PERFORM . . . UNTIL . . . is suddenly satisfied in the middle of executing the PERFORMed paragraph?

6.61   What is an edit program?

6.62   What is hard copy?

6.63   What is the purpose of the ADD statement?

6.64   Distinguish between the effects of default truncation and the ROUNDED option when fractional results are obtained during computer arithmetic.

6.65   What is meant by "overflow"?

6.66   Explain the use of the ON SIZE ERROR clause in arithmetic statements.

6.67   What can be done to make an ON SIZE ERROR routine unnecessary in a program?

6.68   Give guidelines for writing an ON SIZE ERROR routine.

6.69   Where can numeric edited data items be used in arithmetic statements?

6.70   Explain the purpose of the MULTIPLY statement. How does its syntax differ from that of ADD and SUBTRACT?

6.71   What is the purpose of the DIVIDE statement?

6.72   Define: (*a*) quotient, (*b*) remainder.

6.73   What happens in COBOL if you attempt to divide by zero?

6.74   What are some of the advantages of using the COMPUTE statement?

6.75   Give the five binary operators used in the COMPUTE statement.

6.76   What is meant by "unary minus"?

6.77   What is the role of parentheses in the COMPUTE statement?

6.78   What is the default order of operations if parentheses are not used?

6.79   What are some of the frequent mistakes in using COMPUTE?

6.80   Discuss what can be done in COBOL to make arithmetic computations as efficient as possible.

6.81   When may literals be safely used in a program?

6.82   What technique can be used to replace literals in the PROCEDURE DIVISION? When should it be used? Why does it make programs easier to modify later on?

Solved Problems

6.83   Explain the sentence: "Most business algorithms involve repeating an input-process-output cycle until end of file".

An *algorithm* is an unambiguous, detailed set of steps for carrying out some task or solving a problem. Typical business problems involve processing all the logical records in an input file. These problems thus are built around a *main loop*, in which (1) the next logical record is input; (2) the logical record just input is processed; and (3) if appropriate, the results of processing the logical record are output. Steps 1 through 3 are repeated until an end of file is encountered while attempting to execute step 1.

6.84   A program is to read an input file of sales history records and append them to an already existing file. Show how to open both these files.

> OPEN   INPUT   SALES-HISTORY-TRANSACTIONS
>   EXTEND   SALES-HISTORY-MASTER

The EXTEND option allows new records to be appended to the end of an already existing, sequentially organized file.

6.85   In Problem 6.84, suppose it is desired to delete all previous file contents and replace them with totally new records. Give the OPEN statement.

> OPEN   INPUT   SALES-HISTORY-TRANSACTIONS
>   OUTPUT   SALES-HISTORY-MASTER

When an already existing, sequential file is opened OUTPUT, all previously existing logical records are deleted and a totally new version of the file is created by WRITING logical records into it.

6.86   What is wrong with the following PROCEDURE DIVISION?

> FD   INPUT-FILE...
> 01   INPUT-RECORD...
>
> FD   REPORT-FILE...
> 01   REPORT-LINE...
>
> PROCEDURE DIVISION.
>
>   MOVE SPACES TO INPUT-RECORD
>   WRITE REPORT-LINE FROM WS-HEADING-LINE
>   AFTER ADVANCING PAGE
>   OPEN   INPUT   INPUT-FILE
>   OUTPUT   REPORT-FILE

Two common errors are illustrated:
   (1)   MOVE SPACES TO INPUT-RECORD accesses the logical record area for a file *before the file is opened*. This always causes serious errors, since file buffers are not yet available to the program.
   (2)   WRITE REPORT-LINE FROM ... accesses the logical record area before the file is opened (since WRITE...FROM... is the equivalent of a MOVE statement followed by a WRITE statement) and (even worse?) attempts to output a record before the file is opened. This latter mistake will cause a program ABEND.

6.87   OPEN, READ, WRITE, and CLOSE all move a 2-byte "status key" into the FILE STATUS area for the file (assuming a FILE STATUS area has been defined for the file). What status key value indicates successful execution of any of these I/O statements?

   In IBM OS/VS COBOL, "00" always indicates successful completion of an I/O statement. Either PIC XX or PIC 99 may be used for the status key.

6.88   What is wrong with:

> 05   FILE-STATUS-AREA   PIC XX.
> . . . .
> OPEN   INPUT   SAMPLE-FILE
> IF FILE-STATUS-AREA EQUAL 00 ...

A status key area defined PIC XX is a nonnumeric; hence, a nonnumeric literal should be used:

> IF FILE-STATUS-AREA EQUAL "00" ...

6.89   What could cause a CLOSE statement to fail (and set FILE STATUS area to a nonzero code)?

If the file had STANDARD LABELS, a hardware failure could cause uncorrectable I/O errors during label processing. Another possibility is that the file might not have been successfully opened, in which case it could not be successfully closed.

6.90   Show how to close three files, minimizing (*a*) execution time, (*b*) bytes of memory.

(*a*)   CLOSE   INVENTORY-TRANSACTION-FILE
                  INVENTORY-MASTER-FILE
                  INVENTORY-UPDATE-FILE

When many files are closed with one CLOSE statement, execution time is minimized (although extra computer memory is required).

(*b*)   CLOSE   INVENTORY-TRANSACTION-FILE
        CLOSE   INVENTORY-MASTER-FILE
        CLOSE   INVENTORY-UPDATE-FILE

Closing each file individually conserves memory but takes longer.

6.91   Suppose a program is to process two files on the same tape (a multifile tape). It opens the first file, processes it, then closes it and opens the second file. Write the two OPEN and one CLOSE statements.

OPEN   INPUT   FIRST-FILE-ON-TAPE
. . . .
CLOSE   FIRST-FILE-ON-TAPE   WITH   NO   REWIND
OPEN   INPUT   SECOND-FILE-ON-TAPE

6.92   When a program sequentially processes a multivolume file, the operating system normally handles *automatic volume switching*. Explain how this works for (*a*) an input file, (*b*) an output file.

(*a*)   The program begins reading logical records with the first volume of the multivolume file. If there are 500 logical records on the first volume, the execution of the 501st READ causes an automatic volume switch, in which the operating system (i) ensures that the second volume of the file is properly mounted, (ii) processes any standard label records for the second volume, and (iii) makes the first logical record from the second volume available to the program.

(*b*)   When a multivolume file is opened output, the file is positioned at the beginning of the first volume. The program then begins writing logical records on the first volume. When the program executes a WRITE statement but there is no more file space left on the first volume, the operating system automatically (i) finishes any standard label processing for the first volume, (ii) begins standard label processing for the second volume, and (iii) writes the logical record in the beginning of the file space on the second volume.

6.93   Relate the CLOSE . . . UNIT statement to automatic volume switching.

We have seen (Problem 6.92) how the operating system initiates automatic volume switching when an *end of volume* is encountered during normal file processing. The CLOSE . . . UNIT statement can be used to *force* volume switching at an arbitrary point in the program. This can be useful when a multivolume file is being created, because it allows the program directly to control how many logical records are written on each volume.

6.94   What is wrong with the following?

```
OPEN  INPUT  SAMPLE-FILE
READ SAMPLE-FILE
    AT  END
        MOVE "T" TO END-OF-FILE-SW
MOVE SAMPLE-RECORD TO OUTPUT-AREA
WRITE OUTPUT-RECORD
    FROM OUTPUT-AREA
```

There are several errors. (1) No period marks the end of the AT END clause. (2) WRITE OUTPUT-RECORD . . . is executed without opening an output file. (3) The program fails to test for end of file before attempting to "MOVE SAMPLE-RECORD TO OUTPUT-AREA". If end of file occurs, there is no SAMPLE-RECORD to process (and the program winds up processing a *garbage record*).

6.95   In the PROCEDURE DIVISION below, the intent is to copy a file of 80-byte card records onto a disk file. Correct any errors.

```
PROCEDURE DIVISION.

    OPEN  INPUT  CARD-FILE
    MOVE "NO" TO END-OF-FILE
    PERFORM COPY-A-RECORD
        UNTIL END-OF-FILE EQUAL "YES"
    CLOSE DISK-FILE
        .
COPY-A-RECORD.

    READ CARD-FILE
        AT END  MOVE "YES" TO END-OF-FILE
    MOVE CARD-RECORD TO DISK-RECORD
    WRITE DISK-RECORD
```

The errors, in order of occurrence, are: (1) DISK-FILE not OPENed; (2) CARD-FILE not CLOSEd; (3) STOP RUN missing; (4) period after AT END . . . missing; (5) lacks a test for end of file before attempting to MOVE and WRITE a card record. The corrected version is:

```
PROCEDURE DIVISION.

    OPEN  INPUT    CARD-FILE
          OUTPUT   DISK-FILE
    MOVE "NO" TO END-OF-FILE
    PERFORM COPY-A-RECORD
        UNTIL END-OF-FILE EQUAL "YES"
    CLOSE CARD-FILE
          DISK-FILE
    STOP RUN
        .
COPY-A-RECORD.

    READ CARD-FILE
        AT END  MOVE "YES" TO END-OF-FILE
        .
    IF END-OF-FILE EQUAL "NO"
        MOVE CARD-RECORD TO DISK-RECORD
        WRITE DISK-RECORD
        .
```

6.96   Assuming that all files have been OPENed, etc., what is wrong with the following?

> WRITE SAMPLE-OUTPUT-RECORD
> FROM WS-OUTPUT-RECORD-AREA
>
> COMMENT -- DISPLAY RECORD JUST WRITTEN:
> *   FOR DEBUGGING
>
> DISPLAY SAMPLE-OUTPUT-RECORD

After a WRITE statement has been executed, the record description (SAMPLE-OUTPUT-RECORD) no longer refers to the logical record just written. Instead, it refers to a *new* logical record space in a file buffer, which can be used to construct the next logical record to be written. Hence the DISPLAY statement displays garbage, *not* the record just written.

6.97   Correct the error discussed in Problem 6.96.

Since the WRITE...FROM... option was used, the correction is merely to substitute

> DISPLAY WS-OUTPUT-RECORD-AREA

(After execution of the WRITE statement, WS-OUTPUT-RECORD-AREA still contains the logical record just written.)

If Problem 6.96 had involved a simple WRITE..., i.e.,

> WRITE SAMPLE-OUTPUT-RECORD
> DISPLAY SAMPLE-OUTPUT-RECORD

the correction would be equally easy:

> DISPLAY SAMPLE-OUTPUT-RECORD
> WRITE SAMPLE-OUTPUT-RECORD

6.98   What error occurs in the following?

> FD   INPUT-FILE
> .   RECORD CONTAINS 50 TO 200 CHARACTERS
> . . . .
> OPEN   INPUT   INPUT-FILE
> READ INPUT-FILE
>   INTO WS-INPUT-RECORD-AREA
>   AT END...

READ...INTO... may not be used with variable-length records (see Appendix C for COBOL '80 considerations).

6.99   Show how to correct the error in Problem 6.98.

> FD   INPUT-FILE
>   RECORD CONTAINS 50 TO 200 CHARACTERS
> . . . .
> OPEN   INPUT   INPUT-FILE
> READ INPUT-FILE
>   AT END...
> MOVE INPUT-RECORD TO WS-INPUT-RECORD-AREA

For variable-length records, use READ...followed by MOVE... in place of READ...INTO.... Similarly, use MOVE...followed by WRITE..., instead of WRITE...FROM....

6.100 What is wrong with the following?

```
        READ SAMPLE-INPUT-FILE
            AT END
                MOVE "YES" TO END-OF-FILE
                WRITE REPORT-LINE
                    FROM WS-TOTAL-LINE
                    AT END-OF-PAGE
                        ADD 1 TO NUMBER-OF-PAGES
```

All statements in an AT END ... routine must be imperative. Here, WRITE ... AT END-OF-PAGE ... is conditional. This causes a syntax error.

6.101 Correct the error in Problem 6.100.

If it is necessary to execute a conditional statement where the rules call for an imperative statement, put the conditional statement in a paragraph and then use the PERFORM statement (which is imperative) to execute that paragraph.

```
        READ SAMPLE-INPUT-FILE
            AT END
                PERFORM AT-END-ROUTINE

    . . . . . . . . . . . . . . . . . . . . . . . . .

    AT-END-ROUTINE.

        MOVE "YES" TO END-OF-FILE
        WRITE REPORT-LINE
            FROM WS-TOTAL-LINE
            AT END OF PAGE
                ADD 1 TO NUMBER-OF-PAGES
```

6.102 It is desired to produce an "80/80 listing" of a deck of cards, whereby an exact copy of each card is printed on 80 columns of the paper. Each logical page should reproduce precisely ten cards; should have a heading line which contains a title, the page number, the date in both mmyydd and Julian forms, and the time of the computer run; and should have a footing with the message "SO FAR__CARDS WERE PRINTED". Comment on how the program of Fig. 6-13 accomplishes the task.

```
00001           IDENTIFICATION DIVISION.
00002           PROGRAM-ID. CARDLIST.
00003           AUTHOR.   LARRY NEWCOMER.
00004           INSTALLATION.  PENN STATE UNIVERSITY--YORK CAMPUS.
00005           DATE-WRITTEN.  MAY 1983.
00006           DATE-COMPILED. MAY  9,1983.
00007           SECURITY.   NONE.
00008       *   CARDLIST PRODUCES AN 80/80 LISTING OF CARD CONTENTS.
00009       *   ITS PURPOSE HERE IS TO ILLUSTRATE VARIOUS FORMS OF
00010       *   WRITE ... BEFORE/AFTER ADVANCING ... WITH THE LINAGE
00011       *   CLAUSE.
00012           ENVIRONMENT DIVISION.
00013           CONFIGURATION SECTION.
00014           SOURCE-COMPUTER. IBM-370.
00015           OBJECT-COMPUTER. IBM-370.
00016           INPUT-OUTPUT SECTION.
00017           FILE-CONTROL.
00018               SELECT CARD-FILE          ASSIGN TO CARDS.
00019               SELECT PRINT-FILE         ASSIGN TO PRINTER.
00020           DATA DIVISION.
```

Fig. 6-13

```
00021          FILE SECTION.
00022          FD   CARD-FILE
00023               RECORD CONTAINS 80 CHARACTERS
00024               LABEL RECORDS ARE OMITTED
00025               .
00026          01   CARD-INPUT                    PIC X(80).

00028     *    -------------------------------------------------
00029          FD   PRINT-FILE
00030               RECORD CONTAINS 132 CHARACTERS
00031               LABEL RECORDS ARE OMITTED
00032               LINAGE IS 13
00033                   WITH FOOTING AT 11
00034                   LINES AT TOP 2
00035                   LINES AT BOTTOM 2
00036               .
00037
00038          01   PRINT-LINE                    PIC X(132).
00039     *    -------------------------------------------------

00041          WORKING-STORAGE SECTION.
00042
00043     *    -------------------------------------------------
00044          01   WS-DATE-AND-TIME-AREAS.
00045               05   WS-REGULAR-DATE.
00046                    10   WS-YY           PIC 99.
00047                    10   WS-MM           PIC 99.
00048                    10   WS-DD           PIC 99.
00049     *    -------------------------------------------------
00050
00051          01   PROGRAM-SWITCHES-AND-COUNTERS.
00052               05   END-OF-CARDS-SWITCH   PIC X(3).
00053               05   WS-PAGE-NUMBER        PIC S9(3)      COMP-3.
00054               05   WS-CARD-COUNT         PIC S9(3)      COMP-3.
00055          01   WS-LINE-AREA.
00056               05   WS-CARD-AREA          PIC X(80).
00057               05   FILLER                PIC X(52)      VALUE SPACES.
00058
00059     *    ------------------------------------------------------
00060          01   WS-HEADING-AREA.
00061               05   FILLER                PIC X(6)       VALUE "DATE ".
00062               05   HEADING-MM            PIC Z9.
00063               05   FILLER                PIC X          VALUE "/".
00064               05   HEADING-DD            PIC 99.
00065               05   FILLER                PIC X          VALUE "/".
00066               05   HEADING-YY            PIC 99.
00067               05   FILLER                PIC X(9)       VALUE ", JULIAN ".
00068               05   HEADING-JULIAN        PIC Z9B999.
00069               05   FILLER                PIC X(7)       VALUE ", TIME ".
00070               05   HEADING-TIME          PIC 99B99B99B99.
00071               05   FILLER                PIC X(6)       VALUE " PAGE ".
00072               05   WS-HEADING-PAGE-NUMBER PIC ZZ9.
00073               05   FILLER                PIC X(76)      VALUE SPACES.
00074     *    ------------------------------------------------------
00075
00076          01   WS-FOOTING-AREA.
00077               05   FILLER                PIC X(7)       VALUE "SO FAR ".
00078               05   WS-FOOTING-COUNT      PIC ZZ9.
00079               05   FILLER                PIC X(122)
00080                                          VALUE " CARDS WERE PRINTED".

00082          PROCEDURE DIVISION.

00084               MOVE "NO " TO END-OF-CARDS-SWITCH
00085               MOVE ZERO  TO WS-PAGE-NUMBER
00086                             WS-CARD-COUNT
```

Fig. 6-13 *(cont.)*

```
00087
00088            ACCEPT WS-REGULAR-DATE        FROM DATE
00089            ACCEPT HEADING-JULIAN         FROM DAY
00090            ACCEPT HEADING-TIME           FROM TIME
00091
00092            MOVE WS-MM                    TO HEADING-MM
00093            MOVE WS-DD                    TO HEADING-DD
00094            MOVE WS-YY                    TO HEADING-YY
00095
00096            OPEN     INPUT                CARD-FILE
00097                     OUTPUT               PRINT-FILE
00098
00099            PERFORM INPUT-A-RECORD
00100
00101            PERFORM PRODUCE-PAGE-HEADING
00102
00103            PERFORM PRODUCE-80-80-LISTING
00104                UNTIL END-OF-CARDS-SWITCH IS EQUAL TO "YES"
00105
00106            CLOSE    CARD-FILE
00107                     PRINT-FILE
00108            STOP RUN
00109            .

00111        INPUT-A-RECORD.
00112
00113            READ CARD-FILE RECORD
00114                INTO WS-CARD-AREA
00115                AT END
00116                    MOVE "YES" TO END-OF-CARDS-SWITCH
00117            .

00119        PRODUCE-80-80-LISTING.
00120
00121            ADD 1 TO WS-CARD-COUNT
00122
00123            WRITE PRINT-LINE
00124                FROM WS-LINE-AREA
00125                AFTER  ADVANCING 1 LINE
00126                AT END-OF-PAGE
00127                    PERFORM PRODUCE-PAGE-FOOTING
00128                    PERFORM PRODUCE-PAGE-HEADING
00129            .
00130
00131            PERFORM INPUT-A-RECORD
00132            .

00134        PRODUCE-PAGE-HEADING.
00135
00136            ADD 1 TO WS-PAGE-NUMBER
00137            MOVE WS-PAGE-NUMBER TO WS-HEADING-PAGE-NUMBER
00138            WRITE PRINT-LINE
00139                FROM WS-HEADING-AREA
00140                AFTER ADVANCING PAGE
00141            .
00142
00143        PRODUCE-PAGE-FOOTING.
00144
00145            MOVE WS-CARD-COUNT TO WS-FOOTING-COUNT
00146
00147            WRITE PRINT-LINE
00148                FROM WS-FOOTING-AREA
00149                AFTER ADVANCING 2 LINES
00150            .
```

Fig. 6-13 (cont.)

(1) Just as the program starts by reading the first card (immediately after opening the files), so it should start by printing the heading at the top of the first page. Putting the page heading routine in its own paragraph allows it to be performed at the beginning of the PROCEDURE DIVISION and again, as necessary, in the AT END-OF-PAGE routine of PRODUCE-80-80-LISTING. Since printing begins at the top of the first logical page, END-OF-PAGE is *not* detected on the first WRITE to the file. Line 101 of Fig. 6-13 ensures that the first page will have a heading.

(2) The system checks for footing overflow before it checks for page overflow. When the 10th card is printed (on line 11, because of the one-line heading), footing overflow is recognized and the AT END-OF-PAGE routine is executed, causing a footing to be printed, then a heading to be printed at the start of a new logical page. Thus, when the 11th card is to be printed, the paper is already positioned at the top of a page, and page overflow will not occur. We see that using a footing area at the end of the page *heads off* any page overflows by writing a heading line *at the top of a new page*.

(3) The LINAGE value (line 32 of Fig. 6-13) is determined as follows. Since the heading requires 1 line and we desire 10 cards per page, the LINAGE value must be at least 11 (without the page footing). If the footing is to be printed AFTER ADVANCING 2 LINES, then these 2 additional lines bring the page body size to 13. Figure 6-14 shows a sample printed page.

```
DATE    5/09/83, JULIAN 83 129, TIME 13 08 12 41 PAGE    2
CARD   11
CARD   12
CARD   13
CARD   14
CARD   15
CARD   16
CARD   17
CARD   18
CARD   19
CARD   20
SO FAR  20 CARDS WERE PRINTED
```

Fig. 6-14

(4) Apropos lines 88–90 of Fig. 6-13. HEADING-JULIAN and HEADING-TIME are edited fields in WS-HEADING-AREA. The regular date is accepted into WS-REGULAR-DATE because the system keeps the date in the form yymmdd (this is the most convenient form if it is desired to sort by date; the year has the greatest influence). The month, day, and year subfields are moved separately into the heading area (see lines 92–94), so that they can be rearranged.

6.103 The program of Fig. 6-15 is the same as that of Fig. 6-13, except that it has "WITH DEBUGGING MODE" specified in the SOURCE-COMPUTER paragraph, and DISPLAY statements have been added to the PROCEDURE DIVISION to help debug the program. What would be output by these DISPLAY statements?

```
00084          PROCEDURE DIVISION.

00086              MOVE "NO " TO END-OF-CARDS-SWITCH
00087              MOVE ZERO  TO WS-PAGE-NUMBER
00088                         WS-CARD-COUNT
00089
00090              ACCEPT WS-REGULAR-DATE       FROM DATE
00091              ACCEPT HEADING-JULIAN        FROM DAY
00092              ACCEPT HEADING-TIME          FROM TIME
00093
00094      D      DISPLAY "STARTING VALUE OF END-OF-CARDS-SWITCH="
00095      D          END-OF-CARDS-SWITCH
00096      D      DISPLAY "STARTING VALUE OF WS-PAGE-NUMBER AND CARD-COUNT="
00097      D          WS-PAGE-NUMBER  WS-CARD-COUNT
00098      D      DISPLAY "VALUE OF WS-REGULAR-DATE=" WS-REGULAR-DATE
```

Fig. 6-15

```
00099      D      DISPLAY "VALUE OF HEADING-TIME="      HEADING-TIME
00100      D      DISPLAY "VALUE OF JULIAN DATE="       HEADING-JULIAN
00101
00102
00103             MOVE WS-MM                     TO HEADING-MM
00104             MOVE WS-DD                     TO HEADING-DD
00105             MOVE WS-YY                     TO HEADING-YY
00106
00107             OPEN    INPUT                  CARD-FILE
00108                     OUTPUT                 PRINT-FILE
00109
00110             PERFORM INPUT-A-RECORD
00111
00112             PERFORM PRODUCE-PAGE-HEADING
00113
00114             PERFORM PRODUCE-80-80-LISTING
00115                 UNTIL END-OF-CARDS-SWITCH IS EQUAL TO "YES"
00116
00117             CLOSE   CARD-FILE
00118                     PRINT-FILE
00119             STOP RUN
00120             .

00122         INPUT-A-RECORD.
00123
00124             READ CARD-FILE RECORD
00125                 INTO WS-CARD-AREA
00126                 AT END
00127                     MOVE "YES" TO END-OF-CARDS-SWITCH
00128             .
00129      D      DISPLAY "JUST READ THE FOLLOWING CARD: " WS-CARD-AREA
00130      D      DISPLAY "END-OF-CARDS-SWITCH IS: " END-OF-CARDS-SWITCH
00131      D      .
00132

00134         PRODUCE-80-80-LISTING.
00135
00136             ADD 1 TO WS-CARD-COUNT
00137
00138             WRITE PRINT-LINE
00139                 FROM WS-LINE-AREA
00140                 AFTER  ADVANCING 1 LINE
00141                 AT END-OF-PAGE
00142                     PERFORM PRODUCE-PAGE-FOOTING
00143                     PERFORM PRODUCE-PAGE-HEADING
00144             .
00145
00146             PERFORM INPUT-A-RECORD
00147             .

00149         PRODUCE-PAGE-HEADING.
00150
00151      D      DISPLAY "** ENTERING PRODUCE-PAGE-HEADING, CARD COUNT="
00152      D          WS-CARD-COUNT
00153
00154             ADD 1 TO WS-PAGE-NUMBER
00155             MOVE WS-PAGE-NUMBER TO WS-HEADING-PAGE-NUMBER
00156             WRITE PRINT-LINE
00157                 FROM WS-HEADING-AREA
00158                 AFTER ADVANCING PAGE
00159             .
00160
00161         PRODUCE-PAGE-FOOTING.
00162
00163      D      DISPLAY "** ENTERING PRODUCE-PAGE-FOOTING, CARD COUNT="
00164      D          WS-CARD-COUNT
```

Fig. 6-15 (*cont.*)

```
00165
00166          MOVE WS-CARD-COUNT TO WS-FOOTING-COUNT
00167
00168          WRITE PRINT-LINE
00169              FROM WS-FOOTING-AREA
00170              AFTER ADVANCING 2 LINES
00171              .
```

Fig. 6-15   *(cont.)*

See Fig. 6-16. Notice that the IBM OS/VS COBOL compiler removes the operational sign from DISPLAYed numeric fields *if they are positive*; thus, WS-CARD-COUNT prints in readable form. Note also that COMP-3 numbers are converted to USAGE DISPLAY for purposes of printing with the DISPLAY statement.

Study this use of DISPLAY and its accompanying output well: it can save you much valuable debugging time. Observe in particular how Fig. 6-16 reflects the order in which the computer executed the statements of the program.

```
STARTING VALUE OF END-OF-CARDS-SWITCH=NO
STARTING VALUE OF WS-PAGE-NUMBER AND CARD-COUNT=000000
VALUE OF WS-REGULAR-DATE=830509
VALUE OF HEADING-TIME=13 14 00 72
VALUE OF JULIAN DATE=83 129
JUST READ THE FOLLOWING CARD: CARD     1
END-OF-CARDS-SWITCH IS: NO
** ENTERING PRODUCE-PAGE-HEADING, CARD COUNT=000
JUST READ THE FOLLOWING CARD: CARD     2
END-OF-CARDS-SWITCH IS: NO
JUST READ THE FOLLOWING CARD: CARD     3
END-OF-CARDS-SWITCH IS: NO
JUST READ THE FOLLOWING CARD: CARD     4
END-OF-CARDS-SWITCH IS: NO
JUST READ THE FOLLOWING CARD: CARD     5
END-OF-CARDS-SWITCH IS: NO
JUST READ THE FOLLOWING CARD: CARD     6
END-OF-CARDS-SWITCH IS: NO
JUST READ THE FOLLOWING CARD: CARD     7
END-OF-CARDS-SWITCH IS: NO
JUST READ THE FOLLOWING CARD: CARD     8
END-OF-CARDS-SWITCH IS: NO
JUST READ THE FOLLOWING CARD: CARD     9
END-OF-CARDS-SWITCH IS: NO
JUST READ THE FOLLOWING CARD: CARD    10
END-OF-CARDS-SWITCH IS: NO
** ENTERING PRODUCE-PAGE-FOOTING, CARD COUNT=010
** ENTERING PRODUCE-PAGE-HEADING, CARD COUNT=010
JUST READ THE FOLLOWING CARD: CARD    11
END-OF-CARDS-SWITCH IS: NO
JUST READ THE FOLLOWING CARD: CARD    12
END-OF-CARDS-SWITCH IS: NO
JUST READ THE FOLLOWING CARD: CARD    13
END-OF-CARDS-SWITCH IS: NO
JUST READ THE FOLLOWING CARD: CARD    14
END-OF-CARDS-SWITCH IS: NO
JUST READ THE FOLLOWING CARD: CARD    15
```

Fig. 6-16

6.104 Show how to move A   PIC SV999 to B   PIC SV9 with rounding.

    COMPUTE B ROUNDED = A

Although less elegant,

    ADD   ZERO   A   GIVING B ROUNDED

would also work.

6.105 Show what is in the receiving field after each of the following MOVEs:

	Sending Field Value	*Receiving Field PICTURE*
(a)	123.456	S9(5)V9(4)
(b)	123.456	S9(5)V9
(c)	"STRING"	X(4) JUSTIFIED RIGHT
(d)	"STRING"	X(4)
(e)	"DOG"	X(5)
(f)	"DOG"	X(5) JUSTIFIED RIGHT
(g)	"DOG"	9(3)
(h)	HIGH-VALUES	9(3)
(i)	HIGH-VALUES	X(3)
(j)	SPACES	9(3)
(k)	ALL "$"	X(5)
(l)	123.456	S99V99
(m)	−123.456	999V999
(n)	−123.456	$$$$.99−
(o)	−123456	$$$$$$.99BCR

(a) 00123ᵥ4560; (b) 00123ᵥ4; (c) "RING"; (d) "STRI"; (e) "DOG*bb*"; (f) "*bb*DOG"; (g) invalid MOVE (mixes alphanumeric and numeric); (h) invalid MOVE (HIGH-VALUES is alphanumeric and may be moved only to a PIC X field); (i) 3 bytes of the highest character in the collating sequence; (j) invalid MOVE (SPACES is alphanumeric and may be moved only to PIC X or PIC A); (k) "$$$$$"; (l) 23ᵥ45 (truncation occurs on both left and right); (m) 123ᵥ456 (results in absolute value, since receiving field is unsigned); (n) $123.45−; (o) $23456.00*b*CR (leftmost digit truncated).

6.106 Given

```
01  A.
    05  B    PIC  X(4)    VALUE "THIS".
    05  C    PIC  X(2)    VALUE "IS".
    05  D    PIC  X(3)    VALUE "FUN".

01  W.
    05  X    PIC  X(3).
    05  Y    PIC  X(2).
    05  Z    PIC  X(3).
```

find the contents of (a) X, (b) Y, and (c) Z, after

MOVE A TO W

COBOL treats group MOVEs as if they were MOVEs of a large PIC X field. Here, A is 9 bytes long and W is 8 bytes long; so the rightmost byte of A (which is the rightmost byte of D) will be truncated:

(a) "THI"   (b) "SI"   (c) "SFU"

6.107 Criticize

```
01  A.
    05  B    PIC  S9(3)V99    COMP-3.
    05  C    PIC  S99         COMP.
    05  D    PIC  S99V9       DISPLAY.
```

MOVE ZEROS TO A

Since A is a group item, it is treated as PIC X DISPLAY, and alphanumeric, DISPLAY zeros are MOVEd to the fields of A. This will work for item D (since it is USAGE DISPLAY), but it will not work for B and C.

The correct method is:

>   MOVE ZEROS TO B C D

which moves zeros to each individual field, automatically converting to the correct USAGE.

6.108 Criticize

> . . . .
>
>   STOP RUN
>   DISPLAY "ALL FILES ARE NOW CLOSED"
> .

The statements are syntactically correct, but the DISPLAY statement *can never be executed*. Once a STOP RUN is executed, the computer ceases to execute instructions from the current program.

6.109 Suppose that the maximum hourly wage for a company is 55.00 dollars per hour. Suppose also that the maximum number of hours allowed per week is 60 (with time-and-a-half paid for anything over 40). If the company has 1000 employees, write a PICTURE for TOTAL-WEEKLY-PAYROLL such that a SIZE ERROR cannot occur.

If an employee works the maximum number of hours at the maximum rate, the employee's weekly pay is

$$(40 \times 55.00) + (20 \times 55.00 \times 1.5) = 3850.00 \text{ dollars}$$

Hence, TOTAL-WEEKLY-PAYROLL cannot exceed

$$1000 \times 3850.00 = 3,850,000.00 \text{ dollars}$$

so that PIC S9(7)V99 would be adequate.

6.110 Express the following algebraic formulas using COMPUTE . . . :

> (a) $a = \dfrac{b}{c} + b - (c \times d)$ (b) $a = \dfrac{b+c}{d} - \dfrac{c}{e+f}$ (c) $d = \dfrac{(a+b)^2}{a-b} + a - (b+c)$

(a)   COMPUTE A = B / C + B − C ∗ D
(b)   COMPUTE A = (B + C) / D − C / (E + F)
(c)   COMPUTE D = (A + B) ∗∗ 2 / (A − B) + A − (B + C)

6.111 A typical calculation for gross pay with overtime is:

>   COMPUTE GROSS-PAY = (HOURS-WORKED − 40) ∗
>   HOURLY-RATE ∗ 1.5 + 40 ∗ HOURLY-RATE

Show how this could be calculated without use of the COMPUTE statement (make up descriptive data-names for any additional data areas you might need).

>   MULTIPLY 40 BY HOURLY-RATE GIVING REGULAR-PAY
>   MULTIPLY HOURLY-RATE BY 1.5 GIVING OVERTIME-RATE
>   SUBTRACT 40 FROM HOURS-WORKED GIVING OVERTIME-HOURS
>   MULTIPLY OVERTIME-RATE BY OVERTIME-HOURS GIVING OVERTIME-PAY
>   ADD REGULAR-PAY OVERTIME-PAY GIVING GROSS-PAY

The COMPUTE statement is easier to write, and it produces a more efficient object program.

In both versions of the calculation, it would have been safer to use program constants, as defined in the WORKING-STORAGE SECTION, instead of the numeric literals 1.5 and 40, for which new values might have to be substituted during the lifetime of the program.

Supplementary Problems

6.112 Write a program which prints "two-up" mailing labels (i.e., two labels across the page). Output a total line showing how many labels were printed. Input is the same as that for Problem 2.36.

    Ans. See Fig. 6-17. The given program processes input records in the logical record area for the file; print lines are built in WORKING-STORAGE, as usual. Sample output is shown in Fig. 6-18.

```
00001              IDENTIFICATION DIVISION.
00002
00003              PROGRAM-ID. MAILING.
00004              AUTHOR.   LARRY NEWCOMER.
00005              INSTALLATION.   PENN STATE UNIVERSITY--YORK CAMPUS.
00006              DATE-WRITTEN.   MAY 1983.
00007              DATE-COMPILED. MAY  9,1983.
00008              SECURITY.   NONE.
00009          *    MAILING PRODUCES PRINTED MAILING LABELS TWO-UP (TWO ACROSS
00010          *    THE PAGE).   IT ALSO PRINTS A COUNT OF THE NUMBER OF LABELS
00011          *    PRODUCED.   BEFORE ACTUALLY PRINTING LABELS, MAILING PRINTS
00012          *    A TEMPLATE WHICH CAN BE USED TO ALIGN THE LABELS IN THE
00013          *    PRINTER.

00015              ENVIRONMENT DIVISION.
00016
00017              CONFIGURATION SECTION.
00018              SOURCE-COMPUTER. IBM-370.
00019              OBJECT-COMPUTER. IBM-370.
00020              INPUT-OUTPUT SECTION.
00021              FILE-CONTROL.
00022                  SELECT MAILING-MASTER          ASSIGN TO MAILING.
00023                  SELECT MAILING-LABEL-FILE      ASSIGN TO LABELS.

00025              DATA DIVISION.
00026
00027              FILE SECTION.
00028
00029              FD  MAILING-MASTER
00030                  RECORD CONTAINS 80 CHARACTERS
00031                  LABEL RECORDS ARE OMITTED
00032                  .
00033              01  MAILING-INPUT.
00034                  05  MAILING-NAME          PIC X(20).
00035                  05  MAILING-ADDRESS       PIC X(20).
00036                  05  MAILING-CITY          PIC X(20).
00037                  05  MAILING-STATE         PIC X(2).
00038                  05  MAILING-ZIP           PIC X(5).
00039                  05  FILLER                PIC X(13).

00041              FD  MAILING-LABEL-FILE
00042                  RECORD CONTAINS 132 CHARACTERS
00043                  LABEL RECORDS ARE OMITTED
00044                  .
00045              01  LABEL-LINE                PIC X(132).

00047              WORKING-STORAGE SECTION.
00048
00049              01  PROGRAM-SWITCHES-AND-COUNTERS.
00050                  05  END-OF-FILE-SW        PIC X(3).
00051                  05  WS-LABEL-COUNT        PIC S9(3)     COMP-3.
00052
00053              01  WS-NAME-LINE.
00054                  05  NAME-1                PIC X(30)     VALUE ALL "*".
00055                  05  FILLER                PIC X(10)     VALUE SPACES.
00056                  05  NAME-2                PIC X(30)     VALUE ALL "*".
```

Fig. 6-17

```
00057                 05   FILLER                         PIC X(62)      VALUE SPACES.
00058
00059         01    WS-ADDRESS-LINE.
00060                 05   ADDRESS-1                       PIC X(30)      VALUE ALL "*".
00061                 05   FILLER                          PIC X(10)      VALUE SPACES.
00062                 05   ADDRESS-2                       PIC X(30)      VALUE ALL "*".
00063                 05   FILLER                          PIC X(62)      VALUE SPACES.
00064
00065         01    WS-CITY-STATE-LINE.
00066                 05   CITY-1                          PIC X(20)      VALUE ALL "*".
00067                 05   FILLER                          PIC X          VALUE SPACES.
00068                 05   STATE-1                         PIC XX         VALUE ALL "*".
00069                 05   FILLER                          PIC X(2)       VALUE SPACES.
00070                 05   ZIP-1                           PIC X(5)       VALUE ALL "*".
00071                 05   FILLER                          PIC X(10)      VALUE SPACES.
00072                 05   CITY-2                          PIC X(20)      VALUE ALL "*".
00073                 05   FILLER                          PIC X          VALUE SPACES.
00074                 05   STATE-2                         PIC XX         VALUE ALL "*".
00075                 05   FILLER                          PIC X(2)       VALUE SPACES.
00076                 05   ZIP-2                           PIC X(5)       VALUE ALL "*".
00077                 05   FILLER                          PIC X(62)      VALUE SPACES.

00079         01    WS-COUNT-LINE.
00080                 05   PRINTED-COUNT                   PIC Z,ZZ9.
00081                 05   FILLER                          PIC X(15)
00082                                                      VALUE " LABELS PRINTED".
00083                 05   FILLER                          PIC X(112)     VALUE SPACES.

00085         PROCEDURE DIVISION.

00087             MOVE "NO " TO END-OF-FILE-SW
00088             MOVE ZERO   TO WS-LABEL-COUNT
00089
00090             OPEN    INPUT                MAILING-MASTER
00091                     OUTPUT               MAILING-LABEL-FILE
00092
00093             PERFORM 030-PRINT-2-LABELS
00094                 2 TIMES
00095
00096             PERFORM 020-PRODUCE-MAILING-LABELS
00097                 UNTIL END-OF-FILE-SW IS EQUAL TO "YES"
00098
00099             PERFORM 040-PRODUCE-COUNT-LINE
00100
00101             CLOSE   MAILING-MASTER
00102                     MAILING-LABEL-FILE
00103             STOP RUN
00104             .

00106         010-INPUT-2-RECORDS.
00107
00108             MOVE SPACES TO WS-NAME-LINE
00109                            WS-ADDRESS-LINE
00110                            WS-CITY-STATE-LINE
00111
00112             READ MAILING-MASTER RECORD
00113                 AT END
00114                     MOVE "YES" TO END-OF-FILE-SW
00115             .
00116             IF END-OF-FILE-SW = "NO"
00117
00118                 ADD 1 TO WS-LABEL-COUNT
00119                 MOVE MAILING-NAME        TO NAME-1
00120                 MOVE MAILING-ADDRESS     TO ADDRESS-1
00121                 MOVE MAILING-CITY        TO CITY-1
00122                 MOVE MAILING-STATE       TO STATE-1
00123                 MOVE MAILING-ZIP         TO ZIP-1
00124
```

Fig. 6-17 (cont.)

```
00125                          READ MAILING-MASTER RECORD
00126                              AT END
00127                                  MOVE "YES" TO END-OF-FILE-SW
00128                          .
00129                      IF END-OF-FILE-SW EQUAL "NO"
00130
00131                          ADD 1 TO WS-LABEL-COUNT
00132                          MOVE MAILING-NAME        TO NAME-2
00133                          MOVE MAILING-ADDRESS     TO ADDRESS-2
00134                          MOVE MAILING-CITY        TO CITY-2
00135                          MOVE MAILING-STATE       TO STATE-2
00136                          MOVE MAILING-ZIP         TO ZIP-2
00137                      .

00139              020-PRODUCE-MAILING-LABELS.
00140
00141                  PERFORM 010-INPUT-2-RECORDS
00142
00143                  PERFORM 030-PRINT-2-LABELS
00144                  .
00145
00146              030-PRINT-2-LABELS.
00147
00148                  WRITE LABEL-LINE
00149                      FROM WS-NAME-LINE
00150                      BEFORE ADVANCING 1 LINE
00151                  WRITE LABEL-LINE
00152                      FROM WS-ADDRESS-LINE
00153                      BEFORE ADVANCING 1 LINE
00154                  WRITE LABEL-LINE
00155                      FROM WS-CITY-STATE-LINE
00156                      BEFORE ADVANCING 2 LINES
00157                  .
00158
00159              040-PRODUCE-COUNT-LINE.
00160
00161              MOVE WS-LABEL-COUNT TO PRINTED-COUNT
00162              WRITE LABEL-LINE
00163                  FROM WS-COUNT-LINE
00164                  AFTER ADVANCING 2 LINES
00165              .
```

Fig. 6-17   (*cont.*)

```
NATHAN CONVERSE                          MIKE PERELMAN
709 N. SIMPSON ST.                       213 E. SOUTH ST.
MIAMI                 FL  10022          HANOVER             MD  23451


BARNEY PERELMAN                          KATHY BUCHER
782 N. SOUTH ST.                         666 W. EAST ST.
NEW YORK              NY  10012          PHILADELPHIA        PA  34256


ABE SHARP
783 S. NORTH ST.
BALTIMORE             MD  22145


    5 LABELS PRINTED
```

Fig. 6-18

6.113   Write a program which calculates sales statistics based on a sample of the monthly sales of retail outlets. Input consists of logical records containing: store identifier, location code, and monthly sales amount. Output consists of a printed report showing a *detail line* containing the information for each store, followed by a final line which gives, for the sample, the *average* sales and the *standard deviation* of sales.

These sample quantities are obtained from the formulas

$$\text{sample total} = s_1 + s_2 + \cdots + s_n$$

$$\text{average} = \frac{\text{sample total}}{n} = \frac{s_1 + s_1 + \cdots + s_n}{n}$$

$$\text{standard deviation} = \sqrt{\frac{n(s_1^2 + s_2^2 + \cdots + s_n^2) - (s_1 + s_2 + \cdots + s_n)^2}{n(n-1)}}$$

where n is the number of stores sampled and s_i is the amount of sales for the ith store.

Ans.   See Fig. 6-19 (typical output in Fig. 6-20). Although not required, this program prints a footing line giving the running total of sales.

```
00001              IDENTIFICATION DIVISION.
00002
00003              PROGRAM-ID. SALESTAT.
00004              AUTHOR.   LARRY NEWCOMER.
00005              INSTALLATION.   PENN STATE UNIVERSITY--YORK CAMPUS.
00006              DATE-WRITTEN.   MAY 1983.
00007              DATE-COMPILED. MAY  9,1983.
00008              SECURITY.   NONE.
00009
00010        *     SALESTAT PRODUCES A LISTING OF MONTHLY SALES BY RETAIL
00011        *     STORE.  IT PRINTS A FINAL LINE SHOWING THE TOTAL SALES,
00012        *     THE AVERAGE SALES, AND THE STANDARD DEVIATION FOR SALES.
00013
00014        *     SALESTAT PROVIDES A GOOD ILLUSTRATION OF THE USE OF
00015        *     THE COMPUTE STATEMENT.
00016
00017              ENVIRONMENT DIVISION.
00018
00019              CONFIGURATION SECTION.
00020              SOURCE-COMPUTER. IBM-370.
00021              OBJECT-COMPUTER. IBM-370.
00022              INPUT-OUTPUT SECTION.
00023              FILE-CONTROL.
00024                  SELECT SALES-FILE          ASSIGN TO SALES.
00025                  SELECT SALES-REPORT        ASSIGN TO SALELIST.
00026
00027              DATA DIVISION.
00028
00029              FILE SECTION.
00030
00031              FD   SALES-FILE
00032                   RECORD CONTAINS 80 CHARACTERS
00033                   LABEL RECORDS ARE OMITTED
00034                   .
00035              01   SALES-INPUT              PIC X(80).

00037              FD   SALES-REPORT
00038                   RECORD CONTAINS 132 CHARACTERS
00039                   LABEL RECORDS ARE OMITTED
00040                   LINAGE IS 10
00041                       WITH FOOTING AT 8
00042                       LINES AT TOP 2
00043                       LINES AT BOTTOM 2
00044                   .
00045
00046              01   SALES-LINE              PIC X(132).

00048              WORKING-STORAGE SECTION.
00049
00050              01   WS-DATE-AND-TIME-AREAS.
00051                   05  WS-REGULAR-DATE.
00052                       10  WS-YY           PIC 99.
00053                       10  WS-MM           PIC 99.
```

Fig. 6-19

```
00054              10  WS-DD                         PIC 99.
00055
00056        01  PROGRAM-SWITCHES-COUNTERS-SUMS.
00057            05  END-OF-SALES-SWITCH      PIC X(3).
00058            05  WS-PAGE-NUMBER           PIC S9(3)      COMP-3.
00059            05  WS-TOTAL-SALES           PIC S9(7)V99   COMP-3.
00060            05  WS-NUMBER-STORES         PIC S9(5)      COMP-3.
00061            05  WS-SUM-SALES-SQUARED     PIC S9(15)V99  COMP-3.
00062
00063        01  WS-SALES-AREA.
00064            05  WS-SALES-STORE-ID        PIC X(5).
00065            05  WS-SALES-LOCATION-CODE   PIC XX.
00066            05  WS-SALES-SALES           PIC S9(6)V99.
00067            05  FILLER                   PIC X(65).
00068
00069        01  WS-LINE-AREA.
00070            05  WS-LINE-STORE-ID         PIC X(5).
00071            05  FILLER                   PIC X(5)       VALUE SPACES.
00072            05  WS-LINE-LOCATION-CODE    PIC XX.
00073            05  FILLER                   PIC X(5)       VALUE SPACES.
00074            05  WS-LINE-SALES            PIC ZZZ,ZZZ.99.
00075            05  FILLER                   PIC X(105)     VALUE SPACES.
00076
00077        01  WS-HEADING-AREA-1.
00078            05  FILLER                   PIC X(1)       VALUE SPACES.
00079            05  FILLER                   PIC X(20)
00080                                         VALUE "SALES STATISTICS".
00081            05  HEADING-MM               PIC Z9.
00082            05  FILLER                   PIC X          VALUE "/".
00083            05  HEADING-DD               PIC 99.
00084            05  FILLER                   PIC X          VALUE "/".
00085            05  HEADING-YY               PIC 99.
00086            05  FILLER                   PIC X(4)       VALUE SPACES.
00087            05  FILLER                   PIC X(6)       VALUE "PAGE ".
00088            05  WS-HEADING-PAGE-NUMBER   PIC ZZ9.
00089            05  FILLER                   PIC X(90)      VALUE SPACES.
00090
00091        01  WS-HEADING-AREA-2.
00092            05  FILLER                   PIC X(8)       VALUE "STORE ID".
00093            05  FILLER                   PIC X(2)       VALUE SPACES.
00094            05  FILLER                   PIC X(12)      VALUE "LOC".
00095            05  FILLER                   PIC X(10)      VALUE "SALES".
00096            05  FILLER                   PIC X(100)     VALUE SPACES.
00097
00098        01  WS-FOOTING-AREA.
00099            05  FILLER                   PIC X(15)      VALUE SPACES.
00100            05  WS-FOOTING-TOTAL         PIC Z,ZZZ,ZZZ.99.
00101            05  FILLER                   PIC X(105)     VALUE " *".
00102
00103        01  WS-FINAL-LINE-1.
00104            05  FILLER                   PIC X(15)      VALUE SPACES.
00105            05  WS-FINAL-TOTAL           PIC Z,ZZZ,ZZZ.99.
00106            05  FILLER                   PIC X(105)     VALUE " **".
00107
00108        01  WS-FINAL-LINE-2.
00109            05  FILLER                   PIC X(10)      VALUE "AVERAGE--".
00110            05  WS-AVERAGE-SALES         PIC ZZZ,ZZZ.99.
00111            05  FILLER                   PIC X(6)       VALUE " SD-- ".
00112            05  WS-SD                    PIC ZZZ,ZZZ.99.
00113            05  FILLER                   PIC X(96)      VALUE SPACES.

00115    PROCEDURE DIVISION.

00117        MOVE "NO " TO END-OF-SALES-SWITCH
00118        MOVE ZERO   TO WS-PAGE-NUMBER
00119                       WS-TOTAL-SALES
```

Fig. 6-19 (*cont.*)

```
00120                              WS-NUMBER-STORES
00121                              WS-SUM-SALES-SQUARED
00122
00123              ACCEPT WS-REGULAR-DATE        FROM DATE
00124
00125              MOVE WS-MM                    TO HEADING-MM
00126              MOVE WS-DD                    TO HEADING-DD
00127              MOVE WS-YY                    TO HEADING-YY
00128
00129              OPEN    INPUT                 SALES-FILE
00130                      OUTPUT                SALES-REPORT
00131
00132              PERFORM GET-SALES-RECORD
00133
00134              PERFORM PRODUCE-PAGE-HEADING
00135
00136              PERFORM PRODUCE-SALES-LINE
00137                  UNTIL END-OF-SALES-SWITCH IS EQUAL TO "YES"
00138
00139              PERFORM PRODUCE-FINAL-LINES
00140
00141              CLOSE   SALES-FILE
00142                      SALES-REPORT
00143              STOP RUN
00144              .

00146          GET-SALES-RECORD.
00147
00148              READ SALES-FILE RECORD
00149                  INTO WS-SALES-AREA
00150                  AT END
00151                      MOVE "YES" TO END-OF-SALES-SWITCH
00152              .
00153


00155          PRODUCE-SALES-LINE.
00156
00157              ADD 1 TO WS-NUMBER-STORES
00158              COMPUTE WS-SUM-SALES-SQUARED =   WS-SUM-SALES-SQUARED
00159                                            + WS-SALES-SALES ** 2
00160
00161              ADD WS-SALES-SALES TO WS-TOTAL-SALES
00162
00163              MOVE WS-SALES-STORE-ID        TO WS-LINE-STORE-ID
00164              MOVE WS-SALES-LOCATION-CODE   TO WS-LINE-LOCATION-CODE
00165              MOVE WS-SALES-SALES           TO WS-LINE-SALES
00166
00167              WRITE SALES-LINE
00168                  FROM WS-LINE-AREA
00169                  AFTER  ADVANCING 2 LINES
00170                  AT END-OF-PAGE
00171                      PERFORM PRODUCE-PAGE-FOOTING
00172                      PERFORM PRODUCE-PAGE-HEADING
00173              .
00174
00175              PERFORM GET-SALES-RECORD
00176              .


00178          PRODUCE-PAGE-HEADING.
00179
00180              ADD 1 TO WS-PAGE-NUMBER
00181              MOVE WS-PAGE-NUMBER TO WS-HEADING-PAGE-NUMBER
00182              WRITE SALES-LINE
00183                  FROM WS-HEADING-AREA-1
00184                  AFTER ADVANCING PAGE
00185              WRITE SALES-LINE
```

Fig. 6-19 *(cont.)*

```
00186                     FROM WS-HEADING-AREA-2
00187                     AFTER ADVANCING 1 LINE
00188                 .
00189
00190     PRODUCE-PAGE-FOOTING.
00191
00192         MOVE WS-TOTAL-SALES TO WS-FOOTING-TOTAL
00193
00194         WRITE SALES-LINE
00195             FROM WS-FOOTING-AREA
00196             AFTER ADVANCING 2 LINES
00197                 .
00198
00199     PRODUCE-FINAL-LINES.
00200
00201         MOVE WS-TOTAL-SALES         TO WS-FINAL-TOTAL
00202         WRITE SALES-LINE
00203             FROM WS-FINAL-LINE-1
00204             AFTER ADVANCING 2 LINES
00205
00206         COMPUTE WS-AVERAGE-SALES = WS-TOTAL-SALES / WS-NUMBER-STORES
00207
00208         COMPUTE WS-SD =((WS-NUMBER-STORES * WS-SUM-SALES-SQUARED
00209                              - WS-TOTAL-SALES ** 2)
00210                     /
00211             (WS-NUMBER-STORES * (WS-NUMBER-STORES - 1))) ** .5
00212
00213         WRITE SALES-LINE
00214             FROM WS-FINAL-LINE-2
00215             AFTER ADVANCING 2 LINES
00216                 .
```

Fig. 6-19 *(cont.)*

```
    SALES STATISTICS       5/09/83     PAGE     1
    STORE ID  LOC          SALES
    00001     AA       1,000.00
    00002     BB       2,000.00
    00003     CC       3,000.00
                       6,000.00 *

    SALES STATISTICS       5/09/83     PAGE     2
    STORE ID  LOC          SALES
    00004     DD       4,000.00
    00005     EE       5,000.00
    00006     FF       6,000.00
                      21,000.00 *

    SALES STATISTICS       5/09/83     PAGE     3
    STORE ID  LOC          SALES
    00007     GG       7,000.00
    00008     HH       8,000.00
                      36,000.00 **
    AVERAGE--   4,500.00 SD--    2,449.49
```

Fig. 6-20

Programming Assignments

6.114 Given principal P, invested in a savings account at an annual interest rate I which is compounded C times during the year, the total amount T accumulated in N years is

$$T = P * \left(1 + \frac{I}{C}\right)^{C*N}$$

Write a COBOL program which inputs P, I, C, and N, and prints a report showing P, I, C, N, and T. Print as many lines as there are sets of input values. Design your own input records and report layout, but use the LINAGE clause to ensure: (i) 20 double-spaced detail lines per logical page, (ii) top and bottom margins of 3 lines each, (iii) report title and column headings at the top of each page body (including page number and date and time of run).

6.115 Write a COBOL program which inputs 80-byte inventory records of the form:

$$
\begin{array}{rl}
\text{columns 1–6} & : \quad \text{item number} \\
\text{7–26} & : \quad \text{item description} \\
\text{27–31} & : \quad \text{quantity on hand} \\
\text{32–38} & : \quad \text{cost (2 decimal places)} \\
\text{rest} & : \quad \text{unused}
\end{array}
$$

Print a report with a line for each item showing:

item #	description	quantity on hand	cost	worth

where worth is (quantity on hand) * cost. At the end of the report, print a final line showing: (1) the total worth of the inventory (i.e., the sum of the worths of all items) and (2) the average cost of an item (sum of worth divided by sum of quantity on hand). Design your own logical page, but include: (i) headings, (ii) a footing area in which current value of the total quantity on hand is printed (cf. Fig. 6-20), and (iii) page number and date and time of run at top of each page.

6.116 A consulting firm has, for each employee, an *internal rate* (what they pay an employee per hour) and an *external rate* (what they charge customers for an hour of that employee's time). Given the following input:

$$
\begin{array}{rl}
\text{columns 1–4} & : \quad \text{employee ID} \\
\text{5–9} & : \quad \text{internal rate (2 decimal places)} \\
\text{10–14} & : \quad \text{external rate (2 decimal places)} \\
\text{15–17} & : \quad \text{weekly hours worked (1 decimal place)}
\end{array}
$$

print a payroll report showing:

employee ID	hours worked	internal rate	payroll amount	external rate	amount charged	gross profit

where

$$
\begin{array}{rcl}
\text{payroll amount} &=& \text{hours * internal rate} \\
\text{amount charged} &=& \text{hours * external rate} \\
\text{gross profit} &=& \text{amount charged} - \text{payroll amount}
\end{array}
$$

At the end of the report, print a line showing the total payroll amount, total amount charged, and the average gross profit per employee. The logical page should include (i) headings, (ii) a footing showing total number of employees processed so far, (iii) page number and date and time of run at the top of each page.

Chapter 7

Program Logic

7.1 Logical Design: Structured Flowcharts

Program logic refers to the order in which the computer executes the statements in a program (as opposed to their physical order in the source listing). A *structured flowchart* is a diagram that depicts the order of operations in an algorithm. Thus, a structured flowchart may be used to design the logic of the problem-solving part of a program, *before* the program is actually written in COBOL (or some other language). If the flowchart is kept up-to-date, reflecting any program changes, it also serves as useful program documentation.

The standard flowchart symbols are given in Fig. 7-1.

	The *terminal symbol*, bearing the word "START" ("STOP" or "END") inside, identifies the beginning (end) of the algorithm. The name of the algorithm may also be written in the block.
	The *process symbol* indicates computer processing of information. The nature of the processing is described within the block.
	The *decision symbol* indicates a computer decision selecting between two alternate logic paths in the algorithm. It is characterized by *two* arrows leaving the block, showing the two alternate logic paths.
	The *predefined process symbol* represents computer processing which is complex enough to require a separate flowchart to describe it. This block contains the name of the separately charted routine.
	The *input/output symbol* indicates an input or output operation.
	The *connector symbol* represents a junction of two or more parts of a flowchart.
	Arrows are used to connect the above blocks in the order in which they are to be executed.

Fig. 7-1

7.2 Program Logic Structures

It can be shown that the logic of any algorithm or computer program can be realized as a combination of just three fundamental *logic structures*.

Sequence Structure

This is the sequential execution of processes or instructions, one after another. In a computer program with sequence structure, the logical order of statements coincides with the physical order. Figure 7-2 flowcharts the sequence structure.

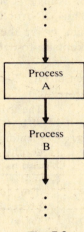

Fig. 7-2

Selection Structure

This structure selects exactly one of two different "branches" (processes or sets of instructions). Which branch is taken depends on the current value of a "condition" which is always either *true* or *false*.

EXAMPLE 7.1 In a payroll program, one set of instructions is needed to calculate gross pay if an employee works 40 hours or less; another set of instructions is needed if an employee works overtime. The selection structure is flowcharted in Fig. 7-3.

The decision symbol must contain a *condition* which is either *true* or *false*. As in the present case, the condition often involves comparing two data items (or a data item and a literal) to determine whether a particular *relationship* (here, "less than or equal to") holds. If the condition is true, the arrow marked YES (or TRUE) is followed in the execution of the selection structure; otherwise, the arrow marked NO (or FALSE) is followed.

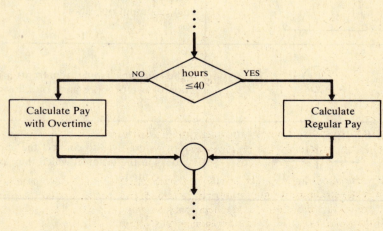

Fig. 7-3

EXAMPLE 7.2 The structured flowchart of Fig. 7-4 combines the sequence structure and the selection structure. Blocks 1, 2, and 9 form a sequence structure, the second part of which (block 2) is *itself* a selection structure (with alternative logic paths through blocks 3 and 4, respectively). Block 4 is a predefined process, representing a (possibly complex) set of procedures defined in another flowchart. Block 3 is the head of yet another selection structure, with alternative paths through block 5 or blocks 6, 7, and 8 (which themselves form a sequence structure).

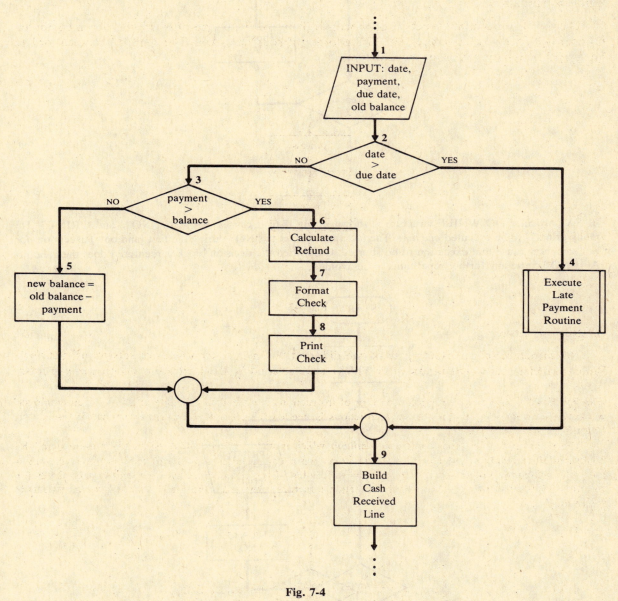

Fig. 7-4

Iteration Structure

The iteration structure is used when a process or group of processes must be *repeated* a certain number of times; it is the structure of a *program loop*.

EXAMPLE 7.3 The version of the iteration structure flowcharted in Fig. 7-5 is commonly called the *DO WHILE structure*. When the structure is entered during execution, the first thing that happens is that a decision is made whether to "repeat" one more time. If the decision is NO (condition for repeating is false), the structure is exited *without execution of Process A*. If the decision is YES (condition for repeating is true), Process A is executed, and the decision whether or not to repeat is made again.

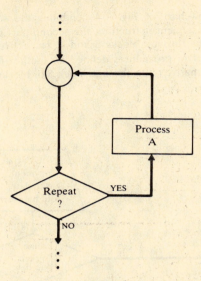

Fig. 7-5

A particular DO WHILE structure is shown in Fig. 7-6; it causes 'Set A to "NO"' and 'PRINT: "This really prints"' to be executed *one time*. The fact that A is set to "NO" during the first (and only) execution *does not* somehow cause that execution to be aborted. Only when the decision block is reentered does the condition A = "NO" cause any further repetitions to be avoided.

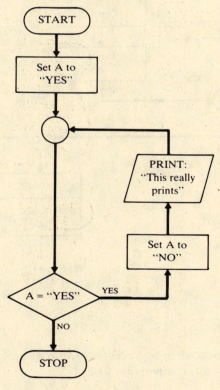

Fig. 7-6

EXAMPLE 7.4 The structured flowchart for the program of Example 2.17 is given in Fig. 7-7; it involves only sequence and iteration structures.

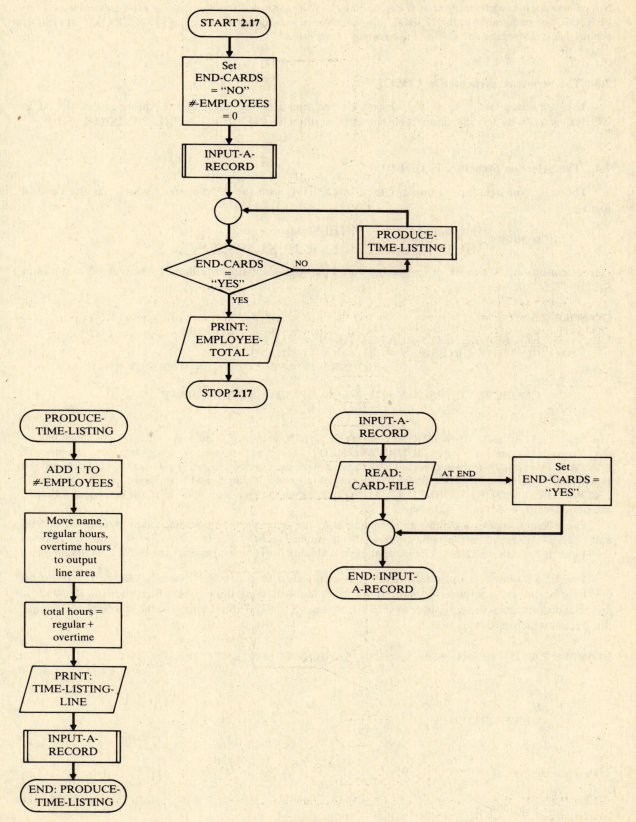

Fig. 7-7

Notice how each predefined process is described in its own appended flowchart; these processes correspond to PERFORMed paragraphs in the COBOL program. Notice also that certain routine PROCEDURE DIVISION actions, such as opening and closing files, are not flowcharted.

7.3   The Sequence Structure in COBOL

The sequence structure is the easiest to program (in any language). Sequence is achieved in COBOL simply by writing one statement after another in the PROCEDURE DIVISION.

7.4   The Selection Structure in COBOL

The selection structure is implemented in COBOL with the *IF statement*, which has the general form

$$\text{IF condition} \begin{Bmatrix} \text{statement-1} \\ \underline{\text{NEXT SENTENCE}} \end{Bmatrix} \begin{bmatrix} \underline{\text{ELSE}} \text{ statement-2} \\ \underline{\text{ELSE NEXT SENTENCE}} \end{bmatrix}.$$

Here, "condition" is a more or less complicated expression or substatement, to be treated in detail in Sections 7.5–7.9.

EXAMPLE 7.5

```
IF   HOURS-WORKED GREATER THAN 40.0
        COMPUTE GROSS-PAY = 40.0 * HOURLY-RATE +
                            (HOURS-WORKED − 40.0) * 1.5 * HOURLY-RATE
ELSE
        COMPUTE GROSS-PAY = HOURS-WORKED * HOURLY-RATE
```

The "condition" is "HOURS-WORKED GREATER THAN 40.0". It has the value true or false depending on the current contents of HOURS-WORKED. If the condition is true, "statement-1" ("COMPUTE . . . 40.0 * . . .") is executed, and the computer then goes on to execute whatever statement follows the period which ends the IF statement. If the condition is false, "statement-1" is ignored, and "statement-2" ("COMPUTE . . . HOURS-WORKED * . . .) is executed; then the computer goes on to the statement following the period which ends the IF statement.

The indentation illustrated, though not required by the compiler, is an essential coding standard. The "IF" and "ELSE" are typed in the same column; the IF-routine and the ELSE-routine are respectively indented under the "IF" and the "ELSE". A (structured) period should *always* be used to mark the end of each IF statement.

The ELSE clause is optional. When it is omitted, a true condition causes "statement-1" to be executed before the computer goes on to the statement following the period which ends the IF; while a false condition causes the computer to *skip* "statement-1" and go immediately to the statement following the period which ends the IF.

EXAMPLE 7.6   It is *never necessary* to specify "ELSE NEXT SENTENCE", since

```
IF . . .
        PERFORM . . .
ELSE
        NEXT SENTENCE

    WRITE . . .
```

is identical in effect to

```
IF . . .
        PERFORM . . .

    WRITE . . .
```

With either formulation, PERFORM . . . , and then WRITE . . . , is executed if the condition is true; while just WRITE . . . is executed if the condition is false.

Nevertheless, "ELSE NEXT SENTENCE" is sometimes *convenient*; see Example 7.25.

EXAMPLE 7.7

```
IF AMOUNT-SOLD IS GREATER THAN SALES-QUOTA
    NEXT SENTENCE
ELSE
    MOVE "YES" TO SEND-MOTIVATING-LETTER-SWITCH
    SUBTRACT AMOUNT-SOLD FROM SALES-QUOTA GIVING AMOUNT-UNDER-QUOTA

WRITE REPORT-LINE
    FROM WS-SALES-PERFORMANCE-LINE
```

If AMOUNT-SOLD is greater than SALES-QUOTA, "NEXT SENTENCE" is executed, causing the computer *to go on to the statement which follows the period ending the IF statement* ("WRITE REPORT-LINE . . ."). If AMOUNT-SOLD is not greater than SALES-QUOTA, then the computer ignores the IF-part and goes on to the ELSE-part, executing "MOVE . . ." and "SUBTRACT . . ." before going on to WRITE . . . .

Observe the serious consequences of omitting the period at the end of the IF statement: The WRITE statement becomes part of ELSE . . . , and so a report line is printed only for underquota salespeople, instead of for all salespeople as intended.

EXAMPLE 7.8 It is *never necessary* to specify "NEXT SENTENCE" in the IF-part of an IF statement: one can always negate the condition and interchange the IF-part with the ELSE-part. After this is done, the ELSE-part consists of "NEXT SENTENCE" and can be dropped (see Example 7.6).

Applying this technique to Example 7.7, we obtain:

```
IF AMOUNT-SOLD IS NOT GREATER THAN SALES-QUOTA
    MOVE "YES" TO SEND-MOTIVATING-LETTER-SWITCH
    SUBTRACT AMOUNT-SOLD FROM SALES-QUOTA GIVING AMOUNT-UNDER-QUOTA

WRITE REPORT-LINE
    FROM WS-SALES-PERFORMANCE-LINE
```

A minor flaw in the IF statement—and in its equivalent, Example 7.7—is that it results in a "motivating letter" being sent when the amount under quota is *zero*. The fix is easy:

```
IF AMOUNT-SOLD IS LESS THAN SALES-QUOTA
```

7.5   Selection Structure: Class Condition

The *class condition* can be used to determine whether a data item contains alphabetic or numeric data. The syntax of the condition is:

$$\text{identifier IS } [\underline{\text{NOT}}] \begin{Bmatrix} \underline{\text{NUMERIC}} \\ \underline{\text{ALPHABETIC}} \end{Bmatrix}$$

The "NUMERIC" and "NOT NUMERIC" tests may be applied only to data items that have either alphanumeric ("X") or numeric ("SV9") PICTURES, and have USAGE DISPLAY (or COMP-3, if the PICTURE is numeric and if COMP-3 is available). The "ALPHABETIC" and "NOT ALPHABETIC" tests may be applied only to data items that have either alphabetic ("A") or alphanumeric ("X") PICTURES, and USAGE DISPLAY.

The condition

```
identifier IS NUMERIC
```

is true if and only if the item contains only the digits 0 through 9. If the PICTURE includes an operational sign (PIC "S"), the item must also contain a valid operational sign to be numeric. If the PICTURE is unsigned, the item must *not* contain an operational sign.

The condition

identifier IS ALPHABETIC

is true if and only if the item contains only the letters A through Z and/or blank spaces.

The main use of the class test is to *validate* input fields in records which were keyed by human beings. The program which validates the data should produce descriptive error messages with enough information to allow the errors to be corrected.

EXAMPLE 7.9

```
    IF PARTIAL-PAYMENT-AMOUNT  NUMERIC
        SUBTRACT PARTIAL-PAYMENT-AMOUNT FROM OLD-BALANCE GIVING
            NEW-BALANCE
    ELSE
        MOVE OLD-BALANCE TO NEW-BALANCE
        MOVE "YES" TO UNPROCESSED-PAYMENT-SWITCH
```

PARTIAL-PAYMENT-AMOUNT, an input field typed by a human being, is validated with the class test before being used in a calculation. OLD-BALANCE is not validated, because it comes from a disk file created by a computer program. If a program is properly designed and fully debugged, files created by the program may be assumed to hold correct data (since, presumably, the program validated all data placed in the file).

7.6 Selection Structure: Relation Condition

The syntax of the *relation condition* is:

$$\text{operand-1 IS [\underline{NOT}]} \begin{cases} \underline{\text{GREATER THAN}} \\ > \\ \underline{\text{LESS THAN}} \\ < \\ \underline{\text{EQUAL}} \text{ TO} \\ = \end{cases} \text{operand-2}$$

Barring certain forbidden combinations (see Example 7.13), "operand-1" and "operand-2" may each be a data item, a literal, or an arithmetic expression (such as would be allowed on the right-hand side of a COMPUTE statement).

EXAMPLE 7.10

● IF A + B ** 2 LESS THAN (A − C) * (A + B)
Any arithmetic expressions that are valid in a COMPUTE statement are valid in a relation condition.

● IF EMPLOYEE-ID-NUMBER EQUAL HIGH-VALUES
Figurative constants are often used in relations.

● IF GROSS-PAY GREATER THAN 900.00
Use of a numeric literal in a relation condition.

● IF INPUT-RECORD-CODE = "A"
Use of a nonnumeric literal in a relation condition; use of algebraic "=" sign.

● IF A NOT GREATER THAN B
IF C NOT LESS THAN D
In COBOL, the relations "less than or equal to ($\leq$)" and "greater than or equal to ($\geq$)" must be expressed as the negation of the opposite relation.

● IF INPUT-RECORD-CODE NOT EQUAL "C"
"IS" and "TO" are optional words in a relation condition.

In COBOL, what does it mean to say that one data item is less than another?

Numeric comparisons.   The USAGEs and the sizes of the PICTUREs do *not* affect the results of the comparison, which are based strictly on the algebraic values of the items. Decimal points are automatically aligned for purposes of the comparison. (The same rules which improve the efficiency of calculations will improve the efficiency of numeric comparisons; see Section 6.18.)

EXAMPLE 7.11   Given

```
01   SAMPLE-DATA-ITEMS.
     05   A   PIC S9999V99   COMP-3    VALUE +25.67.
     05   B   PIC S99V999    COMP      VALUE +25.670.
     05   C   PIC 99V99      DISPLAY   VALUE 25.67.
     05   D   PIC S99V99               VALUE −99.00.
```

A, B, and C are all considered *equal* (they all contain the algebraic value +25.67). D is less than each of A, B, and C, since it is negative.

Nonnumeric comparisons.   Here, "is less than" is defined by the collating sequence in effect during program execution (Sections 4.3 and 4.4). A nonnumeric comparison is effected *one byte at a time*, *working left to right* through the two items being compared. If they match byte for byte the whole way through, they are considered *equal*. If there is a mismatch at some position, the result is determined by the relative order of the nonmatching bytes in the collating sequence. If the two items being compared are of different lengths, the shorter one is considered to be extended with blanks on the right.

EXAMPLE 7.12

(*a*)   "CAB" is less than "CAT" because although the first two bytes match, the third bytes are different, and "B" is less than (precedes) "T" in the collating sequence.

(*b*)   "CAB" is equal to "CAB*bb*", since "CAB" (the shorter item) is considered to be extended with two blanks on the right for purposes of the comparison.

(*c*)   "COB" is greater than "CAT" because a mismatch occurs in the second position, and "O" is greater than "A" in the collating sequence. Notice that "B" and "T" never even get compared, since the result is already determined at the second byte.

(*d*)   "CAB" is less than "CABBY" because "CAB" is considered to be extended with two blanks on the right for purposes of the comparison, and the first mismatch occurs at the first of these two blanks ("CAB*bb*" against "CABBY"). Since blank is less than "B" in the collating sequence, "CAB" is less than "CABBY".

It is seen that nonnumeric comparisons preserve the usual alphabetical order.

EXAMPLE 7.13   As with the MOVE statement, it is forbidden to mix certain nonnumeric and numeric operands in a relation condition. In particular, watch out for the following:

(1)   Numeric items which are COMP or COMP-3 may *only* be compared with other numeric items (which may be DISPLAY, COMP, or COMP-3).

(2)   Two literals or figurative constants may *not* be compared.

(3)   Numeric items with USAGE DISPLAY *may* be compared with alphanumeric (PIC X) items—but *results may be different than expected*. If you think such a comparison must be made, first consult your vendor manual.

7.7   Selection Structure: Sign Condition

The *sign condition* may be used only with a numeric operand; its syntax is

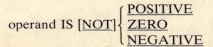

operand IS [NOT] {POSITIVE / ZERO / NEGATIVE}

EXAMPLE 7.14

●   IF CURRENT-BALANCE IS POSITIVE

The condition is true only if the balance is greater than zero. An exact equivalent is:

        IF CURRENT-BALANCE IS GREATER THAN ZERO

●   IF CURRENT-BALANCE – PAYMENT-AMOUNT IS NOT NEGATIVE

Use of an arithmetic expression in a sign condition; equivalent to:

        IF CURRENT-BALANCE – PAYMENT-AMOUNT IS NOT LESS THAN ZERO

●   IF NUMBER-OVERDUE-ACCOUNTS IS ZERO

Equivalent to:

        IF NUMBER-OVERDUE-ACCOUNTS IS EQUAL TO ZERO

●   IF 12.34 IS POSITIVE

Invalid: literals or figurative constants may not be used as the single operand in a sign condition.

●   IF PERIMETER-SIZE – 12.54 IS NOT NEGATIVE

Literals/figurative constants are allowed as part of an arithmetic expression in a sign condition.

7.8   Selection Structure: Condition-Name Condition

The *condition-name condition* may be used in the PROCEDURE DIVISION as a convenient, descriptive replacement for a relation condition. A given data item may have one or more *condition-names* associated with it; each is defined in the DATA DIVISION, *immediately after* the said item, via a special level-88 entry of the form

$$88 \quad \text{condition-name} \left\{ \begin{array}{l} \underline{\text{VALUE}} \text{ IS} \\ \underline{\text{VALUES}} \text{ ARE} \end{array} \right\} \text{literal-1} \left[\left\{ \begin{array}{l} \underline{\text{THROUGH}} \\ \underline{\text{THRU}} \end{array} \right\} \text{literal-2} \right]$$

$$\left[\text{literal-3} \left[\left\{ \begin{array}{l} \underline{\text{THROUGH}} \\ \underline{\text{THRU}} \end{array} \right\} \text{literal-4} \right] \right] \dots$$

The condition-name condition is then expressed as follows: "condition-name" is *true* if and only if the *data item* in question contains the value specified by the VALUE IS . . . clause.

EXAMPLE 7.15 Let us consider the performance of a certain task (*a*) without, and (*b*) with, use of condition-name conditions.

```
(a)      01  CUSTOMER-UPDATE-RECORD.
             05  CUSTOMER-UPDATE-CODE        PIC X.
             05  UPDATE-CUSTOMER-NAME        PIC X(20).
             05  UPDATE-CUSTOMER-ADDRESS     PIC X(30).
         . . . . . . . . . . . . . . . . . . . . . .
         01  WS-END-OF-FILE-SW               PIC X(3).
         . . . . . . . . . . . . . . . . . . . . . .
             READ CUSTOMER-UPDATE-FILE
                 AT END
                     MOVE "YES" TO WS-END-OF-FILE-SW

             IF WS-END-OF-FILE-SW NOT EQUAL "YES"
                 IF CUSTOMER-UPDATE-CODE EQUAL "A"
                     PERFORM ADD-NEW-CUSTOMER-ROUTINE
                 ELSE IF  CUSTOMER-UPDATE-CODE EQUAL "D"
                     PERFORM DELETE-A-CUSTOMER-ROUTINE
                 ELSE IF  CUSTOMER-UPDATE-CODE EQUAL "C"
                     PERFORM CHANGE-NAME-ADDRESS-ROUTINE
                 ELSE
                     PERFORM INVALID-UPDATE-CODE-ROUTINE
```

The first byte of CUSTOMER-UPDATE-RECORD contains a code which indicates whether the update record contains information about a new customer to be added to the CUSTOMER-MASTER-FILE, a customer to be deleted from the file, or a customer whose name/address should be changed on the file. This code is tested by a series of IF statements which determine the appropriate paragraph to PERFORM in order to process the incoming transaction record. We make the following observations:

(1) The code values appear as literals in the IF statements; if these values have to be changed, the programmer must search through the entire PROCEDURE DIVISION to find all occurrences of the literals.

(2) 'CUSTOMER-UPDATE-CODE EQUAL "C"' does not convey much information about what it *means* when the code is equal to "C".

(b)
```
      01  CUSTOMER-UPDATE-RECORD.
          05   CUSTOMER-UPDATE-CODE                PIC X.
              88   ADD-NEW-CUSTOMER-TRANSACTION           VALUE "A".
              88   DELETE-CUSTOMER-TRANSACTION            VALUE "D".
              88   CHANGE-ADDRESS-TRANSACTION            VALUE "C".
          05   UPDATE-CUSTOMER-NAME               PIC X(20).
          05   UPDATE-CUSTOMER-ADDRESS            PIC X(30).

      . . . . . . . . . . . . . . . . . . . . . . . . . . .

      01  WS-END-OF-FILE-SW                       PIC X(3).
          88   NO-MORE-TRANSACTION-RECORDS            VALUE "YES".
          88   TRANSACTION-RECORD-WAS-INPUT          VALUE "NO".

      . . . . . . . . . . . . . . . . . . . . . . . . . . .

      READ CUSTOMER-UPDATE-FILE
          AT END
              MOVE "YES" TO WS-END-OF-FILE-SW


      IF TRANSACTION-RECORD-WAS-INPUT
          IF ADD-NEW-CUSTOMER-TRANSACTION
              PERFORM ADD-NEW-CUSTOMER-ROUTINE
          ELSE IF DELETE-CUSTOMER-TRANSACTION
              PERFORM DELETE-A-CUSTOMER-ROUTINE
          ELSE IF CHANGE-ADDRESS-TRANSACTION
              PERFORM CHANGE-NAME-ADDRESS-ROUTINE
          ELSE
              PERFORM INVALID-UPDATE-CODE-ROUTINE
```

The VALUE clause is required for a level-88 item, but *no other clauses are allowed*. This makes sense, because a condition-name is associated with a particular *value* of the data item under which it is defined.

Observe how the relation conditions of (a) above are here replaced by condition-name conditions; e.g.,

IF CUSTOMER-UPDATE-CODE EQUAL "A"

is replaced by the exactly equivalent

IF ADD-NEW-CUSTOMER-TRANSACTION

Three major benefits accrue from this use of condition-name conditions:

(1) With no literals used in PROCEDURE DIVISION IF and PERFORM statements, the program is easier to modify if the meaning of the input codes or the codes themselves change. All that needs to be modified is the level-88 entries in the DATA DIVISION.

(2) Condition-names can be made descriptive of the condition they represent. Thus, "CHANGE-ADDRESS-TRANSACTION" conveys more meaning to a reader than does 'CUSTOMER-UPDATE-CODE EQUAL "C"'.

(3) A condition-name can simply represent a rather complicated relation condition.

EXAMPLE 7.16

```
01   TRANSCRIPT-RECORD.
     05   TRANSCRIPT-STUDENT-ID              PIC X(9).
     05   TRANSCRIPT-YEAR-ATTENDING          PIC 9.
 88       FRESHMAN                                    VALUE 1.
 88       SOPHOMORE                                   VALUE 2.
 88       JUNIOR                                      VALUE 3.
 88       SENIOR                                      VALUE 4.
 88       UNDERGRADUATE                               VALUE 1 THRU 4.
 88       GRADUATE                                    VALUE 5 THRU 9.
     05   TRANSCRIPT-CREDITS-COMPLETED       PIC 99.
     05   TRANSCRIPT-GRADE-POINT-AVERAGE     PIC 9V9.
 88       HIGHEST-DISTINCTION                         VALUE 3.8 THRU 4.0.
 88       HIGH-DISTINCTION                            VALUE 3.5 THRU 3.7.
 88       NOT-GRADUATING                              VALUE 0.0 THRU 1.9.
     05   TRANSCRIPT-STUDENT-NAME            PIC X(30).
```

. . . .

The use of the THRU option allows a *range* of values to be specified for a condition-name. The UNDER-GRADUATE condition is true if TRANSCRIPT-YEAR-ATTENDING has a value between 1 and 4 inclusive, etc.

Some programmers prefer to type level number 88 in the A margin (as above), to make it stand out; others prefer to indent normally [as in Example 7.15(*b*)].

Notice how much more simple and understandable would be

IF SENIOR AND HIGH-DISTINCTION

than the equivalent relation condition

IF TRANSCRIPT-YEAR-ATTENDING EQUAL 4 AND
    TRANSCRIPT-GRADE-POINT-AVERAGE NOT LESS THAN 3.5 AND
    TRANSCRIPT-GRADE-POINT-AVERAGE NOT GREATER THAN 3.7

EXAMPLE 7.17   More than one range of values can be specified for a given condition-name:

```
05   LOCATION-CODE       PIC XX.
88   PHILADELPHIA                    VALUE "AA" THRU "AC"
                                     "B7"  "D5"
                                     "E3" THRU "E5".
```

Given the above definition,

IF PHILADELPHIA

may be used instead of the cumbersome

IF   (LOCATION-CODE NOT LESS THAN "AA"
              AND NOT GREATER THAN "AC")
    OR   (LOCATION-CODE EQUAL "B7" OR "D5")
    OR   (LOCATION-CODE NOT LESS THAN "E3"
              AND NOT GREATER THAN "E5")

EXAMPLE 7.18   Given the definitions

```
01   END-OF-FILE-SWITCH      PIC XXX.
     88   NO-MORE-RECORDS              VALUE "YES".
     88   MORE-RECORDS                 VALUE "NO".
```

we point out two beginner's errors.

● READ SAMPLE-FILE
      AT END
          MOVE "YES" TO NO-MORE-RECORDS

(in place of: MOVE "YES" TO END-OF-FILE-SWITCH). *The condition-name is not the data item, but the representation of a relation condition involving the data item.* The statement

      MOVE "YES" TO NO-MORE-RECORDS

makes precisely as much sense as:

      MOVE "YES" TO (END-OF-FILE-SWITCH IS EQUAL TO "YES")

●   IF NO-MORE-RECORDS IS EQUAL TO "YES"

NO-MORE-RECORDS is *already* a relation condition (in condensed form); what is intended is

      IF NO-MORE-RECORDS

or

      IF END-OF-FILE-SWITCH IS EQUAL TO "YES"

7.9 Logical Operators and Compound Conditions

The unary logical operator "NOT" can be used to negate a *simple condition* (a class, relation, sign, or condition-name condition), provided the simple condition does not itself contain a "NOT".

EXAMPLE 7.19

●   IF NOT A IS LESS THAN B

The condition that is being negated is "A IS LESS THAN B"; so a clearer rendering of the IF statement would be

      IF NOT (A IS LESS THAN B)

Either form is logically equivalent to

      IF A IS NOT LESS THAN B

This last version, with the "NOT" embedded in the simple condition, is preferred for class, sign, and relation conditions.

●   IF NOT RECORD-IN-BUFFER

"RECORD-IN-BUFFER" *must* be a condition-name. If RECORD-IN-BUFFER is true, NOT RECORD-IN-BUFFER is false; if RECORD-IN-BUFFER is false, NOT RECORD-IN-BUFFER is true.

In addition to being negated, simple conditions can be combined, using the logical operators AND and OR, to form *compound conditions*. The truth value of "condition-1 AND condition-2" depends on the truth values of condition-1 and condition-2 as shown in Fig. 7-8.

condition-1	condition-2	condition-1 AND condition-2
true	true	true
true	false	false
false	true	false
false	false	false

Fig. 7-8

Note that when two conditions are ANDed together, the resulting compound condition is true only when both original conditions are true.

When two conditions are ORed together, the compound condition has the truth table of Fig. 7-9.

condition-1	condition-2	condition-1 OR condition-2
true	true	true
true	false	true
false	true	true
false	false	false

Fig. 7-9

Note that the compound condition is false only when both original conditions are false.

EXAMPLE 7.20

●   IF HOURS-WORKED NUMERIC AND HOURS-WORKED GREATER THAN 40.0

The compound condition is true if and only if both simple conditions are true. This particular condition could cause trouble. In IBM OS/VS COBOL, relation conditions are evaluated before class conditions. Thus, if HOURS-WORKED is *not* numeric, the evaluation of "HOURS-WORKED GREATER THAN 40.0" could cause a program ABEND. The difficulty may be eliminated by using two IF statements:

```
IF HOURS-WORKED NUMERIC
    IF HOURS-WORKED GREATER THAN 40.0
```

Now the relation condition is evaluated only when HOURS-WORKED is known to be numeric.

●   IF HOURS-WORKED NOT NUMERIC OR HOURLY-RATE NOT NUMERIC
        PERFORM ERROR-ROUTINE
  ELSE
        PERFORM CALCULATE-PAY

If at least one of the simple conditions is true, the compound condition is true. Thus, ERROR-ROUTINE is PERFORMed if either or both of HOURS-WORKED and HOURLY-RATE are not numeric; if both fields are numeric, CALCULATE-PAY is PERFORMed.

●   IF HOURS-WORKED NUMERIC AND HOURLY-RATE NUMERIC
        PERFORM CALCULATE-PAY
  ELSE
        PERFORM ERROR-ROUTINE

Exactly equivalent to the foregoing. You should verify (by means of truth tables) that the opposite (i.e., negation) of "A OR B" is "(NOT A) AND (NOT B)", and the opposite of "A AND B" is "(NOT A) OR (NOT B)".

●   IF RECORD-WAS-INPUT AND BALANCE-DUE IS POSITIVE

Here, a condition-name condition and a sign condition are ANDed.

●   IF ON-HAND NOT LESS THAN 1 OR ON-HAND NOT GREATER THAN 500
        PERFORM ADJUST-QUANTITY-ONHAND

Faulty coding. The intent was (we guess) to execute PERFORM ADJUST-QUANTITY-ONHAND if the contents of ON-HAND are not between 1 and 500, inclusive. However, a bit of reflection will show that the compound condition is *always* true (the only way it could be false is if ON-HAND is both less than 1 and greater than 500—an impossibility); hence the PERFORM is *always* executed. The correct coding is:

```
IF ON-HAND LESS THAN 1 OR ON-HAND GREATER THAN 500
    PERFORM ADJUST-QUANTITY-ONHAND
```

More than one logical operator may be used to form a compound condition. When *the same* logical operator is repeated, parentheses are unnecessary in the compound condition (since the result is always the same, regardless of the order of the applications of the single operator). When *different* logical operators are used, the order of their evaluation should be explicitly indicated by parentheses.

EXAMPLE 7.21

-     IF   INPUT-YEAR IS GREATER THAN 80
      AND   INPUT-YEAR IS LESS THAN 84
      AND   INPUT-MONTH IS NOT LESS THAN 1
      AND   INPUT-MONTH IS NOT GREATER THAN 12
      AND   INPUT-DAY IS NOT LESS THAN 1
      AND   INPUT-DAY IS NOT GREATER THAN 31
          PERFORM PROCESS-VALID-DATE
    ELSE
          PERFORM PROCESS-INVALID-DATE

Note that each simple condition is typed on its own line, and that the conditions and logical operators are aligned for readability. *All* six simple conditions must be true in order for the compound condition to be true. Thus, in order to execute PERFORM PROCESS-VALID-DATE, the year must be between 81 and 83 inclusive, the month must be between 1 and 12, and the day must be between 1 and 31. While this test detects most errors in the date field, it will let some errors slip through (e.g., 09/31/83).

-     IF   TIME-CARD-EMPLOYEE-NUMBER NOT NUMERIC
      OR TIME-CARD-REGULAR-HOURS NOT NUMERIC
      OR TIME-CARD-OVERTIME-HOURS NOT NUMERIC
         MOVE "YES" TO INVALID-NUMERIC-FIELDS-SW

This routine validates numeric fields in TIME-CARD-RECORD. Note how each simple condition is typed on its own line, with operators aligned for readability. Since "OR" is used, the compound condition will be true if one or more of the simple conditions is true.

-     IF   (NOT SPECIAL-TERMS-REQUESTED)
        AND (CREDIT-UNSATISFACTORY
            OR PURCHASE-AMOUNT GREATER THAN CREDIT-LIMIT)

"SPECIAL-TERMS-REQUESTED" and "CREDIT-UNSATISFACTORY" must be condition-names. The sequence of evaluations is: (i) SPECIAL-TERMS-REQUESTED is evaluated; (ii) the result of (i) is negated; (iii) PURCHASE-AMOUNT GREATER THAN CREDIT-LIMIT is evaluated; (iv) CREDIT-UNSATIS-FACTORY is evaluated; (v) the results of (iii) and (iv) are ORed together; (vi) the results of (ii) and (v) are ANDed together.

-     IF   (NEW-CUSTOMER
          AND (CUSTOMER-ID-ON-FILE OR
             CUSTOMER-ID NOT NUMERIC))
        OR
       (OLD-CUSTOMER
          AND (CUSTOMER-ID-NOT-ON-FILE
             OR DAYS-PAYMENT-LATE GREATER THAN 90))

If compound conditions become this complicated, it is a *good sign that the program should be partially or totally redesigned.*

    If parentheses are not used (or if conditions are at the same level of parentheses), logical expressions are evaluated in the following order: (1) arithmetic expressions which appear in relation conditions; (2) simple conditions in the order: relation, class, condition-name, sign; (3) negated simple conditions, in the foregoing order; (4) AND; (5) OR. If two subconditions are equal according to this ordering, then they are evaluated left to right.

    If the above rules seem complicated, there is a simple way to eliminate even the remotest possibility of an error due to incorrect evaluation of a complex logical expression: ***use parentheses.***

EXAMPLE 7.22   Without parentheses, the third compound condition of Example 7.21 reads

> IF NOT SPECIAL-TERMS-REQUESTED
>   AND CREDIT-UNSATISFACTORY
>   OR   PURCHASE-AMOUNT GREATER THAN CREDIT-LIMIT

The order of evaluation is as follows: (i) PURCHASE-AMOUNT GREATER THAN CREDIT-LIMIT (relation condition); (ii) SPECIAL-TERMS-REQUESTED (condition-name condition, left to right); (iii) CREDIT-UNSATISFACTORY (condition-name condition, left to right); (iv) NOT (ii) (negated simple condition); (v) (iv) AND (iii) (AND before OR); (vi) (v) OR (i). The result is the same as if the following parentheses were used:

> IF   ((NOT SPECIAL-TERMS-REQUESTED)
>   AND   CREDIT-UNSATISFACTORY)
>   OR   (PURCHASE-AMOUNT GREATER THAN CREDIT-LIMIT)

Thus, the parentheses in Example 7.21 were necessary to achieve the desired result (which differs from the above).

7.10   Abbreviation of Compound Relation Conditions

A generalized simple relation condition has the form:

> subject relational-operator object

A compound relation condition combines two or more simple relation conditions by means of the logical operators AND and OR:

$$\text{subject relational-operator object} \begin{Bmatrix} \text{AND} \\ \text{OR} \end{Bmatrix} \text{subject relational-operator object}$$

If the *relational-operator is the same* for two or more simple relation conditions in a compound relation condition, the relational-operator need not be repeated. Likewise, if the *subject is the same* in several simple relations of a compound relation, the subject need not be repeated. The object must always be written for each simple relation condition.

EXAMPLE 7.23

●   IF A EQUAL B OR A EQUAL C OR A EQUAL D
has both a repeated subject (data item "A") and a repeated relational-operator ("EQUAL"). The repetitions of both subject and relational-operator could be omitted, yielding

> IF A EQUAL B OR C OR D

Of course, the *first* instance of the subject and relational-operator must be indicated.

●   IF A EQUAL B AND A EQUAL C OR A GREATER THAN D
may be abbreviated

> IF A EQUAL B AND C OR GREATER THAN D

If the relational-operator (or the subject) is missing from a simple relation condition, the *last* relational-operator (subject) appearing in the compound condition is understood.

●   IF SAMPLE-ITEM NOT EQUAL 10.5 OR OTHER-ITEM OR 3.0
is an abbreviation of

> IF SAMPLE-ITEM NOT EQUAL 10.5
>   OR SAMPLE-ITEM NOT EQUAL OTHER-ITEM
>   OR SAMPLE-ITEM NOT EQUAL 3.0

Abbreviated compound relation conditions should be used only when clarity is not jeopardized. When in doubt, *use parentheses* and *don't abbreviate.*

7.11   Nested and Linear IF Statements

Structured algorithms built by combining sequence, selection, and iteration structures often have selection structures *inside* selection structures. We say that the COBOL implementation of such an algorithm contains *nested* IF statements. When nested IFs are used, indentation should scrupulously reflect the relationships among the various IF statements.

EXAMPLE 7.24

```
IF    ADD-NEW-MASTER-RECORD
      IF MASTER-ALREADY-EXISTS
          PERFORM DUPLICATE-RECORD-ERROR
ELSE
          PERFORM CREATE-NEW-MASTER-RECORD
ELSE
      IF CHANGE-EXISTING-MASTER-RECORD
          IF MASTER-ALREADY-EXISTS
              PERFORM MAKE-CHANGES-TO-MASTER
          ELSE
              PERFORM RECORD-NOT-FOUND-ERROR
```

Note how each nested IF statement is indented, and how ELSE clauses are always aligned with their corresponding IF. There is generally no problem in interpreting a nested IF when *each* IF statement has an associated ELSE clause. However, this is not required: "IF CHANGE-EXISTING-MASTER-RECORD" has no paired ELSE.

EXAMPLE 7.25   When interpreting a nested IF, the COBOL compiler pairs each ELSE clause with the first preceding IF that has not already been paired with an ELSE (if such an unpaired IF does not exist, there must be a syntax error). This rule can cause problems when nested IFs are written with ELSE clauses omitted:

```
IF TRANSACTION-WAS-READ
    IF PAYMENT-AMOUNT NUMERIC
        SUBTRACT PAYMENT-AMOUNT FROM CURRENT-BALANCE
ELSE
        MOVE "FINAL" TO TOTAL-LINE-HEADING
        PERFORM PRODUCE-FINAL-TOTAL-LINE
```

Here the compiler pairs "ELSE..." with "IF PAYMENT-AMOUNT NUMERIC" (rather than with "IF TRANSACTION-WAS-READ", as the programmer appears to have wanted). Thus the statements will be executed as follows:

```
IF TRANSACTION-WAS-READ
    IF PAYMENT-AMOUNT NUMERIC
        SUBTRACT PAYMENT-AMOUNT FROM CURRENT-BALANCE
    ELSE
        MOVE "FINAL" TO TOTAL-LINE-HEADING
        PERFORM PRODUCE-FINAL-TOTAL-LINE
```

The nested IF as written above is incorrect, since the final total line is produced any time a nonnumeric payment is input as part of a transaction record. The original intent was to print the final total line when no more transaction records could be input (i.e., at end of file).

To prevent such errors, some installations require that every nested IF statement be written with an associated ELSE clause (even if it is just "ELSE NEXT SENTENCE"):

```
IF TRANSACTION-WAS-READ
    IF PAYMENT-AMOUNT NUMERIC
        SUBTRACT PAYMENT-AMOUNT FROM CURRENT-BALANCE
    ELSE
        NEXT SENTENCE
ELSE
    MOVE "FINAL" TO TOTAL-LINE-HEADING
    PERFORM PRODUCE-FINAL-TOTAL-LINE
```

"ELSE NEXT SENTENCE", if executed, takes the computer to the statement after the period.

Occasionally a program must repeatedly test the same field to determine which of a series of values it contains. A special form of nested IF, called a *linear IF*, can be used in such a case.

EXAMPLE 7.26

```
IF TRANSACTION-CODE EQUAL 1
    PERFORM CREATE-NEW-MASTER-RECORD
ELSE
    IF TRANSACTION-CODE EQUAL 2
        PERFORM DELETE-MASTER-RECORD
    ELSE
        IF TRANSACTION-CODE EQUAL 3
            PERFORM CHANGE-EXISTING-MASTER-RECORD
        ELSE
            PERFORM INVALID-TRANSACTION-CODE-ROUTINE
```

This series of tests of TRANSACTION-CODE is better coded as a linear IF:

```
IF TRANSACTION-CODE EQUAL 1
    PERFORM CREATE-NEW-MASTER-RECORD
ELSE IF TRANSACTION-CODE EQUAL 2
    PERFORM DELETE-MASTER-RECORD
ELSE IF TRANSACTION-CODE EQUAL 3
    PERFORM CHANGE-EXISTING-MASTER-RECORD
ELSE
    PERFORM INVALID-TRANSACTION-CODE-ROUTINE
```

In the linear IF, each successive ELSE clause is typed aligned under the initial IF, and each successive IF clause is typed *on the same line* as the preceding ELSE. The actions to be carried out for each IF are indented on separate lines as usual. Notice that the very last ELSE clause is not followed by an IF. The statement(s) associated with this last ELSE are executed only if the data item being tested contains *none* of the values checked in the preceding relation conditions. Notice also that one and only one paragraph will be PERFORMed—which one it is depends solely on the contents of TRANSACTION-CODE.

EXAMPLE 7.27 The linear IF can be used to code a fourth program logic structure, the *case structure*. The case structure is never *necessary*, but it is available in some languages as a programming *convenience*. The case structure causes the execution of *exactly one* of a set of routines, depending on the value of a control data item which is tested within the structure. The case structure can be flowcharted in a number of ways, one of which we illustrate in Fig. 7-10, a flowchart of Example 7.26. (See Appendix C for the case structure in COBOL '80.)

7.12   Iteration Structure: PERFORM Statement

The PERFORM statement allows a PROCEDURE DIVISION paragraph or SECTION to be executed zero, one, or more times. It has four formats.

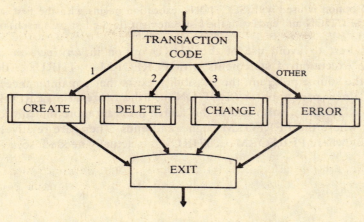

Fig. 7-10

Simple PERFORM

The simplest version of the PERFORM statement is:

$$\underline{PERFORM}\ procedure\text{-}name\text{-}1\ \left[\left\{\begin{array}{c}\underline{THROUGH}\\\underline{THRU}\end{array}\right\}\ procedure\text{-}name\text{-}2\right]$$

Each "procedure-name" must be either a paragraph or a SECTION name.

EXAMPLE 7.28

```
        PERFORM SAMPLE-PARAGRAPH
        COMPUTE...
    . . . . . . . . . . . . . . . . . . . . . . . . . .
     SAMPLE-PARAGRAPH.
        ADD...
        MOVE...
        SUBTRACT...
      .
     NEXT-PARAGRAPH.
        OPEN...
        MOVE...
      .
```

The PERFORM statement causes *all* the statements in SAMPLE-PARAGRAPH to be executed in normal sequential fashion. After execution of SUBTRACT..., the computer moves on to the statement immediately following the PERFORM (COMPUTE...).

When a SECTION (which may consist of many paragraphs) is PERFORMed, the statements are executed beginning with the first statement of the first paragraph and ending with the last statement of the last paragraph.

EXAMPLE 7.29   Given the paragraphs defined in Example 7.28,

```
        PERFORM SAMPLE-PARAGRAPH THRU NEXT-PARAGRAPH
        COMPUTE...
    . . . . . . . . . . . . . . . . . . . . . . . . . .
```

causes the computer to begin executing the statements in SAMPLE-PARAGRAPH in sequential fashion, starting with ADD .... Execution continues, statement after statement, paragraph after paragraph, until the last statement in the "THRU" paragraph is executed (MOVE...), at which point the computer resumes normal sequential execution of instructions at the statement immediately following the PERFORM (COMPUTE...).

When the THRU option is used with SECTIONs, execution begins with the first statement (in the first paragraph) of the first SECTION and ends with the last statement (in the last paragraph) of the last SECTION.

In general, it is best to avoid use of the THRU option in *any version* of the PERFORM statement. Since the execution of statements with PERFORM . . . THRU . . . depends upon their physical position in the source program, the possibility exists that a maintenance programmer might inadvertently insert a new paragraph or SECTION into the range of a PERFORM . . . THRU . . . . Use of PERFORM . . . THRU . . . also makes the source program more difficult to understand, since one must remember where the PERFORM begins and ends. There are relatively few situations in COBOL programming where PERFORM . . . THRU . . . is actually needed; so, avoiding it should be no hardship.

TIMES Version

The next-simplest version of the PERFORM statement is:

$$\underline{\text{PERFORM}} \text{ procedure-name-1} \left[\left\{ \begin{matrix} \underline{\text{THROUGH}} \\ \underline{\text{THRU}} \end{matrix} \right\} \text{procedure-name-2} \right] \left\{ \begin{matrix} \text{dentifier-1} \\ \text{integer-1} \end{matrix} \right\} \underline{\text{TIMES}}$$

The THRU option has exactly the same role in defining the range of statements to be PERFORMed as it does for the simple PERFORM. Again, we do not recommend its use. When identifier-1 is used, it must be a numeric, integer, elementary item (e.g., PIC S9, with no decimal point). Identifier-1 or integer-1 indicates the *number of times* that the specified range of statements should be executed before the computer goes on to the statement immediately following the PERFORM. If identifier-1 or integer-1 is negative or zero, the indicated range of statements *is not performed at all* and the computer immediately goes on to the next statement.

EXAMPLE 7.30

```
05   WS-NUMBER-OF-TEMPLATES      PIC 99.
. . . . . . . . . . . . . . . . . . . . . . .
ACCEPT  WS-NUMBER-OF-TEMPLATES FROM OPERATOR-OPTIONS-DEVICE
. . . . . . . . . . . . . . . . . . . . . . .
PERFORM PRINT-CHECK-ALIGNMENT-TEMPLATE
        WS-NUMBER-OF-TEMPLATES TIMES
```

Here, a numeric data item is used to indicate the desired number of iterations. OPERATOR-OPTIONS-DEVICE must be defined in the SPECIAL-NAMES paragraph of the ENVIRONMENT DIVISION. Note that if the operator enters zero for WS-NUMBER-OF-TEMPLATES, the PERFORM statement will cause *zero* performs of PRINT-CHECK-ALIGNMENT-TEMPLATE.

Despite its simplicity, PERFORM . . . TIMES is not too frequently utilized in COBOL programs, because the number of iterations is seldom known in advance. More often we need to repeat the execution of a routine until some condition arises which indicates that the iterations may cease (e.g., end of file).

UNTIL Version

The syntax is:

$$\underline{\text{PERFORM}} \text{ procedure-name-1} \left[\left\{ \begin{matrix} \underline{\text{THROUGH}} \\ \underline{\text{THRU}} \end{matrix} \right\} \text{procedure-name-2} \right] \underline{\text{UNTIL}} \text{ condition-1}$$

The effect of PERFORM . . . UNTIL . . . is described in the structured flowchart of Fig. 7-11.

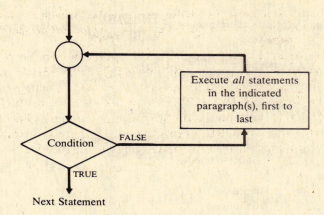

Fig. 7-11

Comparing with Fig. 7-5, we recognize the DO WHILE structure (with a negated condition). Hence, all the characteristics pointed out in Example 7.3 are shared by PERFORM . . . UNTIL . . . . Once more, we discourage the use of the THRU option.

EXAMPLE 7.31

●   MOVE "NO" TO NO-MORE-SWITCH
       PERFORM PRINT-A-MESSAGE
          UNTIL NO-MORE-SWITCH EQUAL "YES"

    . . . .

      PRINT-A-MESSAGE.
         WRITE PRINT-LINE
           FROM WS-MESSAGE-LINE

An "infinite loop": once set to "NO", NO-MORE-SWITCH will never contain "YES", and so the WRITE . . . of PRINT-A-MESSAGE will be repeated endlessly. In practice, most operating systems set limits on how long a given program may use the CPU and on how many printed lines it may produce; if either limit is exceeded, the program automatically ABENDs.

●   PERFORM DETERMINE-NEW-BALANCE
         UNTIL ALL-TRANSACTIONS-PROCESSED
"ALL-TRANSACTIONS-PROCESSED" must be a condition-name (and the condition-name condition must become *true* at some point during the iteration of DETERMINE-NEW-BALANCE).

●   PERFORM LIST-SUBASSEMBLIES
       UNTIL   ALL-ITEMS-LISTED
         OR   LINES-REMAINING IS NEGATIVE
         OR   TOTAL-ASSEMBLY-TIME IS GREATER THAN 20.0
Any compound condition that might be used in an IF statement may also be used in PERFORM . . . UNTIL . . . . Here, a condition-name condition (ALL-ITEMS-LISTED), a sign condition, and a relation condition are connected by means of the logical operator OR. Note how this example is typed.

VARYING Version

    This version of the PERFORM statement is the most complicated syntactically, but it is often useful when working with tables (see Chapter 10) or when writing loops that repeat the execution of a paragraph, with the contents of a certain data item changing in a controlled manner with each repetition. The general format of PERFORM . . . VARYING . . . is displayed in Fig. 7-12 (index-names are discussed in Chapter 10; don't worry about them for now).

$$\underline{\text{PERFORM}} \text{ procedure-name-1 } \left[\begin{Bmatrix} \underline{\text{THROUGH}} \\ \underline{\text{THRU}} \end{Bmatrix} \text{ procedure-name-2} \right]$$

$$\underline{\text{VARYING}} \begin{Bmatrix} \text{identifier-1} \\ \text{index-name-1} \end{Bmatrix} \underline{\text{FROM}} \begin{Bmatrix} \text{literal-2} \\ \text{identifier-2} \\ \text{index-name-2} \end{Bmatrix}$$

$$\underline{\text{BY}} \begin{Bmatrix} \text{literal-3} \\ \text{identifier-3} \end{Bmatrix} \underline{\text{UNTIL}} \text{ condition-1}$$

$$\left[\underline{\text{AFTER}} \begin{Bmatrix} \text{identifier-4} \\ \text{index-name-4} \end{Bmatrix} \underline{\text{FROM}} \begin{Bmatrix} \text{literal-5} \\ \text{identifier-5} \\ \text{index-name-5} \end{Bmatrix} \right.$$

$$\left. \underline{\text{BY}} \begin{Bmatrix} \text{literal-6} \\ \text{identifier-6} \end{Bmatrix} \underline{\text{UNTIL}} \text{ condition-2} \right]$$

$$\left[\underline{\text{AFTER}} \begin{Bmatrix} \text{identifier-7} \\ \text{index-name-7} \end{Bmatrix} \underline{\text{FROM}} \begin{Bmatrix} \text{literal-8} \\ \text{identifier-8} \\ \text{index-name-8} \end{Bmatrix} \right.$$

$$\left. \underline{\text{BY}} \begin{Bmatrix} \text{literal-9} \\ \text{identifier-9} \end{Bmatrix} \underline{\text{UNTIL}} \text{ condition-3} \right]$$

Fig. 7-12

EXAMPLE 7.32

```
        PERFORM ASSIGN-MAILBOXES
            VARYING MAILBOX-NUMBER FROM 1 BY 1
            UNTIL ALL-EMPLOYEES-PROCESSED
. . . . . . . . . . . . . . . . . . . . . . . . . . . . . . . .
    ASSIGN-MAILBOXES.
        READ EMPLOYEE-MASTER-FILE
            INTO WS-EMPLOYEE-RECORD
            AT END
                MOVE "YES" TO ALL-EMPLOYEES-PROCESSED-SW

        IF ANOTHER-EMPLOYEE-INPUT
            MOVE MAILBOX-NUMBER TO WS-OUTPUT-MAILBOX-NUMBER
            MOVE WS-EMPLOYEE-NAME TO WS-OUTPUT-NAME
            WRITE MAILBOX-LIST-LINE
                FROM WS-OUTPUT-LINE
```

This routine is designed to assign company mailboxes (numbered 1, 2, 3, etc.) to company employees. The VARYING version of PERFORM is used to control the MAILBOX-NUMBER to be assigned to the employee currently being processed. MAILBOX-NUMBER is initially set to the "FROM" value, 1. The UNTIL condition is then evaluated, and if it is *false*, the paragraph ASSIGN-MAILBOXES is performed. ASSIGN-MAILBOXES reads an employee record and, if end of file was not encountered, prints a line showing the employee's name and the current contents of MAILBOX-NUMBER. After the last statement in ASSIGN-MAILBOXES is executed, the data item MAILBOX-NUMBER has the "BY" value, 1, added to it, increasing the contents of MAILBOX-NUMBER to 2. Then the UNTIL condition is reevaluated, etc. After the last employee has been processed (and assigned mailbox #n, if there are n employees in all), ALL-EMPLOYEES-PROCESSED becomes *true* ("YES") and the computer skips to the first statement following the PERFORM.

In this example, the FROM value and the BY value happened to be equal. Figure 7-13 is the structured flowchart corresponding to the more general

    PERFORM SAMPLE-PARAGRAPH
        VARYING SAMPLE-ITEM FROM VALUE-A BY VALUE-B
        UNTIL SAMPLE-CONDITION

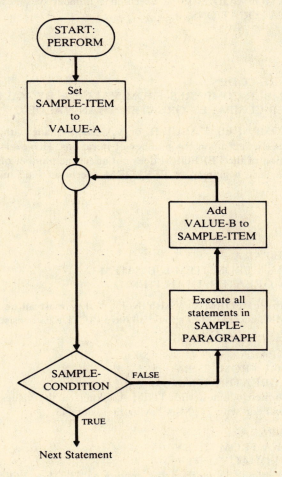

Fig. 7-13

EXAMPLE 7.33 "PERFORM SAMPLE-PARA 10 TIMES" may be rewritten as

    PERFORM SAMPLE-PARA
        VARYING NUMBER-OF-TIMES FROM 1 BY 1
        UNTIL NUMBER-OF-TIMES GREATER THAN 10

or as

    PERFORM SAMPLE-PARA
        VARYING NUMBER-OF-TIMES FROM 1 BY 1
        UNTIL NUMBER-OF-TIMES EQUAL 11

It is critical to understand that

    PERFORM SAMPLE-PARA
        VARYING NUMBER-OF-TIMES FROM 1 BY 1
        UNTIL NUMBER-OF-TIMES IS EQUAL TO 10

will result in SAMPLE-PARA being executed only *nine* times. The reason is easily seen from Fig. 7-13. Similarly,

        PERFORM COMPARE-LOCATION-CODES
            VARYING LOCATION-NUMBER FROM 1 BY 1
            UNTIL LOCATION-NUMBER EQUAL TO MAXIMUM-LOCATIONS

will cause COMPARE-LOCATION-CODES to be executed a number of times which is *one less* than the current contents of MAXIMUM-LOCATIONS.

EXAMPLE 7.34

        PERFORM COMPARE-CODES
            VARYING NUMBER-COMPARES FROM VALUE-A BY VALUE-B
            UNTIL NUMBER-COMPARES GREATER THAN VALUE-C

Any changes in NUMBER-COMPARES, VALUE-B, or VALUE-C made within the COMPARE-CODES paragraph will have the expected effect upon the number of iterations. However, changing the FROM value (VALUE-A) during the execution of the PERFORM does not affect the number of iterations, since the FROM value only plays a part at the very beginning of PERFORM execution (i.e., initializes the contents of the VARYING data item).

EXAMPLE 7.35

        PERFORM SAMPLE-PARA
            VARYING ITEM-A FROM ITEM-B BY ITEM-C
            UNTIL ITEM-A GREATER THAN ITEM-D

When data items are used with PERFORM . . . VARYING . . . , they must all be numeric, elementary items. Thus ITEM-A, ITEM-B, ITEM-C, and ITEM-D should all have PICTUREs consisting of 9s, an optional S, and an optional V.

●   PERFORM SAMPLE-PARA
            VARYING ITEM-A FROM .25 BY .03
            UNTIL ITEM-A GREATER THAN .40
SAMPLE-PARA will be performed 6 times, with ITEM-A taking on the values .25, .28, .31, .34, .37, .40. Execution of the PERFORM will end with ITEM-A having the value .43.

●   PERFORM SAMPLE-PARA
            VARYING ITEM-A FROM .25 BY .03
            UNTIL ITEM-A EQUAL TO .41
This PERFORM results in an infinite loop, since the condition "ITEM-A EQUAL TO .41" is never true (.41 − .25 is not evenly divisible by .03). See Example 7.31.

●   PERFORM SAMPLE-PARA
            VARYING ITEM-A FROM 10 BY −1
            UNTIL ITEM-A IS ZERO
With the BY value negative, ITEM-A will take on the successive values 10, 9, 8, 7, 6, 5, 4, 3, 2, 1, and SAMPLE-PARA will be executed ten times. After the tenth execution, ITEM-A becomes zero, and the computer goes on to the statement immediately following the PERFORM.

When *two* data items are varied in a PERFORM . . . VARYING . . . ,

        PERFORM SAMPLE-PARA
            VARYING ITEM-A FROM ITEM-B BY ITEM-C
                UNTIL ITEM-A GREATER THAN ITEM-D
            AFTER ITEM-E FROM ITEM-F BY ITEM-G
                UNTIL ITEM-E GREATER THAN ITEM-H

execution is as in the structured flowchart Fig. 7-14. It is seen that *for each value of ITEM-A* (in the range

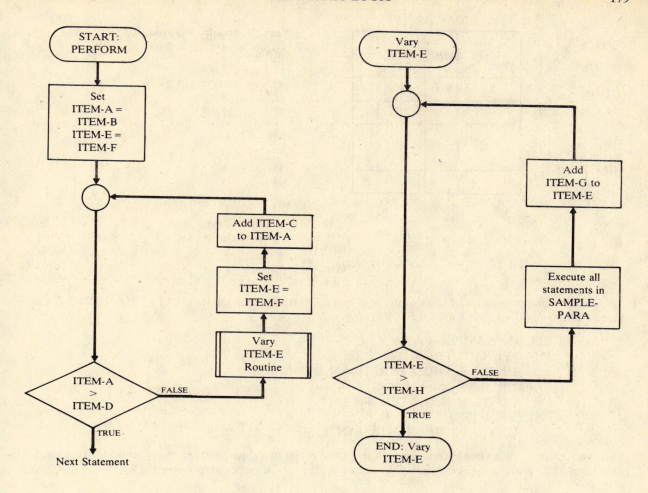

Fig. 7-14

ITEM-B ≤ ITEM-A ≤ ITEM-D), SAMPLE-PARA is executed *for all values of ITEM-E* (in the range ITEM-F ≤ ITEM-E ≤ ITEM-H). Thus, the effect of the PERFORM . . . VARYING . . . is to repeatedly execute SAMPLE-PARA, with

$$\text{total number of iterations}$$
$$= (\text{number of values in range of ITEM-A})$$
$$\times (\text{number of values in range of ITEM-E})$$

EXAMPLE 7.36

      PERFORM CALCULATE-MORTGAGE-PAYMENT
         VARYING PAYMENT-YEAR FROM 83 BY 1
            UNTIL PAYMENT-YEAR GREATER THAN 93
         AFTER PAYMENT-MONTH FROM 1 BY 1
            UNTIL PAYMENT-MONTH GREATER THAN 12

CALCULATE-MORTGAGE-PAYMENT is executed for each value of PAYMENT-YEAR from 83 to 93 inclusive. For each of these 11 values of PAYMENT-YEAR, PAYMENT-MONTH will vary from 1 to 12. The routine therefore calculates $11 \times 12 = 132$ values of the mortgage payment, which might be presented in tabular or linear form (Fig. 7-15).

Month Year	1	2	...	12
83	$xxx			
84				
. .				
93				

Year	Month	Payment
83	1	$xxx
83	2	
. . . .		
83	12	
84	1	
84	2	
. . . .		
84	12	
: : : : : : : : : : : : : : : : : : : :		
93	1	
93	2	
. . . .		
93	12	

(a)   (b)

Fig. 7-15

The maximum number of data items that can be varied in one PERFORM . . . VARYING . . . is three (see Appendix C for COBOL '80):

```
PERFORM SAMPLE-PARA
      VARYING A FROM B BY C
          UNTIL A GREATER THAN D
      AFTER E FROM F BY G
          UNTIL E GREATER THAN H
      AFTER I FROM J BY K
          UNTIL I GREATER THAN L
```

For every value A takes on, E runs through its entire range of values; and for every value E takes on, I runs through its entire range of values. Consequently, the total number of iterations of SAMPLE-PARA is

(number of values of A) × (number of values of E) × (number of values of I)

A structured flowchart is given in Fig. 7-16.

EXAMPLE 7.37

```
PERFORM PRODUCE-TOTAL-INTEREST
      VARYING MORTGAGE-AMOUNT
          FROM 50000 BY 1000
          UNTIL MORTGAGE-AMOUNT GREATER THAN 100000
      AFTER YEARS-TO-REPAY
          FROM 10 BY 1
          UNTIL YEARS-TO-REPAY GREATER THAN 30
      AFTER INTEREST-RATE
          FROM .08 BY .01
          UNTIL INTEREST-RATE GREATER THAN .20
```

This PERFORM statement could be used to generate a report which shows total interest charges for various mortgage amounts at various interest rates with various contract lengths. Mortgage amounts would vary from 50 000 to 100 000 in steps of 1000. For each value of MORTGAGE-AMOUNT, YEARS-TO-REPAY would vary from 10 to 30 in steps of 1. For each value of MORTGAGE-AMOUNT and YEARS-TO-REPAY, INTEREST-RATE would vary from 8% to 20% in steps of 1%. The report might be printed as a linear list or, perhaps better, as a set of 51 tables, each giving total interest for all combinations of contract length and interest rate.

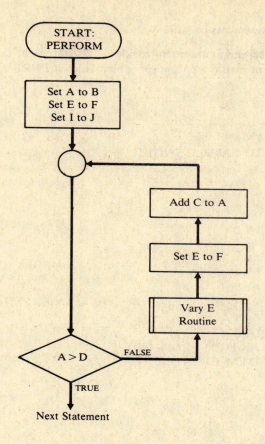

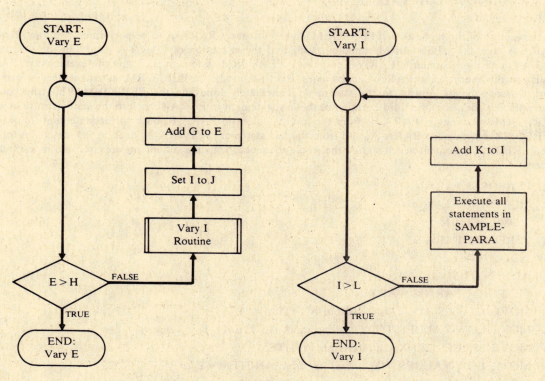

Fig. 7-16

7.13 Nested PERFORM Statements

Just as it is valid to have an IF statement inside an IF statement (Section 7.11), so it is valid to have a PERFORM statement inside a paragraph which is itself PERFORMed.

EXAMPLE 7.38

```
        PERFORM PARA-A
        MOVE "YES" TO SAMPLE-SWITCH
. . . . . . . . . . . . . . . . . . . . . . .
    PARA-A.
        MOVE 1 TO L
        MOVE 2 TO M
        PERFORM PARA-B
        MOVE 3 TO N
        .
. . . . . . . . . . . . . . . . . . . . . .
    PARA-B.
        ADD 1 TO L
        ADD 2 TO M
        PERFORM PARA-C
            VARYING AN-ITEM FROM 1 BY 1
            UNTIL AN-ITEM GREATER THAN 3
        ADD 3 TO P
        .

. . . . . . . . . . . . . . . . . . . . . .
    PARA-C.
        MOVE SPACES TO X
        MOVE LOW-VALUES TO Y
        .
```

The execution of the highest-level PERFORM statement causes PARA-A to be performed one time. However, PARA-A contains a PERFORM statement such that the execution of PARA-A results in the execution of PARA-B one time. Similarly, PARA-B contains a PERFORM statement such that the execution of PARA-B results in the execution of PARA-C *three times*. Recall that when a PERFORM statement finishes executing, control *automatically* returns to the statement immediately following the PERFORM. Thus the computer automatically goes from the third iteration of the last statement in PARA-C back to the statement following the PERFORM statement in PARA-B; from the last statement in PARA-B, back to the statement following the PERFORM statement in PARA-A; and from the last statement in PARA-A, back to the statement following the PERFORM statement which started the whole sequence. Thus the statements are executed in the following order:

1. PERFORM PARA-A
2. MOVE 1 TO L
3. MOVE 2 TO M
4. PERFORM PARA-B
5. ADD 1 TO L
6. ADD 2 TO M
7. PERFORM PARA-C VARYING . . .
8. MOVE SPACES TO X (1st iteration; AN-ITEM = 1)
9. MOVE LOW-VALUES TO Y (1st iteration; AN-ITEM = 1)
10. MOVE SPACES TO X (2nd iteration; AN-ITEM = 2)
11. MOVE LOW-VALUES TO Y (2nd iteration; AN-ITEM = 2)
12. MOVE SPACES TO X (3rd iteration; AN-ITEM = 3)
13. MOVE LOW-VALUES TO Y (3rd iteration; AN-ITEM = 3)

14.   ADD 3 TO P

15.   MOVE 3 TO N

16.   MOVE "YES" TO SAMPLE-SWITCH

The main source of error when using nested PERFORMs involves writing a PERFORM statement which either directly or indirectly PERFORMs itself. When a programming routine *calls itself*, the routine is said to be *recursive*. Recursive PERFORMs are not valid in COBOL (although recursion is possible in other programming languages; e.g., PL/I).

EXAMPLE 7.39

```
PROCEDURE DIVISION.
    OPEN INPUT TEST-FILE
    MOVE "NO" TO END-FILE-SWITCH
    PERFORM READ-AND-VALIDATE
        UNTIL END-FILE-SWITCH EQUAL "YES"
    CLOSE TEST-FILE
    STOP RUN

READ-AND-VALIDATE.
    READ TEST-FILE
        AT END
            MOVE "YES" TO END-FILE-SWITCH

    IF END-FILE-SWITCH EQUAL "NO"
        IF TEST-RECORD-FIELD NUMERIC
            PERFORM VALID-RECORD-PROCESSING
        ELSE
            PERFORM PRODUCE-ERROR-MESSAGE
            PERFORM READ-AND-VALIDATE
```

The very last statement in the paragraph READ-AND-VALIDATE is "PERFORM READ-AND-VALIDATE". Thus, under the right circumstances (TEST-RECORD-FIELD *not* numeric), the PERFORM statement will perform *itself*. This is definitely a programming error, which, in IBM OS/VS COBOL, is likely to show up as an infinite loop.

The programmer evidently thought that if an invalid record is encountered, the proper thing to do is print an error message and proceed to read and process the next record. The strategy is indeed correct—what he or she forgot was that the READ-AND-VALIDATE routine is *already* under control of an earlier PERFORM . . . UNTIL . . . . It is invalid to execute a *second* PERFORM for the paragraph *before the first PERFORM has finished* executing. In this case, PERFORM . . . UNTIL . . . makes the final PERFORM . . . unnecessary, anyway.

EXAMPLE 7.40

```
PROCEDURE DIVISION.
. . . . . . . . . . . . . . . . . . . . .
PARA-A.
    MOVE 1 TO L
    MOVE 2 TO M
    PERFORM PARA-B
    MOVE 3 TO N

    .
. . . . . . . . . . . . . . . . . . . . .
PARA-B.
    ADD 1 TO L
    ADD 2 TO M
    PERFORM PARA-C
    ADD 3 TO P

    .
. . . . . . . . . . . . . . . . . . . . .
```

```
PARA-C.
    MOVE SPACES TO X
    PERFORM PARA-A
    MOVE LOW-VALUES TO Y
```

Here the statement "PERFORM PARA-B" winds up performing itself, but only indirectly, after a series of nested PERFORMs. This is an error likely to manifest itself as an infinite loop. PARA-A contains a PERFORM statement which performs PARA-B (perfectly valid so far). PARA-B contains a PERFORM statement which performs PARA-C (still perfectly valid). PARA-C, however, contains a PERFORM statement which performs PARA-A. *This is invalid* because, during the re-execution of PARA-A, the statement "PERFORM PARA-B" will be executed *while PARA-B is still being PERFORMed.*

To avoid situations like that of Example 7.40 we observe the following

Rule for nested PERFORMs.   A paragraph or SECTION which is being executed under control of a PERFORM statement may not be PERFORMed again until after the controlling PERFORM completely finishes executing.

When control returns from a performed procedure, it is, of course, permissible to perform the procedure again.

7.14   Logical Design: Pseudocode

Pseudocode is often used in place of structured flowcharts to design and document program logic. Because of its similarity to English, pseudocode is sometimes referred to as *structured English.* Since pseudocode is not diagrammatic, it is much easier to produce and to modify than structured flowcharts (which must be carefully drawn).

There is no universal version of pseudocode; the only requirement is that your version be able to represent the three fundamental logic structures: sequence, selection, and iteration. Input, output, and processing of data are described in (condensed) English phrases, and indentation is employed to show the relationships among pseudocode statements.

EXAMPLE 7.41   Sample pseudocode for the basic logic structures:

Sequence
            increment days overdue counter by 1
            compute late charge as 5% of balance due
            build dunning statement for printing

Selection
            if hours worked is greater than 40
            . . . .
            else
            . . . .
            endif

Iteration
            perform until transaction customer ID not equal master customer ID
            . . . .
            endperform

Other approaches are of course possible, so long as they are (1) readily understood and (2) consistent (e.g., if you use perform/endperform for iteration at one place in your pseudocode, use it everywhere).

EXAMPLE 7.42   Give equivalent pseudocode for (*a*) Fig. 7-4, (*b*) Fig. 7-7.

(*a*)   read payment date, payment, due date, old balance
                 if payment date greater than due date
                      call late payment routine
                 else
                      if payment greater than balance
                           calculate refund
                           format check
                           print check
                      else
                           compute new balance as old balance − payment
                      endif
                 endif
                 build cash received line

Note that this pseudocode invokes a predefined process in the statement "call late payment routine". It would also be acceptable to use "perform late payment routine", "execute late payment routine", or any phrase which clearly indicates what is to be done at that point in the algorithm.

(*b*)   set end-cards to "no"
                 set #-employees to zero
                 read card-file at end set end-cards to "yes"
                 perform until end-cards equal "yes"
                      increment #-employees by 1
                      move name, regular hours, and overtime hours to output areas
                      compute total-hours as regular hours + overtime hours
                      print time listing line with name, regular hours, overtime hours, and
                         total hours
                      read card-file at end set end-cards to "yes"
                 endperform
                 print #-employees
                 stop

The pseudocode version is much more compact than the structured flowchart. Notice that pseudocode statements to be repeated in an iteration structure are written between the "perform until..." and "endperform" statements. In the COBOL translation, the statements to be repeated must, of course, be written as a separate paragraph which is "PERFORMed... UNTIL...". (See Appendix C for COBOL '80.)

Most programmers prefer pseudocode to structured flowcharts. Either way, program logic should be designed *before* any COBOL code is written. The PROCEDURE DIVISION should in fact be coded using the pseudocode or structured flowchart as a guide.

Much debugging time can be saved if the pseudocode or structured flowchart is *desk checked* before COBOL coding begins. To desk check means to pretend you are the computer and actually follow the algorithm step by step, processing some test data and producing results. If these results are correct, the algorithm should be correct. If it is then correctly translated into COBOL, the COBOL program should also be correct.

7.15   Logical Design: Decision Tables

Structured flowcharts and pseudocode both can become cumbersome when complicated (e.g., deeply nested) selection structures are required by an algorithm. A *decision table* is a diagram which conveniently summarizes *complicated decision procedures*; more precisely, it is the truth table (Section 7.9) for a set of (complicated) logical statements (called *actions*) which are compounded from a set of simple statements (called *conditions*). The layout of a decision table is shown in Fig. 7-17.

condition stub	conditions
action stub	actions

Fig. 7-17

EXAMPLE 7.43 Figure 7-18 is a decision table pertaining to a credit purchase from a retail store. The condition stub lists three conditions, each of which can be true (yes = "Y") or false (no = "N"). Note that all possible combinations of truth and falsity of the three conditions are represented in the $2^3 = 8$ condition columns. (For n conditions there would be 2^n columns.) The action stub lists three possible actions which can be taken regarding a purchase. (It is accidental that the number of actions equals the number of conditions here.) In each column, an "×" is placed opposite each action which should be taken for that particular combination of truth values. See Problem 7.91 for pseudocode equivalent to this decision table; the decision table is much easier to comprehend than the pseudocode.

Account Active	Y	Y	Y	Y	N	N	N	N
Last Month's Payment Received	Y	Y	N	N	Y	Y	N	N
Purchase Is Within Credit Limit	Y	N	Y	N	Y	N	Y	N
Approve Purchase	×	×	×					
Refer Customer to Credit Office		×	×					
Disapprove Purchase				×	×	×	×	×

Fig. 7-18

Review Questions

7.1   What is meant by "program logic"?

7.2   What are the three basic logic structures?

7.3   What is a structured flowchart? How is it used?

7.4   What is the purpose of each of the standard flowcharting symbols discussed in the text?

7.5   Illustrate how the sequence structure is flowcharted.

7.6   Illustrate how the selection structure is flowcharted.

7.7   Illustrate how the iteration structure can be flowcharted.

7.8   Illustrate how the three basic logic structures can be combined in a flowchart.

7.9   What is a "DO WHILE" structure?

7.10   How is the selection structure implemented in COBOL?

7.11   How may "NEXT SENTENCE" be used?

7.12   Explain the importance of the period in an IF statement.

7.13   Explain the syntax and use of the class condition.

7.14   When is a data item NUMERIC?   ALPHABETIC?

7.15   Which data items should a COBOL program validate?

7.16   What happens if invalid numeric data are used in a calculation or a relation condition?

7.17   When should input data *not* be validated?

7.18   Explain the syntax and use of the relation condition.

7.19   How are the relations "less than or equal to" and "greater than or equal to" implemented in COBOL?

7.20   Explain the rules by which two numeric items are compared in COBOL.

7.21   Explain how nonnumeric items are compared in COBOL.

7.22   What combinations of data items are invalid in relation conditions?

7.23   Explain the syntax and use of the sign condition.

7.24   List three advantages of using condition-name conditions in place of relation conditions.

7.25   How are condition-names defined?

7.26   How does one evaluate a compound condition formed by means of the logical operators AND, OR, NOT?

7.27   When should parentheses be used in compound conditions?

7.28   What rules are followed if parentheses are not used in a compound condition?

7.29   Give the rules for abbreviating compound relation conditions. When should abbreviation be used? When not?

7.30   What is meant by a "nested IF"?

7.31   Explain how IF and ELSE clauses are paired in a nested IF.

7.32   Explain the role of indentation when coding nested IFs.

7.33   Explain the use of NEXT SENTENCE in a nested IF.

7.34   Explain the case structure.

7.35   What is a "linear IF"? Explain how it is used to implement a case structure.

7.36   Discuss the syntaxes of the four varieties of the PERFORM statement.

7.37   Explain the THRU option of PERFORM. Why should it be avoided?

7.38   How is PERFORM . . . UNTIL . . . used to implement the iteration structure?

7.39   What happens if the UNTIL condition becomes true in the middle of the PERFORMance of the paragraph?

7.40   What is an "infinite loop"?

7.41   Is it possible for a paragraph to be PERFORMed zero times? How?

7.42   Discuss the differences between PERFORM . . . VARYING . . . , PERFORM . . . VARYING . . . AFTER . . . , PERFORM . . . VARYING . . . AFTER . . . AFTER . . .

7.43   Discuss the difference between GREATER THAN and EQUAL, with respect to the number of iterations accomplished by a PERFORM . . . UNTIL . . . .

7.44   What is meant by a "nested PERFORM"?

7.45   Give a "Thou Shalt Not" for nested PERFORMs.

7.46   What is "pseudocode", and why is it often preferred over structured flowcharts?

7.47   Write pseudocode and draw a structured flowchart for each PERFORM in Problem 7.42.

7.48   What is a "desk check"?

7.49   Explain the use of decision tables. How are they drawn?

Solved Problems

7.50   Code Fig. 7-19 in COBOL.

```
        IF AGE IS GREATER THAN 12
            MOVE 4.00 TO FARE
        ELSE
            MOVE 3.00 TO FARE
        .

        ADD 1 TO NUMBER-ADMITTED
```

Note the presence of a structured period at the end of the IF . . . ELSE . . . statement.

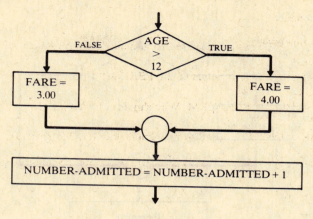

Fig. 7-19

7.51   Code Fig. 7-20 in COBOL.

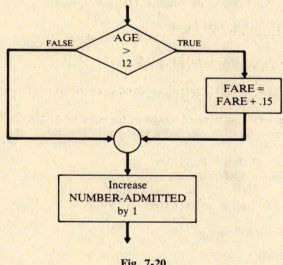

Fig. 7-20

Most COBOL programmers would write

        IF AGE GREATER THAN 12
            ADD .15 TO FARE

        ADD 1 TO NUMBER-ADMITTED

Some shops prefer that every IF have a matching ELSE:

        IF AGE GREATER THAN 12
            ADD .15 TO FARE
        ELSE
            NEXT SENTENCE

        ADD 1 TO NUMBER-ADMITTED

7.52   Code Fig. 7-21 in COBOL.

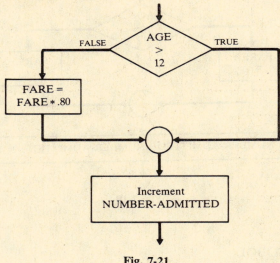

Fig. 7-21

If NEXT SENTENCE is used, the solution is straightforward:

```
IF AGE GREATER THAN 12
    NEXT SENTENCE
ELSE
    COMPUTE FARE = FARE * .80
.
ADD 1 TO NUMBER-ADMITTED
```

Some programmers would find it more elegant to eliminate "NEXT SENTENCE" by negating the condition in Fig. 7-21 and interchanging TRUE and FALSE. This would give the equivalent code

```
IF AGE NOT GREATER THAN 12
    COMPUTE FARE = FARE * .80
.
ADD 1 TO NUMBER-ADMITTED
```

7.53   What is wrong with the following?

```
IF CUSTOMER-TYPE EQUAL "3"
    MOVE ZERO TO SHIPPING-DISCOUNT
ELSE
    PERFORM DETERMINE-SHIPPING-DISCOUNT
ADD SHIPPING-DISCOUNT TO TOTAL-DISCOUNT
PERFORM FORMAT-INVOICE
```

If the indentation correctly indicates the desired processing, then a period is required to end the IF statement, as follows:

```
IF CUSTOMER-TYPE EQUAL "3"
    MOVE ZERO TO SHIPPING-DISCOUNT
ELSE
    PERFORM DETERMINE-SHIPPING-DISCOUNT
.
ADD SHIPPING-DISCOUNT TO TOTAL-DISCOUNT
PERFORM FORMAT-INVOICE
```

Without the period, the ADD and PERFORM statements are considered to be part of the ELSE routine (see Appendix C for COBOL '80).

7.54 Flowchart the program segment of Problem 7.53 (*a*) without, and (*b*) with, the period.

See Fig. 7-22.

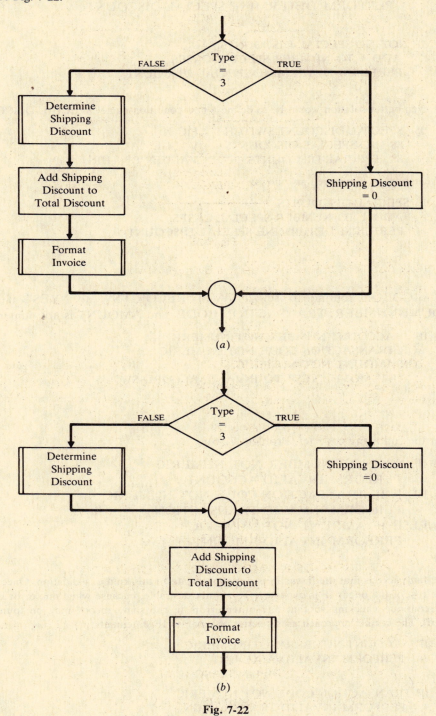

(*a*)

(*b*)

Fig. 7-22

7.55 Rewrite the following IF statement without using NEXT SENTENCE.

```
IF NO-SPECIAL-DISCOUNTS
   NEXT SENTENCE
```

```
ELSE
    ADD 1 TO NUMBER-SPECIAL-CASES
    PERFORM DETERMINE-SPECIAL-DISCOUNT
    .

IF NOT NO-SPECIAL-DISCOUNTS
    ADD 1 TO NUMBER-SPECIAL-CASES
    PERFORM DETERMINE-SPECIAL-DISCOUNT
    .
```

An even better solution would be to define a new condition-name, SPECIAL-DISCOUNTS:

```
05  SPECIAL-DISCOUNT-SWITCH     PIC X.
    88  NO-SPECIAL-DISCOUNTS    VALUE "A".
    88  SPECIAL-DISCOUNTS       VALUE "B" THRU "G".
```

"NOT" can now be eliminated as follows:

```
IF SPECIAL-DISCOUNTS
    ADD 1 TO NUMBER-SPECIAL-CASES
    PERFORM DETERMINE-SPECIAL-DISCOUNT
    .
```

7.56 Write a COBOL routine to set INVALID-RECORD-SW to "YES" if any one of ACCOUNT-NUMBER, TRANSACTION-CODE, and AMOUNT is not numeric.

```
IF    ACCOUNT-NUMBER NOT NUMERIC
   OR TRANSACTION-CODE NOT NUMERIC
   OR AMOUNT NOT NUMERIC
           MOVE "YES" TO INVALID-RECORD-SW
```

7.57 Correct the following code (cf. Problem 7.56):

```
IF ACCOUNT-NUMBER NOT NUMERIC
    PERFORM INVALID-ACCOUNT
ELSE IF TRANSACTION-CODE NOT NUMERIC
    PERFORM INVALID-TRANSACTION
ELSE IF AMOUNT NOT NUMERIC
    PERFORM INVALID-AMOUNT
    .
```

The fault here is that the linear IF is not appropriate to this kind of validation. Once a condition is true, the rest of the linear IF is bypassed. This is not desirable, because when one error is detected, we wish to continue checking so that any other errors in the same record may be found (and hence corrected). The correct approach uses a series of separate IF statements:

```
IF ACCOUNT-NUMBER NOT NUMERIC
    PERFORM INVALID-ACCOUNT
    .

IF TRANSACTION-CODE NOT NUMERIC
    PERFORM INVALID-TRANSACTION
    .

IF AMOUNT NOT NUMERIC
    PERFORM INVALID-AMOUNT
    .
```

7.58 Given the following PICTUREs and contents, tell whether the data item is NUMERIC, ALPHABETIC, or neither:

	PICTURE	Contents
(a)	S99	−82
(b)	XXX	"E T"
(c)	S99	82
(d)	99	82
(e)	99	+82
(f)	XXX	"C3B"
(g)	XXX	"　　"

　　(a) NUMERIC; (b) ALPHABETIC; (c) neither (when PICTURE is signed, contents must be signed); (d) NUMERIC; (e) neither (when PICTURE is unsigned, contents must be unsigned); (f) neither; (g) ALPHABETIC (spaces are allowed).

7.59 Tell whether the following data items should be validated before processing: (a) the amount of a bank deposit as keyed by the teller, (b) the mailing name for a magazine subscriber as keyed by data entry, (c) the amount of a credit purchase for a customer as keyed by a retail clerk, (d) the previous credit balance for the customer in (c) as read from a customer master file on disk, (e) the previous account balance for the account in (a) as read from a customer master file on disk, (f) the quantity of an item ordered by a customer as keyed from a source document by data entry, (g) the price of the item in (f) as read from an inventory master file on disk.

(a) This field is both critically important and keyed input. Hence, the first program which processes it should validate the field.

(b) This field is keyed input, but it is not critically important. The magazine will probably get to the proper destination even if the name is somewhat garbled. Also, a class test for ALPHABETIC data would only detect nonnumeric characters, not misspellings. Hence it is probably not worth validating this field.

(c) Should be validated the first time it is processed, since it is both critical data and keyed input.

(d) Presumably, all data placed in the master file have already been validated; it would be a waste of computer time to revalidate this field.

(e) Same as (d).

(f) Should be validated the first time it is processed.

(g) Same as (d).

7.60 Show the following algebraic relations as they would appear in a COBOL IF statement.

$$(a)\ a + b \le 10 \quad (b)\ 5a \ge \frac{b}{3} \quad (c)\ a \ne b \quad (d)\ \frac{a}{b} \le c \quad (e)\ a \ge b$$

(a)　　　IF A + B NOT GREATER THAN 10

(b)　　　IF 5 * A NOT LESS THAN B / 3

(c)　　　IF A NOT EQUAL TO B

(d)　　　IF A / B NOT GREATER THAN C

(e)　　　IF A NOT LESS THAN B

7.61 Indicate whether item A is less than, equal to, or greater than, item B:

	(a)	(b)	(c)	(d)	(e)	(f)	(g)
A	CAD	+72	HI	−003	−4	+34.5	+34.00
B	COB	0072	HIGH	−3	+4	+34	+34

(a) A < B (alphabetical order preserved); (b) A = B (algebraic comparison); (c) A < B (HI = HI*bb*); (d) A = B (algebraic comparison); (e) A < B (algebraic comparison); (f) A > B (algebraic comparison); (g) A = B (algebraic comparison).

7.62 Rewrite the following statements using sign conditions instead of relation conditions: (a) IF AMOUNT-DUE IS GREATER THAN ZERO ...; (b) PERFORM POST-GENERAL-LEDGER UNTIL LEDGER-ACCOUNT IS EQUAL TO ZERO; (c) IF QUANTITY-ON-HAND IS LESS THAN ZERO ....

(a) IF AMOUNT-DUE IS POSITIVE ...; (b) PERFORM POST-GENERAL-LEDGER UNTIL LEDGER-ACCOUNT IS ZERO; (c) IF QUANTITY-ON-HAND NEGATIVE .... Note the omission of the optional "IS" from (c).

7.63 Rewrite the following data definitions and IF ... PERFORM ... statements to use condition-names in place of relation conditions:

(a)   05 CUSTOMER-ID   PIC X(5).

      IF CUSTOMER-ID NOT LESS THAN ZERO AND NOT GREATER
          THAN "11111"
      PERFORM PROCESS-PREFERRED-CUSTOMER

(b)   05 TRANSACTION-CODE   PIC X.

      IF TRANSACTION-CODE EQUAL "1"
         PERFORM PROCESS-DEPOSIT
      ELSE IF TRANSACTION-CODE EQUAL "2"
         PERFORM PROCESS-WITHDRAWAL

(c)   05 REGION-CODE   PIC X.

      IF REGION-CODE EQUAL "A" OR "B" OR "C"
         PERFORM SHIP-TO-NORTHEAST
      ELSE IF REGION-CODE GREATER THAN "C"
         AND LESS THAN "L"
         PERFORM SHIP-TO-SOUTHEAST
      ELSE IF REGION-CODE EQUAL "M" OR "P"
         PERFORM SHIP-WEST

(d)   05 YEAR-IN-SCHOOL   PIC 99.

      IF YEAR-IN-SCHOOL EQUAL 6
         PERFORM PROCESS-6TH-GRADER
      ELSE IF YEAR-IN-SCHOOL NOT LESS THAN 9 AND NOT
         GREATER THAN 12
      PERFORM PROCESS-HIGH-SCHOOL

(e)   05   DEPRECIATION-TYPE   PIC 9.

             IF DEPRECIATION-TYPE EQUAL 1 OR 2 OR 3
                  PERFORM USE-STRAIGHT-LINE-VALUE
             ELSE IF DEPRECIATION-TYPE EQUAL 4
                  PERFORM USE-DOUBLE-DECLINING-VALUE

                  .

(a)   05   CUSTOMER-ID   PIC X(5).
        88   PREFERRED-CUSTOMER   VALUE ZERO THRU "11111".

        IF PREFERRED-CUSTOMER
             PERFORM PROCESS-PREFERRED-CUSTOMER

             .

(b)   05   TRANSACTION-CODE   PIC X.
        88   DEPOSIT   VALUE "1".
        88   WITHDRAWAL   VALUE "2".

        IF DEPOSIT
             PERFORM PROCESS-DEPOSIT
        ELSE IF WITHDRAWAL
             PERFORM PROCESS-WITHDRAWAL

             .

(c)   05   REGION-CODE   PIC X.
        88   NORTHEAST-REGION   VALUE "A" THRU "C".
        88   SOUTHEAST-REGION   VALUE "D" THRU "K".
        88   WESTERN-REGION   VALUE "M" "P".

        IF NORTHEAST-REGION
             PERFORM SHIP-TO-NORTHEAST
        ELSE IF SOUTHEAST-REGION
             PERFORM SHIP-TO-SOUTHEAST
        ELSE IF WESTERN-REGION
             PERFORM SHIP-WEST

             .

(d)   05   YEAR-IN-SCHOOL   PIC 99.
        88   6TH-GRADE   VALUE 6.
        88   HIGH-SCHOOL   VALUE 9 THRU 12.

        IF 6TH-GRADE
             PERFORM PROCESS-6TH-GRADER
        ELSE IF HIGH-SCHOOL
             PERFORM PROCESS-HIGH-SCHOOL

             .

(e)   05   DEPRECIATION-TYPE   PIC 9.
        88   STRAIGHT-LINE   VALUE 1 THRU 3.
        88   DOUBLE-DECLINING   VALUE 4.

        IF STRAIGHT-LINE
             PERFORM USE-STRAIGHT-LINE-VALUE
        ELSE IF DOUBLE-DECLINING
             PERFORM USE-DOUBLE-DECLINING-VALUE

             .

7.64   Correct the following statements, which misuse condition-names from Problem 7.63.

    (*a*)   IF PREFERRED-CUSTOMER EQUAL "00111"

    (*b*)   IF DEPOSIT
                        MOVE SPACES TO WITHDRAWAL

    (*c*)   IF HIGH-SCHOOL EQUAL 10

    (*a*)   IF CUSTOMER-ID EQUAL "00111"

    A condition-name may not be used in place of a data item anywhere in the program. A condition-name only may abbreviate a specific relation condition.

    (*b*)   IF DEPOSIT
                        MOVE SPACES TO TRANSACTION-CODE

    As in (*a*), the data item must be used in the MOVE statement, not the condition-name.

    (*c*)   IF YEAR-IN-SCHOOL EQUAL 10

    There is no condition-name for the relation 'YEAR-IN-SCHOOL EQUAL 10'; hence the condition must be written out in the IF statement. Alternatively, a condition-name condition could be set up:

            05   YEAR-IN-SCHOOL   PIC 99.
            88   10TH-GRADE   VALUE 10.

            IF 10TH-GRADE

7.65   There is a rule in COBOL which states that the VALUE clause cannot be used in the FILE SECTION. Does this apply to condition-names?

    No, the rule applies to *data items* in the FILE SECTION. The VALUE clause can (and must) be used in the FILE SECTION when defining condition-names (level-88 items).

7.66   Let A, B, C, and D be condition-names. Suppose A and B are true, while C and D are false. Indicate whether the following compound conditions are true or false:

(*a*) A AND B OR A AND C		(*b*) A AND (B OR A) AND C	
(*c*) A AND NOT C OR D		(*d*) A AND NOT (C OR D)	
(*e*) A AND NOT C OR NOT D		(*f*) (A AND NOT C) OR NOT D	
(*g*) A AND NOT (C OR NOT D)		(*h*) A AND C OR B AND D	
(*i*) A AND B AND C		(*j*) A OR B OR C OR D	
(*k*) A OR C AND B OR D		(*l*) (A OR C) AND (B OR D)	
(*m*) A AND C OR B OR D			

(*a*) In the absence of parentheses, ANDs are done first (left to right), followed by ORs. Hence the expression is evaluated as: (A AND B) OR (A AND C). (A AND B) is true; hence, (A AND B) OR . . . is true.

(*b*) The parenthetical expression is evaluated first: (B OR A) is true. Then the ANDs are carried out left to right: A AND (B OR A) is true; this result is then ANDed with C to yield false (the final result).

(*c*) NOT C is evaluated first, producing the result true. A AND NOT C is evaluated next to give true. D is ORed with this result to give true.

(*d*) (C OR D) gives false, so NOT (C OR D) gives true. This is ANDed with A to give true.

(*e*) NOT is done first, from left to right: NOT C gives true; NOT D gives true. A is then ANDed with NOT C to give true. This result is ORed with NOT D to give true.

(f)   (A AND NOT C) OR NOT D   (g)   A AND NOT (C OR NOT D)

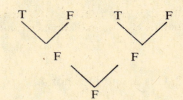

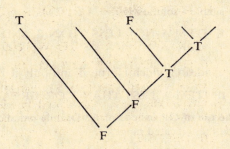

(h)   A AND C OR B AND D   (i)   A AND B AND C

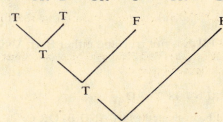

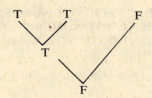

(j)   A OR B   OR   C   OR   D   (k)   A   OR   C AND B   OR   D

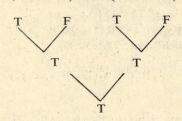

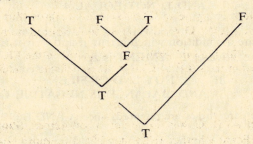

(l)   (A OR C) AND (B OR D)   (m)   A AND C   OR   B   OR   D

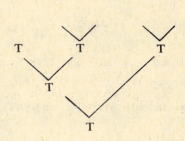

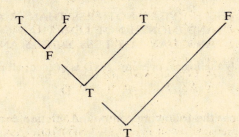

7.67   Let A, B, C, and D be condition-names. Rewrite the following compound conditions with parentheses to show the order in which operations will be carried out:

(a)   NOT A OR B AND NOT C   (b)   NOT A OR NOT B AND NOT C
(c)   A AND C OR B   (d)   A OR B AND C

(a)   (NOT A) OR (B AND (NOT C))   (b)   (NOT A) OR ((NOT B) AND (NOT C))
(c)   (A AND C) OR B   (d)   A OR (B AND C)

7.68   Write a condition which is true if and only if ITEM-A is between 3 and 27 inclusive.

The simplest solution is:

IF ITEM-A NOT LESS THAN 3 AND NOT GREATER THAN 27

7.69   Write a condition which is true if and only if ITEM-A is *not* between 3 and 27 inclusive.

IF ITEM-A LESS THAN 3 OR GREATER THAN 27

Notice the use of OR instead of AND: only *one* of the simple conditions has to be true for ITEM-A to be outside the indicated range.

7.70   Write a condition which is true if and only if any of OLD-BALANCE, PAYMENT, and PAYMENT-DATE are not numeric.

IF   OLD-BALANCE NOT NUMERIC
OR PAYMENT NOT NUMERIC
OR PAYMENT-DATE NOT NUMERIC

7.71   Write a condition which is true if and only if A is 1, B is 2, C is 3, and D is not 4.

IF   A EQUAL 1
AND B EQUAL 2
AND C EQUAL 3
AND D NOT EQUAL 4

7.72   Write a condition which is true if and only if END-OF-FILE is not true and either BALANCE is negative or PAYMENT is zero.

IF   NOT END-OF-FILE
AND (BALANCE IS NEGATIVE OR PAYMENT IS ZERO)

The parentheses are required, since A AND B OR C would be evaluated as (A AND B) OR C.

7.73   Write a condition which is true if and only if YEAR is between 82 and 85, MONTH is between 6 and 8, and DAY is between 5 and 20.

IF   (YEAR NOT LESS THAN 82 AND NOT GREATER THAN 85)
AND (MONTH NOT LESS THAN 6 AND NOT GREATER THAN 8)
AND (DAY NOT LESS THAN 5 AND NOT GREATER THAN 20)

Since only the logical operator AND is needed, all parentheses are optional (although they do improve clarity).

7.74   Show how the following compound relation conditions may be abbreviated:

(*a*)   A NOT EQUAL 1 AND A NOT EQUAL 2 AND A NOT EQUAL 3
(*b*)   A EQUAL 7 OR A EQUAL 8 AND B EQUAL 8
(*c*)   A EQUAL 1 OR A EQUAL 2 AND A EQUAL 3
(*d*)   A EQUAL 1 OR A EQUAL 2 OR A LESS THAN 9 OR B LESS THAN 10
(*e*)   A EQUAL 1 OR A LESS THAN 5 OR A GREATER THAN 8
(*f*)   A EQUAL B AND A LESS THAN C AND A LESS THAN D

(*a*)   A NOT EQUAL 1 AND 2 AND 3
(*b*)   A EQUAL 7 OR 8 AND B EQUAL 8

(c)   A EQUAL 1 OR 2 AND 3 (which can be logically reduced to A EQUAL 1)

(d)   A EQUAL 1 OR 2 OR LESS THAN 9 OR B LESS THAN 10

(e)   A EQUAL 1 OR LESS THAN 5 OR GREATER THAN 8

(f)   A EQUAL B AND LESS THAN C AND D

7.75   Write the following compound relation conditions in unabbreviated form:

(a)   A EQUAL B OR C AND LESS THAN D

(b)   A GREATER THAN B OR D AND C OR LESS THAN B OR D

(c)   A LESS THAN B AND D AND C

(d)   A EQUAL B OR D AND C

(e)   A EQUAL B OR C AND LESS THAN D OR GREATER THAN E

(f)   A NOT EQUAL B OR D AND NOT LESS THAN C AND E

(a)   A EQUAL B OR A EQUAL C AND A LESS THAN D

(b)   A GREATER THAN B OR A GREATER THAN D AND A GREATER THAN C
           OR A LESS THAN B OR A LESS THAN D

(c)   A LESS THAN B AND A LESS THAN D AND A LESS THAN C

(d)   A EQUAL B OR A EQUAL D AND A EQUAL C

(e)   A EQUAL B OR A EQUAL C AND A LESS THAN D OR A GREATER THAN E

(f)   A NOT EQUAL B OR A NOT EQUAL D AND A NOT LESS THAN C AND A NOT
           LESS THAN E

7.76   Revise the following misleading indentation to show how the nested IFs would actually be
           executed:

(a)   IF NOT END-OF-FILE
               IF CREDIT-LINE-OK
                   PERFORM DETERMINE-CREDIT-LIMIT
                   PERFORM PRINT-TERMS
           ELSE
               PERFORM PRINT-FINAL-TOTALS

(b)   IF PAYMENT NOT NUMERIC
               PERFORM INVALID-PAYMENT
               IF DATE2 NOT NUMERIC
                   PERFORM INVALID-DATE2
           ELSE
               PERFORM APPLY-PAYMENT
               IF BALANCE NEGATIVE
                   PERFORM GIVE-REFUND
           ELSE
               PERFORM FILE-BALANCE

(c)   IF A EQUAL B
           MOVE 1 TO A
           MOVE 2 TO B.
           MOVE 3 TO C

```
        IF  B  EQUAL  C
            MOVE  4  TO  D
            IF  C  EQUAL  D
            MOVE  5  TO  E
        ELSE
            MOVE  6  TO  F.
```

(*a*)
```
        IF  NOT  END-OF-FILE
            IF  CREDIT-LINE-OK
                PERFORM  DETERMINE-CREDIT-LIMIT
                PERFORM  PRINT-TERMS
            ELSE
                PERFORM  PRINT-FINAL-TOTALS
```

(*b*)
```
        IF  PAYMENT  NOT  NUMERIC
            PERFORM  INVALID-PAYMENT
            IF  DATE2  NOT  NUMERIC
                PERFORM  INVALID-DATE2
            ELSE
                PERFORM  APPLY-PAYMENT
                IF  BALANCE  NEGATIVE
                    PERFORM  GIVE-REFUND
                ELSE
                    PERFORM  FILE-BALANCE
```

Here, as in (*a*), each ELSE clause is paired with the first preceding unmatched IF.

(*c*)
```
        IF  A  EQUAL  B
            MOVE  1  TO  A
            MOVE  2  TO  B

        MOVE  3  TO  C
        IF  B  EQUAL  C
            MOVE  4  TO  D
            IF  C  EQUAL  D
                MOVE  5  TO  E
            ELSE
                MOVE  6  TO  F
```

Note the importance of the period in changing the meaning of a nested IF. Without the period after "MOVE 2 TO B", the sequence would be executed as follows:

```
        IF  A  EQUAL  B
            MOVE  1  TO  A
            MOVE  2  TO  B
            MOVE  3  TO  C
            IF  B  EQUAL  C
                MOVE  4  TO  D
                IF  C  EQUAL  D
                    MOVE  5  TO  E
                ELSE
                    MOVE  6  TO  F
```

7.77   Rewrite the following without using NEXT SENTENCE; also correct the indentation:

```
IF A EQUAL B
    NEXT SENTENCE
ELSE
    PERFORM PARA-1
    PERFORM PARA-2.
    PERFORM PARA-3


IF A NOT EQUAL B
    PERFORM PARA-1
    PERFORM PARA-2


PERFORM PARA-3
```

7.78   Code the following case structure in a paragraph using a linear IF:

REGION-CODE Value	*Action*
1	PERFORM SHIP-NORTHEAST
2	PERFORM SHIP-SOUTHEAST
3	PERFORM SHIP-NORTHEAST
4	PERFORM SHIP-WEST

```
DETERMINE-SHIPPING.
    IF REGION-CODE EQUAL 1
        PERFORM SHIP-NORTHEAST
    ELSE IF REGION-CODE EQUAL 2
        PERFORM SHIP-SOUTHEAST
    ELSE IF REGION-CODE EQUAL 3
        PERFORM SHIP-NORTHEAST
    ELSE IF REGION-CODE EQUAL 4
        PERFORM SHIP-WEST
    ELSE
        PERFORM INVALID-CODE
```

or, combining cases,

```
DETERMINE-SHIPPING.
    IF REGION-CODE EQUAL 1 OR 3
        PERFORM SHIP-NORTHEAST
    ELSE IF...
```

7.79   Show how to PERFORM the case structure in Problem 7.78.

```
PERFORM DETERMINE-SHIPPING
```

7.80   Rewrite the following using PERFORM ... UNTIL ...:

```
PERFORM GET-INPUT
PERFORM GET-INPUT
PERFORM GET-INPUT
PERFORM GET-INPUT
```

```
PERFORM GET-INPUT
    VARYING TIMES-COUNTER
        FROM 1 BY 1
    UNTIL TIMES-COUNTER GREATER THAN 4
```

7.81   How many times is GET-INPUT performed?

```
PERFORM GET-INPUT
    VARYING TIMES-COUNTER FROM 1 BY 1
    UNTIL TIMES-COUNTER EQUAL 10
```

Nine times.

7.82   How many times is PARA-A performed?

```
MOVE 10 TO TIMES-COUNTER
PERFORM PARA-A TIMES-COUNTER TIMES
. . . . . . . . . . . . . . . . . . . . . . . . . .

PARA-A.
    MOVE 5 TO TIMES-COUNTER
    MOVE P TO Q
    .
```

PARA-A is performed 10 times. Changing the contents of TIMES-COUNTER after the PERFORM . . . TIMES statement starts executing has no effect on the number of iterations.

7.83   How many times is PARA-A performed?

```
PERFORM PARA-A
    VARYING TIMES-COUNTER FROM 1 BY 1
    UNTIL TIMES-COUNTER GREATER THAN 10

. . . . . . . . . . . . . . . . . . . . . . . . . . .

PARA-A.
    MOVE P TO Q
    MOVE 11 TO TIMES-COUNTER
    .
```

PARA-A is performed one time. When PERFORM . . . VARYING . . . UNTIL . . . is used, any change in the VARYING data item, the BY value, or the UNTIL value *does* affect the number of iterations.

7.84   How many times is PARA-A performed?

```
MOVE 11 TO TIMES-COUNTER
PERFORM PARA-A
    UNTIL TIMES-COUNTER GREATER THAN 10
```

PARA-A is not performed at all; the UNTIL condition is evaluated *before* any PERFORMs.

7.85 How many times is PARA-S performed?

```
001        MOVE ZERO TO TIMES-COUNTER
           PERFORM PARA-S
              UNTIL TIMES-COUNTER GREATER THAN 10
. . . . . . . . . . . . . . . . . . . . . . . . . . . . .
           PARA-S.
              ADD 1 TO TIMES-COUNTER
              DISPLAY TIMES-COUNTER
              .
```

Eleven times: TIMES-COUNTER will DISPLAY the values 1, 2, 3, 4, 5, 6, 7, 8, 9, 10, 11.

7.86 Give the values of ITEM for each execution of PARA-A:

(*a*)   PERFORM PARA-A VARYING ITEM FROM 1 BY 2
               UNTIL ITEM GREATER THAN 8

(*b*)   PERFORM PARA-A
               VARYING ITEM FROM 10 BY −3
               UNTIL ITEM LESS THAN −4

(*c*)   PERFORM PARA-A
               VARYING ITEM FROM 2.7 BY −.4
               UNTIL ITEM NEGATIVE

(*d*)   PERFORM PARA-A
               VARYING ITEM FROM 6 BY 2
               UNTIL ITEM EQUAL 11

(*e*)   PERFORM PARA-A
               VARYING ITEM FROM 5 BY 5
               UNTIL ITEM GREATER THAN 25

(*a*) ITEM = 1, 3, 5, 7; execution stops with ITEM = 9.

(*b*) ITEM = 10, 7, 4, 1, −2; execution stops with ITEM = −5.

(*c*) ITEM = 2.7, 2.3, 1.9, 1.5, 1.1, .7, .3; execution stops with ITEM = −.1.

(*d*) ITEM = 6, 8, 10, 12, 14, 16, . . . , until the operating system limit on time and/or records is exceeded. This is an infinite loop.

(*e*) ITEM = 5, 10, 15, 20, 25; execution stops with ITEM = 30.

7.87 Give the values of A and B for which PARA is performed.

```
           PERFORM PARA
              VARYING A FROM 2 BY 2
                 UNTIL A GREATER THAN 8
              AFTER B FROM 5.5 BY −.5
                 UNTIL B LESS THAN 4.0
```

A	2	2	2	2	4	4	4	4	6	6	6	6	8	8	8	8
B	5.5	5.0	4.5	4.0	5.5	5.0	4.5	4.0	5.5	5.0	4.5	4.0	5.5	5.0	4.5	4.0

Execution of the PERFORM statement ends with B = 5.5 and A = 10.

7.88 Give the values of A, B, and C for which PARA is performed.

```
PERFORM PARA
    VARYING A FROM 2 BY 3
        UNTIL A GREATER THAN 7
    AFTER B FROM 5 BY −1
        UNTIL B LESS THAN 3
    AFTER C FROM 1 BY 1
        UNTIL C GREATER THAN 3
```

A	2	2	2	2	2	2	2	2	2	5	5	5	5	5	5	5	5	5
B	5	5	5	4	4	4	3	3	3	5	5	5	4	4	4	3	3	3
C	1	2	3	1	2	3	1	2	3	1	2	3	1	2	3	1	2	3

Execution of the PERFORM statement ends with A = 8, B = 5, and C = 1.

7.89 Explain what is wrong with the following routines:

(*a*)
```
PERFORM PARA-A
    VARYING ITEM-A FROM 1 BY 1 UNTIL ITEM-A GREATER THAN 10
    VARYING ITEM-B FROM 5 BY 2 UNTIL ITEM-B GREATER THAN 20
```

(*b*)
```
            PERFORM PARA-A THRU PARA-C
    . . . . . . . . . . . . . . . . . . . . . .

PARA-C.
    . . . . . . . . . . . . . . . . . . . . . .

PARA-A.
    . . . . . . . . . . . . . . . . . . . . . .
```

(*c*)
```
            PERFORM PRODUCE-REPORT
                UNTIL END-OF-FILE
    . . . . . . . . . . . . . . . . . . . . . .

PRODUCE-REPORT
    IF INPUT-FIELD NUMERIC
        PERFORM PROCESS-IT
    ELSE
        PERFORM INVALID-FIELD
    .
    . . . . . . . . . . . . . . . . . . . . . .
INVALID-FIELD.
    PERFORM WRITE-ERROR-MESSAGE
    PERFORM READ-NEXT-RECORD
    PERFORM PRODUCE-REPORT
    .
```

(*a*) Syntax error; PERFORM with multiple varying items must be written PERFORM . . . VARYING . . . AFTER . . . AFTER . . . .

(*b*) Syntax error: the THRU paragraph (or SECTION) must *physically follow* the first paragraph (SECTION) in the range.

(*c*) Logic error: a recursive PERFORM. The initial PERFORM statement performs PRODUCE-REPORT. Depending on the validity of the input, PRODUCE-REPORT may then PERFORM INVALID-FIELD. INVALID-FIELD then performs PRODUCE-REPORT. It is thus possible for "PERFORM INVALID-FIELD" in PRODUCE-REPORT to be executed again *before* its first execution is finished. Execution of a PERFORM statement which hasn't yet finished a previous execution (because control hasn't returned from the performed paragraph) usually results in an infinite loop.

7.90 Write pseudocode for a program to balance a checkbook. The algorithm inputs the old-balance, followed by a set of transaction-codes ("D" for deposit, "C" for check amount) and amounts, until end-of-file. Output the total-deposits, total-checks, and new-balance.

```
read old-balance
set total-deposits, total-checks to zero
set end-sw to "no"
read transaction-code, amount
    at end set end-sw to "yes"
perform until end-sw = "yes"
    if transaction-code = "D"
        add amount to total-deposits
    else
        if transaction-code = "C"
            add amount to total-checks
        else
            print "invalid transaction code"
        endif
    endif
    read transaction-code, amount
        at end set end-sw = "yes"
endperform
new-balance = old-balance + total-deposits − total-checks
print old-balance, total-deposits, total-checks, new-balance
stop
```

7.91 Write pseudocode to implement the decision table of Fig. 7-18.

```
if account not active
    perform disapprove-purchase
else
    if last month's payment received
        if purchase not greater than credit limit
            perform approve-purchase
        else
            perform approve-purchase
            perform refer-to-credit-office
        endif
    else
        if purchase not greater than credit limit
            perform approve-purchase
            perform refer-to-credit-office
        else
            perform disapprove-purchase
        endif
    endif
endif
```

While the above solution is straightforward, other, more compact, solutions are possible:

```
if account not active
     perform disapprove-purchase
else
     if last payment received and purchase within credit limit
          perform approve-purchase
     else
          if last payment not received and purchase not within credit limit
               perform disapprove-purchase
          else
               perform approve-purchase
               perform refer-to-credit-office
          endif
     endif
endif
```

7.92   Given the following conditions and actions, draw your own decision table for accepting a job in data processing.

<table>
<tr><td>Conditions</td><td></td><td>Actions</td></tr>
<tr><td>(1)</td><td>Salary and benefits acceptable</td><td>(1)</td><td>Accept job</td></tr>
<tr><td>(2)</td><td>Further education/training available</td><td>(2)</td><td>Refuse job</td></tr>
<tr><td>(3)</td><td>Good advancement opportunities</td><td>(3)</td><td>Negotiate for better terms</td></tr>
</table>

See Fig. 7-23 for a possible solution.

Salary	T	T	T	T	F	F	F	F
Education	T	T	F	F	T	T	F	F
Advancement	T	F	T	F	T	F	T	F
Accept	×	×	×	×	×			
Refuse						×	×	×
Negotiate				×	×	×	×	

Fig. 7-23

Supplementary Problems

7.93   Write a program which can be used by a bank to print out a payment schedule for mortgage customers. The program inputs the original principal, the annual interest rate (as a percentage), and the desired monthly payment. The program will print a report listing the following information for each month of the payback period: (i) payment number, (ii) old balance (before this payment), (iii) amount of payment, (iv) amount of payment on principal [= (iii) − (v)], (v) amount of payment for interest [= (ii) × rate/12], (vi) new balance [= (ii) − (iv)]. The program should print 20 double-spaced detail lines per page. Use appropriate column headings, page numbers, run date, etc.   *Ans.*   See Fig. 7-24; sample output in Fig. 7-25.

```
00001              IDENTIFICATION DIVISION.
00002
00003              PROGRAM-ID.  MORTGAGE.
00004
00005              AUTHOR. LARRY NEWCOMER.
00006              INSTALLATION. PENN STATE UNIVERSITY -- YORK CAMPUS.
00007              DATE-WRITTEN.  MAY 1983.
00008              SECURITY.   NONE.
00009
00010              ENVIRONMENT DIVISION.
00011
00012              CONFIGURATION SECTION.
00013              SOURCE-COMPUTER.  IBM-3081.
00014              OBJECT-COMPUTER.  IBM-3081.
00015
00016              INPUT-OUTPUT SECTION.
00017              FILE-CONTROL.
00018
00019                  SELECT TERMS-FILE
00020                      ASSIGN TO TERMS
00021                      ORGANIZATION IS SEQUENTIAL
00022                      ACCESS IS SEQUENTIAL
00023                      .
00024                  SELECT PAYMENT-REPORT
00025                      ASSIGN TO PAYMENTS
00026                      ORGANIZATION IS SEQUENTIAL
00027                      ACCESS IS SEQUENTIAL
00028                      .
00029
00030              DATA DIVISION.
00031
00032              FILE SECTION.
00033
00034              FD  TERMS-FILE
00035                  RECORD CONTAINS 80 CHARACTERS
00036                  LABEL RECORDS ARE OMITTED
00037                  .
00038
00039              01  TERMS-RECORD.
00040                  05  TERMS-PRINCIPAL        PIC S9(7)V99.
00041                  05  TERMS-INTEREST-RATE    PIC SV999.
00042                  05  TERMS-PAYMENT          PIC S9(5)V99.
00043                  05  FILLER                 PIC X(61).
00044
00045              FD  PAYMENT-REPORT
00046                  RECORD CONTAINS 132 CHARACTERS
00047                  LABEL RECORDS ARE OMITTED
00048                      LINAGE IS 60
00049                          WITH FOOTING AT 59
00050                          LINES AT TOP 3
00051                          LINES AT BOTTOM 3
00052                  .
00053
00054              01  PAYMENT-RECORD            PIC X(132).
00055
00056              WORKING-STORAGE SECTION.
00057
00058              01  WS-SWITCHES-AND-COUNTERS.
00059                  05  WS-PAGE-NUMBER         PIC S999        COMP-3.
00060                  05  WS-TERMS-FILE-END-SW   PIC XXX.
00061                      88  EMPTY-TERMS-FILE   VALUE "YES".
00062                  05  WS-FINAL-PAYMENT-SW    PIC XXX.
00063                      88  FINAL-PAYMENT      VALUE "YES".
00064                      88  REGULAR-PAYMENT    VALUE "NO".
00065
00066              01  WS-COMPUTATION-WORK-AREAS.
```

Fig. 7-24

```
00067          05   WS-INTEREST-AMOUNT          PIC S9(5)V99    COMP-3.
00068          05   WS-PAYMENT-AMOUNT           PIC S9(5)V99    COMP-3.
00069          05   WS-BALANCE                  PIC S9(7)V99    COMP-3.
00070          05   WS-PAYMENT-NUMBER           PIC S9(3)       COMP-3.
00071          05   WS-INTEREST-RATE            PIC SV999       COMP-3.
00072          05   WS-PRINCIPAL-AMOUNT         PIC S9(5)V99    COMP-3.
00073
00074      01  WS-DATE.
00075          05   SYSTEM-YY                   PIC 99.
00076          05   SYSTEM-MM                   PIC 99.
00077          05   SYSTEM-DD                   PIC 99.
00078
00079      01  WS-HEADING-LINE-1.
00080          05   FILLER                      PIC X(10)       VALUE SPACES.
00081          05   FILLER                      PIC X(17)
00082                                           VALUE "MORTGAGE PAYMENTS".
00083          05   FILLER                      PIC X(1)        VALUE SPACES.
00084          05   WS-HEADING-MM               PIC Z9.
00085          05   FILLER                      PIC X           VALUE "/".
00086          05   WS-HEADING-DD               PIC 99.
00087          05   FILLER                      PIC X           VALUE "/".
00088          05   WS-HEADING-YY               PIC 99.
00089          05   FILLER                      PIC X(4)        VALUE SPACES.
00090          05   FILLER                      PIC X(5)        VALUE "PAGE ".
00091          05   WS-HEADING-PAGE-NO          PIC ZZ9.
00092          05   FILLER                      PIC X(84)       VALUE SPACES.
00093
00094      01  WS-HEADING-LINE-2.
00095          05   FILLER                      PIC X(10)
00096                                           VALUE "PAYMENT #".
00097          05   FILLER                      PIC X(2)        VALUE SPACES.
00098          05   FILLER                      PIC X(15)
00099                                           VALUE "OLD BALANCE".
00100          05   FILLER                      PIC X(2)        VALUE SPACES.
00101          05   FILLER                      PIC X(10)
00102                                           VALUE "PAYMENT".
00103          05   FILLER                      PIC X(2)        VALUE SPACES.
00104          05   FILLER                      PIC X(10)
00105                                           VALUE "PRINCIPAL".
00106          05   FILLER                      PIC X(2)        VALUE SPACES.
00107          05   FILLER                      PIC X(10)
00108                                           VALUE "INTEREST".
00109          05   FILLER                      PIC X(2)        VALUE SPACES.
00110          05   FILLER                      PIC X(12)
00111                                           VALUE "NEW BALANCE".
00112          05   FILLER                      PIC X(55)       VALUE SPACES.
00113
00114      01  WS-DETAIL-LINE.
00115          05   FILLER                      PIC X(3)        VALUE SPACES.
00116          05   WS-DETAIL-NUMBER            PIC Z9.
00117          05   FILLER                      PIC X(7)        VALUE SPACES.
00118          05   WS-DETAIL-OLD-BAL           PIC Z,ZZZ,ZZZ.99.
00119          05   FILLER                      PIC X(5)        VALUE SPACES.
00120          05   WS-DETAIL-PAYMENT           PIC ZZ,ZZZ.99.
00121          05   FILLER                      PIC X(3)        VALUE SPACES.
00122          05   WS-DETAIL-PRINCIPAL         PIC ZZ,ZZZ.99.
00123          05   FILLER                      PIC X(3)        VALUE SPACES.
00124          05   WS-DETAIL-INTEREST          PIC ZZ,ZZZ.99.
00125          05   FILLER                      PIC X(3)        VALUE SPACES.
00126          05   WS-DETAIL-NEW-BAL           PIC Z,ZZZ,ZZZ.99.
00127          05   FILLER                      PIC X(55)       VALUE SPACES.
00128
00129      PROCEDURE DIVISION.
00130
00131      000-EXECUTIVE-MODULE.
00132
```

Fig. 7-24 *(cont.)*

```
00133                   PERFORM 100-GET-TERMS
00134                   PERFORM 200-PRODUCE-DETAIL-LINE
00135                       UNTIL FINAL-PAYMENT
00136                   PERFORM 300-PRODUCE-FINAL-PAYMENT
00137                   PERFORM 400-TERMINATE
00138                   STOP RUN
00139                       .
00140
00141              100-GET-TERMS.
00142
00143                   MOVE "NO" TO WS-TERMS-FILE-END-SW
00144                                WS-FINAL-PAYMENT-SW
00145                   MOVE ZERO TO WS-PAGE-NUMBER
00146                                WS-PAYMENT-NUMBER
00147                   OPEN    INPUT    TERMS-FILE
00148                           OUTPUT   PAYMENT-REPORT
00149                   READ TERMS-FILE
00150                       AT END
00151                           MOVE "YES" TO WS-TERMS-FILE-END-SW
00152                       .
00153                   IF EMPTY-TERMS-FILE
00154                       MOVE "YES" TO WS-FINAL-PAYMENT-SW
00155                       DISPLAY "*** EMPTY TERMS FILE ***"
00156                   ELSE
00157                       MOVE TERMS-PRINCIPAL      TO WS-BALANCE
00158                       MOVE TERMS-INTEREST-RATE  TO WS-INTEREST-RATE
00159                       MOVE TERMS-PAYMENT        TO WS-PAYMENT-AMOUNT
00160                       ACCEPT WS-DATE FROM DATE
00161                       MOVE SYSTEM-YY            TO WS-HEADING-YY
00162                       MOVE SYSTEM-MM            TO WS-HEADING-MM
00163                       MOVE SYSTEM-DD            TO WS-HEADING-DD
00164                       PERFORM 600-PRODUCE-HEADINGS
00165                       .
00166
00167              200-PRODUCE-DETAIL-LINE.
00168
00169                   ADD 1 TO WS-PAYMENT-NUMBER
00170                   COMPUTE WS-INTEREST-AMOUNT =
00171                       (WS-BALANCE * WS-INTEREST-RATE) / 12
00172                   SUBTRACT WS-INTEREST-AMOUNT FROM WS-PAYMENT-AMOUNT
00173                       GIVING WS-PRINCIPAL-AMOUNT
00174                   IF WS-PRINCIPAL-AMOUNT NOT LESS THAN WS-BALANCE
00175                       MOVE "YES" TO WS-FINAL-PAYMENT-SW
00176                       .
00177                   IF REGULAR-PAYMENT
00178                       MOVE WS-PAYMENT-NUMBER    TO WS-DETAIL-NUMBER
00179                       MOVE WS-BALANCE           TO WS-DETAIL-OLD-BAL
00180                       MOVE WS-PAYMENT-AMOUNT    TO WS-DETAIL-PAYMENT
00181                       MOVE WS-PRINCIPAL-AMOUNT  TO WS-DETAIL-PRINCIPAL
00182                       MOVE WS-INTEREST-AMOUNT   TO WS-DETAIL-INTEREST
00183                       SUBTRACT WS-PRINCIPAL-AMOUNT FROM WS-BALANCE
00184                           GIVING WS-DETAIL-NEW-BAL
00185                                  WS-BALANCE
00186                       PERFORM 500-PRINT-LINE
00187                       .
00188
00189              300-PRODUCE-FINAL-PAYMENT.
00190
00191                   MOVE WS-PAYMENT-NUMBER        TO WS-DETAIL-NUMBER
00192                   MOVE WS-BALANCE               TO WS-DETAIL-OLD-BAL
00193                                                    WS-DETAIL-PRINCIPAL
00194                   ADD WS-BALANCE WS-INTEREST-AMOUNT
00195                       GIVING WS-DETAIL-PAYMENT
00196                   MOVE WS-INTEREST-AMOUNT       TO WS-DETAIL-INTEREST
00197                   MOVE ZERO                     TO WS-DETAIL-NEW-BAL
00198                   PERFORM 500-PRINT-LINE
00199                       .
```

Fig. 7-24 (*cont.*)

```
00200
00201            400-TERMINATE.
00202
00203                CLOSE    TERMS-FILE
00204                         PAYMENT-REPORT
00205                .
00206
00207            500-PRINT-LINE.
00208
00209                WRITE PAYMENT-RECORD
00210                     FROM WS-DETAIL-LINE
00211                     AFTER ADVANCING 2 LINES
00212                     AT END-OF-PAGE
00213                         PERFORM 600-PRODUCE-HEADINGS
00214                .
00215
00216            600-PRODUCE-HEADINGS.
00217
00218                ADD 1 TO WS-PAGE-NUMBER
00219                MOVE WS-PAGE-NUMBER TO WS-HEADING-PAGE-NO
00220                WRITE PAYMENT-RECORD
00221                     FROM WS-HEADING-LINE-1
00222                     AFTER ADVANCING PAGE
00223                WRITE PAYMENT-RECORD
00224                     FROM WS-HEADING-LINE-2
00225                     AFTER ADVANCING 2 LINES
00226                .
```

Fig. 7-24 (*cont.*)

```
          MORTGAGE PAYMENTS   5/09/83    PAGE   1
PAYMENT #    OLD BALANCE      PAYMENT      PRINCIPAL    INTEREST    NEW  BALANCE
    1          6,000.00      1,000.00       950.00       50.00       5,050.00
    2          5,050.00      1,000.00       957.92       42.08       4,092.08
    3          4,092.08      1,000.00       965.90       34.10       3,126.18
    4          3,126.18      1,000.00       973.95       26.05       2,152.23
    5          2,152.23      1,000.00       982.07       17.93       1,170.16
    6          1,170.16      1,000.00       990.25        9.75         179.91
    7            179.91        181.40       179.91        1.49            .00
```

Fig. 7-25

Programming Assignments

7.94   Given the following sales records on a card-type file:

Field	Data type & length
sales ID	X(5)
closing date	X(6) in the form yymmdd
amount this year	S9(4)V99
amount last year	S9(4)V99
unused	57 bytes

Print a report which consists only of an appropriate heading and two lines: (1) sales ID, amount this year, amount last year, and amount of increase over last year, all for the salesperson with the maximum increase in sales; and (2) the same information, but for the salesperson with the minimum increase in sales. [Increase in sales is defined as

$$(\text{amount this year}) - (\text{amount last year})$$

It is possible in (1), and probable in (2), that the increase will be negative; i.e., a decrease.]

7.95   Modify Problem 7.94 so that the program also prints the total sales this year, total sales last year, average sales this year, and average sales last year. Make your output as realistic and usable as possible.

7.96   Modify Problem 7.93 so that the program prints, after every twelfth month, the total principal paid and the total interest paid during the preceding 12-month period. It should also print the total interest paid on the loan at the end of the report.

7.97   Write a validation (or "edit") program for the input file in Problem 7.94. The program should print a report listing *only* those file records which contain a nonnumeric field. Invalid fields should be underlined in the report. Remember that 1, 2, 3, or all 4 fields could be invalid in the same record. Print appropriate report titles, with run date, page numbers, and column headings. Thoroughly test your program for all possible combinations of input records.

Chapter 8

Program Development: The Top-Down, Modular Approach

Up till now the reader has been left to his or her own devices as to how to attack a programming problem. This chapter presents a proven and effective *program development process*, which can benefit beginner and professional alike.

8.1 Step 1: Defining the Problem

The programmer should first acquire and study all design materials produced by any systems analysts who have worked on the project. Such materials include record layout charts, printer spacing charts, and English narrative descriptions of programs. A *programmer/analyst* may have to develop such materials alone.

8.2 Step 2: General Program Design

The next step is to produce a *top-down*, *modular design* of the program and to document it with a *structure chart* (also called a *visual table of contents* (*VTOC*) or *hierarchy chart*). The design is called *modular* because it breaks the program up into pieces, or *modules*, each of which carries out one well-defined function. Each module can be coded as a COBOL paragraph. The design is called *top-down* because it focuses first on the "higher-level" (overall, controlling) functions which the program must carry out, and treats "lower-level" (specific, detailed) functions last.

EXAMPLE 8.1 The *final form* of the structure chart for a sales report program is shown in Fig. 8-1. If each module (box) is to be coded as a COBOL paragraph, the connecting lines indicate which paragraphs will PERFORM which other paragraphs. Note that each module carries a descriptive name which identifies the function of the module, and an identifying number. The hyphenated combination of module number and module name should not exceed the 30-character limit for a COBOL paragraph name. Notice the shaded corner that identifies a module (paragraph) which is *called* (PERFORMed) by more than one other module of the chart; e.g., 230 is called by both 100 and 220. Of course, 230-PRINT-HEADINGS will appear only once in the COBOL source program; we use duplicate modules in the structure chart to keep the chart in hierarchical (*tree*) form.

What went on in the mind of the programmer as he constructed Fig. 8-1 *module by module, from the top down*?

1. The problem at hand is to produce a sales by region report; so I'll place a module at the very top of the structure chart, number it 000, and label it "Produce Sales by Region":

000

```
┌─────────────────┐
│     Produce     │
│  Sales by Region │
└─────────────────┘
```

2. Now, what functions must be carried out in order to produce the sales by region report? There seem to me to be three overall: initializing the program to prepare to process data for the first region, processing individual sales records, and handling final totals at the end of the job. (There is no right or wrong way to break a problem up into individual modules. Although some solutions are better than others, in general there is no unique best solution.) After the identification of the three major functions to be carried out by 000-PRODUCE-SALES-BY-REGION and the separation of those functions into their own modules, the structure chart looks like Fig. 8-2.

212

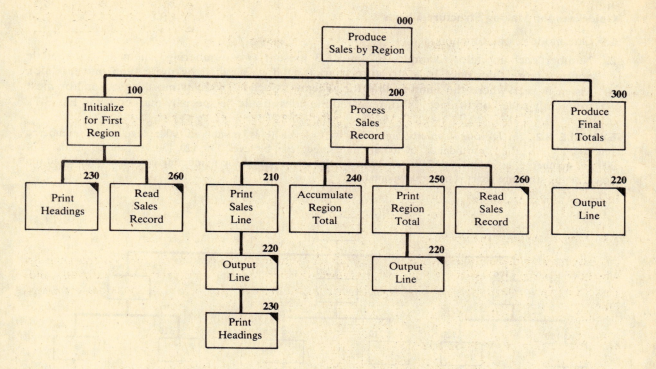

Fig. 8-1

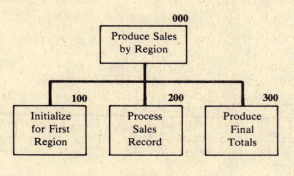

Fig. 8-2

3. Having broken down the module at *level 0* into the major logic-controlling functions of the program, I shall do the same thing for each module at *level 1*. What separately identifiable functions must be carried out in order to initialize processing for the first region? Well, the program will have to print headings to start the report, and must also input the first sales record to tell which region is first. Likewise, to process a sales record the program must (1) print a sales line on the report listing the contents of this sales record; (2) accumulate the region total by adding in the sales amount from this sales record; (3) if necessary, print the region total (if the region has changed); and (4) input the next sales record. Thus I have the modules at *level 2* (modules 230, 260, 210, 240, 250, 260, 220). I now decompose the modules at level 2 into subfunctions to produce modules at level 3, and so on, until all modules contain no nontrivial subfunctions.

The completed structure chart serves as the blueprint for organizing the PROCEDURE division of the program. Experience shows that an attempt to "save time" by skipping this design stage—or trying to code first and design afterwards—will almost surely end up *costing* time in a faulty and inefficient program.

Guidelines for Making Structure Charts

1. One module, one function.

2. Number each module. Examples 8.2 and 8.3 present two numbering schemes. If a module appears more than once in a structure chart (i.e., if it is called by more than one module), assign it everywhere the number that the scheme associates with its most logical and/or most frequently called occurrence. Also, repeated modules should be specially marked (as in Fig. 8-1).

EXAMPLE 8.2 In *horizontal numbering* (Fig. 8-3), level 0 is numbered 000; level 1 is numbered 100, 200, 300, . . . ; the "descendants" of 100 are numbered, level by level, 110, 120, 130, . . . ; the descendants of 200 are numbered, level by level, 210, 220, 230, . . . ; etc. Observe that the numbering can be accomplished top down, as the structure chart is being developed.

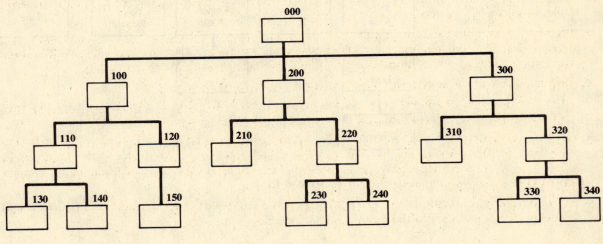

Fig. 8-3

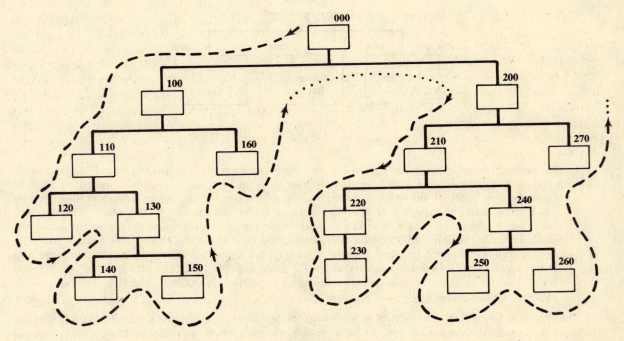

Fig. 8-4

EXAMPLE 8.3 In *vertical numbering* (Fig. 8-4), one does not proceed level by level, but *turns left* (as the chart is viewed) *at every junction*. Thus, numbering the level-0 module 000 and constantly turning left, encounter modules 100, 110, 120, ... At the "end of the line", go back to the last junction and take the *first left not yet taken*. Continue numbering by increments of 10 until all the descendants of 100 are accounted for. Then, beginning at 200 (the first left from 000 not yet taken), use the same rule to number the descendants of 200. And so on. An easy way to do all this is to draw a continuous curve skirting the entire chart (see Fig. 8-4); you can then number along this curve.

Vertical numbering, which tends to keep calling and called modules near one another in the program, is recommended for use on *virtual storage* systems (consult vendor manuals).

3. Develop modules that are *functionally cohesive*, which means that each statement in the module directly contributes to carrying out the single function of the module.

4. Develop modules that are low in *coupling*; in other words, try to minimize the number of data items which are accessed by two or more COBOL paragraphs.

5. A module should require no more than about 50 lines of COBOL coding (i.e., one page of a source listing). Any module larger than one page should be evaluated to see whether some operations may be moved into lower-level modules called by the oversized module.

6. Modules should call only those modules which are *below* their own level.

7. The level-0 *executive module* generally is responsible for calling a level-1 module repeatedly, thus setting up the main program loop. Often this is a "perform until end of file"-type loop.

8. Try to use only one READ module per input file and one WRITE module per output file; the appropriate READ/WRITE module can be called by any module where an input/output operation is needed. An exception occurs in the case of print files, for which one module might WRITE headings and another might WRITE detail lines.

9. If a nonrepeated module becomes trivial (e.g., just a few statements), consider eliminating it and moving its statements into the module which calls it.

8.3   Step 3: Detailed Program Design

Having produced a general blueprint for the program in the form of a structure chart (VTOC), the next step in program development is to design the detailed logic of each module. This can be done using structured flowcharts or pseudocode, as discussed in Chapter 7; however, an even more useful tool is the *hierarchical input-process-output*, or *HIPO, chart*. A single page of a HIPO chart (Fig. 8-5) combines pseudocode description of the detailed logic of one module with an indication of what input or WORKING-STORAGE data items the module needs and what output or WORKING-STORAGE data items the module produces or changes. It should be noted that one and the same data item may appear in both the input and the output blocks (if it is both used and changed by the module). The various HIPO pages are developed from the VTOC in top-down fashion. See Fig. 8-11 for an actual HIPO chart.

When the HIPO chart has been completed, the pseudocode in each process block should be desk checked to locate and correct as many errors as possible *before* module coding and testing begins.

8.4   Step 4: Preparation of a Coding/Testing Plan

The top-down approach can and should be applied to the coding and testing of a program as well as its design. This means:

(1) Higher-level modules are coded first; after these modules have been tested and debugged, lower-level modules can be coded and tested.

(2) A module should not be coded until all modules between it and the executive module (level 000) have been *coded and tested*.

Designer _____	System/Program Name _____	Date _____
Module No. _____	Module Name _____	

Input	Process	Output

Fig. 8-5

(3)   A module that calls other modules which have not yet been coded can be tested using *program stubs*, which simulate the execution of the called modules. A program stub usually consists of just the paragraph name followed by a DISPLAY statement which prints a message showing that the paragraph was performed. Sometimes the stub must also set switches required by the calling module. (See Fig. 8-12, lines 145–158, and Fig. 8-13, lines 193–215.)

Some programmers prefer to code and test modules level by level (i.e., in the sequence of horizontal numbering; see Example 8.2). Others employ the order of vertical numbering (see Example 8.3). So long as rule 2 above is observed, any combination of these two approaches is fine.

EXAMPLE 8.4   A coding/testing plan for the program of Fig. 8-1 follows:

Run	Modules	Test With
1	000	all empty files; stubs 100, 200, 300
2	100, 200, 300	data for a single sales region; stubs 230, 260, 210, 240, 250, 220
3	210, 220, 230, 260	data for two regions
4	240, 250	(*a*) all empty files
		(*b*) data for all regions—includes one region with only one sales record
		(*c*) enough data to cause page overflow

8.5   Step 5: Assemblage of Test Data

Sometimes test data are made up by the programmer, sometimes they can be generated by special programs, and sometimes they are obtained by copying from live files (files actually in use by programs already in production). When the test data have been collected, the programmer should determine the correct output corresponding to those data, so that any discrepancies between it and the actual output can be identified and the program debugged.

Ideally, at the end of the testing process, *each logic path through each module* will have been tested. In particular, test data will have been provided which take every IF... through its "true" routine, while other test data will have invoked the corresponding "false" routine. Every iteration (PERFORM...UNTIL...) will have been tested for zero, one, ... repetitions. For large programs it may be impossible to supply enough data to test all possible logic paths in a reasonable amount of time. In this case, at least the most important and/or frequently used logic paths should be thoroughly tested.

8.6   Step 6: Top-Down Coding and Testing

The program should now be coded and tested, module by module, according to the sequence set up in the coding/testing plan and using the analyzed test data. See Problem 8.30 for an implementation of this step.

8.7   Step 7: Completion of Program Documentation

After the program has been tested and completely debugged, the structure chart, HIPO chart, coding/testing plan, test data, test runs with test output and source listings, etc., should be collected. Any changes in the program made during the testing/debugging process should be incorporated in the VTOC and HIPO. All documents should be saved for use by maintenance programmers assigned to make changes to the program later on.

Review Questions

8.1   Explain the first step in individual program development.

8.2   What is a structure chart (VTOC)? How is it used in general program design?

8.3   What is meant by "top-down design"?

8.4   What is a "module"?

8.5   Define the concept of "level" in a structure chart.

8.6   Compare and contrast horizontal numbering schemes with vertical numbering schemes.

8.7   Explain the importance of the rule "one module, one function".

8.8   Why should modules exhibit high cohesion?   low coupling?

8.9   What is a "mainline" or "executive" module?

8.10   Why is it recommended that only one READ or WRITE statement per file be used in a program? How may this be accomplished?

8.11   Explain the use of HIPOs for detailed program design.

8.12   Discuss what goes in the input, process, and output blocks of a HIPO.

8.13   What is meant by "top-down coding and testing"?

8.14   What is a "program stub"?

8.15   Compare a horizontal approach to top-down coding/testing with a vertical approach.

8.16   What is the aim of program testing? Explain how test data should change during the top-down testing process.

8.17   What is the importance of program documentation? Explain how program *design* tools can later serve as program documentation.

Solved Problems

8.18   Number the modules in Fig. 8-6 (*a*) horizontally, (*b*) vertically.

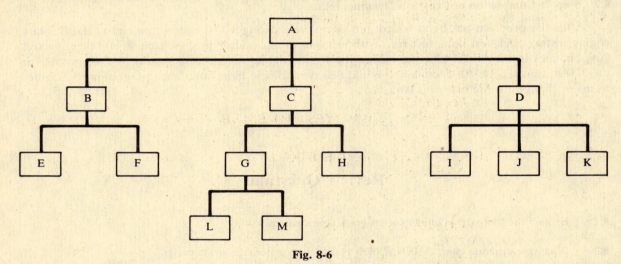

Fig. 8-6

(*a*)   A 000; B 100, E 110, F 120; C 200, G 210, H 220, L 230, M 240; D 300, I 310, J 320, K 330.

(*b*)   A 000; B 100, E 110, F 120; C 200, G 210, L 220, M 230, H 240; D 300, I 310, J 320, K 330.

8.19   Is the following module (COBOL paragraph) highly cohesive?

```
SAMPLE-PARA.
    MOVE SPACES TO SALARIED-MESSAGE-AREA
    MOVE ZEROS  TO TOTAL-SALARY-AMOUNT
    PERFORM READ-TIME-CARD
    ADD TIME-CARD-HOURS TO TOTAL-HOURS
    IF TIME-CARD-ID NOT NUMERIC
        MOVE "YES" TO INVALID-SWITCH

    PERFORM COMPUTE-TAX
    IF LINE-COUNT-ON-REPORT GREATER THAN 30
        PERFORM PRINT-HEADINGS
```

A cohesive module is one in which each statement contributes to the carrying out of one well-defined function. A module that (1) initializes some data items, (2) inputs a record, (3) accumulates a total, (4) validates a field, (5) calculates a payroll tax, and (6) handles printing headings when end of page is reached, is certainly very *low* in cohesion.

8.20   What functions does the executive module perform in a typical business application?

The executive module usually carries out four functions:

```
SAMPLE-EXECUTIVE-MODULE.
    PERFORM INITIALIZATION-MODULE
    PERFORM MAIN-PROCESSING-MODULE
        UNTIL END-OF-FILE
    PERFORM TERMINATION-MODULE
    STOP RUN
```

INITIALIZATION-MODULE gets the program started (opens files, zeros counters and total areas, reads the first logical record, etc.). TERMINATION-MODULE brings the program to an orderly conclusion (prints final totals and report footings, closes files, etc.). MAIN-PROCESSING-MODULE carries out the main purpose of the program (e.g., printing checks, validating an input file, updating a master file, printing a report). If initialization and termination involve relatively little work, they need not be implemented as separate modules but can be coded within the executive module itself.

8.21   Criticize the handling of READ . . . in the following:

```
100-INITIALIZE-PROGRAM
    MOVE ZERO TO . . .
    MOVE SPACES TO . . .
    OPEN . . .
    READ INPUT-FILE
        AT END   MOVE "YES" TO END-FILE-SW

    IF END-FILE-SW NOT EQUAL "YES"
        MOVE A TO B

. . . . . . . . . . . . . . . . . .

210-PRODUCE-REPORT-LINE.
    MOVE . . .
    ADD . . .
    READ INPUT-FILE
        AT END   MOVE "YES" TO END-FILE-SW
```

Here, a separate READ statement is used wherever it is desired to input a logical record. This can be inconvenient if the I/O specifications for the program change, since the maintenance programmer must hunt through the entire program looking for each READ statement. A better approach is to place one READ statement for the file in its own paragraph:

```
100-INITIALIZE-PROGRAM.
    MOVE ZERO TO . . .
    MOVE SPACES TO . . .
    OPEN . . .
    PERFORM GET-INPUT-RECORD
    IF END-FILE-SW NOT EQUAL "YES"
        MOVE A TO B

. . . . . . . . . . . . . . . . . .

210-PRODUCE-REPORT-LINE.
    MOVE . . .
    ADD . . .
    PERFORM GET-INPUT-RECORD
```

. . . .

```
GET-INPUT-RECORD.
    READ INPUT-FILE
        AT END
            MOVE "YES" TO END-FILE-SW
```

.

.

8.22 One of the modules in Fig. 8-1 is almost certainly trivial; identify it.

240-ACCUMULATE-REGION-TOTAL will consist only of an ADD statement, which may easily be incorporated into the calling module, 200-PROCESS-SALES-RECORD.

8.23 Why should test data start out simple?

A brand-new program generally has several bugs. Initially complicated test data will often cause bugs to interact with one another in ways that can be misleading and make the bugs harder to identify. Further on in the testing process, when most of the bugs have been corrected, more complex test data may be used.

8.24 Suppose that A, B, and C are fields in an input record. Make up a set of test values for A, B, and C that will test all the logic paths in the following code:

```
IF A LESS THAN B
    MOVE...
    ADD...
    IF A LESS THAN C
        PERFORM...
    ELSE
        PERFORM...
ELSE
    SUBTRACT...
    IF B EQUAL C
        MOVE...
    ELSE
        PERFORM...
    IF A EQUAL C
        MOVE...
```

Draw the *decision tree* for the nested IFs, Fig. 8-7; the logic paths are given by the paths from the "root" A < B to the "leaves" or endpoints of the tree. There are seen to be five paths, for which appropriate test data are shown in Table 8-1.

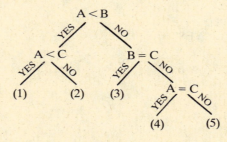

Fig. 8-7

Table 8-1

Path	A	B	C
(1)	1	2	3
(2)	1	2	0
(3)	2	1	1
(4)	2	1	2
(5)	2	1	3

8.25   Many business reporting programs access their information by processing files on tape or disk. These programs are built around a main loop in which a logical record is input and processed, and, if appropriate, the results are output. There are two basic approaches to designing the logic for such a program. In the first approach, the body of the main loop (1) inputs a logical record; (2) checks for end of file; and (3) if end of file has not occurred, processes the logical record just input. Write pseudocode to illustrate this logic for a program which lists the monthly salaries of all salaried employees by reading the employee master file.

```
set end-of-file-switch "off"
open employee-master, report-file
perform until end-of-file-switch is "on" (main loop):
      read employee-master-record
            at end:   set end-of-file-switch "on"
      if end-of-file-switch is "off"
            perform process-employee-record
            perform output-employee-results
      endif
endperform
close employee-master, report-file
stop
```

It is critical in this approach to test for end of file before processing a logical record (see Example 6.10). On some systems the logical record area (FD) for the file still contains the last record read when end of file occurs. In this case, failure to test for end of file before processing a record would result in the last record's being processed twice.

8.26   The second basic approach to the type of program discussed in Problem 8.25 uses a *priming read*, an initial read to the file executed *before* beginning the main program loop. Since a logical record has already been input when the main loop begins executing, the first thing the main loop does is (1) to process a logical record and to output the results; then (2) it reads the next logical record (which will be processed when the loop is repeated back at step 1). The priming read approach has two advantages: (i) no test for end of file is needed inside the loop; and (ii) since the first record is input separately, it can receive special treatment (see Problem 8.27). Rework Problem 8.25 with a priming read.

```
set end-of-file-switch "off"
open employee-master, report-file
read employee-master record (priming read)
      at end:   set end-of-file-switch "on"
. . . (any special processing required for the first
      logical record could be done here)
perform until end-of-file-switch is "on" (main loop):
      perform process-employee-record
      perform output-employee-results
      read employee-master record
            at end:   set end-of-file-switch "on"
endperform
close employee-master, report-file
stop
```

8.27   Show how the approach in Problem 8.25 (no priming read) can be used if the first logical record of a file requires special processing.

```
set end-of-file-switch to "off"
set first-time-switch to "on"
open employee-master, report-file
perform until end-of-file-switch is "on" (main loop):
```

```
            read employee-master record
                 at end:   set end-of-file-switch "on"
            if end-of-file-switch is "off"
                 if first-time-switch is "on"
                      perform first-record-only-processing
                      perform first-record-only-output
                      set first-time-switch "off"
                 else
                      perform process-employee-record
                      perform output-employee-results
                 endif
            endif
       endperform
       close employee-master, report-file
       stop
```

Note the importance of turning the first-time switch off after the first logical record receives its special processing. If this were not done, each record in the file would be treated as if it were the first.

8.28   The priming read technique is especially useful in *control break problems*, where logical records in a file are sorted on one or more *control fields*. When the value in the control field of the current logical record is different from the value in the control field of the previous logical record, a *control break* is said to occur; at this point, special processing may be called for. For example, suppose that the file in Problem 8.25 includes a department number for each employee, and that the file is sorted in ascending sequence on the department number. Print a report for the file which shows not only individual salaries, but the total salary for each department and a grand total.

```
       set eof "off" (end of file switch)
       open files
       zero:   department-total, grand-total
       read employee-master record
            at end:   set eof "on"
       if eof is "off":
            move current-department-# to previous-department-#
       endif

       perform until eof is "on" (main loop):
            if current-department-# not equal previous-department-#
            (this is a control break)
                 perform print-department-total
                 add department-total to grand-total
                 move zero to department-total
                 move current-department-# to previous-department-#
            endif
            perform print-current-employee-salary
            add current-employee-salary to department-total
            read employee-master record
                 at end:   set eof "on"
       endperform

       (end of file should be treated as a control break to
        print last department total)

       perform print-department-total
       add department-total to grand-total
       perform print-grand-total
       close files
       stop
```

Some comments on the above *single-level* (one control field) control break problem:

(1) We have tested for end of file on the first record (priming read). This is not likely to happen, but it is possible (e.g., mistakes in job control language, operator mistakes when the program is run, etc.). Setting previous-department-# to the department # for the first record read ensures that a control break will not erroneously be taken for the first record when the main loop is entered.

(2) Department-total must be reset to zero every time the department # changes (otherwise department-total will accumulate a running total of *all* salaries from *all* departments).

(3) Once a change in control field is recognized, the *next* change in value will be occasioned by a value different from the one which just caused the *current* change. Thus, previous-department-# should be set to current-department-# at every control break.

(4) The grand total can be found most efficiently by adding up the individual department totals. This should be done at every control break.

(5) When end of file occurs, it should be treated as a control break, for there can be no change in control field for the *last* department # in the file. This means that the last department total must be printed at end of file; also, the last department total must be added to the grand total if the grand total is to be correct.

8.29 Suppose that in Problem 8.28 each employee master record also contains a division number, and that the file is sorted first on division number (the *major* control field), and then, within each division, on department number (the *minor* control field). Redesign the logic of Problem 8.28 to print a department total whenever the department number changes (*minor control break*), and a division total whenever the division number changes (*major control break*). The report should have the format of Fig. 8-8.

```
employee salary (division 1000, department 1)
employee salary (division 1000, department 1)
department 1 total
employee salary (division 1000, department 2)
employee salary (division 1000, department 2)
department 2 total
division 1000 total
employee salary (division 2000, department 1)
department 1 total
employee salary (division 2000, department 2)
employee salary (division 2000, department 2)
department 2 total
division 2000 total
grand total
```

Fig. 8-8

```
set eof "off"
open files
zero:  department-total, division-total, grand-total
read employee-master record
    at end:  set eof "on"
if eof is "off":
    move current-department-# to previous-department-#
    move current-division-# to previous-division-#
endif

perform until eof is "on" (main loop):
    if current-division-# not equal previous-division-#
    (this is a major control break)
```

```
          perform handle-department-break
          perform print-division-total
          add division-total to grand-total
          move zero to division-total
          move current-division-# to previous-division-#
     else if current-department-# not equal previous-department-#
     (this is a minor control break)
          perform handle-department-break
     endif
     perform print-current-employee-salary
     add current-employee-salary to department-total
     read employee-master record
          at end:   set eof "on"
endperform

(end of file should be treated as a major control break)

perform handle-department-break
perform print-division-total
add division-total to grand-total
perform print-grand-total
close files
stop
```

Here, "handle-department-break" is defined as follows:

```
handle-department-break:
     perform print-department-total
     add department-total to division-total
     move zero to department-total
     move current-department-# to previous-department-#
```

Comments on the double-level control break algorithm:

(1) Both the major control field and the minor control field should be initialized to the values on the first logical record. This is simple to accomplish if a priming read is used.

(2) The logic of the program's main loop begins by testing for a major control break. Note that because of the initialization of previous-division-# to the first current-division-#, a control break is *not* indicated for the first record in the file.

(3) Major control break processing begins by handling a minor control break. It is a common beginner's mistake to overlook the fact that when the major control field (division #) changes, the last minor control field (department #) totals should be printed and the minor control field totals reset. Consult Fig. 8-8 to make sure you understand why.

(4) After major control break processing handles a minor control break, the major break routine does whatever is appropriate for the change in major control field. Note particularly that previous-division-# is reset to current-division-# during major control break processing, and that major control field totals are reset to zero.

(5) After the main loop tests for a major control break, it should test for a minor control break. Note that this can be done with a linear IF structure. The minor break routine is implemented as a PERFORMed paragraph, since it must be called both from the major break routine and the minor break routine.

(6) The logic of both control break routines is as follows: (i) call next-lower-level control break routine (if any), (ii) print control totals for this break, (iii) add this control total to next-higher-level total, (iv) clear this control total to zero, (v) set this previous-control-field to this current-control-field.

(7) Once again, end of file must be treated as a major control break (otherwise the *last* department and division totals will not be printed and will not be added into the grand total).

8.30   Figure 8-9 is the *systems flowchart*—which diagrams the relationships between the programs and the files—for a (drastically simplified) payroll system. (The symbols for a card file and a disk file are self-evident; the "grand piano lid" symbolizes a print file.) Design, code, and test the edit program for this payroll system.

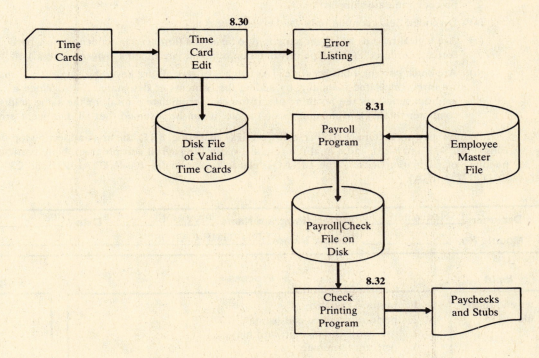

Fig. 8-9

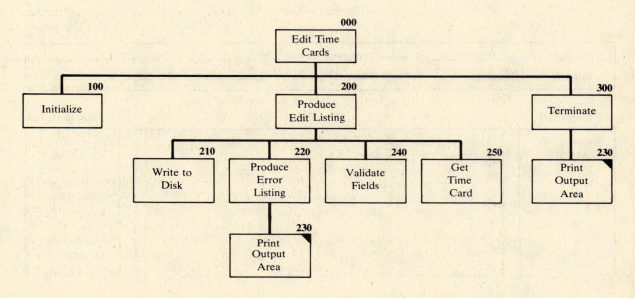

Fig. 8-10

As we know (Example 6.35), the purpose of an edit program is to validate information keyed by data entry. Specifically, an edit program should give the answers to the following questions:

(1) Are numeric fields actually NUMERIC?   alphabetic fields actually ALPHABETIC?   etc.

(2) Are values within the proper range (e.g., day-of-the-month must be between 1 and 31)?

(3) Are the values in a record consistent with one another (e.g., the date received cannot validly precede the date shipped)?

(4) Do coded fields contain only valid code values?

(5) Are logical records which are supposed to be sorted (arranged in sequence) on a particular field correctly ordered? (This type of validation is commonly called a *sequence check*.)

(6) Are batch control totals accurate? [As batches of records are keyed by data entry, *control totals* are often calculated manually, by adding the contents of designated fields. When a computer program processes the resulting file, it too can accumulate a total for the same field(s). If the computer total(s) and manual total(s) agree, it can be assumed that all data were processed.]

We now give a structure chart (Fig. 8-10), a HIPO chart (Fig. 8-11), the first and second top-down test runs (Figs. 8-12 and 8-13), and a final run (Fig. 8-14), for the payroll edit program. Note particularly the handling of pagination *without* the LINAGE clause (see modules 100-INITIALIZE and 230-PRINT-OUTPUT-AREA).

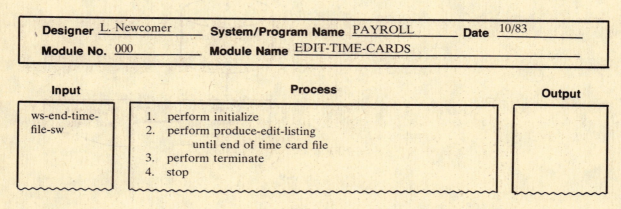

Designer L. Newcomer	System/Program Name PAYROLL	Date 10/83
Module No. 000	Module Name EDIT-TIME-CARDS	

Input

ws-end-time-file-sw

Process

1. perform initialize
2. perform produce-edit-listing
        until end of time card file
3. perform terminate
4. stop

Output

Fig. 8-11.   Page 1

Designer L. Newcomer	System/Program Name PAYROLL	Date 10/83
Module No. 100	Module Name INITIALIZE	

Input

ws-page-size, system date

Process

1. open files
2. move "no" to ws-end-time-file-sw
3. zero: ws-page-number, ws-number-employees, ws-total-hours
4. move ws-page-size to ws-lines-on-page
5. get system date and move to heading

Output

ws-end-time-file-sw, ws-page-number, ws-number-employees, ws-total-hours, ws-lines-on-page, heading

Fig. 8-11.   Page 2

Designer L. Newcomer	System/Program Name PAYROLL	Date 10/83
Module No. 200	Module Name PRODUCE-EDIT-LISTING	

Input	Process	Output

ws-end-time-file-sw, ws-error-detected-sw, time-card-hours	1. perform get-time-card
	2. if a card was read
	    perform validate-fields
	    if record was valid
	        add 1 to ws-number-employees
	        add time-card-hours to ws-total-hours
	        perform write-to-disk
	    else
	        perform produce-error-listing
		ws-number-employees, ws-total-hours

Fig. 8-11.   Page 3

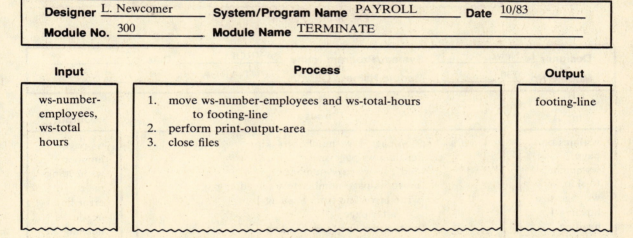

Designer L. Newcomer	System/Program Name PAYROLL	Date 10/83
Module No. 300	Module Name TERMINATE	

Input	Process	Output
ws-number-employees, ws-total hours	1. move ws-number-employees and ws-total-hours to footing-line 2. perform print-output-area 3. close files	footing-line

Fig. 8-11.   Page 4

Designer L. Newcomer	System/Program Name PAYROLL	Date 10/83
Module No. 220	Module Name PRODUCE ERROR LISTING	

Input	Process	Output
time-card, underline	1. move all time card fields to detail-line 2. move detail-line to output-area 3. perform print-output-area 4. move underline to output-area 5. perform print-output-area	detail-line output-area

Fig. 8-11.   Page 5

Designer L. Newcomer	System/Program Name PAYROLL	Date 10/83
Module No. 240	Module Name VALIDATE-FIELDS	

Input	Process	Output

time-card-id, time-card-hours, time-card-date, time-card-department	1. move "no" to error-detected-sw
	2. move spaces to under-line
	3. if time-card-id not numeric
	    set up underline for id
	    set error-detected-sw to "yes"
	4. if time-card-hours not numeric
	    set up underline for hours
	    set error-detected-sw to "yes"
	5. if time-card-date not numeric
	    set up underline for date
	    set error-detected-sw to "yes"
	6. if time-card-department not numeric
	    set up underline for department
	    set error-detected-sw to "yes"
		error-detected-sw, underline

Fig. 8-11. Page 6

Designer L. Newcomer	System/Program Name PAYROLL	Date 10/83
Module No. 230	Module Name PRINT-OUTPUT-AREA	

Input	Process	Output

ws-lines-on-page, ws-number-to-skip, ws-page-size, heading-1, heading-2, output-area	1. if ws-lines-on-page + ws-number-to-skip
	    greater than ws-page-size
	        add 1 to ws-page-number
	        move ws-page-number to ws-heading-page
	        write error-line from heading-1
	            after page
	        write error-line from heading-2
	            after 2 lines
	        move 2 to ws-lines-on-page
	2. Write error-line
	    from output-area
	    after 2 lines
	3. add number of lines skipped to ws-lines-on-page
		ws-page-number, ws-heading-page, error-line, heading-1, heading-2, ws-lines-on-page, output-area

Fig. 8-11. Page 7

Designer L. Newcomer	System/Program Name PAYROLL	Date 10/83
Module No. 210	Module Name WRITE-TO-DISK	

Input	Process	Output
time card	1. move all fields from time card to disk record 2. write disk record	disk record

Fig. 8-11. Page 8

| Designer | L. Newcomer | System/Program Name | PAYROLL | Date | 10/83 |
| Module No. | 250 | Module Name | GET-TIME-CARD | | |

Input	Process	Output
time-card	1. read time-card-file at end: move "yes" to end-time-file-sw	ws-end-time-file-sw

Fig. 8-11.   Page 9

```
00001              IDENTIFICATION DIVISION.
00002
00003              PROGRAM-ID.   TIMEEDIT.
00004
00005              AUTHOR.   LARRY NEWCOMER.
00006              INSTALLATION.   PENN STATE UNIVERSITY -- YORK CAMPUS.
00007
00008              ENVIRONMENT DIVISION.
00009
00010              CONFIGURATION SECTION.
00011              SOURCE-COMPUTER.   IBM-3081 WITH DEBUGGING MODE.
00012              OBJECT-COMPUTER.   IBM-3081.
00013
00014              INPUT-OUTPUT SECTION.
00015              FILE-CONTROL.
00016
00017                  SELECT TIME-CARD-FILE
00018                      ASSIGN TO TIMECARD
00019                      ORGANIZATION IS SEQUENTIAL
00020                      ACCESS IS SEQUENTIAL
00021                      .
00022                  SELECT VALID-TIME-FILE
00023                      ASSIGN TO DISKTIME
00024                      ORGANIZATION IS SEQUENTIAL
00025                      ACCESS IS SEQUENTIAL
00026                      .
00027                  SELECT ERROR-LISTING-FILE
00028                      ASSIGN TO ERRORLOG
00029                      ORGANIZATION IS SEQUENTIAL
00030                      ACCESS IS SEQUENTIAL
00031                      .
00032
00033              DATA DIVISION.
00034
00035              FILE SECTION.
00036
00037              FD  TIME-CARD-FILE
00038                  RECORD CONTAINS 80 CHARACTERS
00039                  LABEL RECORDS ARE OMITTED
00040                  .
00041
00042              01  TIME-CARD-RECORD.
00043                  05  TIME-CARD-ID            PIC X(5).
00044                  05  TIME-CARD-HOURS         PIC 9(2)V9.
00045                  05  TIME-CARD-X-HOURS       REDEFINES TIME-CARD-HOURS
00046                                              PIC X(3).
00047                  05  TIME-CARD-CLOSING-DATE  PIC X(6).
00048                  05  TIME-CARD-DEPARTMENT    PIC X(4).
00049                  05  FILLER                  PIC X(62).
00050
```

Fig. 8-12

```
00051        FD   VALID-TIME-FILE
00052             BLOCK CONTAINS 0 RECORDS
00053             RECORD CONTAINS 23 CHARACTERS
00054             LABEL RECORDS ARE STANDARD
00055             .
00056
00057        01   VALID-TIME-RECORD.
00058             05   VALID-TIME-ID              PIC X(5).
00059             05   VALID-TIME-HOURS           PIC S9(2)V9    COMP-3.
00060             05   VALID-TIME-CLOSING-DATE    PIC X(6).
00061             05   VALID-TIME-DEPARTMENT      PIC X(4).
00062             05   VALID-TIME-EDIT-DATE       PIC X(6).
00063
00064        FD   ERROR-LISTING-FILE
00065             RECORD CONTAINS 132 CHARACTERS
00066             LABEL RECORDS ARE OMITTED
00067             .
00068
00069        01   ERROR-REPORT-LINE              PIC X(132).
00070
00071    WORKING-STORAGE SECTION.
00072
00073        01   PROGRAM-SWITCHES.
00074             05   WS-END-TIME-FILE-SW        PIC X(3).
00075                  88   NO-MORE-RECORDS       VALUE "YES".
00076                  88   RECORD-AVAILABLE      VALUE "NO".
00077             05   WS-ERROR-DETECTED-SW       PIC X(3).
00078                  88   VALID-RECORD          VALUE "NO ".
00079                  88   INVALID-RECORD        VALUE "YES".
00080
00081        01   PROGRAM-COUNTERS.
00082             05   WS-PAGE-NUMBER             PIC S9(3)      COMP-3.
00083             05   WS-NUMBER-EMPLOYEES        PIC S9(5)      COMP-3.
00084             05   WS-NUMBER-TO-SKIP          PIC S9         COMP SYNC.
00085             05   WS-LINES-ON-PAGE           PIC S9(2)      COMP SYNC.
00086
00087        01   PROGRAM-TOTAL-AREAS.
00088             05   WS-TOTAL-HOURS             PIC S9(7)V9    COMP-3.
00089
00090        01   PROGRAM-CONSTANTS.
00091             05   WS-PAGE-SIZE               PIC S9(2)      COMP SYNC
00092                                             VALUE +50.
00093
00094        01   WS-HEADING-LINE-1.
00095             05   FILLER                     PIC X(5)       VALUE SPACES.
00096             05   FILLER                     PIC X(15)
00097                                             VALUE "TIME CARD EDIT".
00098             05   WS-HEADING-MM              PIC Z9.
00099             05   FILLER                     PIC X          VALUE "/".
00100             05   WS-HEADING-DD              PIC 99.
00101             05   FILLER                     PIC X          VALUE "/".
00102             05   WS-HEADING-YY              PIC 99.
00103             05   FILLER                     PIC X(3)       VALUE SPACES.
00104             05   FILLER                     PIC X(5)       VALUE "PAGE ".
00105             05   WS-HEADING-PAGE            PIC ZZ9.
00106             05   FILLER                     PIC X(93)      VALUE SPACES.
00107
00108        01   WS-HEADING-LINE-2.
00109             05   FILLER                     PIC X(7)       VALUE "  ID".
00110             05   FILLER                     PIC X(5)       VALUE "HRS".
00111             05   FILLER                     PIC X(8)       VALUE " DATE".
00112             05   FILLER                     PIC X(112)     VALUE "DEPT".
00113
00114        01   WS-DETAIL-LINE.
00115             05   WS-DETAIL-ID               PIC X(5).
00116             05   FILLER                     PIC X(2)       VALUE SPACES.
```

Fig. 8-12 *(cont.)*

```
00117                    05   WS-DETAIL-HOURS          PIC  X(3).
00118                    05   FILLER                   PIC  X(2)        VALUE SPACES.
00119                    05   WS-DETAIL-DATE           PIC  X(6).
00120                    05   FILLER                   PIC  X(2)        VALUE SPACES.
00121                    05   WS-DETAIL-DEPARTMENT     PIC  X(4).
00122                    05   FILLER                   PIC  X(108)      VALUE SPACES.
00123
00124              01  WS-UNDER-LINE.
00125                    05   WS-UNDER-ID              PIC  X(5).
00126                    05   FILLER                   PIC  X(2)        VALUE SPACES.
00127                    05   WS-UNDER-HOURS           PIC  X(3).
00128                    05   FILLER                   PIC  X(2)        VALUE SPACES.
00129                    05   WS-UNDER-DATE            PIC  X(6).
00130                    05   FILLER                   PIC  X(2)        VALUE SPACES.
00131                    05   WS-UNDER-DEPARTMENT      PIC  X(4).
00132                    05   FILLER                   PIC  X(108)      VALUE SPACES.
00133
00134              PROCEDURE DIVISION.
00135
00136              000-EDIT-TIME-CARDS.
00137
00138                    PERFORM 100-INITIALIZE
00139                    PERFORM 200-PRODUCE-EDIT-LISTING
00140                         UNTIL NO-MORE-RECORDS
00141                    PERFORM 300-TERMINATE
00142                    STOP RUN
00143                    .
00144
00145              100-INITIALIZE.
00146
00147         D      DISPLAY "100 ENTERED"
00148                    .
00149              200-PRODUCE-EDIT-LISTING.
00150
00151         D      DISPLAY "200 ENTERED"
00152         D      MOVE "YES" TO WS-END-TIME-FILE-SW
00153                    .
00154
00155              300-TERMINATE.
00156
00157         D      DISPLAY "300 ENTERED"
00158                    .
```

Fig. 8-12 *(cont.)*

```
00153              PROCEDURE DIVISION.
00154
00155              000-EDIT-TIME-CARDS.
00156
00157                    PERFORM 100-INITIALIZE
00158                    PERFORM 200-PRODUCE-EDIT-LISTING
00159                         UNTIL NO-MORE-RECORDS
00160                    PERFORM 300-TERMINATE
00161                    STOP RUN
00162                    .
00163
00164              100-INITIALIZE.
00165
00166         D      DISPLAY "100 ENTERED"
00167                    OPEN    INPUT    TIME-CARD-FILE
00168                            OUTPUT   VALID-TIME-FILE
00169                                     ERROR-LISTING-FILE
00170                    MOVE "NO" TO              WS-END-TIME-FILE-SW
00171                    MOVE ZERO TO             WS-PAGE-NUMBER
00172                                             WS-NUMBER-EMPLOYEES
```

Fig. 8-13

```
00173                                               WS-TOTAL-HOURS
00174              MOVE WS-PAGE-SIZE TO             WS-LINES-ON-PAGE
00175              ACCEPT WS-SYSTEM-DATE FROM DATE
00176              MOVE SYSTEM-YY TO               WS-HEADING-YY
00177              MOVE SYSTEM-MM TO               WS-HEADING-MM
00178              MOVE SYSTEM-DD TO               WS-HEADING-DD
00179                  .
00180
00181          200-PRODUCE-EDIT-LISTING.
00182
00183      D       DISPLAY "200 ENTERED"
00184              PERFORM 250-GET-TIME-CARD
00185              IF RECORD-AVAILABLE
00186                  PERFORM 240-VALIDATE-FIELDS
00187                  IF VALID-RECORD
00188                      PERFORM 210-WRITE-TO-DISK
00189                  ELSE
00190                      PERFORM 220-PRODUCE-ERROR-LISTING
00191                  .
00192
00193          210-WRITE-TO-DISK.
00194
00195      D       DISPLAY "210 ENTERED"
00196                  .
00197
00198          220-PRODUCE-ERROR-LISTING.
00199
00200      D       DISPLAY "220 ENTERED"
00201                  .
00202
00203          230-PRINT-OUTPUT-AREA.
00204
00205      D       DISPLAY "230 ENTERED"
00206                  .
00207
00208          240-VALIDATE-FIELDS.
00209
00210      D       DISPLAY "240 ENTERED"
00211      D       ON 1 AND EVERY 2
00212      D           MOVE "YES" TO WS-ERROR-DETECTED-SW
00213      D       ELSE
00214      D           MOVE "NO" TO WS-ERROR-DETECTED-SW
00215                  .
00216
00217          250-GET-TIME-CARD.
00218
00219              READ TIME-CARD-FILE
00220                  AT END
00221                      MOVE "YES" TO WS-END-TIME-FILE-SW
00222                  .
00223
00224          300-TERMINATE.
00225
00226      D       DISPLAY "300 ENTERED"
00227              MOVE WS-NUMBER-EMPLOYEES     TO WS-FOOTING-COUNT
00228              MOVE WS-TOTAL-HOURS          TO WS-FOOTING-TOTAL
00229              MOVE WS-FOOTING-LINE         TO WS-OUTPUT-AREA
00230              MOVE WS-SKIP-BEFORE-FOOTING TO WS-NUMBER-TO-SKIP
00231              MOVE WS-FOOTING-LINE         TO WS-OUTPUT-AREA
00232              PERFORM 230-PRINT-OUTPUT-AREA
00233
00234              CLOSE   TIME-CARD-FILE
00235                      VALID-TIME-FILE
00236                      ERROR-LISTING-FILE
00237                  .
```

Fig. 8-13   *(cont.)*

```
00001              IDENTIFICATION DIVISION.
00002
00003              PROGRAM-ID.   TIMEEDIT.
00004
00005              AUTHOR.   LARRY NEWCOMER.
00006              INSTALLATION.   PENN STATE UNIVERSITY -- YORK CAMPUS.
00007
00008              ENVIRONMENT DIVISION.
00009
00010              CONFIGURATION SECTION.
00011              SOURCE-COMPUTER.   IBM-3081 WITH DEBUGGING MODE.
00012              OBJECT-COMPUTER.   IBM-3081.
00013
00014              INPUT-OUTPUT SECTION.
00015              FILE-CONTROL.
00016
00017                  SELECT TIME-CARD-FILE
00018                      ASSIGN TO TIMECARD
00019                      ORGANIZATION IS SEQUENTIAL
00020                      ACCESS IS SEQUENTIAL
00021                      .
00022                  SELECT VALID-TIME-FILE
00023                      ASSIGN TO DISKTIME
00024                      ORGANIZATION IS SEQUENTIAL
00025                      ACCESS IS SEQUENTIAL
00026                      .
00027                  SELECT ERROR-LISTING-FILE
00028                      ASSIGN TO ERRORLOG
00029                      ORGANIZATION IS SEQUENTIAL
00030                      ACCESS IS SEQUENTIAL
00031                      .
00032
00033              DATA DIVISION.
00034
00035              FILE SECTION.
00036
00037              FD   TIME-CARD-FILE
00038                   RECORD CONTAINS 80 CHARACTERS
00039                   LABEL RECORDS ARE OMITTED
00040                   .
00041
00042              01   TIME-CARD-RECORD.
00043                   05   TIME-CARD-ID             PIC X(5).
00044                   05   TIME-CARD-HOURS          PIC 9(2)V9.
00045                   05   TIME-CARD-X-HOURS        REDEFINES TIME-CARD-HOURS
00046                                                 PIC X(3).
00047                   05   TIME-CARD-CLOSING-DATE   PIC X(6).
00048                   05   TIME-CARD-DEPARTMENT     PIC X(4).
00049                   05   FILLER                   PIC X(62).
00050
00051              FD   VALID-TIME-FILE
00052                   BLOCK CONTAINS 0 RECORDS
00053                   RECORD CONTAINS 23 CHARACTERS
00054                   LABEL RECORDS ARE STANDARD
00055                   .
00056
00057              01   VALID-TIME-RECORD.
00058                   05   VALID-TIME-ID           PIC X(5).
00059                   05   VALID-TIME-HOURS        PIC S9(2)V9    COMP-3.
00060                   05   VALID-TIME-CLOSING-DATE PIC X(6).
00061                   05   VALID-TIME-DEPARTMENT   PIC X(4).
00062                   05   VALID-TIME-EDIT-DATE    PIC X(6).
00063
00064              FD   ERROR-LISTING-FILE
00065                   RECORD CONTAINS 132 CHARACTERS
00066                   LABEL RECORDS ARE OMITTED
00067                   .
```

Fig. 8-14

```
00068
00069          01   ERROR-REPORT-LINE              PIC X(132).
00070
00071      WORKING-STORAGE SECTION.
00072
00073          01   PROGRAM-SWITCHES.
00074               05   WS-END-TIME-FILE-SW       PIC X(3).
00075                    88   NO-MORE-RECORDS      VALUE "YES".
00076                    88   RECORD-AVAILABLE     VALUE "NO".
00077               05   WS-ERROR-DETECTED-SW      PIC X(3).
00078                    88   VALID-RECORD         VALUE "NO ".
00079                    88   INVALID-RECORD       VALUE "YES".
00080
00081          01   PROGRAM-COUNTERS.
00082               05   WS-PAGE-NUMBER            PIC S9(3)      COMP-3.
00083               05   WS-NUMBER-EMPLOYEES       PIC S9(5)      COMP-3.
00084               05   WS-NUMBER-TO-SKIP         PIC S9         COMP SYNC.
00085               05   WS-LINES-ON-PAGE          PIC S9(2)      COMP SYNC.
00086
00087          01   PROGRAM-TOTAL-AREAS.
00088               05   WS-TOTAL-HOURS            PIC S9(7)V9    COMP-3.
00089
00090          01   PROGRAM-CONSTANTS.
00091               05   WS-PAGE-SIZE              PIC S9(2)      COMP SYNC
00092                                             VALUE +50.
00093               05   WS-SKIP-BEFORE-HEADING    PIC S9(2)      COMP SYNC
00094                                             VALUE +2.
00095               05   WS-SKIP-BEFORE-FOOTING    PIC S9(2)      COMP SYNC  S.
00096                                             VALUE +4.
00097               05   WS-SKIP-BEFORE-DETAIL     PIC S9(2)      COMP SYNC
00098                                             VALUE +2.
00099               05   WS-SKIP-BEFORE-UNDER      PIC S9(2)      COMP SYNC
00100                                             VALUE +1.
 .     .    .    .      .      .    .    .    .      .    .    .    .
00159      PROCEDURE DIVISION.
00160
00161      000-EDIT-TIME-CARDS.
00162
00163          PERFORM 100-INITIALIZE
00164          PERFORM 200-PRODUCE-EDIT-LISTING
00165              UNTIL NO-MORE-RECORDS
00166          PERFORM 300-TERMINATE
00167          STOP RUN
00168          .
00169
00170      100-INITIALIZE.
00171
00172   D      DISPLAY "100 ENTERED"
00173          OPEN     INPUT   TIME-CARD-FILE
00174                   OUTPUT  VALID-TIME-FILE
00175                           ERROR-LISTING-FILE
00176          MOVE "NO" TO                    WS-END-TIME-FILE-SW
00177          MOVE ZERO TO                    WS-PAGE-NUMBER
00178                                          WS-NUMBER-EMPLOYEES
00179                                          WS-TOTAL-HOURS
00180          MOVE WS-PAGE-SIZE TO            WS-LINES-ON-PAGE
00181          ACCEPT WS-SYSTEM-DATE FROM DATE
00182          MOVE SYSTEM-YY TO              WS-HEADING-YY
00183          MOVE SYSTEM-MM TO              WS-HEADING-MM
00184          MOVE SYSTEM-DD TO              WS-HEADING-DD
00185
00186          .
00187      200-PRODUCE-EDIT-LISTING.
00188
00189   D      DISPLAY "200 ENTERED"
00190          PERFORM 250-GET-TIME-CARD
```

Fig. 8-14 (cont.)

```
00191              IF RECORD-AVAILABLE
00192                  PERFORM 240-VALIDATE-FIELDS
00193                  IF VALID-RECORD
00194                      ADD 1                    TO WS-NUMBER-EMPLOYEES
00195                      ADD TIME-CARD-HOURS TO WS-TOTAL-HOURS
00196                      PERFORM 210-WRITE-TO-DISK
00197                  ELSE
00198                      PERFORM 220-PRODUCE-ERROR-LISTING
00199                  .
00200
00201          210-WRITE-TO-DISK.
00202
00203     D        DISPLAY "210 ENTERED"
00204              MOVE TIME-CARD-ID            TO VALID-TIME-ID
00205              MOVE TIME-CARD-HOURS         TO VALID-TIME-HOURS
00206              MOVE TIME-CARD-CLOSING-DATE TO VALID-TIME-CLOSING-DATE
00207              MOVE TIME-CARD-DEPARTMENT    TO VALID-TIME-DEPARTMENT
00208              MOVE WS-SYSTEM-DATE          TO VALID-TIME-EDIT-DATE
00209              WRITE VALID-TIME-RECORD
00210              .
00211
00212          220-PRODUCE-ERROR-LISTING.
00213
00214     D        DISPLAY "220 ENTERED"
00215              MOVE TIME-CARD-ID            TO WS-DETAIL-ID
00216              MOVE TIME-CARD-X-HOURS       TO WS-DETAIL-HOURS
00217              MOVE TIME-CARD-CLOSING-DATE TO WS-DETAIL-DATE
00218              MOVE TIME-CARD-DEPARTMENT    TO WS-DETAIL-DEPARTMENT
00219
00220              MOVE WS-DETAIL-LINE          TO WS-OUTPUT-AREA
00221              MOVE WS-SKIP-BEFORE-DETAIL   TO WS-NUMBER-TO-SKIP
00222              PERFORM 230-PRINT-OUTPUT-AREA
00223
00224              MOVE WS-UNDER-LINE           TO WS-OUTPUT-AREA
00225              MOVE WS-SKIP-BEFORE-UNDER    TO WS-NUMBER-TO-SKIP
00226              PERFORM 230-PRINT-OUTPUT-AREA
00227              .
00228
00229          230-PRINT-OUTPUT-AREA.
00230
00231     D        DISPLAY "230 ENTERED"
00232              IF WS-LINES-ON-PAGE + WS-NUMBER-TO-SKIP
00233                  GREATER THAN WS-PAGE-SIZE
00234                      ADD 1 TO WS-PAGE-NUMBER
00235                      MOVE WS-PAGE-NUMBER TO WS-HEADING-PAGE
00236                      WRITE ERROR-REPORT-LINE
00237                          FROM WS-HEADING-LINE-1
00238                          AFTER ADVANCING PAGE
00239                      WRITE ERROR-REPORT-LINE
00240                          FROM WS-HEADING-LINE-2
00241                          AFTER ADVANCING WS-SKIP-BEFORE-HEADING LINES
00242                      MOVE WS-SKIP-BEFORE-HEADING TO WS-LINES-ON-PAGE
00243                  .
00244              WRITE ERROR-REPORT-LINE
00245                  FROM WS-OUTPUT-AREA
00246                  AFTER ADVANCING WS-NUMBER-TO-SKIP LINES
00247              ADD WS-NUMBER-TO-SKIP TO WS-LINES-ON-PAGE
00248              .
00249
00250          240-VALIDATE-FIELDS.
00251
00252     D        DISPLAY "240 ENTERED"
00253              MOVE "NO"   TO WS-ERROR-DETECTED-SW
00254              MOVE SPACES TO WS-UNDER-LINE
00255              IF TIME-CARD-ID NOT NUMERIC
00256                  MOVE ALL "-" TO WS-UNDER-ID
00257                  MOVE "YES"   TO WS-ERROR-DETECTED-SW
```

Fig. 8-14 (*cont.*)

```
00258                       .
00259              IF TIME-CARD-HOURS NOT NUMERIC
00260                  MOVE ALL "-" TO WS-UNDER-HOURS
00261                  MOVE "YES"   TO WS-ERROR-DETECTED-SW
00262                       .
00263              IF TIME-CARD-CLOSING-DATE NOT NUMERIC
00264                  MOVE ALL "-" TO WS-UNDER-DATE
00265                  MOVE "YES"   TO WS-ERROR-DETECTED-SW
00266                       .
00267              IF TIME-CARD-DEPARTMENT NOT NUMERIC
00268                  MOVE ALL "-" TO WS-UNDER-DEPARTMENT
00269                  MOVE "YES"   TO WS-ERROR-DETECTED-SW
00270                  .
00271
00272          250-GET-TIME-CARD.
00273
00274              READ TIME-CARD-FILE
00275                  AT END
00276                      MOVE "YES" TO WS-END-TIME-FILE-SW
00277                  .
00278
00279          300-TERMINATE.
00280
00281        D     DISPLAY "300 ENTERED"
00282              MOVE WS-NUMBER-EMPLOYEES       TO WS-FOOTING-COUNT
00283              MOVE WS-TOTAL-HOURS            TO WS-FOOTING-TOTAL
00284              MOVE WS-FOOTING-LINE           TO WS-OUTPUT-AREA
00285              MOVE WS-SKIP-BEFORE-FOOTING TO WS-NUMBER-TO-SKIP
00286              MOVE WS-FOOTING-LINE           TO WS-OUTPUT-AREA
00287              PERFORM 230-PRINT-OUTPUT-AREA
00288
00289              CLOSE   TIME-CARD-FILE
00290                      VALID-TIME-FILE
00291                      ERROR-LISTING-FILE
00292                  .
```

```
       TIME CARD EDIT   5/09/83     PAGE    1
   ID    HRS    DATE     DEPT
1 111   111   111111   1111
-----
11 11   111   111111   1111
-----
111 1   111   111111   1111
-----
11111    11   111111   1111
          ---
11111   1 1   111111   1111
          ---
.
.
.
11111   111   111111   11 1
                       ----
       TIME CARD EDIT   5/09/83     PAGE    2
   ID    HRS    DATE     DEPT
11111   111   111111   111
                       ----

-----   ---   ------   ----

# EMPLOYEES=      2    TOTAL HOURS=        33.3
```

Fig. 8-14 (*cont.*)

Problem 11.22 enhances the above solution.

8.31 For the payroll system of Problem 8.30, give a structure chart for the payroll program.

See Fig. 8-15. The heart of the algorithm is the module which matches valid-time-card logical records (from the disk file produced by the program of Problem 8.30) with the corresponding employee-master-file logical records, which give each employee's pay rate. On the assumption that both files are sorted in ascending sequence by employee ID, the module might be HIPO'd as in Fig. 8-16. (See Problem 11.23 for a complete COBOL program.)

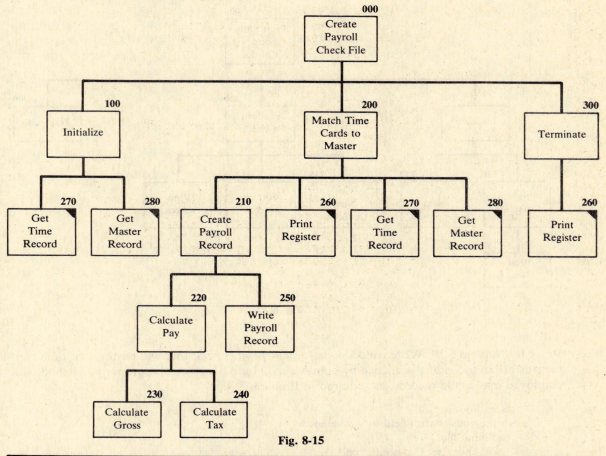

Fig. 8-15

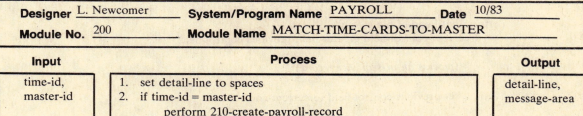

Designer	L. Newcomer	System/Program Name	PAYROLL	Date	10/83
Module No.	200	Module Name	MATCH-TIME-CARDS-TO-MASTER		

Input	Process	Output

time-id, master-id	1. set detail-line to spaces
	2. if time-id = master-id
	        perform 210-create-payroll-record
	        perform 270-get-time-record
	        perform 280-get-master-record
	    else if time-id less than master-id
	        format "unmatched time record" error
	        perform 270-get-time-record
	    else
	        format "inactive employee" message (*unmatched master*)
	        perform 280-get-master-record
	    endif
	3. perform 260-print-register
		detail-line, message-area

Fig. 8-16

8.32   For the payroll system of Problems 8.30 and 8.31, give a structure chart for the check printing program.

See Fig. 8-17. In the COBOL paragraph 100-INITIALIZE, the ACCEPT statement would be used to obtain today's date and the check number to be printed on the first check; subsequent check numbers would be generated by adding 1 for each check. (Example 12.10 gives a complete COBOL program.)

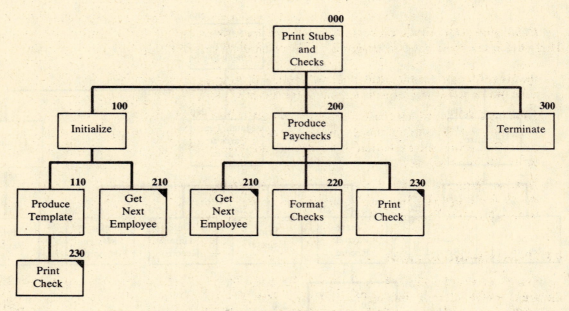

Fig. 8-17

8.33   Refer to Problem 8.30. Write pseudocode for a *sequence check* that will ensure that time card records are in ascending sequence by employee ID (and hence can be properly matched with employee master file records, as required in Problem 8.31).

```
set end-of-file "off"
set previous-control-field to low-values
read input-file
    at end:   set end-of-file "on"

perform until end-of-file is "on"
    if current-control-field greater than previous-control-field

        (process an in-sequence record)

        set previous-control-field to current-control-field
    else
        (current logical record is out of sequence)

        perform record-out-of-sequence-routine
    endif
    read input-file
        at end:   set end-of-file "on"
endperform
```

Note that initializing previous-control-field to low-values guarantees that previous-control-field is less than current-control-field for the first logical record. Note also that every time an in-sequence logical record is processed the data item previous-control-field is set equal to the contents of current-control-field. This prepares previous-control-field for comparison with the *next* logical record in the file.

Chapter 9

Debugging

Debugging refers to the process of identifying the causes of program errors and correcting them. There are three basic types of program errors which must be dealt with:

Syntax errors, or grammatical errors in the use of a programming language (COBOL). They are detected by the compiler as it attempts to translate from COBOL into machine language.

Fatal logic errors, which cause a program to ABEND. They are detected by the hardware and/or operating system during the execution of a test run (i.e., after all syntax errors have been corrected), when the execution of a machine language instruction or an operating system service turns out to be invalid.

Nonfatal logic errors, which are such that the program executes all the way to the STOP RUN, but does not produce the correct output. All syntax errors and fatal logic errors must be removed from a program before the nonfatal logic errors have a chance to manifest themselves.

9.1 Debugging Syntax Errors

Syntax errors are the easiest to debug, because the COBOL compiler prints diagnostic error messages which identify the errors and the COBOL statements in which they occurred. These messages usually appear at the bottom of the source listing; one merely looks up each error and corrects the offending statement so that it conforms to the COBOL rules.

EXAMPLE 9.1 Figure 9-1 is an IBM OS/VS COBOL source listing, showing some syntax errors with diagnostic error messages. Each error message indicates the compiler-generated card number of the statement which is in error, a code which identifies the error and its severity, and an English phrase which attempts to describe the error. Discussion of selected syntax errors follows.

```
00001          IDENTIFICATION DIVISION.
00002
00003          PROGRAM-ID.   SYNTAX.
00004
00005          AUTHOR.   LARRY NEWCOMER.
00006          INSTALLATION.   PENN STATE UNIVERSITY -- YORK CAMPUS.
00007
00008          ENVIRONMENT DIVISION.
00009
00010          CONFIGURATION SECTION.
00011          SOURCE-COMPUTER.   IBM-3081
00012          OBJECT-COMPUTER.   IBM-3081.
00013
00014          INPUT-OUTPUT SECTION.
00015          FILE-CONTROL.
00016
00017              SELECT TIME-CORD-FILE
00018                  ASSIGN TO TIMECARD
00019                  ORGANIZATION IS SEQUENTIAL
00020                  ACCESS IS SEQUENTIAL
00021                  .
00022              SELECT VALID-TIME-FILE
00023                  ASSIGN TO DISKTIME
00024                  ORGANIZATION IS SEQUENTIAL
00025                  ACCESS IS SEQUENTIAL
00026                  .
00027              SELECT ERROR-LISTING-FILE
00028                  ASSIGN TO ERRORLOG
00029                  ORGANIZATION IS SEQUENTIAL
00030                  ACCESS IS SEQUENTIAL
00031                  .
00032
```

Fig. 9-1

239

```
00033          DATA DIVISION.
00034
00035          FILE SECTION.
00036
00037          FD  TIME-CARD-FILE
00038              RECORD CONTAINS 80 CHARACTERS
00039              LABEL RECORDS ARE OMITTED
00040              .
00041
00042          01  TIME-CARD-RECORD.
00043              05  TIME-CARD-ID            PIC S(5).
00044              05  TIME-CARD-HOURS         PIC 9(2)V9.
00045              05  TIME-CARD-X-HOURS       REDFINES TIME-CARD-HOURS
00046                                          PIC X(3).
00047              05  TIME-CARD-CLOSING-DATE  PIC X(6).
00048              05  TIME-CARD-DEPARTMENT    PIC X(4).
00049              05  FILLER                  PIC X(62).
00050
00051          FD  VALID-TIME-FILE
00052              BLOCK CONTAINS 0 RECORDS
00053              RECORD CONTAINS 23 CHARACTERS
00054              LABEL RECORDS ARE STANDARD
00055
00056          01  VALID-TIME-RECORD.
00057              05  VALID-TIME-ID           PIC X(5).
00058              05  VALID-TIME-HOURS        PIC S9(2)V9    COMP-3.
00059              05  VALID-TIME-CLOSING-DATE PIC X(6).
00060              05  VALID-TIME-DEPARTMENT   PIC X(4).
00061              05  VALID-TIME-EDIT-DATE    PIC X(6).
00062
00063          FD  ERROR-LISTING-FILE
00064              RECORD CONTAINS 132 CHARACTERS
00065              LABEL RECORDS ARE OMITTED
00066              .
00067
00068          01  ERROR-REPORT-LINE           PIC X(132).
00069
00070          WORKING-STORAGE SECTION.
00071

         .
         .
         .

00106          01  WS-HEADING-LINE-1.
00107              05  FILLER              PIC X(5)       VALUE SPACES.
00108              05  FILLER              PIC X(15)
00109                                      VALUE "TIME CARD EDIT".
00110              05  WS-HEADING-MM       PIC Z9.
00111              05  FILLER              PIC X          VALUE "//".
00112              05  WS-HEADING-DD       PIC 99.
00113              05  FILLER              PIC X          VALUE "/".
00114              05  WS-HEADING-YY       PIC 99.
00115              05  FILLER              PIC X(3)       VALUE SPACES.
00116              05  FILLER              PIC X(5)       VALUE "PAGE ".
00117              05  WS-HEADING-PAGE     PIC ZZ9.
00118              05  FILLER              PIC X(93)      VALUE SPACES.
         .
         .
         .

00135
00136          01  WS-UNDER-LINE.
00137              05  WS-UNDER-ID         PIC X(5).
00138              05  FILLER              PIC X(2)       VALUE SPICES.
00139              05  WS-UNDER-HOURS      PIC X(3).
00140              05  FILLER              PIC X(2)       VALUE SPACES.
00141              05  WS-UNDER-DATE       PIC X(6).
00142              05  FILLER              PIC X(2)       VALUE SPACES.
00143              05  WS-UNDER-DEPARTMENT PIC X(4).
00144              05  FILLER              PIC X(108)     VALUE SPACES.
         .
         .
         .

00158          PROCEDURE DIVISION.
00159
00160          000-EDIT-TIME-CARDS.
00161
00162              PERFORM 100-INITIALIZE
00163              PERFORM 200-PRODUCE-EDIT-LISTING
00164                  UNTIL NO-MORE-RECORDS
00165              PERFORM 300-TERMINATE
00166              STOP RUN
00167              .
00168
00169          100-INITIALIZE.
00170
00171      D       DISPLAY "100 ENTERED"
00172              OPEN    INPUT    TIME-CARD-FILE
00173                      OUTPUT   VALID-TIME-FILE
00174                               ERROR-LISTING-FILE
00175              MOVE "NO" TO              WS-END-TIME-FILE-SW
00176              MOVE ZERO TO              WS-PAGE-NUMBER
00177                                       WS-NUMBER-EMPLOYEES
00178                                       WS-TOTAL-HOURS
00179              MOVE WS-PAGE-SIZE TO      WS-LINES-ON-PAGE
00180              ACCEPT WS-SYSTEM-DATE FROM DATE
00181              MOVE SYSTEM-YY TO         WS-HEADING-YY
```

Fig. 9-1 *(cont.)*

```
00182                    MOVE SYSTEM-MM TO            WS-HEADING-MM
00183                    MOVE SYSTEM-DD TO            WS-HEADING-DD
00184
00185                        .
00186            200-PRODUCE-EDIT-LISTING.
00187
00188          D    DISPLAY "200 ENTERED"
00189               PERFORM 250-GET-TIME-CARD
00190               IF RECORD-AVAILABLE
00191                    PERFORM 240 VALIDATE-FIELDS
00192                    IF VALID-RECORD EQUAL "YES"
00193                        ADD 1                 TO WS-NUMBER-EMPLOYEES
00194                        ADD TIME-CARD-HOURS TO WS-TOTAL-HOURS
00195                        PERFORM 210-WRITE-TO-DISK
00196                    ELSE
00197                        PERFORM 220-PRODUCE-ERROR-LISTING
00198                        .
00199
00200            210-WRITE-TO-DISK.
00201
00202          D    DISPLAY "210 ENTERED"
00203               MOVE TIME-CARD-ID           TO VALID-TIME-ID
00204               MOVE TIME-CARD-HOURS        TO VALID-TIME-HOURS
00205               MOVE TIME-CARD-CLOSING-DATE TO VALID-TIME-CLOSING-DATE
00206               MOVE TIME-CARD-DEPARTMENT   TO VALID-TIME-DEPARTMENT
00207               MOVE WS-SYSTEM-DATE         TO VALID-TIME-EDIT-DATE
00208               WRITE VALID-TIME-FILE
00209                        .
```

```
CARD    ERROR MESSAGE

 12     IKF1043I-W    END OF SENTENCE SHOULD PRECEDE OBJECT-COMPUTER . ASSUMED PRESENT.
 40     IKF1056I-E    FILE-NAME NOT DEFINED IN A SELECT. DESCRIPTION IGNORED.
 56     IKF1043I-W    END OF SENTENCE SHOULD PRECEDE 01 . ASSUMED PRESENT.
111     IKF2126I-C    VALUE CLAUSE LITERAL TOO LONG. TRUNCATED TO PICTURE SIZE.
138     IKF1017I-E    SPICES INVALID IN VALUE CLAUSE. SKIPPING TO NEXT CLAUSE.
172     IKF3001I-E    TIME-CARD-FILE NOT DEFINED. DELETING TILL LEGAL ELEMENT FOUND.
191     IKF3001I-E    240 NOT DEFINED. STATEMENT DISCARDED.
191     IKF3001I-E    VALIDATE-FIELDS NOT DEFINED.
192     IKF4030I-E    FOUND ´ EQUAL ´ AFTER CONDITION. EXPECT ´OR´, ´AND´ OR VERB TO IMMEDIATELY FOLLOW
                      CONDITION. DELETING TILL ONE OF THESE IS FOUND.
194     IKF3001I-E    TIME-CARD-HOURS NOT DEFINED. SUBSTITUTING TALLY .
203     IKF3001I-E    TIME-CARD-ID NOT DEFINED. DISCARDED.
204     IKF3001I-E    TIME-CARD-HOURS NOT DEFINED. DISCARDED.
205     IKF3001I-E    TIME-CARD-CLOSING-DATE NOT DEFINED. DISCARDED.
206     IKF3001I-E    TIME-CARD-DEPARTMENT NOT DEFINED. DISCARDED.
```

Fig. 9-1   (*cont.*)

Card 12.   In IBM OS/VS COBOL, message codes which end in "W" (IKF1043I-W) indicates a *warning*. This means that the error was slight and the compiler was able to correct it. In this case, the programmer forgot the period ending the SOURCE-COMPUTER paragraph; the compiler assumed the period was there, anyway. The compiler *is* able to translate statements which produce warning messages.

Card 111.   In IBM OS/VS COBOL, message codes which end in "C" (IKF2126I-C) indicate *conditional errors*. These errors are more severe than warnings, but the compiler is still able to "guess" at what the programmer wanted. It is this "guess" which is used to translate the statement, but the probability that the translation is what the programmer *intended* is not nearly so high as with a warning. In this case, the VALUE clause constant was bigger than the PICTURE size; so the compiler truncated the constant (VALUE "/ /" is truncated to "/", to fit into PIC X).

Card 192.   In IBM OS/VS COBOL, message codes which end in "E" (IKF4030I-E) indicate *severe errors*. In this case, the compiler cannot even guess at what the statement is supposed to mean; hence, it cannot translate the statement into machine language. As a result, there is no working object program with which to make a test run. Notice that in this instance the English error message does not tell the programmer what is truly wrong with the statement. The real error is that the programmer used a condition-name ("VALID-RECORD") instead of the data item ("WS-ERROR-DETECTED-SW") in a relation condition ('VALID-RECORD EQUAL "YES" ').

Card 40.   This syntax error illustrates the fact that diagnostic error messages do not always refer to the line number of the statement which actually causes the error. Here, line 40 is a structured period ending the FD for TIME-CARD-FILE. The error message says: FILE-NAME NOT DEFINED IN A SELECT. Although the error message refers to line 40, the real problem is a typographical error in line 17, which reads "SELECT TIME-CORD-FILE".

Cards 194, 203, 204, 205, 206.   Owing to the card-40 error, the entire FD and level-01 record description for TIME-CARD-FILE is not processed by the compiler. Hence, any PROCEDURE DIVISION references to the fields in TIME-CARD-RECORD constitute syntax errors. The error message says that the items are "NOT DEFINED"; and, from the point of view of the compiler, they are not—even though the programmer has defined them in lines 42–49 of the DATA DIVISION.

9.2   Debugging Fatal Logic Errors

When a fatal logic error causes a program to ABEND, the operating system cancels the execution of the rest of the program. Furthermore, *if the job control language for the program requests it*, the operating system will print a *termination dump* (on a printer file specified in the job control language). Termination dumps supply one or both of the following kinds of information, useful for debugging fatal logic errors:

Memory dump.   A memory dump shows the contents of computer memory at the time the fatal error occurred. Often the cause of the error can be determined by studying the contents of critical data items.

Program trace.   A program trace records all instructions executed by the computer prior to and at the time of the ABEND. For instance, the compiler-generated line number for each statement might be printed just before the machine language translation of the statement is executed.

On some computer systems, only a *standard operating system hexadecimal dump* is available; this is a memory dump printed as a series of base-16 numbers. The serious COBOL programmer should learn at least enough *assembler language* to be able to interpret system memory dumps. Other computer systems offer *symbolic dumps*, wherein the contents of some or all DATA DIVISION items are printed upon ABEND (a memory dump), along with a program trace; data items are printed in DISPLAY format and are labeled with their COBOL names.

9.3   Debugging Nonfatal Logic Errors

While syntax errors produce error messages and fatal logic errors produce termination dumps, nonfatal logic errors are more difficult to debug, for no particular statement is spotlighted as the culprit. It is left to the programmer's ingenuity to determine what is going wrong and why.

There are some COBOL language features which were specifically designed to help the programmer identify nonfatal logic errors. Because these special statements and techniques are *also* quite useful in providing information regarding the state of program execution prior to a fatal logic error (see Example 9.6), they are presented in the independent Sections 9.4–9.6.

9.4   Obtaining Program Trace Information

One way to obtain program trace information is to place at the beginning of each PROCEDURE DIVISION paragraph a debugging line (with a "D" in column 7) containing a DISPLAY statement. Whenever the paragraph is entered, the DISPLAY statement is executed, printing a message which serves as a program trace datum.

EXAMPLE 9.2

```
        SOURCE-COMPUTER. IBM-3081  WITH DEBUGGING MODE.
. . . . . . . . . . . . . . . . . . . . . . . . . . . . . . . .
        PROCEDURE DIVISION.
  D     DISPLAY "PROGRAM EXECUTION BEGINNING"
. . . . . . . . . . . . . . . . . . . . . . . . . . . . . . . .
```

```
     PARA-ONE.
D      DISPLAY "PARA-ONE BEING ENTERED"
 . . . . . . . . . . . . . . . . . . . . . . . . . . . . .
     PARA-TWO.
D      DISPLAY "PARA-TWO BEING ENTERED"
 . . . . . . . . . . . . . . . . . . . . . . . . . . . . . .
```

When the program is fully debugged, WITH DEBUGGING MODE can be removed from the SOURCE-COMPUTER paragraph. All lines with a "D" in column 7 will then be treated as comments, thus eliminating the trace output.

IBM OS/VS COBOL also provides a special statement whose purpose is to produce a program trace:

READY TRACE

causes the line number of each paragraph name (or the paragraph name itself, depending on specifications in the job control language when the program was compiled) to be printed out whenever the paragraph is executed. Since paragraphs in a loop may be executed many times, there is a companion statement,

RESET TRACE

which turns the tracing feature off. READY TRACE and RESET TRACE may be executed as many times as desired in a program.

EXAMPLE 9.3 The PROCEDURE DIVISION of Fig. 9-2 uses READY TRACE; sample output is shown at the bottom. READY/RESET TRACE is not available with all compilers. In IBM OS/VS COBOL, READY TRACE prints its output on the special system file SYSOUT; therefore, a job-control-language statement for this file must be present when READY TRACE is used (otherwise, the program will ABEND). Note that this trace prints out the COBOL paragraph *name* just before the first statement in the paragraph is executed. Under different job control language, it could print out the compiler-generated *line number* instead.

```
00070          PROCEDURE DIVISION.

00072          *---------------------------------------
00073               READY TRACE
00074          *---------------------------------------
00075
00076               MOVE "NO " TO END-OF-CARDS-SWITCH
00077               MOVE ZERO TO TOTAL-SALES
00078
00079               OPEN   INPUT              CARD-FILE
00080                      OUTPUT             PRINT-FILE
00081
00082               PERFORM 100-INPUT-A-RECORD
00083
00084               PERFORM 200-PRODUCESALES-LISTING
00085                   UNTIL END-OF-CARDS-SWITCH IS EQUAL TO "YES"
00086
00087               WRITE PRINT-LINE
00088                   FROM SALES-TOTAL-LINE
00089
00090               CLOSE   CARD-FILE
00091                       PRINT-FILE
00092               STOP RUN
00093               .

00095          100-INPUT-A-RECORD.
00096
00097               READ CARD-FILE RECORD
00098                   INTO WORKING-SALES-CARD
00099                   AT END
00100                       MOVE "YES" TO END-OF-CARDS-SWITCH
00101               .
```

Fig. 9-2

```
00103              200-PRODUCESALES-LISTING.
00104
00105              ADD WORKING-SALES-AMOUNT  TO TOTAL-SALES
00106
00107              MOVE WORKING-SALES-ID        TO LISTING-SALES-ID
00108              MOVE WORKING-CUSTOMER-ID     TO LISTING-CUSTOMER-ID
00109              MOVE WORKING-SALES-AMOUNT    TO LISTING-SALES-AMOUNT
00110
00111              WRITE PRINT-LINE
00112                  FROM SALES-LISTING-LINE
00113
00114              PERFORM 100-INPUT-A-RECORD
00115              .
```

```
100-INPUT-A-RECORD  ,200-PRODUCESALES-LISTING  ,100-INPUT-A-RECORD  ,200-PRODUCESALES-LISTING  ,
100-INPUT-A-RECORD  ,200-PRODUCESALES-LISTING  ,100-INPUT-A-RECORD  ,200-PRODUCESALES-LISTING  ,
100-INPUT-A-RECORD  ,200-PRODUCESALES-LISTING  ,100-INPUT-A-RECORD  ,200-PRODUCESALES-LISTING  ,
100-INPUT-A-RECORD  ,
```

Fig. 9-2 *(cont.)*

A powerful supplement to READY/RESET TRACE is furnished by the following IBM OS/VS COBOL extension to ANS COBOL:

$$\underline{ON} \begin{Bmatrix} \text{integer-1} \\ \text{identifier-1} \end{Bmatrix} \left[\underline{AND\ EVERY} \begin{Bmatrix} \text{integer-2} \\ \text{identifier-2} \end{Bmatrix} \right] \left[\underline{UNTIL} \begin{Bmatrix} \text{integer-3} \\ \text{identifier-3} \end{Bmatrix} \right]$$

imperative statement

$$\left[\begin{matrix} \underline{ELSE} \\ \text{imperative statement} \end{matrix} \right]$$

EXAMPLE 9.4

SOURCE-COMPUTER. IBM-3081 WITH DEBUGGING MODE.

. . . .

PROCEDURE DIVISION.

. . . .

        PERFORM PARA-A
            UNTIL SOME-CONDITION-OR-OTHER

        . . . .

    PARA-A.
    D   ON 1 AND EVERY 2 UNTIL 9
    D   READY TRACE
    D   ELSE
    D   RESET TRACE
    D   .
            . . . .

READY TRACE is executed the first time, third time, fifth time, seventh time, and ninth time PARA-A is entered. RESET TRACE is executed (instead of READY TRACE) for all other executions of PARA-A. Note the use of "D" in column 7 for all debugging statements (including the structured period at the end of the ON statement). Thus these statements are translated by the compiler only when WITH DEBUGGING MODE is specified in the SOURCE-COMPUTER paragraph.

   A few more samples of correct ON statements:

●   ON 3 AND EVERY 5 READY TRACE ELSE RESET TRACE.

●   ON 1 READY TRACE ELSE RESET TRACE.

- ON 1 AND EVERY 2 DISPLAY INPUT-RECORD.

- ON 1 AND EVERY 2
        DISPLAY INPUT-RECORD
        READY TRACE
    ELSE
        RESET TRACE

9.5 Dumping Data Items During Program Execution

The simplest way to obtain *dynamic memory dump* information is to insert debugging lines with DISPLAY statements into the program. Whenever a DISPLAY statement is executed, it will print the contents of the indicated data item. It is a good idea to DISPLAY every input record just after the READ, and every output record just before the WRITE.

EXAMPLE 9.5

```
        SOURCE-COMPUTER. IBM-3081  WITH DEBUGGING MODE.
        . . . . . . . . . . . . . . . . . . . . . . . . . . . . . .
        PROCEDURE DIVISION.
        . . . . . . . . . . . . . . . . . . . .
            READ INPUT-FILE
                AT END MOVE "YES" TO END-FILE-SW

    D       DISPLAY "INPUT RECORD IS:" INPUT-REC
        . . . . . . . . . . . . . . . . . . . . . . . . . . .
    D       DISPLAY "OUTPUT RECORD IS:" OUTPUT-REC
            WRITE OUTPUT-REC
        . . . . . . . . . . . . . . . . . . . . . . . . . . .
            ADD 1 TO SAMPLE-COUNTER
    D       DISPLAY "SAMPLE-COUNTER AFTER INCREMENTING:" SAMPLE-COUNTER
        . . . . . . . . . . . . . . . . . . . . . . . . . . . . . . . . .
```

Note the use of nonnumeric literals in the DISPLAY statements to *label* the debugging output. These labels also provide program trace information, since they indicate where the computer was executing instructions in the program when the DISPLAY output was produced. Output from the above statements might look like:

    INPUT RECORD IS:0003A789108264
    OUTPUT RECORD IS:172A12 CARTONSB97634900000
    SAMPLE-COUNTER AFTER INCREMENTING:0007

Remember: when DISPLAY is used in IBM OS/VS COBOL, a job-control-language statement must be supplied to define the printer file SYSOUT, or the program will ABEND.

Many versions of COBOL include a statement that prints out not only the contents of a data item but also the COBOL name for the data item; the syntax is

$$\underline{\text{EXHIBIT}} \begin{Bmatrix} \underline{\text{NAMED}} \\ \underline{\text{CHANGED NAMED}} \\ \underline{\text{CHANGED}} \end{Bmatrix} \begin{Bmatrix} \text{identifier-1} \\ \text{literal-1} \end{Bmatrix} \begin{bmatrix} \text{identifier-2} \\ \text{literal-2} \end{bmatrix} \dots$$

EXHIBIT NAMED . . . prints out the contents of each data item together with the COBOL name of the item, in the form: cobol-name = contents.

EXHIBIT CHANGED NAMED . . . prints out the COBOL name of the item followed by its current contents, *provided* the contents have changed since the last time this particular EXHIBIT statement was executed.

EXHIBIT CHANGED... prints out the contents of the indicated data item, provided they have changed since the last time this EXHIBIT statement was executed; it does *not* print the COBOL name of the item.

In IBM OS/VS COBOL, a job-control-language statement must be supplied to define the SYSOUT printer file when any form of EXHIBIT... is used.

EXAMPLE 9.6 READY TRACE and EXHIBIT NAMED statements have been added to the program of Fig. 9-3 to aid in debugging an ABEND. The debugging output, Fig. 9-4, illustrates how READY TRACE and EXHIBIT... outputs are intermixed on the SYSOUT print file, how EXHIBIT... automatically starts a new line if all information won't fit on one line, and how EXHIBIT... and READY TRACE output provide a useful "history" of what occurred during program execution. Compare the printed report at the bottom of Fig. 9-3 with the debugging output to make sure you follow the logic of the program as it processed each input record. The last paragraph executed (according to the trace) is 200-PRODUCE-TIME-LISTING. Notice that the computer got at least as far as the EXHIBIT statement in this paragraph, since the contents of WORKING-REGULAR-HOURS and WORKING-OVERTIME-HOURS appear on the debugging output. We can deduce that the ABEND occurred during execution of the COMPUTE statement on line 116, because the output from the EXHIBIT statement shows that WORKING-OVERTIME-HOURS contains *blanks*. This ABEND, then, was due not to the program but to *invalid input data*. The program should be redesigned so that it edits (validates) the input data before attempting to process them.

```
00001              IDENTIFICATION DIVISION.
00002
00003              PROGRAM-ID.  TIMELIST.
00004
00005              AUTHOR.    LARRY NEWCOMER.
00006              INSTALLATION.   PENN STATE UNIVERSITY, YORK CAMPUS.
00007
00008              DATE-COMPILED. MAY  9,1983.

00011              ENVIRONMENT DIVISION.

00013              CONFIGURATION SECTION.

00015              SOURCE-COMPUTER.  IBM-3081 WITH DEBUGGING MODE.
00016              OBJECT-COMPUTER.  IBM-3081.

00018              INPUT-OUTPUT SECTION.

00020              FILE-CONTROL.

00022                  SELECT CARD-FILE          ASSIGN TO CARDS.
00023                  SELECT PRINT-FILE         ASSIGN TO PRINTER.

00025              DATA DIVISION.

00027              FILE SECTION.

00029              FD  CARD-FILE
00030                  RECORD CONTAINS 80 CHARACTERS
00031                  LABEL RECORDS ARE OMITTED
00032                  .
00033
00034              01  TIME-CARD-INPUT           PIC X(80).

00036              FD  PRINT-FILE
00037                  RECORD CONTAINS 132 CHARACTERS
00038                  LABEL RECORDS ARE OMITTED
00039                  .
00040
00041              01  PRINT-LINE                PIC X(132).

00043              WORKING-STORAGE SECTION.
```

Fig. 9-3

```
00045              01   END-OF-CARDS-SWITCH          PIC X(3).

00047              01   WORKING-TIME-CARD.
00048
00049                   05   WORKING-NAME            PIC X(20).
00050                   05   WORKING-REGULAR-HOURS   PIC 99.
00051                   05   WORKING-OVERTIME-HOURS  PIC 99.
00052                   05   FILLER                  PIC X(56).

00054              01   TIME-LISTING-LINE.
00055
00056                   05   LISTING-NAME            PIC X(20).
00057                   05   FILLER                  PIC X(5)        VALUE SPACES.
00058                   05   LISTING-REGULAR-HOURS   PIC 99.
00059                   05   FILLER                  PIC X(5)        VALUE SPACES.
00060                   05   LISTING-OVERTIME-HOURS  PIC 99.
00061                   05   FILLER                  PIC X(5)        VALUE SPACES.
00062                   05   LISTING-TOTAL-HOURS     PIC 999.
00063                   05   FILLER                  PIC X(85)       VALUE SPACES.

00065              01   EMPLOYEE-TOTAL-LINE.
00066
00067                   05   FILLER                  PIC X(25)
00068                                                VALUE "NUMBER OF EMPLOYEES IS".
00069                   05   NUMBER-OF-EMPLOYEES     PIC 999.
00070                   05   FILLER                  PIC X(104)      VALUE SPACES.

00072              PROCEDURE DIVISION.

00074       D      READY TRACE
00075
00076              MOVE "NO " TO END-OF-CARDS-SWITCH
00077              MOVE ZERO   TO NUMBER-OF-EMPLOYEES
00078
00079              OPEN     INPUT               CARD-FILE
00080                       OUTPUT              PRINT-FILE
00081
00082              PERFORM 100-INPUT-A-RECORD
00083
00084              PERFORM 200-PRODUCE-TIME-LISTING
00085                  UNTIL END-OF-CARDS-SWITCH IS EQUAL TO "YES"
00086
00087              WRITE PRINT-LINE
00088                  FROM EMPLOYEE-TOTAL-LINE
00089
00090              CLOSE    CARD-FILE
00091                       PRINT-FILE
00092              STOP RUN
00093                  .

00095          100-INPUT-A-RECORD.
00096
00097              READ CARD-FILE RECORD
00098                  INTO WORKING-TIME-CARD
00099                  AT END
00100                      MOVE "YES" TO END-OF-CARDS-SWITCH
00101                  .
00102       D      EXHIBIT NAMED WORKING-TIME-CARD
00103       D                    END-OF-CARDS-SWITCH
00104       D          .

00106          200-PRODUCE-TIME-LISTING.
00107
00108              ADD 1 TO NUMBER-OF-EMPLOYEES
00109
00110              MOVE WORKING-NAME            TO LISTING-NAME
```

Fig. 9-3 *(cont.)*

```
00111                    MOVE WORKING-REGULAR-HOURS  TO LISTING-REGULAR-HOURS
00112                    MOVE WORKING-OVERTIME-HOURS TO LISTING-OVERTIME-HOURS
00113
00114         D          EXHIBIT NAMED WORKING-REGULAR-HOURS
00115         D                        WORKING-OVERTIME-HOURS
00116                    COMPUTE LISTING-TOTAL-HOURS =  WORKING-REGULAR-HOURS
00117                                               + WORKING-OVERTIME-HOURS
00118
00119                    WRITE PRINT-LINE
00120                       FROM TIME-LISTING-LINE
00121
00122                    PERFORM 100-INPUT-A-RECORD
00123                    .
```

PRINTED REPORT:


```
ABEL FRED                40      03      043
BAKER SUE                30      00      030
CHARLIE CHUCK            40      12      052
PERELMAN BARNEY          40      15      055
PERELMAN MIKE            03      00      003
```

Fig. 9-3 *(cont.)*


```
100-INPUT-A-RECORD ,
WORKING-TIME-CARD = ABEL FRED            4003           END-OF-CARDS-SWITCH
 = NO
200-PRODUCE-TIME-LISTING ,
WORKING-REGULAR-HOURS = 40 WORKING-OVERTIME-HOURS = 03
100-INPUT-A-RECORD ,
WORKING-TIME-CARD = BAKER SUE            3000           END-OF-CARDS-SWITCH
 = NO
200-PRODUCE-TIME-LISTING ,
WORKING-REGULAR-HOURS = 30 WORKING-OVERTIME-HOURS = 00
100-INPUT-A-RECORD ,
WORKING-TIME-CARD = CHARLIE CHUCK        4012           END-OF-CARDS-SWITCH
 = NO
200-PRODUCE-TIME-LISTING ,
WORKING-REGULAR-HOURS = 40 WORKING-OVERTIME-HOURS = 12
100-INPUT-A-RECORD ,
WORKING-TIME-CARD = PERELMAN BARNEY      4015           END-OF-CARDS-SWITCH
 = NO
200-PRODUCE-TIME-LISTING ,
WORKING-REGULAR-HOURS = 40 WORKING-OVERTIME-HOURS = 15
100-INPUT-A-RECORD ,
WORKING-TIME-CARD = PERELMAN MIKE        0300           END-OF-CARDS-SWITCH
 = NO
200-PRODUCE-TIME-LISTING ,
WORKING-REGULAR-HOURS = 03 WORKING-OVERTIME-HOURS = 00
100-INPUT-A-RECORD ,
WORKING-TIME-CARD = TROUBLE TOM          40             END-OF-CARDS-SWITCH
 = NO
200-PRODUCE-TIME-LISTING ,
WORKING-REGULAR-HOURS = 40 WORKING-OVERTIME-HOURS =
```

Fig. 9-4

9.6 DECLARATIVES and the
USE FOR DEBUGGING Statement

ANS Standard COBOL provides for special debugging routines, called *DECLARATIVES*, which must be written at the very beginning of the PROCEDURE DIVISION. Such routines are unique in that they are executed not as part of the normal program logic, but only if triggered by certain special events.

EXAMPLE 9.7

```
PROCEDURE DIVISION.
DECLARATIVES.
DECLARATIVE-SECTION-1 SECTION.
. . . . . . . . . . . . . . . . . . . . .

DECLARATIVE-SECTION-2 SECTION.

. . . . . . . . . . . . . . . . . . .

END DECLARATIVES.
. . . (normal PROCEDURE DIVISION statements)
```

Note the header "DECLARATIVES" and the final line "END DECLARATIVES" (typed in the A margin).

Each DECLARATIVE SECTION should begin with a *USE* statement, which defines when the DECLARATIVE SECTION is to be executed. The general format for DEBUGGING DECLARATIVES is displayed in Fig. 9-5.

USE FOR DEBUGGING

$$\text{ON} \begin{Bmatrix} \text{[ALL REFERENCES OF] identifier-1} \\ \text{file-name-1} \\ \text{procedure-name-1} \\ \underline{\text{ALL PROCEDURES}} \end{Bmatrix} \begin{bmatrix} \text{[ALL REFERENCES OF] identifier-2} \\ \text{file-name-2} \\ \text{procedure-name-2} \\ \underline{\text{ALL PROCEDURES}} \end{bmatrix} \dots$$

Fig. 9-5

EXAMPLE 9.8

```
PROCEDURE DIVISION.
DECLARATIVES.
CHECK-COUNTER SECTION.
    USE FOR DEBUGGING
        ON ALL REFERENCES OF NUMBER-CUSTOMERS-BILLED

    EXHIBIT NAMED NUMBER-CUSTOMERS-BILLED
    EXHIBIT NAMED CURRENT-CUSTOMER-ID

END DECLARATIVES.
. . . . . . . . . . . . . . . . . . . . . . .
```

Here, the "ON ALL REFERENCES OF identifier-1" option has been used. The SECTION (in this case, the two EXHIBIT NAMED statements) would be executed just before each WRITE of "identifier-1", and just after any other COBOL statement explicitly involving "identifier-1".

Other variations of USE FOR DEBUGGING . . . are exemplified below.

● ON identifier-1   (ON SAMPLE-OUTPUT-RECORD)
"Identifier-1" would normally be the COBOL record name for an output file. The DECLARATIVE is executed just before each WRITE statement for the file (e.g., before WRITE SAMPLE-OUTPUT-RECORD).

● ON file-name-1   (ON EMPLOYEE-MASTER-FILE)
The DECLARATIVE is executed *after* any OPEN, CLOSE, or READ statements for the indicated file.

- ON procedure-name-1   (ON 200-PRODUCE-MAILING-LABELS)

"Procedure-name-1" is a paragraph or SECTION name in the PROCEDURE DIVISION. The DECLARA-TIVE is executed *before* each execution of the named procedure.

- ON ALL PROCEDURES

The DECLARATIVE is executed *before* each execution of all paragraphs and SECTIONS (except the DECLARATIVE SECTIONS themselves).

As with other debugging lines, DEBUGGING DECLARATIVES are translated into the machine-language object program only if **WITH DEBUGGING MODE** is specified in the SOURCE-COMPUTER paragraph.

When a DEBUGGING DECLARATIVE is executed, the system places valuable information in a special data area named DEBUG-ITEM. DEBUG-ITEM, a COBOL reserved word, is *not* defined by the programmer in the DATA DIVISION; it has the COBOL layout indicated in Fig. 9-6.

```
01  DEBUG-ITEM.
    05  DEBUG-LINE      PIC X(6).
    05  FILLER          PIC X        VALUE SPACES.
    05  DEBUG-NAME      PIC X(30).
    05  FILLER          PIC X        VALUE SPACES.
    05  DEBUG-SUB-1     PIC S9999    SIGN IS LEADING SEPARATE CHARACTER.
    05  FILLER          PIC X        VALUE SPACES.
    05  DEBUG-SUB-2     PIC S9999    SIGN IS LEADING SEPARATE CHARACTER.
    05  FILLER          PIC X        VALUE SPACES.
    05  DEBUG-SUB-3     PIC S9999    SIGN IS LEADING SEPARATE CHARACTER.
    05  FILLER          PIC X        VALUE SPACES.
    05  DEBUG-CONTENTS  PIC X(n).
```

Fig. 9-6

Contents of the level-05 fields will be as follows:

(1) DEBUG-LINE is set to the compiler-generated line number of the statement which caused the DECLARATIVE to be executed.

(2) DEBUG-NAME is set to the first 30 characters of the name causing the DECLARATIVE to be executed.

(3) DEBUG-SUB-1, DEBUG-SUB-2, and DEBUG-SUB-3 are set to the current subscript values for the DEBUG-NAME item, *if* it is part of a table (see Chapter 10); otherwise, these parts of DEBUG-ITEM are left blank.

(4) DEBUG-CONTENTS is set to the contents of the data item (whose name is in DEBUG-NAME) which caused the DECLARATIVE to be executed. If the DECLARATIVE is being executed because of a USE FOR DEBUGGING ON procedure-name, DEBUG-NAME contains the procedure-name and DEBUG-CONTENTS is set to a short English phrase which describes what kind of procedure is involved.

DEBUG-ITEM contains so much useful information that a simple DISPLAY DEBUG-ITEM or EXHIBIT DEBUG-ITEM is often all that is needed in the DECLARATIVE SECTION.

EXAMPLE 9.9 We reconsider the ABEND of Example 9.6, this time using a DECLARATIVE as a debugging tool. The new PROCEDURE DIVISION is shown in Fig. 9-7, with lines 74–88 setting up the DECLARATIVE. When several conditions are specified in one ON clause, the occurrence of any one of them will cause the DECLARATIVE to be executed. Notice that all the DECLARATIVE does is to EXHIBIT DEBUG-ITEM. The sample output, Fig. 9-8, shows how much information this simple statement produces. (The format of Fig. 9-8 follows Fig. 9-6, with blanks for the DEBUG-SUBs and with "PERFORM LOOP" as the DEBUG-CONTENTS of 200-PRODUCE-TIME-LISTING.) We infer that the program got at least as far as line 124 (the last line to show up in the debugging output), and that at this time WORKING-OVERTIME-HOURS contained blanks. Since line 125 in the COBOL program is blank and line 126 uses WORKING-OVERTIME-HOURS (which then contains SPACES) in a calculation, the mystery of the ABEND is cleared up (see Example 9.6).

```
00072          PROCEDURE DIVISION.

00074          DECLARATIVES.
00075
00076          IDENTIFY-ABEND SECTION.
00077
00078              USE FOR DEBUGGING
00079                  ON ALL REFERENCES OF WORKING-TIME-CARD
00080                     ALL REFERENCES OF WORKING-REGULAR-HOURS
00081                     ALL REFERENCES OF WORKING-OVERTIME-HOURS
00082                     ALL REFERENCES OF 200-PRODUCE-TIME-LISTING
00083              .
00084
00085              EXHIBIT NAMED DEBUG-ITEM
00086              .
00087
00088          END DECLARATIVES.
00089
00090
00091              MOVE "NO " TO END-OF-CARDS-SWITCH
00092              MOVE ZERO   TO NUMBER-OF-EMPLOYEES
00093
00094              OPEN    INPUT            CARD-FILE
00095                      OUTPUT           PRINT-FILE
00096
00097              PERFORM 100-INPUT-A-RECORD
00098
00099              PERFORM 200-PRODUCE-TIME-LISTING
00100                  UNTIL END-OF-CARDS-SWITCH IS EQUAL TO "YES"
00101
00102              WRITE PRINT-LINE
00103                  FROM EMPLOYEE-TOTAL-LINE
00104
00105              CLOSE   CARD-FILE
00106                      PRINT-FILE
00107              STOP RUN
00108              .

00110          100-INPUT-A-RECORD.
00111
00112              READ CARD-FILE RECORD
00113                  INTO WORKING-TIME-CARD
00114                  AT END
00115                      MOVE "YES" TO END-OF-CARDS-SWITCH
00116              .

00118          200-PRODUCE-TIME-LISTING.
00119
00120              ADD 1 TO NUMBER-OF-EMPLOYEES
00121
00122              MOVE WORKING-NAME            TO LISTING-NAME
00123              MOVE WORKING-REGULAR-HOURS  TO LISTING-REGULAR-HOURS
00124              MOVE WORKING-OVERTIME-HOURS TO LISTING-OVERTIME-HOURS
00125
00126              COMPUTE LISTING-TOTAL-HOURS =  WORKING-REGULAR-HOURS
00127                                          + WORKING-OVERTIME-HOURS
00128
00129              WRITE PRINT-LINE
00130                  FROM TIME-LISTING-LINE
00131
00132              PERFORM 100-INPUT-A-RECORD
00133              .
```

Fig. 9-7

```
DEBUG-ITEM = 000112 WORKING-TIME-CARD              ABEL FRED           4003

DEBUG-ITEM = 000099 200-PRODUCE-TIME-LISTING       PERFORM LOOP
DEBUG-ITEM = 000123 WORKING-REGULAR-HOURS          40
DEBUG-ITEM = 000124 WORKING-OVERTIME-HOURS         03
DEBUG-ITEM = 000126 WORKING-REGULAR-HOURS          40
DEBUG-ITEM = 000126 WORKING-OVERTIME-HOURS         03
DEBUG-ITEM = 000112 WORKING-TIME-CARD              BAKER SUE           3000

DEBUG-ITEM = 000099 200-PRODUCE-TIME-LISTING       PERFORM LOOP
DEBUG-ITEM = 000123 WORKING-REGULAR-HOURS          30
DEBUG-ITEM = 000124 WORKING-OVERTIME-HOURS         00
DEBUG-ITEM = 000126 WORKING-REGULAR-HOURS          30
DEBUG-ITEM = 000126 WORKING-OVERTIME-HOURS         00
DEBUG-ITEM = 000112 WORKING-TIME-CARD              CHARLIE CHUCK       4012

DEBUG-ITEM = 000099 200-PRODUCE-TIME-LISTING       PERFORM LOOP
DEBUG-ITEM = 000123 WORKING-REGULAR-HOURS          40
DEBUG-ITEM = 000124 WORKING-OVERTIME-HOURS         12
DEBUG-ITEM = 000126 WORKING-REGULAR-HOURS          40
DEBUG-ITEM = 000126 WORKING-OVERTIME-HOURS         12
DEBUG-ITEM = 000112 WORKING-TIME-CARD              PERELMAN BARNEY     4015

DEBUG-ITEM = 000099 200-PRODUCE-TIME-LISTING       PERFORM LOOP
DEBUG-ITEM = 000123 WORKING-REGULAR-HOURS          40
DEBUG-ITEM = 000124 WORKING-OVERTIME-HOURS         15
DEBUG-ITEM = 000126 WORKING-REGULAR-HOURS          40
DEBUG-ITEM = 000126 WORKING-OVERTIME-HOURS         15
DEBUG-ITEM = 000112 WORKING-TIME-CARD              PERELMAN MIKE       0300

DEBUG-ITEM = 000099 200-PRODUCE-TIME-LISTING       PERFORM LOOP
DEBUG-ITEM = 000123 WORKING-REGULAR-HOURS          03
DEBUG-ITEM = 000124 WORKING-OVERTIME-HOURS         00
DEBUG-ITEM = 000126 WORKING-REGULAR-HOURS          03
DEBUG-ITEM = 000126 WORKING-OVERTIME-HOURS         00
DEBUG-ITEM = 000112 WORKING-TIME-CARD              TROUBLE TOM         40

DEBUG-ITEM = 000099 200-PRODUCE-TIME-LISTING       PERFORM LOOP
DEBUG-ITEM = 000123 WORKING-REGULAR-HOURS          40
DEBUG-ITEM = 000124 WORKING-OVERTIME-HOURS
```

Fig. 9-8

Review Questions

9.1   What is program testing?   program debugging?

9.2   Discuss the three types of errors that can occur during program testing.

9.3   What are diagnostic error messages?

9.4   Discuss the differences between W-level, C-level, and E-level syntax errors.

9.5   What is a memory dump? Differentiate between hexadecimal and symbolic dumps.

9.6   What is a program trace? How is it useful in debugging?

9.7   What information is typically provided in a symbolic dump?

9.8   How may DISPLAY statements be used for debugging?

9.9   Describe the actions of READY TRACE and RESET TRACE.

9.10   Describe the syntax and use of the ON statement.

9.11   Discuss the syntax and use of the EXHIBIT statement.

9.12   What is the format of output from EXHIBIT NAMED . . .?

9.13   What are DECLARATIVES?

9.14   How do DECLARATIVES differ from other statements in the PROCEDURE DIVISION?

9.15   Discuss effect of the SOURCE-COMPUTER paragraph on DECLARATIVES and lines with "D" in column 7.

9.16   Discuss the effects of the following in a USE FOR DEBUGGING statement: (*a*) ON ALL REFERENCES . . . , (*b*) ON file-name, (*c*) ON procedure-name, and (*d*) ON ALL PROCEDURES.

9.17   Discuss the contents of DEBUG-ITEM and how they may be used.

Solved Problems

9.18   Debug the following program, which contains nonfatal logic errors. You are given a source listing (Fig. 9-9), test output (Fig. 9-10), and debugging output from a DEBUGGING DECLARATIVE (Fig. 9-11). The output is incorrect because (i) the count of employees should be 006, not 012; (ii) for no employee does the sum of regular and overtime hours equal total hours worked (i.e., the columns of Fig. 9-10 do not add correctly).

```
00001          IDENTIFICATION DIVISION.
00002
00003          PROGRAM-ID.  TIMELIST.
00004
00005          AUTHOR.    LARRY NEWCOMER.
00006          INSTALLATION.   PENN STATE UNIVERSITY--YORK CAMPUS.
00007
00008          DATE-WRITTEN.   MAY 1983.
00009          DATE-COMPILED. MAY  9,1983.
00011      *    TIMELIST PRINTS ONE LINE FOR EACH EMPLOYEE SHOWING:
00012      *    NUMBER OF REGULAR HOURS WORKED, NUMBER OF OVERTIME
00013      *    HOURS WORKED, AND TOTAL HOURS WORKED.  AT THE END OF THE
00014      *    REPORT, IT ALSO PRINTS A COUNT OF THE NUMBER OF
00015      *    EMPLOYEES PROCESSED.   INPUT IS FROM A DECK OF TIME
00016      *    CARDS, KEPT IN SEQUENCE BY EMPLOYEE NAME.

00018          ENVIRONMENT DIVISION.

00020          CONFIGURATION SECTION.

00022          SOURCE-COMPUTER.  IBM-3081 WITH DEBUGGING MODE.
00023          OBJECT-COMPUTER.  IBM-3081.
```

Fig. 9-9

```
00025          INPUT-OUTPUT SECTION.

00027          FILE-CONTROL.

00029              SELECT CARD-FILE          ASSIGN TO CARDS.
00030              SELECT PRINT-FILE         ASSIGN TO PRINTER.

00032          DATA DIVISION.

00034          FILE SECTION.

00036          FD  CARD-FILE
00037              RECORD CONTAINS 80 CHARACTERS
00038              LABEL RECORDS ARE OMITTED
00039              .
00040
00041          01  TIME-CARD-INPUT           PIC X(80).

00043          FD  PRINT-FILE
00044              RECORD CONTAINS 132 CHARACTERS
00045              LABEL RECORDS ARE OMITTED
00046              .
00047
00048          01  PRINT-LINE                PIC X(132).

00050          WORKING-STORAGE SECTION.

00052          01  END-OF-CARDS-SWITCH       PIC X(3).

00054          01  WORKING-TIME-CARD.
00055
00056              05  WORKING-NAME          PIC X(20).
00057              05  WORKING-REGULAR-HOURS PIC 99.
00058              05  WORKING-OVERTIME-HOURS PIC 99.
00059              05  FILLER                PIC X(56).

00061          01  TIME-LISTING-LINE.
00062
00063              05  LISTING-NAME          PIC X(20).
00064              05  FILLER                PIC X(5)      VALUE SPACES.
00065              05  LISTING-REGULAR-HOURS PIC 99.
00066              05  FILLER                PIC X(5)      VALUE SPACES.
00067              05  LISTING-OVERTIME-HOURS PIC 99.
00068              05  FILLER                PIC X(5)      VALUE SPACES.
00069              05  LISTING-TOTAL-HOURS   PIC 999.
00070              05  FILLER                PIC X(85)     VALUE SPACES.

00072          01  EMPLOYEE-TOTAL-LINE.
00073
00074              05  FILLER                PIC X(25)
00075                                        VALUE "NUMBER OF EMPLOYEES IS".
00076              05  NUMBER-OF-EMPLOYEES   PIC 999.
00077              05  FILLER                PIC X(104)    VALUE SPACES.
00079          PROCEDURE DIVISION.

00081          DECLARATIVES.
00082
00083          CHECK-LOGIC SECTION.
00084
00085              USE FOR DEBUGGING
00086                  ON ALL REFERENCES OF NUMBER-OF-EMPLOYEES
00087                     ALL REFERENCES OF WORKING-REGULAR-HOURS
00088                     ALL REFERENCES OF WORKING-OVERTIME-HOURS
00089                     ALL REFERENCES OF LISTING-TOTAL-HOURS
00090              .
00091              EXHIBIT NAMED DEBUG-ITEM
```

Fig. 9-9 (*cont.*)

```
00092          .
00093
00094      END DECLARATIVES.

00096          MOVE "NO " TO END-OF-CARDS-SWITCH
00097          MOVE ZERO TO NUMBER-OF-EMPLOYEES
00098
00099          OPEN     INPUT              CARD-FILE
00100                   OUTPUT             PRINT-FILE
00101
00102          PERFORM INPUT-A-RECORD
00103
00104          PERFORM PRODUCE-TIME-LISTING
00105              UNTIL END-OF-CARDS-SWITCH IS EQUAL TO "YES"
00106
00107          WRITE PRINT-LINE
00108              FROM EMPLOYEE-TOTAL-LINE
00109
00110          CLOSE    CARD-FILE
00111                   PRINT-FILE
00112          STOP RUN
00113          .

00115      INPUT-A-RECORD.
00116
00117          READ CARD-FILE
00118              INTO WORKING-TIME-CARD
00119              AT END
00120                  MOVE "YES" TO END-OF-CARDS-SWITCH
00121          .

00123      PRODUCE-TIME-LISTING.
00124
00125      *             INCREMENT COUNTER EACH TIME AN EMPLOYEE IS PROCESSED
00126
00127          ADD 2 TO NUMBER-OF-EMPLOYEES
00128
00129      *             MOVE DATA FROM INPUT CARD TO AREA WHERE LINE IS BUILT
00130
00131          MOVE WORKING-NAME            TO LISTING-NAME
00132          MOVE WORKING-REGULAR-HOURS   TO LISTING-REGULAR-HOURS
00133          MOVE WORKING-OVERTIME-HOURS  TO LISTING-OVERTIME-HOURS
00134
00135      *             CALCULATE TOTAL HOURS BY ADDING REGULAR, OVERTIME
00136      *             NOTE THAT RESULT IS PLACED IN TIME-LISTING-LINE.
00137
00138          ADD WORKING-REGULAR-HOURS WORKING-REGULAR-HOURS
00139              GIVING LISTING-TOTAL-HOURS
00140
00141          WRITE PRINT-LINE
00142              FROM TIME-LISTING-LINE
00143
00144          PERFORM INPUT-A-RECORD
00145          .
```

Fig. 9-9 (*cont.*)

```
ABEL FRED                       40    03    080
BAKER SUE                       30    00    060
CHARLIE CHUCK                   40    12    080
PERELMAN BARNEY                 40    15    080
PERELMAN MIKE                   03    00    006
TROUBLE TOM                     40    10    080
NUMBER OF EMPLOYEES IS     012
```

Fig. 9-10

```
DEBUG-ITEM = 000097  NUMBER-OF-EMPLOYEES                          000
DEBUG-ITEM = 000127  NUMBER-OF-EMPLOYEES                          002
DEBUG-ITEM = 000132  WORKING-REGULAR-HOURS                        40
DEBUG-ITEM = 000133  WORKING-OVERTIME-HOURS                       03
DEBUG-ITEM = 000138  WORKING-REGULAR-HOURS                        40
DEBUG-ITEM = 000138  LISTING-TOTAL-HOURS                          080
DEBUG-ITEM = 000127  NUMBER-OF-EMPLOYEES                          004
DEBUG-ITEM = 000132  WORKING-REGULAR-HOURS                        30
DEBUG-ITEM = 000133  WORKING-OVERTIME-HOURS                       00
DEBUG-ITEM = 000138  WORKING-REGULAR-HOURS                        30
DEBUG-ITEM = 000138  LISTING-TOTAL-HOURS                          060
DEBUG-ITEM = 000127  NUMBER-OF-EMPLOYEES                          006
DEBUG-ITEM = 000132  WORKING-REGULAR-HOURS                        40
DEBUG-ITEM = 000133  WORKING-OVERTIME-HOURS                       12
DEBUG-ITEM = 000138  WORKING-REGULAR-HOURS                        40
DEBUG-ITEM = 000138  LISTING-TOTAL-HOURS                          080
DEBUG-ITEM = 000127  NUMBER-OF-EMPLOYEES                          008
DEBUG-ITEM = 000132  WORKING-REGULAR-HOURS                        40
DEBUG-ITEM = 000133  WORKING-OVERTIME-HOURS                       15
DEBUG-ITEM = 000138  WORKING-REGULAR-HOURS                        40
DEBUG-ITEM = 000138  LISTING-TOTAL-HOURS                          080
DEBUG-ITEM = 000127  NUMBER-OF-EMPLOYEES                          010
DEBUG-ITEM = 000132  WORKING-REGULAR-HOURS                        03
DEBUG-ITEM = 000133  WORKING-OVERTIME-HOURS                       00
DEBUG-ITEM = 000138  WORKING-REGULAR-HOURS                        03
DEBUG-ITEM = 000138  LISTING-TOTAL-HOURS                          006
DEBUG-ITEM = 000127  NUMBER-OF-EMPLOYEES                          012
DEBUG-ITEM = 000132  WORKING-REGULAR-HOURS                        40
DEBUG-ITEM = 000133  WORKING-OVERTIME-HOURS                       10
DEBUG-ITEM = 000138  WORKING-REGULAR-HOURS                        40
DEBUG-ITEM = 000138  LISTING-TOTAL-HOURS                          080
```

Fig. 9-11

The following is one way to debug the program:

1. We begin with the number-of-employees counter. Our debugging output EXHIBIT DEBUG-ITEM on ALL REFERENCES OF NUMBER-OF-EMPLOYEES. We find that NUMBER-OF-EMPLOYEES was set to zero at line 97.

2. The next reference to NUMBER-OF-EMPLOYEES was at line 127, when it became 002. How did it skip from 000 to 002 without taking on the value 001?

3. Looking at line 127, we find:

    ADD 2 TO NUMBER-OF-EMPLOYEES

    This line is supposed to increment the counter every time an employee record is input; clearly, we should be adding 1, not 2. What we have, then, is *merely* a typographical error in the COBOL program. Observe, however, that this error is not caught by the compiler (the syntax of line 127 is correct), and it does not cause a program ABEND. This type of error must be found *by the programmer* during *program testing*.

4. We now turn to the total-hours-worked column. Our debugging output shows us the contents of WORKING-REGULAR-HOURS and WORKING-OVERTIME-HOURS during the execution of the MOVE statements in lines 132 and 133. For example, for the first employee, regular hours is 40 and overtime hours is 03.

5. The next reference to WORKING-REGULAR-HOURS is on line 138, which also references LISTING-TOTAL-HOURS, the incorrect field. Notice that WORKING-OVERTIME-HOURS does not appear to be referenced on line 138, and that LISTING-TOTAL-HOURS is always twice the value of WORKING-REGULAR-HOURS.

6. Examining the statement on line 138 of the program, we find

    ADD WORKING-REGULAR-HOURS   WORKING-REGULAR-HOURS
        GIVING LISTING-TOTAL-HOURS

    instead of the obviously intended

ADD WORKING-REGULAR-HOURS   WORKING-OVERTIME-HOURS
GIVING LISTING-TOTAL-HOURS

This is another "silly" mistake which does not cause a syntax error or program ABEND.

9.19   Debug the following program, which contains an infinite loop. Source listing, test output, and debugging output are provided in Figs. 9-12, 9-13, and 9-14, respectively.

```
00001              IDENTIFICATION DIVISION.
00002
00003              PROGRAM-ID.  TIMELIST.
00004
00005              AUTHOR.   LARRY NEWCOMER.
00006              INSTALLATION.   PENN STATE UNIVERSITY--YORK CAMPUS.
00007
00008              DATE-WRITTEN.   MAY 1983.
00009              DATE-COMPILED.  MAY  9,1983.
00011         *    TIMELIST PRINTS ONE LINE FOR EACH EMPLOYEE SHOWING:
00012         *    NUMBER OF REGULAR HOURS WORKED, NUMBER OF OVERTIME
00013         *    HOURS WORKED, AND TOTAL HOURS WORKED. AT THE END OF THE
00014         *    REPORT, IT ALSO PRINTS A COUNT OF THE NUMBER OF
00015         *    EMPLOYEES PROCESSED.   INPUT IS FROM A DECK OF TIME
00016         *    CARDS, KEPT IN SEQUENCE BY EMPLOYEE NAME.

00018         ENVIRONMENT DIVISION.

00020         CONFIGURATION SECTION.

00022         SOURCE-COMPUTER.  IBM-3081 WITH DEBUGGING MODE.
00023         OBJECT-COMPUTER.  IBM-3081.

00025         INPUT-OUTPUT SECTION.

00027         FILE-CONTROL.

00029             SELECT CARD-FILE          ASSIGN TO CARDS.
00030             SELECT PRINT-FILE         ASSIGN TO PRINTER.

00032         DATA DIVISION.

00034         FILE SECTION.

00036         FD   CARD-FILE
00037              RECORD CONTAINS 80 CHARACTERS
00038              LABEL RECORDS ARE OMITTED
00039              .
00040
00041         01   TIME-CARD-INPUT          PIC X(80).

00043         FD   PRINT-FILE
00044              RECORD CONTAINS 132 CHARACTERS
00045              LABEL RECORDS ARE OMITTED
00046              .
00047
00048         01   PRINT-LINE               PIC X(132).

00050         WORKING-STORAGE SECTION.

00052         01   END-OF-CARDS-SWITCH      PIC X(3).

00054         01   WORKING-TIME-CARD.
00055
00056              05   WORKING-NAME           PIC X(20).
00057              05   WORKING-REGULAR-HOURS  PIC 99.
00058              05   WORKING-OVERTIME-HOURS PIC 99.
00059              05   FILLER                 PIC X(56).
```

Fig. 9-12

```
00061          01   TIME-LISTING-LINE.
00062
00063               05   LISTING-NAME              PIC X(20).
00064               05   FILLER                    PIC X(5)          VALUE SPACES.
00065               05   LISTING-REGULAR-HOURS     PIC 99.
00066               05   FILLER                    PIC X(5)          VALUE SPACES.
00067               05   LISTING-OVERTIME-HOURS    PIC 99.
00068               05   FILLER                    PIC X(5)          VALUE SPACES.
00069               05   LISTING-TOTAL-HOURS       PIC 999.
00070               05   FILLER                    PIC X(85)          VALUE SPACES.

00072          01   EMPLOYEE-TOTAL-LINE.
00073
00074               05   FILLER                    PIC X(25)
00075                                              VALUE "NUMBER OF EMPLOYEES IS".
00076               05   NUMBER-OF-EMPLOYEES       PIC 999.
00077               05   FILLER                    PIC X(104)         VALUE SPACES.

00079          PROCEDURE DIVISION.

00081          DECLARATIVES.
00082
00083          CHECK-LOGIC SECTION.
00084
00085               USE FOR DEBUGGING
00086                    ON ALL REFERENCES OF NUMBER-OF-EMPLOYEES
00087                       ALL REFERENCES OF WORKING-REGULAR-HOURS
00088                       ALL REFERENCES OF WORKING-OVERTIME-HOURS
00089                       ALL REFERENCES OF LISTING-TOTAL-HOURS
00090                    .
00091               EXHIBIT NAMED DEBUG-ITEM
00092                    .
00093
00094          END DECLARATIVES.

00096      D   READY TRACE
00097
00098               MOVE "NO " TO END-OF-CARDS-SWITCH
00099               MOVE ZERO TO NUMBER-OF-EMPLOYEES
00100
00101               OPEN     INPUT               CARD-FILE
00102                        OUTPUT              PRINT-FILE
00103
00104               PERFORM INPUT-A-RECORD
00105
00106               PERFORM PRODUCE-TIME-LISTING
00107                    UNTIL END-OF-CARDS-SWITCH IS EQUAL TO "YES"
00108
00109               WRITE PRINT-LINE
00110                    FROM EMPLOYEE-TOTAL-LINE
00111
00112               CLOSE    CARD-FILE
00113                        PRINT-FILE
00114               STOP RUN
00115                    .

00117          INPUT-A-RECORD.
00118
00119               READ CARD-FILE
00120                    INTO WORKING-TIME-CARD
00121                    AT END
00122                         MOVE "YES" TO END-OF-CARDS-SWITCH
00123                    .
```

Fig. 9-12 (*cont.*)

```
00125          PRODUCE-TIME-LISTING.
00126
00127     *             INCREMENT COUNTER EACH TIME AN EMPLOYEE IS PROCESSED
00128
00129          ADD 2 TO NUMBER-OF-EMPLOYEES
00130
00131     *             MOVE DATA FROM INPUT CARD TO AREA WHERE LINE IS BUILT
00132
00133          MOVE WORKING-NAME             TO LISTING-NAME
00134          MOVE WORKING-REGULAR-HOURS  TO LISTING-REGULAR-HOURS
00135          MOVE WORKING-OVERTIME-HOURS TO LISTING-OVERTIME-HOURS
00136
00137     *             CALCULATE TOTAL HOURS BY ADDING REGULAR, OVERTIME
00138     *             NOTE THAT RESULT IS PLACED IN TIME-LISTING-LINE.
00139
00140          ADD WORKING-REGULAR-HOURS WORKING-REGULAR-HOURS
00141             GIVING LISTING-TOTAL-HOURS
00142
00143          WRITE PRINT-LINE
00144             FROM TIME-LISTING-LINE
00145
00146          .
```

Fig. 9-12   (*cont.*)

```
ABEL FRED                     40     03     080
ABEL FRED                     40     03     080
ABEL FRED                     40     03     080
ABEL FRED                     40     03     080
  .
  .
  .
```

Fig. 9-13

```
DEBUG-ITEM = 000099 NUMBER-OF-EMPLOYEES                          000
INPUT-A-RECORD ,PRODUCE-TIME-LISTING ,
DEBUG-ITEM = 000129 NUMBER-OF-EMPLOYEES                          002
DEBUG-ITEM = 000134 WORKING-REGULAR-HOURS                        40
DEBUG-ITEM = 000135 WORKING-OVERTIME-HOURS                       03
DEBUG-ITEM = 000140 WORKING-REGULAR-HOURS                        40
DEBUG-ITEM = 000140 LISTING-TOTAL-HOURS                          080
PRODUCE-TIME-LISTING ,
DEBUG-ITEM = 000129 NUMBER-OF-EMPLOYEES                          004
DEBUG-ITEM = 000134 WORKING-REGULAR-HOURS                        40
DEBUG-ITEM = 000135 WORKING-OVERTIME-HOURS                       03
DEBUG-ITEM = 000140 WORKING-REGULAR-HOURS                        40
DEBUG-ITEM = 000140 LISTING-TOTAL-HOURS                          080
PRODUCE-TIME-LISTING ,
DEBUG-ITEM = 000129 NUMBER-OF-EMPLOYEES                          006
DEBUG-ITEM = 000134 WORKING-REGULAR-HOURS                        40
DEBUG-ITEM = 000135 WORKING-OVERTIME-HOURS                       03
DEBUG-ITEM = 000140 WORKING-REGULAR-HOURS                        40
DEBUG-ITEM = 000140 LISTING-TOTAL-HOURS                          080
  .
  .
  .
```

Fig. 9-14

Illustrative debugging procedure:

1. Check the test output: it appears that the first record input is being printed over and over.

2. Check the debugging output, which includes a READY TRACE and a display of DEBUG-ITEM on ALL REFERENCES OF NUMBER-OF-EMPLOYEES, WORKING-REGULAR-HOURS, WORKING-OVERTIME-HOURS, and LISTING-TOTAL-HOURS. If we abstract the TRACE output, we find:

    > INPUT-A-RECORD, PRODUCE-TIME-LISTING,
    > PRODUCE-TIME-LISTING,
    > PRODUCE-TIME-LISTING,
    > . . .

    Clearly, PRODUCE-TIME-LISTING is being executed over and over again.

3. Checking DEBUG-ITEM output for each execution of PRODUCE-TIME-LISTING, we find that WORKING-REGULAR-HOURS and WORKING-OVERTIME-HOURS never change —confirmation that the same record is being processed over and over.

4. Checking the program, we find that lines 106–107 contain

    > PERFORM PRODUCE-TIME-LISTING
    >   UNTIL END-OF-CARDS-SWITCH IS EQUAL TO "YES"

5. Checking lines 125–146, we find that PRODUCE-TIME-LISTING does not change END-OF-CARDS-SWITCH, nor does it PERFORM any paragraph which does. In short, there is no way for the PERFORM...UNTIL... ever to end. It is also apparent that PRODUCE-TIME-LISTING processed the same record over and over, since the routine does not provide for the input of a new logical record.

6. Both problems can be corrected by adding the statement

    > PERFORM INPUT-A-RECORD

    at the end of the PRODUCE-TIME-LISTING paragraph. INPUT-A-RECORD will set END-OF-CARDS-SWITCH at end of file and will also input the next logical record for the next execution of PRODUCE-TIME-LISTING.

Chapter 10

Table Handling

The notion of an array of similar data items, or *table*, has already been encountered in Sections 5.14 and 7.12 (see Examples 7.36 and 7.37). We develop the subject in detail in the present chapter. Consideration will be restricted to one- and two-dimensional tables; however, the reader should have no trouble in extending our treatment of the latter to three-dimensional tables—the highest dimension provided for in COBOL (see Appendix C for COBOL '80).

10.1 One-Dimensional Tables: the OCCURS Clause

The format for defining one-dimensional, fixed-length tables is:

> level-number   data-name <u>OCCURS</u> integer TIMES

The OCCURS clause may be used at any level *except* level-01. To be able to specify "integer", the programmer must know the size of the table in advance. Since this is not always certain, the usual practice is to set aside enough entries to accommodate the *maximum* table size which will ever be needed during the useful life of the program.

EXAMPLE 10.1

- ```
  01   MONTHLY-SALES-TABLE.
     05   MONTHLY-SALES        PIC S9(7)V99           COMP-3
                               OCCURS 12 TIMES.
  ```

With certainty, there are 12 months in a year.

- ```
  01   MONTHLY-SALES-INFORMATION.
     05   SALESPERSON-DATA     OCCURS 400 TIMES.
        10   SALES-ID          PIC X(4).
        10   SALES-NAME        PIC X(20).
        10   MONTHLY-SALES     PIC S9(5)V99           COMP-3.
        10   QUOTA-AMOUNT      PIC S9(5)V99           COMP-3.
  ```

Here, a group item, SALESPERSON-DATA, is repeated: there will be 400 entries in the table, each entry consisting of a block of the four level-10 subfields. Thus, an entry will be $4 + 20 + 4 + 4 = 32$ bytes long (see Section 5.18), and the entire table, MONTHLY-SALES-INFORMATION, will be $400 \times 32 = 12\,800$ bytes long. The table size, 400, represents a "safe guess" as to the maximum number of sales people ever to be processed during the life of the program.

One-dimensional (or higher-dimensional) tables may be defined as part of records in the FILE SECTION or in WORKING-STORAGE.

10.2 Subscripts

Given that the OCCURS clause defines many table entries (with identical descriptions), how does the programmer inform the compiler *which* entry is being referenced in a PROCEDURE DIVISION statement? The simplest way is to use a *subscript*, which is a *positive integer* (in the form of a numeric literal or a numeric data item), which is written in parentheses after the name of the tabulated item.

261

EXAMPLE 10.2 The following code employs four subscripts to sum the entries of a table.

```
01   QUARTERLY-SALES.
     05   QUARTER-TOTAL        PIC S9(7)V99                COMP-3
                               OCCURS 4 TIMES.

. . . . . . . . . . . . . . . . .
     PROCEDURE DIVISION.
. . . . . . . . . . . . . . .
         ADD QUARTER-TOTAL (1)
             QUARTER-TOTAL (2)
             QUARTER-TOTAL (3)
             QUARTER-TOTAL (4)
                               GIVING YEARLY-TOTAL
```

The real utility of tables and subscripts arises from the fact that a *variable* integer data item may be used as a subscript; the current value of the item indicates which table entry is to be processed. Very often a data item used as a subscript is controlled through a PERFORM . . . VARYING statement.

EXAMPLE 10.3

```
01   TOTAL-AREAS.
     05   LAST-YEARS-TOTAL   PIC S9(9)V99   COMP-3.
     05   THIS-YEARS-TOTAL   PIC S9(9)V99   COMP-3.

. . . . . . . . . . . . . . . . . . . . .
01   SUBSCRIPT-AREAS.
     05   MONTH              PIC S9(2)      COMP SYNC.

. . . . . . . . . . . . . . . . . . . . .
01   SALES-INFORMATION.
     05   MONTHLY-SALES      OCCURS 12 TIMES.
          10   LAST-YEAR     PIC S9(7)V99   COMP-3.
          10   THIS-YEAR     PIC S9(7)V99   COMP-3.

. . . . . . . . . . . . . . . . . . . . .
         MOVE ZERO TO LAST-YEARS-TOTAL
                      THIS-YEARS-TOTAL
         PERFORM CALCULATE-YEARLY-TOTALS
             VARYING MONTH FROM 1 BY 1
                 UNTIL MONTH GREATER THAN 12

. . . . . . . . . . . . . . . . . . . . .
     CALCULATE-YEARLY-TOTALS.
         ADD LAST-YEAR (MONTH) TO LAST-YEARS-TOTAL
         ADD THIS-YEAR (MONTH) TO THIS-YEARS-TOTAL
```

Here, from a table of 12 values of the group item MONTHLY-SALES, the 12 values of the elementary item LAST-YEAR, and those of the elementary item THIS-YEAR, are separately summed by use of the variable subscript MONTH.

In IBM OS/VS COBOL, the most efficient way to define a numeric data item for use as a subscript is PIC S9(n) COMP SYNC. Subscripts are *required* for all data items at or subordinate to an OCCURS clause.

10.3 Manipulation of One-Dimensional Tables

Loading (Initializing) a Table to Zero

Frequently, it is desired to initialize all entries in a table to the same value; say, zero. Because the VALUE clause may not be used for data items which are part of a table, the MOVE statement provides a simple means to set a table to zero.

EXAMPLE 10.4   Defining a 50-entry table by

```
01   SALES-FIGURES-BY-STATE.
     05   STATE-SALES            OCCURS 50 TIMES.
          10   STATE-ID          PIC X(2).
          10   SALES-AMOUNT      PIC S9(5)V99      COMP-3.
```

we indicate an incorrect, and the correct, way to zero the table.

●   MOVE ZEROS TO SALES-FIGURES-BY-STATE

is valid insofar as SALES-FIGURES-BY-STATE is not a table entry (it is not described with an OCCURS clause and is not subordinate to an OCCURS clause), and so does not require a subscript. But, since it is a group item, PIC X DISPLAY zeros will be moved into the entire table; in particular, into the 50 occurrences of SALES-AMOUNT, which is a COMP-3 item. Thus, a logic error is incurred.

●   PERFORM ZERO-SALES-AMOUNT
             VARYING STATE-SALES-SUB
             FROM 1 BY 1
             UNTIL STATE-SALES-SUB GREATER THAN 50

```
ZERO-SALES-AMOUNT.
     MOVE ZERO TO SALES-AMOUNT (STATE-SALES-SUB)
     MOVE SPACES TO STATE-ID (STATE-SALES-SUB)
```

The correct procedure is to define a subscript (STATE-SALES-SUB) whereby the subfields of the table may be individually cleared in a PERFORMed paragraph.

EXAMPLE 10.5

```
01   EMPLOYEE-DATA-TABLE.
     05   EMPLOYEE-INFORMATION       OCCURS 500 TIMES.
          10   SOCIAL-SEC-NUMBER     PIC 9(9).
          10   EMPLOYEE-SALARY       PIC S9(3)V99.
```

Since all table fields are DISPLAY, we can zero the entire table with one statement:

    MOVE ZEROS TO EMPLOYEE-DATA-TABLE

Loading with the VALUE Clause

If each table entry must be initialized to its own unique value, the VALUE clause may be used to set up a series of individual data items which can then be REDEFINED as a table. (The detour is necessary because the VALUE clause may not be directly applied to table entries.) The VALUE clause may be used in this way only for WORKING-STORAGE items.

EXAMPLE 10.6

```
01   VALID-STATUS-CODES-TABLE.
     05   VALID-STATUS-VALUES.
          10   FILLER          PIC X(3)      VALUE "A07".
          10   FILLER          PIC X(3)      VALUE "A2K".
          10   FILLER          PIC X(3)      VALUE "B03".
          10   FILLER          PIC X(3)      VALUE "C99".
     05   STATUS-CODE          REDEFINES VALID-STATUS-VALUES
                               PIC X(3)
                               OCCURS 4 TIMES.
```

VALID-STATUS-VALUES consists of four elementary items, all PIC X(3), that are initialized with the VALUE clause. Note that we do not bother to give these data items names, but use the reserved word FILLER instead. VALID-STATUS-VALUES is then REDEFINED as a table, STATUS-CODE, in such manner that the four PIC X(3) items in STATUS-CODE and the four PIC X(3) items in VALID-STATUS-VALUES are one and the same (i.e., they occupy exactly the same memory locations). This means that STATUS-CODE (1) has the starting value "A07", STATUS-CODE (2) has the starting value "A2K", etc. The statements that actually process the table will, of course, refer to STATUS-CODE, not VALID-STATUS-VALUES.

EXAMPLE 10.7 Example 10.6 used the VALUE clause to initialize a table with elementary entries; we now initialize a table with group entries.

```
01   SHIPPING-INSTRUCTIONS-TABLE.
     05   SHIPPING-CODES-VALUES.
          10   FILLER              PIC X(2)     VALUE "A3".
          10   FILLER              PIC X(20)    VALUE "U.S. MAIL".
          10   FILLER              PIC X(2)     VALUE "A8".
          10   FILLER              PIC X(20)    VALUE "UPS".
          10   FILLER              PIC X(2)     VALUE "C3".
          10   FILLER              PIC X(20)    VALUE "FEDERAL EXPRESS".
     05   CODES-AND-INSTRUCTIONS   REDEFINES SHIPPING-CODES-VALUES
                                   OCCURS 3 TIMES.
          10   SHIPPING-CODE         PIC X(2).
          10   SHIPPING-INSTRUCTION  PIC X(20).
```

Again, the table entries are first defined as elementary items with the name FILLER and the appropriate PIC, USAGE, and VALUE clauses. Note that SHIPPING-CODES-VALUES consists of a PIC X(2) item, followed by a PIC X(20) item, followed by a second PIC X(2) item, etc. CODES-AND-INSTRUCTIONS then REDEFINES SHIPPING-CODES-VALUES as a 3-entry table, where each entry consists of a PIC X(2) SHIPPING-CODE followed by a PIC X(20) SHIPPING-INSTRUCTION. Because of the VALUE clauses, SHIPPING-CODE (1) has the starting value "A3", SHIPPING-INSTRUCTION (1) has the starting value "U.S. MAIL"; SHIPPING-CODE (2) has the starting value "A8", SHIPPING-INSTRUCTION (2) has the starting value "UPS"; etc. Example 10.20 applies this technique to a table with numeric entries.

Loading with the READ Statement

There are two major disadvantages to initializing WORKING-STORAGE tables by REDEFINING items with the VALUE clause: (1) as tables become large and/or complex, this approach becomes extremely awkward and requires much DATA DIVISION coding; (2) if the initial values for table entries must be changed, the COBOL program itself must be modified and recompiled. An effective way to avoid these difficulties is to keep starting table values on a sequential disk or tape file. When the program begins execution, it can READ the initial values into the appropriate table areas. If the starting table values must be changed, this can be done simply by modifying the file.

EXAMPLE 10.8 The status codes table of Example 10.6 could be initialized from a file in the following manner:

```
FD   STATUS-CODE-FILE ...
01   STATUS-CODE-RECORD.
     05   STATUS-CODE-VALUE      PIC X(3).
     . . . . . . . . . . . . . . . . . . .

WORKING-STORAGE SECTION.
     . . . . . . . . . . . . . . . . . . .

01   VALID-STATUS-CODES-TABLE.
     05   STATUS-CODE           PIC X(3)   OCCURS 400 TIMES.
     05   NUMBER-OF-CODES       PIC S9(3)  COMP SYNC.
     . . . . . . . . . . . . . . . . . . .

PROCEDURE DIVISION.
     OPEN INPUT STATUS-CODE-FILE
     MOVE "NO" TO END-STATUS-FILE-SW
     PERFORM LOAD-STATUS-TABLE
          VARYING NUMBER-OF-CODES FROM 1 BY 1
          UNTIL      END-STATUS-FILE-SW EQUAL "YES"
               OR  NUMBER-OF-CODES GREATER THAN 400
```

```
          IF NUMBER-OF-CODES GREATER THAN 400
              MOVE 400 TO NUMBER-OF-CODES
              DISPLAY "TABLE FILE TOO LARGE--MODIFY, RECOMPILE COBOL TABLE"
                  UPON OPERATOR-MESSAGE-DEVICE
          ELSE
              SUBTRACT 1 FROM NUMBER-OF-CODES
          .

          CLOSE STATUS-CODE-FILE

      . . . . . . . . . . . . . . . . . . . . . . . .

      LOAD-STATUS-TABLE.
          READ STATUS-CODE-FILE
              AT END
                  MOVE "YES" TO END-STATUS-FILE-SW
          .

          IF END-STATUS-FILE-SW EQUAL "NO"
              MOVE STATUS-CODE-VALUE TO STATUS-CODE (NUMBER-OF-CODES)
          .
```

Note how NUMBER-OF-CODES is used to count how many table entries are actually input from the file. Note, too, that the PERFORM...VARYING loop which inputs the status code values stops either on end of file *or* if NUMBER-OF-CODES exceeds the size of the table as declared in the OCCURS clause (400, in this case). An IF statement following the PERFORM...VARYING... then tests NUMBER-OF-CODES, and if the maximum table size has been exceeded, a message is displayed for the operator, indicating that the OCCURS clause must be changed and the program recompiled. Observe that if end of file occurs, the last value of NUMBER-OF-CODES corresponds to the end of file, not to a STATUS-CODE-VALUE. Hence, NUMBER-OF-CODES must be decremented by 1 after the PERFORM...VARYING... stops on end of file. In any case, NUMBER-OF-CODES will correctly indicate the number of table entries loaded for any particular program run.

Maintaining a count of the number of active entries in a table is an extremely common table handling technique.

Summing Table Entries

In addition to Example 10.3, we give one further example.

EXAMPLE 10.9 Suppose that it is desired to accumulate the sum of the employee salaries in the table of Example 10.5:

```
01   EMPLOYEE-DATA-TABLE.
     05   EMPLOYEE-INFORMATION          OCCURS 500 TIMES.
          10   SOCIAL-SEC-NUMBER        PIC 9(9).
          10   EMPLOYEE-SALARY          PIC S9(3)V99    COMP-3.
     05   NUMBER-ACTIVE-EMPLOYEES       PIC S9(3)       COMP.
     . . . . . . . . . . . . . . . . . . . . . . . .

     MOVE ZERO TO TOTAL-SALARIES
     PERFORM TOTAL-EMPLOYEE-SALARIES
         VARYING EMPLOYEE-SUB
         FROM 1 BY 1
         UNTIL EMPLOYEE-SUB GREATER THAN NUMBER-ACTIVE-EMPLOYEES
     . . . . . . . . . . . . . . . . . . . . . . . .

 TOTAL-EMPLOYEE-SALARIES.
     ADD EMPLOYEE-SALARY (EMPLOYEE-SUB) TO TOTAL-SALARIES
     .
```

Here we do not add up all 500 entries, for although the table is defined to accommodate a maximum of 500 employees, it may actually contain data for fewer than 500. The data item NUMBER-ACTIVE-EMPLOYEES (which is not itself part of the table) is used to keep track of how many employees are actually represented in the table. It is assumed that the routines which add new employees to the table or remove employees from the table also maintain this count. NUMBER-ACTIVE-EMPLOYEES becomes the stopping value for the PERFORM statement which controls the addition of employee salaries.

Table Look-Up with PERFORM

In a *look-up* or *search* operation, the entries in a table are systematically compared to a given value until an entry is found which matches the given value or until that value is determined not to be in the table. The simplest table search algorithm is the *sequential* or *linear* search, in which the first entry is examined, then the second entry, then the third, and so on, until the desired entry is found or until the end of the table is reached. Most versions of COBOL provide a special SEARCH statement (see Section 10.8) for programming a sequential search. However, it can also be coded with a PERFORM loop.

EXAMPLE 10.10   Given the table of Example 10.6 and a known value in INPUT-STATUS-CODE PIC X(3), determine whether INPUT-STATUS-CODE is valid by looking it up in VALID-STATUS-CODES-TABLE.

```
01   VALID-STATUS-CODES-TABLE.
     05   STATUS-CODE               PIC X(3)
                                    OCCURS 40 TIMES.
. . . . . . . . . . . . . . . . . . . . . . . . .

CHECK-STATUS-CODE.
     PERFORM LOOK-UP-STATUS
     IF VALID-STATUS-SW EQUAL "YES"
     . . . (process valid status code)
     ELSE
     . . . (handle invalid status code)
. . . . . . . . . . . . . . . . . . . . .

LOOK-UP-STATUS.
     MOVE "NO" TO VALID-STATUS-SW
     PERFORM CHECK-ENTRY
         VARYING STATUS-CODE-SUBSCRIPT FROM 1 BY 1
         UNTIL    STATUS-CODE-SUBSCRIPT GREATER THAN 40
              OR VALID-STATUS-SW EQUAL "YES"

CHECK-ENTRY.
     IF STATUS-CODE (STATUS-CODE-SUBSCRIPT) EQUAL INPUT-STATUS-CODE
         MOVE "YES" TO VALID-STATUS-SW
```

LOOK-UP-STATUS first sets VALID-STATUS-SW to "NO". CHECK-ENTRY is then performed, with STATUS-CODE-SUBSCRIPT [defined PIC S9(5) COMP SYNC] varying from 1 up to the number of table entries. If at any point the entry corresponding to the current value of STATUS-CODE-SUBSCRIPT is equal to INPUT-STATUS-CODE, VALID-STATUS-SW is set to "YES", thus stopping execution of the PERFORM . . . UNTIL . . . . If no table entry is equal to INPUT-STATUS-CODE, VALID-STATUS-SW remains set to "NO".

Observe that if the sixth entry (say) is equal to INPUT-STATUS-CODE, the PERFORM . . . stops with STATUS-CODE-SUBSCRIPT equal to *seven* (cf. Fig. 7-14). This shortcoming can be remedied as follows:

```
LOOK-UP-STATUS.
     MOVE 1 TO STATUS-CODE-SUBSCRIPT
     MOVE "YES" TO VALID-STATUS-SW
     PERFORM CHECK-ENTRY
         UNTIL VALID-STATUS-SW EQUAL "NO"
              OR STATUS-CODE (STATUS-CODE-SUBSCRIPT) EQUAL
                   INPUT-STATUS-CODE

CHECK-ENTRY.
```

```
        IF STATUS-CODE-SUBSCRIPT EQUAL 40
            MOVE "NO" TO VALID-STATUS-SW
        ELSE
            ADD 1 TO STATUS-CODE-SUBSCRIPT
```

Now if STATUS-CODE-SUBSCRIPT ever points to an entry which is equal to INPUT-STATUS-CODE, the UNTIL condition becomes true and execution of the PERFORM statement halts immediately without incrementing STATUS-CODE-SUBSCRIPT, which thus points to the desired table entry).

EXAMPLE 10.11　A common reason for table searching is to *decode* coded input fields for printing on reports. We illustrate with a table similar to that of Example 10.7:

```
    01  SHIPPING-INSTRUCTIONS-TABLE.
        05  CODES-AND-INSTRUCTIONS      OCCURS 18 TIMES.
            10  SHIPPING-CODE           PIC X(2).
            10  SHIPPING-INSTRUCTION    PIC X(30).
    . . . . . . . . . . . . . . . . . . . . . . . . . .
        MOVE "YES" TO FOUND-CODE-SW
        MOVE 1 TO SHIPPING-SUBSCRIPT
        PERFORM CHECK-ENTRY
            UNTIL      SHIPPING-CODE (SHIPPING-SUBSCRIPT) EQUAL INPUT-CODE
                    OR FOUND-CODE-SW EQUAL "NO"
        IF FOUND-CODE-SW EQUAL "YES"
            MOVE SHIPPING-INSTRUCTION (SHIPPING-SUBSCRIPT) TO
                PRINTED-SHIPPING-MESSAGE
        ELSE
            MOVE "*** INVALID SHIPPING CODE ***" TO
                PRINTED-SHIPPING-MESSAGE

    . . . . . . . . . . . . . . . . . . . . . . . . . .
        CHECK-ENTRY.
            IF SHIPPING-SUBSCRIPT EQUAL 18
                MOVE "NO" TO FOUND-CODE-SW
            ELSE
                ADD 1 TO SHIPPING-SUBSCRIPT
```

If the INPUT-CODE is found in the SHIPPING-INSTRUCTIONS-TABLE, the SHIPPING-INSTRUCTION corresponding to the SHIPPING-CODE that matches INPUT-CODE is moved to a printer output area. If the INPUT-CODE is not in the table, an error message is printed on the report. This technique allows input records to contain only a 2-byte code, yet provides the entire 30-byte shipping instruction on the printed report.

10.4　Two-Dimensional Tables

When an item with an OCCURS clause in its definition has a subordinate item which also has an OCCURS clause, we say that the subordinate table is *two-dimensional*.

EXAMPLE 10.12

```
    01  FREIGHT-CHARGES-TABLE.
        05  WEIGHT-RANGE            OCCURS 3 TIMES.
            10  WEIGHT-LIMIT        PIC S9(3)           COMP-3.
            10  DESTINATION         OCCURS 3 TIMES.
                15  FREIGHT-CHARGE  PIC S9(3)V99        COMP-3.
```

WEIGHT-RANGE is a table with 3 entries, each entry consisting of the fields WEIGHT-LIMIT and DESTINATION. DESTINATION, however, is itself a table with 3 entries (each entry consisting of a FREIGHT-CHARGE value). Thus, the subordinate table DESTINATION contains $3 \times 3 = 9$ items; see

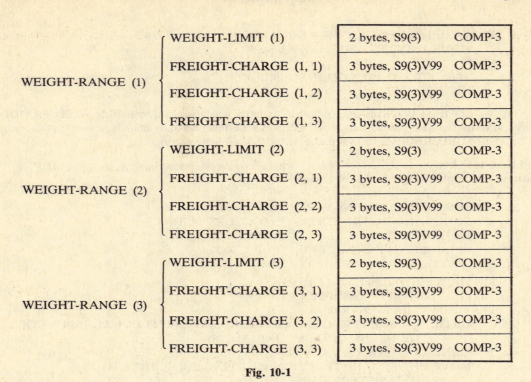

	WEIGHT-LIMIT (1)	2 bytes, S9(3)	COMP-3
WEIGHT-RANGE (1)	FREIGHT-CHARGE (1, 1)	3 bytes, S9(3)V99	COMP-3
	FREIGHT-CHARGE (1, 2)	3 bytes, S9(3)V99	COMP-3
	FREIGHT-CHARGE (1, 3)	3 bytes, S9(3)V99	COMP-3
	WEIGHT-LIMIT (2)	2 bytes, S9(3)	COMP-3
WEIGHT-RANGE (2)	FREIGHT-CHARGE (2, 1)	3 bytes, S9(3)V99	COMP-3
	FREIGHT-CHARGE (2, 2)	3 bytes, S9(3)V99	COMP-3
	FREIGHT-CHARGE (2, 3)	3 bytes, S9(3)V99	COMP-3
	WEIGHT-LIMIT (3)	2 bytes, S9(3)	COMP-3
WEIGHT-RANGE (3)	FREIGHT-CHARGE (3, 1)	3 bytes, S9(3)V99	COMP-3
	FREIGHT-CHARGE (3, 2)	3 bytes, S9(3)V99	COMP-3
	FREIGHT-CHARGE (3, 3)	3 bytes, S9(3)V99	COMP-3

Fig. 10-1

Fig. 10-1. Observe that the number of subscripts needed to reference an item in the table is equal to the number of OCCURS clauses that apply to the item. The first subscript refers to the highest-level OCCURS clause; the second, to the next-highest-level; etc. For this particular two-dimensional table, the two subscripts have the same range of values; that, of course, will not be true in general. In Fig. 10-1, multiple subscripts are separated by a comma plus a space; the comma is optional.

EXAMPLE 10.13 If STUDENT-TRANSCRIPT, defined below, is a logical record for a student master file, what is the logical record length?

```
01   STUDENT-TRANSCRIPT.
    05   STUDENT-ID                PIC X(9).
    05   STUDENT-NAME              PIC X(25).
    05   SEMESTERS-ATTENDED        PIC S9            COMP-3.
    05   SEMESTER-INFORMATION      OCCURS 8 TIMES.
        10   GRADE-POINT-AVERAGE   PIC S9V99         COMP-3.
        10   NUMBER-COURSES        PIC S9            COMP-3.
        10   COURSE-INFO           OCCURS 6 TIMES.
            15   COURSE-ID         PIC X(5).
            15   NUMBER-CREDITS    PIC S9V9          COMP-3.
            15   GRADE             PIC S9            COMP-3.
```

COURSE-ID is 5 bytes, and (Section 5.18) NUMBER-CREDITS is 2 bytes and GRADE is 1 byte; hence, one COURSE-INFO entry is 8 bytes long. Since COURSE-INFO OCCURS 6 TIMES, the entire COURSE-INFO table is 48 bytes long. One SEMESTER-INFORMATION entry consists of an entire COURSE-INFO table, plus NUMBER-COURSES (1 byte) and GRADE-POINT-AVERAGE (2 bytes); so one SEMESTER-INFORMATION entry is 51 bytes. Since there are 8 entries, the entire SEMESTER-INFORMATION table requires 408 bytes. To this we must add space for STUDENT-ID (9 bytes), STUDENT-NAME (25 bytes), and SEMESTERS-ATTENDED (1 byte), giving a total record length of 443 bytes.

It should be noted that the definition of STUDENT-TRANSCRIPT presupposes a loading of the table such that COURSE-INFO (i, j) refers to the jth course *taken by the student* during the ith semester *of the student's enrollment* (i.e., if the table were displayed in matrix form, the matrix would be packed toward the upper left corner). The number of semesters taken by the student will be stored in the counter SEMESTER-ATTENDED, and the counter NUMBER-COURSES (k) will store the number of courses taken by the student during the kth semester of his or her enrollment. These counters indicate exactly which of the $8 \times 6 = 48$ COURSE-INFO memory locations contain active data.

EXAMPLE 10.14   Calculate the average semester performance for a student whose information is currently in the logical record STUDENT-TRANSCRIPT of Example 10.13.

```
        MOVE ZERO TO GRADE-POINT-TOTAL
        PERFORM ADD-UP-SEMESTER-AVERAGES
            VARYING SEMESTER-SUB FROM 1 BY 1
            UNTIL SEMESTER-SUB GREATER THAN SEMESTERS-ATTENDED
        DIVIDE SEMESTERS-ATTENDED INTO GRADE-POINT-TOTAL
            GIVING AVERAGE-SEMESTER-GRADE

        . . . . . . . . . . . . . . . . . . . . .

    ADD-UP-SEMESTER-AVERAGES.
        ADD GRADE-POINT-AVERAGE (SEMESTER-SUB) TO GRADE-POINT-TOTAL
```

10.5   Manipulation of Two-Dimensional Tables

Loading to Zero

Since two subscripts are involved, PERFORM . . . VARYING . . . AFTER . . . is employed.

EXAMPLE 10.15   In the following, it is assumed that all six table entries are currently active.

```
    01  SALES-AMOUNTS.
        05  REGION-TOTALS            OCCURS 2 TIMES.
            10  DEPARTMENT-TOTALS     OCCURS 3 TIMES.
                15  SALES             PIC S9(5)V99  COMP.

    . . . . . . . . . . . . . . . . . . . . . . . .

    01  SUBSCRIPTS.
        05  REGION-NUMBER            PIC S9(5)  COMP SYNC.
        05  DEPARTMENT-NUMBER        PIC S9(5)  COMP SYNC.

    . . . . . . . . . . . . . . . . . . . . . . .

        PERFORM ZERO-SALES-AMOUNTS
            VARYING REGION-NUMBER FROM 1 BY 1
                UNTIL REGION-NUMBER GREATER THAN 2
            AFTER DEPARTMENT-NUMBER FROM 1 BY 1
                UNTIL DEPARTMENT-NUMBER GREATER THAN 3

        . . . . . . . . . . . . . . . . . . . . .

    ZERO-SALES-AMOUNTS.
        MOVE ZERO TO SALES (REGION-NUMBER DEPARTMENT-NUMBER)
```

Summation of Entries

EXAMPLE 10.16   Calculate total credits to date for the student of Example 10.13.

```
        . . . . . . . . . . . . . . . . . . .

    05  TOTAL-CREDITS    PIC S9(3)V9    COMP-3.
        . . . . . . . . . . . . . . . . . . .

        MOVE ZERO TO TOTAL-CREDITS
        PERFORM ACCUMULATE-TOTAL-CREDITS
            VARYING SEMESTER-NUMBER FROM 1 BY 1
                UNTIL SEMESTER-NUMBER GREATER THAN SEMESTERS-ATTENDED
            AFTER COURSE-NUMBER FROM 1 BY 1
                UNTIL COURSE-NUMBER GREATER THAN
                    NUMBER-COURSES (SEMESTER-NUMBER)

        . . . . . . . . . . . . . . . . . . . . .
```

```
            ACCUMULATE-TOTAL-CREDITS.
                ADD NUMBER-CREDITS (SEMESTER-NUMBER COURSE-NUMBER)
                    TO TOTAL-CREDITS
```

where the subscripts are defined as:

```
        01  SUBSCRIPTS.
            05  SEMESTER-NUMBER      PIC S9(5)  COMP SYNC.
            05  COURSE-NUMBER        PIC S9(5)  COMP SYNC.
```

Note especially the subscripting of NUMBER-COURSES in the PERFORM statement. Because NUMBER-COURSES OCCURS 8 TIMES as part of the SEMESTER-INFORMATION table, it must be subscripted; each time SEMESTER-NUMBER is incremented, the value of NUMBER-COURSES (SEMESTER-NUMBER) changes accordingly.

EXAMPLE 10.17 In Examples 10.13 and 10.14, the contents of GRADE-POINT-AVERAGE, part of the SEMESTER-INFORMATION table, were treated as though input data. Suppose that it was necessary to *calculate* GRADE-POINT-AVERAGE from the COURSE-INFO table: this could be done, for each semester, by summing grade times number of credits over all courses taken during the semester and dividing the sum by the total number of credits for the semester. The COBOL coding would involve a nested PERFORM . . . VARYING . . . structure, as shown below, where the subscripts are as defined in Example 10.16 and where TOTAL-GRADE-POINTS and TOTAL-CREDITS are numeric items in WORKING-STORAGE.

```
        PERFORM CALCULATE-SEMESTER-AVERAGE
            VARYING SEMESTER-NUMBER FROM 1 BY 1
                UNTIL SEMESTER-NUMBER GREATER THAN SEMESTERS-ATTENDED
    . . . . . . . . . . . . . . . . . . . . . . . . . . . .
        CALCULATE-SEMESTER-AVERAGE.
            MOVE ZERO TO TOTAL-GRADE-POINTS
                        TOTAL-CREDITS
            PERFORM TOTAL-SEMESTER-COURSES
                VARYING COURSE-NUMBER FROM 1 BY 1
                    UNTIL COURSE-NUMBER GREATER THAN
                        NUMBER-COURSES (SEMESTER-NUMBER)
            DIVIDE TOTAL-CREDITS INTO TOTAL-GRADE-POINTS
                GIVING GRADE-POINT-AVERAGE (SEMESTER-NUMBER)

        TOTAL-SEMESTER-COURSES.
            ADD NUMBER-CREDITS (SEMESTER-NUMBER COURSE-NUMBER)
                TO TOTAL-CREDITS
            COMPUTE TOTAL-GRADE-POINTS = TOTAL-GRADE-POINTS +
                GRADE (SEMESTER-NUMBER COURSE-NUMBER) *
                    NUMBER-CREDITS (SEMESTER-NUMBER COURSE-NUMBER)
```

Conversion of Input Data to Subscripts

For the tables so far considered, the subscripts have been generated with PERFORM . . . VARYING . . . . Sometimes, however, it is desired to obtain subscripts values by conversion of input data.

The simplest conversion is no conversion—the case when the input data are (by design) suitable "as is".

EXAMPLE 10.18 Suppose data entry personnel have keyed the following (DISPLAY) fields:

```
        FD  SALES-INPUT-FILE . . .
        01  SALES-RECORD.
            05  REGION-ID           PIC 9(1).
            05  DEPARTMENT-ID       PIC 9(2).
            05  SALES-AMOUNT        PIC S9(4)V99.
```

Using REGION-ID and DEPARTMENT-ID as subscripts, create a table of total sales by region and department:

```
01   TOTAL-SALES-AMOUNTS-TABLE.
     05   REGION                       OCCURS 7 TIMES.
          10   DEPARTMENT              OCCURS 12 TIMES.
               15   TOTAL-SALES-AMOUNT PIC S9(5)V99  COMP.
     05   REGION-LIMIT                 PIC S9(2)      COMP SYNC  VALUE + 7.
     05   DEPARTMENT-LIMIT             PIC S9(2)      COMP SYNC  VALUE + 12.
```

The following code would work (it is assumed that TOTAL-SALES-AMOUNT entries are already zeroed):

```
     . . . . . . . . . . . . . . . . . . . .
          OPEN  INPUT  SALES-INPUT-FILE
          MOVE "NO" TO END-FILE-SW
          PERFORM GET-SALES-RECORD
          PERFORM ACCUMULATE-SALES-TOTALS
               UNTIL END-FILE-SW EQUAL "YES"
          CLOSE SALES-INPUT-FILE
     . . . . . . . . . . . . . . . . . . . .

     GET-SALES-RECORD.
          READ SALES-INPUT-FILE
               AT END
                    MOVE "YES" TO END-FILE-SW


     ACCUMULATE-SALES-TOTALS.
          IF REGION-ID NOT NUMERIC OR DEPARTMENT-ID NOT NUMERIC OR
               SALES-AMOUNT NOT NUMERIC
                    PERFORM INVALID-NUMBER-ROUTINE
          ELSE IF REGION-ID LESS THAN 1 OR GREATER THAN REGION-LIMIT
               PERFORM REGION-OUT-OF-RANGE-ROUTINE
          ELSE IF DEPARTMENT-ID LESS THAN 1 OR GREATER THAN
               DEPARTMENT-LIMIT
               PERFORM DEPARTMENT-OUT-OF-RANGE-ROUTINE
          ELSE
               ADD SALES-AMOUNT TO
                    TOTAL-SALES-AMOUNT (REGION-ID DEPARTMENT-ID)


          PERFORM  GET-SALES-RECORD
     .
```

Note the checks on the input items used as subscripts: most versions of COBOL *do not provide any automatic warning* when a subscripted reference falls outside the actual table.

Actual conversion of input data can be accomplished with a linear IF, provided the number of values is relatively small, or with table look-up. Example 10.19 illustrates both techniques.

EXAMPLE 10.19 Rework Example 10.18 if the table is to be 3×15 (instead of 7×12) and if the alphanumeric input fields are given by

```
01   SALES-RECORD.
     05   REGION-ID          PIC  X(3).
     05   DEPARTMENT-ID      PIC  X(5).
     05   SALES-AMOUNT       PIC  S9(4)V99.
```

We may use a one-dimensional table to convert DEPARTMENT-ID to the subscript DEPARTMENT-NUMBER:

```
01   DEPARTMENT-ID-TABLE.
     05   VALID-DEPARTMENT-ID     OCCURS 15 TIMES
                                  PIC X(5).
```

The first entry in DEPARTMENT-ID-TABLE will be converted to the value 1 of DEPARTMENT-NUMBER; the second entry to the value 2; and so forth. Thus, we can obtain DEPARTMENT-NUMBER by looking up DEPARTMENT-ID in the table. This look-up, together with the linear IF structure that converts REGION-ID into the subscript REGION-NUMBER, is shown in the revised accumulation routine for the problem:

```
ACCUMULATE-SALES-TOTAL.
    MOVE "NO" TO ERROR-SW
    IF REGION-ID EQUAL "XYZ"
        MOVE 1 TO REGION-NUMBER
    ELSE IF REGION-ID EQUAL "ABC"
        MOVE 2 TO REGION-NUMBER
    ELSE IF REGION-ID EQUAL "GHF"
        MOVE 3 TO REGION-NUMBER
    ELSE
        MOVE "YES" TO ERROR-SW
    .

    MOVE 1 TO DEPARTMENT-NUMBER
    PERFORM LOOKUP-DEPARTMENT
        UNTIL ERROR-SW EQUAL "YES" OR
            DEPARTMENT-ID EQUAL
                VALID-DEPARTMENT-ID (DEPARTMENT-NUMBER)
    IF SALES-AMOUNT NOT NUMERIC
        MOVE "YES" TO ERROR-SW
    .

    IF ERROR-SW EQUAL "YES"
        PERFORM INVALID-INPUT-ROUTINE
    ELSE
        ADD SALES-AMOUNT TO
            TOTAL-SALES-AMOUNT (REGION-NUMBER DEPARTMENT-NUMBER)

    PERFORM GET-SALES-RECORD
    .

. . . . . . . . . . . . . . . . . . . . . . . . . . . . .
LOOKUP-DEPARTMENT.
    IF DEPARTMENT-NUMBER EQUAL DEPARTMENT-LIMIT
        MOVE "YES" TO ERROR-SW
    ELSE
        ADD 1 TO DEPARTMENT-NUMBER
    .
```

In a more realistic program, the values of REGION-ID would not be written as constants, but would be WORKING-STORAGE data items VALUEd to the desired contents; e.g.,

```
05  REGION-ONE-ID    PIC X(3)    VALUE "XYZ".
```

If the REGION-ID is not recognized, an error switch is set. Similarly, if DEPARTMENT-ID is not found in the table of valid IDs, the same error switch is set. The error switch is also set if SALES-AMOUNT is not numeric.

Loading with the VALUE Clause

As with one-dimensional tables (see Section 10.3), it is possible to initialize a two-dimensional table by REDEFINING an area whose structure matches that of the table. Again, this technique is not recommended if the table is likely to be changed during the useful life of the program.

EXAMPLE 10.20 An initialization of the table of Example 10.12:

```
01  FREIGHT-CHARGES-AREA.
    05  FREIGHT-CHARGE-VALUES.
```

```
          10  FILLER.
               15  FILLER     PIC S9(3)        COMP-3       VALUE +50.
               15  FILLER     PIC S9(3)V99     COMP-3       VALUE +1.50.
               15  FILLER     PIC S9(3)V99     COMP-3       VALUE +2.75.
               15  FILLER     PIC S9(3)V99     COMP-3       VALUE +2.25.
          10  FILLER.
               15  FILLER     PIC S9(3)        COMP-3       VALUE +100.
               15  FILLER     PIC S9(3)V99     COMP-3       VALUE +3.00.
               15  FILLER     PIC S9(3)V99     COMP-3       VALUE +4.23.
               15  FILLER     PIC S9(3)V99     COMP-3       VALUE +4.16.
          10  FILLER.
               15  FILLER     PIC S9(3)        COMP-3       VALUE +999.
               15  FILLER     PIC S9(3)V99     COMP-3       VALUE +3.50.
               15  FILLER     PIC S9(3)V99     COMP-3       VALUE +5.45.
               15  FILLER     PIC S9(3)V99     COMP-3       VALUE +5.20.
      05  FREIGHT-CHARGES-TABLE REDEFINES FREIGHT-CHARGE-VALUES.
          10  WEIGHT-RANGE                   OCCURS 3 TIMES.
               15  WEIGHT-LIMIT          PIC S9(3)  COMP-3.
               15  DESTINATION           OCCURS 3 TIMES.
                    20  FREIGHT-CHARGE   PIC S9(3)V99  COMP-3.
```

Loading with the READ Statement

This procedure—and its advantages—is analogous to that for one-dimensional tables (see Section 10.3).

EXAMPLE 10.21   The table of Example 10.12 is to be loaded from the input file

```
FD  TABLE-VALUES-FILE...
01  TABLE-VALUES-RECORD.
    05  WEIGHT-VALUE        PIC S9(3)           COMP-3.
    05  FREIGHT-VALUE       PIC S9(3)V99        COMP-3.
                            OCCURS 3 TIMES.
```

i.e., each TABLE-VALUES-RECORD is to be placed into WEIGHT-RANGE entry, such that WEIGHT-VALUE is put in WEIGHT-LIMIT and the three FREIGHT-VALUEs are put in the three FREIGHT-CHARGEs.

The following coding will do the job.

```
          . . . . . . . . . . . . . . . . . . . . .
          OPEN  INPUT  TABLE-VALUES-FILE
          MOVE "NO" TO END-FILE-SW
          MOVE 1 TO NUMBER-WEIGHT-ENTRIES
          PERFORM GET-TABLE-RECORD
          PERFORM LOAD-TABLE
               UNTIL END-FILE-SW EQUAL "YES" OR NUMBER-WEIGHT-ENTRIES
                    GREATER THAN SIZE-OF-WEIGHT-TABLE
          IF END-FILE-SW EQUAL "NO"
               DISPLAY "FREIGHT-CHARGES-TABLE TOO SMALL: CHANGE PROGRAM"
                    UPON OPERATOR-MESSAGE-DEVICE
          .
          .
          SUBTRACT 1 FROM NUMBER-WEIGHT-ENTRIES
          CLOSE TABLE-VALUES-FILE
          . . . . . . . . . . . . . . . . . . . . .
      GET-TABLE-RECORD.
          READ TABLE-VALUES-FILE
               AT END
                    MOVE "YES" TO END-FILE-SW
```

```
LOAD-TABLE.
    MOVE WEIGHT-VALUE TO WEIGHT-LIMIT (NUMBER-WEIGHT-ENTRIES)
    PERFORM MOVE-FREIGHT-CHARGES
        VARYING NUMBER-FREIGHT-CHARGES FROM 1 BY 1
            UNTIL NUMBER-FREIGHT-CHARGES GREATER THAN
                SIZE-OF-FREIGHT-TABLE
    PERFORM GET-TABLE-RECORD
    ADD 1 TO NUMBER-WEIGHT-ENTRIES
    .

MOVE-FREIGHT-CHARGES.
    MOVE FREIGHT-VALUE (NUMBER-FREIGHT-CHARGES) TO
        FREIGHT-CHARGE (NUMBER-WEIGHT-ENTRIES NUMBER-FREIGHT-CHARGES)
    .
```

in which the two subscripts and their limits are defined in WORKING-STORAGE:

```
01   TABLE-DIMENSIONS.
     05   NUMBER-WEIGHT-ENTRIES      PIC S9(5)   COMP SYNC.
     05   NUMBER-FREIGHT-CHARGES     PIC S9(5)   COMP SYNC.
     05   SIZE-OF-WEIGHT-TABLE       PIC S9(5)   COMP SYNC   VALUE +3.
     05   SIZE-OF-FREIGHT-TABLE      PIC S9(5)   COMP SYNC   VALUE +3.
```

Note that every effort has been made to make the program as flexible and easy to change as possible. Thus the number of active weight entries is calculated (as the number of logical records in the input file), so that the program may properly adapt to between 1 and 3 WEIGHT-RANGE entries. Further, SIZE-OF-WEIGHT-TABLE and SIZE-OF-FREIGHT-TABLE appear in the code as data items, so that if the size of a table must be changed, only the relevant OCCURS and VALUE clauses need be modified. (See Prob. 10.78 for a more efficient solution.)

10.6   Variable-Length Tables:
The OCCURS ... DEPENDING ... Clause

Up until now we have been defining tables with a *fixed* number of entries, usually setting aside enough space for the *maximum* predicted number of entries and keeping a *counter* of the actual number of *active* entries. There is, in COBOL, no way to conserve main memory when a table is not completely filled. However, when tables are output to disk or tape, COBOL does provide a mechanism whereby only the active entries become part of the logical record, thus conserving space on the disk or tape.

EXAMPLE 10.22   Consider the file

```
FD   PRODUCT-MASTER-FILE ...
01   PRODUCT-MASTER-RECORD.
     05   PRODUCT-ID                PIC X(5).
     05   PRODUCT-DESCRIPTION       PIC X(20).
     05   NUMBER-OF-SUPPLIERS       PIC S9(2)   COMP.
     05   SUPPLIER-INFORMATION      OCCURS 1 TO 50 TIMES
                                    DEPENDING ON NUMBER-OF-SUPPLIERS.
          10   SUPPLIER-ID          PIC X(4).
          10   SUPPLIER-NAME        PIC X(20).
          10   SUPPLIER-PRICE       PIC S9(3)V99   COMP-3.
          10   SUPPLIER-TERMS       PIC X(2).
```

The OCCURS ... DEPENDING ... clause indicates to the compiler that although the maximum table size is 50 entries, the *active* table size (the effective size on disk or tape) is determined by the contents of NUMBER-OF-SUPPLIERS, which can range from 1 to 50.

When a *variable-length table* (as defined by an OCCURS ... DEPENDING ... clause) is part of a logical record, the file perforce consists of variable-length records (Chapter 5).

The syntax of the OCCURS . . . DEPENDING . . . clause for variable-length tables is:

<u>OCCURS</u> integer-1 <u>TO</u> integer-2 TIMES
<u>DEPENDING</u> ON data-name

where "integer-1" must be at least 1 and less than "integer-2". "Data-name" is a numeric item (with any USAGE) that, during execution, may assume integral values between integer-1 and integer-2, inclusive. It is the current value of "data-name" which determines how many table entries are currently active (and therefore how much space is required for the variable-length logical record on auxiliary storage). Note that a variable-length table must always have at least one entry (see Appendix C for COBOL '80).

When a variable-length table occurs in a record, it is required to be the *last* field in the record. If tables are nested, only the *highest-level* table may be variable-length; in other words, an OCCURS . . . DEPENDING . . . clause may not be subordinate to any other OCCURS clause.

Moving Variable-Length Tables

If it is desired to copy a variable-length table from one data area to another, the values of the two DEPENDING items must be set equal *before the MOVE is executed*. (See Appendix C for COBOL '80 modifications.)

EXAMPLE 10.23   The following shows the correct way to place into WORKING-STORAGE a logical record that contains a variable-length table:

```
FD   ASSEMBLY-FILE...
01   ASSEMBLY-RECORD.
     05  ITEM-ID                     PIC X(6).
     05  NUMBER-SUBASSEMBLIES        PIC S9(2)      COMP.
     05  SUBASSEMBLY-INFO            OCCURS 1 TO 25 TIMES
                                     DEPENDING ON
                                          NUMBER-SUBASSEMBLIES.
         10  SUBPART-ID              PIC X(6).
         10  WAREHOUSE-LOCATION      PIC XX.
         10  QUANTITY-AVAILABLE      PIC S9(5)      COMP-3.

. . . . . . . . . . . . . . . . . . . . . . . .

WORKING-STORAGE SECTION.
01   WS-ASSEMBLY-RECORD.
     05  WS-ITEM-ID                  PIC X(6).
     05  WS-NUMBER-SUBASSEMBLIES     PIC S9(2)      COMP.
     05  WS-SUBASSEMBLY-INFO         OCCURS 1 TO 25 TIMES
                                     DEPENDING ON
                                          WS-NUMBER-SUBASSEMBLIES.
         10  WS-SUBPART-ID           PIC X(6).
         10  WS-WAREHOUSE-LOCATION   PIC XX.
         10  WS-QUANTITY-AVAILABLE   PIC S9(5)      COMP-3.

. . . . . . . . . . . . . . . . . . . . . . . .

READ ASSEMBLY-FILE   AT END...
MOVE NUMBER-SUBASSEMBLIES          TO WS-NUMBER-SUBASSEMBLIES
MOVE ASSEMBLY-RECORD               TO WS-ASSEMBLY-RECORD
```

Note that a simple "READ ASSEMBLY-FILE INTO WS-ASSEMBLY-RECORD . . ." would not do the job, since it is equivalent to

```
READ ASSEMBLY-FILE...
MOVE ASSEMBLY-RECORD TO WS-ASSEMBLY-RECORD
```

which would *not* equate WS-NUMBER-SUBASSEMBLIES to NUMBER-SUBASSEMBLIES before the MOVE was executed. The result of the MOVE would likely be truncation or padding of WS-ASSEMBLY-RECORD, depending on the prior contents of WS-NUMBER-SUBASSEMBLIES.

Expanding or Contracting Tables

Active entries may be added to or deleted from a variable-length table, provided the TIMES limits in the OCCURS clause are not violated. If an entry is to be added, the value of the DEPENDING item should be increased by 1; if an entry is to be deleted, the value of the DEPENDING item should be decreased by 1.

Changes to a variable-length table which affect the table size should not be made in the logical record input buffer (where they could disrupt any succeeding logical records in a blocked file). Such changes may be made to a WORKING-STORAGE copy of the input record or in a logical record output buffer.

EXAMPLE 10.24   To add the information from

```
FD   TRANSACTION-FILE . . .
01   TRANSACTION-RECORD.
     05   INPUT-ITEM-ID                PIC X(6).
     05   INPUT-SUBPART-ID             PIC X(6).
     05   INPUT-WAREHOUSE-LOCATION     PIC XX.
     05   INPUT-QUANTITY-AVAILABLE     PIC S9(5).
```

to the WS-ASSEMBLY-RECORD of Example 10.23, we would code as follows:

```
ADD 1 TO WS-NUMBER-SUBASSEMBLIES
MOVE INPUT-SUBPART-ID TO
    WS-SUBPART-ID (WS-NUMBER-SUBASSEMBLIES)
MOVE INPUT-WAREHOUSE-LOCATION TO
    WS-WAREHOUSE-LOCATION (WS-NUMBER-SUBASSEMBLIES)
MOVE INPUT-QUANTITY-AVAILABLE TO
    WS-QUANTITY-AVAILABLE (WS-NUMBER-SUBASSEMBLIES)
```

Note that the DEPENDING item is incremented by 1 *first*, thereby expanding the table to accommodate the new entry. The DEPENDING item then serves as a subscript that locates the new entry at the *end* of the table (the easiest place to put it; see Example 10.37 for a different approach).

EXAMPLE 10.25   Suppose that INPUT-SUBPART-ID identifies a subassembly that is to be removed from the WS-ASSEMBLY-RECORD of Example 10.23.

(*a*)   In a *logical deletion*, we move spaces (or some other *deletion code*) into the table entry that matches INPUT-SUBPART-ID; the spaces will mark the entry as inactive to any program that will process the table. However, we do not decrement WS-NUMBER-SUBASSEMBLIES, since the entry has not been *physically* removed.

```
            MOVE "YES" TO ENTRY-IN-TABLE
            MOVE 1 TO TABLE-SUBSCRIPT
            PERFORM LOCATE-SUBPART
                UNTIL ENTRY-IN-TABLE EQUAL "NO"
                OR INPUT-SUBPART-ID EQUAL
                    WS-SUBPART-ID (TABLE-SUBSCRIPT)
            IF ENTRY-IN-TABLE EQUAL "NO"
                PERFORM ERROR-ROUTINE
            ELSE
                MOVE SPACES TO WS-SUBPART-ID (TABLE-SUBSCRIPT)
            . . . . . . . . . . . . . . . . . . . .
        LOCATE-SUBPART.
            IF TABLE-SUBSCRIPT EQUAL WS-NUMBER-SUBASSEMBLIES
                MOVE "NO" TO ENTRY-IN-TABLE
            ELSE
                ADD 1 TO TABLE-SUBSCRIPT
```

With spaces in WS-SUBPART-ID (j), any future program that processes the table will also ignore WS-WAREHOUSE-LOCATION (j) and WS-QUANTITY-AVAILABLE (j).

(*b*) In a *physical deletion*, we move all the entries that follow the one matching INPUT-SUBPART-ID up one position (toward the head of the table). The DEPENDING item is decremented by 1, since one entry has been physically deleted.

```
            MOVE "YES" TO ENTRY-IN-TABLE
            MOVE 1 TO TABLE-SUBSCRIPT
            PERFORM LOCATE-SUBPART
                UNTIL ENTRY-IN-TABLE EQUAL "NO"
                    OR INPUT-SUBPART-ID EQUAL
                        WS-SUBPART-ID (TABLE-SUBSCRIPT)
            IF ENTRY-IN-TABLE EQUAL "NO"
                PERFORM ERROR-ROUTINE
            ELSE
                PERFORM MOVE-UP-TABLE-ENTRIES
                    VARYING MOVING-SUBSCRIPT FROM TABLE-SUBSCRIPT BY 1
                        UNTIL MOVING-SUBSCRIPT EQUAL WS-NUMBER-SUBASSEMBLIES
                SUBTRACT 1 FROM WS-NUMBER-SUBASSEMBLIES


        . . . . . . . . . . . . . . . . . . . . . .

        LOCATE-SUBPART.
            IF TABLE-SUBSCRIPT EQUAL WS-NUMBER-SUBASSEMBLIES
                MOVE "NO" TO ENTRY-IN-TABLE
            ELSE
                ADD 1 TO TABLE-SUBSCRIPT

        MOVE-UP-TABLE-ENTRIES.
            ADD 1 MOVING-SUBSCRIPT GIVING MOVING-SUBSCRIPT-PLUS-1
            MOVE WS-SUBASSEMBLY-INFO (MOVING-SUBSCRIPT-PLUS-1) TO
                WS-SUBASSEMBLY-INFO (MOVING-SUBSCRIPT)
```

Note how PERFORM LOCATE-SUBPART UNTIL . . . sets TABLE-SUBSCRIPT to the position number of the entry to be deleted (if the entry exists in the table). All entries between TABLE-SUBSCRIPT and the end of the table (at WS-NUMBER-SUBASSEMBLIES) must be moved up one position to contract the table over the deleted item. This is done in MOVE-UP-TABLE-ENTRIES, where the entry at MOVING-SUBSCRIPT + 1 is moved to the entry at MOVING-SUBSCRIPT. MOVING-SUBSCRIPT is varied from TABLE-SUBSCRIPT to WS-NUMBER-SUBASSEMBLIES −1 (remember that when EQUAL rather than GREATER THAN is employed in a PERFORM . . . VARYING . . . UNTIL . . . , the last value of the VARYING item for which the paragraph is actually performed is *one less* than the indicated stopping value). This is necessary because the positions of the entries to be moved are specified by MOVING-SUBSCRIPT *plus one*. Since a subscript cannot be an expression, it is necessary to define an extra data item, MOVING-SUBSCRIPT-PLUS-1, in which to compute MOVING-SUBSCRIPT + 1. After all appropriate entries have been moved up one position, the DEPENDING item is decremented by 1 to indicate that the table now has one fewer entry. Physical deletion is preferable to logical deletion for variable-length tables, since it decreases the amount of auxiliary storage space required to hold the table.

10.7   Indexes

When subscripts are used to identify table entries, the compiler must generate machine language instructions to convert the subscript value to the actual memory address of the desired entry. *Indexes* are COBOL data items which can be used in place of subscripts to make machine-language address calculations more efficient (see Problems 10.74 and 10.75). An index value is a *displacement* into a table; i.e., a number which when added to the starting address of the table yields the address of a desired entry. Indexes are more efficient than subscripts, and should be used whenever possible.

Indexes to be used in place of subscripts for a given table are defined in the OCCURS clause which defines the table; they do not require any separate definition (unlike subscripts). The syntax of the OCCURS clause when indexes are defined is as shown in Fig. 10-2.

OCCURS integer-1 [TO integer-2] TIMES
[DEPENDING ON data-name-1]
[INDEXED BY index-name-1 [index-name-2] . . .]

Fig. 10-2

"Index-name-1", "index-name-2", etc., become available for use in place of subscripts when accessing table entries.

EXAMPLE 10.26

```
01   SALES-FIGURES-BY-STATE.
     05   STATE-SALES            OCCURS 50 TIMES
                                 INDEXED BY STATE-NUMBER.
     10   STATE-ID              PIC X(2).
     10   SALES-AMOUNT          PIC S9(5)V99   COMP-3.
```

Here the table from Example 10.4 is defined with an index. The index STATE-NUMBER is now available for use in place of STATE-SALES-SUB. Note that an index is associated with a *particular table*; STATE-NUMBER should not be used to access any other table unless that table has exactly the same structure (PICTUREs, USAGEs, levels, number of entries, etc.) as STATE-SALES. Note too that no further definition of STATE-NUMBER is needed (or allowed).

Indexes *cannot* be manipulated in the same ways as subscripts. An index can be initialized or changed only with (1) a SET statement, (2) a PERFORM statement; or (3) a SEARCH statement (see Section 10.8).

The SET statement can be used to initialize an index to the value of another index, a numeric data item, or a numeric literal. Conversely, the SET statement can be used to set a numeric data item to the current value of an index. The syntax is:

$$\underline{\text{SET}} \begin{Bmatrix} \text{index-name-1} \\ \text{data-name-1} \end{Bmatrix} \begin{bmatrix} \text{index-name-2} \\ \text{data-name-2} \end{bmatrix} \cdots \underline{\text{TO}} \begin{Bmatrix} \text{index-name-3} \\ \text{identifier-3} \\ \text{literal} \end{Bmatrix}$$

EXAMPLE 10.27

●   SET STATE-NUMBER TO 3
The SET statement converts the value "3" to the displacement for the third entry in STATE-SALES (see Example 10.26).

●   SET STATE-NUMBER TO SOME-OTHER-INDEX
If SOME-OTHER-INDEX points to the *k*th entry in SOME-OTHER-TABLE, STATE-NUMBER is made to point to the *k*th entry in STATE-SALES.

●   SET STATE-NUMBER TO A-SUBSCRIPT
STATE-NUMBER is made to point to the table entry whose position number is currently in A-SUBSCRIPT. A-SUBSCRIPT might be defined:

```
05   A-SUBSCRIPT      PIC S9(5)      COMP SYNC.
```

●   SET A-SUBSCRIPT TO STATE-NUMBER
The position number corresponding to the displacement currently stored in STATE-NUMBER is moved to A-SUBSCRIPT.

A SET statement must also be used to increment or decrement indexes:

$$\underline{\text{SET}} \text{ index-name-1 [index-name-2]} \cdots \begin{Bmatrix} \underline{\text{UP BY}} \\ \underline{\text{DOWN BY}} \end{Bmatrix} \begin{Bmatrix} \text{data-name} \\ \text{literal} \end{Bmatrix}$$

(MOVE . . . , ADD . . . , or SUBTRACT . . . *may not be used* with indexes.)

EXAMPLE 10.28

●   SET STATE-NUMBER DOWN BY 1

The displacement in STATE-NUMBER is decremented by the length of a table entry, so that STATE-NUMBER points to the preceding entry in the table.

●   SET STATE-NUMBER UP BY A-SUBSCRIPT

STATE-NUMBER is incremented by the displacement value which will cause it to point ahead a number of entries equal to the current contents of A-SUBSCRIPT (e.g., if STATE-NUMBER starts out pointing to the third entry and A-SUBSCRIPT contains the value 5, then STATE-NUMBER will wind up pointing to the eighth entry).

Indexes can be used in PERFORM statements and IF conditions exactly as any integer data item.

EXAMPLE 10.29   Find the total amount of sales in Example 10.26.

```
01   SALES-FIGURES-BY-STATE.
     05   STATE-SALES          OCCURS 50 TIMES INDEXED BY STATE-NUMBER.
          10   STATE-ID        PIC X(2).
          10   SALES-AMOUNT    PIC S9(5)V99    COMP-3.
. . . . . . . . . . . . . . . . . . . . . . . . . . .

     MOVE ZERO TO TOTAL-SALES
     PERFORM ADD-UP-STATE-SALES
          VARYING STATE-NUMBER FROM 1 BY 1
          UNTIL STATE-NUMBER GREATER THAN 50
. . . . . . . . . . . . . . . . . . . . . . . . .
 ADD-UP-STATE-SALES.
     ADD SALES-AMOUNT (STATE-NUMBER) TO TOTAL-SALES
 .
```

Note that STATE-NUMBER is used *exactly like a subscript*. In fact, it is only by looking at the OCCURS clause that one can tell that it is *not* a subscript. Nevertheless, the *index* STATE-NUMBER yields more efficient machine language.

EXAMPLE 10.30   In Example 10.10, recode LOOK-UP-STATUS with an index instead of a subscript.

```
LOOK-UP-STATUS.
    SET STATUS-TABLE-INDEX TO 1
    MOVE "YES" TO VALID-STATUS-SW
    PERFORM CHECK-ENTRY
        UNTIL VALID-STATUS-SW EQUAL "NO"
            OR STATUS-CODE (STATUS-TABLE-INDEX) EQUAL INPUT-STATUS-CODE
 .
CHECK-ENTRY.
    IF STATUS-TABLE-INDEX EQUAL 40
        MOVE "NO" TO VALID-STATUS-SW
    ELSE
        SET STATUS-TABLE-INDEX UP BY 1
 .
```

The index must be SET; otherwise, it might just as well be a subscript.

EXAMPLE 10.31   Example 10.18, with indexes instead of subscripts:

```
FD   SALES-INPUT-FILE . . .
. . . . . . . . . . . . . . . . . . . . . . . . . . .
01   TOTAL-SALES-AMOUNTS-TABLE.
     05   REGION                          OCCURS 7 TIMES
                                          INDEXED BY REGION-INDEX.
```

```
    10   DEPARTMENT                OCCURS 12 TIMES
                                   INDEXED BY DEPARTMENT-INDEX.
    15   TOTAL-SALES-AMOUNT        PIC S9(5)V99  COMP.
. . . . . . . . . . . . . . . . .
ELSE
    SET REGION-INDEX TO REGION-ID
    SET DEPARTMENT-INDEX TO DEPARTMENT-ID
    ADD SALES-AMOUNT TO TOTAL-SALES (REGION-INDEX DEPARTMENT-INDEX)

PERFORM GET-SALES-RECORD
```

Relative Indexing

An index may have a numeric literal (and *only* a numeric literal) added to or subtracted from it to point to an entry relative to the current value of the index. This is often convenient when moving table entries around within the table.

EXAMPLE 10.32 Suppose that it is desired to move the entry at position K to position $K - 5$. With subscripting, we would define:

```
01   TABLE-SUBSCRIPTS.
    05   K                PIC S9(5)   COMP SYNC.
    05   K-MINUS-FIVE     PIC S9(5)   COMP SYNC.
. . . . . . . . . . . . . . . . . . . . . . .
    SUBTRACT 5 FROM K GIVING K-MINUS-FIVE
    MOVE TABLE-ENTRY (K) TO TABLE-ENTRY (K-MINUS-FIVE)
```

With indexing, we could use the much simpler:

```
    SET TABLE-INDEX TO K
    MOVE TABLE-ENTRY (TABLE-INDEX) TO TABLE-ENTRY (TABLE-INDEX − 5)
```

10.8   Sequential Table Search and the SEARCH Verb

Previous Sections have illustrated how to program a table search with a PERFORM loop. However, ANS COBOL provides a special SEARCH verb which is both easier to use and more efficient. If a table has n entries, a sequential (linear) search examines them in the order $k, k + 1, k + 2, \ldots, n - 1, n$. (Ordinarily, $k = 1$.) The sequential SEARCH statement has the syntax indicated in Fig. 10-3. "Identifier-1" must be the name of the table to the searched (i.e., the data item described with the OCCURS clause). The AT END clause specifies what is to be done if the search "fails" (i.e., if none of the WHEN conditions is true during the search).

$$\underline{\text{SEARCH}}\text{ identifier-1 } \left[\underline{\text{VARYING}} \begin{Bmatrix} \text{identifier-2} \\ \text{index-name-1} \end{Bmatrix}\right]$$
$$[\text{AT }\underline{\text{END}}\text{ imperative-statement(s)-1}]$$
$$\underline{\text{WHEN}}\text{ condition-1} \begin{Bmatrix} \text{imperative-statement(s)-2} \\ \underline{\text{NEXT SENTENCE}} \end{Bmatrix}$$
$$\left[\underline{\text{WHEN}}\text{ condition-2} \begin{Bmatrix} \text{imperative-statement(s)-3} \\ \underline{\text{NEXT SENTENCE}} \end{Bmatrix}\right] \ldots$$

Fig. 10-3

EXAMPLE 10.33 Do Example 10.10, using SEARCH . . . instead of PERFORM . . . .

```
01   VALID-STATUS-CODES-TABLE.
    05   STATUS-CODE              PIC X(3)
                                  OCCURS 40 TIMES
                                  INDEXED BY VALID-CODE-INDEX.
. . . . . . . . . . . . . . . . . . . . .
```

```
LOOK-UP-STATUS.
    SET VALID-CODE-INDEX TO 1
    SEARCH STATUS-CODE
        AT END
            MOVE "NO" TO INPUT-CODE-OK-SW
        WHEN INPUT-STATUS-CODE EQUAL STATUS-CODE (VALID-CODE-INDEX)
            MOVE "YES" TO INPUT-CODE-OK-SW
```

Note that a table must be defined *with an index* if the SEARCH verb is to be applied. The programmer must SET the SEARCH index to the entry at which the SEARCH is to begin (usually 1). The SEARCH statement above works as follows:

(1) Since the VARYING option is not specified, the SEARCH uses the *first* index defined for the STATUS-CODE table. In this case, the first (and only) index is VALID-CODE-INDEX.

(2) The value of the SEARCH index is compared to the number of entries in the table (here 40). If the index exceeds the table size, the AT END statement(s) are executed, and then execution continues with the first statement after the period which marks the end of the SEARCH statement.

(3) If the index does not exceed the table size, the WHEN conditions are evaluated (in the order in which they are written). The first WHEN condition which is true causes its associated statements to be executed. At this point, the SEARCH is over (and execution continues with the first statement following the period which marks the end of the SEARCH statement).

(4) If *no* WHEN condition is true, the SEARCH index is incremented by one entry, and execution of the SEARCH statement resumes back at step 2 above.

EXAMPLE 10.34 Using SEARCH . . . VARYING . . . , we can scan *parallel tables*, tables whose corresponding entries contain data about the same entity. Suppose we have the following parallel tables:

```
01   DEDUCTION-CODES-TABLE.
    05   DEDUCT-CODE              PIC X
                                  OCCURS 30 TIMES
                                  INDEXED BY CODE-INDEX.


01   DEDUCTIONS-INFO-TABLE.
    05   PAYROLL-DEDUCTIONS       OCCURS 30 TIMES
                                  INDEXED BY INFO-INDEX.
        10   DEDUCT-DESCRIPTION   PIC X(25).
        10   DEDUCT-AMOUNT        PIC S99V99    COMP-3.
```

where DEDUCT-CODE (k) corresponds to PAYROLL-DEDUCTIONS (k). Given an input PAYROLL-CODE, we process payroll deductions with a SEARCH . . . VARYING . . . :

```
SET CODE-INDEX TO 1
SET INFO-INDEX TO 1
SEARCH DEDUCT-CODE
    VARYING INFO-INDEX
    AT END
        MOVE "YES" TO PAYROLL-ERROR-SW
    WHEN DEDUCT-CODE (CODE-INDEX) EQUAL PAYROLL-CODE
        MOVE DEDUCT-DESCRIPTION (INFO-INDEX) TO OUTPUT-AREA
        SUBTRACT DEDUCT-AMOUNT (INFO-INDEX) FROM NET-PAY
```

Since the two tables have different structures, two indexes are necessary. When the VARYING option specifies an index that belongs to a table other than the SEARCH table, (i) the *first* index specified for the SEARCH table (CODE-INDEX) is incremented during the SEARCH; and (ii) every time the first index for the SEARCH table is incremented, so is the VARYING index (INFO-INDEX), Thus the VARYING index "trails along" with the SEARCH index, so that they will always point to corresponding entries, provided they have been SET to the same value before the SEARCH is executed.

If a table has more than one index defined for it, and VARYING . . . names an index other than the first, that index is used in the SEARCH.

Since SEARCH . . . is geared to only one OCCURS clause at a time, special coding must be used to search fully a two-dimensional table. It usually suffices to put the SEARCH statement in a PERFORMed paragraph, letting the PERFORM statement VARY the first index (the second is varied by the SEARCH statement).

EXAMPLE 10.35   To locate INPUT-COURSE   PIC X(5) in the table

```
01   STUDENT-TRANSCRIPT.
     05   STUDENT-ID                 PIC  X(9).
     05   SEMESTERS-ATTENDED         PIC  S9          COMP.
     05   SEMESTER-INFORMATION       OCCURS  1 TO 8 TIMES
                                     DEPENDING ON SEMESTERS-ATTENDED
                                     INDEXED BY SEMESTER-INDEX.
          10   SEMESTER-DATE         PIC  X(6).
          10   NUMBER-COURSES        PIC  S9          COMP.
          10   COURSE-INFO           OCCURS 6 TIMES
                                     INDEXED BY COURSE-INDEX.
               15   COURSE-ID        PIC  X(5).
               15   CREDITS          PIC  S9V9        COMP-3.
               15   GRADE            PIC  S9          COMP-3.
```

we code as follows:

. . . .

```
        MOVE "NO" TO FOUND-IT-SW
        PERFORM LOCATE-COURSE
            VARYING SEMESTER-INDEX FROM 1 BY 1
                UNTIL SEMESTER-INDEX GREATER THAN SEMESTERS-ATTENDED
                    OR FOUND-IT-SW EQUAL "YES"
        IF FOUND-IT-SW EQUAL "YES"
            SET SEMESTER-INDEX DOWN BY 1
            PERFORM PROCESS-COURSE-INFO
        ELSE
            PERFORM COURSE-NOT-FOUND-ERROR
```

. . . .

```
        LOCATE-COURSE.
            SET COURSE-INDEX TO 1
            SEARCH COURSE-INFO
                WHEN COURSE-INDEX GREATER THAN
                    NUMBER-COURSES (SEMESTER-INDEX)
                    NEXT SENTENCE
                WHEN COURSE-ID (SEMESTER-INDEX COURSE-INDEX)
                    EQUAL INPUT-COURSE
                    MOVE "YES" TO FOUND-IT-SW
```

Comments:

(1) The SEARCH statement is performed over and over as SEMESTER-INDEX is varied from 1 up to SEMESTERS-ATTENDED, its full range of possible values.

(2) COURSE-INDEX is SET to 1 each time LOCATE-COURSE is performed; hence the entire COURSE-INFO table is searched for each value of SEMESTER-INDEX.

(3) COURSE-INFO, the name of the searched table, is *not* subscripted or indexed in the SEARCH statement, even though it is an entry in the SEMESTER-INFORMATION table and so would normally be subscripted or indexed.

(4) The lack of an AT END clause is *not* a problem here. If the end of the COURSE-INFO table is encountered for a particular value of SEMESTER-INDEX, execution would continue with the statement following the SEARCH, which in this case is the end of the paragraph. But coming to the

end of LOCATE-COURSE causes the PERFORM statement to increment SEMESTER-INDEX and perform the paragraph again, thus searching the next semester's COURSE-INFO, as desired.

(5) The first WHEN clause tests for the *logical end* of the COURSE-INFO table. If this condition is true, NEXT SENTENCE causes execution to proceed to the end of the paragraph, with SEMESTER-INDEX being incremented as in (4) above.

(6) If the second WHEN condition becomes true, FOUND-IT-SW is set to "YES". However the PERFORM ... VARYING ... *first* increments SEMESTER-INDEX, *then* evaluates the UNTIL condition ('FOUND-IT-SW EQUAL "YES" ').

> SET SEMESTER-INDEX DOWN BY 1

undoes the extra incrementation.

10.9 Binary Table Search and the SEARCH ALL Verb

The *binary search* algorithm is more efficient than the sequential search for tables that are *relatively large* and are *sorted in ascending or descending sequence* on some table field, called the *key*. The larger the table, the greater the superiority of the binary search to the sequential search. A binary search begins by examining (*probing*) the "middle" entry (suitably interpreted if the number of entries is even). If the desired item is at the middle entry, the search ends. If the desired item is greater (i.e., has a greater key-value) than the middle entry, it must lie in the higher half of the table (for a table sorted in ascending sequence); likewise, if the desired item is less than the middle entry, it must lie in the lower half of the table. In either case, half the table may be eliminated from further consideration.

The search continues by examining the middle entry of the half still under consideration, and applies the same procedure, thereby cutting the remaining table half in half. Eventually, only one entry is left; either it is the desired entry or the desired entry is *not in the table*.

Binary searching is programmed in COBOL using the SEARCH ALL statement (Fig. 10-4). "Identifier-1" must be the name of the table (defined with an OCCURS clause) to be searched; it must not be subscripted or indexed in the SEARCH-ALL clause itself. The AT END clause functions as it did for a sequential search, being executed only if the binary search fails for the indicated table. If the WHEN condition becomes true during the search, its associated statement(s) are executed and the search ends. Note that the WHEN condition must be of the form shown in Fig. 10-4.

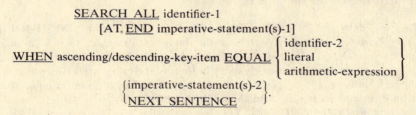

$$
\begin{aligned}
&\underline{\text{SEARCH ALL}}\ \text{identifier-1}\\
&\quad [\underline{\text{AT END}}\ \text{imperative-statement(s)-1}]\\
&\underline{\text{WHEN}}\ \text{ascending/descending-key-item}\ \underline{\text{EQUAL}}
\left\{
\begin{array}{l}
\text{identifier-2}\\
\text{literal}\\
\text{arithmetic-expression}
\end{array}
\right\}\\
&\qquad
\left\{
\begin{array}{l}
\text{imperative-statement(s)-2}\\
\underline{\text{NEXT SENTENCE}}
\end{array}
\right\}.
\end{aligned}
$$

Fig. 10-4

After the AT END statement(s) or the WHEN statement(s) are executed (or after the AT END condition occurs but no AT END clause is specified), execution continues with the statement immediately following the period which ends the SEARCH ALL statement.

When a table is to be processed with SEARCH ALL, its OCCURS clause must include an ASCENDING/DESCENDING KEY subclause (Fig. 10-5). It is important to understand that this subclause does not cause the table to be sorted; it merely tells which field the table is sorted on.

$$
\begin{aligned}
&\underline{\text{OCCURS}}\ \text{integer-1}\ [\underline{\text{TO}}\ \text{integer-2}]\ \text{TIMES}\\
&\quad [\underline{\text{DEPENDING}}\ \text{ON data-name-1}]\\
&\quad
\left\{
\begin{array}{l}
\underline{\text{ASCENDING}}\\
\underline{\text{DESCENDING}}
\end{array}
\right\}\ \text{KEY IS data-name-2}\\
&\quad [\underline{\text{INDEXED}}\ \text{BY index-name-1 [index-name-2] ...]}
\end{aligned}
$$

Fig. 10-5

EXAMPLE 10.36 Let it be desired to retrieve the job description for INPUT-JOB-CODE   PIC X(3) from the following table:

```
01  JOB-CODES-TABLE.
    05   NUMBER-JOB-CODES        PIC S9(5)    COMP SYNC.
    05   JOB-CODES-MEANINGS      OCCURS 1 TO 100 TIMES
                                 DEPENDING ON NUMBER-JOB-CODES
                                 ASCENDING KEY IS JOB-CODE
                                 INDEXED BY JOB-CODE-INDEX.
         10   JOB-CODE           PIC X(3).
         10   JOB-DESCRIPTION    PIC X(35).
```

Assuming the table is already sorted in ascending sequence according to JOB-CODE, we can use a binary search:

```
SEARCH ALL JOB-CODES-MEANINGS
    AT END
        MOVE "** INVALID JOB CODE **" TO OUTPUT-JOB-DESCRIPTION
    WHEN JOB-CODE (JOB-CODE-INDEX) EQUAL INPUT-JOB-CODE
        MOVE JOB-DESCRIPTION (JOB-CODE-INDEX) TO OUTPUT-JOB-DESCRIPTION
```

Some remarks:

(1)   The table name, as defined with an OCCURS clause, must occur in SEARCH ALL without a subscript or index.

(2)   The VARYING clause is not valid with SEARCH ALL: SEARCH ALL always varies the *first index* defined for the table being searched. There is no need to initialize the index when SEARCH ALL is used.

(3)   In order for SEARCH ALL to work correctly, the table must already be sorted as described in the KEY clause. If the table is not sorted correctly, no warnings or error messages are given—the SEARCH ALL simply produces incorrect results! In particular, if the present table had been *fixed-length*, lacking the DEPENDING subclause, some of the 100 entries would almost surely have been inactive (garbage), thus making the table as a whole unsorted. The results of the SEARCH ALL would then also have been garbage. See Problems 10.76 and 10.77 for how to program a sort of an unsorted table.

(4)   The order of the subclauses within the OCCURS clause is invariable in IBM OS/VS COBOL (i.e., they must be written in the order shown in Fig. 10-5).

EXAMPLE 10.37   The data in INPUT-JOB-CODE PIC X(3)   and   INPUT-JOB-DESCRIPTION PIC X(35) are to be inserted as a new entry in the table of Example 10.36. To maintain the table in ascending sequence on JOB-CODE, we must search the table for the first entry which is greater (in key-value) than the new entry, then place the new entry in front of it. If no entry exists which is greater than the new entry, then the new entry should be placed at the end of the table. If an entry equal to the new entry is found in the table, an error condition exists and should be dealt with.

We wish to test for JOB-CODE *GREATER THAN* ..., but the WHEN clause of SEARCH ALL ... only provides for JOB-CODE *EQUAL* .... Therefore, we are forced to use SEARCH ... rather than SEARCH ALL ..., even though the table is sorted:

```
SET JOB-CODE-INDEX TO 1
SEARCH JOB-CODES-MEANINGS
    AT END
        ADD 1 TO NUMBER-JOB-CODES
        SET JOB-CODE-INDEX TO NUMBER-JOB-CODES
        MOVE INPUT-JOB-CODE TO JOB-CODE (JOB-CODE-INDEX)
        MOVE INPUT-JOB-DESCRIPTION TO
            JOB-DESCRIPTION (JOB-CODE-INDEX)
    WHEN
        JOB-CODE (JOB-CODE-INDEX) EQUAL INPUT-JOB-CODE
            PERFORM DUPLICATE-CODE-ERROR
    WHEN
```

```
        JOB-CODE (JOB-CODE-INDEX) GREATER THAN INPUT-JOB-CODE
            ADD 1 TO NUMBER-JOB-CODES
            PERFORM MOVE-ENTRIES-UP
                VARYING MOVE-INDEX
                    FROM NUMBER-JOB-CODES BY −1
                    UNTIL MOVE-INDEX EQUAL JOB-CODE-INDEX
            MOVE INPUT-JOB-CODE TO JOB-CODE (JOB-CODE-INDEX)
            MOVE INPUT-JOB-DESCRIPTION TO
                JOB-DESCRIPTION (JOB-CODE-INDEX)
```

```
. . . . . . . . . . . . . . . . . . . . . . . . . .
    MOVE-ENTRIES-UP.
        MOVE JOB-CODES-MEANINGS (MOVE-INDEX − 1) TO
            JOB-CODES-MEANINGS (MOVE-INDEX)
```

Comments:

(1)   The INDEXED subclause in Example 10.36 is changed to

```
        INDEXED BY JOB-CODE-INDEX
                   MOVE-INDEX.
```

(2)   If the SEARCH results in an AT END condition, we know that the new entry is greater than all existing entries. Thus, we add it to the end of the table by (i) incrementing the DEPENDING item, (ii) moving the new information into the new last entry created by (i).

(3)   If the SEARCH locates an entry equal to the new one, we PERFORM an error routine.

(4)   If the SEARCH determines a value of JOB-CODE-INDEX for which JOB-CODE exceeds INPUT-JOB-CODE, then we create a new last position in the table by incrementing NUMBER-JOB-CODES (see Fig. 10-6). The last entry in the table, now at NUMBER-JOB-CODES − 1, is moved to the new position; its place is taken by the entry at NUMBER-JOB-CODES − 2; ...; the entry at JOB-CODE-INDEX is moved to JOB-CODE-INDEX + 1; and, the PERFORM having finished, the input data are moved to JOB-CODE-INDEX. Note that the reverse ordering of the moves was essential: if we tried to start by moving the data at JOB-CODE-INDEX forward, the result would be that those data obliterated all succeeding entries in the table.

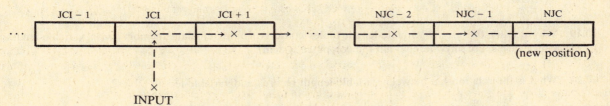

Fig. 10-6

Review Questions

10.1   Give several examples of business tables.

10.2   Discuss the factors involved in determining the maximum size of a table.

10.3   Explain the use of tables in processing *coded* information.

10.4   What is meant by "expanding a code through a table-lookup"?

10.5   What is a subscript? How should it be defined?

10.6   Where in the DATA DIVISION can tables be defined?

10.7   Discuss the use of the VALUE clause to initialize WORKING-STORAGE tables.

10.8   Under what conditions will "MOVE ZEROS TO ENTIRE-TABLE" work correctly?

10.9   When should MOVE statements in a PERFORMed paragraph be used to initialize table entries?

10.10   Discuss the importance of keeping a count of the number of active entries for most tables. When is such a count *not* needed?

10.11   Why is it often better to input initial table values from a file rather than use VALUE and REDEFINES?

10.12   How are two-dimensional tables defined?

10.13   Explain the rules for subscripting or indexing two-dimensional table entries.

10.14   Discuss the use of PERFORM ... VARYING ... AFTER ... with two-dimensional tables.

10.15   Explain how input data can serve as a subscript. When might this be useful?

10.16   Why is it important to validate input fields used as subscripts?

10.17   Discuss how alphanumeric input fields can be translated into subscript values.

10.18   Explain what is meant by "nested OCCURS clauses". What is the limit on OCCURS nesting in COBOL?

10.19   Why doesn't the use of variable-length tables conserve computer main memory? Can variable-length tables save space anywhere within the computer system?

10.20   What is the relationship between variable-length records and variable-length tables?

10.21   Discuss the placement of the DEPENDING item within a logical record. Can it follow the variable-length table?

10.22   Give the restrictions on nested OCCURS clauses when variable-length tables are involved.

10.23   Why might a variable-length table be defined in WORKING-STORAGE? Does this save any computer memory?

10.24   Discuss the pitfalls involved in moving variable-length tables.

10.25   Why can't READ ... INTO ... and WRITE ... FROM ... be used with records containing variable-length tables?

10.26   Discuss two methods for deleting an entry from a table.

10.27　Discuss the role of a *deletion code* when logically deleting table entries. What implications does logical deletion have for other programs that process the table?

10.28　Discuss the algorithm for contracting a table when physical deletion is used.

10.29　What is an index? When should indexes be used? How are they defined?

10.30　Compare index values with subscript values.

10.31　What is *address calculation*?

10.32　What table(s) should any given index be used with?

10.33　List the three ways in which indexes may be initialized or modified.

10.34　Discuss the use of the SET statement. What is its syntax?

10.35　Discuss how indexes may be used in the PERFORM statement; in IF statements.

10.36　What is *relative indexing*? Discuss its use.

10.37　Is there an equivalent of relative indexing for subscripts?

10.38　Explain the sequential search algorithm.

10.39　Discuss the SEARCH statement. What is its syntax? Explain (*a*) VARYING . . . , (*b*) AT END . . . , (*c*) WHEN . . . , (*d*) initializing the SEARCH index.

10.40　Discuss the importance of the order in which WHEN clauses are written for SEARCH . . . .

10.41　What are *parallel tables*. How do they relate to the VARYING option of SEARCH . . . ?

10.42　Discuss how SEARCH . . . or SEARCH ALL . . . can be applied to two-dimensional tables.

10.43　Explain the binary search algorithm. What is the precondition for a binary search to work properly?

10.44　Discuss the relative efficiency of sequential versus binary searching. When might each be used?

10.45　Discuss the SEARCH ALL statement. How does it differ from the SEARCH statement?

10.46　Explain the use of ASCENDING/DESCENDING KEY . . . .

10.47　SEARCH ALL . . . should not be used with a fixed-length table unless it is "full". Why not?

10.48　Describe an algorithm for inserting an entry into a sorted table.

10.49　Describe an algorithm for physically deleting a table entry.

Solved Problems

10.50 What is wrong with the following table definitions?

(a) 01 DECK-OF-CARDS   PIC X(2)
                                          OCCURS 52 TIMES.

(b) 01 DECK-OF-CARDS.
         05 POKER-HAND   OCCURS 1 TO 10 TIMES
                                          DEPENDING ON NUMBER-OF-PLAYERS.
             10 CARDS   OCCURS 5 TIMES.
                 15 RANK   PIC XX.
                 15 SUIT   PIC X.
         05 NUMBER-OF-PLAYERS   PIC S9(5) COMP SYNC.

(c) 01 POKER-HAND.
         05 CARD   OCCURS 5 TIMES
                                           INDEXED BY CARD-INDEX
                                           ASCENDING KEY IS RANK.
             10 RANK   PIC XX.
             10 SUIT   PIC X.

(d) 01 POKER-TABLE.
         05 NUMBER-OF-PLAYERS   PIC S9(4) COMP SYNC.
         05 POKER-HAND   OCCURS 1 TO 10 TIMES
                                           DEPENDING ON NUMBER-OF-PLAYERS
                                           INDEXED BY HAND-INDEX.
             10 NUMBER-DEALT   PIC S9(4) COMP SYNC.
             10 CARDS   OCCURS 1 TO 7 TIMES
                                           DEPENDING ON NUMBER-DEALT
                                           INDEXED BY CARD-INDEX.
                 15 RANK   PIC XX.
                 15 SUIT   PIC X.

(a) The OCCURS clause may not be used at level 01.

(b) A data item (NUMBER-OF-PLAYERS) follows a variable-length table in a record description.

(c) INDEXED BY ... should *follow* ASCENDING KEY ... (under IBM OS/VS COBOL).

(d) An OCCURS ... DEPENDING ... clause is subordinate to another OCCURS .... It would be correct to use:

             10 CARDS   OCCURS 7 TIMES
                           INDEXED BY CARD-INDEX.

i.e., a *fixed-length* table may be subordinate to a variable-length (or to a fixed-length) table.

10.51 Comment on the following table:

         01 BASEBALL-TEAM
             05 STARTING-PLAYER   OCCURS 9 TIMES
                                          INDEXED BY PLAYER-INDEX.
                 10 PLAYER-NAME   PIC X(25).
                 10 PLAYER-POSITION   PIC X(5).
                 10 BATTING-AVERAGE   PIC SV999   COMP-3.

This table will always hold exactly nine active entries. Usually, the number of active entries in a table will change, either during the execution of the program processing the table or at some point during the useful life of the program.

10.52 Define a table to hold the number of lines of COBOL produced per week by each programmer at an installation. Currently the shop employs 55 programmers. Next year, they plan to hire 15 more; then 10% more per year after that. The useful life of the program processing the table is estimated to be four years.

```
01  PROGRAMMER-PRODUCTIVITY.
    05  NUMBER-OF-PROGRAMMERS        PIC S9(5)  COMP SYNC.
    05  PROGRAMMER-DATA              OCCURS 1 TO 94 TIMES
                                     DEPENDING ON
                                         NUMBER-OF-PROGRAMMERS
                                     INDEXED BY PROGRAMMER-INDEX.
        10  PROGRAMMER-ID            PIC X(2).
        10  LINES-OF-COBOL           PIC S9(3)  COMP-3.
```

The first year the program is used, the company will have $55 + 15 = 70$ programmers; the 2nd year, $70 \times 1.10 = 77$; 3rd year, $77 \times 1.10 = 85$; 4th year, $85 \times 1.10 = 94$. Thus, we use a variable-length table, with a maximum of 94 entries.

10.53 Using the table in Problem 10.51, write code to DISPLAY the position with the lowest batting average.

As a second index will be useful, modify the INDEXED subclause to read: INDEXED BY PLAYER-INDEX LOWEST-INDEX. Then:

```
SET LOWEST-INDEX TO 1
PERFORM FIND-LOWEST-AVERAGE
    VARYING PLAYER-INDEX FROM 2 BY 1
        UNTIL PLAYER-INDEX GREATER THAN 9
DISPLAY PLAYER-POSITION (LOWEST-INDEX)
 . . . . . . . . . . . . . . . . . . . . . . . .
FIND-LOWEST-AVERAGE.
    IF BATTING-AVERAGE (PLAYER-INDEX) LESS THAN
        BATTING-AVERAGE (LOWEST-INDEX)
            SET LOWEST-INDEX TO PLAYER-INDEX
    .
```

10.54 If, in Problem 10.53, there is a tie for lowest average, will the program DISPLAY the first one found or the last one found?

Since the relational operator "LESS THAN" is used, the first low average found will be DISPLAYed.

10.55 Modify Problem 10.53 to DISPLAY the last one found in case of a tie for lowest average.

Use "NOT GREATER THAN" instead of "LESS THAN" in FIND-LOWEST-AVERAGE.

10.56 Decode INPUT-LOCATION-CODE PIC X(3) into OUTPUT-LOCATION PIC X(30), using the information in the following parallel tables:

```
01  LOCATION-CODE-TABLE.
    05  LOCATION-CODE                PIC X(3)
                                     OCCURS 80 TIMES
                                     ASCENDING KEY
                                         LOCATION-CODE
                                     INDEXED BY CODE-INDEX.
```

```
01   LOCATION-DESCRIPTION-TABLE.
    05   LOCATION-DESCRIPTION        PIC X(30)
                                      OCCURS 80 TIMES
                                      INDEXED BY
                                          DESCRIPTION-INDEX.
```

Since the entries in the two tables correspond, we could use (assuming that LOCATION-CODE-TABLE really *is* sorted on LOCATION-CODE):

```
SEARCH ALL LOCATION-CODE
    AT END
        MOVE "** UNKNOWN LOCATION **" TO OUTPUT-LOCATION
    WHEN
        LOCATION-CODE (CODE-INDEX) EQUAL INPUT-LOCATION-CODE
            SET DESCRIPTION-INDEX TO CODE-INDEX
            MOVE LOCATION-DESCRIPTION (DESCRIPTION-INDEX)
                TO OUTPUT-LOCATION
```

10.57   Rework Problem 10.56 if the location code table is not sorted.

Now we must use the sequential search:

```
SET CODE-INDEX
    DESCRIPTION-INDEX TO 1
SEARCH LOCATION-CODE
    VARYING DESCRIPTION-INDEX
    AT END
        MOVE "** UNKNOWN LOCATION **" TO OUTPUT-LOCATION
    WHEN
        LOCATION-CODE (CODE-INDEX) EQUAL INPUT-LOCATION-CODE
            MOVE LOCATION-DESCRIPTION (DESCRIPTION-INDEX)
                TO OUTPUT-LOCATION
```

Because the VARYING item pertains to another table, it is incremented along with the SEARCH index (the first index for the SEARCH table); thus CODE-INDEX and DESCRIPTION-INDEX always point to corresponding entries.

10.58   In COBOL, what happens if the value of a subscript or index drops below 1 (the first table entry) or exceeds the current table size?

Memory areas "preceding" or "following" the table may be violated. If there is the slightest chance that a subscript/index value could be invalid, the program should check it before using it to access a table.

10.59   Criticize the following:

```
01   PROJECT-ASSIGNMENTS.
    05   PROJECT-VALUES.
        10   FILLER      PIC X(11)      VALUE "MARYX250100".
        10   FILLER      PIC X(11)      VALUE "MIKE2A70553".
        10   FILLER      PIC X(11)      VALUE "JOHNRS20050".
    05   PROGRAMMER-INFO            REDEFINES PROJECT-VALUES
                                     OCCURS 3 TIMES
                                     INDEXED BY PROGRAMMER-INDEX.
        10   FIRST-NAME      PIC X(4).
        10   PROJECT-CODE    PIC X(3).
        10   HOURS-WORKED    PIC S9(3)V9      COMP-3.
```

(1) The VALUE clauses do not match the description of a table entry: HOURS-WORKED is supposed to be a COMP-3 field, but the VALUE clauses have it as DISPLAY.

(2) Since the information in this table will probably change frequently, the use of VALUE and REDEFINES to initialize the table is a very poor choice. It would be much better to keep the table information on a disk file, where it could easily be changed and from which the table values could be input as needed.

(3) Since the number of programmers is subject to change, there should be a counter associated with the table which indicates the number of active entries. Such a counter would usually be defined as a level-05 item under PROJECT-ASSIGNMENTS.

10.60 Correct PROJECT-VALUES in Problem 10.59 to meet objection (1).

```
05   PROJECT-VALUES.
     10   FILLER  PIC X(7)          VALUE "MARYX25".
     10   FILLER  PIC S9(3)V9  COMP-3  VALUE +10.0.
     10   FILLER  PIC X(7)          VALUE "MIKE2A7".
     10   FILLER  PIC S9(3)V9  COMP-3  VALUE +55.3.
     10   FILLER  PIC X(7)          VALUE "JOHNRS2".
     10   FILLER  PIC S9(3)V9  COMP-3  VALUE +5.0.
```

10.61 (a) Would the following work for the tables in Problem 10.56?

MOVE SPACES TO LOCATION-CODE-TABLE
                          LOCATION-DESCRIPTION-TABLE

(b) Would the following work for the table in Problem 10.52?

MOVE SPACES TO PROGRAMMER-DATA

(a) Yes, since all entries are PIC X(m) DISPLAY.

(b) No. First, PROGRAMMER-DATA would require a subscript or index when used in a MOVE statement. Second, the tabulated fields are PIC X(2) and PIC S9(3) COMP-3, so that a blanket MOVE cannot properly initialize both.

10.62 Write code to set PROGRAMMER-ID and LINES-OF-COBOL in Problem 10.52 to spaces and zeros, respectively.

```
PERFORM CLEAR-PROGRAMMER-DATA
     VARYING PROGRAMMER-INDEX FROM 1 BY 1
        UNTIL PROGRAMMER-INDEX GREATER THAN
           NUMBER-OF-PROGRAMMERS

. . . . . . . . . . . . . . . . . . . . . . . .

CLEAR-PROGRAMMER-DATA.
     MOVE SPACES  TO  PROGRAMMER-ID (PROGRAMMER-INDEX)
     MOVE ZEROS   TO  LINES-OF-COBOL (PROGRAMMER-INDEX)
```

10.63 Define a table to hold up to one hundred PART-ID PIC X(5) and QUANTITY PIC S9(4) COMP entries for each of up to twenty WAREHOUSE-LOCATION PIC X(3) entries.

```
01   WAREHOUSE-CONTENTS.
     05   NUMBER-LOCATIONS        PIC S9(5)  COMP SYNC.
     05   LOCATION-DATA           OCCURS 1 TO 20 TIMES
                                  DEPENDING ON NUMBER-LOCATIONS
                                  INDEXED BY LOCATION-INDEX.
```

```
10   WAREHOUSE-LOCATION    PIC X(3).
10   NUMBER-PARTS          PIC S9(5)  COMP.
10   PARTS-DATA            OCCURS 100 TIMES
                           INDEXED  BY PART-INDEX.
     15   PART-ID          PIC X(5).
     15   QUANTITY         PIC S9(4)  COMP.
```

Though one might like to define PARTS-DATA as "OCCURS 1 TO 100 TIMES DEPENDING ON NUMBER-PARTS", a variable-length table may not be made part of any other table.

10.64 Which data names from Problem 10.63 might occur in (*a*) a SEARCH ALL statement? (*b*) a SEARCH statement?

(*a*) None, since there are no ASCENDING/DESCENDING KEY clauses; (*b*) LOCATION-DATA and PARTS-DATA (note that a table must be indexed to be used in SEARCH or SEARCH ALL statements).

10.65 Write each data name in Problem 10.63 as it must appear in a MOVE statement.

WAREHOUSE-CONTENTS; NUMBER-LOCATIONS; LOCATION-DATA (LOCATION-INDEX); WAREHOUSE-LOCATION (LOCATION-INDEX); NUMBER-PARTS (LOCATION-INDEX); PARTS-DATA (LOCATION-INDEX PART-INDEX); PART-ID (LOCATION-INDEX PART-INDEX); QUANTITY (LOCATION-INDEX PART-INDEX).

10.66 Show how to add 10% to each QUANTITY entry for the table in Problem 10.63.

```
PERFORM ADD-TEN-PERCENT
    VARYING LOCATION-INDEX FROM 1 BY 1
        UNTIL LOCATION-INDEX GREATER THAN NUMBER-LOCATIONS
    AFTER PART-INDEX FROM 1 BY 1
        UNTIL PART-INDEX GREATER THAN
            NUMBER-PARTS (LOCATION-INDEX)
. . . . . . . . . . . . . . . . . . . . . . . . . . . . .
ADD-TEN-PERCENT.
    COMPUTE QUANTITY (LOCATION-INDEX PART-INDEX) =
        QUANTITY (LOCATION-INDEX PART-INDEX) * 1.10
```

Note that NUMBER-PARTS must be indexed as shown, it being a table entry.

10.67 Write code to DISPLAY *all* warehouse locations which store the item identified by INPUT-PART-ID   PIC X(5). Use the table in Problem 10.63.

```
PERFORM FIND-WHERE-PART-IS
    VARYING LOCATION-INDEX FROM 1 BY 1
        UNTIL LOCATION-INDEX GREATER THAN NUMBER-LOCATIONS
. . . . . . . . . . . . . . . . . . . . . . . . . . . . .
FIND-WHERE-PART-IS.
    SET PART-INDEX TO 1
    SEARCH PARTS-DATA
        AT END
            NEXT SENTENCE
        WHEN
            INPUT-PART-ID EQUAL
                PART-ID (LOCATION-INDEX PART-INDEX)
                    DISPLAY WAREHOUSE-LOCATION (LOCATION-INDEX)
```

10.68 We are given the following logical records:

```
FD   SHIPPING-FILE...
01   SHIPPING-RECORD.
     05   CUSTOMER-ID          PIC X(6).
     05   PRODUCT-ID           PIC X(4).
     05   SHIPPING-CLASS       PIC S9(2).
     05   WEIGHT-CLASS         PIC S9(2).
     05   SHIP-TO-ADDRESS      PIC X(50).
```

Suppose that a shipping charge table has been defined and loaded in WORKING-STORAGE:

```
01   SHIPPING-CHARGE-TABLE.
     05   NUMBER-SHIPPING-CLASSES     PIC S9(5)  COMP SYNC.
     05   SHIPPING-CLASS-ENTRY        OCCURS 30 TIMES
                                      INDEXED BY SHIPPING-INDEX.
          10   NUMBER-WEIGHT-CLASSES  PIC S9(5)  COMP.
          10   WEIGHT-CLASS-ENTRY     OCCURS 15 TIMES
                                      INDEXED BY WEIGHT-INDEX.
               15   SHIPPING-CHARGE   PIC S9(3)V99  COMP-3.
```

Assuming that SHIPPING-CLASS is defined as an integer between 1 and 30, and that WEIGHT-CLASS is defined as an integer between 1 and 15, write code to set CUSTOMER-SHIP-CHARGE to the appropriate shipping charge. If the charge cannot be located, set CUSTOMER-SHIP-CHARGE to zero.

```
IF SHIPPING-CLASS LESS THAN 1 OR GREATER THAN
    NUMBER-SHIPPING-CLASSES
        MOVE ZERO TO CUSTOMER-SHIP-CHARGE
ELSE IF WEIGHT-CLASS LESS THAN 1 OR GREATER THAN
    NUMBER-WEIGHT-CLASSES (SHIPPING-CLASS)
        MOVE ZERO TO CUSTOMER-SHIP-CHARGE
ELSE
    MOVE SHIPPING-CHARGE (SHIPPING-CLASS WEIGHT-CLASS)
        TO CUSTOMER-SHIP-CHARGE
```

10.69 Revise Problem 10.68 to use indexes instead of subscripts.

```
IF SHIPPING-CLASS LESS THAN 1 OR GREATER THAN
    NUMBER-SHIPPING-CLASSES
        MOVE ZERO TO CUSTOMER-SHIP-CHARGE
ELSE
    SET SHIPPING-INDEX TO SHIPPING-CLASS
    IF WEIGHT-CLASS LESS THAN 1 OR GREATER THAN
        NUMBER-WEIGHT-CLASSES (SHIPPING-INDEX)
            MOVE ZERO TO CUSTOMER-SHIP-CHARGE
    ELSE
        SET WEIGHT-INDEX TO WEIGHT-CLASS
        MOVE SHIPPING-CHARGE (SHIPPING-INDEX WEIGHT-INDEX)
            TO CUSTOMER-SHIP-CHARGE
```

10.70 What is wrong with the following, and how may it be corrected?

```
SET A-TABLE-INDEX TO 10
SEARCH A-TABLE
    AT END NEXT SENTENCE
```

WHEN A-TABLE-ENTRY (A-TABLE-INDEX) EQUAL SPACES
    SEARCH ALL ANOTHER-TABLE
        WHEN ANOTHER-KEY (ANOTHER-INDEX) EQUAL ZERO
    PERFORM WHOOPEE

It is permissible to start a sequential search at any point in a table; so, provided A-TABLE has at least 10 entries, the SET statement is correct. However, the WHEN clause must contain *imperative* statements only, and SEARCH ALL . . . is classified as a *conditional* statement. Proper coding is:

```
SET A-TABLE-INDEX TO 10
SEARCH A-TABLE
    AT END NEXT SENTENCE
    WHEN A-TABLE-ENTRY (A-TABLE-INDEX) EQUAL SPACES
        PERFORM SEARCH-ANOTHER
  . . . . . . . . . . . . . . . . . . . . . . .
SEARCH-ANOTHER.
    SEARCH ALL ANOTHER-TABLE
        WHEN ANOTHER-KEY (ANOTHER-INDEX) EQUAL ZERO
            PERFORM WHOOPEE
```

10.71 Problem 10.68 is changed so that SHIPPING-CLASS is PIC X(4), WEIGHT-CLASS is PIC X(3), and SHIPPING-CHARGE-TABLE includes a level-10 entry SHIPPING-CLASS-ID PIC X(4) and a level-15 entry WEIGHT-CLASS-ID PIC X(3). Rewrite the code to convert the alphanumeric input to the proper indexes.

```
SET SHIPPING-INDEX TO 1
SEARCH SHIPPING-CLASS-ENTRY
    AT END
        MOVE ZERO TO CUSTOMER-SHIP-CHARGE
    WHEN
        SHIPPING-CLASS-ID (SHIPPING-INDEX) EQUAL
            SHIPPING-CLASS
                PERFORM LOCATE-WEIGHT-CLASS
  . . . . . . . . . . . . . . . . . . . . . . .
LOCATE-WEIGHT-CLASS.
    SET WEIGHT-INDEX TO 1
    SEARCH WEIGHT-CLASS-ENTRY
        AT END
            MOVE ZERO TO CUSTOMER-SHIP-CHARGE
        WHEN
            WEIGHT-CLASS-ID (SHIPPING-INDEX WEIGHT-INDEX)
                EQUAL WEIGHT-CLASS
                    MOVE SHIPPING-CHARGE (SHIPPING-INDEX WEIGHT-INDEX)
                        TO CUSTOMER-SHIP-CHARGE
```

10.72 Given the table (cf. Problem 10.68)

```
01  SHIPPING-TABLE.
    05  NUMBER-CLASSES          PIC S9(5)  COMP SYNC.
    05  CLASS-ENTRY             OCCURS 1 TO 80 TIMES
                                DEPENDING ON NUMBER-CLASSES
                                ASCENDING KEY CLASS-ID
                                INDEXED BY CLASS-INDEX.
        10  CLASS-ID            PIC X(4).
```

```
        10   NUMBER-WEIGHTS      PIC S9(5)  COMP.
        10   WEIGHT-ENTRY        OCCURS 15 TIMES
                                 DESCENDING KEY WEIGHT-ID
                                 INDEXED BY WEIGHT-INDEX.
             15   WEIGHT-ID      PIC X(3).
             15   CHARGE         PIC S9(3)V99  COMP-3.
```

revise the code in Problem 10.71 so that it uses binary search when possible and halts any sequential searches when the search index exceeds the number of active table entries.

```
        SEARCH ALL CLASS-ENTRY
            AT END
                MOVE ZERO TO CUSTOMER-SHIP-CHARGE
            WHEN
                CLASS-ID (CLASS-INDEX) EQUAL SHIPPING-CLASS
                    PERFORM LOCATE-WEIGHT-CLASS

    . . . . . . . . . . . . . . . . . . .

    LOCATE-WEIGHT-CLASS.
        SET WEIGHT-INDEX TO 1
        SEARCH WEIGHT-ENTRY
            AT END
                MOVE ZERO TO CUSTOMER-SHIP-CHARGE
            WHEN
                WEIGHT-INDEX GREATER THAN NUMBER-WEIGHTS (CLASS-INDEX)
                    MOVE ZERO TO CUSTOMER-SHIP-CHARGE
            WHEN
                WEIGHT-ID (CLASS-INDEX WEIGHT-INDEX) EQUAL WEIGHT-CLASS
                    MOVE CHARGE (CLASS-INDEX WEIGHT-INDEX)
                        TO CUSTOMER-SHIP-CHARGE
```

Note that this is a more efficient solution than that in Problem 10.71.

10.73 Why isn't SEARCH ALL . . . used to search the WEIGHT-ENTRY table in Problem 10.72?

Because it is a fixed-length table which is not always filled; i.e., NUMBER-WEIGHTS is not always 15. Therefore, the table as a whole is not actually sorted.

10.74 Given the tables in Problem 10.56, (*a*) what is actually moved to DESCRIPTION-INDEX by "SET DESCRIPTION-INDEX TO 1"? (*b*) what is added to DESCRIPTION-INDEX by "SET DESCRIPTION-INDEX UP BY 1"?

(*a*) Zero: An index represents the *displacement* into the table needed to reach the desired entry. Entry *one* is zero bytes beyond the start of the table.

(*b*) Thirty: Indexes are incremented/decremented by multiples of the length of an entry—one entry length for every table position to be skipped over.

10.75 Contrast the machine-language address calculations required for subscripting and for indexing a one-dimensional table.

When K is a subscript, it is the position number of an entry:

$$\text{address ENTRY (K)} = \text{address-start-of-table} + (K - 1) * \text{entry-length}$$

When K is an index, it is a displacement from the start of the table:

$$\text{address ENTRY (K)} = \text{address-start-of-table} + K$$

10.76 What if it is desired to do binary searching of a table which is originally sorted? One solution, if the table values are being input from a file, is to do an *insertion sort*, in which each entry is placed in its proper position in the partially completed table as the entry is input from the file. Apply this technique to:

```
FD   INPUT-FILE...
01   INPUT-RECORD.
     05   INPUT-CODE            PIC X(3).
     05   INPUT-DESCRIPTION     PIC X(35).

01   JOB-CODES-TABLE.
     05   NUMBER-CODES          PIC S9(5) COMP SYNC.
     05   CODE-ENTRY            OCCURS 1 TO 100 TIMES
                                DEPENDING ON NUMBER-CODES
                                ASCENDING KEY IS JOB-CODE
                                INDEXED BY CODE-INDEX
                                             MOVE-INDEX.
          10   JOB-CODE         PIC X(3).
          10   JOB-DESCRIPTION  PIC X(35).

     BUILD-TABLE.
         OPEN  INPUT  INPUT-FILE
         MOVE "NO" TO END-FILE-SW
         PERFORM GET-NEXT-RECORD
         IF END-FILE-SW EQUAL "NO"
             MOVE 1 TO NUMBER-CODES
             MOVE INPUT-CODE        TO JOB-CODE (1)
             MOVE INPUT-DESCRIPTION TO JOB-DESCRIPTION (1)
             PERFORM GET-NEXT-RECORD
             PERFORM INSERT-IN-SORTED-ORDER
                 UNTIL END-FILE-SW EQUAL "YES" OR NUMBER-CODES
                     EQUAL 100
         ELSE
             PERFORM FILE-EMPTY-ERROR
         .
         IF END-FILE-SW NOT EQUAL "YES"
             PERFORM TABLE-TOO-SMALL-ERROR
         .
         CLOSE INPUT-FILE
. . . . . . . . . . . . . . . . . . . . . . . . . . .
     INSERT-IN-SORTED-ORDER.
         (routine as in Example 10.37)
```

10.77 Another (inefficient) table sort is the *bubble sort*, in which pairs of adjacent entries are compared and swapped (interchanged) if they are out of relative sequence. Obviously, if one moves through the table comparing and swapping often enough, the table will eventually become sorted. Write code to perform a bubble sort on the table of Problem 10.76, which must be assumed already built.

   We define one more index for the table, STOP-INDEX, as well as two data items, HAD-TO-SWAP and HOLD-ENTRY, which are PIC X(3) and PIC X(38), respectively.

```
     SET STOP-INDEX TO NUMBER-CODES
     SET STOP-INDEX DOWN BY 1
     MOVE "YES" TO HAD-TO-SWAP
     PERFORM MAKE-A-PASS
         UNTIL STOP-INDEX NOT GREATER THAN ZERO
             OR HAD-TO-SWAP EQUAL "NO"
```

. . . .

```
            MAKE-A-PASS.
                MOVE "NO" TO HAD-TO-SWAP
                PERFORM COMPARE-AND-SWAP
                    VARYING CODE-INDEX FROM 1 BY 1
                    UNTIL CODE-INDEX GREATER THAN STOP-INDEX
                SET STOP-INDEX DOWN BY 1
                    .

            . . . . . . . . . . . . . . . . . . . . . . . . . . .

            COMPARE-AND-SWAP.
                IF JOB-CODE (CODE-INDEX) GREATER THAN
                    JOB-CODE (CODE-INDEX + 1)
                        MOVE "YES" TO HAD-TO-SWAP
                        MOVE CODE-ENTRY (CODE-INDEX) TO HOLD-ENTRY
                        MOVE CODE-ENTRY (CODE-INDEX + 1) TO
                            CODE-ENTRY (CODE-INDEX)
                        MOVE HOLD-ENTRY TO CODE-ENTRY (CODE-INDEX + 1)
```

10.78 Give a more efficient way to load the table in Example 10.21.

Since TABLE-VALUES-RECORD has *exactly* the same layout as a WEIGHT-RANGE entry in the FREIGHT-CHARGES-TABLE, a *group MOVE* could be used to move the entire entry in one statement. Thus, LOAD-TABLE could be written as follows (eliminating the need for MOVE-FREIGHT-CHARGES):

```
            LOAD-TABLE.
                MOVE TABLE-VALUES-RECORD TO
                    WEIGHT-RANGE (NUMBER-WEIGHT-ENTRIES)
                ADD 1 TO NUMBER-WEIGHT-ENTRIES
                PERFORM GET-TABLE-RECORD
```

Chapter 11

Sequential File Processing

By now, we are thoroughly familiar with (1) creating and (2) retrieving logical records from a file whose ORGANIZATION IS SEQUENTIAL; we also know (3) the use of the FILE STATUS area in detecting errors in the processing of sequential files. One further illustration of this last follows.

EXAMPLE 11.1 On IBM systems, a status code of "00" indicates successful completion, "10" indicates end of file, "30" indicates a permanent hardware I/O error, and "92" indicates a program logic error. Thus, if the FILE STATUS clause of the SELECT statement names the WORKING-STORAGE item STATUS-CODE-AREA   PIC XX, we might have in the PROCEDURE DIVISION:

```
        OPEN  INPUT  ANY-SEQUENTIAL-FILE
        IF STATUS-CODE-AREA NOT EQUAL "00"
            DISPLAY "CANNOT OPEN FILE--ABORTING RUN"
            MOVE "YES" TO PROGRAM-ABORT-SW
            .
  . . . . . . . . . . . . . . . . . . . . . . . . .
        READ ANY-SEQUENTIAL-FILE
        IF STATUS-CODE-AREA NOT EQUAL "00"
            IF STATUS-CODE-AREA EQUAL "10"
                MOVE "YES" TO END-FILE-SW
            ELSE IF STATUS-CODE-AREA EQUAL "30"
                DISPLAY "HARDWARE ERROR READING FILE"
                MOVE "YES" TO IGNORE-RECORD-SW
            .
  . . . . . . . . . . . . . . . . . . . . . . . . .
        CLOSE ANY-SEQUENTIAL-FILE
        IF STATUS-CODE-AREA NOT EQUAL "00"
            DISPLAY "CLOSE FAILED--RUN DIAGNOSTIC ON FILE"
            .
```

11.1 Sequential File Updating

Sequentially organized master files are almost always kept sorted on a key field (cf. Section 10.9)—a fact that becomes critically important when the file is *updated*. The logical records containing information to be added to or removed from the master file are usually incorporated in a separate sequential file, the *transaction file*. Each transaction file record specifies the key of a master file record which is to be added, changed, or deleted; the transaction file itself is sorted on this same key. A typical sequential file update is flowcharted in Fig. 11-1; it involves the following steps:

1. *Either* source documents are collected over a period of time until the whole *batch* is keyed into a sequential disk transaction file; *or* transactions are keyed into online terminals as they occur, but the program which communicates with the terminals, rather than processing these transactions, simply collects them in a "batch" on a sequential disk transaction file.

2. In either event, we have a sequential transaction file, which is now validated and sorted into the same sequence as the master file to be updated. Transactions in error must be corrected and recycled back to step 1.

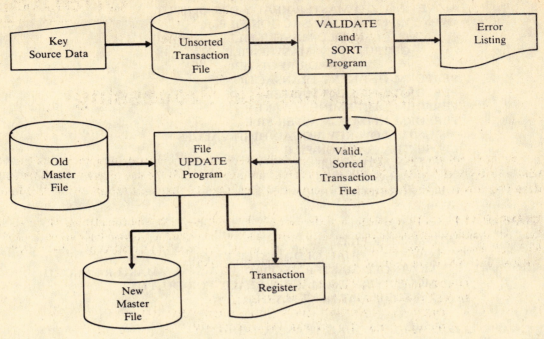

Fig. 11-1

3. The validated and sorted transactions are now input to a sequential file update program. This program also retrieves the existing master file records, makes the indicated changes, and creates a *new master file* which is up-to-date. The *old master file* is preserved in this process.

4. The old master file and the transaction file are retained in a safe place for *backup* purposes. If anything happens to the new master file, it can be recreated just by running the update program again. This is known as the *grandparent, parent, child* method of backup, since as many "generations" of transaction and old master files can be saved as desired.

5. The sequential file update program executed in step 3 usually produces a printed report, called a *transaction register*, which lists the results of applying each transaction to the master file. Note that although a transaction may be valid in and of itself, it may be in error with respect to the master file (e.g., it is possible to have a correctly specified delete transaction for a master file record that doesn't exist). Such errors must be corrected and recycled back to step 1.

11.2   The Balanced-Line Algorithm

Figure 11-2 delineates, in COBOL-like pseudocode, one of the most effective methods of matching the records in a sorted transaction file against the records in a sorted master file, the so-called *balanced-line algorithm*. The algorithm properly handles more than one transaction record per master record, a common situation when transactions are batched over a period of time. It should be noted that all details of processing record fields have been left to lower-level modules. Hence the high-level modules could be used in many different programs for different applications.

The heart of the algorithm is found in the UPDATE-MASTER-FILE paragraph. LOW-KEY is always set equal to the smaller of TRANSACTION-KEY and OLD-MASTER-KEY. If OLD-MASTER-RECORD's key is less than or equal to TRANSACTION-KEY ("LOW-KEY EQUAL OLD-MASTER-KEY"), then OLD-MASTER-RECORD is moved to WS-NEW-MASTER-RECORD, a WORKING-STORAGE area where records for the new master file are built. MASTER-READY-FOR-OUTPUT is a program switch which tells whether there are active data in this record construction area. The reader should verify (by desk checking) that it is impossible for

```
BALANCED-LINE.
    MOVE "NO" TO MASTER-READY-FOR-OUTPUT
    OPEN   INPUT     TRANSACTION-FILE
                     OLD-MASTER-FILE
           OUTPUT    NEW-MASTER-FILE
                     ERROR-REGISTER
    PERFORM GET-NEXT-TRANSACTION
    PERFORM GET-NEXT-MASTER
    PERFORM DETERMINE-LOW-KEY
    PERFORM UPDATE-MASTER-FILE
        UNTIL LOW-KEY EQUAL HIGH-VALUES
    CLOSE TRANSACTION-FILE
        OLD-MASTER-FILE
        NEW-MASTER-FILE
        ERROR-REGISTER
    STOP RUN
.

UPDATE-MASTER-FILE.
    IF LOW-KEY EQUAL OLD-MASTER-KEY
        MOVE OLD-MASTER-RECORD TO WS-NEW-MASTER-RECORD
        MOVE "YES" TO MASTER-READY-FOR-OUTPUT
        PERFORM GET-NEXT-MASTER
.

    IF LOW-KEY EQUAL TRANSACTION-KEY
        PERFORM PROCESS-A-TRANSACTION
            UNTIL LOW-KEY NOT EQUAL TRANSACTION-KEY
.

    IF MASTER-READY-FOR-OUTPUT EQUAL "YES"
        WRITE NEW-MASTER-RECORD FROM WS-NEW-MASTER-RECORD
        MOVE "NO" TO MASTER-READY-FOR-OUTPUT
.

    PERFORM DETERMINE-LOW-KEY
.

PROCESS-A-TRANSACTION.
    IF TRANSACTION-CODE-IS-ADD
        IF MASTER-READY-FOR-OUTPUT EQUAL "YES"
            PERFORM DUPLICATE-KEY-ERROR
        ELSE
            PERFORM MOVE-TRANS-INFO-TO-WS-NEW-MASTER
            MOVE "YES" TO MASTER-READY-FOR-OUTPUT
    ELSE IF TRANSACTION-CODE-IS-CHANGE
        IF MASTER-READY-FOR-OUTPUT EQUAL "NO"
            PERFORM NO-MASTER-TO-CHANGE-ERROR
        ELSE
            PERFORM APPLY-TRANS-TO-WS-NEW-MASTER
    ELSE IF TRANSACTION-CODE-IS-DELETE
        IF MASTER-READY-FOR-OUTPUT EQUAL "NO"
            PERFORM NO-MASTER-TO-DELETE-ERROR
        ELSE
            MOVE "NO" TO MASTER-READY-FOR-OUTPUT
    ELSE
        PERFORM INVALID-TRANS-CODE-ERROR
.

    PERFORM GET-NEXT-TRANSACTION
.
```

Fig. 11-2

```
         DETERMINE-LOW-KEY
             IF TRANSACTION-KEY IS LESS THAN OLD-MASTER-KEY
                 MOVE TRANSACTION-KEY TO LOW-KEY
             ELSE
                 MOVE OLD-MASTER-KEY TO LOW-KEY


         GET-NEXT-TRANSACTION.
             READ TRANSACTION-FILE
                 AT END
                     MOVE HIGH-VALUES TO TRANSACTION-KEY


         GET-NEXT-MASTER.
             READ OLD-MASTER-FILE
                 AT END
                     MOVE HIGH-VALUES TO OLD-MASTER-KEY
```

Fig. 11-2 *(cont.)*

"MOVE OLD-MASTER-RECORD TO WS-NEW-MASTER-RECORD" to be executed when there is *already* an active record being built in the WS-NEW-MASTER-RECORD area. As soon as the OLD-MASTER-RECORD is moved into the new master record construction area, the next old master record is read into the OLD-MASTER-FILE input buffer.

The next step is to determine if there are any transactions which should be applied to the contents of WS-NEW-MASTER-RECORD. As long as TRANSACTION-KEY remains equal to the current value of LOW-KEY, transaction records apply to the same master and are input and processed. Note that it is PERFORM PROCESS-A-TRANSACTION UNTIL... which allows the algorithm to handle more than one transaction per master record.

All appropriate transactions having been applied, the algorithm outputs the record from WS-NEW-MASTER-RECORD to NEW-MASTER-FILE (assuming there is an active record in the construction area). Then the MASTER-READY-FOR-OUTPUT switch is turned back off.

Finally, after the possible input of a new OLD-MASTER-RECORD and/or one or more new TRANSACTION-RECORDs, DETERMINE LOW-KEY is performed again before UPDATE-MASTER-FILE is repeated.

EXAMPLE 11.2   Table 11-1 records the application of the balanced-line algorithm to the test files:

TRANSACTION-FILE: 15, 20, 20, 60
OLD-MASTER-FILE: 10, 20, 30, 60, 70

Step-by-step notes:

1. The algorithm begins by reading the first record from each file and determining the lowest key; the new master record construction area is empty.

2. "LOW-KEY EQUAL OLD-MASTER-KEY" is true; so the old master record is copied to the new master construction area, the switch is turned on to indicate that the work area contains a record, and the *next* old master record is input.

3. "LOW-KEY EQUAL TRANSACTION-KEY" is false; so no transactions are processed. Since MASTER-READY-FOR-OUTPUT EQUAL "YES", the contents of the work area (10) are written to the new master file and the master ready switch is turned off.

4. DETERMINE-LOW-KEY compares 15 with 20, choosing 15.

5. For the 2nd execution of UPDATE-MASTER-FILE, LOW-KEY is not equal to OLD-MASTER-KEY; no old master record is input. Since LOW-KEY *is* equal to TRANSACTION-KEY, PERFORM PROCESS-A-TRANSACTION is executed, processing transaction 15. Note that if it is not an add transaction, it will be treated as an error, since MASTER-READY switch is "NO". Assuming it is an add, the transaction information is moved to the work area and MASTER-READY is turned on.

Table 11-1

	Execution of UPDATE-MASTER-FILE	LOW-KEY	Value in TRANSACTION-RECORD	Value in OLD-MASTER-RECORD	Value in WORKING-STORAGE NEW-MASTER Area	Ready Switch
1.	first	10	15	10	empty	NO
2.	first	10	15	20	10	YES
3.	first	10	15	20	empty	NO
4.	first	15	15	20	empty	NO
5.	second	15	15	20	15	YES
6.	second	15	20 (1st)	20	15	YES
7.	second	15	20 (1st)	20	empty	NO
8.	second	20	20 (1st)	20	empty	NO
9.	third	20	20 (1st)	30	20	YES
10.	third	20	20 (1st)	30	20 (changed)	YES
11.	third	20	20 (2nd)	30	20 (changed)	YES
12.	third	20	20 (2nd)	30	20 (changed twice)	YES
13.	third	20	60	30	20 (changed twice)	YES
14.	third	20	60	30	empty	NO
15.	third	30	60	30	empty	NO
16.	fourth	30	60	30	30	YES
17.	fourth	30	60	60	empty	NO
18.	fourth	60	60	60	empty	NO
19.	fifth	60	60	60	60	YES
20.	fifth	60	60	70	60	NO
21.	fifth	60	HIGH-VALUES	70	60	NO
22.	fifth	70	HIGH-VALUES	70	60	NO
23.	sixth	70	HIGH-VALUES	HIGH-VALUES	70	YES
24.	sixth	70	HIGH-VALUES	HIGH-VALUES	empty	NO
25.	sixth	HIGH-VALUES	HIGH-VALUES	HIGH-VALUES	empty	NO

6.   PROCESS-A-TRANSACTION now inputs the next transaction record.

7.   Since LOW-KEY ≠ TRANSACTION-KEY, PROCESS-A-TRANSACTION is not performed again at this time. Instead, the algorithm checks the MASTER-READY switch, which is on; so 15 is written to the new master file and the switch set off.

8.   DETERMINE-LOW-KEY compares 20 with 20, choosing 20.

9.   Beginning the third execution of UPDATE-MASTER-FILE, LOW-KEY equals OLD-MASTER-KEY; so the old master record is moved to the work area, the switch set on, and the next old master record input.

10. Since LOW-KEY also equals TRANSACTION-KEY, PROCESS-A-TRANSACTION is performed, causing the first 20-transaction to be processed. Note that if it is an add, we detect a duplicate key, since MASTER-READY is on; assuming it is a change, we apply the changes to old master record 20, which is in the work area.

11. The next transaction record is input.

12. Since LOW-KEY still equals the new TRANSACTION-KEY, PROCESS-A-TRANSACTION is performed again, causing old master record 20 in the work area to be modified a second time (supposing a change transaction).

13. The next transaction record is input.

14. Since LOW-KEY no longer equals TRANSACTION-KEY, the algorithm goes on to check MASTER-READY. Since the switch is on, the changed record in the work area (20) is output to the new master file, and the switch is turned off.

15. DETERMINE-LOW-KEY compares 60 and 30, choosing 30.

16. Beginning the fourth execution of UPDATE-MASTER-FILE, LOW-KEY equals OLD-MASTER-KEY; so the old master record is moved to the work area, the switch set on, and the next old master record input.

17. Since LOW-KEY ≠ TRANSACTION-KEY, no transactions are processed. Since MASTER-READY is on, the contents of the work area (record 30) are output to the new master file, and MASTER-READY turned off.

18. DETERMINE-LOW-KEY compares 60 with 60, choosing 60.

19. Beginning the fifth execution of UPDATE-MASTER-FILE, LOW-KEY equals OLD-MASTER-KEY; so the old master record is moved to the work area and the switch set on. The next old master record is input.

20. Since LOW-KEY = TRANSACTION-KEY, the current transaction is processed. On the assumption that it is a deletion, MASTER-READY is turned off.

21. The next transaction is input; this causes end of file, which sets TRANSACTION-KEY to HIGH-VALUES. Since LOW-KEY ≠ TRANSACTION-KEY, PROCESS-A-TRANSACTION is not performed again. Because MASTER-READY was turned off by the deletion, the contents of the work area are *not* output to the new master file.

22. DETERMINE-LOW-KEY compares HIGH-VALUES and 70, choosing 70.

23. Beginning the sixth execution of UPDATE-MASTER-FILE, LOW-KEY = OLD-MASTER-KEY; so the old master record is moved to the work area, MASTER-READY set on, and the next old master record input. This causes end of file, setting OLD-MASTER-KEY to HIGH-VALUES.

24. Since LOW-KEY ≠ TRANSACTION-KEY, PROCESS-A-TRANSACTION is not performed. Since MASTER-READY is "YES", the contents of the work area (record 70) are output to the new master file, and MASTER-READY turned off.

25. DETERMINE-LOW-KEY compares HIGH-VALUES with HIGH-VALUES, choosing HIGH-VALUES. Since LOW-KEY now equals HIGH-VALUES, no more repetitions of UPDATE-MASTER-FILE are performed. The results are:

NEW-MASTER-FILE: 10, 15(added), 20(changed twice), 30, 70

Note that record 60 has been properly deleted.

EXAMPLE 11.3 Using the balanced-line algorithm, write a sequential file update for the following accounts receivable master file:

```
01  AR-CUSTOMER-MASTER-RECORD.
    05  AR-CUSTOMER-ID        PIC X(4).
    05  AR-CUSTOMER-NAME      PIC X(20).
    05  AR-NUMBER-INVOICES    PIC S9(2)        COMP-3.
```

```
      05   AR-INVOICE-DATA              OCCURS 1 TO 15 TIMES
                                        DEPENDING ON AR-NUMBER-INVOICES
                                        ASCENDING KEY IS AR-INVOICE-DATE.
          10   AR-INVOICE-ID            PIC X(5).
          10   AR-INVOICE-DATE.
              15   AR-INVOICE-YY        PIC 99.
              15   AR-INVOICE-MM        PIC 99.
              15   AR-INVOICE-DD        PIC 99.
          10   AR-INVOICE-AMOUNT   PIC S9(5)V99      COMP-3.
```

The master file, and also the transaction file, is sorted by customer ID. There are three types of transaction record:

Delete a customer record from the master file—

> columns 1–4 : customer ID
> column   5 : transaction code "1"
> columns 6–80: unused

Add a new customer record to the master file—

> columns 1–4 : customer ID
> column   5 : transaction code "2"
> columns 6–25 : customer name
> columns 26–30: invoice ID
> columns 31–36: invoice date (yymmdd)
> columns 37–43: amount (DISPLAY)
> columns 44–80: unused

Change existing invoice data—

> columns 1–4 : customer ID
> column   5 : transaction code "3"
> column   6 : invoice code ("I", "P", or "A")
> columns 7–11 : invoice ID
> columns 12–17: invoice date (yymmdd)
> columns 18–24: amount [S9(5)V99   DISPLAY]
> columns 25–80: unused

Code "I" directs that a new entry be inserted in the invoice data table (keeping the table sorted by invoice date). Code "A" calls for the replacement of the amount in the table by the amount from the transaction record. Code "P" signals the application of a payment to the invoice amount. If the invoice amount is *zero* after the payment is subtracted, physically delete the entire invoice data entry; if it is *negative*, effect the deletion and also write a record to a sequential CREDIT-FILE having the fields CUSTOMER-ID, CUSTOMER-NAME, INVOICE-ID, INVOICE-DATE (yymmdd), and CREDIT-BALANCE [S9(5)V99   COMP-3]. If a master record is left with no invoices, delete it from the file. In addition to the NEW-AR-CUSTOMER-MASTER-FILE and the CREDIT-FILE, output an ERROR-REPORT that includes page headings (with page number and run date) for each page, *all* transaction fields for each record in error, and an English phrase describing the error. The following errors should be covered: (1) transaction code "1" and customer ID not in file; (2) transaction code "2" and customer ID already in file; (3) code "3" and customer ID not in file; (4) code "3I" and invoice ID already in invoice table; (5) code "3A" and invoice ID not in invoice table; (6) code "3P" and invoices ID not in invoice table *or* transaction invoice date does not match master invoice date; (7) transaction invoice date or invoice amount not numeric.

One solution is given in Fig. 11-3 below.

```
00001            IDENTIFICATION DIVISION.
00002
00003            PROGRAM-ID.   SEQUPDAT.
00004
00005            AUTHOR.   LARRY NEWCOMER.
00006            INSTALLATION. PENN STATE UNIVERSITY, YORK CAMPUS.
```

Fig. 11-3

```
00007
00008          DATE-WRITTEN.  MAY 1983.
00009          DATE-COMPILED. MAY  9,1983.
00011          SECURITY. NONE.
00012
00013     *      SEQUENTIAL FILE UPDATE USING THE BALANCED LINE
00014     *      ALGORITHM.   INPUT:   OLD MASTER FILE
00015     *                            TRANSACTION FILE
00016     *                   OUTPUT: NEW MASTER FILE
00017     *                            ERROR REPORT
00018     *                            CREDIT FILE

00020          ENVIRONMENT DIVISION.

00022          CONFIGURATION SECTION.
00023          SOURCE-COMPUTER.  IBM-3081.
00024          OBJECT-COMPUTER.  IBM-3081.

00026          INPUT-OUTPUT SECTION.

00028          FILE-CONTROL.
00029
00030              SELECT OLD-MASTER-FILE
00031                  ASSIGN TO OLDMAST
00032                  ORGANIZATION IS SEQUENTIAL
00033                  ACCESS IS SEQUENTIAL
00034                  .
00035
00036              SELECT TRANSACTION-FILE
00037                  ASSIGN TO TRANS
00038                  ORGANIZATION IS SEQUENTIAL
00039                  ACCESS IS SEQUENTIAL
00040                  .
00041
00042              SELECT NEW-MASTER-FILE
00043                  ASSIGN TO NEWMAST
00044                  ORGANIZATION IS SEQUENTIAL
00045                  ACCESS IS SEQUENTIAL
00046                  .
00047
00048              SELECT CREDIT-FILE
00049                  ASSIGN TO CREDITS
00050                  ORGANIZATION IS SEQUENTIAL
00051                  ACCESS IS SEQUENTIAL
00052                  .
00053
00054              SELECT ERROR-REPORT
00055                  ASSIGN TO ERRORLOG
00056                  ORGANIZATION IS SEQUENTIAL
00057                  ACCESS IS SEQUENTIAL
00058                  .
00059

00061          DATA DIVISION.

00063          FILE SECTION.
00064
00065     *
00066     * ----------------------------------------------------------
00067     *
00068     *    USE OF VARIABLE-LENGTH RECORDS TO SAVE DISK/TAPE SPACE
00069     *
00070     * ----------------------------------------------------------
00071     *
00072          FD  OLD-MASTER-FILE
00073              BLOCK CONTAINS O RECORDS
```

Fig. 11-3 (*cont.*)

```
00074                    RECORD CONTAINS 41 TO 251 CHARACTERS
00075                    LABEL RECORDS ARE STANDARD
00076                    .
00077
00078        01   OM-AR-CUSTOMER-RECORD.
00079             05   OM-AR-CUSTOMER-ID       PIC X(4).
00080             05   OM-AR-CUSTOMER-NAME     PIC X(20).
00081             05   OM-AR-NUMBER-INVOICES   PIC S9(2)        COMP-3.
00082        *
00083        *    -------------------------------------------------------
00084        *
00085        *    VARIABLE-LENGTH TABLE DEFINED WITHIN LOGICAL RECORD
00086        *
00087        *    -------------------------------------------------------
00088        *
00089             05   OM-AR-INVOICE-DATA      OCCURS 1 TO 15 TIMES
00090                                          DEPENDING ON
00091                                              OM-AR-NUMBER-INVOICES
00092                                          .
00093                  10   OM-INVOICE-ID      PIC X(5).
00094                  10   OM-INVOICE-DATE.
00095                       15   OM-INVOICE-YY    PIC 99.
00096                       15   OM-INVOICE-MM    PIC 99.
00097                       15   OM-INVOICE-DD    PIC 99.
00098                  10   OM-INVOICE-AMOUNT    PIC S9(5)V99    COMP-3.
00099
00100        FD   TRANSACTION-FILE
00101             RECORD CONTAINS 80 CHARACTERS
00102             LABEL RECORDS ARE OMITTED
00103             .
00104
00105        01   TRANSACTION-RECORD.
00106             05   TRANS-SORT-KEY.
00107                  10   TRANS-CUSTOMER-ID   PIC X(4).
00108                  10   TRANS-CODE          PIC X.
00109                       88   DELETION-TRANSACTION          VALUE "1".
00110                       88   ADD-TRANSACTION               VALUE "2".
00111                       88   CHANGE-TRANSACTION            VALUE "3".
00112             05   TRANS-VARIABLE-AREA      PIC X(75).
00113        *
00114        *    -------------------------------------------------------
00115        *
00116        *    USE OF REDEFINES TO DESCRIBE THE VARIOUS FORMS OF
00117        *    TRANSACTION RECORDS
00118        *
00119        *    -------------------------------------------------------
00120        *
00121             05   TRANS-ADD-AREA          REDEFINES TRANS-VARIABLE-AREA.
00122                  10   ADD-CUSTOMER-NAME  PIC X(20).
00123                  10   ADD-INVOICE-ID     PIC X(5).
00124                  10   ADD-INVOICE-DATE   PIC 9(6).
00125                  10   ADD-AMOUNT         PIC S9(5)V99.
00126                  10   FILLER             PIC X(37).
00127             05   TRANS-CHANGE-AREA       REDEFINES TRANS-VARIABLE-AREA.
00128                  10   TRANS-INVOICE-CODE PIC X.
00129                       88   INSERTION-CODE               VALUE "I".
00130                       88   ADJUSTMENT-CODE              VALUE "A".
00131                       88   PAYMENT-CODE                 VALUE "P".
00132                  10   CHANGE-INVOICE-ID   PIC X(5).
00133                  10   CHANGE-INVOICE-DATE PIC X(6).
00134                  10   CHANGE-AMOUNT       PIC S9(5)V99.
00135                  10   CHANGE-AMOUNT-X     REDEFINES CHANGE-AMOUNT
00136                                           PIC X(7).
00137                  10   FILLER              PIC X(56).
00138
00139
00140        FD   NEW-MASTER-FILE
00141             BLOCK CONTAINS 0 RECORDS
```

Fig. 11-3 (cont.)

```
00142                        RECORD CONTAINS 41 TO 251 CHARACTERS
00143                        LABEL RECORDS ARE STANDARD
00144                            .
00145
00146                01   NM-AR-CUSTOMER-RECORD.
00147                        05   NM-AR-CUSTOMER-ID        PIC X(4).
00148                        05   NM-AR-CUSTOMER-NAME      PIC X(20).
00149                        05   NM-AR-NUMBER-INVOICES    PIC S9(2)        COMP-3.
00150                        05   NM-AR-INVOICE-DATA       OCCURS 1 TO 15 TIMES
00151                                                      DEPENDING ON
00152                                                          NM-AR-NUMBER-INVOICES
00153                                                      .
00154                            10   NM-INVOICE-ID        PIC X(5).
00155                            10   NM-INVOICE-DATE.
00156                                15   NM-INVOICE-YY    PIC 99.
00157                                15   NM-INVOICE-MM    PIC 99.
00158                                15   NM-INVOICE-DD    PIC 99.
00159                            10   NM-INVOICE-AMOUNT    PIC S9(5)V99    COMP-3.
00160
00161            FD   CREDIT-FILE
00162                    BLOCK CONTAINS 0 RECORDS
00163                    RECORD CONTAINS 39 CHARACTERS
00164                    LABEL RECORDS ARE STANDARD
00165                        .
00166
00167            01   CREDIT-BALANCE-RECORD.
00168                    05   CREDIT-CUSTOMER-ID       PIC X(4).
00169                    05   CREDIT-CUSTOMER-NAME     PIC X(20).
00170                    05   CREDIT-INVOICE-ID        PIC X(5).
00171                    05   CREDIT-INVOICE-DATE      PIC 9(6).
00172                    05   CREDIT-BALANCE           PIC 9(5)V99     COMP-3.
00173
00174            FD   ERROR-REPORT
00175                    RECORD CONTAINS 132 CHARACTERS
00176                    LABEL RECORDS ARE OMITTED
00177                    LINAGE IS 60
00178                        WITH FOOTING AT 59
00179                        LINES AT TOP 3
00180                        LINES AT BOTTOM 3
00181                        .
00182
00183            01   ERROR-REPORT-LINE               PIC X(132).

00185            WORKING-STORAGE SECTION.

00187            01   WS-SWITCHES-AND-WORK-AREAS.
00188                    05   WS-PAGE-NUMBER           PIC S9(3)       COMP-3.
00189                    05   LOW-KEY                  PIC X(4).
00190                    05   MAXIMUM-TABLE-SIZE       PIC S9(3)       COMP-3
00191                                                                  VALUE +15.
00192                    05   MASTER-READY             PIC X(3).
00193                        88   MASTER-RECORD-PRESENT            VALUE "YES".
00194                        88   NO-MASTER-RECORD                 VALUE "NO ".
00195                    05   SYSTEM-DATE.
00196                        10   SYSTEM-YY            PIC 99.
00197                        10   SYSTEM-MM            PIC 99.
00198                        10   SYSTEM-DD            PIC 99.
00199                    05   WS-DIFFERENCE            PIC S9(5)V99    COMP-3.
00200
00201       *
00202       * -----------------------------------------------------------------
00203       *
00204       *     ERROR MESSAGE TEXT DEFINED AS PROGRAM CONSTANTS RATHER
00205       *     THAN USING NON-NUMERIC LITERALS IN PROCEDURE DIVISION
00206       *
00207       * -----------------------------------------------------------------
00208       *
```

Fig. 11-3   *(cont.)*

```
00209          01   WS-ERROR-MESSAGE-AREAS.
00210               05   ADD-ERROR-MESSAGE          PIC X(42)
00211                                               VALUE "DUPLICATE KEY--NO ADD".
00212               05   CHANGE-ERROR-MESSAGE       PIC X(42)
00213                                               VALUE "KEY NOT FOUND--NO CHANGE".
00214               05   DELETION-ERROR-MESSAGE     PIC X(42)
00215                                               VALUE "KEY NOT FOUND--NO DELETE".
00216               05   INVALID-TRANS-CODE-MESSAGE
00217                                               PIC X(42)
00218                                               VALUE "INVALID CODE--NO ACTION".
00219               05   INVALID-CHANGE-CODE-MESSAGE
00220                                               PIC X(42)
00221                                               VALUE "INVALID CHANGE--IGNORED".
00222               05   ADJUST-ERROR-MESSAGE       PIC X(42)
00223                                               VALUE "INVOICE NOT FOUND".
00224               05   INVALID-FIELDS-MESSAGE     PIC X(42)
00225                                               VALUE "INVALID AMOUNT/DATE".
00226               05   NO-PAYMENT-INVOICE-MESSAGE
00227                                               PIC X(42)
00228                                   VALUE "NO INVOICE--PAYMENT NOT CREDITED".
00229               05   DUPLICATE-INVOICE-MESSAGE
00230                                               PIC X(42)
00231                                     VALUE "DUPLICATE INVOICE--IGNORED".
00232               05   TABLE-OVERFLOW-MESSAGE   PIC X(42)
00233                                               VALUE ">15 INVOICES--IGNORED".
00234
00235     *
00236     * -----------------------------------------------------------
00237     *
00238     *    WORKING-STORAGE AREA USED IN BALANCED LINE ALGORITHM
00239     *    TO CONSTRUCT NEW-MASTER-FILE RECORD WITH ALL
00240     *    TRANSACTIONS APPLIED
00241     *
00242     * -----------------------------------------------------------
00243     *
00244          01   WS-AR-CUSTOMER-RECORD.
00245               05   WS-AR-CUSTOMER-ID         PIC X(4).
00246               05   WS-AR-CUSTOMER-NAME       PIC X(20).
00247               05   WS-AR-NUMBER-INVOICES     PIC S9(2)       COMP-3.
00248               05   WS-AR-INVOICE-DATA        OCCURS 1 TO 15 TIMES
00249                                              DEPENDING ON
00250                                                  WS-AR-NUMBER-INVOICES
00251                                              ASCENDING KEY IS
00252                                                  WS-INVOICE-DATE
00253                                              INDEXED BY WS-INDEX
00254                                                  WS-INDEX-2
00255                                                  .
00256                    10   WS-INVOICE-ID        PIC X(5).
00257                    10   WS-INVOICE-DATE.
00258                         15   WS-INVOICE-YY   PIC 99.
00259                         15   WS-INVOICE-MM   PIC 99.
00260                         15   WS-INVOICE-DD   PIC 99.
00261                    10   WS-INVOICE-AMOUNT    PIC S9(5)V99    COMP-3.
00262
00263
00264          01   WS-ERROR-PAGE-TITLE.
00265               05   FILLER                    PIC X(20)       VALUE SPACES.
00266               05   FILLER                    PIC X(25)
00267                                              VALUE "TRANSACTION ERROR LOG".
00268               05   FILLER                    PIC X(5)        VALUE "PAGE ".
00269               05   WS-ERROR-PAGE-NUMBER      PIC ZZ9.
00270               05   FILLER                    PIC XX          VALUE SPACES.
00271               05   WS-ERROR-PAGE-DATE.
00272                    10   WS-ERROR-MM          PIC Z9.
00273                    10   FILLER               PIC X           VALUE "/".
00274                    10   WS-ERROR-DD          PIC 99.
00275                    10   FILLER               PIC X           VALUE "/".
```

Fig. 11-3   (cont.)

```
00276                   10   WS-ERROR-YY            PIC 99.
00277              05   FILLER                       PIC X(69)         VALUE SPACES.
00278
00279         01   WS-ERROR-HEADING.
00280              05   FILLER                       PIC X(9)          VALUE "CUSTOMER".
00281              05   FILLER                       PIC X(5)          VALUE "CODE".
00282              05   FILLER                       PIC X(118)
00283                                                VALUE "REST OF TRANSACTION".
00284
00285         01   WS-ERROR-LINE.
00286              05   WS-ERROR-CUSTOMER-ID         PIC X(4).
00287              05   FILLER                       PIC X(5)          VALUE SPACES.
00288              05   WS-ERROR-CODE                PIC X.
00289              05   FILLER                       PIC X(4)          VALUE SPACES.
00290              05   WS-ERROR-REST-OF-TRAN        PIC X(75).
00291              05   FILLER                       PIC X(1)          VALUE SPACES.
00292              05   WS-ERROR-MESSAGE             PIC X(42).
00293

00295         PROCEDURE DIVISION.

00297    *
00298    * -----------------------------------------------------------
00299    *
00300    *     COBOL IMPLEMENTATION OF BALANCED LINE ALGORITHM
00301    *     FOR SEQUENTIAL FILE UPDATE
00302    *
00303    * -----------------------------------------------------------
00304    *
00305         000-SEQUENTIAL-FILE-UPDATE.
00306
00307             MOVE "NO" TO MASTER-READY
00308             MOVE ZERO TO WS-PAGE-NUMBER
00309             ACCEPT SYSTEM-DATE FROM DATE
00310             MOVE SYSTEM-YY TO WS-ERROR-YY
00311             MOVE SYSTEM-MM TO WS-ERROR-MM
00312             MOVE SYSTEM-DD TO WS-ERROR-DD
00313             OPEN    INPUT               OLD-MASTER-FILE
00314                                         TRANSACTION-FILE
00315                     OUTPUT              NEW-MASTER-FILE
00316                                         CREDIT-FILE
00317                                         ERROR-REPORT
00318             PERFORM 170-PRINT-ERROR-REPORT-HEADING
00319             PERFORM 030-READ-TRANSACTION
00320             PERFORM 040-READ-MASTER
00321             PERFORM 050-DETERMINE-LOW-KEY
00322             PERFORM 010-UPDATE-MASTER-FILE
00323                 UNTIL LOW-KEY EQUAL HIGH-VALUES
00324
00325             CLOSE   OLD-MASTER-FILE
00326                     TRANSACTION-FILE
00327                     NEW-MASTER-FILE
00328                     CREDIT-FILE
00329                     ERROR-REPORT
00330             STOP RUN
00331             .
00332
00333         010-UPDATE-MASTER-FILE.
00334
00335             IF LOW-KEY EQUAL OM-AR-CUSTOMER-ID
00336    *
00337    * -----------------------------------------------------------
00338    *
00339    *     ILLUSTRATES MOVING VARIABLE-LENGTH TABLE
00340    *
00341    * -----------------------------------------------------------
00342    *
```

Fig. 11-3 (*cont.*)

```
00343                     MOVE OM-AR-NUMBER-INVOICES TO WS-AR-NUMBER-INVOICES
00344                     MOVE OM-AR-CUSTOMER-RECORD TO WS-AR-CUSTOMER-RECORD
00345                     MOVE "YES" TO MASTER-READY
00346                     PERFORM 040-READ-MASTER
00347                 .
00348             IF LOW-KEY EQUAL TRANS-CUSTOMER-ID
00349                 PERFORM 020-PROCESS-TRANSACTIONS
00350                     UNTIL LOW-KEY NOT EQUAL TRANS-CUSTOMER-ID
00351                 .
00352             IF MASTER-RECORD-PRESENT
00353                 PERFORM 060-WRITE-NEW-MASTER-RECORD
00354                 MOVE "NO" TO MASTER-READY
00355                 .
00356             PERFORM 050-DETERMINE-LOW-KEY
00357                 .
00358
00359         020-PROCESS-TRANSACTIONS.
00360
00361     *
00362     * ---------------------------------------------------------------
00363     *
00364     *     NOTE THAT THIS VERSION OF THE BALANCED LINE ALGORITHM
00365     *     VALIDATES ALL TRANSACTIONS BEFORE APPLYING THEM
00366     *
00367     * ---------------------------------------------------------------
00368     *
00369             IF ADD-TRANSACTION
00370                 IF MASTER-RECORD-PRESENT
00371                     MOVE ADD-ERROR-MESSAGE TO WS-ERROR-MESSAGE
00372                     PERFORM 070-WRITE-ERROR-LINE
00373                 ELSE
00374                     IF ADD-INVOICE-DATE NUMERIC AND ADD-AMOUNT NUMERIC
00375                         PERFORM 080-MOVE-TRANS-TO-MASTER-AREA
00376                         MOVE "YES" TO MASTER-READY
00377                     ELSE
00378                         MOVE INVALID-FIELDS-MESSAGE TO WS-ERROR-MESSAGE
00379                         PERFORM 070-WRITE-ERROR-LINE
00380             ELSE IF CHANGE-TRANSACTION
00381                 IF NO-MASTER-RECORD
00382                     MOVE CHANGE-ERROR-MESSAGE TO WS-ERROR-MESSAGE
00383                     PERFORM 070-WRITE-ERROR-LINE
00384                 ELSE
00385                     IF    CHANGE-INVOICE-DATE NUMERIC
00386                         AND CHANGE-AMOUNT NUMERIC
00387                         PERFORM APPLY-TRANSACTION-TO-MASTER
00388                     ELSE
00389                         MOVE INVALID-FIELDS-MESSAGE TO WS-ERROR-MESSAGE
00390                         PERFORM 070-WRITE-ERROR-LINE
00391             ELSE IF DELETION-TRANSACTION
00392                 IF NO-MASTER-RECORD
00393                     MOVE DELETION-ERROR-MESSAGE TO WS-ERROR-MESSAGE
00394                     PERFORM 070-WRITE-ERROR-LINE
00395                 ELSE
00396                     MOVE "NO" TO MASTER-READY
00397             ELSE
00398                 MOVE INVALID-TRANS-CODE-MESSAGE TO WS-ERROR-MESSAGE
00399                 PERFORM 070-WRITE-ERROR-LINE
00400                 .
00401             PERFORM 030-READ-TRANSACTION
00402                 .
00403
00404         030-READ-TRANSACTION.
00405
00406             READ TRANSACTION-FILE
00407                 AT END
00408                     MOVE HIGH-VALUES TO TRANS-CUSTOMER-ID
00409                 .
```

Fig. 11-3 *(cont.)*

```
00410
00411                    040-READ-MASTER.
00412
00413                        READ OLD-MASTER-FILE
00414                            AT END
00415                                MOVE HIGH-VALUES TO OM-AR-CUSTOMER-ID
00416                        .
00417
00418                    050-DETERMINE-LOW-KEY.
00419
00420                        IF TRANS-CUSTOMER-ID IS LESS THAN OM-AR-CUSTOMER-ID
00421                            MOVE TRANS-CUSTOMER-ID TO LOW-KEY
00422                        ELSE
00423                            MOVE OM-AR-CUSTOMER-ID TO LOW-KEY
00424                        .
00425
00426                    060-WRITE-NEW-MASTER-RECORD.
00427
00428                *
00429                * -------------------------------------------------------------
00430                *
00431                *    CHECK FOR VARIABLE-LENGTH DEPENDING ON ITEM = ZERO
00432                *    BEFORE WRITING LOGICAL RECORD TO FILE
00433                *
00434                * -------------------------------------------------------------
00435                *
00436                        IF WS-AR-NUMBER-INVOICES POSITIVE
00437                            MOVE WS-AR-NUMBER-INVOICES TO NM-AR-NUMBER-INVOICES
00438                            MOVE WS-AR-CUSTOMER-RECORD TO NM-AR-CUSTOMER-RECORD
00439                            WRITE NM-AR-CUSTOMER-RECORD
00440                        .
00441
00442                    070-WRITE-ERROR-LINE.
00443
00444                        MOVE TRANS-CUSTOMER-ID        TO WS-ERROR-CUSTOMER-ID
00445                        MOVE TRANS-CODE               TO WS-ERROR-CODE
00446                        MOVE TRANS-VARIABLE-AREA      TO WS-ERROR-REST-OF-TRAN
00447                        WRITE ERROR-REPORT-LINE
00448                            FROM WS-ERROR-LINE
00449                            AFTER ADVANCING 2 LINES
00450                            AT END-OF-PAGE
00451                                PERFORM 170-PRINT-ERROR-REPORT-HEADING
00452                        .
00453
00454                    080-MOVE-TRANS-TO-MASTER-AREA.
00455
00456                        MOVE TRANS-CUSTOMER-ID    TO WS-AR-CUSTOMER-ID
00457                        MOVE ADD-CUSTOMER-NAME    TO WS-AR-CUSTOMER-NAME
00458                        MOVE 1                    TO WS-AR-NUMBER-INVOICES
00459                        MOVE ADD-INVOICE-ID       TO WS-INVOICE-ID (1)
00460                        MOVE ADD-INVOICE-DATE     TO WS-INVOICE-DATE (1)
00461                        MOVE ADD-AMOUNT           TO WS-INVOICE-AMOUNT (1)
00462                        .
00463
00464                    APPLY-TRANSACTION-TO-MASTER.
00465
00466                        IF INSERTION-CODE
00467                            PERFORM 090-INSERT-NEW-INVOICE
00468                        ELSE IF ADJUSTMENT-CODE
00469                            PERFORM 130-ADJUST-AN-INVOICE
00470                        ELSE IF PAYMENT-CODE
00471                            PERFORM 140-APPLY-PAYMENT
00472                        ELSE
00473                            MOVE INVALID-CHANGE-CODE-MESSAGE TO WS-ERROR-MESSAGE
00474                            PERFORM 070-WRITE-ERROR-LINE
00475                        .
00476
```

Fig. 11-3 *(cont.)*

```
00477        090-INSERT-NEW-INVOICE.
00478
00479    *
00480    *  -------------------------------------------------------
00481    *
00482    *     CHECK FOR TABLE OVERFLOW BEFORE INSERTING NEW INVOICE
00483    *
00484    *  -------------------------------------------------------
00485    *
00486          IF WS-AR-NUMBER-INVOICES EQUAL MAXIMUM-TABLE-SIZE
00487              MOVE TABLE-OVERFLOW-MESSAGE TO WS-ERROR-MESSAGE
00488              PERFORM 070-WRITE-ERROR-LINE
00489          ELSE
00490    *
00491    *  -------------------------------------------------------
00492    *
00493    *     ILLUSTRATES USE OF SEQUENTIAL SEARCH
00494    *
00495    *  -------------------------------------------------------
00496    *
00497              SET WS-INDEX TO 1
00498              SEARCH WS-AR-INVOICE-DATA
00499                 AT END
00500                     PERFORM 100-LOCATE-AND-MOVE
00501                 WHEN WS-INVOICE-ID (WS-INDEX) EQUAL CHANGE-INVOICE-ID
00502                     MOVE DUPLICATE-INVOICE-MESSAGE TO WS-ERROR-MESSAGE
00503                     PERFORM 070-WRITE-ERROR-LINE
00504              .
00505
00506        100-LOCATE-AND-MOVE.
00507
00508          SET WS-INDEX TO 1
00509          SEARCH WS-AR-INVOICE-DATA
00510             AT END
00511                 ADD 1 TO WS-AR-NUMBER-INVOICES
00512                 PERFORM 120-MOVE-IN-NEW-ENTRY
00513             WHEN WS-INVOICE-DATE (WS-INDEX) GREATER THAN
00514                 CHANGE-INVOICE-DATE
00515                 ADD 1 TO WS-AR-NUMBER-INVOICES
00516                 PERFORM 110-MOVE-ENTRIES-DOWN
00517                     VARYING WS-INDEX-2 FROM WS-AR-NUMBER-INVOICES
00518                     BY -1
00519                     UNTIL WS-INDEX-2 EQUAL WS-INDEX
00520                 PERFORM 120-MOVE-IN-NEW-ENTRY
00521          .
00522
00523        110-MOVE-ENTRIES-DOWN.
00524
00525          MOVE WS-AR-INVOICE-DATA (WS-INDEX-2 - 1) TO
00526              WS-AR-INVOICE-DATA (WS-INDEX-2)
00527          .
00528
00529        120-MOVE-IN-NEW-ENTRY.
00530
00531          MOVE CHANGE-INVOICE-ID    TO WS-INVOICE-ID (WS-INDEX)
00532          MOVE CHANGE-INVOICE-DATE  TO WS-INVOICE-DATE (WS-INDEX)
00533          MOVE CHANGE-AMOUNT        TO WS-INVOICE-AMOUNT (WS-INDEX)
00534          .
00535
00536        130-ADJUST-AN-INVOICE.
00537
00538          SET WS-INDEX TO 1
00539          SEARCH WS-AR-INVOICE-DATA
00540             AT END
00541                 MOVE ADJUST-ERROR-MESSAGE TO WS-ERROR-MESSAGE
00542                 PERFORM 070-WRITE-ERROR-LINE
00543             WHEN WS-INVOICE-ID (WS-INDEX) EQUAL CHANGE-INVOICE-ID
```

Fig. 11-3 *(cont.)*

```
00544                          MOVE CHANGE-AMOUNT TO WS-INVOICE-AMOUNT (WS-INDEX)
00545                      .
00546
00547          140-APPLY-PAYMENT.
00548
00549              SET WS-INDEX TO 1
00550              SEARCH WS-AR-INVOICE-DATA
00551                  AT END
00552                      MOVE NO-PAYMENT-INVOICE-MESSAGE TO WS-ERROR-MESSAGE
00553                      PERFORM 070-WRITE-ERROR-LINE
00554                  WHEN WS-INVOICE-ID (WS-INDEX) EQUAL CHANGE-INVOICE-ID
00555                      PERFORM 150-CALCULATE-BALANCE
00556                  .
00557
00558          150-CALCULATE-BALANCE.
00559
00560              SUBTRACT CHANGE-AMOUNT FROM WS-INVOICE-AMOUNT (WS-INDEX)
00561                  GIVING WS-INVOICE-AMOUNT (WS-INDEX)
00562                      WS-DIFFERENCE
00563      *
00564      * ------------------------------------------------------------
00565      *
00566      *     IF OVERPAID, WRITE CUSTOMER INFORMATION TO CREDIT FILE
00567      *
00568      * ------------------------------------------------------------
00569      *
00570              IF WS-DIFFERENCE NEGATIVE
00571                  MOVE TRANS-CUSTOMER-ID      TO CREDIT-CUSTOMER-ID
00572                  MOVE WS-AR-CUSTOMER-NAME    TO CREDIT-CUSTOMER-NAME
00573                  MOVE CHANGE-INVOICE-ID      TO CREDIT-INVOICE-ID
00574                  MOVE CHANGE-INVOICE-DATE    TO CREDIT-INVOICE-DATE
00575                  MOVE WS-DIFFERENCE          TO CREDIT-BALANCE
00576                  WRITE CREDIT-BALANCE-RECORD
00577                  .
00578      *
00579      * ------------------------------------------------------------
00580      *
00581      *     IF OVERPAID OR PAID OUT, REMOVE INVOICE FROM TABLE
00582      *
00583      * ------------------------------------------------------------
00584      *
00585              IF WS-DIFFERENCE NOT POSITIVE
00586                  PERFORM 160-REMOVE-INVOICE
00587                      VARYING WS-INDEX FROM WS-INDEX BY 1
00588                      UNTIL WS-INDEX GREATER THAN WS-AR-NUMBER-INVOICES
00589                  SUBTRACT 1 FROM WS-AR-NUMBER-INVOICES
00590                  .
00591
00592          160-REMOVE-INVOICE.
00593
00594              MOVE WS-AR-INVOICE-DATA (WS-INDEX + 1) TO
00595                  WS-AR-INVOICE-DATA (WS-INDEX)
00596                  .
00597
00598          170-PRINT-ERROR-REPORT-HEADING.
00599
00600              ADD 1 TO WS-PAGE-NUMBER
00601              MOVE WS-PAGE-NUMBER TO WS-ERROR-PAGE-NUMBER
00602              WRITE ERROR-REPORT-LINE
00603                  FROM WS-ERROR-PAGE-TITLE
00604                  AFTER ADVANCING PAGE
00605              WRITE ERROR-REPORT-LINE
00606                  FROM WS-ERROR-HEADING
00607                  AFTER ADVANCING 2 LINES
00608                  .
```

Fig. 11-3   (cont.)

11.3   Updating in Place

When sequentially organized master files are stored on disk, it is possible to update logical records without creating a new master file: this is done by reading the records into main memory, making changes to them, then writing them back to the exact disk locations from which they were originally input. See the systems flowchart, Fig. 11-4. The process is subject to the following restrictions: (i) records may not be added to the file; (ii) deletions must be done *logically* (by flagging records with a deletion code); (iii) the length of a logical record may not be changed; (iv) the file must be OPENed I-O (see Chapter 6).

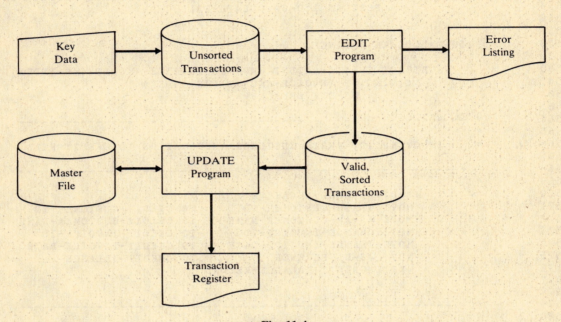

Fig. 11-4

In COBOL, the REWRITE verb is used to output a logical record to the same disk location from which it was just READ. Its format is

REWRITE record-name [FROM identifier]

EXAMPLE 11.4

```
FD   MASTER-FILE
01   MASTER-RECORD ...
 . . . . . . . . . . . . . . . . . . . . . . . . . . . . . . . . .
     OPEN  I-O  MASTER-FILE
     READ MASTER-FILE   AT END ...
     PERFORM MAKE-CHANGES-TO-MASTER-RECORD
     REWRITE MASTER-RECORD
```

Note that in order to do an update in place, the file must be OPENed I-O, which allows the READ statement to function for input as it normally would, and the REWRITE statement to be used to output a logical record to the physical disk location used by *the most recent READ*.

Review Questions

11.1   What are (*a*) file creation, (*b*) file retrieval, (*c*) file maintenance (updating)?

11.2   Discuss the three operations which must be carried out as part of file maintenance.

11.3   What is the purpose of a FILE STATUS area? How is it defined and used?

11.4   Define: (*a*) master file, (*b*) transaction file, (*c*) key (field).

11.5   Give the sequence of steps involved in a typical sequential file update.

11.6   Explain the terms "old master file" and "new master file".

11.7   Discuss the "grandparent, parent, child" method of backup.

11.8   What is a transaction register?

11.9   Draw a systems flowchart for a typical sequential file update.

11.10   Explain the balanced-line algorithm, using pseudocode.

11.11   What is meant by an "update in place"?

11.12   Contrast OPENing a file (*a*) INPUT, (*b*) OUTPUT, (*c*) I-O.

11.13   What limitations must be placed on a sequential file update in place?

11.14   Explain the use of the REWRITE verb.

11.15   Draw a systems flowchart for a sequential file update in place.

11.16   State one advantage and one disadvantage of an update in place vis a vis the classical (old master/new master) approach. (*Hint*: Consider unchanged records and the matter of backup.)

Solved Problems

11.17   What is the difference between *file updating* and *record updating*?

"File updating" refers to file maintenance, in which logical records are added to a file, deleted from a file, and/or have their contents changed. "Record updating" refers to the process of making changes to logical records *during file updating*.

11.18   What is wrong with the following sequential-file-update test data?

TRANSACTION-FILE: 4, 23, 15, 12, 30, 50
MASTER-FILE: 10, 20, 30, 40, 50, 60, 70

The transaction file must be *sorted* into the same key-sequence as the master file. The transaction records must contain the key for the master file record they are attempting to update.

11.19 With reference to Problem 11.12, give a fourth OPEN option.

OPEN EXTEND, whereby new records may be added to the end of the file, using the WRITE verb.

11.20 How many generations of transaction and old master files should be saved, and for how long, when using grandparent, parent, child backup?

There is no single answer: the importance of the application and the data to the business, legal requirements as dictated by government, accounting requirements, etc., all must be weighed.

11.21 How is backup handled when files are updated in place?

A copy of the file can be made before the transactions are applied. This copy can be saved along with the transactions and used to reconstruct the master file in case of mishap.

11.22 Problems 8.30 and 8.31 form what is in effect a sequential file update sequence, where Problem 8.30 is the edit program and Problem 8.31 performs the file update. Revise Problem 8.30 to use a table of the number of days in each month to validate the date field on the input time cards. (Ignore turn-of-the-century and leap-year special cases.)

A partial COBOL program is given in Fig. 11-5. Lines 110–126 define the date table, and lines 269–290 and 299–312 do the input checking.

```
(THE FOLLOWING TABLE IS IN WORKING-STORAGE) . . .

00110      01  WS-VALID-DATES-TABLE.
00111          05  VALID-DAYS-PER-MONTH-VALUES.
00112              10  FILLER           PIC 99           VALUE 31.
00113              10  FILLER           PIC 99           VALUE 28.
00114              10  FILLER           PIC 99           VALUE 31.
00115              10  FILLER           PIC 99           VALUE 30.
00116              10  FILLER           PIC 99           VALUE 31.
00117              10  FILLER           PIC 99           VALUE 30.
00118              10  FILLER           PIC 99           VALUE 31.
00119              10  FILLER           PIC 99           VALUE 31.
00120              10  FILLER           PIC 99           VALUE 30.
00121              10  FILLER           PIC 99           VALUE 31.
00122              10  FILLER           PIC 99           VALUE 30.
00123              10  FILLER           PIC 99           VALUE 31.
00124          05  DAYS-PER-MONTH       REDEFINES VALID-DAYS-PER-MONTH-VALUES
00125                                   PIC 99
00126                                   OCCURS 12 TIMES.
     .
     .
     .
(THE FOLLOWING ARE THE RELEVANT PROCEDURE DIVISION PARAGRAPHS) . . .

00269          240-VALIDATE-FIELDS.
00270
00271              MOVE "NO"   TO WS-ERROR-DETECTED-SW
00272              MOVE SPACES TO WS-UNDER-LINE
00273              IF TIME-CARD-ID NOT NUMERIC
00274                  MOVE ALL "-" TO WS-UNDER-ID
00275                  MOVE "YES"   TO WS-ERROR-DETECTED-SW
00276              .
00277              IF TIME-CARD-HOURS NOT NUMERIC
00278                  MOVE ALL "-" TO WS-UNDER-HOURS
00279                  MOVE "YES"   TO WS-ERROR-DETECTED-SW
00280              .
00281              IF TIME-CARD-CLOSING-DATE NOT NUMERIC
00282                  MOVE ALL "-" TO WS-UNDER-DATE
```

Fig. 11-5

```
00283                          MOVE "YES"   TO WS-ERROR-DETECTED-SW
00284                     ELSE
00285                          PERFORM 260-VALIDATE-DATE
00286                     .
00287                     IF TIME-CARD-DEPARTMENT NOT NUMERIC
00288                          MOVE ALL "-" TO WS-UNDER-DEPARTMENT
00289                          MOVE "YES"   TO WS-ERROR-DETECTED-SW
00290                     .
00298
00299                260-VALIDATE-DATE.
00300
00301                     IF TIME-CARD-CLOSING-YR GREATER THAN SYSTEM-YY
00302                          MOVE ALL "-" TO WS-UNDER-YR
00303                          MOVE "YES" TO WS-ERROR-DETECTED-SW
00304                     .
00305                     IF TIME-CARD-CLOSING-MO LESS THAN 1 OR GREATER THAN 12
00306                          MOVE ALL "-" TO WS-UNDER-MO
00307                          MOVE "YES" TO WS-ERROR-DETECTED-SW
00308                     ELSE IF TIME-CARD-CLOSING-DAY LESS THAN 1 OR
00309                          GREATER THAN DAYS-PER-MONTH (TIME-CARD-CLOSING-MO)
00310                               MOVE ALL "-" TO WS-UNDER-DAY
00311                               MOVE "YES" TO WS-ERROR-DETECTED-SW
00312                     .
```

Fig. 11-5   (*cont.*)

11.23 Give complete COBOL coding for Problem 8.31. Use a tax table lookup to compute payroll tax, and update the employee master file (in place) by adding gross pay, tax amount, and net pay to year-to-date fields within the employee master record.

See Fig. 11-6. The tax computation is found in lines 112–137 and 331–343; the update, in lines 234, 256, and 309–315.

```
00001                IDENTIFICATION DIVISION.
00002
00003                PROGRAM-ID.   PAYROLL.
00004
00005                AUTHOR.   LARRY NEWCOMER.
00006                INSTALLATION.   PENN STATE UNIVERSITY -- YORK CAMPUS.
00007
00008                ENVIRONMENT DIVISION.
00009
00010                CONFIGURATION SECTION.
00011                SOURCE-COMPUTER.   IBM-3081.
00012                OBJECT-COMPUTER.   IBM-3081.
00013
00014                INPUT-OUTPUT SECTION.
00015                FILE-CONTROL.
00016
00017                     SELECT VALID-TIME-FILE
00018                          ASSIGN TO DISKTIME
00019                          ORGANIZATION IS SEQUENTIAL
00020                          ACCESS IS SEQUENTIAL
00021                     .
00022                     SELECT EMPLOYEE-MASTER-FILE
00023                          ASSIGN TO EMPMAST
00024                          ORGANIZATION IS SEQUENTIAL
00025                          ACCESS IS SEQUENTIAL
00026                     .
00027                     SELECT PAYROLL-CHECK-FILE
00028                          ASSIGN TO PAYCHECK
00029                          ORGANIZATION IS SEQUENTIAL
00030                          ACCESS IS SEQUENTIAL
00031                     .
```

Fig. 11-6

```
00032                    SELECT PAYROLL-REGISTER-FILE
00033                        ASSIGN TO REGISTER
00034                        ORGANIZATION IS SEQUENTIAL
00035                        ACCESS IS SEQUENTIAL
00036                        .
00037
00038            DATA DIVISION.
00039
00040            FILE SECTION.
00041
00042            FD   VALID-TIME-FILE
00043                 BLOCK CONTAINS 0 RECORDS
00044                 RECORD CONTAINS 80 CHARACTERS
00045                 LABEL RECORDS ARE STANDARD
00046                 .
00047
00048            01   VALID-TIME-RECORD.
00049                 05   VALID-TIME-ID            PIC X(5).
00050                 05   VALID-TIME-HOURS         PIC S9(2)V9.
00051                 05   VALID-TIME-CLOSING-DATE  PIC X(6).
00052                 05   VALID-TIME-DEPARTMENT    PIC X(4).
00053                 05   VALID-TIME-EDIT-DATE     PIC X(6).
00054                 05   FILLER                   PIC X(56).
00055
00056            FD   EMPLOYEE-MASTER-FILE
00057                 BLOCK CONTAINS 0 RECORDS
00058                 RECORD CONTAINS 80 CHARACTERS
00059                 LABEL RECORDS ARE STANDARD
00060                 .
00061
00062            01   EMPLOYEE-MASTER-RECORD.
00063                 05   EMPLOYEE-MASTER-ID       PIC X(5).
00064                 05   EMPLOYEE-MASTER-NAME     PIC X(20).
00065                 05   EMPLOYEE-MASTER-RATE     PIC S9(3)V99.
00066                 05   EMPLOYEE-MASTER-YTD-GROSS
00067                                               PIC 9(7)V99.
00068                 05   EMPLOYEE-MASTER-YTD-TAX PIC 9(6)V99.
00069                 05   EMPLOYEE-MASTER-YTD-NET PIC 9(7)V99.
00070                 05   FILLER                   PIC X(24).
00071
00072            FD   PAYROLL-CHECK-FILE
00073                 BLOCK CONTAINS 0 RECORDS
00074                 RECORD CONTAINS 66 CHARACTERS
00075                 LABEL RECORDS ARE STANDARD
00076                 .
00077
00078            01   PAYROLL-CHECK-RECORD.
00079                 05   PAYROLL-ID               PIC X(5).
00080                 05   PAYROLL-HOURS            PIC S9(2)V9.
00081                 05   PAYROLL-DATE             PIC X(6).
00082                 05   PAYROLL-DEPARTMENT       PIC X(4).
00083                 05   PAYROLL-RATE             PIC S9(3)V99.
00084                 05   PAYROLL-NAME             PIC X(20).
00085                 05   PAYROLL-GROSS            PIC S9(6)V99.
00086                 05   PAYROLL-TAX              PIC S9(5)V99.
00087                 05   PAYROLL-NET              PIC S9(6)V99.
00088
00089            FD   PAYROLL-REGISTER-FILE
00090                 RECORD CONTAINS 132 CHARACTERS
00091                 LABEL RECORDS ARE OMITTED
00092                 .
00093
00094            01   ERROR-REPORT-LINE            PIC X(132).
00095
00096            WORKING-STORAGE SECTION.
00097
```

Fig. 11-6 *(cont.)*

```
00098          01    PROGRAM-SWITCHES.
00099                05    WS-END-TIME-FILE-SW         PIC X(3).
00100                      88    NO-MORE-TIMES         VALUE "YES".
00101                      88    TIME-AVAILABLE        VALUE "NO".
00102                05    WS-END-MASTER-FILE-SW       PIC X(3).
00103                      88    NO-MORE-MASTERS       VALUE "YES".
00104                      88    MASTER-AVAILABLE      VALUE "NO ".
00105
00106          01    PROGRAM-COUNTERS.
00107                05    WS-PAGE-NUMBER             PIC S9(3)          COMP-3.
00108                05    WS-NUMBER-EMPLOYEES        PIC S9(5)          COMP-3.
00109                05    WS-NUMBER-TO-SKIP          PIC S9             COMP SYNC.
00110                05    WS-LINES-ON-PAGE           PIC S9(2)          COMP SYNC.
00111
00112    *     -------------------------------------------------------
00113    *
00114    *     TAX TABLE IS USED TO LOOKUP TAX-RATE.  NOTE HOW ENTRIES
00115    *     ARE ARRANGED IN TABLE.  LAST ENTRY = ZERO GUARANTEES
00116    *     SEARCH WILL ALWAYS SUCCEED.  ALTHOUGH WE USE THE VALUE
00117    *     AND REDEFINES CLAUSES TO LOAD THIS TABLE.
00118    *     IT COULD ALSO BE INPUT FROM A FILE.
00119    *
00120    *     -------------------------------------------------------
00121
00122          01    TAX-DATA.
00123                05    TAX-TABLE-VALUES.
00124                      10    FILLER         PIC S9(3)V99 COMP-3 VALUE +800.00.
00125                      10    FILLER         PIC SV999    COMP-3 VALUE +.25.
00126                      10    FILLER         PIC S9(3)V99 COMP-3 VALUE +500.00.
00127                      10    FILLER         PIC SV999    COMP-3 VALUE +.15.
00128                      10    FILLER         PIC S9(3)V99 COMP-3 VALUE +300.00.
00129                      10    FILLER         PIC SV999    COMP-3 VALUE +.08.
00130                      10    FILLER         PIC S9(3)V99 COMP-3 VALUE ZERO.
00131                      10    FILLER         PIC SV999    COMP-3 VALUE +.05.
00132                05    TAX-TABLE          REDEFINES TAX-TABLE-VALUES
00133                                         OCCURS 4 TIMES
00134                                         INDEXED BY TAX-INDEX.
00135                      10    LOWER-LIMIT    PIC S9(3)V99 COMP-3.
00136                      10    TAX-RATE       PIC SV999    COMP-3.
00137
00138          01    PROGRAM-TOTAL-AREAS.
00139                05    WS-TOTAL-HOURS            PIC S9(7)V9        COMP-3.
00140
00141          01    PROGRAM-COMPUTATION-AREAS.
00142                05    WS-GROSS-PAY              PIC S9(7)V99       COMP-3.
00143                05    WS-NET-PAY               PIC S9(7)V99       COMP-3.
00144                05    WS-TAX                   PIC S9(5)V99       COMP-3.
00145
00146          01    PROGRAM-CONSTANTS.
00147                05    WS-PAGE-SIZE              PIC S9(2)          COMP SYNC
00148                                               VALUE +50.
00149                05    WS-SKIP-BEFORE-HEADING   PIC S9(2)          COMP SYNC
00150                                               VALUE +2.
00151                05    WS-SKIP-BEFORE-FOOTING   PIC S9(2)          COMP SYNC
00152                                               VALUE +4.
00153                05    WS-SKIP-BEFORE-DETAIL    PIC S9(2)          COMP SYNC
00154                                               VALUE +2.
00155                05    WS-UNMATCHED-TIME-MESSAGE
00156                                               PIC X(30)
00157                                               VALUE "EMPLOYEE NOT ON FILE".
00158                05    WS-UNMATCHED-MASTER-MESSAGE
00159                                               PIC X(30)
00160                                               VALUE "INACTIVE THIS PAY PERIOD".
00161                05    WS-OVERTIME-POINT        PIC S99V9          COMP-3
00162                                               VALUE +40.0.
00163                05    WS-OVERTIME-FACTOR       PIC S9V9           COMP-3
00164                                               VALUE +1.5.
```

Fig. 11-6 (cont.)

```
00165
00166          01   WS-SYSTEM-DATE.
00167               05    SYSTEM-YY              PIC 99.
00168               05    SYSTEM-MM              PIC 99.
00169               05    SYSTEM-DD              PIC 99.
00170
00171          01   WS-HEADING-LINE-1.
00172               05    FILLER                 PIC X(2)          VALUE SPACES.
00173               05    FILLER                 PIC X(18)
00174                                            VALUE "PAYROLL REGISTER".
00175               05    WS-HEADING-MM          PIC Z9.
00176               05    FILLER                 PIC X             VALUE "/".
00177               05    WS-HEADING-DD          PIC 99.
00178               05    FILLER                 PIC X             VALUE "/".
00179               05    WS-HEADING-YY          PIC 99.
00180               05    FILLER                 PIC X(3)          VALUE SPACES.
00181               05    FILLER                 PIC X(5)          VALUE "PAGE ".
00182               05    WS-HEADING-PAGE        PIC ZZ9.
00183               05    FILLER                 PIC X(93)         VALUE SPACES.
00184
00185          01   WS-HEADING-LINE-2.
00186               05    FILLER                 PIC X(7)          VALUE "  ID".
00187               05    FILLER                 PIC X(5)          VALUE "HRS".
00188               05    FILLER                 PIC X(8)          VALUE " DATE".
00189               05    FILLER                 PIC X(6)          VALUE "DEPT".
00190               05    FILLER                 PIC X(8)          VALUE " RATE".
00191               05    FILLER                 PIC X(98)         VALUE "NET PAY".
00192
00193          01   WS-DETAIL-LINE.
00194               05    WS-DETAIL-ID           PIC X(5).
00195               05    FILLER                 PIC X(1)          VALUE SPACES.
00196               05    WS-DETAIL-HOURS        PIC ZZ.9.
00197               05    FILLER                 PIC X(2)          VALUE SPACES.
00198               05    WS-DETAIL-DATE         PIC X(6).
00199               05    FILLER                 PIC X(2)          VALUE SPACES.
00200               05    WS-DETAIL-DEPARTMENT   PIC X(4).
00201               05    FILLER                 PIC X(2)          VALUE SPACES.
00202               05    WS-DETAIL-RATE         PIC ZZZ.99.
00203               05    FILLER                 PIC X(2)          VALUE SPACES.
00204               05    WS-DETAIL-REMARKS.
00205                     10   WS-DETAIL-PAY     PIC ZZZ,ZZZ.99.
00206                     10   FILLER            PIC X(88).
00207
00208          01   WS-FOOTING-LINE.
00209               05    FILLER                 PIC X(12)
00210                                            VALUE "# EMPLOYEES=".
00211               05    WS-FOOTING-COUNT       PIC ZZ,ZZ9.
00212               05    FILLER                 PIC X(3)          VALUE SPACES.
00213               05    FILLER                 PIC X(12)
00214                                            VALUE "TOTAL HOURS=".
00215               05    WS-FOOTING-TOTAL       PIC Z,ZZZ,ZZZ.9.
00216               05    FILLER                 PIC X(88)         VALUE SPACES.
00217
00218          01   WS-OUTPUT-AREA              PIC X(132).
00219
00220          PROCEDURE DIVISION.
00221
00222          CREATE-PAYROLL-CHECK-FILE.
00223
00224               PERFORM 100-INITIALIZE
00225               PERFORM 200-MATCH-TIME-CARDS-TO-MASTER
00226                    UNTIL NO-MORE-TIMES AND NO-MORE-MASTERS
00227               PERFORM 300-TERMINATE
00228               STOP RUN
00229               .
00230
```

Fig. 11-6 (*cont.*)

```
00231          100-INITIALIZE.
00232
00233              OPEN     INPUT     VALID-TIME-FILE
00234                       I-O       EMPLOYEE-MASTER-FILE
00235                       OUTPUT    PAYROLL-REGISTER-FILE
00236                                 PAYROLL-CHECK-FILE
00237              MOVE "NO" TO                 WS-END-TIME-FILE-SW
00238                                           WS-END-MASTER-FILE-SW
00239              MOVE ZERO TO                 WS-PAGE-NUMBER
00240                                           WS-NUMBER-EMPLOYEES
00241                                           WS-TOTAL-HOURS
00242              MOVE WS-PAGE-SIZE TO         WS-LINES-ON-PAGE
00243              ACCEPT WS-SYSTEM-DATE FROM DATE
00244              MOVE SYSTEM-YY TO            WS-HEADING-YY
00245              MOVE SYSTEM-MM TO            WS-HEADING-MM
00246              MOVE SYSTEM-DD TO            WS-HEADING-DD
00247
00248              PERFORM 270-GET-TIME-RECORD
00249              PERFORM 280-GET-MASTER-RECORD
00250              .
00251          B-MATCH-TIME-CARDS-TO-MASTER.
00252
00253              MOVE SPACES TO WS-DETAIL-LINE
00254              IF VALID-TIME-ID EQUAL EMPLOYEE-MASTER-ID
00255                  PERFORM 210-CREATE-PAYROLL-REC
00256                  PERFORM 215-UPDATE-MASTER-FILE
00257                  PERFORM 270-GET-TIME-RECORD
00258                  PERFORM 280-GET-MASTER-RECORD
00259              ELSE IF VALID-TIME-ID LESS THAN EMPLOYEE-MASTER-ID
00260                  MOVE WS-UNMATCHED-TIME-MESSAGE
00261                                           TO WS-DETAIL-REMARKS
00262                  MOVE VALID-TIME-ID       TO WS-DETAIL-ID
00263                  MOVE VALID-TIME-HOURS    TO WS-DETAIL-HOURS
00264                  MOVE VALID-TIME-CLOSING-DATE
00265                                           TO WS-DETAIL-DATE
00266                  MOVE VALID-TIME-DEPARTMENT
00267                                           TO WS-DETAIL-DEPARTMENT
00268                  MOVE WS-SKIP-BEFORE-DETAIL
00269                                           TO WS-NUMBER-TO-SKIP
00270                  MOVE WS-DETAIL-LINE      TO WS-OUTPUT-AREA
00271                  PERFORM 270-GET-TIME-RECORD
00272              ELSE
00273                  MOVE WS-UNMATCHED-MASTER-MESSAGE
00274                                           TO WS-DETAIL-REMARKS
00275                  MOVE EMPLOYEE-MASTER-ID     TO WS-DETAIL-ID
00276                  MOVE EMPLOYEE-MASTER-RATE   TO WS-DETAIL-RATE
00277                  MOVE WS-SKIP-BEFORE-DETAIL TO WS-NUMBER-TO-SKIP
00278                  MOVE WS-DETAIL-LINE         TO WS-OUTPUT-AREA
00279                  PERFORM 280-GET-MASTER-RECORD
00280              .
00281              PERFORM 260-PRINT-REGISTER
00282              .
00283
00284          210-CREATE-PAYROLL-REC.
00285
00286              MOVE VALID-TIME-ID             TO WS-DETAIL-ID
00287              MOVE VALID-TIME-HOURS          TO WS-DETAIL-HOURS
00288              MOVE VALID-TIME-CLOSING-DATE   TO WS-DETAIL-DATE
00289              MOVE VALID-TIME-DEPARTMENT     TO WS-DETAIL-DEPARTMENT
00290              MOVE EMPLOYEE-MASTER-RATE      TO WS-DETAIL-RATE
00291              MOVE WS-SKIP-BEFORE-DETAIL     TO WS-NUMBER-TO-SKIP
00292
00293              PERFORM 220-CALCULATE-PAY
00294              MOVE WS-NET-PAY               TO WS-DETAIL-PAY
00295              PERFORM 250-WRITE-PAYROLL-RECORD
00296              MOVE WS-DETAIL-LINE TO WS-OUTPUT-AREA
```

Fig. 11-6 (*cont.*)

```
00297          ADD 1                        TO WS-NUMBER-EMPLOYEES
00298          ADD VALID-TIME-HOURS         TO WS-TOTAL-HOURS
00299      .
00300
00301      220-CALCULATE-PAY.
00302
00303          PERFORM 230-CALCULATE-GROSS
00304          PERFORM 240-CALCULATE-TAX
00305          SUBTRACT WS-TAX FROM WS-GROSS-PAY
00306              GIVING WS-NET-PAY
00307          .
00308
00309      215-UPDATE-MASTER-FILE.
00310
00311          ADD WS-TAX          TO EMPLOYEE-MASTER-YTD-TAX
00312          ADD WS-GROSS-PAY TO EMPLOYEE-MASTER-YTD-GROSS
00313          ADD WS-NET-PAY      TO EMPLOYEE-MASTER-YTD-NET
00314          REWRITE EMPLOYEE-MASTER-RECORD
00315          .
00316
00317      230-CALCULATE-GROSS.
00318
00319          IF VALID-TIME-HOURS GREATER THAN WS-OVERTIME-POINT
00320              COMPUTE WS-GROSS-PAY =
00321                  (WS-OVERTIME-POINT * EMPLOYEE-MASTER-RATE)
00322              +  ((VALID-TIME-HOURS - WS-OVERTIME-POINT)
00323                      * EMPLOYEE-MASTER-RATE * WS-OVERTIME-FACTOR)
00324          ELSE
00325              COMPUTE WS-GROSS-PAY =
00326                  VALID-TIME-HOURS * EMPLOYEE-MASTER-RATE
00327          .
00328
00329      240-CALCULATE-TAX
00330
00331      * ------------------------------------------------------
00332      *
00333      *   USE SEQUENTIAL SEARCH TO LOOKUP TAX RATE IN TAX TABLE
00334      *   (DUE TO DESIGN OF TABLE, AT END... CONDITION CAN'T OCCUR)
00335      *
00336      * ------------------------------------------------------
00337
00338          SET TAX-INDEX TO 1
00339          SEARCH TAX-TABLE
00340              WHEN WS-GROSS-PAY GREATER THAN LOWER-LIMIT (TAX-INDEX)
00341                  COMPUTE WS-TAX =
00342                      WS-GROSS-PAY * TAX-RATE (TAX-INDEX)
00343          .
00344
00345      250-WRITE-PAYROLL-RECORD.
00346
00347          MOVE VALID-TIME-ID            TO PAYROLL-ID
00348          MOVE VALID-TIME-HOURS         TO PAYROLL-HOURS
00349          MOVE VALID-TIME-CLOSING-DATE  TO PAYROLL-DATE
00350          MOVE VALID-TIME-DEPARTMENT    TO PAYROLL-DEPARTMENT
00351          MOVE EMPLOYEE-MASTER-RATE     TO PAYROLL-RATE
00352          MOVE EMPLOYEE-MASTER-NAME     TO PAYROLL-NAME
00353          MOVE WS-GROSS-PAY             TO PAYROLL-GROSS
00354          MOVE WS-TAX                   TO PAYROLL-TAX
00355          MOVE WS-NET-PAY               TO PAYROLL-NET
00356          WRITE PAYROLL-CHECK-RECORD
00357          .
00358
00359      260-PRINT-REGISTER.
00360
00361          IF WS-LINES-ON-PAGE + WS-NUMBER-TO-SKIP
00362              GREATER THAN WS-PAGE-SIZE
```

Fig. 11-6   (cont.)

```
00363                         ADD 1 TO WS-PAGE-NUMBER
00364                         MOVE WS-PAGE-NUMBER TO WS-HEADING-PAGE
00365                         WRITE ERROR-REPORT-LINE
00366                             FROM WS-HEADING-LINE-1
00367                             AFTER ADVANCING PAGE
00368                         WRITE ERROR-REPORT-LINE
00369                             FROM WS-HEADING-LINE-2
00370                             AFTER ADVANCING WS-SKIP-BEFORE-HEADING LINES
00371                         MOVE WS-SKIP-BEFORE-HEADING TO WS-LINES-ON-PAGE
00372                     .
00373                 WRITE ERROR-REPORT-LINE
00374                     FROM WS-OUTPUT-AREA
00375                     AFTER ADVANCING WS-NUMBER-TO-SKIP LINES
00376                 ADD WS-NUMBER-TO-SKIP TO WS-LINES-ON-PAGE
00377                 .
00378
00379             270-GET-TIME-RECORD.
00380
00381                 READ VALID-TIME-FILE
00382                     AT END
00383                         MOVE "YES" TO WS-END-TIME-FILE-SW
00384                         MOVE HIGH-VALUES TO VALID-TIME-ID
00385                 .
00386
00387             280-GET-MASTER-RECORD.
00388
00389                 READ EMPLOYEE-MASTER-FILE
00390                     AT END
00391                         MOVE "YES" TO WS-END-MASTER-FILE-SW
00392                         MOVE HIGH-VALUES TO EMPLOYEE-MASTER-ID
00393                 .
00394
00395             300-TERMINATE.
00396
00397                 MOVE WS-NUMBER-EMPLOYEES      TO WS-FOOTING-COUNT
00398                 MOVE WS-TOTAL-HOURS           TO WS-FOOTING-TOTAL
00399                 MOVE WS-FOOTING-LINE          TO WS-OUTPUT-AREA
00400                 MOVE WS-SKIP-BEFORE-FOOTING TO WS-NUMBER-TO-SKIP
00401                 MOVE WS-FOOTING-LINE          TO WS-OUTPUT-AREA
00402             PERFORM 260-PRINT-REGISTER
00403
00404                 CLOSE    VALID-TIME-FILE
00405                          EMPLOYEE-MASTER-FILE
00406                          PAYROLL-CHECK-FILE
00407                          PAYROLL-REGISTER-FILE
00408                 .
```

Fig. 11-6 (*cont.*)

Chapter 12

File Sorting and Merging

File sorting involves rearranging the *logical records in a file* which resides on an auxiliary storage device. This is in contrast to table sorting, in which *parts of a single logical record* (i.e., the table) are rearranged. File sorts are easily programmed using the COBOL verb "SORT".

12.1 The Vocabulary of File Sorting

The fields within a logical record on which the file is arranged or *sorted* are called *control fields* or sort *keys*. The records in a file may be arranged in *ascending* or *descending* sequence on any given key. IBM OS/VS COBOL allows for simultaneous sorting of a file on up to 12 different keys, in any combination of ascending and descending sequences. When sorting is done on multiple keys, the most important key field is called the *major key* and the least important is called the *minor key*; the remaining, *intermediate keys*—and the minor key, too—effect sorts *within* each value of the major key. Consequently, if attention is focused only on an intermediate or the minor key, the file as a whole will not appear sorted.

EXAMPLE 12.1 Table 12-1 displays a three-key sort of a sales file. The major sort is ascending; the intermediate sort, within the major sort, is descending; the minor sort, within the intermediate sort, is ascending.

Table 12-1

Department # (Major Key)	Salesperson # (Intermediate Key)	Customer # (Minor Key)	Sales Amount (Not a Key Field)
101	7823	10925	1,000.98
101	7823	27832	2,000.00
101	7823	59838	1,500.00
101	6345	20782	1,200.32
101	6345	48793	5,000.00
101	3287	10925	3,003.43
206	8291	27832	1,305.50
206	8291	40058	2,783.45
206	5094	39840	5,672.34
206	5094	60291	3,476.52
206	4925	27832	4,000.00
206	4925	30618	2,987.50
206	3920	10071	4,526.98

12.2 Use of the SORT Statement

The SORT statement, whose syntax is given in Fig. 12-1, is written in the PROCEDURE DIVISION. Along with it, a fictitious *sort file* must be set up; this "file" must have a SELECT statement in the ENVIRONMENT DIVISION and a sort file description entry (or "SD"), similar to a file description entry ("FD"), in the DATA DIVISION. The record descriptions for the sort file define the key fields on which sorting will be done. The logical record area for the sort file is used for passing records back and forth between the COBOL program and a prewritten *sort/merge utility program*, which does the actual sorting. Utility programs come with the operating system.

324

SORT file-name-1

    ON $\left\{\begin{array}{l}\underline{\text{ASCENDING}}\\\underline{\text{DESCENDING}}\end{array}\right\}$ KEY data-name-1 [data-name-2] . . .

    $\left[\text{ON }\left\{\begin{array}{l}\underline{\text{ASCENDING}}\\\underline{\text{DESCENDING}}\end{array}\right\}\text{ KEY data-name-3 [data-name-4] . . .}\right]$ . . .

    [COLLATING $\underline{\text{SEQUENCE}}$ IS alphabet-name]

    $\left\{\begin{array}{l}\underline{\text{USING}}\text{ file-name-2 [file-name-3] . . .}\\[6pt]\underline{\text{INPUT PROCEDURE}}\text{ IS section-name-1}\left[\left\{\begin{array}{l}\underline{\text{THROUGH}}\\\underline{\text{THRU}}\end{array}\right\}\text{section-name-2}\right]\end{array}\right\}$

    $\left\{\begin{array}{l}\underline{\text{GIVING}}\text{ file-name-4}\\[6pt]\underline{\text{OUTPUT PROCEDURE}}\text{ IS section-name-3}\left[\left\{\begin{array}{l}\underline{\text{THROUGH}}\\\underline{\text{THRU}}\end{array}\right\}\text{section-name-4}\right]\end{array}\right\}$

Fig. 12-1

EXAMPLE 12.2

. . . .

```
ENVIRONMENT DIVISION.
INPUT-OUTPUT SECTION.
FILE-CONTROL.
    SELECT MORTGAGE-PAYMENT-FILE
        ASSIGN TO MORTRECV
        ORGANIZATION IS SEQUENTIAL
        ACCESS IS SEQUENTIAL
        .

    SELECT PAYMENT-SORT-FILE
        ASSIGN TO SORTWK
        .
```

. . . .

```
DATA DIVISION.
FILE SECTION.
FD  MORTGAGE-PAYMENT-FILE
    BLOCK CONTAINS 0 CHARACTERS
    RECORD CONTAINS 23 CHARACTERS
    LABEL RECORDS ARE STANDARD
    .

01  MORTGAGE-PAYMENT-RECORD.
    05  MORTGAGE-ACCOUNT-ID         PIC X(6).
    05  MORTGAGE-DUE-DATE           PIC X(6).
    05  MORTGAGE-PAID-DATE          PIC X(6).
    05  MORTGAGE-AMOUNT             PIC S9(3)V99.

SD  PAYMENTS-SORT-FILE
    RECORD CONTAINS 23 CHARACTERS
    .

01  SORT-RECORD.
    05  SORT-ACCOUNT-ID             PIC X(6).
    05  SORT-DUE-DATE               PIC X(6).
    05  SORT-PAID-DATE              PIC X(6).
    05  SORT-AMOUNT                 PIC S9(3)V99.
```

. . . .

```
PROCEDURE DIVISION.
```

. . . .

```
SORT PAYMENTS-SORT-FILE
    ON ASCENDING KEY SORT-ACCOUNT-ID
    ON ASCENDING KEY SORT-PAID-DATE
    INPUT PROCEDURE IS SCREEN-PAYMENT-RECORDS
    OUTPUT PROCEDURE IS PRODUCE-QUARTERLY-REPORT
    . . . . . . . . . . . . . . . . . . . . . .
SCREEN-PAYMENT-RECORDS SECTION.
    . . . . . . . . . . . . . . . . . . . . . .
PRODUCE-QUARTERLY-REPORT SECTION.
    . . . . . . . . . . . . . . . . . . . . . .
```

Here, MORTGAGE-PAYMENT-FILE is the actual file on disk which is to be sorted in ascending sequence by paid date (minor key) within account ID (major key). PAYMENTS-SORT-FILE is the sort file. Note:

(1) For a sort file, the SELECT statement has the simplified form

> <u>SELECT</u> sort-file-name
> <u>ASSIGN TO</u> assignment-name-comment

Because the sort "file" is not really a file, the ASSIGN TO name is treated as comments. *No* job control language is required for further definition of the sort file.

(2) Job control or command language statements *are* usually needed if the SORT statement is properly to invoke the sort/merge utility. The reader should determine what is required at his or her installation.

(3) PAYMENTS-SORT-FILE is defined in the DATA DIVISION through an SD:

> <u>SD</u>   sort-file-name
> [<u>RECORD</u> CONTAINS [integer-1 <u>TO</u>] integer-2 CHARACTERS]
> $\left[\underline{\text{DATA}} \left\{ \begin{array}{l} \underline{\text{RECORD}} \text{ IS} \\ \underline{\text{RECORDS}} \text{ ARE} \end{array} \right\} \text{data-name} \right]$

(4) SORT-RECORD (level-01) provides a description of the records to be sorted and serves as the buffer in which records are passed back and forth between the sort utility and the program.

(5) The SORT statement names the sort file, not the actual file. The ASCENDING/DESCENDING KEY clauses define the sort key fields in *major-to-minor order*; these data items must be included in the sort file record description. The SORT begins by executing the INPUT PROCEDURE.

(6) The INPUT PROCEDURE must be a SECTION. SCREEN-PAYMENT-RECORDS contains a program loop that will READ each logical record from MORTGAGE-PAYMENT-FILE, move it into SORT-RECORD, and then "give" it to the sort utility by executing a RELEASE statement. When the SORT statement is executed, the INPUT PROCEDURE is in effect performed once.

(7) When the INPUT PROCEDURE finishes executing, the sort utility automatically sorts the logical records which have been RELEASEd to it. When sorting is completed, the OUTPUT PROCEDURE (PRODUCE-QUARTERLY-REPORT) is automatically performed once.

(8) The OUTPUT PROCEDURE must also be a COBOL SECTION. It is written to request that the sort utility "give back" (into SORT-RECORD) the next logical record in sorted sequence. This is done by executing a RETURN statement within the OUTPUT PROCEDURE. The OUTPUT PROCEDURE can then process the record (in this case, it would print a line of the report). Like the INPUT PROCEDURE, PRODUCE-QUARTERLY-REPORT will contain a loop whereby the entire sorted file will be RETURNed from the sort utility, one record at a time.

(9) When the OUTPUT PROCEDURE finishes executing, program execution continues with the statement immediately following the SORT statement.

Since INPUT PROCEDUREs RELEASE logical records to the sort utility one at a time, they may be used to *screen* or *preprocess* the records *before they are sorted*. Indeed, if there is no need to screen or preprocess the records to be sorted, the INPUT PROCEDURE can be eliminated; the sort utility can "get" the records to be sorted directly from an actual file. This option is indicated with the USING clause of the SORT statement.

EXAMPLE 12.3 Suppose it is desired to print mailing labels from a customer master file sorted by customer number; we wish to send letters only to those customers who have not made a purchase during the last 8 months. In order to cut down mailing costs, the labels should be sorted by zip code. Since, presumably, most customers will have been active during the last 8 months, an INPUT PROCEDURE could be used to RELEASE for sorting *only* those customer records for customers in the mailing.

Furthermore, the sort file records could be defined to consist of *only* the name and address fields from the customer master records, and the INPUT PROCEDURE could be written to move only these fields to the sort file record area before RELEASing the sort record. The sort would then take less computer time, since smaller records were being sorted.

EXAMPLE 12.4 Suppose that a customer master file includes last year's total purchases and this year's total purchases. It is desired to print a customer list in descending sequence according to the percentage change from last year to this year. To this end, a percentage change field could be described as part of the sort file record description. An INPUT PROCEDURE could be used to input a customer master record; to *calculate* the percentage change value; and then to move this value, along with other *needed* customer master information, to the sort record, for RELEASE to the sort utility.

We emphasize that, when an INPUT PROCEDURE is used, the records to be sorted *need not correspond to the records in any actual file* (e.g., there was no percentage change field in the master records). On the other hand, when USING... is elected, the SD should exactly reflect the PICTUREs, USAGEs, and structures of the records in the USING file.

Just as INPUT PROCEDUREs preprocess unsorted records, OUTPUT PROCEDUREs post-process sorted records. If postprocessing is not required, the GIVING option may be employed to direct the sort utility to place the sorted records directly on the GIVING file.

EXAMPLE 12.5 If the MORTGAGE-PAYMENT-FILE of Example 12.2 were used to update the mortgage master file, the edit program that validated and sorted the mortgage payments might contain:

```
SORT PAYMENTS-SORT-FILE
    ON ASCENDING KEY SORT-ACCOUNT-ID
    INPUT PROCEDURE IS VALIDATE-PAYMENT-RECORDS
    GIVING VALID-TRANS-FILE
```

where VALID-TRANS-FILE is an actual file, with a regular SELECT statement and FD.

It should be mentioned that a COBOL program may contain any number of SORT (or MERGE) statements, provided only that there be no nesting of the statements.

Having surveyed the overall function of the SORT statement, we devote the remainder of this section to a closer look at its separate clauses and various options.

ASCENDING/DESCENDING KEY Clause

The purpose of these clauses is to identify the positions of the keys within the records to be sorted. In the case of variable-length records, it is required that each key field be in exactly the same position within all records.

EXAMPLE 12.6 Consider the file

```
SD  PARTS-SORT-FILE
    RECORD CONTAINS 12 TO 22 CHARACTERS.


01    MADE-PART-RECORD.
    05    MADE-PART-ID                  PIC X(6).
    05    QUANTITY-ON-HAND              PIC S9(5)  COMP-3.
    05    MADE-WAREHOUSE-CODE           PIC X(3).
01  BOUGHT-PART-RECORD.
    05    BOUGHT-PART-ID                PIC X(6).
```

```
05    BOUGHT-QUANTITY-ON-HAND          PIC S9(5)   COMP-3.
05    BOUGHT-WAREHOUSE-CODE            PIC X(3).
05    SUPPLIER-ID                      PIC X(7).
05    SUPPLIER-PRICE                   PIC S9(3)V99   COMP-3.
```

The record length is 12 for MADE-PART-RECORD and 22 for BOUGHT-PART-RECORD; however, as required, PART-ID occupies the same position in both records (bytes 1–6), as does WAREHOUSE-CODE (bytes 10–12). Hence, the SORT statement for the file might read either

```
SORT PARTS-SORT-FILE
    ASCENDING KEY MADE-PART-ID
    DESCENDING KEY MADE-WAREHOUSE-CODE
    INPUT PROCEDURE IS SCREEN-PARTS
    OUTPUT PROCEDURE IS PRINT-REPORT
```

or

```
SORT PARTS-SORT-FILE
    ASCENDING KEY BOUGHT-PART-ID
    DESCENDING KEY BOUGHT-WAREHOUSE-CODE
    INPUT PROCEDURE IS SCREEN-PARTS
    OUTPUT PROCEDURE IS PRINT-REPORT
```

COLLATING SEQUENCE Clause

This is analogous to the PROGRAM COLLATING SEQUENCE clause, discussed in Section 4.3; however, the collating sequence specified for a SORT need not be the same as that specified for comparing alphanumeric items in the PROCEDURE DIVISION. "Alphabet-name" (Fig. 12-1) must be defined in SPECIAL-NAMES (Section 4.4). COLLATING SEQUENCE . . . is usually omitted from SORT, putting the default collating sequence in effect.

INPUT PROCEDURE: RELEASE . . .
OUTPUT PROCEDURE: RETURN . . .

When an INPUT PROCEDURE is used, it must contain at least one RELEASE statement:

RELEASE record-name [FROM data-name]

The RELEASE statement is very similar to the WRITE statement; it may, in fact, be thought of as the WRITE of a sort file record to the sort utility, which collects all such records for sorting when the INPUT PROCEDURE is over. The FROM option functions similarly to WRITE . . . FROM . . . .

EXAMPLE 12.7   In Example 12.6, the coding for SCREEN-PARTS might involve:

```
IF MADE-PART
    RELEASE MADE-PART-RECORD
        FROM INPUT-RECORD
ELSE
    MOVE INPUT-ID TO BOUGHT-PART-ID
    MOVE INPUT-QUANTITY TO BOUGHT-QUANTITY-ON-HAND
    MOVE INPUT-CODE TO BOUGHT-WAREHOUSE-CODE
    MOVE INPUT-SUPPLIER TO SUPPLIER-ID
    MOVE INPUT-PRICE TO SUPPLIER-PRICE
    RELEASE BOUGHT-PART-RECORD
```

Every OUTPUT PROCEDURE must contain at least one RETURN statement, which signals the sort utility to place the next logical record of the sorted sequence in the sort file record area:

RETURN sort-file-name RECORD [INTO data-name]
    AT END imperative-statement

The RETURN statement is very similar to a READ statement, and RETURN ... INTO ... functions like READ ... INTO .... Furthermore, the AT END (of sort file) clause functions exactly like AT END with a READ.

SORT ... USING ... GIVING ...

When neither pre- nor postprocessing of logical records is necessary, SORT ... USING ... GIVING ... can be employed. However, it is more efficient to execute the sort utility as a *stand-alone program* (rather than invoking it from COBOL). In a COBOL SORT, the USING and GIVING files must be *closed* when the SORT statement executes.

SORT ... INPUT PROCEDURE ... GIVING ...

When INPUT (and/or OUTPUT) PROCEDUREs are used, the PROCEDURE DIVISION should be structured as in Example 12.8.

EXAMPLE 12.8

```
PROCEDURE DIVISION.
    SORT ...
        ON ...
        INPUT PROCEDURE IS SCREEN-INPUT
        OUTPUT PROCEDURE IS PRINT-REPORT
    STOP RUN
    .
SCREEN-INPUT SECTION.
. . . . . . . . . . . . . . . . . . . . . . . . . . . .
PRINT-REPORT SECTION.
. . . . . . . . . . . . . . . . . . . . . . . . . . . .
END-SORT-PROCEDURES SECTION.
A-PARAGRAPH.
. . . . . . . . . . . . . . . . . . . . . . . . . . . .
B-PARAGRAPH.
. . . . . . . . . . . . . . . . . . . . . . . . . . . .
```

Note that the SORT verb is placed in the executive module, immediately followed by STOP RUN. A STOP RUN during an INPUT/OUTPUT PROCEDURE would produce unpredictable results and, in OS/VS COBOL, a program ABEND.

Note also "END-SORT-PROCEDURES SECTION"; without this header, A-PARAGRAPH and B-PARAGRAPH would belong to the PRINT-REPORT SECTION. If the program is such that SCREEN-INPUT or PRINT-REPORT *performs* either of these "outside" paragraphs (as is legal under IBM OS/VS COBOL), a better choice of header would be "PERFORMED-PARAGRAPHS SECTION", or the like. See Problem 12.32 for more on the use of PERFORM in INPUT/OUTPUT PROCEDUREs.

A typical application of SORT ... INPUT PROCEDURE ... GIVING ... would be in an edit program.

EXAMPLE 12.9 Revamp the edit program of Problems 11.22 and 8.30 by including a SORT which uses an INPUT PROCEDURE to screen invalid records and employs the GIVING option to place the valid, sorted transactions on a disk file.

See Fig. 12-2, paying particular attention to the structure of the PROCEDURE DIVISION. The entire original PROCEDURE DIVISION (of which only a part is given in Fig. 11-5) has become the INPUT PROCEDURE for the SORT. The original WRITE statement (not included in Fig. 11-5, but see line 209 of Fig. 8-14) which transferred a validated transaction to disk has been replaced with a RELEASE statement which gives the validated transaction to the sort utility. The sort utility will create the VALID-TIME-FILE in response to the GIVING option. Note that the GIVING file *must be closed* when the SORT is executed, since the sort utility automatically OPENs and CLOSEs the USING/GIVING files.

```
00014                    INPUT-OUTPUT SECTION.
00015                    FILE-CONTROL.
00016
00017                        SELECT TIME-CARD-FILE
00018                            ASSIGN TO TIMECARD
00019                            ORGANIZATION IS SEQUENTIAL
00020                            ACCESS IS SEQUENTIAL
00021                            .
00022           *
00023           *        ----------------------------------------------------
00024           *
00025           *        TO DO A COBOL SORT, ONE MUST DEFINE A SELECT STATEMENT
00026           *        FOR THE "SORT FILE", WHICH IS NOT ACTUALLY A FILE LIKE
00027           *        OTHER DATA FILES IN THE PROGRAM, BUT RATHER REPRESENTS
00028           *        THE AREA IN WHICH THE SORT/MERGE UTILITY WILL REARRANGE
00029           *        THE RECORDS TO BE SORTED.
00030           *
00031           *        ----------------------------------------------------
00032           *
00033                        SELECT SORTING-TIME-CARD-FILE
00034                            ASSIGN TO SORTWK
00035                            .
00036                        SELECT VALID-TIME-FILE
00037                            ASSIGN TO DISKTIME
00038                            ORGANIZATION IS SEQUENTIAL
00039                            ACCESS IS SEQUENTIAL
00040                            .
00041                        SELECT ERROR-LISTING-FILE
00042                            ASSIGN TO ERRORLOG
00043                            ORGANIZATION IS SEQUENTIAL
00044                            ACCESS IS SEQUENTIAL
00045                            .
00046
00047                    DATA DIVISION.
00048
00049                    FILE SECTION.
00050
00051                    FD   TIME-CARD-FILE
00052                        RECORD CONTAINS 80 CHARACTERS
00053                        LABEL RECORDS ARE OMITTED
00054                        .
00055
00056                    01   TIME-CARD-RECORD.
00057                        05   TIME-CARD-ID             PIC X(5).
00058                        05   TIME-CARD-HOURS          PIC 9(2)V9.
00059                        05   TIME-CARD-X-HOURS        REDEFINES TIME-CARD-HOURS
00060                                                      PIC X(3).
00061                        05   TIME-CARD-CLOSING-DATE.
00062                            10   TIME-CARD-CLOSING-MO       PIC 99.
00063                            10   TIME-CARD-CLOSING-DAY      PIC 99.
00064                            10   TIME-CARD-CLOSING-YR       PIC 99.
00065                        05   TIME-CARD-DEPARTMENT    PIC X(4).
00066                        05   FILLER                 PIC X(62).
00067
00068           *        ----------------------------------------------------
00069           *
00070           *        THE "SORT FILE" MUST BE DEFINED WITH AN "SD" RATHER
00071           *        THAN AN "FD".  THE "SD" DEFINES THE RECORD LAYOUT FOR
00072           *        THE RECORDS TO BE SORTED.  IT REPRESENTS THE MEMORY
00073           *        AREA FROM WHICH THE SORT/MERGE UTILITY PICKS UP ANY
00074           *        RECORDS TO BE SORTED, AND TO WHICH THE UTILITY RETURNS
00075           *        RECORDS (ONE AT A TIME) AFTER THEY HAVE BEEN REARRANGED.
00076           *
00077           *        ----------------------------------------------------
00078           *
```

Fig. 12-2

```
00079            SD   SORTING-TIME-CARD-FILE
00080                 RECORD CONTAINS 23 CHARACTERS
00081                 .
00082
00083            01   VALID-TIME-RECORD.
00084                 05   VALID-TIME-ID            PIC X(5).
00085                 05   VALID-TIME-HOURS         PIC S9(2)V9    COMP-3.
00086                 05   VALID-TIME-CLOSING-DATE  PIC X(6).
00087                 05   VALID-TIME-DEPARTMENT    PIC X(4).
00088                 05   VALID-TIME-EDIT-DATE     PIC X(6).
00089
00090            FD   VALID-TIME-FILE
00091                 BLOCK CONTAINS 0 RECORDS
00092                 RECORD CONTAINS 23 CHARACTERS
00093                 LABEL RECORDS ARE STANDARD
00094                 .
00095
00096            01   SORTED-VALID-RECORD          PIC X(23).
00097
00098
00099            FD   ERROR-LISTING-FILE
00100                 RECORD CONTAINS 132 CHARACTERS
00101                 LABEL RECORDS ARE OMITTED
00102                 .
00103
00104            01   ERROR-REPORT-LINE            PIC X(132).
00105
00106        WORKING-STORAGE SECTION.

00215        PROCEDURE DIVISION.
00216
00217        *    -------------------------------------------------
00218        *
00219        *    THE SORT VERB MUST NAME THE "SORT FILE" WHICH HAS BEEN
00220        *    PREVIOUSLY DEFINED.  IT ALSO INDICATES THE KEY(S) ON
00221        *    WHICH SORTING IS TO BE DONE (THE SORT KEY(S) MUST BE
00222        *    PART OF THE SORT FILE RECORD DESCRIPTION), AND WHETHER
00223        *    THE SORT IS TO BE ASCENDING/DESCENDING ON EACH FIELD.
00224        *    IN THIS CASE THE ENTIRE EDIT PROGRAM IS MADE AN
00225        *    INPUT PROCEDURE TO THE SORT.   THE SORTED RECORDS
00226        *    WILL AUTOMATICALLY BE PLACED ON THE "GIVING" FILE.
00227        *
00228        *    -------------------------------------------------
00229        *
00230             SORT SORTING-TIME-CARD-FILE
00231                 ON ASCENDING KEY VALID-TIME-ID
00232                 INPUT PROCEDURE IS 000-EDIT-TIME-CARDS
00233                 GIVING VALID-TIME-FILE
00234             STOP RUN
00235                 .
00236
00237        000-EDIT-TIME-CARDS SECTION.
00238
00239             PERFORM 100-INITIALIZE
00240             PERFORM 200-PRODUCE-EDIT-LISTING
00241                 UNTIL NO-MORE-RECORDS
00242             PERFORM 300-TERMINATE
00243             .
00244
00245        PERFORMED-PARAGRAPHS SECTION.
00246
00247        100-INITIALIZE.
00248
00249             OPEN    INPUT    TIME-CARD-FILE
00250                     OUTPUT   ERROR-LISTING-FILE
00251             MOVE "NO" TO                      WS-END-TIME-FILE-SW
```

Fig. 12-2 *(cont.)*

```
00252                    MOVE ZERO TO                    WS-PAGE-NUMBER
00253                                                    WS-NUMBER-EMPLOYEES
00254                                                    WS-TOTAL-HOURS
00255                    MOVE WS-PAGE-SIZE TO            WS-LINES-ON-PAGE
00256                    ACCEPT WS-SYSTEM-DATE FROM DATE
00257                    MOVE SYSTEM-YY TO               WS-HEADING-YY
00258                    MOVE SYSTEM-MM TO               WS-HEADING-MM
00259                    MOVE SYSTEM-DD TO               WS-HEADING-DD
00260
00261                        .
00262                200-PRODUCE-EDIT-LISTING.
00263
00264                    PERFORM 250-GET-TIME-CARD
00265                    IF RECORD-AVAILABLE
00266                        PERFORM 240-VALIDATE-FIELDS
00267                        IF VALID-RECORD
00268                            ADD 1                   TO WS-NUMBER-EMPLOYEES
00269                            ADD TIME-CARD-HOURS TO WS-TOTAL-HOURS
00270                            PERFORM 210-RELEASE-TO-SORT
00271                        ELSE
00272                            PERFORM 220-PRODUCE-ERROR-LISTING
00273                        .
00274
00275                210-RELEASE-TO-SORT.
00276
00277           *    -------------------------------------------------
00278           *
00279           *    RELEASE A RECORD TO THE SORT/MERGE UTILIITY FOR SORTING.
00280           *    THIS IS DONE BY MOVING THE RECORD INTO THE SORT FILE
00281           *    BUFFER AREA, THEN "RELEASING" THE RECORD.
00282           *
00283           *    -------------------------------------------------
00284
00285                    MOVE TIME-CARD-ID              TO VALID-TIME-ID
00286                    MOVE TIME-CARD-HOURS           TO VALID-TIME-HOURS
00287                    MOVE TIME-CARD-CLOSING-DATE TO VALID-TIME-CLOSING-DATE
00288                    MOVE TIME-CARD-DEPARTMENT      TO VALID-TIME-DEPARTMENT
00289                    MOVE WS-SYSTEM-DATE            TO VALID-TIME-EDIT-DATE
00290                    RELEASE VALID-TIME-RECORD
00291                        .
00292
00293                220-PRODUCE-ERROR-LISTING.
00294
00295                    MOVE TIME-CARD-ID              TO WS-DETAIL-ID
00296                    MOVE TIME-CARD-X-HOURS         TO WS-DETAIL-HOURS
00297                    MOVE TIME-CARD-CLOSING-DATE TO WS-DETAIL-DATE
00298                    MOVE TIME-CARD-DEPARTMENT      TO WS-DETAIL-DEPARTMENT
00299
00300                    MOVE WS-DETAIL-LINE            TO WS-OUTPUT-AREA
00301                    MOVE WS-SKIP-BEFORE-DETAIL     TO WS-NUMBER-TO-SKIP
00302                    PERFORM 230-PRINT-OUTPUT-AREA
00303
00304                    MOVE WS-UNDER-LINE             TO WS-OUTPUT-AREA
00305                    MOVE WS-SKIP-BEFORE-UNDER      TO WS-NUMBER-TO-SKIP
00306                    PERFORM 230-PRINT-OUTPUT-AREA
00307                        .
00308
00309                230-PRINT-OUTPUT-AREA.
00310
00311                    IF WS-LINES-ON-PAGE + WS-NUMBER-TO-SKIP
00312                        GREATER THAN WS-PAGE-SIZE
00313                            ADD 1 TO WS-PAGE-NUMBER
00314                            MOVE WS-PAGE-NUMBER TO WS-HEADING-PAGE
00315                            WRITE ERROR-REPORT-LINE
00316                                FROM WS-HEADING-LINE-1
00317                                AFTER ADVANCING PAGE
00318                            WRITE ERROR-REPORT-LINE
00319                                FROM WS-HEADING-LINE-2
```

Fig. 12-2 (cont.)

```
00320                                    AFTER ADVANCING WS-SKIP-BEFORE-HEADING LINES
00321                             MOVE WS-SKIP-BEFORE-HEADING TO WS-LINES-ON-PAGE
00322                         .
00323                    WRITE ERROR-REPORT-LINE
00324                        FROM WS-OUTPUT-AREA
00325                        AFTER ADVANCING WS-NUMBER-TO-SKIP LINES
00326                    ADD WS-NUMBER-TO-SKIP TO WS-LINES-ON-PAGE
00327                        .
00328
00329              240-VALIDATE-FIELDS.
00330
00331                    MOVE "NO"    TO WS-ERROR-DETECTED-SW
00332                    MOVE SPACES TO WS-UNDER-LINE
00333                    IF TIME-CARD-ID NOT NUMERIC
00334                        MOVE ALL "-" TO WS-UNDER-ID
00335                        MOVE "YES"   TO WS-ERROR-DETECTED-SW
00336                        .
00337                    IF TIME-CARD-HOURS NOT NUMERIC
00338                        MOVE ALL "-" TO WS-UNDER-HOURS
00339                        MOVE "YES"   TO WS-ERROR-DETECTED-SW
00340                        .
00341                    IF TIME-CARD-CLOSING-DATE NOT NUMERIC
00342                        MOVE ALL "-" TO WS-UNDER-DATE
00343                        `MOVE "YES"   TO WS-ERROR-DETECTED-SW
00344                    ELSE
00345                        PERFORM 260-VALIDATE-DATE
00346                        .
00347                    IF TIME-CARD-DEPARTMENT NOT NUMERIC
00348                        MOVE ALL "-" TO WS-UNDER-DEPARTMENT
00349                        MOVE "YES"   TO WS-ERROR-DETECTED-SW
00350                        .
00351
00352              250-GET-TIME-CARD.
00353
00354                    READ TIME-CARD-FILE
00355                        AT END
00356                            MOVE "YES" TO WS-END-TIME-FILE-SW
00357                        .
00358
00359              260-VALIDATE-DATE.
00360
00361                    IF TIME-CARD-CLOSING-YR GREATER THAN SYSTEM-YY
00362                        MOVE ALL "-" TO WS-UNDER-YR
00363                        MOVE "YES" TO WS-ERROR-DETECTED-SW
00364                        .
00365                    IF TIME-CARD-CLOSING-MO LESS THAN 1 OR GREATER THAN 12
00366                        MOVE ALL "-" TO WS-UNDER-MO
00367                        MOVE "YES" TO WS-ERROR-DETECTED-SW
00368                    ELSE IF TIME-CARD-CLOSING-DAY LESS THAN 1 OR
00369                        GREATER THAN DAYS-PER-MONTH (TIME-CARD-CLOSING-MO)
00370                            MOVE ALL "-" TO WS-UNDER-DAY
00371                            MOVE "YES" TO WS-ERROR-DETECTED-SW
00372                        .
00373
00374              300-TERMINATE.
00375
00376                    MOVE WS-NUMBER-EMPLOYEES      TO WS-FOOTING-COUNT
00377                    MOVE WS-TOTAL-HOURS           TO WS-FOOTING-TOTAL
00378                    MOVE WS-FOOTING-LINE          TO WS-OUTPUT-AREA
00379                    MOVE WS-SKIP-BEFORE-FOOTING TO WS-NUMBER-TO-SKIP
00380                    MOVE WS-FOOTING-LINE          TO WS-OUTPUT-AREA
00381                    PERFORM 230-PRINT-OUTPUT-AREA
00382
00383                    CLOSE   TIME-CARD-FILE
00384                            ERROR-LISTING-FILE
00385                        .
```

Fig. 12-2 (cont.)

SORT...USING...OUTPUT PROCEDURE...

This version may be used to sort and then process an *entire file*, when there is no need for screening or preprocessing of logical records (e.g., printing mailing labels).

EXAMPLE 12.10 Problem 8.32 concerned the check printing program for the payroll system whose edit program has been treated in Problem 11.22 and Example 12.9. Revise Problem 8.32 to print the checks alphabetically by employee name (instead of by employee number, the order of records on PAYROLL-DISK-FILE).

See Fig. 12-3; comment lines 156–160 refer to the "original program" that is implied by the structure chart in Fig. 8-17 but not displayed in Problem 8.32.

```
 .
 .
 .
00022                    SELECT PAYROLL-DISK-FILE
00023                        ASSIGN TO PAYDISK
00024                        ORGANIZATION IS SEQUENTIAL
00025                        ACCESS IS SEQUENTIAL
00026                        .
00027                    SELECT SORT-CHECK-FILE
00028                        ASSIGN TO SORTUTIL
00029                        .
00030                    SELECT PAYCHECK-FILE
00031                        ASSIGN TO CHECKS
00032                        ORGANIZATION IS SEQUENTIAL
00033                        ACCESS IS SEQUENTIAL
00034                        .
00035
00036             DATA DIVISION.
00037
00038             FILE SECTION.
00039
00040             FD   PAYROLL-DISK-FILE
00041                  BLOCK CONTAINS 0 RECORDS
00042                  RECORD CONTAINS 80 CHARACTERS
00043                  LABEL RECORDS ARE STANDARD
00044                      .
00045
00046         *    ----------------------------------------------------
00047         *    NOTE THAT PAYROLL-CHECK-RECORD NEED NOT BE FULLY
00048         *    DESCRIBED WITH SORT...USING...
00049         *    ----------------------------------------------------
00050
00051             01   PAYROLL-CHECK-RECORD          PIC X(80).
00052
00053             SD   SORT-CHECK-FILE
00054                  RECORD CONTAINS 80 CHARACTERS
00055                      .
00056
00057             01   SORT-CHECK-RECORD.
00058                  05   PAYROLL-ID               PIC X(5).
00059                  05   PAYROLL-HOURS            PIC S9(2)V9.
00060                  05   PAYROLL-DATE             PIC X(6).
00061                  05   PAYROLL-DEPARTMENT       PIC X(4).
00062                  05   PAYROLL-RATE             PIC S9(3)V99.
00063                  05   PAYROLL-NAME.
00064                       10   PAYROLL-INITIALS    PIC X(4).
00065                       10   PAYROLL-LAST-NAME   PIC X(16).
00066                  05   PAYROLL-GROSS            PIC S9(6)V99.
00067                  05   PAYROLL-TAX              PIC S9(5)V99.
00068                  05   PAYROLL-NET              PIC S9(6)V99.
00069                  05   FILLER                   PIC X(14).
00070
00071             FD   PAYCHECK-FILE
00072                  RECORD CONTAINS 132 CHARACTERS
```

Fig. 12-3

```
00073                    LABEL RECORDS ARE OMITTED
00074                .
00075
00076            01  PAYCHECK-LINE                 PIC X(132).
00077
00078            WORKING-STORAGE SECTION.
 .
 .
 .
00152            PROCEDURE DIVISION.
00153
00154        *   -------------------------------------------------
00155        *   THE SORT STATEMENT IS PLACED IN THE HIGHEST LEVEL
00156        *   MODULE.  THE REST OF THE ORIGINAL PROGRAM
00157        *   BECOMES THE OUTPUT PROCEDURE, WITH ONLY THE FOLLOWING
00158        *   CHANGES NECESSARY:  1) PAYROLL-DISK-FILE MUST NOT BE
00159        *   OPENED SINCE IT IS THE USING FILE, AND 2) "READ
00160        *   PAYROLL-DISK-FILE" BECOMES "RETURN SORT-CHECK-FILE"
00161        *   -------------------------------------------------
00162
00163            SORT SORT-CHECK-FILE
00164                ON ASCENDING KEY PAYROLL-LAST-NAME
00165                USING PAYROLL-DISK-FILE
00166                OUTPUT PROCEDURE IS PRINT-STUBS-AND-CHECKS
00167            STOP RUN
00168                .
00169
00170            PRINT-STUBS-AND-CHECKS SECTION.
00171
00172            PERFORM 100-INITIALIZE
00173            PERFORM 200-PRODUCE-PAYCHECKS
00174                UNTIL NO-MORE-RECORDS
00175            PERFORM 300-TERMINATE
00176                .
00177        *-------------------------------
00178            PERFORMED-PARAGRAPHS SECTION.
00179        *-------------------------------
00180            100-INITIALIZE.
00181
00182            OPEN    OUTPUT  PAYCHECK-FILE
00183            MOVE "NO" TO                WS-END-DISK-FILE-SW
00184            MOVE ZERO TO                WS-NUMBER-EMPLOYEES
00185                                        WS-TOTAL-HOURS
00186            ACCEPT WS-TODAYS-DATE FROM DATE
00187            MOVE SYSTEM-YY               TO WS-YY
00188            MOVE SYSTEM-MM               TO WS-MM
00189            MOVE SYSTEM-DD               TO WS-DD
00190            ACCEPT WS-CHECK-NUMBER
00191                FROM STARTING-CHECK-NUMBER-DEVICE
00192
00193            PERFORM 110-PRODUCE-TEMPLATE
00194            PERFORM 210-GET-NEXT-EMPLOYEE
00195                .
00196
00197            110-PRODUCE-TEMPLATE.
00198
00199            MOVE ALL "*" TO WS-STUB-ID
00200                            WS-STUB-NAME
00201                            WS-STUB-DATE
00202                            WS-CHECK-NAME
00203            PERFORM 230-PRINT-CHECK
00204                WS-NUMBER-OF-TEMPLATES TIMES
00205                .
00206
00207            200-PRODUCE-PAYCHECKS.
00208
```

Fig. 12-3 *(cont.)*

```
00209                    PERFORM 220-FORMAT-CHECKS
00210                    PERFORM 230-PRINT-CHECK
00211                    ADD PAYROLL-HOURS                TO WS-TOTAL-HOURS
00212                    ADD 1                            TO WS-NUMBER-EMPLOYEES
00213                                                        WS-CHECK-NUMBER
00214                    PERFORM 210-GET-NEXT-EMPLOYEE
00215
00216
00217                210-GET-NEXT-EMPLOYEE.
00218
00219                    RETURN SORT-CHECK-FILE
00220                        AT END
00221                            MOVE "YES" TO WS-END-DISK-FILE-SW
00222                    .
00223
00224                220-FORMAT-CHECKS.
00225
00226                    MOVE PAYROLL-ID                 TO WS-STUB-ID
00227                    MOVE PAYROLL-NAME               TO WS-STUB-NAME
00228                                                       WS-CHECK-NAME
00229                    MOVE PAYROLL-DEPARTMENT         TO WS-STUB-DEPARTMENT
00230                    MOVE PAYROLL-DATE               TO WS-STUB-DATE
00231                    MOVE PAYROLL-HOURS              TO WS-STUB-HOURS
00232                    MOVE PAYROLL-RATE               TO WS-STUB-RATE
00233                    MOVE PAYROLL-GROSS              TO WS-STUB-GROSS
00234                    MOVE PAYROLL-TAX                TO WS-STUB-TAX
00235                    MOVE PAYROLL-NET                TO WS-STUB-NET
00236                                                       WS-CHECK-AMOUNT
00237                    .
00238
00239                230-PRINT-CHECK.
00240
00241                    WRITE PAYCHECK-LINE
00242                        FROM WS-STUB-LINE-1
00243                        AFTER ADVANCING WS-SKIP-BEFORE-STUB-1 LINES
00244                    WRITE PAYCHECK-LINE
00245                        FROM WS-STUB-LINE-2
00246                        AFTER ADVANCING WS-SKIP-BEFORE-STUB-2 LINES
00247                    WRITE PAYCHECK-LINE
00248                        FROM WS-CHECK-LINE-1
00249                        AFTER ADVANCING WS-SKIP-BEFORE-CHECK-1 LINES
00250                    WRITE PAYCHECK-LINE
00251                        FROM WS-CHECK-LINE-2
00252                        AFTER ADVANCING WS-SKIP-BEFORE-CHECK-2 LINES
00253                    .
00254
00255                300-TERMINATE.
00256
00257                    CLOSE   PAYCHECK-FILE
00258                    .
```

Fig. 12-3 *(cont.)*

SORT... INPUT PROCEDURE... OUTPUT PROCEDURE...

EXAMPLE 12.11 In Fig. 12-4, we illustrate INPUT/OUTPUT PROCEDUREs with an *indexed file* creation program; such files are very popular for applications where random file processing is necessary. The most efficient way to create indexed files is to build them sequentially, placing the records in the file in sorted order by key. An INPUT PROCEDURE is used to detect invalid transaction records and prevent them from being sorted; then an OUTPUT PROCEDURE actually creates the indexed file. Notice that the INPUT and OUTPUT PROCEDUREs look like two separate programs: each begins by opening files and initializing switches, then performs a main processing paragraph until end-of-data, and then closes files and finishes. This is not surprising, for the two "routines" are executed independently of each other under the control of the SORT verb.

```
00015           INPUT-OUTPUT SECTION.
00016
00017           FILE-CONTROL.
00018
00019               SELECT CREATION-INFO-FILE
00020                   ASSIGN TO CREATE
00021                   ORGANIZATION IS SEQUENTIAL
00022                   ACCESS IS SEQUENTIAL
00023                   .
00024               SELECT SORTED-TRANS-FILE
00025                   ASSIGN TO SORTWK
00026                   .
00027               SELECT PRICING-MASTER-FILE
00028                   ASSIGN TO PRICES
00029                   ORGANIZATION IS INDEXED
00030                   ACCESS IS SEQUENTIAL
00031                   RECORD KEY IS PRICING-ITEM-ID
00032                   FILE STATUS IS MASTER-STATUS-CODE
00033                   .
00034               SELECT ERROR-LOG
00035                   ASSIGN TO ERRORS
00036                   ORGANIZATION IS SEQUENTIAL
00037                   ACCESS IS SEQUENTIAL
00038                   .
00039
00040           DATA DIVISION.
00041
00042           FILE SECTION.
00043
00044           FD  CREATION-INFO-FILE
00045               RECORD CONTAINS 80 CHARACTERS
00046               LABEL RECORDS ARE OMITTED
00047               .
00048           01  CREATION-RECORD.
00049               05  CREATION-ITEM-ID          PIC X(5).
00050               05  CREATION-ITEM-DESCRIPTION
00051                                             PIC X(25).
00052               05  CREATION-PRICE            PIC 9(5)V99.
00053               05  CREATION-PRICE-X          REDEFINES CREATION-PRICE
00054                                             PIC X(7).
00055               05  CREATION-QUANTITY         PIC 9(5).
00056               05  CREATION-QUANTITY-X       REDEFINES CREATION-QUANTITY
00057                                             PIC X(5).
00058               05  FILLER                    PIC X(38).
00059
00060           SD  SORTED-TRANS-FILE
00061               RECORD CONTAINS 80 CHARACTERS
00062               .
00063           01  TRANS-RECORD.
00064               05  TRANSACT-ITEM-ID          PIC X(5).
00065               05  TRANSACT-ITEM-DESCRIPTION
00066                                             PIC X(25).
00067               05  TRANSACT-PRICE            PIC S9(5)V99.
00068               05  TRANSACT-PRICE-X          REDEFINES TRANSACT-PRICE
00069                                             PIC X(7).
00070               05  TRANSACT-QUANTITY         PIC S9(5).
00071               05  TRANSACT-QUANTITY-X       REDEFINES TRANSACT-QUANTITY
00072                                             PIC X(5).
00073               05  FILLER                    PIC X(38).
00074
00075           FD  PRICING-MASTER-FILE
00076               RECORD CONTAINS 37 CHARACTERS
00077               LABEL RECORDS ARE STANDARD
00078               .
00079           01  PRICING-RECORD.
00080               05  PRICING-ITEM-ID           PIC X(5).
```

Fig. 12-4

```
00081            05   PRICING-ITEM-DESCRIPTION
00082                                           PIC X(25).
00083            05   PRICING-QUANTITY-ONHAND PIC S9(5)        COMP-3.
00084            05   PRICING-PRICE            PIC S9(5)V99     COMP-3.
00085
00086       FD   ERROR-LOG
00087            RECORD CONTAINS 132 CHARACTERS
00088            LABEL RECORDS ARE OMITTED
00089            LINAGE IS 60 LINES
00090                WITH FOOTING AT 59
00091                LINES AT TOP 3
00092                LINES AT BOTTOM 3
00093            .
00094
00095       01   ERROR-LINE                    PIC X(132).
00096
00097       WORKING-STORAGE SECTION.
00098
00099       01   PROGRAM-SWITCHES.
00100            05   WS-END-CREATION-SW        PIC X(3).
00101                88   NO-MORE-RECORDS       VALUE "YES".
00102                88   MORE-RECORDS          VALUE "NO".
00103            05   WS-VALID-TRANS-SW         PIC X(3).
00104                88   VALID-TRANS           VALUE "YES".
00105                88   INVALID-TRANS         VALUE "NO".
00106            05   MASTER-STATUS-CODE        PIC XX.
00107
00108       01   PROGRAM-COUNTERS.
00109            05   WS-PAGE-NUMBER            PIC S9(3)        COMP-3.
00110
00111       01   SYSTEM-DATE-AREA.
00112            05   SYSTEM-YY                 PIC 99.
00113            05   SYSTEM-MM                 PIC 99.
00114            05   SYSTEM-DD                 PIC 99.
00115
00116       01   PROGRAM-CONSTANTS.
00117            05   WS-MESSAGES.
00118                10   WS-INVALID-FIELDS-MSG             PIC X(30)
00119                                           VALUE "INVALID FIELDS".
00120                10   WS-FILE-FULL-MSG                  PIC X(30)
00121                                           VALUE "FILE FULL--NO ADD".
00122                10   WS-DUPLICATE-MESSAGE              PIC X(30)
00123                                           VALUE "DUPLICATE KEY--NO ADD".
00124
00125
00126       01   WS-HEADING-LINE-1.
00127            05   FILLER                    PIC X(3)         VALUE SPACES.
00128            05   FILLER                    PIC X(32)
00129                                  VALUE "PRICING FILE CREATION ERROR LOG".
00130            05   WS-MM                     PIC Z9.
00131            05   FILLER                    PIC X            VALUE "/".
00132            05   WS-DD                     PIC 99.
00133            05   FILLER                    PIC X            VALUE "/".
00134            05   WS-YY                     PIC 99.
00135            05   FILLER                    PIC X(2)         VALUE SPACES.
00136            05   FILLER                    PIC X(5)         VALUE "PAGE ".
00137            05   WS-HEADING-PAGE           PIC ZZ9.
00138            05   FILLER                    PIC X(79)        VALUE SPACES.
00139
00140       01   WS-HEADING-LINE-2.
00141            05   FILLER                    PIC X(10)        VALUE "ITEM-ID".
00142            05   FILLER                    PIC X(27)
00143                                  VALUE "DESCRIPTION".
00144            05   FILLER                    PIC X(9)         VALUE "PRICE".
00145            05   FILLER                    PIC X(86)        VALUE "QUANTITY".
00146
```

Fig. 12-4 (*cont.*)

```
00147          01  WS-DETAIL-LINE.
00148              05   WS-DETAIL-ITEM-ID        PIC X(5).
00149              05   FILLER                   PIC X(5)        VALUE SPACES.
00150              05   WS-DETAIL-DESCRIPTION     PIC X(25).
00151              05   FILLER                   PIC X(2)        VALUE SPACES.
00152              05   WS-DETAIL-PRICE          PIC X(7).
00153              05   FILLER                   PIC X(2)        VALUE SPACES.
00154              05   WS-DETAIL-QUANTITY       PIC X(5).
00155              05   FILLER                   PIC X(2)        VALUE SPACES.
00156              05   WS-DETAIL-MESSAGE        PIC X(79).
00157
00158          PROCEDURE DIVISION.
00159
00160              SORT SORTED-TRANS-FILE
00161                  ON ASCENDING KEY TRANSACT-ITEM-ID
00162                  INPUT PROCEDURE IS 000-SCREEN-TRANSACTIONS
00163                  OUTPUT PROCEDURE IS 001-CREATE-PRICING-MASTER
00164              STOP RUN
00165                  .
00166
00167          000-SCREEN-TRANSACTIONS SECTION.
00168
00169              OPEN OUTPUT ERROR-LOG
00170              OPEN INPUT  CREATION-INFO-FILE
00171              MOVE "NO" TO WS-END-CREATION-SW
00172
00173              ACCEPT SYSTEM-DATE-AREA  FROM DATE
00174              MOVE SYSTEM-MM  TO WS-MM
00175              MOVE SYSTEM-DD  TO WS-DD
00176              MOVE SYSTEM-YY  TO WS-YY
00177
00178              MOVE ZERO        TO WS-PAGE-NUMBER
00179
00180              PERFORM 170-PRINT-HEADINGS
00181              PERFORM 180-GET-NEXT-TRANS
00182
00183              PERFORM 100-GENERATE-PRICING-RECORD
00184                  UNTIL NO-MORE-RECORDS
00185
00186              CLOSE    CREATION-INFO-FILE
00187                  .
00188
00189          001-CREATE-PRICING-MASTER SECTION.
00190
00191              OPEN OUTPUT PRICING-MASTER-FILE
00192              MOVE "NO" TO WS-END-CREATION-SW
00193              PERFORM 140-RETURN-NEXT-TRANS
00194              PERFORM 120-PRODUCE-MASTER-REC
00195                  UNTIL NO-MORE-RECORDS
00196              CLOSE    PRICING-MASTER-FILE
00197                       ERROR-LOG
00198                  .
00199
00200          PERFORMED-PARAGRAPHS SECTION.
00201
00202          100-GENERATE-PRICING-RECORD.
00203
00204              PERFORM 110-VALIDATE-TRANS
00205              IF VALID-TRANS
00206                  PERFORM 125-RELEASE-TO-SORT
00207              ELSE
00208                  MOVE WS-INVALID-FIELDS-MSG  TO WS-DETAIL-MESSAGE
00209                  PERFORM 130-PRODUCE-ERROR-LOG
00210                  .
00211              PERFORM 180-GET-NEXT-TRANS
00212                  .
```

Fig. 12-4   (cont.)

```
00213
00214        110-VALIDATE-TRANS.
00215
00216            IF    CREATION-PRICE NOT NUMERIC
00217               OR CREATION-QUANTITY NOT NUMERIC
00218                   MOVE "NO" TO WS-VALID-TRANS-SW
00219            ELSE
00220                   MOVE "YES" TO WS-VALID-TRANS-SW
00221            .
00222
00223        120-PRODUCE-MASTER-REC.
00224
00225            MOVE TRANSACT-ITEM-ID     TO PRICING-ITEM-ID
00226            MOVE TRANSACT-ITEM-DESCRIPTION
00227                TO PRICING-ITEM-DESCRIPTION
00228            MOVE TRANSACT-PRICE  ·    TO PRICING-PRICE
00229            MOVE TRANSACT-QUANTITY  TO PRICING-QUANTITY-ONHAND
00230            PERFORM 150-WRITE-MASTER-RECORD
00231            IF MASTER-STATUS-CODE NOT EQUAL "00"
00232                MOVE WS-DUPLICATE-MESSAGE   TO WS-DETAIL-MESSAGE
00233                PERFORM 130-PRODUCE-ERROR-LOG
00234            .
00235            PERFORM 140-RETURN-NEXT-TRANS
00236            .
00237
00238        125-RELEASE-TO-SORT.
00239
00240            RELEASE TRANS-RECORD
00241                FROM CREATION-RECORD
00242            .
00243
00244        130-PRODUCE-ERROR-LOG.
00245
00246            MOVE TRANSACT-ITEM-ID          TO WS-DETAIL-ITEM-ID
00247            MOVE TRANSACT-ITEM-DESCRIPTION
00248                                  TO WS-DETAIL-DESCRIPTION
00249            MOVE TRANSACT-PRICE-X     TO WS-DETAIL-PRICE
00250            MOVE TRANSACT-QUANTITY-X    TO WS-DETAIL-QUANTITY
00251            PERFORM 160-PRINT-DETAIL-LINE
00252            .
00253
00254        140-RETURN-NEXT-TRANS.
00255
00256            RETURN SORTED-TRANS-FILE
00257                AT END
00258                   MOVE "YES" TO WS-END-CREATION-SW
00259            .
00260
00261
00262        150-WRITE-MASTER-RECORD.
00263
00264            WRITE PRICING-RECORD
00265            .
00266
00267        160-PRINT-DETAIL-LINE.
00268
00269            WRITE ERROR-LINE
00270                FROM WS-DETAIL-LINE
00271                AFTER ADVANCING 2 LINES
00272                AT END-OF-PAGE
00273                   PERFORM 170-PRINT-HEADINGS
00274            .
00275
00276        170-PRINT-HEADINGS.
00277
00278            ADD 1 TO WS-PAGE-NUMBER
```

Fig. 12-4   (*cont.*)

```
00279              MOVE WS-PAGE-NUMBER              TO WS-HEADING-PAGE
00280              WRITE ERROR-LINE
00281                  FROM WS-HEADING-LINE-1
00282                  AFTER ADVANCING PAGE
00283              WRITE ERROR-LINE
00284                  FROM WS-HEADING-LINE-2
00285                  AFTER ADVANCING 2 LINES
00286              .
00287
00288          180-GET-NEXT-TRANS.
00289
00290              READ CREATION-INFO-FILE
00291                  AT END
00292                      MOVE "YES" TO WS-END-CREATION-SW
00293              .
00294
```

Fig. 12-4   *(cont.)*

Sorting on a Group Item

The efficiency of a multikey sort can be improved by grouping the key fields together and sorting on the group item. This technique may apply when the keys to be grouped are (i) *mutually adjacent* within the record; (ii) all alphanumeric or unsigned numeric, with USAGE DISPLAY; (iii) all ascending or all descending; (iv) arranged from major key (first in the group) to minor key (last in the group).

EXAMPLE 12.12

```
    SD   SORT-FILE...
    01   SORT-RECORD.
         05   SORT-KEYS.
              10   REGION-ID          PIC X(4).
              10   DEPARTMENT-ID      PIC X(7).
              10   SALESPERSON-ID     PIC X(3).
         05   REGION-NAME             PIC X(10).
         05   DEPARTMENT-NAME         PIC X(20).
         05   SALESPERSON-NAME        PIC X(15).
    . . . . . . . . . . . . . . . . . . . . . . . . . . . . . . . . . . . . .
         SORT SORT-FILE
              ON ASCENDING KEY SORT-KEYS
    . . . . . . . . . . . . . . . . . . . . . . . . . . . . . . . . . . . . .
```

12.3   File Merging with the MERGE Verb

Merging is the combination of two or more *already sorted* files into one sorted file. One speaks of an "*n*-way merge" if *n* files are being combined; under IBM OS/VS COBOL, $n \leq 8$. The same system utility which does file sorting usually also handles file merging. Since both sorting and merging involve *ordering* the records in files, the concepts of key fields; ascending versus descending sequence; and major, intermediate, and minor keys apply to both.

The syntax of the MERGE statement (Fig. 12-5) is very similar to that of the SORT statement. In order to do either a sort or merge, the programmer must define a special sort/merge file with a restricted form of the SELECT statement in the ENVIRONMENT DIVISION and an SD in the DATA DIVISION. Aside from the SORT/MERGE statements themselves, the COBOL requirements for sorting and merging are *identical*.

The MERGE statement must define the key fields on which the files to be merged are *already sorted* and on which the resulting merged file is to be ordered. The keys are written in major-to-minor sequence, just as in the SORT statement.

$$\underline{\text{MERGE}} \text{ file-name-1}$$

$$\text{ON} \left\{ \begin{array}{l} \underline{\text{ASCENDING}} \\ \underline{\text{DESCENDING}} \end{array} \right\} \text{KEY data-name-1 [data-name-2]} \dots$$

$$\left[\text{ON} \left\{ \begin{array}{l} \underline{\text{ASCENDING}} \\ \underline{\text{DESCENDING}} \end{array} \right\} \text{KEY data-name-3 [data-name-4]} \dots \right]$$

$$\text{[COLLATING } \underline{\text{SEQUENCE}} \text{ IS alphabet-name]}$$

$$\underline{\text{USING}} \text{ file-name-2 file-name-3 [file-name-4]} \dots$$

$$\left\{ \begin{array}{l} \underline{\text{GIVING}} \text{ file-name-5} \\ \underline{\text{OUTPUT PROCEDURE}} \text{ IS section-name-1} \left[\left\{ \begin{array}{l} \underline{\text{THROUGH}} \\ \underline{\text{THRU}} \end{array} \right\} \text{section-name-2} \right] \end{array} \right\}$$

Fig. 12-5

Notice that no INPUT PROCEDURE is allowed with MERGE. The USING files (those to be merged according to the ASCENDING/DESCENDING KEY specifications) must be closed at the time the MERGE is executed, since the MERGE statement automatically opens them. When the MERGE operation is completed, MERGE automatically closes them.

The GIVING option specifies that the merged records are to be written directly to the indicated file. The GIVING file must be closed when the MERGE is executed, since the sort/merge utility automatically opens the file, writes the merged records into it, then closes the file again.

The OUTPUT PROCEDURE functions exactly as in the SORT statement.

File A	File B	File C	Merged File
20	10	5	5
40	30	25	10
60	50	35	20
80	70		25
	90		30
			35
			40
			50
			60
			70
			80
			90

Fig. 12-6

EXAMPLE 12.13 To merge the files shown in Fig. 12-6, we would code:

```
ENVIRONMENT DIVISION.
. . . . . . . . . . . . . . . . . . . . . . . .
    SELECT FILE-A ASSIGN TO ...
    SELECT FILE-B ASSIGN TO ...
    SELECT FILE-C ASSIGN TO ...
    SELECT MERGE-FILE
        ASSIGN TO SORTWK.
. . . . . . . . . . . . . . . . . . . . . . . .

DATA DIVISION.

FILE SECTION.

FD   FILE-A ...
01   RECORD-A ...

FD   FILE-B ...
01   RECORD-B ...
```

```
    FD   FILE-C
    01   RECORD-C...

    SD   MERGE-FILE
         RECORD CONTAINS...
    01   MERGE-RECORD.
         05   MERGE-KEY-1...
         05   DATA-FIELD-1...
         05   MERGE-KEY-2...
         05   DATA-FIELD-2...
    . . . . . . . . . . . . . . . . . . . . . . . . . . . .
    PROCEDURE DIVISION.

        MERGE MERGE-FILE
            ON ASCENDING KEY MERGE-KEY-1
            ON DESCENDING KEY MERGE-KEY-2
            USING FILE-A   FILE-B   FILE-C
            OUTPUT PROCEDURE IS PROCESS-MERGED-RECORDS
        STOP RUN
    .

    PROCESS-MERGED-RECORDS SECTION.
    . . . . . . . . . . . . . . . . . . . . . . . . . . . .
    PERFORMED-PARAGRAPHS SECTION.
    GET-MERGED-RECORD.
        RETURN MERGE-FILE
            AT END...
    .
```

The above program would remain valid with the MERGE verb replaced by the SORT verb; this substitution would be *essential* if the files to be ordered were not already sorted. Of course, since they *are* sorted, MERGE will be much more efficient than SORT.

Note that when more than one USING file is specified for a SORT, all records from all files are combined and sorted. We thus have a technique for merging *unsorted* files.

Review Questions

12.1   Distinguish between file sorting and table sorting.

12.2   Explain: key field, ascending sort, descending sort, major key, intermediate key, minor key.

12.3   Explain the relationship between the system sort/merge utility and the COBOL SORT and MERGE statements.

12.4   What is a "sort file"?

12.5   Explain the restrictions on the SELECT and SD entries when defining a sort/merge file.

12.6   Explain the purpose of the RELEASE and RETURN statements.

12.7   Give several examples of when an INPUT PROCEDURE might be useful.

12.8   Give several examples of when an OUTPUT PROCEDURE might be useful.

12.9   Give an example of when an INPUT PROCEDURE might construct the records it releases to the sort/merge utility.

12.10 Explain any restrictions on the sort keys when variable-length records are to be sorted.

12.11 Explain the purpose of the COLLATING SEQUENCE clause in the SORT and MERGE statements.

12.12 Why are USING . . . GIVING . . . sorts not common in COBOL programs?

12.13 Discuss the structure of the PROCEDURE DIVISION when SORT or MERGE is used.

12.14 Discuss the series of events which occurs when a SORT statement is executed.

12.15 What happens if a STOP RUN is executed within an INPUT or OUTPUT procedure?

12.16 Discuss the relationship between an INPUT and OUTPUT procedure under control of a SORT.

12.17 Explain how grouping of sort key fields can improve sorting efficiency. What restrictions apply to this technique?

12.18 Differentiate between file sorting and file merging.

12.19 Give some examples of when file merging might be used.

12.20 What is meant by a three-way merge?

12.21 Why must the USING or GIVING files be closed before a SORT or MERGE is executed?

12.22 How should a merge operation be programmed if the files to be merged are not already sorted?

Solved Problems

12.23 (*a*) Identify the major, intermediate, and minor keys in the record fields below. (*b*) Which keys are ascending, and which descending?

Name	Region	Number-of-Accounts
PERELMAN	10	5
SNYDER	10	5
ABEL	10	3
CONVERSE	10	3
FOLKERS	20	8
GETZ	20	8
BAKER	20	4

(*a*) Major key, region; intermediate key, number-of-accounts; minor key, name.

(*b*) Region and name are ascending; number-of-accounts is descending.

12.24 In addition to the sort/merge utility, what other utility programs are typically available on a computer system.

Programs to copy files, to print file contents, to list all files on a particular disk pack or tape, to attempt to recover files from a damaged pack or tape, etc.

12.25 What is the difference between the COBOL definitions of a sort file and a merge file?

    None. Both require a restricted form of SELECT and both require an SD. There is no way to tell whether a "sort" file is to be used with SORT or MERGE, except by looking at the actual statement in the PROCEDURE DIVISION.

12.26 What is the proper form of the ASSIGN TO name for a sort/merge file?

    Any legal name will do, since the ASSIGN TO name is just treated as comments.

12.27 Tell whether the following would be likely to involve USING, INPUT PROCEDURE, GIVING, and/or OUTPUT PROCEDURE: (*a*) a program to print mailing labels for all records on a customer mailing tape; (*b*) a program to calculate and print the grade point averages for all nondegree students at a university; (*c*) a program to make a backup copy of an accounts payable check file, which shall be sorted by general ledger number rather than by check number; (*d*) an edit program which produces a disk file of sorted and validated transactions.

(*a*) USING with OUTPUT PROCEDURE (to format, print report).

(*b*) INPUT PROCEDURE (to select only nondegree students) with OUTPUT PROCEDURE (to calculate and print averages).

(*c*) USING with GIVING (in real life, one would probably run the sort/merge utility as a stand-alone program rather than invoke it through COBOL).

(*d*) INPUT PROCEDURE (to filter out invalid transactions) with GIVING.

12.28 What is wrong with the following?

```
SD   ANY-SORT-FILE
     BLOCK CONTAINS 10 RECORDS
     RECORD CONTAINS 200 CHARACTERS
     LABEL RECORDS ARE STANDARD
```

    Only the RECORD CONTAINS... and DATA RECORDS ARE... clauses are allowed in a sort/merge file definition (SD): BLOCK CONTAINS... and LABEL RECORDS... clauses are invalid.

12.29 Write a program that sorts sales records on average sales per customer, as calculated by an INPUT PROCEDURE.

```
     SELECT SALES-FILE ASSIGN TO...
     SELECT SORT-FILE ASSIGN TO ANYTHING.
     . . . . . . . . . . . . . . . . . . . . . . . . . . . .
     FD   SALES-FILE...
     01   SALES-RECORD.
          05   SALESPERSON-ID          PIC X(7).
          05   TOTAL-SALES             PIC S9(5)V99   COMP.
          05   NUMBER-CUSTOMERS        PIC S9(3)      COMP.
     SD   SORT-FILE
          RECORD-CONTAINS...
     01   SORT-RECORD.
          05   SORT-SALES-ID           PIC X(7).
          05   SORT-TOTAL-SALES        PIC S9(5)V99   COMP.
          05   SORT-NUMBER-CUSTOMERS   PIC S9(3)      COMP.
          05   SORT-AVERAGE-SALES      PIC S9(5)V99   COMP.
     . . . . . . . . . . . . . . . . . . . . . . . . . . . .
```

```
          SORT SORT-FILE
              ON DESCENDING KEY SORT-AVERAGE-SALES
              INPUT PROCEDURE IS CALCULATE-AVERAGE
              OUTPUT PROCEDURE IS PRINT-REPORT
          STOP RUN


      CALCULATE-AVERAGE SECTION.
          OPEN   INPUT   SALES-FILE
          MOVE "NO" TO END-FILE-SW
          PERFORM GET-SALES-RECORD
          PERFORM RELEASE-A-RECORD
              UNTIL END-FILE-SW EQUAL "YES"
          CLOSE SALES-FILE
          .
      PRINT-REPORT SECTION.
      . . . . . . . . . . . . . . . . . . . . . . . . . . .
      PERFORMED-PARAGRAPHS SECTION.

      GET-SALES-RECORD.
          READ SALES-FILE
              AT END   MOVE "YES" TO END-FILE-SW

      RELEASE-A-RECORD.
          MOVE SALESPERSON-ID       TO SORT-SALES-ID
          MOVE TOTAL-SALES          TO SORT-TOTAL-SALES
          MOVE NUMBER-CUSTOMERS  TO SORT-NUMBER-CUSTOMERS
          DIVIDE TOTAL-SALES BY NUMBER-CUSTOMERS
              GIVING SORT-AVERAGE-SALES
          RELEASE SORT-RECORD
          PERFORM GET-SALES-RECORD
          .
```

12.30 The normal EBCDIC collating sequence places the digits 0–9 after the letters A–Z. Make a sort that places 0–9 before A–Z.

```
          . . . . . . . . . . . . . . . . . . . . . . . .
          SPECIAL-NAMES.
              CUSTOMER-SORT-ORDER IS "0" THRU "9"
                                      "A" THRU "Z"
          . . . . . . . . . . . . . . . . . . . . . .
              SORT SORT-FILE
                  ON ASCENDING KEY WHATEVER
                  COLLATING SEQUENCE IS CUSTOMER-SORT-ORDER
                  INPUT PROCEDURE IS SCREEN-THEM
                  OUTPUT PROCEDURE IS PROCESS-THEM
```

12.31 Discuss how one can properly sort date fields.

Dates defined as PIC X(6) or PIC 9(6) can be sorted correctly if the six characters in the date are arranged yymmdd (year, month, day) rather than the usual mmddyy (month, day, year). "yymmdd" preserves the proper major-to-minor order within the date field. The other approach is to use the Julian date, yyddd (Section 6.6). Neither of these techniques, unmodified, will produce proper results when the century changes.

12.32 Certain COBOL compilers do not allow an INPUT/OUTPUT PROCEDURE to PERFORM a paragraph located outside the INPUT/OUTPUT SECTION proper. Assuming such a compiler, rewrite the INPUT PROCEDURE of Problem 12.29.

```
CALCULATE-AVERAGE SECTION.
    OPEN  INPUT  SALES-FILE
    MOVE "NO" TO END-FILE-SW
    PERFORM GET-SALES-RECORD
    PERFORM RELEASE-A-RECORD
        UNTIL END-FILE-SW EQUAL "YES"
    CLOSE SALES-FILE
    GO TO CALCULATE-AVERAGE-EXIT
    .
GET-SALES-RECORD.
. . . . . . . . . . . . . . . . . . . . . . . . . . . . . .
RELEASE-A-RECORD.
. . . . . . . . . . . . . . . . . . . . . . . . . . . . . .
CALCULATE-AVERAGE-EXIT.
    EXIT.
PRINT-REPORT SECTION.
. . . . . . . . . . . . . . . . . . . . . . . . . . . . . .
```

GO TO . . . , an instruction widely used in nonstructured COBOL, is needed in the above coding to prevent GET-SALES-RECORD and RELEASE-A-RECORD, now within the SECTION, from being executed one more time after SALES-FILE has been CLOSEd. "EXIT" is a do-nothing statement which merely allows CALCULATE-AVERAGE-EXIT to serve as the ending paragraph for the SECTION.

12.33 Redefine the following sort record for more efficient sorting:

```
SD   SORT-FILE . . .
01       SORT-REC.
    05   EMPLOYEE-ID          PIC X(4).
    05   NAME                 PIC X(20).
    05   DEPT                 PIC XX.
    05   NUMBER-DEPENDENTS    PIC S9        COMP-3.
    05   HOURLY-RATE          PIC S9(2)V99  COMP.
. . . . . . . . . . . . . . . . . . . . . . . . . . . .
    SORT SORT-FILE
        ON DESCENDING KEY HOURLY-RATE
        ON ASCENDING KEY DEPT
        ON ASCENDING KEY EMPLOYEE-ID
```

```
SD   SORT-FILE . . .
01       SORT-REC.
    05   SORT-KEYS.
        10  DEPT             PIC XX.
        10  EMPLOYEE-ID      PIC X(4).
    05   NAME                 PIC X(20).
    05   NUMBER-DEPENDENTS    PIC S9        COMP-3.
    05   HOURLY-RATE          PIC S9(2)V99  COMP.
. . . . . . . . . . . . . . . . . . . . . . . . . . . .
    SORT SORT-FILE
        ON DESCENDING KEY HOURLY-RATE
        ON ASCENDING KEY SORT-KEYS
```

12.34 How should the following two files be merged?

        File A: 10, 5, 18, 17, 23   File B: 20, 30, 40, 50

Since file A is not sorted, the files would have to be merged using the SORT statement:

```
SORT SORT-FILE
    ON . . .
    USING  FILE-A  FILE-B
    OUTPUT PROCEDURE IS . . .
```

12.35 What is wrong with the following?

                PROCEDURE DIVISION.
                    OPEN   INPUT   FILE-A
                            FILE-B
                    MERGE MERGE-WORK-FILE
                        ON ASCENDING KEY MERGE-KEY
                        USING FILE-A
                            FILE-B
                    OUTPUT PROCEDURE IS PROCESS-RECORDS

The USING option requires that the USING files be *closed* when the SORT or MERGE statement is executed (since the sort/merge utility automatically opens them).

Programming Assignments

12.36 Write a harassment program for a collection agency.

Input.   Cards containing account number (columns 1–6); name (columns 11–30); amount owed (columns 31–37, 2 decimal places).

Output.   Print a report: start on a new page and have a title and appropriate headings. Print the account number, name, and amount owed across the page. Make your own layout. Sort the accounts in descending order of amount owed. At the end, print the total number of accounts and the total amount owed.

12.37 Write a program to help the university track down students with unpaid parking fines.

Input.   Cards will contain student ID [X(9)], name [X(20)], and amount owed [9(2)V9(2)].

Output.   Print a report with a title and appropriate headings. Print student information across the page. The report should list the student with the largest fine first, the smallest fine last. At the end of the report, print the total number of students owing money, the total amount owed, and the average amount owed.

12.38 Write a program that produces an order error report and a master order file.

Input.

Field Name	Characteristics	Position
Customer Number	9(6)	1–6
Customer Name	X(20)	11–30
Item Number	X(6)	31–36
Order Number	X(5)	38–42
Order Date	9(6)	44–49
Order Quantity	9(3)	51–53
Price	999V99	55–59

Cards will not be in any particular order. Define customer number, order number, and item number as alphanumeric.

Output.   (1) A report which contains information from those cards which show errors. Validate that the customer number, item number, order number, date, quantity, and price are numeric, and that the price is greater than zero. (2) A master order file on disk, which should be in order by customer number, with item numbers in order for each customer. There will be one record in this file for each customer. The layout for this file will be

Field Name	Characteristics	Position
Customer Number	X(6)	1–6
Customer Name	X(20)	7–26
Number of Orders	9 (COMP-3)	27

followed by data for each order:

Item Number	X(6)
Order Number	X(5)
Date	9(6)
Quantity	9(3)
Price	999V99

There will be at most 4 orders for any customer, and the total record length will be 127 bytes.

Process.   Validate input records, printing a report of error cards. Sort the valid cards in order by item number within customer number. Use the sorted records to produce the master file on disk. If there are more than 4 orders for a customer, only the first 4 will be included in the master. Print error messages for extra orders and ignore those cards.

12.39   Update with today's orders the master file created in Problem 12.38. You may want to use the balanced-line algorithm discussed in Chapter 11.

Input.   (1) A master order file with the layout given in Problem 12.38, but having variable-length records. A record will only be as long as needed to hold the number of orders it contains. Records which contain 1 order will be 52 characters long; those with 4 orders will be 127 characters. This will be a disk file. (2) A transaction order file having the same layout as in Problem 12.38. This is a card file.

Output.   (1) The updated master order file. (2) A transaction register, a printed report that will show the changes which were made to the master and will display error messages for orders that did not update the master.

Process.   The master file will be in order by item number within customer number; sort the order file so that it will be in that same order (all order cards are previously validated, contain numerics). In the update routine:

> if there is an order for a customer who is not in the master, print an error message and
> > ignore that order.
>
> if customer number on an order matches an existing master, then
> > if the ordered item is already in the master, update that item by adding the order
> > > quantity to the quantity in the master, and change the order date in the master to
> > > today's date.
> >
> > if the ordered item is not in the master, print an error message if there is no room to add
> > > the item to the master. If there is room, add it to the master, inserting it so that the
> > > orders remain in order of item number. **Warning:**   Be sure to write out all masters
> > > which are read in, even if there are no orders for a customer.

COBOL Reserved Words

Reserved Word	ANS COBOL '74	CODASYL COBOL '80 only	IBM OS/VS COBOL
ACCEPT	×	—	×
ACCESS	×	—	×
ACTUAL	—	—	×
ADD	×	—	×
ADVANCING	×	—	×
AFTER	×	—	×
ALL	×	—	×
ALPHABET	—	×	—
ALPHABETIC	×	—	×
ALPHANUMERIC	—	×	—
ALPHANUMERIC-EDITED	—	×	—
ALSO	×	—	×
ALTER	×	—	×
ALTERNATE	×	—	×
AND	×	—	×
ANY	—	×	—
APPLY	—	—	×
ARE	×	—	×
AREA	×	—	×
AREAS	×	—	×
ASCENDING	×	—	×
ASSIGN	×	—	×
AT	×	—	×
AUTHOR	×	—	×
BASIS	—	×	—
BEFORE	×	—	×
BEGINNING	—	—	×
BINARY	—	×	—
BIT	—	×	—
BITS	—	×	—
BLANK	×	—	×
BLOCK	×	—	×
BOOLEAN	—	×	—
BOTTOM	×	—	×
BY	×	—	×
CALL	×	—	×
CANCEL	×	—	×
CBL	—	—	×
CD	×	—	×
CF	×	—	×
CH	×	—	×
CHANGED	—	—	×
CHARACTER	×	—	×
CHARACTERS	×	—	×

Reserved Word	ANS COBOL '74	CODASYL COBOL '80 only	IBM OS/VS COBOL
CLOCK-UNITS	×	–	–
CLOSE	×	–	×
COBOL	×	–	–
CODE	×	–	×
CODE-SET	×	–	×
COLLATING	×	–	×
COLUMN	×	–	×
COMMA	×	–	×
COMMIT	–	×	–
COMMON	–	×	–
COMMUNICATION	×	–	×
COMP	×	–	×
COMP-1	–	–	×
COMP-2	–	–	×
COMP-3	–	–	×
COMP-4	–	–	×
COMPUTATIONAL	×	–	×
COMPUTATIONAL-1	–	–	×
COMPUTATIONAL-2	–	–	×
COMPUTATIONAL-3	–	–	×
COMPUTATIONAL-4	–	–	×
COMPUTE	×	–	×
CONFIGURATION	×	–	×
CONNECT	–	×	–
CONSOLE	–	–	×
CONTAINS	×	–	×
CONTENT	–	×	–
CONTINUE	–	×	–
CONTROL	×	–	×
CONTROLS	×	–	×
CONVERTING	–	×	–
COPY	×	–	×
CORE-INDEX	–	–	×
CORR	×	–	×
CORRESPONDING	×	–	×
COUNT	×	–	×
CSP	–	–	×
CURRENCY	×	–	×
CURRENT	–	×	–
CURRENT-DATE	–	–	×
C01	–	–	×
C02	–	–	×
C03	–	–	×
C04	–	–	×
C05	–	–	×
C06	–	–	×
C07	–	–	×
C08	–	–	×
C09	–	–	×
C10	–	–	×
C11	–	–	×
C12	–	–	×
DATA	×	–	×
DATE	×	–	×
DATE-COMPILED	×	–	×
DATE-WRITTEN	×	–	×
DAY	×	–	×

Reserved Word	ANS COBOL '74	CODASYL COBOL '80 only	IBM OS/VS COBOL
DAY-OF-WEEK	–	×	–
DB	–	×	–
DB-ACCESS-CONTROL-KEY	–	×	–
DB-DATA-NAME	–	×	–
DB-EXCEPTION	–	×	–
DB-RECORD-NAME	–	×	–
DB-SET-NAME	–	×	–
DB-STATUS	–	×	–
DE	×	–	×
DEBUG	–	–	×
DEBUG-CONTENTS	×	–	×
DEBUG-ITEM	×	–	×
DEBUG-LINE	×	–	×
DEBUG-NAME	×	–	×
DEBUG-SUB-1	×	–	×
DEBUG-SUB-2	×	–	×
DEBUG-SUB-3	×	–	×
DEBUGGING	×	–	×
DECIMAL-POINT	×	–	×
DECLARATIVES	×	–	×
DELETE	×	–	×
DELIMITED	×	–	×
DELIMITER	×	–	×
DEPENDING	×	–	×
DESCENDING	×	–	×
DESTINATION	×	–	×
DETAIL	×	–	×
DISABLE	×	–	×
DISCONNECT	–	×	–
DIS	–	–	×
DISPLAY	×	–	×
DISPLAY-n	–	×	–
DISPLAY-ST	–	–	×
DIVIDE	×	–	×
DIVISION	×	–	×
DOWN	×	–	×
DUPLICATE	–	×	–
DUPLICATES	×	–	×
DYNAMIC	×	–	×
EGI	×	–	×
EJECT	–	–	×
ELSE	×	–	×
EMI	×	–	×
EMPTY	–	×	–
ENABLE	×	–	×
END	×	–	×
END-ADD	–	×	–
END-CALL	–	×	–
END-COMPUTE	–	×	–
END-DELETE	–	×	–
END-DIVIDE	–	×	–
END-EVALUATE	–	×	–
END-IF	–	×	–
END-MULTIPLY	–	×	–
END-OF-PAGE	×	–	×
END-PERFORM	–	×	–
END-READ	–	×	–

Reserved Word	ANS COBOL '74	CODASYL COBOL '80 only	IBM OS/VS COBOL
END-RECEIVE	–	×	–
END-RETURN	–	×	–
END-REWRITE	–	×	–
END-SEARCH	–	×	–
END-START	–	×	–
END-STRING	–	×	–
END-SUBTRACT	–	×	–
END-UNSTRING	–	×	–
END-WRITE	–	×	–
ENDING	–	–	×
ENTER	×	–	×
ENTRY	–	–	×
ENVIRONMENT	×	–	×
EOP	×	–	×
EQUAL	×	–	×
EQUALS	–	×	–
ERASE	–	×	–
ERROR	×	–	×
ESI	×	–	×
EVALUATE	–	×	–
EVERY	×	–	×
EXAMINE	–	–	×
EXCEEDS	–	×	–
EXCEPTION	×	–	×
EXCLUSIVE	–	×	–
EXHIBIT	–	–	×
EXIT	×	–	×
EXOR	–	×	–
EXTEND	×	–	×
EXTERNAL	–	×	–
FALSE	–	×	–
FD	×	–	×
FILE	×	–	×
FILE-CONTROL	×	–	×
FILE-LIMIT	–	–	×
FILE-LIMITS	–	–	×
FILLER	×	–	×
FINAL	×	–	×
FIND	–	×	–
FINISH	–	×	–
FIRST	×	–	×
FOOTING	×	–	×
FOR	×	–	×
FREE	–	×	–
FROM	×	–	×
FUNCTION	–	×	–
GENERATE	×	–	×
GET	–	×	–
GIVING	×	–	×
GLOBAL	–	×	–
GO	×	–	×
GREATER	×	–	×
GROUP	×	–	×
HEADING	×	–	×
HIGH-VALUE	×	–	×
HIGH-VALUES	×	–	×

Reserved Word	ANS COBOL '74	CODASYL COBOL '80 only	IBM OS/VS COBOL
I-O	×	–	×
I-O-CONTROL	×	–	×
ID	–	–	×
IDENTIFICATION	×	–	×
IF	×	–	×
IN	×	–	×
INDEX	×	–	×
INDEX-n	–	×	–
INDEXED	×	–	×
INDICATE	×	–	×
INITIAL	×	–	×
INITIALIZE	–	×	×
INITIATE	×	–	×
INPUT	×	–	×
INPUT-OUTPUT	×	–	×
INSERT	–	–	×
INSPECT	×	–	×
INSTALLATION	×	–	×
INTO	×	–	×
INVALID	×	–	×
IS	×	–	×
JUST	×	–	×
JUSTIFIED	×	–	×
KEEP	–	×	–
KEY	×	–	×
LABEL	×	–	×
LAST	×	–	×
LD	–	×	–
LEADING	×	–	×
LEAVE	–	–	×
LEFT	×	–	×
LENGTH	×	–	×
LESS	×	–	×
LIMIT	×	–	×
LIMITS	×	–	×
LINAGE	×	–	×
LINAGE-COUNTER	×	–	×
LINE	×	–	×
LINE-COUNTER	×	–	×
LINES	×	–	×
LINKAGE	×	–	×
LOCALLY	–	×	–
LOCK	×	–	×
LOW-VALUE	×	–	×
LOW-VALUES	×	–	×
MEMBER	–	×	–
MEMORY	×	–	×
MERGE	×	–	×
MESSAGE	×	–	×
MODE	×	–	×
MODIFY	–	×	–
MODULES	×	–	×
MORE-LABELS	–	–	×
MOVE	×	–	×

Reserved Word	ANS COBOL '74	CODASYL COBOL '80 only	IBM OS/VS COBOL
MULTIPLE	×	–	×
MULTIPLY	×	–	×
NAMED	–	–	×
NATIVE	×	–	×
NEGATIVE	×	–	×
NEXT	×	–	×
NO	×	–	×
NOMINAL	–	×	×
NOT	×	–	×
NOTE	–	–	×
NULL	–	×	–
NUMBER	×	–	×
NUMERIC	×	–	×
NUMERIC-EDITED	–	×	–
OBJECT-COMPUTER	×	–	×
OCCURS	×	–	×
OF	×	–	×
OFF	×	–	×
OMITTED	×	–	×
ON	×	–	×
OPEN	×	–	×
OPTIONAL	×	–	×
OR	×	–	×
ORDER	–	×	–
ORGANIZATION	×	–	×
OTHER	–	×	–
OTHERWISE	–	–	×
OUTPUT	×	–	×
OVERFLOW	×	–	×
OWNER	–	×	–
PACKED-DECIMAL	–	×	–
PADDING	–	×	–
PAGE	×	–	×
PAGE-COUNTER	×	–	×
PASSWORD	–	–	×
PERFORM	×	–	×
PF	×	–	×
PH	×	–	×
PIC	×	–	×
PICTURE	×	–	×
PLUS	×	–	×
POINTER	×	–	×
POSITION	×	–	×
POSITIONING	–	–	×
POSITIVE	×	–	×
PRINTING	×	–	–
PRIOR	–	×	–
PROCEDURE	×	–	×
PROCEDURES	×	–	×
PROCEED	×	–	×
PROCESSING	–	–	×
PROGRAM	×	–	×
PROGRAM-ID	×	–	×
PROTECTED	–	×	–
PURGE	–	×	–

Reserved Word	ANS COBOL '74	CODASYL COBOL '80 only	IBM OS/VS COBOL
QUEUE	×	–	×
QUOTE	×	–	×
QUOTES	×	–	×
RANDOM	×	–	×
RD	×	–	×
READ	×	–	×
READY	–	–	×
REALM	–	×	–
REALMS	–	×	–
RECEIVE	×	–	×
RECONNECT	–	×	–
RECORD	×	–	×
RECORD-NAME	–	×	–
RECORD-OVERFLOW	–	–	×
RECORDS	×	–	×
REDEFINES	×	–	×
REEL	×	–	×
REFERENCE	–	×	–
REFERENCES	×	–	×
RELATIVE	×	–	×
RELEASE	×	–	×
RELOAD	–	–	×
REMAINDER	×	–	×
REMARKS	–	–	×
REMOVAL	×	–	×
RENAMES	×	–	×
REORG-CRITERIA	–	–	×
REPEATED	–	×	–
REPLACE	–	×	–
REPLACING	×	–	×
REPORT	×	–	×
REPORTING	×	–	×
REPORTS	×	–	×
REREAD	–	–	×
RERUN	×	–	×
RESERVE	×	–	×
RESET	×	–	×
RETAINING	–	×	–
RETRIEVAL	–	×	–
RETURN	×	–	×
RETURN-CODE	–	–	×
REVERSED	×	–	×
REWIND	×	–	×
REWRITE	×	–	×
RF	×	–	×
RH	×	–	×
RIGHT	×	–	×
ROLLBACK	–	×	–
ROUNDED	–	–	×
RUN	×	–	×
SAME	×	–	×
SD	×	–	×
SEARCH	×	–	×
SECTION	×	–	×
SECURITY	×	–	×
SEEK	–	–	×

Reserved Word	ANS COBOL '74	CODASYL COBOL '80 only	IBM OS/VS COBOL
SEGMENT	×	–	×
SEGMENT-LIMIT	×	–	×
SELECT	×	–	×
SELECTIVE	–	–	×
SEND	×	–	×
SENTENCE	×	–	×
SEPARATE	×	–	×
SEQUENCE	×	–	×
SEQUENTIAL	×	–	×
SET	×	–	×
SETS	–	×	–
SIGN	×	–	×
SIZE	×	–	×
SKIP-1	–	–	×
SKIP-2	–	–	×
SKIP-3	–	–	×
SORT	×	–	×
SORT-CORE-SIZE	–	–	×
SORT-FILE-SIZE	–	–	×
SORT-MERGE	×	–	×
SORT-MESSAGE	–	–	×
SORT-MODE-SIZE	–	–	×
SORT-RETURN	–	–	×
SOURCE	×	–	×
SOURCE-COMPUTER	×	–	×
SPACE	×	–	×
SPACES	×	–	×
SPECIAL-NAMES	×	–	×
STANDARD	×	–	×
STANDARD-1	×	–	×
STANDARD-2	–	×	–
START	×	–	×
STATUS	×	–	×
STOP	×	–	×
STORE	–	–	×
STRING	×	–	×
SUB-QUEUE-1	×	–	×
SUB-QUEUE-2	×	–	×
SUB-QUEUE-3	×	–	×
SUB-SCHEMA	–	×	–
SUBTRACT	×	–	×
SUM	×	–	×
SUPPRESS	×	–	×
SYMBOLIC	×	–	×
SYNC	×	–	×
SYNCHRONIZED	×	–	×
SYSIN	–	–	×
SYSOUT	–	–	×
SYSPUNCH	–	–	×
S01	–	–	×
S02	–	–	×
TABLE	×	–	×
TALLY	–	–	×
TALLYING	×	–	×
TAPE	×	–	×
TENANT	–	×	–
TERMINAL	×	–	×

Reserved Word	ANS COBOL '74	CODASYL COBOL '80 only	IBM OS/VS COBOL
TERMINATE	×	–	×
TEST	–	×	–
TEXT	×	–	×
THAN	×	–	×
THEN	–	–	×
THROUGH	×	–	×
THRU	×	–	×
TIME	×	–	×
TIME-OF-DAY	–	–	×
TIMES	×	–	×
TO	×	–	×
TOP	×	–	×
TOTALED	–	–	×
TOTALING	–	–	×
TRACE	–	–	×
TRACK-AREA	–	–	×
TRACK-LIMIT	–	–	×
TRACKS	–	–	×
TRAILING	×	–	×
TRANSFORM	–	–	×
TRUE	–	×	–
TYPE	×	–	×
UNEQUAL	–	×	–
UNIT	×	–	×
UNSTRING	×	–	×
UNTIL	×	–	×
UP	×	–	×
UPDATE	–	×	–
UPON	×	–	×
UPSI-0	–	–	×
UPSI-1	–	–	×
UPSI-2	–	–	×
UPSI-3	–	–	×
UPSI-4	–	–	×
UPSI-5	–	–	×
UPSI-6	–	–	×
UPSI-7	–	–	×
USAGE	×	–	×
USAGE-MODE	–	×	–
USE	×	–	×
USING	×	–	×
VALUE	×	–	×
VALUES	×	–	×
VARYING	×	–	×
WHEN	×	–	×
WHEN-COMPILED	–	–	×
WITH	×	–	×
WITHIN	–	×	–
WORDS	×	–	×
WORKING-STORAGE	×	–	×
WRITE	×	–	×
WRITE-ONLY	–	–	×
ZERO	×	–	×
ZEROES	×	–	×
ZEROS	×	–	×

Reserved Word	ANS COBOL '74	CODASYL COBOL '80 only	IBM OS/VS COBOL
+	×	–	×
–	×	–	×
*	×	–	×
/	×	–	×
**	×	–	×
<	×	–	×
>	×	–	×
=	×	–	×

Collating Sequences

Ascending EBCDIC Sequence

Decimal Representation	Bit Configuration	Symbol	Meaning
0	00000000		
74	01001010	¢	cent sign
75	01001011	.	period, decimal point
76	01001100	<	less than sign
77	01001101	(	left parenthesis
78	01001110	+	plus sign
79	01001111	|	vertical bar, logical OR
80	01010000	&	ampersand
90	01011010	!	exclamation point
91	01011011	$	dollar sign
92	01011100	*	asterisk
93	01011101	)	right parenthesis
94	01011110	;	semicolon
95	01011111	¬	logical NOT
96	01100000	−	minus, hyphen
97	01100001	/	slash
107	01101011	,	comma
108	01101100	%	percent sign
109	01101101	_	underscore
110	01101110	>	greater than sign
111	01101111	?	question mark
122	01111010	:	colon
123	01111011	#	number sign
124	01111100	@	at sign

Ascending EBCDIC Sequence (*cont.*)

Decimal Representation	Bit Configuration	Symbol	Meaning
125	01111101	'	apostrophe, prime
126	01111110	=	equals sign
127	01111111	"	quotation marks
129	10000001	a	
130	10000010	b	
131	10000011	c	
132	10000100	d	
133	10000101	e	
134	10000110	f	
135	10000111	g	
136	10001000	h	
137	10001001	i	
145	10010001	j	
146	10010010	k	
147	10010011	l	
148	10010100	m	
149	10010101	n	
150	10010110	o	
151	10010111	p	
152	10011000	q	
153	10011001	r	
162	10100010	s	
163	10100011	t	
164	10100100	u	
165	10100101	v	
166	10100110	w	
167	10100111	x	
168	10101000	y	
169	10101001	z	
193	11000001	A	

Ascending EBCDIC Sequence (*cont.*)

Decimal Representation	Bit Configuration	Symbol	Meaning
194	11000010	B	
195	11000011	C	
196	11000100	D	
197	11000101	E	
198	11000110	F	
199	11000111	G	
200	11001000	H	
201	11001001	I	
209	11010001	J	
210	11010010	K	
211	11010011	L	
212	11010100	M	
213	11010101	N	
214	11010110	O	
215	11010111	P	
216	11011000	Q	
217	11011001	R	
226	11100010	S	
227	11100011	T	
228	11100100	U	
229	11100101	V	
230	11100110	W	
231	11100111	X	
232	11101000	Y	
233	11101001	Z	
240	11110000	0	
241	11110001	1	
242	11110010	2	
243	11110011	3	
244	11110100	4	

Ascending EBCDIC Sequence (*cont.*)

Decimal Representation	Bit Configuration	Symbol	Meaning
245	11110101	5	
246	11110110	6	
247	11110111	7	
248	11111000	8	
249	11111001	9	

Ascending ASCII Sequence

Decimal Representation	Bit Configuration	Symbol	Meaning
0	00000000		null
32	00100000	SP	space
33	00100001	|	logical OR
34	00100010	"	quotation mark
35	00100011	#	number sign
36	00100100	$	dollar sign
37	00100101	%	percent
38	00100110	&	ampersand
39	00100111	'	apostrophe, prime
40	00101000	(	opening parenthesis
41	00101001	)	closing parenthesis
42	00101010	*	asterisk
43	00101011	+	plus
44	00101100	,	comma
45	00101101	-	hyphen, minus
46	00101110	.	period, decimal point
47	00101111	/	slant
48	00110000	0	
49	00110001	1	
50	00110010	2	
51	00110011	3	

Ascending ASCII Sequence (*cont.*)

Decimal Representation	Bit Configuration	Symbol	Meaning
52	00110100	4	
53	00110101	5	
54	00110110	6	
55	00110111	7	
56	00111000	8	
57	00111001	9	
58	00111010	:	colon
59	00111011	;	semicolon
60	00111100	<	less than
61	00111101	=	equals
62	00111110	>	greater than
63	00111111	?	question mark
64	01000000	@	commercial AT
65	01000001	A	
66	01000010	B	
67	01000011	C	
68	01000100	D	
69	01000101	E	
70	01000110	F	
71	01000111	G	
72	01001000	H	
73	01001001	I	
74	01001010	J	
75	01001011	K	
76	01001100	L	
77	01001101	M	
78	01001110	N	
79	01001111	O	
80	01010000	P	
81	01010001	Q	

Ascending ASCII Sequence (*cont.*)

Decimal Representation	Bit Configuration	Symbol	Meaning
82	01010010	R	
83	01010011	S	
84	01010100	T	
85	01010101	U	
86	01010110	V	
87	01010111	W	
88	01011000	X	
89	01011001	Y	
90	01011010	Z	
91	01011011	[	opening bracket
92	01011100	\	reverse slant
93	01011101	]	closing bracket
94	01011110	^	circumflex, logical NOT
95	01011111	_	underscore
96	01100000	`	grave accent
97	01100001	a	
98	01100010	b	
99	01100011	c	
100	01100100	d	
101	01100101	e	
102	01100110	f	
103	01100111	g	
104	01101000	h	
105	01101001	i	
106	01101010	j	
107	01101011	k	
108	01101100	l	
109	01101101	m	
110	01101110	n	
111	01101111	o	

Ascending ASCII Sequence (*cont.*)

Decimal Representation	Bit Configuration	Symbol	Meaning
112	01110000	p	
113	01110001	q	
114	01110010	r	
115	01110011	s	
116	01110100	t	
117	01110101	u	
118	01110110	v	
119	01110111	w	
120	01111000	x	
121	01111001	y	
122	01111010	z	
123	01111011	{	opening brace
124	01111100	¦	vertical line
125	01111101	}	closing brace
126	01111110	~	tilde

Appendix C

COBOL '80 Considerations

Recently, the CODASYL and ANSI committees have been working on a new version of COBOL for the 1980s. As first made public, in 1981, the proposed COBOL '80 standards embodied changes which would have made some COBOL '74 programs incompatible with COBOL '80. At present, the new standards are undergoing further revision, constructive criticism, and debate.

Following are *some* of the more important changes which *may* become official.

1. The restriction to just 3 subscripts (or indexes) and 3 levels of nested OCCURS clauses has been relaxed (to 48).
2. Substrings of a data item may be defined in PROCEDURE DIVISION statements: "DATA-ITEM (3:7)" indicates the seven bytes of DATA-ITEM which start with the third byte.
3. The DEPENDING ON item for an OCCURS...DEPENDING ON... table may have a zero value (indicating zero table entries).
4. An item which REDEFINES another may be *shorter than* the item being redefined.
5. "ACCEPT...FROM DAY-OF-WEEK" produces the appropriate integer between 1 and 7.
6. The word "TO" is now allowed in:

        ADD ITEM-A TO ITEM-B GIVING ITEM-C

7. The MOVE statement may be used to move an edited item to a nonedited numeric item, the editing being *undone* during the process.
8. Variable-length records are now permitted with READ...INTO..., RETURN...INTO..., WRITE ...FROM..., and RELEASE...FROM....
9. The description of the contents of the DEBUG-ITEM special register has been changed, thereby affecting "USE FOR DEBUGGING DECLARATIVES".
10. When the DEPENDING ON item is part of a variable-length record which is a receiving field, the *maximum* possible value of the DEPENDING ON item (rather than its current value) is used to determine the length of the receiving field.
11. There are two new CLASS conditions: ALPHABETIC-UPPER and ALPHABETIC-LOWER. The ALPHABETIC condition now covers both upper and lower case.
12. The ALTER statement has been deleted from the language.
13. Evaluation of a compound conditional expression terminates as soon as a final truth value for the expression can be determined. Thus, if "A" is false in "IF A AND B AND C...", "B" and "C" will not be evaluated, since it is immediately known that the entire expression must be false.
14. The definition of PERFORM has been expanded to allow the statements which are to be performed to be specified *in-line*:

        PERFORM UNTIL FLAG-IS-SET
            MOVE EMPLOYEE-NAME TO DETAIL-LINE-NAME
            ADD 1 TO NUMBER-PRINTED
            WRITE DETAIL-LINE...
            PERFORM SOME-CALCULATION
            ADD EMPLOYEE-AMOUNT TO TOTAL-AMOUNT
        END-PERFORM

The rules for performing the indicated statements are the same as they would be if the statements were placed in a separate paragraph (say, PARA-A) and the following were used:

        PERFORM PARA-A UNTIL FLAG-IS-SET

Note that when the statements to be performed are specified in-line: (1) no paragraph or SECTION is named in the PERFORM statement; and (2) a new statement, END-PERFORM, is required to designate the end of the group of statements involved in the PERFORM.

15. PERFORM . . . UNTIL . . . has been expanded to allow specification of whether the UNTIL condition should be tested *before* or *after* the indicated statements or paragraphs are performed:

>   PERFORM SAMPLE-PARAGRAPH
>   WITH TEST AFTER
>   UNTIL WE-ARE-DONE

or

>   PERFORM WITH TEST BEFORE
>   UNTIL TEST-IS-SATISFIED
>   ADD . . .
>   MOVE . . .
>   READ . . .
>   END-PERFORM

With TEST AFTER, the indicated statements are performed at least once, even if the condition is initially true (DO UNTIL); with TEST BEFORE (the default), the indicated statements are *not* executed when the condition is initially true (DO WHILE).

16. The IF statement is terminated with a new, END-IF statement rather than with a period:

>   IF A EQUAL B
>   ADD . . .
>   MOVE . . .
>   END-IF

or

>   IF X NOT EQUAL Y
>   MOVE . . .
>   PERFORM . . .
>   ELSE
>   ADD . . .
>   READ . . .
>   END-IF

17. A new statement, EVALUATE . . . , has been added to COBOL to implement the case structure. We illustrate by revising Example 7.26:

>   EVALUATE TRANSACTION-CODE
>   WHEN 1 PERFORM CREATE-NEW-MASTER-RECORD
>   WHEN 2 PERFORM DELETE-MASTER-RECORD
>   WHEN 3 PERFORM CHANGE-EXISTING-MASTER-RECORD
>   WHEN OTHER
>   PERFORM INVALID-TRANSACTION-CODE-ROUTINE
>   END-EVALUATE

Note the error-trapping WHEN OTHER clause and the explicit termination END-EVALUATE.

Index

Catalog

If you are interested in a list of SCHAUM'S
OUTLINE SERIES send your name
and address, requesting your free catalog, to:

SCHAUM'S OUTLINE SERIES, Dept. C
McGRAW-HILL BOOK COMPANY
1221 Avenue of Americas
New York, N.Y. 10020